economics
today

the macro view

THIRTEENTH EDITION

The Addison-Wesley Series in Economics

economics today

the macro view

THIRTEENTH EDITION

Roger LeRoy Miller

Institute for University Studies, Arlington, Texas

Boston   San Francisco   New York
London   Toronto   Sydney   Tokyo   Singapore   Madrid
Mexico City   Munich   Paris   Cape Town   Hong Kong   Montreal

Editor-in-Chief: Denise Clinton
Acquisitions Editor: Roxanne Hoch
Senior Development Editor: Rebecca Ferris-Caruso
Managing Editor: James Rigney
Senior Production Supervisor: Katherine Watson
Executive Marketing Manager: Stephen Frail
Senior Media Producer: Melissa Honig
Design Manager: Regina Hagen Kolenda
Executive Producer, Technology: Michelle Neil

Cover Designer: Regina Hagen Kolenda
Digital Assets Manager: Jason Miranda
Supplements Production Coordinator: Kirsten Dickerson
Senior Manufacturing Buyer: Hugh Crawford
Senior Media Buyer: Ginny Michaud
Cover Images: © PictureQuest and Masterfile
Production House: Orr Book Services
Compostion: Nesbitt Graphics, Inc.

Photo Credits

Pages 1 and 12, © Ariel Skelley/CORBIS; Pages 25 and 42, © Photodisc/Getty Images; Pages 48 and 71, © Photodisc/Getty Images; Pages 77 and 93, ©Photodisc/Getty Images; Pages 98 and 118, © AFP/Getty Images; Pages 123 and 139, © Photodisc/Getty Images; Pages 145 and 163, © Ralf-Finn Hestoft/CORBIS; Pages 168 and 190, © Brand X Pictures/Getty Images; Pages 196 and 215, © Photodisc/Getty Images; Pages 220 and 235, © Royalty-Free/CORBIS; Pages 240 and 259, ©Royalty-Free/CORBIS;

Pages 263 and 285, © Ed Kashi/CORBIS; Pages 292 and 306, © AFP/Getty Images; Pages 314 and 331, © Getty Images; Pages 336 and 357, © Tim McGuire/CORBIS; Pages 362 and 385, © Reuters/CORBIS; Pages 390 and 408, © James Leynse/CORBIS; Pages 416 and 436, © Jonathan Ernst/Reuters/CORBIS; Pages 441 and 458, © Enzo & Paolo Ragazzini/CORBIS; Pages 777 and 793, © AFP/Getty Images; Pages 799 and 821, © Alan Schein Photography/CORBIS.

Library of Congress Cataloging-in-Publication Data

Miller, Roger LeRoy.
   Economics today/Roger LeRoy Miller—13th ed.
     p.cm.
   Includes bibliographical references and index.
   ISBN 0-321-27883-6 (main edition (hard cover) : alk. paper) —
   ISBN 0-321-27886-0 (the micro view (soft cover) : alk. paper) —
   ISBN 0-321-27885-2 (the macro view (soft cover) : alk. paper)
   I. Economics. 2. Microeconomics. 3. Macroeconomics. I. Title.
HB171.5.M642 2006
330—dc22   2004028936

ISBN: 0-321-27885-2
2 3 4 5 6 7 8 9 10—QWD—09 08 07 06 05

Dedication

To Joe Csizmazia,

If you keep training
so well, I will never
catch up with you in the
Boulder Mountain Tour.

Your friend,
— R. L. M.

Contents in Brief

Contents in Detail

Chapter 6   TAXES, TRANSFERS, AND PUBLIC SPENDING   123

PART II   INTRODUCTION TO MACROECONOMICS AND ECONOMIC GROWTH   145

Chapter 7   THE MACROECONOMY: UNEMPLOYMENT, INFLATION, AND DEFLATION   145

Chapter 8   MEASURING THE ECONOMY'S PERFORMANCE   168

Chapter 9   GLOBAL ECONOMIC GROWTH AND DEVELOPMENT

PART III   REAL GDP DETERMINATION AND FISCAL POLICY

Chapter 10   REAL GDP AND THE PRICE LEVEL IN THE LONG RUN

Chapter 14 DEFICIT SPENDING AND THE PUBLIC DEBT   314

PART IV MONEY, STABILIZATION, AND GROWTH   336

Chapter 15 MONEY, BANKING, AND CENTRAL BANKING   336

Chapter 19 POLICIES AND PROSPECTS FOR GLOBAL ECONOMIC GROWTH   441

PART VIII   GLOBAL ECONOMICS

Chapter 33 COMPARATIVE ADVANTAGE AND THE OPEN ECONOMY   777

Chapter 34   EXCHANGE RATES AND THE BALANCE OF PAYMENTS   799

Acknowledgments

I am the most fortunate of economics textbook writers, for I receive the benefit of literally hundreds of suggestions from those of you who use *Economics Today*. I continue to be fully appreciative of the constructive criticisms that you offer. There are some professors who have been asked by my publisher to participate in a more detailed reviewing process of this edition. I list them below. I hope that each one of you so listed accepts my sincere appreciation for the fine work that you have done.

Carlos Aguilar, El Paso Community College
Bruce W. Bellner, Ohio State University, Marion
Daniel K. Benjamin, Clemson University
Margaret M. Dalton, Frostburg State University
Diana Denison, Red Rocks Community College
Diana Fortier, Waubonsee Community College

M. James Kahiga, Georgia Perimeter College
Daniel Mizak, Frostburg State University
Judy Roobian-Mohr, Columbus State Community College
Paul Seidenstat, Temple University

Diane L. Stehman, Northeastern Illinois University
Anthony Uremovic, Joliet Junior College
David VanHoose, Baylor University
Mark A. Wilkening, Blinn College

I also thank the reviewers of previous editions:

Cinda J. Adams
Esmond Adams
John Adams
Bill Adamson
John R. Aidem
Mohammed Akacem
E. G. Aksoy
M. C. Alderfer
John Allen
Ann Al-Yasiri
Charles Anderson
Leslie J. Anderson
Fatma W. Antar
Mohammad Ashraf
Aliakbar Ataiifar
Leonard Atencio
John M. Atkins
Glen W. Atkinson
Thomas R. Atkinson
James Q. Aylesworth
John Baffoe-Bonnie
Kevin Baird
Charley Ballard
Maurice B. Ballabon
G. Jeffrey Barbour
Daniel Barszcz
Robin L. Bartlett
Kari Battaglia
Robert Becker
Charles Beem
Glen Beeson
Charles Berry
Abraham Bertisch
John Bethune
R.A. Blewett
Scott Bloom
M. L. Bodnar
Mary Bone
Karl Bonnhi
Thomas W. Bonsor
John M. Booth
Wesley F. Booth
Thomas Borcherding
Melvin Borland
Tom Boston
Barry Boyer
Maryanna Boynton
Ronald Brandolini
Fenton L. Broadhead
Elba Brown
William Brown
Michael Bull
Maureen Burton

Conrad P. Caligaris
Kevin Carey
James Carlson
Robert Carlsson
Dancy R. Carr
Scott Carson
Doris Cash
Thomas H. Cate
Richard J. Cebula
Catherine Chanbers
K. Merry Chambers
Richard Chapman
Ronald Cherry
Young Back Choi
Marc Chopin
Carol Cies
Joy L. Clark
Curtis Clarke
Gary Clayton
Marsha Clayton
Dale O. Cloninger
Warren L. Coats
Ed Coen
Pat Conroy
James Cox
Stephen R. Cox
Eleanor D. Craig
Peggy Crane
Jerry Crawford
Joanna Cruse
John P. Cullity
Will Cummings
Thomas Curtis
Andrew J. Dane
Mahmoud Davoudi
Edward Dennis
Carol Dimamro
William Dougherty
Barry Duman
Diane Dumont
Floyd Durham
G. B. Duwaji
James A. Dyal
Ishita Edwards
Robert P. Edwards
Alan E. Ellis
Mike Ellis
Steffany Ellis
Frank Emerson
Carl Enomoto
Zaki Eusufzai
Sandy Evans
John L. Ewing-Smith

Frank Falero
Frank Fato
Abdollah Ferdowsi
Grant Ferguson
David Fletcher
James Foley
John Foreman
Ralph G. Fowler
Arthur Friedberg
Peter Frost
Tom Fullerton
E. Gabriel
James Gale
Byron Gangnes
Steve Gardner
Peter C. Garlick
Neil Garston
Alexander Garvin
Joe Garwood
Doug Gehrke
J. P. Gilbert
Otis Gilley
Frank Glesber
Jack Goddard
Michael Goode
Allen C. Goodman
Richard J. Gosselin
Paul Graf
Edward Greenberg
Gary Greene
Nicholas Grunt
William Gunther
Kwabena Gyimah-Brempong
Demos Hadjiyanis
Martin D. Haney
Mehdi Haririan
Ray Harvey
E. L. Hazlett
Sanford B. Helman
William Henderson
John Hensel
Robert Herman
Gus W. Herring
Charles Hill
John M. Hill
Morton Hirsch
Benjamin Hitchner
Charles W. Hockert
R. Bradley Hoppes
James Horner
Grover Howard
Nancy Howe-Ford

Yu-Mong Hsiao
Yu Hsing
James Hubert
Joseph W. Hunt Jr.
Scott Hunt
John Ifediora
R. Jack Inch
Christopher Inya
Tomotaka Ishimine
E. E. Jarvis
Parvis Jenab
Allan Jenkins
Mark Jensen
S. D. Jevremovic
J. Paul Jewell
Frederick Johnson
David Jones
Lamar B. Jones
Paul A. Joray
Daniel A. Joseph
Craig Justice
Septimus Kai Kai
Devajyoti Kataky
Timothy R. Keely
Ziad Keilany
Norman F. Keiser
Randall G. Kesselring
Alan Kessler
E. D. Key
Saleem Khan
M. Barbara Killen
Bruce Kimzey
Philip G. King
Terrence Kinal
E. R. Kittrell
David Klingman
Charles Knapp
Jerry Knarr
Faik Koray
Janet Koscianski
Marie Kratochvil
Peter Kressler
Michael Kupilik
Larry Landrum
Margaret Landman
Richard LaNear
Keith Langford
Anthony T. Lee
Loren Lee
Bozena Leven
Donald Lien
George Lieu
Stephen E. Lile

Lawrence W. Lovick
Marty Ludlum
G. Dirk Mateer
Robert McAuliffe
James C. McBrearty
Howard J. McBride
Bruce McClung
John McDowell
E. S. McKuskey
James J. McLain
John L. Madden
Mary Lou Madden
Glen Marston
John M. Martin
Paul J. Mascotti
James D. Mason
Paul M. Mason
Tom Mathew
Warren Matthews
Warren T. Matthews
Akbar Marvasti
G. Hartley Mellish
Mike Melvin
Diego Mendez-Carbajo
Dan C. Messerschmidt
Michael Metzger
Herbert C. Milikien
Joel C. Millonzi
Glenn Milner
Khan Mohabbat
Thomas Molloy
Margaret D. Moore
William E. Morgan
Stephen Morrell
Irving Morrissett
James W. Moser
Thaddeaus Mounkurai
Martin F. Murray
Densel L. Myers
George L. Nagy
Solomon Namala
Jerome Neadly
James E. Needham
Claron Nelson
Douglas Nettleton
Gerald T. O'Boyle
Gregory Okoro
Richard E. O'Neill
Lucian T. Orlowski
Diane S. Osborne
Melissa A. Osborne
James O'Toole
Jan Palmer

Zuohong Pan
Gerald Parker
Ginger Parker
Randall E. Parker
Kenneth Parzych
Norm Paul
Wesley Payne
Raymond A. Pepin
Martin M. Perline
Timothy Perri
Jerry Petr
Bruce Pietrykowski
Maurice Pfannesteil
James Phillips
Raymond J. Phillips
I. James Pickl
Dennis Placone
Mannie Poen
William L. Polvent
Robert Posatko
Renée Prim
Robert W. Pulsinelli
Rod D. Raehsler
Kambriz Raffiee
Sandra Rahman
Jaishankar Raman
John Rapp
Richard Rawlins
Gautam Raychaudhuri
Ron Reddall
Mitchell Redlo
Charles Reichhelu
Robert S. Rippey
Charles Roberts
Ray C. Roberts
Richard Romano
Duane Rosa
Richard Rosenberg
Larry Ross
Barbara Ross-Pfeiffer
Philip Rothman
John Roufagalas
Stephen Rubb
Henry Ryder
Patricia Sanderson
Thomas N. Schaap
William A. Schaeffer
William Schaniel
David Schauer
A. C. Schlenker
David Schlow
Scott J. Schroeder
William Scott

Dan Segebarth	Phil Smith	Rebecca Summary	William N. Trumbull	Wylie Whalthall	Whitney Yamamura
Swapan Sen	Steve Smith	Joseph L. Swaffar	Arianne K. Turner	James H. Wheeler	Donald Yankovic
Augustus Shackelford	William Doyle Smith	Thomas Swanke	Kay Unger	Everett E. White	Alex Yguado
Richard Sherman Jr.	Lee Spector	Frank D. Taylor	John Vahaly	Michael D. White	Paul Young
Liang-rong Shiau	George Spiva	Daniel Teferra	Jim Van Beek	Mark A. Wilkening	Shik Young
David Shorow	Richard L. Sprinkle	Lea Templer	Lee J. Van Scyoc	Raburn M. Williams	Mohammed Zaheer
Vishwa Shukla	Alan Stafford	Gary Theige	Roy Van Til	James Willis	Ed Zajicek
R. J. Sidwell	Herbert F. Steeper	Dave Thiessen	Craig Walker	George Wilson	Paul Zarembka
David E. Sisk	Columbus Stephens	Robert P. Thomas	Robert F. Wallace	Travis Wilson	William J. Zimmer Jr.
Alden Smith	William Stine	Deborah Thorsen	Henry C. Wallich	Mark Wohar	
Garvin Smith	Allen D. Stone	Richard Trieff	Milledge Weathers	Ken Woodward	
Howard F. Smith	Osman Suliman	George Troxler	Robert G. Welch	Tim Wulf	
Lynn A. Smith	J. M. Sullivan	William T. Trulove	Terence West	Peter R. Wyman	

When I undertake a major revision of *Economics Today*, I start the process almost immediately after I've published the previous edition. So, what you are about to read has its roots in editorial meetings that started almost three years ago.

I am fortunate to have an incredibly imaginative and knowledgeable editorial team at Addison-Wesley, with which I have worked during these last several years. They include Adrienne D'Ambrosio, Rebecca Ferris-Caruso, Roxanne Hoch, and Denise Clinton. Of course, they have accused me of monopolizing their time. In any event, I thank them for all of the meetings, phone calls, e-mails, and faxes that, if properly recorded, would fill up more pages than the resulting text.

On the design and production side, I feel fortunate to have worked with John Orr of Orr Book Services. I thank his staff and him for their creative and professional services as well as Katherine Watson, my production manager at Addison-Wesley, and Regina Kolenda, my talented designer. I also very much appreciate the efforts of Jason Miranda and Kirsten Dickerson in coordinating the production process of the many print supplements.

I had more than my deserved amount of constant comments and criticisms from my colleagues David VanHoose and Dan Benjamin. I hope they will accept this sentence of appreciation in the manner in which it is offered—with utmost sincerity.

I have been blessed with a powerhouse of talented colleagues who have created or revised the extensive supplements package. So, thank you David VanHoose of Baylor University for the Study Guides; Andrew J. Dane of Angelo State University for the Instructor's Manual; Debbie Mullin of the University of Colorado at Colorado Springs for the PowerPoint slides; Judy Roobian-Mohr, Columbus State Community College for Test Bank 1; Diane L. Stehman of Northeastern Illinois University for Test Bank 2; and G. Dirk Mateer of Penn State University for his critical role as editor of Test Bank 3 overseeing top-notch question contributions from Susan Glanz of St. Joseph's University and Bruce W. Bellner of Ohio State University, Marion, Marie Duggan of Keene State College, Teresa Laughlin of Pomona College, Debbie Mullin of the University of Colorado at Colorado Springs, Densel L. Myers of Oklahoma City Community College, and David Schlow of Penn State University.

I also must extend my gratitude to the multimedia developers who created and refined all of the online services for this edition of *Economics Today*. At Addison-Wesley, Melissa Honig and Michelle Neil deftly coordinated the efforts of the content and multimedia developers. I am especially appreciative of the efforts of the MyEconLab content development team. Key contributors include Scott Hunt of Columbus State Community College, Daniel Mizak of Frostburg State University, and Margaret M. Dalton of Frostburg State University.

Finally, Sue Jasin probably could teach a course in economics after typing, retyping, and even retyping again various drafts of this revision. Thank you, Sue, for everything, including the many weekends you worked on this project.

I welcome comments and ideas from professors and students. After all, by the time you read this, I will already be working on the next edition.

R. L. M.

Miller's Economics Today—
real-life economics for today's students

I have always challenged myself to deliver a textbook for principles of economics that would motivate students to take what they learn in this course into everyday life. I believe that the key to achieving this goal is to illustrate economic theory through attention-grabbing issues and applications that students are eager to read and discuss.

Clear presentation of theory ... examples, examples, and more examples ... plenty of opportunities to practice

One of the major challenges economics instructors face today is the unprecedented level of diversity in their principles classroom. Students arrive in their first economics course with widely divergent skill sets, math abilities, academic interests, and personal backgrounds. Some students plan to major in economics, although many take the course to fulfill a college requirement.

If you accept the premise, as I do, that all students learn better when they're motivated through applications that tap into their personal interests, you will understand why I include such a breadth of examples—domestic and international, corporate and policy, consumer and celebrity—and why I update them in each new edition to make sure they stay current with students' interests. Each page offers instructors a new opportunity to connect with students, and a chance for students to connect economics to the world around them.

Balanced attention to a full range of modern and traditional theories

And, as in previous editions, **Economics Today** provides balanced treatment of macroeconomic theories— including classical, Keynesian, monetarist, and real-business-cycle approaches—and it explores the arguments and evidence promoting active, discretionary versus passive, rules-based policymaking. In the realm of microeconomics, the text considers both time-tested approaches to perfect and imperfect competition, as well as more recent developments relating to information products and network effects.

In essence, my goals haven't changed since I wrote the first edition, but now I know that my priorities are in line with what students need. Millions of students have used my textbook. Feedback from those students and their instructors has convinced me that **Economics Today** focuses on what matters most: user friendliness; clear, modern theory; examples, examples, examples; and unlimited opportunities to practice via problem sets and online pedagogy.

Roger LeRoy Miller

Roger LeRoy Miller

A significant revision—the latest public debates, a new Chapter 14, and recent data throughout

Building on the success of previous editions, the Thirteenth Edition offers thoroughly updated coverage throughout. Every example, table, and graph has been revised to reflect the most recent data available. You'll find major new material incorporating the latest public debates, research, and data in every part of the text, including:

▶ **New Chapter 14, "Deficit Spending and the Public Debt,"** addresses one of today's foremost public policy issues—the implications of higher deficits and a growing public debt. This timely chapter helps students understand why higher federal deficits may or may not pose problems for the U.S. economy. Major topics include the challenge of measuring the federal budget deficit; effects of government budget deficits on aggregate demand; and ways to reduce the government budget deficit.

▶ **Updated treatment of regulation and antitrust in Chapter 28** gives students the background required to evaluate the effects of regulatory and antitrust actions by U.S. and foreign policymakers. The chapter contrasts the benefits and costs of regulation, covers modern pricing techniques such as product versioning and bundling, and explains how U.S. and foreign policymakers have reacted differently to these pricing mechanisms.

▶ **Detailed coverage of the issue of labor outsourcing in Chapter 29** keys students in on this topic that has generated much public debate. Examples from both U.S. and foreign perspectives show why outsourcing has mixed near-term effects on wages and employment in U.S. labor markets but is beneficial on net for U.S. workers in the long run.

▶ **Enhanced coverage of labor union issues in Chapter 30** emphasizes the significant shift in U.S. unionization from manufacturing to services and highlights global unionization trends. The chapter provides complete coverage of the factors accounting for recent trends in and economic effects of labor unions. The discussion shows that unions are fundamental institutions in many nations, even though U.S. unionization rates are falling.

▶ **Expanded coverage of the role of international trade organizations in Chapter 33** highlights the increasing importance of regional trade blocs in affecting global trade flows and broadens the scope of coverage of the institutional framework governing world trade.

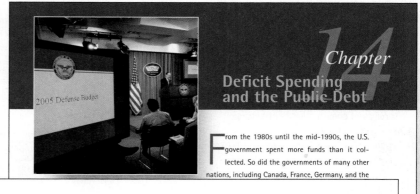

Chapter
14
Deficit Spending and the Public Debt

From the 1980s until the mid-1990s, the U.S. government spent more funds than it collected. So did the governments of many other nations, including Canada, France, Germany, and the

CHAPTER 29 *The Labor Market: Demand, Supply, and Outsourcing* **695**

ment and wages in the United States? Who loses and who gains from outsourcing? Let's consider each of these questions in turn.

Wage and Employment Effects of Outsourcing

Equilibrium wages and levels of employment in U.S. labor markets are determined by the demands for and supplies of labor in those markets. As you have learned, one of the determinants of the market demand for labor is the price of a substitute input. Availability of a lower-priced substitute, you also learned, causes the demand for labor to fall. Thus the *immediate* economic effects of labor outsourcing are straightforward. When a home industry's firms can obtain *foreign* labor services that are a close substitute for *home* labor services, the demand for labor services provided by foreign workers will increase. The demand for labor services provided by home workers will decrease. What this economic reasoning ultimately implies for U.S. labor markets, however, depends on whether we view the United States as the "home" country or the "foreign" country.

U.S. Labor Market Effects of Outsourcing by U.S. Firms. To begin, let's view the United States as the home country. Developments in computer, communications, and transportation technologies have enabled an increasing number of U.S. firms to regard the labor of foreign workers as a close substitute for labor provided by U.S. workers. Take a look at Figure 29-5. Panel (a) depicts demand and supply curves in the U.S. market for workers who handle calls for technical support for U.S. manufacturers of personal computers. Suppose that before technological change makes foreign labor substitutable for U.S. labor, point E_1 is the initial equilibrium. At this point, the market wage rate in this U.S. labor market is $19 per hour.

FIGURE 29-5
Outsourcing of U.S. Computer Technical-Support Services
Initially, the market wage for U.S. workers providing technical support for customers of U.S. computer manufacturers is $19 per hour at point E_1 in panel (a), while the market wage for Indian workers who provide the same service is $8 per hour in panel (b). This gives U.S. firms an incentive to substitute away from U.S. workers to Indian workers. The market demand for U.S. labor decreases in panel (a), generating a new equilibrium at point E_2 at a lower U.S. market wage and employment level. The market demand for Indian labor increases in panel (b), bringing about higher wages and employment at point E_2.

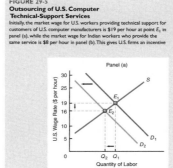

Demonstrating economic principles with examples from today's headlines

Economics Today captures interest through the infusion of dozens of new cases and 145 examples that reflect the vitality of economics—all selected to hold students' attention and to drive home the application of the theory just presented. Hard-hitting boxed features apply concepts to real-world situations. New examples throughout the text give immediate, common-sense reinforcement to economic concepts.

NEW "Economics Front and Center" Case Studies

These all-new cases—one in each chapter—place students in real-world situations requiring them to apply what they have studied in the chapter. The case in Chapter 3, for example, asks students to analyze the effects of a tornado on the supply and demand for the services of construction contractors.

Other cases include:

▶ Holding Out for a Better Salary Offer in an Improved Job Climate

▶ Confronting the Temptation to Collude in the Airline Industry

▶ Outsourcing Can Be a Win-Win Situation

Many new real-life examples highlight domestic topics and events

Effectively demonstrating economic principles, these new thought-provoking examples appear throughout the book, including:

▶ When Incomes Rise, It's Easier to Believe Butter Isn't Margarine

▶ The Low Present Value of a Volunteer Soldier's Pay Package

▶ Is Krispy Kreme Trying to Bake Too Many Doughnuts?

▶ Why You Pay a Different Price to Attend College Than Many of Your Fellow Students

Many added examples dealing with important policy questions

Students are exposed to policy questions on both domestic and international fronts in over 20 policy examples. This strong policy perspective helps students understand why economic concepts are important to them as citizens who seek to evaluate public debates surrounding the issues of the day. "Policy Examples" include:

▶ Does Imposing the Ultimate Legal Penalty Deter Homicides?

▶ How Pushing Prices Lower Can Violate Antitrust Laws

▶ State Government Spending Takes Off—Especially in One State

▶ The Discount Window Is Open, So Where Are the Banks?

CASE STUDY: Economics Front and Center

The Economics of a Tornado Cleanup Can Hit Close to Home

An early spring tornado has just rolled through a midwestern town, and more than 500 structures have experienced at least moderate damage. After recovering from the initial shock, one couple, the Richardsons, realize that they are lucky to have only blown-out windows and large holes in their roof, which they quickly cover with plastic sheeting. When they try to find a construction contractor to make permanent repairs, however, they do not feel so lucky any more. Most phone calls to contractors are producing either busy signals or unanswered voice mail messages. The few contractors who respond say that they are overwhelmed with requests for work and cannot possibly begin the Richardsons' repairs for at

nearly 25 percent higher than the usual prices charged to replace windows and a roof. How can demand and supply analysis explain the situation that the Richardsons are facing?

Points to Analyze

1. Has the structural damage inflicted on this town by the tornado resulted in changes in the demand for and supply of the services of construction contractors or changes in the quantities demanded and

relo-

EXAMPLE

Is Krispy Kreme Trying to Bake Too Many Doughnuts?

In 1937, the founder of Krispy Kreme Doughnuts, Vernon Rudolph, purchased a secret yeast-raised doughnut recipe from a French chef in New Orleans and opened a doughnut shop in Winston-Salem, North Carolina. Gradually, Krispy Kreme outlets spread across the southern tier of the United States. Then, in 2000, Krispy Kreme became a publicly traded company and embarked on a major expansion across most of the rest of the country.

The company calls many of its newest outlets "factory stores." These outlets are equipped with costly doughnut-making machinery that can churn out tens of thousands of doughnuts each day. An aim of the expansion strategy has been to reduce the long-run average cost of producing doughnuts. Some locales now have so many Krispy Kreme outlets in clo

urated" with doughnuts. Stores in these areas end up throwing away numerous one- and two-day-old doughnuts, which raises average costs of ingredients, labor, electricity, and wear and tear on machinery. For this reason, critics of Krispy Kreme's expansion strategy contend that the result has been higher long-run average costs for the company as a whole. The firm, they argue, has expanded beyond its minimum efficient scale.

For Critical Analysis

How might Krispy Kreme continue to expand geographically into the four states that currently lack outlets while at the same time reducing its overall nationwide scale of doughnut

---

Policy EXAMPLE

Does Imposing the Ultimate Legal Penalty Deter Homicides?

Figure 1-1 on the following page shows that a drop in the annual number of legally sanctioned executions in the United States between the late 1950s and early 1980s was accompanied by an increase in the U.S. murder rate. When the number of executions rose during the 1990s and early 2000s, the U.S. murder rate declined.

The extent to which the threat of receiving a death penalty actually contributes to lower murder rates depends on a host of other incentives, however. For instance, if more states reduce the chances of a convicted murderer receiving the death penalty, the disincentive to committing murders is reduced. In contrast, the disincentive effects of the death penalty are likely to be greater if prison conditions improve, thereby making the death penalty a much less desirable alternative punishment.

Economists have found that when these and other factors are taken into account, every *additional* legally sanctioned execution is associated with about five to six fewer homicides. Each judicial *reduction* of a death-penalty sentence to imprisonment is associated with the occurrence of one to two additional murders. Thus both the execution rate and the rate at which death-penalty sentences are reduced to long-term imprisonment have incentive effects on people contemplating murder.

For Critical Analysis

Why do you suppose that careful economic studies of the effects of the death penalty on homicide rates take into account whether people who committed murders might have been under the influence of alcohol or drugs?

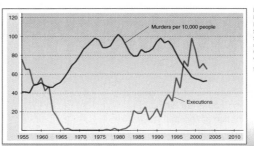

FIGURE 1-1
Murder Rates and Executions in the United States Since 1955
Since the mid-1950s, there has been an apparent negative relationship between the number of death-penalty sentences carried out and the U.S. murder rate.

Source: U.S. Department of Justice.

Economic stimulus for your classroom

International examples emphasize today's global economy

This edition features more than 40 international examples that broaden students' perspectives by showing that economic principles are applicable in other cultures and institutional environments. New "International Examples" include:

▶ The IMF's Cost to Taxpayers Is Surely "Not One Dime"

▶ Manufacturing Jobs Disappear Worldwide

▶ Hidden Costs of "Free" Canadian Health Care

▶ The European Union Starts a Food Fight

"E-Commerce Examples" explore the impact of advances in information technology

This edition's 15 new "E-Commerce Examples" demonstrate how advances in information technology are affecting virtually every area of the economy and students' personal lives. "E-Commerce Examples" include:

▶ Divorce Court Moves to the Internet

▶ U.S. Web Sellers Find Themselves Collecting Europe's Taxes

▶ Internet Packaging Tracking Cuts Marginal Costs at Federal Express

▶ Why Market Entries Have Been Followed by Market Exits at Online Auction Sites

Students get many opportunities to "think like economists"

At the end of each of this book's boxed examples, students are asked to "think like economists" as they answer **For Critical Analysis** questions. These probing questions are effective tools for sharpening students' analytical skills. Suggested answers to all questions are found in the *Instructor's Manual.*

International E X A M P L E

Hidden Costs of "Free" Canadian Health Care

Because physicians are unwilling to provide as many services as people wish to purchase at below-market fees dictated by the Canadian government, long waiting lists are a fixture of the Canadian system. The average waiting time to see a specialist after referral by a general practitioner is more than four months. Individuals experiencing debilitating back pain often must wait at least a year for neurosurgery. Even people diagnosed with life-threatening cancers typically have to wait six weeks before they have an initial examination by a cancer specialist.

The high opportunity costs associated with long waits for officially approved health care have led to the establishment of private health care clinics on Native American reservations, where physicians can legally accept private payments. (It is il-legal for Canadians to purchase private health insurance to pay for care received on these reservations, however.) In addition, rather than wait for years to obtain elective surgeries, about 20,000 Canadians fly to India each year at their own expense and pay physicians in that country to perform surgeries such as hip replacements. In actuality, the "free" Canadian health care system is very costly to that nation's residents.

For Critical Analysis
Why do you suppose that many Canadians who wish to have MRI scans travel to the United States and pay for scans out of their own pockets instead of waiting three months for a "free" MRI scan in Canada?

E-Commerce E X A M P L E

Divorce Court Moves to the Internet

At Web sites such as CompleteCase.com and LegalZoom.com, a couple desiring to amicably dissolve their marriage can pro-vide sufficient information to obtain fully completed legal di-vorce papers for fees ranging from $250 to $300. For another $50 to $100, they can also obtain all the information required to file their papers with a court to end their marriage legally. These online prices are much lower than the fees of $2,000 or so that divorce lawyers typically charge simply to fill out and process the same required legal forms.

When there are no child-custody or property-division is-sues to iron out, it is often in a couple's self-interest to bypass traditional lawyers to obtain a divorce. Not surprisingly, the total number of do-it-yourself divorces arranged online has more than doubled each year since Web-based preparers of di-vorce papers began operating in the early 2000s.

For Critical Analysis
Under what types of circumstances might a self-interested marriage partner be willing to pay an attorney much more than $2,000 to handle legal issues associated with obtaining a divorce?

For Critical Analysis
Under what types of circumstances might a self-interested marriage partner be willing to pay an attorney much more than $2,000 to handle legal issues associated with obtaining a divorce?

Provocative applications engage students in every chapter

Economics Today is based on the belief that students learn more when they are involved and engaged. The current applications in this book—all new to this edition—get students' attention right at the beginning of each chapter.

New chapter-opening issues present compelling examples . . .

Each chapter-opening issue whets student interest in core chapter concepts with a compelling example. These openers engage students up front and involve them in the chapter material. New chapter-opening issues include:

▶ Increasing Obesity Rates Among U.S. Children
▶ Supply and Demand in the Market for Economics Instructors
▶ The Market for Online Music
▶ Collusive Price Fixing by Top Fashion-Modeling Agencies

. . . which are linked to corresponding chapter-end "Issues and Applications"

Located at the end of every chapter, the two-page "Issues and Applications" sections offer a more in-depth discussion of the issue introduced at the beginning of the chapter. These capstone applications feature current issues designed to encourage students to apply economic concepts to real-world situations. Each "Issues and Applications" concludes with "For Critical Analysis" questions, "Web Resources," and a suggested "Research Project" that give students opportunities for in-depth discussion and exploration of the application. (Suggested answers to critical thinking questions appear in the *Instructor's Manual.*)

Chapter 1
The Nature of Economics

Thirty years ago, only about 5 percent of all U.S. residents between the ages of 2 and 19 were sufficiently overweight to be classified as "obese." Since then, however, the obesity rate among U.S. children and adolescents has increased to more than 15 percent. Why are there so many more obese children and adolescents? It is tempting to look first to the medical profession for an answer to this question. Most individuals who become overweight, however, consciously *choose* to consume more calories than they use up through daily exercise. Increasingly, therefore, society is looking to *economists*, who specialize in understanding how people make self-interested decisions in response to incentives—that is, rewards, or inducements—they face, to develop a better understanding of why the rate of obesity among U.S. children has increased.

LEARNING OBJECTIVES

After reading this chapter, you should be able to:

1. Discuss the difference between microeconomics and macroeconomics
2. Evaluate the role that rational self-interest plays in economic analysis
3. Explain why economics is a science
4. Distinguish between positive and normative economics

Media Resources

Refer to the end of the chapter for a full listing of the multimedia learning materials available in MyEconLab.

I

Issues and Applications
Applying Economics to the Problem of Childhood Obesity

According to current medical standards, more than 65 percent of the U.S. population is overweight. This figure is about 20 percentage points higher than was true in 1980. More than 30 percent of the population is extremely overweight, or obese, which is more than double the 1980 figure.

It appears likely that even more people will be overweight or obese in future years people are getting heavier at younger ages. As noted before, more than 15 percent children and adolescents are obese today, compared to about 5 percent in the 1970s. dy mass is gained, it is difficult to shed. Thus many of these children will probably obese and confront the associated health problems later when they reach maturity.

t Home

alories than they e fastest eat rela- such as hamburg- me watching tel- burning calories ts activities.
hers—have taken ren's food intake y parents are not y once did. In the s, but today more the home. These eir children from nds for exercise. bout 8 percent of e obese, whereas t among children d, economists es- are roughly twice home moms.

Schools Contribute to a Feeding Frenzy

Parents who choose to allocate more time to working than to overseeing their children entrust other caregivers—usually administrators and employees at day-care centers, preschools, and elementary and secondary schools—with providing that supervision. When it comes to planning a child's schedule, however, most caregivers have little incentive to include daily exercise that would burn off children's calories.

Furthermore, more than 25 percent of U.S. elementary schools give students access to vending machines with snacks, and 16 percent have contracts for delivery of lunch items from fast-food providers. Vending machines are present in 67 percent of middle schools and 96 percent of high schools. Furthermore, more than 25 percent of all middle schools and high schools contract with fast-food purveyors to provide a portion of the foods sold on school premises. Schools often earn a share of the profits from sales of snacks and fast-food lunches. Therefore, a number of school administrators have a strong economic incentive to encourage children to consume *more*, not fewer, high-calorie snacks and fast-food items.

Study tools guide students through each chapter

Economics Today provides a finely tuned teaching and learning system. Acknowledging that students learn in different ways and at different speeds, each of the following features has been carefully crafted to provide a sound structure to ground the student.

▶ **"Did You Know That . . . ?" questions use current data to engage students in chapter topics**
Each chapter starts with a provocative question to engage students and to lead them into the content of the chapter. This new "Did You Know That . . .?" from Chapter 1 uses data about young Italians to show students how self-interest and incentives can be underpinnings for economic decisions.

Did You Know That . . . more than half of all Italians aged 20 to 29 live with their parents? A labor law contributes to this state of affairs. Under the law, firing a worker who has been on a company's payroll longer than a three-month probationary period exposes the company to the risk that a judge will rule that the company did not have "just" cause to dismiss the employee. In this event, the company must reinstate the employee, reimburse the employee for back wages, and pay a fine to the government. Rather than expose themselves to this risk, the owners of many Italian companies have determined that it is in their self-interest *not* to keep new employees on their payrolls longer than three months. This response to Italy's labor law makes it difficult for many young Italians to earn steady incomes that would permit them to live independently from their parents.

"Learning Objectives" begin each chapter
A clear, numbered list of learning objectives on the first page of the chapter focuses students' studies.

▶ **Chapter-ending "Summary Discussion of Learning Objectives" reviews objectives**
To encourage students to retain important concepts, every chapter ends with a concise yet thorough summary of the key concepts. Each "Summary Discussion" paragraph is numbered to match its corresponding chapter-opening "Learning Objective."

SUMMARY DISCUSSION of Learning Objectives

1. **The Problem of Scarcity, Even for the Affluent:** Scarcity is very different from poverty. No one can obtain all one desires from nature without sacrifice. Thus even the richest people face scarcity because they have to make choices among alternatives. Despite their high levels of income or wealth, affluent people, like everyone else, want more than they can have (in terms of goods, power, prestige, and so on).

2. **Why Economists Consider Individuals' Wants but Not Their "Needs":** Goods are all things from which individuals derive satisfaction. Economic goods are those for which the desired quantity exceeds the amount that is directly available from nature at a zero price. To economists, the term *need* is undefinable, whereas humans have unlimited *wants*, which are defined as the goods and services on which we place a positive value.

3. **Why Scarcity Leads People to Evaluate Opportunity Costs:** We measure the opportunity cost of anything by the highest-valued alternative that one must give up to obtain it. The trade-offs we face as individuals and as a society can be represented by a production possibilities curve (PPC), and moving from one point on a PPC to another entails incurring an opportunity cost. The reason is that along a PPC, all currently available resources and technology are being used, so obtaining more of one good requires shifting resources to production of that good and away from production of another. That is, there is an opportunity cost of allocating scarce resources toward producing one good instead of another good.

4. **Why Obtaining Increasing Increments of a Good Requires Giving Up More and More Units of Other Goods:** Typically, resources are specialized. Thus, when society allocates additional resources to producing more and more of a single good, it must increasingly employ resources that would be better suited for producing other goods. As a result, the law of increasing relative cost holds. Each additional unit of a good can be obtained only by giving up more and more of other goods, which means that the production possibilities curve that society faces is bowed outward.

5. **The Trade-Off Between Consumption Goods and Capital Goods:** If we allocate more resources to producing capital goods today, then, other things being equal, the economy will grow faster than it would have otherwise. Thus the production possibilities curve will shift outward by a larger amount in the future, which means that we can have more consumption goods in the future. The trade-off, however, is that producing more capital goods today entails giving up consumption goods today.

6. **Absolute Advantage versus Comparative Advantage:** A person has an absolute advantage if she can produce more of a specific good than someone else who uses the same amount of resources. Nevertheless, the individual may be better off producing a different good if she has a comparative advantage in producing that good, meaning that she can produce the good at a lower opportunity cost than someone else. By specializing in producing the good for which she has a comparative advantage, she assures herself of reaping gains from specialization in the form of a higher income.

CONCEPTS in Brief

- Scarcity exists because human wants always exceed what can be produced with the limited resources and time that nature makes available.
- We use scarce resources, such as land, labor, physical and human capital, and entrepreneurship, to produce economic goods—goods that are desired but are not directly obtainable from nature to the extent demanded or desired at a zero price.
- Wants are unlimited; they include all material desires and all nonmaterial desires, such as love, affection, power, and prestige.
- The concept of need is difficult to define objectively for every person; consequently, we simply consider every person's wants to be unlimited. In a world of scarcity, satisfaction of one want necessarily means nonsatisfaction of one or more other wants.

To test your understanding of the concepts covered in this section, go to the Online Review at www.myeconlab.com/miller.

▲ **"Concepts in Brief" offer review of each chapter section**
Encouraging students to review after reading each major section, "Concepts in Brief" summarize the main points of the section to reinforce learning and to encourage rereading of any difficult material. To further test their understanding of the concepts covered, students are encouraged to go to the Online Review at www.myeconlab.com/miller. Please turn to page xxix of this Preface for details on **MyEconLab.**

A variety of chapter-end "Problems"
At the end of each chapter students will find a variety of interesting "Problems" that offer many opportunities to test knowledge and review chapter concepts. Answers for all odd-numbered problems are provided at the back of the textbook.

Superb integration of online resources

Get Ahead of the Curve

Refer to the end of the chapter for a full listing of the multimedia learning materials available in MyEconLab.

"Media Resources" icons at the beginning of each chapter

These helpful prompts remind students to go to the end of the chapter for a full list of the multimedia materials available at **MyEconLab,** the full-featured online homework and tutorial system that accompanies *Economics Today.*

Chapter-end "Media Resources" sections correlated to MyEconLab

These helpful sections at the end of each chapter detail the many media resources—animations, videos, audio clips, and web links—available specifically for that chapter, which students can access by registering at **www.myeconlab.com/miller.**

URLs in the margins guide students to topic-related Web sites

Notes in the margins offer Web addresses—linking students to interesting Web sites that illustrate chapter topics and give students the opportunity to build their economic research skills as they access the latest information on the national and global economy.

"Economics on the Net" activities

These activities are designed to build student research skills and reinforce key concepts. The activities guide students to a Web site and provide structured assignments for both individual and group work.

If your exam were tomorrow, would you be ready? For each chapter, MyEconLab Practice Tests and Study Plans pinpoint which sections you have mastered and which ones you need to study. That way, you are more efficient with your study time, and you are better prepared for your exams.

Here is how it works:

1. Register and log in to www.myeconlab.com/miller.
2. Click on "Take a Test" and select Test A for this chapter.
3. Take the diagnostic test and MyEconLab will grade it automatically and create a personalized Study Plan, so you see which sections of the chapter you should study further.
4. The Study Plan will serve up additional practice problems and tutorials to help you master the specific areas where you need to focus. By practicing online, you can track your progress in the Study Plan.
5. After you have mastered the sections, "Take a Test" and select Test B for this chapter. Take the test, and see how you do!

In addition to Practice Tests and your personalized Study Plan, you'll find the following media resources in MyEconLab:

1. *Graphs in Motion* animation of Figure A-8.
2. Videos featuring the author, Roger LeRoy Miller, on the following subjects:
   ● The Difference Between Microeconomics and Macroeconomics
   ● Rational Self-Interest and the Rationality Assumption
   ● Positive versus Normative Economics
3. Links to the Web sites cited in the marginal Internet Resources, Issues and Applications feature, and Economics on the Net activity.
4. Audio clips of all key terms, additional practice problems, and a PDF version of the material from the print Study Guide.
5. eThemes of the Times, which is a New York Times article to help you understand the real-world applications

Go to www.econtoday.com/chap02 to find out from the World Trade Organization how much international trade takes place. Under "Resources," click on "Trade statistics."

COMPARATIVE ADVANTAGE AND TRADE AMONG NATIONS

Though most of our analysis of absolute advantage, comparative advantage, and specialization has dealt with individuals, it is equally applicable to nations. First consider the United States. The Plains states have a comparative advantage in the production of grains and other agricultural goods. Relative to the Plains states, the states to the north and east tend to specialize in industrialized production, such as automobiles. Not surprisingly, grains are shipped from the Plains states to the northern states, and automobiles are shipped in the reverse direction. Such specialization and trade allow for higher incomes and standards of living. If both the Plains states and the northern states were separate nations, the same analysis would still hold, but we would call it international trade. Indeed, the European Union (EU) is comparable to the United States in area and population, but instead of one nation, the EU has 25. What U.S. residents call *interstate* trade, Europeans call *international* trade. There is no difference, however, in the economic results—both yield greater economic efficiency and higher average incomes.

ECONOMICS ON THE NET

The U.S. Nursing Shortage For some years media stories have discussed a shortage of qualified nurses in the United States. This application explores some of the factors that have caused the quantity of newly trained nurses demanded to tend to exceed the quantity of newly trained nurses supplied.

Title: Nursing Shortage Resource Web Link

Navigation: Go to the Nursing Shortage Resource Web Link at www.econtoday.com/chap03, and click on *Enrollment Increase Insufficient to Meet the Projected Increase in Demand for New Nurses.*

Application Read the discussion, and answer the following questions.

1. Since 1995, what has happened to the demand for new nurses in the United States? What has happened to the supply of new nurses? Why has the result been a shortage?

2. If there is a free market for the skills of new nurses, what can you predict is likely to happen to the wage rate earned by individuals who have just completed their nursing training?

For Group Study and Analysis Discuss the pros and cons of high schools and colleges trying to factor predictions about future wages into student career counseling. How might this potentially benefit students? What problems might high schools and colleges face in trying to assist students in evaluating the future earnings prospects of various jobs?

Get Ahead of the Curve

MyEconLab:
The new standard in personalized online learning

MyEconLab—the innovative, resource-packed online homework and tutorial system that is packaged with every new copy of **Economics Today**—puts students in control of their own learning through a suite of study and practice tools correlated with the online, interactive version of the textbook and other media tools. Within **MyEconLab's** structured environment, students practice what they learn, test their understanding, and then pursue a Study Plan that MyEconLab generates for them based on their performance on practice tests.

At the core of MyEconLab are the following features:

Practice Tests—Practice tests for each chapter of the textbook enable students to test their understanding and identify the areas in which they need to do further work. Many practice test questions ask students to work with graphs: interpreting them, manipulating them, and even drawing them. Instructors can let students use the supplied pre-built tests or create their own tests.

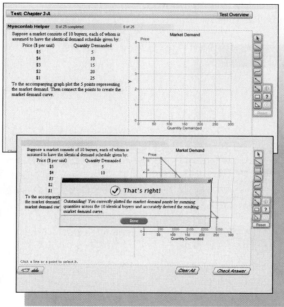

Personalized Study Plan—Using a student's performance on a practice test, a personal Study Plan MyEconLab generates shows where further study is needed. This study plan directs students to a series of additional exercises, including many graphing questions.

Additional Practice Exercises—Using their personalized study plan, students find additional exercises for each topic. These additional practice exercises, which are keyed to each section of the textbook, provide extensive practice and link students to the eText with animated graphs and to other tutorial instruction resources.

Tutorial Instruction—Launched from the additional practice exercises, tutorial instruction is provided in the form of solutions to problems, step-by-step explanations, and other media-based explanations.

Powerful Graphing Tool—Students can draw a graph, and **MyEconLab's** powerful graphing application will evaluate and grade it. Integrated into the practice tests and additional practice exercises, the graphing tool lets students manipulate and even draw graphs so that they get a better feel for how the concepts, numbers, and graphs are connected.

For additional MyEconLab resources, please turn the page ▶

Many time-saving tools for instructors:

MyEconLab provides flexible tools that enable instructors to easily and effectively customize online course materials to suit their needs. Instructors can create and assign tests, quizzes, or graded homework assignments. **MyEconLab** saves time by automatically grading all questions and tracking results in an online grade book. **MyEconLab** can even grade assignments that require students to draw a graph. Test Banks can also be used within **MyEconLab,** giving instructors ample material from which they can create assignments.

Once registered for **MyEconLab,** instructors have access to downloadable supplements such as instructor's manuals, PowerPoint® lecture notes, and Test Banks. Instructors can direct their students to the "Ask the Author" feature that allows them to connect directly with the author via e-mail.

For more information about **MyEconLab,** or to request an Instructor Access Code, visit **http://www.myeconlab.com.**

Get Ahead of the Curve

PLUS many additional MyEconLab resources

▶ **eText**—The entire textbook in electronic format with an audio clip for each glossary item.

▶ **eStudy guide**—The entire *Study Guide* in electronic format and printable.

▶ **Econ Tutor Center**—Staffed by qualified, experienced college economics instructors! The Econ Tutor Center is open five days a week, seven hours a day. Tutors can be reached by phone, fax, e-mail, or White Board technology. The Econ Tutor Center hours are designed to meet your students' study schedules, with evening hours Sunday through Thursday. Students receive one-on-one tutoring on examples, related exercises, and problems.

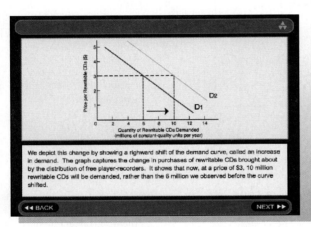

▶ **Animated figures**—145 figures from the textbook presented in step-by-step animations with audio explanations of the action.

▶ **Economics in Motion Animations**—In-depth animations of ten key economic ideas from the textbook—guiding students through precise graphical presentations with detailed audio explanations. A "Content Guide" in each animation allows students to zero in on ideas with which they are struggling.

▶ **Video clips**—Author Roger LeRoy Miller stresses key points in every chapter and further clarifies concepts that students find most difficult to grasp.

▶ **Audio clips**—Featuring an upbeat introduction to each chapter, discussing chapter topics, and focusing student attention on the most critical concepts.

▶ **Glossary Flashcards**—Every key term is available as a flashcard, allowing students to quiz themselves on vocabulary from one or more chapters at a time.

MyEconLab content resources:

▶ **Weekly News**—Featuring a new microeconomic and macroeconomic current events article with discussion questions posted online weekly by Andrew J. Dane of Angelo State University. Students can test their knowledge of current events in a five-question quiz posted each week. Instructor answer keys are available.

▶ **Economics and Your Everyday Life**—An online booklet offering numerous practical applications of economics and guidance for analyzing economic news.

▶ **eThemes of the Times**—Archived articles from *The New York Times*, correlated to each textbook chapter and paired with critical thinking questions.

▶ **Research Navigator**—Extensive help on the research process and four exclusive databases of accredited and reliable source material including The *New York Times*, The *Financial Times*, and peer-reviewed journals.

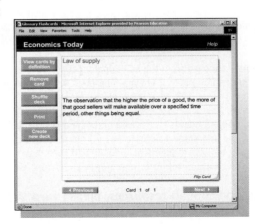

Essential teaching tools to help busy instructors maximize their time

Test Bank I—This Test Bank provides more than 3,750 multiple-choice and 250 short-essay questions with answers. Revised by Judy Roobian-Mohr of Columbus State Community College and Michael Goode of Central Piedmont Community College, the questions have undergone extensive classroom testing for a number of years.

Test Bank 2—Revised by Diane L. Stehman of Northeastern Illinois University, this Test Bank includes more than 3,250 multiple-choice and 250 short-essay questions. All questions have been class-tested by many professors, including Clark G. Ross, coauthor of the National Competency Test for economics majors for the Educational Testing Service in Princeton, New Jersey.

Test Bank 3—This Test Bank features 3,250 test questions expertly assembled from a team of contributors by G. Dirk Mateer of Penn State University. *Test Bank 3* incorporates the best question-writing tactics and time-tested approaches of a number of dedicated and experienced instructors, including lead contributor Susan Glanz of St. Joseph's University and contributors Bruce W. Bellner of Ohio State University–Marion, Marie Duggan of Keene State College, Teresa Laughlin of Pomona College, Debbie Mullin of the University of Colorado at Colorado Springs, Densel L. Myers of Oklahoma City Community College, and David Schlow of Penn State University.

Instructor's Manual—Prepared by Andrew J. Dane of Angelo State University, the *Instructor's Manual* provides a new section featuring lecture-ready examples presented in the same format as the in-text examples. It also includes the following materials:

- ▶ Chapter overviews, objectives, and outlines
- ▶ Points to emphasize for instructors who wish to stress theory
- ▶ Answers to "Issues and Applications" critical thinking questions
- ▶ Further questions for class discussion
- ▶ Answers to all end-of-chapter problems (even and odd)
- ▶ Detailed step-by-step analyses of the end-of-chapter problems
- ▶ Suggested answers to "Economics Front and Center" case questions
- ▶ Annotated answers to selected student learning questions
- ▶ Selected references

Instructor's Resource Disk with PowerPoint Lecture Presentation.

Compatible with Windows and Macintosh computers, this CD-ROM provides numerous resources. The PowerPoint® Lecture Presentation was developed by Jeff Caldwell, Steve Smith, and Mark Mitchell of Rose State College and revised by Debbie Mullin of the University of Colorado at Colorado Springs. The PowerPoint® Lecture Presentation features graphs from the text and outlines key terms, concepts, and figures. For added convenience, the CD-ROM also includes Microsoft Word files for the entire content of the *Instructor's Manual* and computerized test bank files of *Test Banks 1, 2,* and *3*. The easy-to-use testing software (TestGen with QuizMaster for Windows and Macintosh) is a valuable test preparation tool that allows professors to view, edit, and add questions. *You will have 10,750 questions at your fingertips!*

Four-Color Overhead Transparencies—One hundred of the most important graphs from the textbook are reproduced as full-color transparency acetates. Many contain multiple overlays.

Proven resources guarantee student success—available for convenient packaging with this text

In addition to access to **MyEconLab,** the student's ultimate online tool, which is automatically packaged with each text, the following supplementary materials are available to aid and enhance students' mastery of concepts:

Micro-View and Macro-View Study Guides

Written by Roger LeRoy Miller and updated by David VanHoose, these valuable guides offer the practice and review students need to excel in this course. They have been thoroughly revised to take into account the significant changes in many of the chapters of the Thirteenth Edition. Each *Study Guide* is firmly oriented toward helping students learn what they need to know to succeed in the course—and in life. Electronic versions of the *Study Guides* are available on **MyEconLab.**

Economist.com Edition

The premier online source of economic news analysis, **Economist.com** provides your students with insight and opinion on current economic events. Through an agreement between Addison-Wesley and *The Economist,* students can receive a low-cost subscription to this premium Web site for three months, including the complete text of the current issue of *The Economist* and access to *The Economist's* searchable archives. Other features include Web-only weekly articles, news feeds with current world and business news, and stock market and currency data. Professors who adopt this special edition will receive a complimentary one-year subscription to **Economist.com.**

Wall Street Journal Edition

When packaged with the Miller text, Addison-Wesley offers students a reduced cost, 10- or 15-week subscription to the *Wall Street Journal* print edition and the *Wall Street Journal Interactive Edition.* Adopting professors will receive a complimentary one-year subscription to both the print and interactive versions.

Financial Times Edition

Featuring international news and analysis from journalists in more than 50 countries, *The Financial Times* will provide your students with insights and perspectives on economic developments around the world. For a small charge, a 15-week subscription to *The Financial Times* can be included with each new textbook. Adopting professors will receive a complimentary one-year subscription, as well as access to the online edition at **FT.com.**

The Dismal Scientist Edition

The Dismal Scientist provides real-time monitoring of the global economy allowing your students to go beyond theory and into application. For a nominal fee, a three-month subscription to *The Dismal Scientist* can be included with each new textbook. Each subscription includes complete access to all of *The Dismal Scientist's* award winning features. Professors adopting a book on this list receive a complimentary one-year subscription.

Pearson Choice Alternate Editions

With ever-increasing demands on time and resources, today's college faculty and students want greater value, innovation, and flexibility in products designed to meet teaching and learning goals. We've responded to that need by creating **PearsonChoices,** a unique program that allows faculty and students to choose from a range of text and media formats that match their teaching and learning styles—and, in the case of students, their budget.

Books à la Carte Edition

For today's student on the go, we've created highly portable versions of the **Economics Today** textbooks that are three-hole punched. Students can take only what they need to class, incorporate their own notes—and save money! Each *Books à la Carte* text arrives with a laminated study card, perfect for students to use when preparing for exams, plus access to **MyEconLab.**

MyEconLab Xpress Edition

The *Xpress Edition* contains access to all **MyEconLab** resources—including the eText—and a laminated study card. Students receive all the critical course content and powerful study tools included in **MyEconLab** at approximately half the cost of the full print textbook.

Chapter 1
The Nature of Economics

Thirty years ago, only about 5 percent of all U.S. residents between the ages of 2 and 19 were sufficiently overweight to be classified as "obese." Since then, however, the obesity rate among U.S. children and adolescents has increased to more than 15 percent. Why are there so many more obese children and adolescents? It is tempting to look first to the medical profession for an answer to this question. Most individuals who become overweight, however, consciously *choose* to consume more calories than they use up through daily exercise. Increasingly, therefore, society is looking to *economists*, who specialize in understanding how people make self-interested decisions in response to incentives—that is, rewards, or inducements—they face, to develop a better understanding of why the rate of obesity among U.S. children has increased.

LEARNING OBJECTIVES

After reading this chapter, you should be able to:

1. Discuss the difference between microeconomics and macroeconomics
2. Evaluate the role that rational self-interest plays in economic analysis
3. Explain why economics is a science
4. Distinguish between positive and normative economics

Media Resources

Refer to the end of the chapter for a full listing of the multimedia learning materials available in MyEconLab.

... more than half of all Italians aged 20 to 29 live with their parents? A labor law contributes to this state of affairs. Under the law, firing a worker who has been on a company's payroll longer than a three-month probationary period exposes the company to the risk that a judge will rule that the company did not have "just" cause to dismiss the employee. In this event, the company must reinstate the employee, reimburse the employee for back wages, and pay a fine to the government. Rather than expose themselves to this risk, the owners of many Italian companies have determined that it is in their self-interest *not* to keep new employees on their payrolls longer than three months. This response to Italy's labor law makes it difficult for many young Italians to earn steady incomes that would permit them to live independently from their parents.

In this chapter, you will learn why studying the nature of self-interested responses to **incentives** is the starting point for analyzing choices people make in all walks of life. After all, just as Italian companies have responded to legal incentives they face by limiting new workers' terms of employment, how much time you end up devoting to your study of economics depends in part on incentives established by your instructor's system of determining your grade. As you will see, self-interest and incentives are the underpinnings for all the decisions you and others around you make each day.

Incentives
Rewards for engaging in a particular activity.

THE POWER OF ECONOMIC ANALYSIS

Simply knowing that self-interest and incentives are central to any decision-making process is not sufficient for predicting the choices that people will actually make. You also have to develop a framework that will allow you to analyze solutions to each economic problem—whether you are trying to decide how much to study, which courses to take, whether to finish school, or whether the U.S. government should send troops abroad or raise taxes. The framework that you will learn in this text is the *economic way of thinking*.

This framework gives you power—the power to reach informed conclusions about what is happening in the world. You can, of course, live your life without the power of economic analysis as part of your analytical framework. Indeed, most people do. But economists believe that economic analysis can help you make better decisions concerning your career, your education, financing your home, and other important matters. In the business world, the power of economic analysis can help you increase your competitive edge as an employee or as the owner of a business. As a voter, for the rest of your life you will be asked to make judgments about policies that are advocated by political parties. Many of these policies will deal with questions related to international economics, such as whether the U.S. government should encourage or discourage immigration, prevent foreigners from investing in domestic TV stations and newspapers, or restrict other countries from selling their goods here.

Finally, just as taking an art, music, or literature appreciation class increases the pleasure you receive when you view paintings, listen to concerts, or read novels, taking an economics course will increase your understanding when watching the news on TV or reading articles in the newspaper or at Web sites.

DEFINING ECONOMICS

What is economics exactly? Some cynics have defined *economics* as "common sense made difficult." But common sense, by definition, should be within everyone's grasp. You will encounter in the following pages numerous examples that show that economics is, in fact, pure and simple common sense.

Economics is part of the social sciences and as such seeks explanations of real events. All social sciences analyze human behavior, as opposed to the physical sciences, which generally analyze the behavior of electrons, atoms, and other nonhuman phenomena.

> *Economics is the study of how people allocate their limited resources in an attempt to satisfy their unlimited wants. As such, economics is the study of how people make choices.*

To understand this definition fully, two other words need explaining: *resources* and *wants*. **Resources** are things that have value and, more specifically, are used to produce things that satisfy people's wants. **Wants** are all of the things that people would purchase if they had unlimited income.

Whenever an individual, a business, or a nation faces alternatives, a choice must be made, and economics helps us study how those choices are made. For example, you have to choose how to spend your limited income. You also have to choose how to spend your limited time. You may have to choose how much of your company's limited funds to spend on advertising and how much to spend on new-product research. In economics, we examine situations in which individuals choose how to do things, when to do things, and with whom to do them. Ultimately, the purpose of economics is to explain choices.

Economics
The study of how people allocate their limited resources to satisfy their unlimited wants.

Resources
Things used to produce other things to satisfy people's wants.

Wants
What people would buy if their incomes were unlimited.

MICROECONOMICS VERSUS MACROECONOMICS

Economics is typically divided into two types of analysis: **microeconomics** and **macroeconomics.**

> *Microeconomics is the part of economic analysis that studies decision making undertaken by individuals (or households) and by firms. It is like looking through a microscope to focus on the small parts of our economy.*

> *Macroeconomics is the part of economic analysis that studies the behavior of the economy as a whole. It deals with economywide phenomena such as changes in unemployment, the general price level, and national income.*

Microeconomics
The study of decision making undertaken by individuals (or households) and by firms.

Macroeconomics
The study of the behavior of the economy as a whole, including such economywide phenomena as changes in unemployment, the general price level, and national income.

Microeconomic analysis, for example, is concerned with the effects of changes in the price of gasoline relative to that of other energy sources. It examines the effects of new taxes on a specific product or industry. If price controls were reinstituted in the United States, how individual firms and consumers would react to them would be in the realm of microeconomics. The effects of higher wages brought about by an effective union strike would also be analyzed using the tools of microeconomics.

In contrast, issues such as the rate of inflation, the amount of economywide unemployment, and the yearly growth in the output of goods and services in the nation all fall into the realm of macroeconomic analysis. In other words, macroeconomics deals with **aggregates,** or totals—such as total output in an economy.

Be aware, however, of the blending of microeconomics and macroeconomics in modern economic theory. Modern economists are increasingly using microeconomic analysis—the study of decision making by individuals and by firms—as the basis of macroeconomic analysis. They do this because even though in macroeconomic analysis aggregates are being examined, those aggregates are the result of choices made by individuals and firms.

Aggregates
Total amounts or quantities; aggregate demand, for example, is total planned expenditures throughout a nation.

Go to www.econtoday.com/chap01 to access the eCommerce Info Center and explore whether it is in a consumer's self-interest to shop on the Internet. Click on "To e-shoppers."

THE ECONOMIC PERSON: RATIONAL SELF-INTEREST

Economists assume that individuals act *as if* motivated by self-interest and respond predictably to opportunities for gain. This central insight of economics was first clearly articulated by Adam Smith in 1776. Smith wrote in his most famous book, *An Inquiry into the*

Nature and Causes of the Wealth of Nations, that "it is not from the benevolence of the butcher, the brewer, or the baker that we expect our dinner, but from their regard to their own interest." Thus the typical person about whom economists make behavioral predictions is assumed to act as though motivated by self-interest. Because monetary benefits and costs of actions are often the most easily measured, economists make behavioral predictions about individuals' responses to opportunities to increase their wealth, measured in money terms. Is it possible to apply the theory of rational self-interest to explain why many couples who mutually desire to end their marriages now use online divorce services?

E-Commerce EXAMPLE

Divorce Court Moves to the Internet

At Web sites such as CompleteCase.com and LegalZoom.com, a couple desiring to amicably dissolve their marriage can provide sufficient information to obtain fully completed legal divorce papers for fees ranging from $250 to $300. For another $50 to $100, they can also obtain all the information required to file their papers with a court to end their marriage legally. These online prices are much lower than the fees of $2,000 or so that divorce lawyers typically charge simply to fill out and process the same required legal forms.

When there are no child-custody or property-division issues to iron out, it is often in a couple's self-interest to bypass traditional lawyers to obtain a divorce. Not surprisingly, the total number of do-it-yourself divorces arranged online has more than doubled each year since Web-based preparers of divorce papers began operating in the early 2000s.

For Critical Analysis
Under what types of circumstances might a self-interested marriage partner be willing to pay an attorney much more than $2,000 to handle legal issues associated with obtaining a divorce?

The Rationality Assumption

Rationality assumption
The assumption that people do not intentionally make decisions that would leave them worse off.

The **rationality assumption** of economics, simply stated, is as follows:

> *We assume that individuals do not intentionally make decisions that would leave them worse off.*

The distinction here is between what people may think—the realm of psychology and psychiatry and perhaps sociology—and what they do. Economics does *not* involve itself in analyzing individual or group thought processes. Economics looks at what people actually do in life with their limited resources. It does little good to criticize the rationality assumption by stating, "Nobody thinks that way" or "I never think that way" or "How unrealistic! That's as irrational as anyone can get!"

Take the example of driving. When you consider passing another car on a two-lane highway with oncoming traffic, you have to make very quick decisions: You must estimate the speed of the car that you are going to pass, the speed of the oncoming cars, the distance between your car and the oncoming cars, and your car's potential rate of acceleration. If we were to apply a model to your behavior, we would use the rules of calculus. In actual fact, you and most other drivers in such a situation do not actually think of using the rules of calculus, but to predict your behavior, we could make the prediction *as if* you understood the rules of calculus.

How could experiments seeking to determine whether students are willing to trade coffee mugs for chocolate bars have led some researchers to question the rationality assumption?

EXAMPLE

Using Coffee Mugs to Attack the Rationality Assumption

Some researchers have challenged the rationality assumption based on results from numerous repetitions of the following experiment: Everyone in a group of university students is asked whether they would prefer to have a coffee mug or an identically priced chocolate bar. After recording the typical response that about half of the students prefer the chocolate bar, the experimenter randomly gives half of the students coffee mugs and the other half chocolate bars. Then the experimenter invites students who did not receive a preferred item to trade with other students who also failed to receive an item they desired. Only about half the students will have received their preferred items, so on average the other half should make trades. But in experiment after experiment, fewer than 10 percent typically do. According to some researchers, this provides evidence of irrational attachment to goods—and a contradiction to the rationality assumption of economics.

John List of the University of Maryland conducted the same experiment with people who commonly trade sports memorabilia, such as baseball cards, professional players' au-

tographs, and the like. In repeated experiments with these groups, about half of those who randomly received undesired coffee mugs and chocolate bars readily engaged in trades. Perhaps because they were less likely to suspect hidden motives by the experimenter, people who commonly engage in trade were more willing to do so. Thus the coffee mug-chocolate bar trading experiments have only shown that *inexperienced* traders are less likely to readily exchange items, while experienced traders are more likely to do so. The experiments have not disproved the rationality assumption.

For Critical Analysis
Why might it be rational for someone to be hesitant to trade a coffee mug for a more desirable chocolate bar when an experimenter offers an opportunity to do so? (Hint: Imagine yourself in the described experiment, and suppose that you have never before met either the person conducting the experiment or the other students participating in the experiment.)

Responding to Incentives

If it can be assumed that individuals never intentionally make decisions that would leave them worse off, then almost by definition they will respond to changes in incentives. Indeed, much of human behavior can be explained in terms of how individuals respond to changing incentives over time.

Schoolchildren are motivated to do better by a variety of incentive systems, ranging from gold stars and certificates of achievement when they are young, to better grades with accompanying promises of a "better life" as they get older. Of course, negative incentives affect our behavior, too. Punishments and other forms of negative incentives can raise the cost of engaging in criminal activities, for instance. This is why policymakers sometimes turn to economists for help with understanding the effects that alternative forms of punishment, such as the death penalty, are likely to have on crime rates. Does the death penalty actually affect murder rates?

Policy EXAMPLE

Does Imposing the Ultimate Legal Penalty Deter Homicides?

Figure 1-1 on the following page shows that a drop in the annual number of legally sanctioned executions in the United States between the late 1950s and early 1980s was accompa-

nied by an increase in the U.S. murder rate. When the number of executions rose during the 1990s and early 2000s, the U.S. murder rate declined.

The extent to which the threat of receiving a death penalty actually contributes to lower murder rates depends on a host of other incentives, however. For instance, if more states reduce the chances of a convicted murderer receiving the death penalty, the disincentive to committing murders is reduced. In contrast, the disincentive effects of the death penalty are likely to be greater if prison conditions improve, thereby making the death penalty a much less desirable alternative punishment.

Economists have found that when these and other factors are taken into account, every *additional* legally sanctioned execution is associated with about five to six fewer homicides. Each

judicial *reduction* of a death-penalty sentence to imprisonment is associated with the occurrence of one to two additional murders. Thus both the execution rate and the rate at which death-penalty sentences are reduced to long-term imprisonment have incentive effects on people contemplating murder.

For Critical Analysis
Why do you suppose that careful economic studies of the effects of the death penalty on homicide rates take into account whether people who committed murders might have been under the influence of alcohol or drugs?

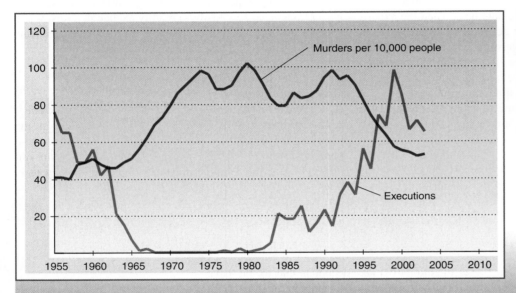

FIGURE 1-1
Murder Rates and Executions in the United States Since 1955
Since the mid-1950s, there has been an apparent negative relationship between the number of death-penalty sentences carried out and the U.S. murder rate.

Source: U.S. Department of Justice.

Defining Self-Interest

Self-interest does not always mean increasing one's wealth measured in dollars and cents. We assume that individuals seek many goals, not just increased wealth measured in monetary terms. Thus the self-interest part of our economic-person assumption includes goals relating to prestige, friendship, love, power, helping others, creating works of art, and many other matters. We can also think in terms of enlightened self-interest, whereby individuals, in the pursuit of what makes them better off, also achieve the betterment of others around them. In brief, individuals are assumed to want the right to further their goals by making decisions about how things around them are used. The head of a charitable organization will usually not turn down an additional contribution, because accepting it yields control over how those funds are used, even if it is for other people's benefit.

Thus charitable acts are not ruled out by self-interest. Giving gifts to relatives can be considered a form of charity that is nonetheless in the self-interest of the giver. But how efficient is such gift giving?

EXAMPLE

The Perceived Value of Gifts

Every holiday season, aunts, uncles, grandparents, mothers, and fathers give gifts to their college-aged loved ones. Joel Waldfogel, an economist at Yale University, surveyed several thousand college students after Christmas to find out the value of holiday gifts. He found that compact discs and outerwear (coats and jackets) had a perceived intrinsic value about equal to their actual cash equivalent. By the time he got down the list to socks, underwear, and cosmetics, the students' valu-

ation was only about 85 percent of the cash value of the gift. He found out that aunts, uncles, and grandparents gave the "worst" gifts and friends, siblings, and parents gave the "best."

For Critical Analysis
What argument could you use against the idea of substituting cash or gift certificates for physical gifts?

CONCEPTS in Brief

- Economics is a social science that involves the study of how individuals choose among alternatives to satisfy their wants, which are what people would buy if their incomes were unlimited.

- Microeconomics, the study of the decision-making processes of individuals (or households) and firms, and macroeconomics, the study of the performance of the economy as a whole, are the two main branches into which the study of economics is divided.

- In economics, we assume that people do not intentionally make decisions that will leave them worse off. This is known as the rationality assumption.

- Self-interest is not confined to material well-being but also involves any action that makes a person feel better off, such as having more friends, love, power, affection, or providing more help to others.

To test your understanding of the concepts covered in this section, go to the Online Review at www.myeconlab.com/miller.

ECONOMICS AS A SCIENCE

Economics is a social science that employs the same kinds of methods used in other sciences, such as biology, physics, and chemistry. Like these other sciences, economics uses models, or theories. Economic **models,** or **theories,** are simplified representations of the real world that we use to help us understand, explain, and predict economic phenomena in the real world. There are, of course, differences between sciences. The social sciences—especially economics—make little use of laboratory experiments in which changes in variables are studied under controlled conditions. Rather, social scientists, and especially economists, usually have to test their models, or theories, by examining what has already happened in the real world.

Models, or theories
Simplified representations of the real world used as the basis for predictions or explanations.

Models and Realism

At the outset it must be emphasized that no model in *any* science, and therefore no economic model, is complete in the sense that it captures *every* detail or interrelationship that exists. Indeed, a model, by definition, is an abstraction from reality. It is conceptually impossible to construct a perfectly complete realistic model. For example, in physics we cannot account for every molecule and its position and certainly not for every atom and subparticle. Not only is such a model impossibly expensive to build, but working with it would be impossibly complex.

The nature of scientific model building is that the model should capture only the *essential* relationships that are sufficient to analyze the particular problem or answer the particular question with which we are concerned. *An economic model cannot be faulted as unrealistic simply because it does not represent every detail of the real world.* A map of a city that shows only major streets is not necessarily unrealistic if, in fact, all you need to know is how to pass through the city using major streets. As long as a model is able to shed light on the *central* issue at hand or forces at work, it may be useful.

A map is the quintessential model. It is always a simplified representation. It is always unrealistic. But it is also useful in making predictions about the world. If the model—the map—predicts that when you take Campus Avenue to the north, you always run into the campus, that is a prediction. If our goal is to explain observed behavior, the simplicity or complexity of the model we use is irrelevant. If a simple model can explain observed behavior in repeated settings just as well as a complex one, the simple model has some value and is probably easier to use.

Assumptions

Every model, or theory, must be based on a set of assumptions. Assumptions define the set of circumstances in which our model is most likely to be applicable. When scientists predicted that sailing ships would fall off the edge of the earth, they used the *assumption* that the earth was flat. Columbus did not accept the implications of such a model because he did not accept its assumptions. He assumed that the world was round. The real-world test of his own model refuted the flat-earth model. Indirectly, then, it was a test of the assumption of the flat-earth model.

Is it possible to use our knowledge about assumptions to understand why driving directions sometimes contain very few details?

EXAMPLE

Getting Directions

Assumptions are a shorthand for reality. Imagine that you have decided to drive from your home in San Diego to downtown San Francisco. Because you have never driven this route, you decide to get directions from the local office of the American Automobile Association (AAA).

When you ask for directions, the travel planner could give you a set of detailed maps that shows each city through which you will travel—Oceanside, San Clemente, Irvine, Anaheim, Los Angeles, Bakersfield, Modesto, and so on—and then, opening each map, show you exactly how the freeway threads through each of these cities. You would get a nearly complete description of reality because the AAA travel planner will not have used many simplifying assumptions. It is more likely,

however, that the travel planner will simply say, "Get on Interstate 5 going north. Stay on it for about 500 miles. Follow the signs for San Francisco. After crossing the toll bridge, take any exit marked 'Downtown.'" By omitting all of the trivial details, the travel planner has told you all that you really need and want to know. The models you will be using in this text are similar to the simplified directions on how to drive from San Diego to San Francisco—they focus on what is relevant to the problem at hand and omit what is not.

For Critical Analysis
In what way do small talk and gossip represent the use of simplifying assumptions?

The *Ceteris Paribus* Assumption: All Other Things Being Equal. Everything in the world seems to relate in some way to everything else in the world. It would be impossible to isolate the effects of changes in one variable on another variable if we always had to worry about the many other variables that might also enter the analysis. Like other sciences, economics uses the **ceteris paribus assumption.** *Ceteris paribus* means "other things constant" or "other things equal."

Consider an example taken from economics. One of the most important determinants of how much of a particular product a family buys is how expensive that product is relative to other products. We know that in addition to relative prices, other factors influence decisions about making purchases. Some of them have to do with income, others with tastes, and yet others with custom and religious beliefs. Whatever these other factors are, we hold them constant when we look at the relationship between changes in prices and changes in how much of a given product people will purchase.

Ceteris paribus [KAY-ter-us PEAR-uh-bus] assumption
The assumption that nothing changes except the factor or factors being studied.

Deciding on the Usefulness of a Model

We generally do not attempt to determine the usefulness, or "goodness," of a model merely by evaluating how realistic its assumptions are. Rather, we consider a model "good" if it yields usable predictions and implications for the real world. In other words, can we use the model to predict what will happen in the world around us? Does the model provide useful implications of how things happen in our world?

Once we have determined that the model does predict real-world phenomena, the scientific approach to the analysis of the world around us requires that we consider evidence. Evidence is used to test the usefulness of a model. This is why we call economics an **empirical** science, *empirical* meaning that evidence (data) is looked at to see whether we are right. Economists are often engaged in empirically testing their models.

Empirical
Relying on real-world data in evaluating the usefulness of a model.

Consider two competing models for the way students act when doing complicated probability problems to choose the best gambles. One model predicts that based on the assumption of rational self-interest, students who are paid more money for better performance will perform better on average during the experiment. A competing model might be that students whose last names start with the letters *A* through *L* will do better than students with last names starting with *M* through *Z,* regardless of how much they are paid. Presumably, the model that consistently predicts more accurately is the model that we would normally choose if we wanted to understand the world. In this example, the "alphabet" model did not work well: The first letter of the last name of the students who actually did the experiment at UCLA was irrelevant in predicting how well they would perform the mathematical calculations necessary to choose the correct gambles. On average, students who received higher cash payments for better gambles did choose a higher percentage of better gambles. Thus the model based on rational self-interest predicted well.

Models of Behavior, Not Thought Processes

Take special note of the fact that economists' models do not relate to the way people *think;* they relate to the way people *act,* to what they do in life with their limited resources. Models tend to generalize human behavior. Normally, the economist does not attempt to predict how people will think about a particular topic, such as a higher price of oil products, accelerated inflation, or higher taxes. Rather, the task at hand is to predict how people will behave, which may be quite different from what they *say* they will do (much to the consternation of poll takers and market researchers). The people involved in examining thought processes are psychologists and psychiatrists, not typically economists.

If you ask people whether they like the routines in their lives, they usually say that they don't. But, then, why do so many people stick to so many routines in their day-to-day existences?

**Economics
Front and Center**

To see why thought processes regarding the pros and cons of sticking to a routine schedule ultimately amount to making choices about *actions* that are in one's self-interest, contemplate the case study,

Confronting a New Week—And Assessing Self-Interest,
on page 11.

E X A M P L E

The Costs and Benefits of Being Stuck in a Rut

Following a routine entails engaging in a customary or regular course of procedure from day to day. Routine is boring, and in random surveys, people claim to avoid it whenever possible. Nevertheless, there are benefits to routine scheduling of daily activities. People who work for a living are more likely to stick to set routines. Following similar daily and weekly routines can also allow spouses to spend more time together. Therefore, even though people consistently say in surveys that they avoid following routines, we can predict that married people with jobs are in fact likely, *ceteris paribus*, to follow relatively systematic daily schedules. In fact, studies of how people budget their time provide evidence supporting these predictions.

One *ceteris paribus* qualification concerning these predictions is extremely important. Irrespective of a person's involvement in the workplace or marital status, a key factor influencing just how much an individual tends to follow a routine is the person's income. Higher-income people have a greater ability than lower-income individuals to purchase more varied schedules in the form of evening dinners and weekend trips. Consequently, their schedules tend to include more nonroutine activities.

For Critical Analysis
What other factors, besides involvement in the workplace, marital status, and income, do you think are likely to influence whether an individual tends to follow a daily routine?

POSITIVE VERSUS NORMATIVE ECONOMICS

Economics uses *positive analysis,* a value-free approach to inquiry. No subjective or moral judgments enter into the analysis. Positive analysis relates to statements such as "If A, then B." For example, "If the price of gasoline goes up relative to all other prices, then the amount of it that people will buy will fall." That is a positive economic statement. It is a statement of *what is.* It is not a statement of anyone's value judgment or subjective feelings. For many problems analyzed in the hard sciences such as physics and chemistry, the analyses are considered to be virtually value-free. After all, how can someone's values enter into a theory of molecular behavior? But economists face a different problem. They deal with the behavior of individuals, not molecules. That makes it more difficult to stick to what we consider to be value-free or **positive economics** without reference to our feelings.

When our values are interjected into the analysis, we enter the realm of **normative economics,** involving *normative analysis.* A positive economic statement is "If the price of gas rises, people will buy less." If we add to that analysis the statement "so we should not allow the price to go up," we have entered the realm of normative economics—we have expressed a value judgment. In fact, any time you see the word *should,* you will know that values are entering into the discussion. Just remember that positive statements are concerned with *what is,* whereas normative statements are concerned with *what ought to be.*

Each of us has a desire for different things. That means that we have different values. When we express a value judgment, we are simply saying what we prefer, like, or desire. Because individual values are diverse, we expect—and indeed observe—people expressing widely varying value judgments about how the world ought to be.

A Warning: Recognize Normative Analysis

It is easy to define positive economics. It is quite another matter to catch all unlabeled normative statements in a textbook, even though an author goes over the manuscript many times before it is printed. Therefore, do not get the impression that a textbook author will be able to keep all personal values out of the book. They will slip through. In fact, the very

Positive economics
Analysis that is *strictly* limited to making either purely descriptive statements or scientific predictions; for example, "If A, then B." A statement of *what is.*

Normative economics
Analysis involving value judgments about economic policies; relates to whether things are good or bad. A statement of *what ought to be.*

choice of which topics to include in an introductory textbook involves normative economics. There is no value-free way to decide which topics to use in a textbook. The author's values ultimately make a difference when choices have to be made. But from your own standpoint, you might want to be able to recognize when you are engaging in normative as opposed to positive economic analysis. Reading this text will help equip you for that task.

CONCEPTS in Brief

- A model, or theory, uses assumptions and is by nature a simplification of the real world. The usefulness of a model can be evaluated by bringing empirical evidence to bear on its predictions.

- Models are not necessarily deficient simply because they are unrealistic and use simplifying assumptions, because every model in every science requires simplification compared to the real world.

- Most models use the *ceteris paribus* assumption that all other things are held constant, or equal.

- Positive economics is value-free and relates to statements that can be refuted, such as "If A, then B." Normative economics involves people's values, and normative statements typically contain the word *should*.

To test your understanding of the concepts covered in this section, go to the Online Review at **www.myeconlab.com/miller.**

CASE STUDY: Economics Front and Center

Confronting a New Week—And Assessing Self-Interest

Stevenson, a first-semester college sophomore, awakens to a sunny Monday morning. As the cobwebs clear from his mind, he realizes that another week is beginning. Today he will face the same schedule as last Monday, and his schedule will be the same next Monday and the Monday after that. Furthermore, his basic schedule for the rest of the week will be essentially identical to last week's schedule and to the schedule for several weeks to come. He is sick of all this routine, and the thought of getting up to confront the same routine today and the rest of the week is almost unbearable. He contemplates sleeping in, skipping classes, and taking a one- or two-day mini-vacation.

Stevenson has observed, however, that his fellow students who attend all their classes each and every day and stick to a regular study schedule typically earn the highest grades and land the best jobs. In addition, a fellow student whom he hopes may eventually become his "significant other" will be at his 9 A.M. class.

The class meeting could prove his only opportunity to suggest studying together at the library a couple of nights each week. Stevenson does not have sufficient funds on hand to suggest discussing common interests over dinner at a nice restaurant.

What principle will guide Stevenson in deciding whether to stay stuck in a rut on this particular Monday? The answer, of course, is self-interest. The issue Stevenson faces now is determining how to *act* in his own self-interest.

Points to Analyze

1. *What are the advantages and disadvantages to Stevenson of following his regular routine this week?*

2. *If Stevenson's roommate interrupts his thoughts to repay a $100 loan he had extended last week, how might this influence his decision about where his self-interest will lead him on this particular Monday?*

Applying Economics to the Problem of Childhood Obesity

Concepts Applied
- Decision Making
- Rational Self-Interest
- Incentives

A ccording to current medical standards, more than 65 percent of the U.S. population is overweight. This figure is about 20 percentage points higher than was true in 1980. More than 30 percent of the population is extremely overweight, or obese, which is more than double the 1980 figure.

It appears likely that even more people will be overweight or obese in future years because people are getting heavier at younger ages. As noted before, more than 15 percent of U.S. children and adolescents are obese today, compared to about 5 percent in the 1970s. Once body mass is gained, it is difficult to shed. Thus many of these children will probably remain obese and confront the associated health problems later when they reach maturity.

Like Most Things, Obesity Begins at Home

Children who gain weight consume more calories than they use up each day. Those who gain weight the fastest eat relatively larger amounts of high-calorie foods, such as hamburgers and french fries. They also spend more time watching television and playing video games rather than burning calories by playing in parks and participating in sports activities.

Traditionally, parents—in particular, mothers—have taken responsibility for making choices about children's food intake and the scope of their outdoor activities. Today parents are not allocating as much time to these duties as they once did. In the 1960s, fewer than half of all mothers had jobs, but today more than three-fourths of mothers work outside the home. These mothers have less time to spend keeping their children from eating too much or taking them to playgrounds for exercise. This undoubtedly helps explain why only about 8 percent of children whose mothers have never worked are obese, whereas the obesity rate rises to more than 17 percent among children whose mothers have worked full-time. Indeed, economists estimate that children with working mothers are roughly twice as likely to be obese as children with stay-at-home moms.

Schools Contribute to a Feeding Frenzy

Parents who choose to allocate more time to working than to overseeing their children entrust other caregivers—usually administrators and employees at day-care centers, preschools, and elementary and secondary schools—with providing that supervision. When it comes to planning a child's schedule, however, most caregivers have little incentive to include daily exercise that would burn off children's calories.

Furthermore, more than 25 percent of U.S. elementary schools give students access to vending machines with snacks, and 16 percent have contracts for delivery of lunch items from fast-food providers. Vending machines are present in 67 percent of middle schools and 96 percent of high schools. Furthermore, more than 25 percent of all middle schools and high schools contract with fast-food purveyors to provide a portion of the foods sold on school premises. Schools often earn a share of the profits from sales of snacks and fast-food lunches. Therefore, a number of school administrators have a strong economic incentive to encourage children to consume *more,* not fewer, high-calorie snacks and fast-food items.

Incentives, Incentives, Incentives

Incentives matter for children and adults alike. Children naturally have an incentive to consume sweet snacks and lunch on the best-tasting foods. Many children also prefer watching television or playing computer games in climate-controlled surroundings to working up a sweat on a playground. Parents increasingly have incentives to spend less time regulating their children's diets and activities. Few caregivers of children have an incentive to encourage exercise, and many have a strong financial incentive to encourage the consumption of high-calorie food and drinks.

Although children can engage in more activities while seated than in years past, they have always enjoyed eating sweets and lounging on sofas. What have changed are mainly the incentives faced by adult supervisors, who fail to encourage children to eat more healthful foods and to get more exercise. Parental choices about time allocations and school choices about daily schedules and availability of vending machines and fast-food items at schools are all economic decisions made in light of the incentives faced by parents and caregivers. Reducing the rate of child obesity, therefore, will require changes in the economic incentives confronting these adult supervisors of children.

For Critical Analysis

1. From an economic standpoint, is it possible that some parents effectively make a choice to have bigger, more expensive houses *and* overweight children? (Hint: To be able to purchase more expensive houses, parents must spend more time earning incomes and less time rearing their children.)
2. How might bans on the sale and consumption of snacks and fast foods on school grounds, which several states have begun to adopt, affect the incentives of children who have a taste for such items? (Hint: If there are convenience stores on busy streets within walking distance of schools with such bans, how are at least some students likely to respond?)

Web Resources

1. For basic facts and figures about child obesity, go to the link to the American Obesity Association's Web site at **www.econtoday.com/chap01**.
2. To learn about various ways states and the federal government are trying to combat child obesity, click on the link to the National Center for Chronic Disease Prevention and Health Promotion, available at **www.econtoday.com/chap01**.

Research Project

Health difficulties related to obesity clearly pose problems for an obese individual. From an economic standpoint, why might society at large care about a greater incidence of health problems resulting from increases in the rate of obesity among children? If one takes the stand that higher child obesity rates are a social problem, what are two possible actions that society might take to change the incentives of parents and caregivers in ways that might reverse the upward trend in child obesity? If your proposed actions require government spending, who would finance these expenditures?

SUMMARY DISCUSSION of Learning Objectives

1. **Microeconomics versus Macroeconomics:** In general, economics is the study of how individuals make choices to satisfy wants. Economics is usually divided into microeconomics, which is the study of individual decision making by households and firms, and macroeconomics, which is the study of nationwide phenomena, such as inflation and unemployment.

2. **Self-Interest in Economic Analysis:** Rational self-interest is the assumption that individuals never intentionally make decisions that would leave them worse off. Instead, they are motivated primarily by their self-interest, keeping in mind that self-interest can relate to monetary and nonmonetary objectives, such as love, prestige, and helping others.

3. **Economics as a Science:** Like other scientists, economists use models, or theories, that are simplified representations of the real world to analyze and make predictions about the real world. Economic models are never

completely realistic because by definition they are simplifications using assumptions that are not directly testable. Nevertheless, economists can subject the predictions of economic theories to empirical tests in which real-world data are used to decide whether or not to reject the predictions.

4. **Positive and Normative Economics:** Positive economics deals with *what is,* whereas normative economics deals with *what ought to be.* Positive economic statements are of the "if . . . then" variety; they are descriptive and predictive and are not related to what "should" happen. By contrast, whenever statements embodying values are made, we enter the realm of normative economics, or how individuals and groups think things ought to be.

KEY TERMS AND CONCEPTS

aggregates (3)

ceteris paribus assumption (9)

economics (3)

empirical (9)

incentives (2)

macroeconomics (3)

microeconomics (3)

models, or theories (7)

normative economics (10)

positive economics (10)

rationality assumption (4)

resources (3)

wants (3)

PROBLEMS

Answers to the odd-numbered problems appear at the back of the book.

1-1. Define economics. Explain briefly how the economic way of thinking—in terms of rational, self-interested people responding to incentives—relates to each of the following situations.

    a. A student deciding whether to purchase a textbook for a particular class

    b. Government officials seeking more funding for mass transit through higher taxes

    c. A municipality taxing hotel guests to obtain funding for a new sports stadium

1-2. Some people claim that the "economic way of thinking" does not apply to issues such as health care. Explain how economics does apply to this issue by developing a "model" of an individual's choice.

1-3. Does the phrase "unlimited wants and limited resources" apply to both a low-income household and a middle-income household? Can the same phrase be applied to a very high-income household?

1-4. In a single sentence, contrast microeconomics and macroeconomics. Next, categorize each of the following issues as either a microeconomic issue, a macroeconomic issue, or not an economic issue.

    a. The national unemployment rate

    b. The decision of a worker to work overtime or not

    c. A family's choice of having a baby

    d. The rate of growth of the money supply

    e. The national government's budget deficit

    f. A student's allocation of study time across two subjects

1-5. One of your classmates, Sally, is a hardworking student, serious about her classes, and conscientious about her grades. Sally is also involved, however, in volunteer activities and an extracurricular sport. Is Sally displaying rational behavior? Based on what you read in this chapter, construct an argument supporting the conclusion that she is.

1-6. You have 10 hours in which to study for both a French test and an economics test. Construct a model to determine your allocation of study hours. Include as assumptions the points you "gain" from an hour of study time in each subject and your desired outcome on each test.

1-7. Suppose that a model constructed in answer to Problem 1-6 indicates that the student will earn 15 percentage points on an examination in each course for every hour spent studying. Suppose that you are taking these courses and desire to earn an "A" (90 percent) in economics and merely to pass (60 percent) in French. How much time does this model indicate that you should study each subject before taking the examinations?

1-8. Suppose you followed the model you constructed in Problem 1-6. Explain how you would "grade" the model.

1-9. Which of the following predictions appears to follow from a model based on the assumption that rational, self-interested individuals respond to incentives?

a. For every 10 points Myrna must earn in order to pass her economics course and meet her graduation requirements, she will study one additional hour for her economics test next week.

b. A coin toss will best predict Leonardo's decision about whether to purchase an expensive business suit or an inexpensive casual outfit to wear next week when he interviews for a high-paying job he is seeking.

c. Celeste, who uses earnings from her regularly scheduled hours of part-time work to pay for her room and board at college, will decide to buy a newly released DVD this week only if she is able to work two additional hours.

1-10. Consider two models for estimating, in advance of an election, the shares of votes that will go to rival candidates. According to one model, pollsters' surveys of a randomly chosen set of registered voters before an election can be used to forecast the percentage of votes that each candidate will receive. This first model relies on the assumption that unpaid survey respondents will give truthful responses about how they will vote and that they will actually cast a ballot in the election. The other model uses prices of financial assets (legally binding I.O.U.s) issued by the Iowa Electronic Market, operated by the University of Iowa, to predict electoral outcomes. The final payments received by owners of these assets, which can be bought or sold during the weeks and days preceding an election, depend on the shares of votes the candidates actually end up receiving. This second model assumes that owners of these assets wish to earn the highest possible returns, and it

indicates that the market prices of these assets provide an indication of the percentage of votes that each candidate will actually receive on the day of the election.

a. Which of these two models for forecasting electoral results is more firmly based on the rationality assumption of economics?

b. How would an economist evaluate which is the better model for forecasting electoral outcomes?

1-11. Write a sentence contrasting positive and normative economic analysis.

1-12. Based on your answer to Problem 1-11, categorize each of the following conclusions as being the result of positive analysis or normative analysis.

a. A higher minimum wage will reduce employment opportunities for minimum wage workers.

b. Increasing the earnings of minimum wage employees is desirable, and raising the minimum wage is the best way to accomplish this.

c. Everyone should enjoy open access to health care.

d. Heath care subsidies will increase the consumption of health care.

1-13. Consider the following statements, based on a positive economic analysis that assumes that all other things remain constant. For each, list one other thing that might change and thus offset the outcome stated.

a. Increased demand for laptop computers will drive up their price.

b. Falling gasoline prices will result in additional vacation travel.

c. A reduction of income tax rates will result in more people working.

1-14. Alan Greenspan, chairman of the U.S. Federal Reserve, referred to the high stock market prices of the late 1990s as a result of "irrational exuberance." Counter this statement by considering the rationality of stock market investors.

ECONOMICS ON THE NET

The Usefulness of Studying Economics This application helps you see how accomplished people benefited from their study of economics. It also explores ways in which these people feel others of all walks of life can gain from learning more about the economics field.

Title: How Taking an Economics Course Can Lead to Becoming an Economist

Navigation: Go to www.econtoday.com/chap01 to visit the Federal Reserve Bank of Minneapolis home page. To access economists in *The Region* on their student experiences and the need for economic literacy, under Publications, click on *The Region*. Select the *Index by Issues*. Click on *December 1998,* and select the last article of the issue, Economists in *The Region* on Their Student Experiences and the Need for Economic Literacy.

Application Read the interviews of the six economists, and answer the following questions.

1. Based on your reading, what economists do you think other economists regard as influential? What educational institutions do you think are the most influential in economics?

2. Which economists do you think were attracted to microeconomics and which to macroeconomics?

For Group Study and Analysis Divide the class into three groups, and assign the groups the Blinder, Yellen, and Rivlin interviews. Have each group use the content of its assigned interview to develop a statement explaining why the study of economics is important, regardless of a student's chosen major.

Media
Resources

If your exam were tomorrow, would you be ready? For each chapter, MyEconLab Practice Tests and Study Plans pinpoint which sections you have mastered and which ones you need to study. That way, you are more efficient with your study time, and you are better prepared for your exams.

Here is how it works:

1. Register and log in to www.myeconlab.com/miller.
2. Click on "Take a Test" and select Test A for this chapter.
3. Take the diagnostic test and MyEconLab will grade it automatically and create a personalized Study Plan, so you see which sections of the chapter you should study further.
4. The Study Plan will serve up additional practice problems and tutorials to help you master the specific areas where you need to focus. By practicing online, you can track your progress in the Study Plan.
5. After you have mastered the sections, "Take a Test" and select Test B for this chapter. Take the test, and see how you do!

In addition to Practice Tests and your personalized Study Plan, you'll find the following media resources in MyEcon-Lab:

1. *Graphs in Motion* animation of Figure A-8.
2. Videos featuring the author, Roger LeRoy Miller, on the following subjects:
   ● The Difference Between Microeconomics and Macroeconomics
   ● Rational Self-Interest and the Rationality Assumption
   ● Positive versus Normative Economics
3. Links to the Web sites cited in the marginal Internet Resources, Issues and Applications feature, and Economics on the Net activity.
4. Audio clips of all key terms, additional practice problems, and a PDF version of the material from the print Study Guide.
5. eThemes of the Times, which is a New York Times article to help you understand the real-world applications of what you are learning.

   www.myeconlab.com/miller.

Get Ahead of the Curve

Reading and Working with Graphs

A graph is a visual representation of the relationship between variables. In this appendix, we'll stick to just two variables: an **independent variable,** which can change in value freely, and a **dependent variable,** which changes only as a result of changes in the value of the independent variable. For example, if nothing else is changing in your life, your weight depends on your intake of calories. The independent variable is caloric intake and the dependent variable is weight.

A table is a list of numerical values showing the relationship between two (or more) variables. Any table can be converted into a graph, which is a visual representation of that list. Once you understand how a table can be converted to a graph, you will understand what graphs are and how to construct and use them.

Consider a practical example. A conservationist may try to convince you that driving at lower highway speeds will help you conserve gas. Table A-1 shows the relationship between speed—the independent variable—and the distance you can go on a gallon of gas at that speed—the dependent variable. This table does show a pattern. As the data in the first column get larger in value, the data in the second column get smaller.

Now let's take a look at the different ways in which variables can be related.

DIRECT AND INVERSE RELATIONSHIPS

Two variables can be related in different ways, some simple, others more complex. For example, a person's weight and height are often related. If we measured the height and weight of thousands of people, we would surely find that taller people tend to weigh more than shorter people. That is, we would discover that there is a **direct relationship** between height and weight. By this we simply mean that an *increase* in one variable is usually associated with an *increase* in the related variable. This can easily be seen in panel (a) of Figure A-1.

Let's look at another simple way in which two variables can be related. Much evidence indicates that as the price of a specific commodity rises, the amount purchased decreases—there is an **inverse relationship** between the variable's price per unit and

Independent variable
A variable whose value is determined independently of, or outside, the equation under study.

Dependent variable
A variable whose value changes according to changes in the value of one or more independent variables.

TABLE A-1
Gas Mileage as a Function of Driving Speed

Miles per Hour	Miles per Gallon
45	25
50	24
55	23
60	21
65	19
70	16
75	13

Direct relationship
A relationship between two variables that is positive, meaning that an increase in one variable is associated with an increase in the other and a decrease in one variable is associated with a decrease in the other.

Inverse relationship
A relationship between two variables that is negative, meaning that an increase in one variable is associated with a decrease in the other and a decrease in one variable is associated with an increase in the other.

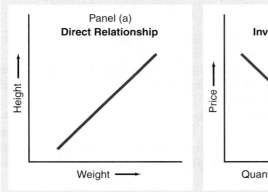
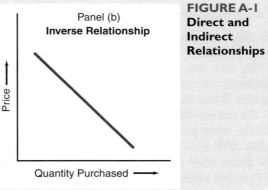

FIGURE A-1
Direct and Indirect Relationships

Panel (a) — Direct Relationship — Height / Weight

Panel (b) — Inverse Relationship — Price / Quantity Purchased

FIGURE A-2
Horizontal Number Line

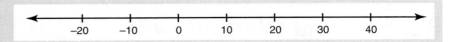

Number line
A line that can be divided into segments of equal length, each associated with a number.

FIGURE A-3
Vertical Number Line

quantity purchased. Such a relationship would indicate that for higher and higher prices, smaller and smaller quantities would be purchased. We see this relationship in panel (b) of Figure A-1 on the previous page.

CONSTRUCTING A GRAPH

Let us now examine how to construct a graph to illustrate a relationship between two variables.

A Number Line

The first step is to become familiar with what is called a **number line.** One is shown in Figure A-2. There are two things that you should know about it.

1. The points on the line divide the line into equal segments.
2. The numbers associated with the points on the line increase in value from left to right; saying it the other way around, the numbers decrease in value from right to left. However you say it, what you're describing is formally called an *ordered set of points*.

On the number line, we have shown the line segments—that is, the distance from 0 to 10 or the distance between 30 and 40. They all appear to be equal and, indeed, are each equal to $\frac{1}{2}$ inch. When we use a distance to represent a quantity, such as barrels of oil, graphically, we are *scaling* the number line. In the example shown, the distance between 0 and 10 might represent 10 barrels of oil, or the distance from 0 to 40 might represent 40 barrels. Of course, the scale may differ on different number lines. For example, a distance of 1 inch could represent 10 units on one number line but 5,000 units on another. Notice that on our number line, points to the left of 0 correspond to negative numbers and points to the right of 0 correspond to positive numbers.

Of course, we can also construct a vertical number line. Consider the one in Figure A-3. As we move up this vertical number line, the numbers increase in value; conversely, as we descend, they decrease in value. Below 0 the numbers are negative, and above 0 the numbers are positive. And as on the horizontal number line, all the line segments are equal. This line is divided into segments such that the distance between -2 and -1 is the same as the distance between 0 and 1.

Combining Vertical and Horizontal Number Lines

By drawing the horizontal and vertical lines on the same sheet of paper, we are able to express the relationships between variables graphically. We do this in Figure A-4.

We draw them (1) so that they intersect at each other's 0 point and (2) so that they are perpendicular to each other. The result is a set of coordinate axes, where each line is called an *axis*. When we have two axes, they span a *plane*.

For one number line, you need only one number to specify any point on the line; equivalently, when you see a point on the line, you know that it represents one number or one value. With a coordinate value system, you need two numbers to specify a single point in the plane; when you see a single point on a graph, you know that it represents two numbers or two values.

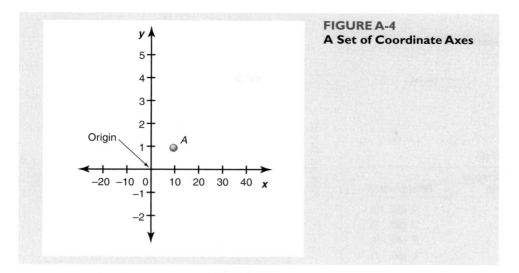

FIGURE A-4
A Set of Coordinate Axes

The basic things that you should know about a coordinate number system are that the vertical number line is referred to as the **y axis,** the horizontal number line is referred to as the **x axis,** and the point of intersection of the two lines is referred to as the **origin.**

Any point such as *A* in Figure A-4 represents two numbers—a value of *x* and a value of *y*. But we know more than that: We also know that point *A* represents a positive value of *y* because it is above the *x* axis, and we know that it represents a positive value of *x* because it is to the right of the *y* axis.

Point *A* represents a "paired observation" of the variables *x* and *y*; in particular, in Figure A-4, *A* represents an observation of the pair of values *x* = 10 and *y* = 1. Every point in the coordinate system corresponds to a paired observation of *x* and *y*, which can be simply written (*x*, *y*)—the *x* value is always specified first and then the *y* value. When we give the values associated with the position of point *A* in the coordinate number system, we are in effect giving the coordinates of that point. *A*'s coordinates are *x* = 10, *y* = 1, or (10, 1).

y axis
The vertical axis in a graph.

x axis
The horizontal axis in a graph.

Origin
The intersection of the *y* axis and the *x* axis in a graph.

GRAPHING NUMBERS IN A TABLE

Consider Table A-2. Column 1 shows different prices for T-shirts, and column 2 gives the number of T-shirts purchased per week at these prices. Notice the pattern of these numbers. As the price of T-shirts falls, the number of T-shirts purchased per week increases. Therefore, an inverse relationship exists between these two variables, and as soon as we represent it on a graph, you will be able to see the relationship. We can graph this relationship using a coordinate number system—a vertical and horizontal number line for each of these two variables. Such a graph is shown in panel (b) of Figure A-5 on the next page.

In economics, it is conventional to put dollar values on the *y* axis. We therefore construct a vertical number line for price and a horizontal number line, the *x* axis, for quantity of T-shirts purchased per week. The resulting coordinate system allows the plotting of each of the paired observation points; in panel (a), we repeat Table A-2, with a column added expressing these points in paired-data (*x*, *y*) form. For example, point *J* is the paired observation (30, 9). It indicates that when the price of a T-shirt is $9, 30 will be purchased per week.

If it were possible to sell parts of a T-shirt ($\frac{1}{2}$ or $\frac{1}{20}$ of a shirt), we would have observations at every possible price. That is, we would be able to connect our paired observations, represented as lettered points. Let's assume that we can make T-shirts perfectly divisible so that the

TABLE A-2
T-Shirts Purchased

(1) Price of T-Shirts	(2) Number of T-Shirts Purchased per Week
$10	20
9	30
8	40
7	50
6	60
5	70

FIGURE A-5
Graphing the Relationship Between T-Shirts Purchased and Price

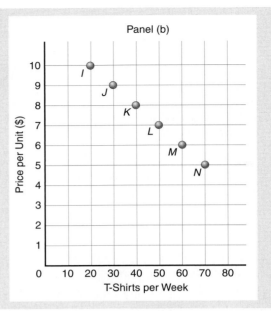

Panel (b)

Panel (a)

Price per T-Shirt	T-Shirts Purchased per Week	Point on Graph
$10	20	I (20, 10)
9	30	J (30, 9)
8	40	K (40, 8)
7	50	L (50, 7)
6	60	M (60, 6)
5	70	N (70, 5)

linear relationship shown in Figure A-5 also holds for fractions of dollars and T-shirts. We would then have a line that connects these points, as shown in the graph in Figure A-6.

In short, we have now represented the data from the table in the form of a graph. Note that an inverse relationship between two variables shows up on a graph as a line or curve that slopes *downward* from left to right. (You might as well get used to the idea that economists call a straight line a "curve" even though it may not curve at all. Much of economists' data turn out to be curves, so they refer to everything represented graphically, even straight lines, as curves.)

FIGURE A-6
Connecting the Observation Points

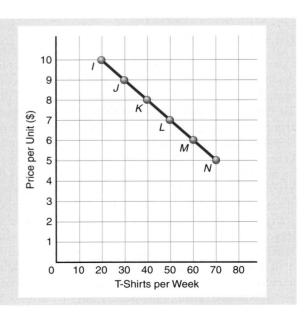

THE SLOPE OF A LINE (A LINEAR CURVE)

An important property of a curve represented on a graph is its *slope*. Consider Figure A-7, which represents the quantities of shoes per week that a seller is willing to offer at different prices. Note that in panel (a) of Figure A-7, as in Figure A-5, we have expressed the coordinates of the points in parentheses in paired-data form.

The **slope** of a line is defined as the change in the *y* values divided by the corresponding change in the *x* values as we move along the line. Let's move from point *E* to point *D* in panel (b) of Figure A-7. As we move, we note that the change in the *y* values, which is the change in price, is +$20, because we have moved from a price of $20 to a price of $40 per pair. As we move from *E* to *D*, the change in the *x* values is +80; the number of pairs of shoes willingly offered per week rises from 80 to 160 pairs. The slope calculated as a change in the *y* values divided by the change in the *x* values is therefore

> **Slope**
> The change in the *y* value divided by the corresponding change in the *x* value of a curve; the "incline" of the curve.

$$\frac{20}{80} = \frac{1}{4}$$

It may be helpful for you to think of slope as a "rise" (movement in the vertical direction) over a "run" (movement in the horizontal direction). We show this abstractly in Figure A-8 (page 22). The slope is the amount of rise divided by the amount of run. In the example in Figure A-8, and of course in Figure A-7, the amount of rise is positive and so is the amount of run. That's because it's a direct relationship. We show an inverse relationship in Figure A-9 (page 22). The slope is still equal to the rise divided by the run, but in this case the rise and the run have opposite signs because the curve slopes downward. That means that the slope is negative and that we are dealing with an inverse relationship.

Now let's calculate the slope for a different part of the curve in panel (b) of Figure A-7. We will find the slope as we move from point *B* to point *A*. Again, we note that the slope, or rise over run, from *B* to *A* equals

$$\frac{20}{80} = \frac{1}{4}$$

A specific property of a straight line is that its slope is the same between any two points; in other words, the slope is constant at all points on a straight line in a graph.

FIGURE A-7
A Positively Sloped Curve

Panel (a)

Price per Pair	Pairs of Shoes Offered per Week	Point on Graph
$100	400	A (400,100)
80	320	B (320, 80)
60	240	C (240, 60)
40	160	D (160, 40)
20	80	E (80, 20)

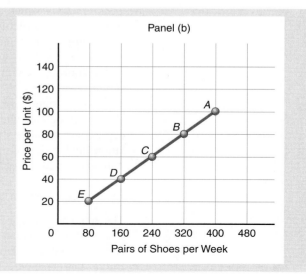

FIGURE A-8
Figuring Positive Slope

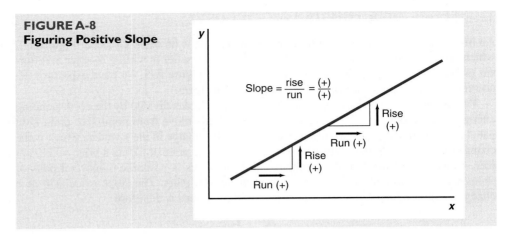

FIGURE A-9
Figuring Negative Slope

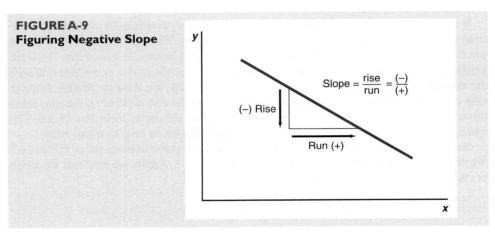

We conclude that for our example in Figure A-7 on the previous page, the relationship between the price of a pair of shoes and the number of pairs of shoes willingly offered per week is *linear,* which simply means "in a straight line," and our calculations indicate a constant slope. Moreover, we calculate a direct relationship between these two variables, which turns out to be an upward-sloping (from left to right) curve. Upward-sloping curves have positive slopes—in this case, the slope is $+\frac{1}{4}$.

We know that an inverse relationship between two variables shows up as a downward-sloping curve—rise over run will be negative because the rise and run have opposite signs, as shown in Figure A-9. When we see a negative slope, we know that increases in one variable are associated with decreases in the other. Therefore, we say that downward-sloping curves have negative slopes. Can you verify that the slope of the graph representing the relationship between T-shirt prices and the quantity of T-shirts purchased per week in Figure A-6 on page 20 is $-\frac{1}{10}$?

Slopes of Nonlinear Curves

The graph presented in Figure A-10 indicates a *nonlinear* relationship between two variables, total profits and output per unit of time. Inspection of this graph indicates that at first, increases in output lead to increases in total profits; that is, total profits rise as output increases. But beyond some output level, further increases in output cause decreases in total profits.

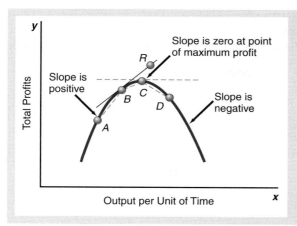

FIGURE A-10
The Slope of a Nonlinear Curve

Can you see how this curve rises at first, reaches a peak at point *C*, and then falls? This curve relating total profits to output levels appears mountain-shaped.

Considering that this curve is nonlinear (it is obviously not a straight line), should we expect a constant slope when we compute changes in *y* divided by corresponding changes in *x* in moving from one point to another? A quick inspection, even without specific numbers, should lead us to conclude that the slopes of lines joining different points in this curve, such as between *A* and *B*, *B* and *C*, or *C* and *D*, will *not* be the same. The curve slopes upward (in a positive direction) for some values and downward (in a negative direction) for other values. In fact, the slope of the line between any two points on this curve will be different from the slope of the line between any two other points. Each slope will be different as we move along the curve.

Instead of using a line between two points to discuss slope, mathematicians and economists prefer to discuss the slope *at a particular point*. The slope at a point on the curve, such as point *B* in the graph in Figure A-10, is the slope of a line *tangent* to that point. A tangent line is a straight line that touches a curve at only one point. For example, it might be helpful to think of the tangent at *B* as the straight line that just "kisses" the curve at point *B*.

To calculate the slope of a tangent line, you need to have some additional information besides the two values of the point of tangency. For example, in Figure A-10, if we knew that the point *R* also lay on the tangent line and we knew the two values of that point, we could calculate the slope of the tangent line. We could calculate rise over run between points *B* and *R*, and the result would be the slope of the line tangent to the one point *B* on the curve.

A P P E N D I X   S U M M A R Y

1. Direct relationships involve a dependent variable changing in the same direction as the change in the independent variable.

2. Inverse relationships involve the dependent variable changing in the opposite direction of the change in the independent variable.

3. When we draw a graph showing the relationship between two economic variables, we are holding all other things constant (the Latin term for which is *ceteris paribus*).

4. We obtain a set of coordinates by putting vertical and horizontal number lines together. The vertical line is called the *y* axis; the horizontal line, the *x* axis.

5. The slope of any linear (straight-line) curve is the change in the *y* values divided by the corresponding change in

the x values as we move along the line. Otherwise stated, the slope is calculated as the amount of rise over the amount of run, where rise is movement in the vertical direction and run is movement in the horizontal direction.

6. The slope of a nonlinear curve changes; it is positive when the curve is rising and negative when the curve is falling. At a maximum or minimum point, the slope of the nonlinear curve is zero.

KEY TERMS AND CONCEPTS

dependent variable (17)

direct relationship (17)

independent variable (17)

inverse relationship (17)

number line (18)

origin (19)

slope (21)

x axis (19)

y axis (19)

PROBLEMS

Answers to the odd-numbered problems appear at the back of the book.

A-1. Explain which is the independent variable and which is the dependent variable for each of the following examples.

   a. Once you determine the price of a notebook at the college bookstore, you will decide how many notebooks to buy.

   b. You will decide how many credit hours to register for this semester once the university tells you how many work-study hours you will be assigned.

   c. You anticipate earning a higher grade on your next economics exam grade because you studied more hours in the weeks preceding the exam.

A-2. For each of the following items, state whether a direct or an inverse relationship is likely to exist.

   a. The number of hours you study for an exam and your exam score

   b. The price of pizza and the quantity purchased

   c. The number of games the university basketball team won *last* year and the number of season tickets sold *this* year

A-3. Review Figure A-4, and then state whether each of the following paired observations is on, above, or below the x axis and on, to the left of, or to the right of the y axis.

   a. $(-10, 4)$

   b. $(20, -2)$

   c. $(10, 0)$

A-4. State whether each of the following functions is linear or nonlinear.

   a. $y = 5x$

   b. $y = 5x^2$

   c. $y = 3 + x$

   d. $y = -3x$

A-5. Given the function $y = 5x$, complete the following schedule and plot the curve.

y	x
	-4
	-2
	0
	2
	4

A-6. Given the function $y = 5x^2$, complete the following schedule and plot the curve.

y	x
	-4
	-2
	0
	2
	4

A-7. Calculate the slope of the function you graphed in Problem A-5.

A-8. Indicate at each ordered pair whether the slope of the curve you plotted in Problem A-6 is positive, negative, or zero.

A-9. State whether each of the following functions implies a positive or negative relationship between x and y.

   a. $y = 5x$

   b. $y = 3 + x$

   c. $y = -3x$

Chapter 2
Scarcity and the World of Trade-Offs

Since the early 2000s, law enforcement officials have noticed three disturbing trends concerning bank robberies. First, an increasing number of bank robberies are committed by women. Second, bank robberies in general are on an upswing—thieves of both genders are robbing more banks. Third, an increasing percentage of bank robbers are never caught. All three trends are linked to a common factor: Since the war on terrorism began in 2001, a greater share of the nation's law enforcement resources has been devoted to antiterrorism efforts. This has left fewer resources available to combat lesser crimes, such as bank robberies. In this chapter, you will learn about the fundamental trade-offs that society faces in the allocation of *all* scarce resources, including those relating to law enforcement.

LEARNING OBJECTIVES

After reading this chapter, you should be able to:

1. Evaluate whether even affluent people face the problem of scarcity
2. Understand why economics considers individuals' "wants" but not their "needs"
3. Explain why the scarcity problem induces individuals to consider opportunity costs
4. Discuss why obtaining increasing increments of any particular good typically entails giving up more and more units of other goods
5. Explain why society faces a trade-off between consumption goods and capital goods
6. Distinguish between absolute and comparative advantage

Media Resources

Refer to the end of the chapter for a full listing of the multimedia learning materials available in MyEconLab.

. . . a typical individual who commutes by automobile to and from a job in the 68 largest U.S. cities spends the equivalent of almost two more full workdays on the road each year, compared with a decade ago? A key reason is that the average amount of time that commuters spend at a complete stop in traffic each year has increased from just over 34 hours ten years ago to more than 50 hours today

The additional hours that people devote to commuting every year could otherwise be allocated to leisure activities with family or friends or perhaps simply staying in bed a few more minutes each morning. For many people, some of the hours stuck on highways and city streets could otherwise be spent on the job, where the average U.S. worker currently earns about $16 per hour. Every hour spent sitting in traffic imposes a cost on a commuter because time, like all other resources, is scarce.

SCARCITY

Scarcity
A situation in which the ingredients for producing the things that people desire are insufficient to satisfy all wants.

Whenever individuals or communities cannot obtain everything they desire simultaneously, they must make choices. Choices occur because of *scarcity*. **Scarcity** is the most basic concept in all of economics. Scarcity means that we do not ever have enough of everything, including time, to satisfy our *every* desire. Scarcity exists because human wants always exceed what can be produced with the limited resources and time that nature makes available.

What Scarcity Is Not

Scarcity is not a shortage. After a hurricane hits and cuts off supplies to a community, TV newscasts often show people standing in line to get minimum amounts of cooking fuel and food. A news commentator might say that the line is caused by the "scarcity" of these products. But cooking fuel and food are always scarce—we cannot obtain all that we want at a zero price. Therefore, do not confuse the concept of scarcity, which is general and all-encompassing, with the concept of shortages as evidenced by people waiting in line to obtain a particular product.

Scarcity is not the same thing as poverty. Scarcity occurs among the poor and among the rich. Even the richest person on earth faces scarcity because available time is limited. Low income levels do not create more scarcity. High income levels do not create less scarcity.

Scarcity is a fact of life, like gravity. And just as physicists did not invent gravity, economists did not invent scarcity—it existed well before the first economist ever lived. It has existed at all times in the past and will exist at all times in the future.

Scarcity and Resources

Production
Any activity that results in the conversion of resources into products that can be used in consumption.

Scarcity exists because resources are insufficient to satisfy our every desire. Resources are the inputs used in the production of the things that we want. **Production** can be defined as virtually any activity that results in the conversion of resources into products that can be used in consumption. Production includes delivering things from one part of the country to another. It includes taking ice from an ice tray to put it in your soft-drink glass. The resources used in production are called *factors of production,* and some economists use the terms *resources* and *factors of production* interchangeably. The total quantity of all resources that an economy has at any one time determines what that economy can produce.

Factors of production can be classified in many ways. Here is one such classification:

1. *Land.* **Land** encompasses all the nonhuman gifts of nature, including timber, water, fish, minerals, and the original fertility of land. It is often called the *natural resource.*
2. *Labor.* **Labor** is the *human resource,* which includes all productive contributions made by individuals who work, such as Web page designers, ballet dancers, and professional football players.
3. *Physical capital.* **Physical capital** consists of the factories and equipment used in production. It also includes improvements to natural resources, such as irrigation ditches.
4. *Human capital.* **Human capital** is the economic characterization of the education and training of workers. How much the nation produces depends not only on how many hours people work but also on how productive they are, and that in turn depends in part on education and training. To become more educated, individuals have to devote time and resources, just as a business has to devote resources if it wants to increase its physical capital. Whenever a worker's skills increase, human capital has been improved.
5. *Entrepreneurship.* The factor of production known as **entrepreneurship** (actually a subdivision of labor) involves human resources that perform the functions of organizing, managing, and assembling the other factors of production to create and operate business ventures. Entrepreneurship also encompasses taking risks that involve the possibility of losing large sums of wealth on new ventures. It includes new methods of doing common things and generally experimenting with any type of new thinking that could lead to making more money income. Without entrepreneurship, virtually no business organization could operate.

Land
The natural resources that are available from nature. Land as a resource includes location, original fertility and mineral deposits, topography, climate, water, and vegetation.

Labor
Productive contributions of humans who work, involving both mental and physical activities.

Physical capital
All manufactured resources, including buildings, equipment, machines, and improvements to land that is used for production.

Human capital
The accumulated training and education of workers.

Entrepreneurship
The factor of production involving human resources that perform the functions of raising capital, organizing, managing, assembling other factors of production, and making basic business policy decisions. The entrepreneur is a risk taker.

Goods versus Economic Goods

Goods are defined as all things from which individuals derive satisfaction or happiness. Goods therefore include air to breathe and the beauty of a sunset as well as food, cars, and MP3 players.

Economic goods are a subset of all goods—they are scarce goods about which we must constantly make decisions regarding their best use. By definition, the desired quantity of an economic good exceeds the amount that is directly available at a zero price. Virtually every example we use in economics concerns economic goods—cars, DVD players, computers, socks, baseball bats, and corn. Weeds are a good example of *bads*—goods for which the desired quantity is much *less* than what nature provides at a zero price.

Sometimes you will see references to "goods and services." **Services** are tasks that are performed for someone else, such as laundry, Internet access, hospital care, restaurant meal preparation, car polishing, psychological counseling, and teaching. One way of looking at services is thinking of them as *intangible goods.*

Goods
All things from which individuals derive satisfaction or happiness.

Economic goods
Goods that are scarce, for which the quantity demanded exceeds the quantity supplied at a zero price.

Services
Mental or physical labor or help purchased by consumers. Examples are the assistance of physicians, lawyers, dentists, repair personnel, housecleaners, educators, retailers, and wholesalers; things purchased or used by consumers that do not have physical characteristics.

WANTS AND NEEDS

Wants are not the same as needs. Indeed, from the economist's point of view, the term *needs* is objectively undefinable. When someone says, "I need some new clothes," there is no way to know whether that person is stating a vague wish, a want, or a lifesaving necessity. If the individual making the statement were dying of exposure in a northern country during the winter, we might argue that indeed the person does need clothes—perhaps not new ones, but at least some articles of warm clothing. Typically, however, the term *need* is used very casually in conversation. What people mean, usually, is that they desire something that they do not currently have.

Humans have unlimited wants. Just imagine if every single material want that you might have were satisfied. You can have all of the clothes, cars, houses, DVDs, yachts, and other things that you want. Does that mean that nothing else could add to your total level of happiness? Probably not, because you might think of new goods and services that you could obtain, particularly as they came to market. You would also still be lacking in fulfilling all of your wants for compassion, friendship, love, affection, prestige, musical abilities, sports abilities, and so on.

In reality, every individual has competing wants but cannot satisfy all of them, given limited resources. This is the reality of scarcity. Each person must therefore make choices. Whenever a choice is made to produce or buy something, something else that is also desired is not produced or not purchased. In other words, in a world of scarcity, every want that ends up being satisfied causes one or more other wants to remain unsatisfied or to be forfeited.

CONCEPTS in Brief

- Scarcity exists because human wants always exceed what can be produced with the limited resources and time that nature makes available.

- We use scarce resources, such as land, labor, physical and human capital, and entrepreneurship, to produce economic goods—goods that are desired but are not directly obtainable from nature to the extent demanded or desired at a zero price.

- Wants are unlimited; they include all material desires and all nonmaterial desires, such as love, affection, power, and prestige.

- The concept of need is difficult to define objectively for every person; consequently, we simply consider every person's wants to be unlimited. In a world of scarcity, satisfaction of one want necessarily means nonsatisfaction of one or more other wants.

To test your understanding of the concepts covered in this section, go to the Online Review at www.myeconlab.com/miller.

SCARCITY, CHOICE, AND OPPORTUNITY COST

The natural fact of scarcity implies that we must make choices. One of the most important results of this fact is that every choice made (or not made, for that matter) means that some opportunity had to be sacrificed. Every choice involves giving up an opportunity to produce or consume something else.

Consider a practical example. Every choice you make to study one more hour of economics requires that you give up the opportunity to engage in any of the following activities: study more of another subject, listen to music, sleep, browse at a local store, read a novel, or work out at the gym. The most highly valued of these opportunities is forgone also if you choose to study economics an additional hour.

Because there were so many alternatives from which to choose, how could you determine the value of what you gave up to engage in that extra hour of studying economics? First of all, no one else can tell you the answer because only *you* can put a value on the alternatives forgone. Only you know the value of another hour of sleep or of an hour looking for the latest DVDs. That means that only you can determine the highest-valued, next-best alternative that you had to sacrifice in order to study economics one more hour. Only you can determine the value of the next-best alternative.

For instance, when faced with alternative methods of moving from their parents' homes to their college dormitories, not all students will view the same methods as the next-best alternative. How has this given entrepreneurs an opportunity to profit from providing online mechanisms for arranging college moves?

E-Commerce EXAMPLE

Making the Big Move to College a Next-Best Alternative

If you live on campus, think back to your first days of college. Recall stuffing many of your personal items into your parent's car, perhaps a luggage-rack container on top of the car, and maybe even a trailer behind the car. In addition, remember all the efforts entailed in finding a parking place within walking distance of the dormitory and carrying everything to your room.

Now consider an alternative way to move into a college dorm room that is available to today's students: purchasing goods and services provided by AllDorm.com. At this Web site, which offers 6,000 common dorm room items, new students can buy items and arrange for advance delivery directly to their rooms.

For many students, moving numerous personal items from their home is the next-best alternative to paying AllDorm.com to handle delivery of desired items ahead of time. This is why AllDorm.com, which was founded by four college sophomores, now earns revenues of $25 million per year.

For Critical Analysis
Why might a student view purchasing the goods and services offered by AllDorm.com as the next-best alternative to moving all of her personal items to campus on her own?

The value of the next-best alternative is called **opportunity cost.** The opportunity cost of any action is the value of what is given up—the next-highest-ranked alternative—because a choice was made. When you study one more hour, there may be many alternatives available for the use of that hour, but assume that you can do only one other thing in that hour—your next-highest-ranked alternative. What is important is the choice that you would have made if you hadn't studied one more hour. Your opportunity cost is the *next-highest-ranked* alternative, not *all* alternatives.

Opportunity cost
The highest-valued, next-best alternative that must be sacrificed to obtain something or to satisfy a want.

In economics, cost is always a forgone opportunity.

One way to think about opportunity cost is to understand that when you choose to do something, you lose something else. What you lose is being able to engage in your next-highest-valued alternative. The cost of your choice is what you lose, which is by definition your next-highest-valued alternative. This is your opportunity cost.

What do you think happens to the amount of time school bands play at basketball games when schools can receive large payments for short advertisements piped through their public address (PA) systems?

EXAMPLE

Why Today's College Bands Get Less Playing Time

With 25 seconds left in the college basketball game, the home team has scored and now trails by only one point. Following theft of the in-bound pass by the visiting team, the home team calls time out. The home pep band's director is preparing to lead a rousing chorus of the school sports fight song to get the crowd behind the team as it prepares to try to score a last-

second basket to win the game. But then the band director hears over her headset the words, "Sorry, but we've got one more commercial to do before the end of the game, so you can't play now." As the scoreboard flashes the name of a local bank, the gymnasium's 110-decibel sound system blares out a prerecorded voice describing the bank's low-interest loans and top-notch customer service. The commercial ends just before play resumes. Then a subdued crowd and the silent pep band watch the star player buckle under pressure and dribble the ball out of bounds just as time expires.

Across the nation, college athletic departments have discovered that each minute of time in front of crowds of thousands of fans can be worth as much as $15,000 to advertisers. When the opportunity cost of each minute of time taken by school songs played by pep bands amounts to thousands of dollars, it is little surprise that college bands are getting less playing time at sporting events. Many bands now fight to work

in 15-second snippets of school songs called "shorts" just before play resumes following timeouts that now are commonly allocated fully to commercial messages. At a number of colleges, however, even 15-second slots of time can command advertising revenues. Consequently, pep bands' "shorts" are also being heard less frequently at many college games.

For Critical Analysis
If the average minute of time at a college game can generate $10,000 in advertising revenues, what is the opportunity cost of a 15-second pep-band "short"?

THE WORLD OF TRADE-OFFS

Whenever you engage in any activity using any resource, even time, you are *trading off* the use of that resource for one or more alternative uses. The value of the trade-off is represented by the opportunity cost. The opportunity cost of studying economics has already been mentioned—it is the amount of the next-best alternative. When you think of any alternative, you are thinking of trade-offs.

Let's consider a hypothetical example of a trade-off between the results of spending time studying economics and history. For the sake of this argument, we will assume that additional time studying either economics or history will lead to a higher grade in the subject studied more. One of the best ways to examine this trade-off is with a graph. (If you would like a refresher on graphical techniques, study Appendix A at the end of Chapter 1 before going on.)

Graphical Analysis

In Figure 2-1, the expected grade in history is measured on the vertical axis of the graph, and the expected grade in economics is measured on the horizontal axis. We simplify the world and assume that you have a maximum of 12 hours per week to spend studying these two subjects and that if you spend all 12 hours on economics, you will get an A in the course. You will, however, fail history. Conversely, if you spend all of your 12 hours studying history, you will get an A in that subject, but you will flunk economics. Here the trade-off is a special case: one to one. A one-to-one trade-off means that the opportunity cost of receiving one grade higher in economics (for example, improving from a C to a B) is one grade lower in history (falling from a C to a D).

The Production Possibilities Curve (PPC)

The graph in Figure 2-1 illustrates the relationship between the possible results that can be produced in each of two activities, depending on how much time you choose to devote to each activity. This graph shows a representation of a **production possibilities curve (PPC)**.

Consider that you are producing a grade in economics when you study economics and a grade in history when you study history. Then the line that goes from A on one axis to A on the other axis therefore becomes a production possibilities curve. It is defined as the maximum quantity of one good or service that can be produced, given that a specific quantity of another is produced. It is a curve that shows the possibilities available for increasing the output of one good or service by reducing the amount of another. In the example in

Economics Front and Center

To consider how new technologies are affecting the opportunity costs that students face when deciding how to allocate their time, examine the case study, **Missing Class but Catching the Lecture,** on page 41.

Production possibilities curve (PPC)
A curve representing all possible combinations of total output that could be produced assuming (1) a fixed amount of productive resources of a given quality and (2) the efficient use of those resources.

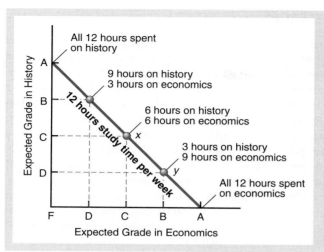

FIGURE 2-1
Production Possibilities Curve for Grades in History and Economics (Trade-Offs)
We assume that only 12 hours can be spent per week on studying. If the student is at point x, equal time (6 hours a week) is spent on both courses, and equal grades of C will be received. If a higher grade in economics is desired, the student may go to point y, thereby receiving a B in economics but a D in history. At point y, 3 hours are spent on history and 9 hours on economics.

Figure 2-1, your time for studying was limited to 12 hours per week. The two possible outputs were your grade in history and your grade in economics. The particular production possibilities curve presented in Figure 2-1 is a graphical representation of the opportunity cost of studying one more hour in one subject. It is a *straight-line production possibilities curve,* which is a special case. (The more general case will be discussed next.) If you decide to be at point x in Figure 2-1, you will devote 6 hours of study time to history and 6 hours to economics. The expected grade in each course will be a C. If you are more interested in getting a B in economics, you will go to point y on the production possibilities curve, spending only 3 hours on history but 9 hours on economics. Your expected grade in history will then drop from a C to a D.

Note that these trade-offs between expected grades in history and economics are the result of *holding constant* total study time as well as all other factors that might influence a student's ability to learn, such as computerized study aids. Quite clearly, if you wished to spend more total time studying, it would be possible to have higher grades in both economics and history. In that case, however, we would no longer be on the specific production possibilities curve illustrated in Figure 2-1. We would have to draw a new curve, farther to the right, to show the greater total study time and a different set of possible trade-offs.

CONCEPTS in Brief

- Scarcity requires us to choose. Whenever we choose, we lose the next-highest-valued alternative.

- Cost is always a forgone opportunity.

- Another way to look at opportunity cost is the trade-off that occurs when one activity is undertaken rather than the next-best alternative activity.

- A production possibilities curve (PPC) graphically shows the trade-off that occurs when more of one output is obtained at the sacrifice of another. The PPC is a graphical representation of, among other things, opportunity cost.

To test your understanding of the concepts covered in this section, go to the Online Review at www.myeconlab.com/miller.

THE CHOICES SOCIETY FACES

The straight-line production possibilities curve presented in Figure 2-1 can be generalized to demonstrate the related concepts of scarcity, choice, and trade-offs that our entire nation faces. As you will see, the production possibilities curve is a simple but powerful economic model because it can demonstrate these related concepts. The example we will use is the choice between the production of digital cameras and pocket personal computers (pocket PCs). We assume for the moment that these are the only two goods that can be produced in the nation. Panel (a) of Figure 2-2 gives the various combinations of digital cameras and pocket PCs that are possible. If all resources are devoted to camera production, 50 million per year can be produced. If all resources are devoted to production of pocket PCs, 60 million per year can be produced. In between are various possible combinations. These combinations are plotted as points *A, B, C, D, E, F,* and *G* in panel (b) of Figure 2-2. If these points are connected with a smooth curve, the nation's production possibilities curve is shown, demonstrating the trade-off between the production of digital cameras and pocket PCs. These trade-offs occur *on* the PPC.

Go to www.econtoday.com/chap02 for one perspective, offered by the National Center for Policy Analysis, on whether society's production decisions should be publicly or privately coordinated.

Notice the major difference in the shape of the production possibilities curves in Figure 2-1 on page 31, and Figure 2-2. In Figure 2-1, there is a constant trade-off between grades in economics and in history. In Figure 2-2, the trade-off between digital camera production and pocket PC production is not constant, and therefore the PPC is a *bowed* curve. To understand why the production possibilities curve for a society is typically bowed outward, you must understand the assumptions underlying the PPC.

FIGURE 2-2
Society's Trade-Off Between Digital Cameras and Pocket PCs
The production of digital cameras and pocket PCs is measured in millions of units per year. The various combinations are given in panel (a) and plotted in panel (b). Connecting the points *A–G* with a relatively smooth line gives the society's production possibilities curve for digital cameras and pocket PCs. Point *R* lies outside the production possibilities curve and is therefore unattainable at the point in time for which the graph is drawn. Point *S* lies inside the production possibilities curve and therefore entails unemployed or underemployed resources.

Panel (a)		
Combination	Digital Cameras (millions per year)	Pocket PCs (millions per year)
A	50.0	0
B	48.0	10
C	45.0	20
D	40.0	30
E	33.0	40
F	22.5	50
G	0.0	60

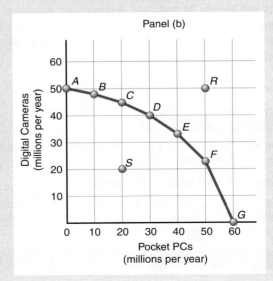

Panel (b)

Assumptions Underlying the Production Possibilities Curve

When we draw the curve that is shown in Figure 2-2, we make the following assumptions:

1. Resources are fully employed.
2. We are looking at production over a specific time period—for example, one year.
3. The resource inputs, in both quantity and quality, used to produce digital cameras or pocket PCs are fixed over this time period.
4. Technology does not change over this time period.

Technology is defined as society's pool of applied knowledge concerning how goods and services can be produced by managers, workers, engineers, scientists, and artisans, using land, physical and human capital, and entrepreneurship. You can think of technology as the formula or recipe used to combine factors of production. (When better formulas are developed, more production can be obtained from the same amount of resources.) The level of technology sets the limit on the amount and types of goods and services that we can derive from any given amount of resources. The production possibilities curve is drawn under the assumption that we use the best technology that we currently have available and that this technology doesn't change over the time period under study.

The land available to a town with established borders is an example of a fixed resource that is fully employed and used with available technology along a production possibilities curve. Why do you suppose that deciding how to allocate a fixed amount of land recently posed "grave" problems for a town in France?

Technology
Society's pool of applied knowledge concerning how goods and services can be produced.

International EXAMPLE

Making Death Illegal—At Least, Inside City Limits

Le Lavandou, France, a Riviera community known for breathtaking views of a rocky coastline along a clear-blue section of the Mediterranean Sea, recently drew international ridicule when it passed a law that appeared aimed at regulating death. Specifically, the law stated, "It is forbidden without a cemetery plot to die on the territory of the commune."

Of course, it is not possible for a law to prevent someone from dying inside a town. The purpose of the law was to indicate a permissible choice along a production possibilities curve. Land is a scarce resource with many alternative uses, so trade-offs involving different productive uses of land arise everywhere on the planet where people establish communities. Le Lavandou is no exception. The town's cemetery filled up, and the townspeople had to decide whether to allocate more land to cemetery plots, thereby providing a service for

deceased individuals and for their family and friends, or to continue allocating remaining land resources to the production of other goods and services. The point of the legal requirement was to emphasize that the town had decided not to incur an opportunity cost by allocating more space to cemetery plots.

Nonetheless, it was still true that someone who happened to die in Le Lavandou without first buying an existing cemetery plot was technically breaking the law.

For Critical Analysis
What is likely to happen to the opportunity cost of cemetery services as the world's population continues to increase and spread over available land resources?

Being off the Production Possibilities Curve

Look again at panel (b) of Figure 2-2. Point *R* lies *outside* the production possibilities curve and is *impossible* to achieve during the time period assumed. By definition, the PPC indicates the *maximum* quantity of one good given some quantity of the other.

It is possible, however, to be at point *S* in Figure 2-2 on page 32. That point lies beneath the production possibilities curve. If the nation is at point *S*, it means that its resources are not being fully utilized. This occurs, for example, during periods of unemployment. Point *S* and all such points inside the PPC are always attainable but imply unemployed or under-employed resources.

Efficiency

The production possibilities curve can be used to define the notion of efficiency. Whenever the economy is operating on the PPC, at points such as *A, B, C,* or *D*, we say that its production is efficient. Points such as *S* in Figure 2-2, which lie beneath the PPC, are said to represent production situations that are not efficient.

Efficiency can mean many things to many people. Even in economics, there are different types of efficiency. Here we are discussing *productive efficiency*. An economy is productively efficient whenever it is producing the maximum output with given technology and resources.

A simple commonsense definition of efficiency is getting the most out of what we have. Clearly, we are not getting the most out of what we have if we are at point *S* in panel (b) of Figure 2-2 on page 32. We can move from point *S* to, say, point *C*, thereby increasing the total quantity of digital cameras produced without any decrease in the total quantity of pocket PCs produced. Alternatively, we can move from point *S* to point *E*, for example, and have both more digital cameras and more pocket PCs. Point *S* is called an **inefficient point**, which is defined as any point below the production possibilities curve.

The Law of Increasing Relative Cost

In the example in Figure 2-1 on page 31, the trade-off between a grade in history and a grade in economics was one to one. The trade-off ratio was constant. That is, the production possibilities curve was a straight line. The curve in Figure 2-2 on page 32 is a more general case. We have re-created the curve in Figure 2-2 as Figure 2-3. Each combination, *A* through *G*, of digital cameras and pocket PCs is represented on the production possibilities curve. Starting with the production of zero pocket PCs, the nation can produce 50 mil-

Efficiency
The case in which a given level of inputs is used to produce the maximum output possible. Alternatively, the situation in which a given output is produced at minimum cost.

Inefficient point
Any point below the production possibilities curve at which the use of resources is not generating the maximum possible output.

FIGURE 2-3
The Law of Increasing Relative Cost
Consider equal increments of production of pocket PCs, as measured on the horizontal axis. All of the horizontal arrows—*aB, bC,* and so on—are of equal length (10 million). The opportunity cost of going from 50 million pocket PCs per year to 60 million (*Ff*) is much greater than going from zero units to 10 million (*Aa*). The opportunity cost of each additional equal increase in production of pocket PCs rises.

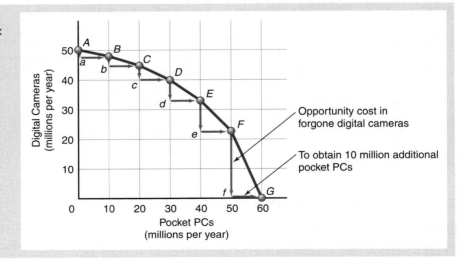

lion digital cameras with its available resources and technology. When we increase production of pocket PCs from zero to 10 million per year, the nation has to give up in digital cameras an amount shown by that first vertical arrow, *Aa*. From panel (a) of Figure 2-2 on page 32 you can see that this is 2 million per year (50 million minus 48 million). Again, if we increase production of pocket PCs by 10 million units per year, we go from *B* to *C*. In order to do so, the nation has to give up the vertical distance *Bb*, or 3 million digital cameras per year. By the time we go from 50 million to 60 million pocket PCs, to obtain that 10 million increase, we have to forgo the vertical distance *Ff*, or 22.5 million digital cameras. In other words, we see that the opportunity cost of the last 10 million pocket PCs has increased to 22.5 million digital cameras, compared to 2 million digital comeras for an equivalent increase in pocket PCs when we started with none at all being produced.

What we are observing is called the **law of increasing relative cost.** When society takes more resources and applies them to the production of any specific good, the opportunity cost increases for each additional unit produced. The reason that as a nation we face the law of increasing relative cost (shown as a production possibilities curve that is bowed outward) is that certain resources are better suited for producing some goods than they are for other goods. Generally, resources are not *perfectly* adaptable for alternative uses. When increasing the output of a particular good, producers must use less suitable resources than those already used in order to produce the additional output. Hence the cost of producing the additional units increases. With respect to our hypothetical example here, at first the optical imaging specialists at digital camera firms would shift over to producing pocket PCs. After a while, though, lens-crafting technicians, workers who normally build cameras, and others would be asked to help design and manufacture pocket PC components. Clearly, they would be less effective in making pocket PCs than the people who specialize in this task.

As a rule of thumb, *the more specialized the resources, the more bowed the production possibilities curve.* At the other extreme, if all resources are equally suitable for digital camera production or production of pocket PCs, the curves in Figures 2-2 and 2-3 would approach the straight line shown in our first example in Figure 2-1 on page 31.

Law of increasing relative cost
The observation that the opportunity cost of additional units of a good generally increases as society attempts to produce more of that good. This accounts for the bowed-out shape of the production possibilities curve.

CONCEPTS in Brief

- Trade-offs are represented graphically by a production possibilities curve showing the maximum quantity of one good or service that can be produced, given a specific quantity of another, from a given set of resources over a specified period of time—for example, one year.

- A PPC is drawn holding the quantity and quality of all resources fixed over the time period under study.

- Points outside the production possibilities curve are unattainable; points inside are attainable but represent an inefficient use or underuse of available resouces.

- Because many resources are better suited for certain productive tasks than for others, society's production possibilities curve is bowed outward, following the law of increasing relative cost.

To test your understanding of the concepts covered in this section, go to the Online Review at www.myeconlab.com/miller.

ECONOMIC GROWTH AND THE PRODUCTION POSSIBILITIES CURVE

Over any particular time period, a society cannot be outside the production possibilities curve. Over time, however, it is possible to have more of everything. This occurs through economic growth. (An important reason for economic growth, capital accumulation, is discussed next. A more complete discussion of why economic growth occurs appears in Chapter 9.) Figure 2-4 on the following page shows the production possibilities curve for

FIGURE 2-4
Economic Growth Allows for More of Everything
If the nation experiences economic growth, the production possibilities curve between digital cameras and pocket PCs will move out as shown. This takes time, however, and it does not occur automatically. This means, therefore, that we can have more digital cameras and more pocket PCs only after a period of time during which we have experienced economic growth.

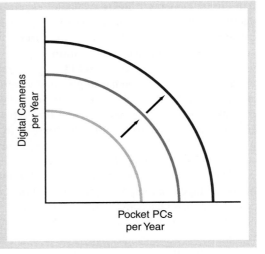

digital cameras and pocket PCs shifting outward. The two additional curves shown represent new choices open to an economy that has experienced economic growth. Such economic growth occurs because of many things, including increases in the number of workers and productive investment in equipment.

Scarcity still exists, however, no matter how much economic growth there is. At any point in time, we will always be on some production possibilities curve; thus we will always face trade-offs. The more we want of one thing, the less we can have of others.

If a nation experiences economic growth, the production possibilities curve between digital cameras and pocket PCs will move outward, as shown in Figure 2-4. This takes time and does not occur automatically. One reason it will occur involves the choice about how much to consume today.

THE TRADE-OFF BETWEEN THE PRESENT AND THE FUTURE

Consumption
The use of goods and services for personal satisfaction.

The production possibilities curve and economic growth can be used to examine the trade-off between present **consumption** and future consumption. When we consume today, we are using up what we call consumption or consumer goods—food and clothes, for example.

Why We Make Capital Goods

Why would we be willing to use productive resources to make things—capital goods—that we cannot consume directly? For one thing, capital goods enable us to produce larger quantities of consumer goods or to produce them less expensively than we otherwise could. Before fish are "produced" for the market, equipment such as fishing boats, nets, and poles is produced first. Imagine how expensive it would be to obtain fish for market without using these capital goods. Catching fish with one's hands is not an easy task. The price per fish would be very high if capital goods weren't used.

Forgoing Current Consumption

Whenever we use productive resources to make capital goods, we are implicitly forgoing current consumption. We are waiting for some time in the future to consume the fruits that will be reaped from the use of capital goods. In effect, when we forgo current consumption to invest in capital goods, we are engaging in an economic activity that is forward-looking—we do not get instant utility or satisfaction from our activity. Indeed, if we were to produce only consumer goods now and no capital goods, our capacity to produce consumer goods in the future would suffer. Here we see a trade-off.

The Trade-Off Between Consumption Goods and Capital Goods

To have more consumer goods in the future, we must accept fewer consumer goods today. In other words, an opportunity cost is involved. Every time we make a choice for more goods today, we incur an opportunity cost of fewer goods tomorrow, and every time we make a choice of more goods in the future, we incur an opportunity cost of fewer goods today. With the resources that we don't use to produce consumer goods for today, we invest in capital goods that will produce more consumer goods for us later. The trade-off is shown in Figure 2-5. On the left in panel (a), you can see this trade-off depicted as a production possibilities curve between capital goods and consumption goods.

Assume that we are willing to give up $1 trillion worth of consumption today. We will be at point *A* in the left-hand diagram of panel (a). This will allow the economy to grow. We will have more future consumption because we invested in more capital goods today. In the right-hand diagram of panel (a), we see two goods represented, food and entertainment. The production possibilities curve will move outward if we collectively decide to restrict consumption each year and invest in capital goods.

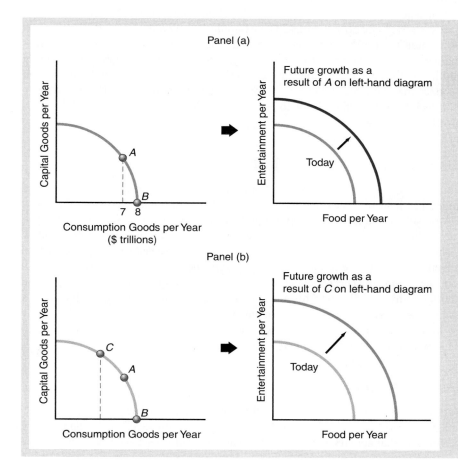

FIGURE 2-5
Capital Goods and Growth
In panel (a), the nation chooses not to consume $1 trillion, so it invests that amount in capital goods. In panel (b), it chooses even more capital goods (point *C*). The PPC moves even more to the right on the right-hand diagram in panel (b) as a result.

In panel (b), we show the results of our willingness to forgo even more current consumption. We move to point *C*, where we have many fewer consumer goods today but produce many more capital goods. This leads to more future growth in this simplified model, and thus the production possibilities curve in the right-hand side of panel (b) shifts outward more than it did in the right-hand side of panel (a).

In other words, the more we give up today, the more we can have tomorrow, provided, of course, that the capital goods are productive in future periods.

CONCEPTS in Brief

- The use of capital requires using productive resources to produce capital goods that will later be used to produce consumer goods.

- A trade-off is involved between current consumption and capital goods or, alternatively, between current consumption and future consumption. The more we invest in capital goods today, the greater the amount of consumer goods we can produce in the future and the smaller the amount of consumer goods we can produce today.

To test your understanding of the concepts covered in this section, go to the Online Review at www.myeconlab.com/miller.

SPECIALIZATION AND GREATER PRODUCTIVITY

Specialization
The division of productive activities among persons and regions so that no one individual or one area is totally self-sufficient. An individual may specialize, for example, in law or medicine. A nation may specialize in the production of coffee, computers, or cameras.

Specialization involves working at a relatively well-defined, limited endeavor, such as accounting or teaching. It involves a division of labor among different individuals and regions. Most individuals do specialize. For example, you could change the oil in your car if you wanted to. Typically, though, you take your car to a garage and let the mechanic change the oil. You benefit by letting the garage mechanic specialize in changing the oil and in doing other repairs on your car. The specialist normally will get the job finished sooner than you could and has the proper equipment to make the job go more smoothly. Specialization usually leads to greater productivity, not only for each individual but also for the nation.

Absolute Advantage

Absolute advantage
The ability to produce more units of a good or service using a given quantity of labor or resource inputs. Equivalently, the ability to produce the same quantity of a good or service using fewer units of labor or resource inputs.

Specialization occurs because different individuals and different nations have different skills. Sometimes it seems that some individuals are better at doing everything than anyone else. A president of a large company might be able to type better than any of the typists, file faster than any of the file clerks, and wash windows faster than any of the window washers. The president has an **absolute advantage** in all of these endeavors—if he were to spend a given amount of time in one of these activities, he could produce more than anyone else in the company. The president does not, however, spend his time doing those other activities. Why not? Because his absolute advantage in undertaking the president's managerial duties is even greater. The president specializes in one particular task in spite of having an absolute advantage in all tasks. Indeed, absolute advantage is irrelevant in predicting how he uses his time; only *comparative advantage* matters.

Comparative Advantage

Comparative advantage
The ability to produce a good or service at a lower opportunity cost compared to other producers.

Comparative advantage is the ability to perform an activity *at a lower opportunity cost*. You have a comparative advantage in one activity whenever you have a lower opportunity cost of performing that activity. Comparative advantage is always a *relative* concept. You may be able to change the oil in your car; you might even be able to change it faster than the local mechanic. But if the opportunity cost you face by changing the oil exceeds the mechanic's opportunity cost, the mechanic has a comparative advantage in changing the oil. The mechanic faces a lower opportunity cost for that activity.

You may be convinced that everybody can do everything better than you. In this extreme situation, do you still have a comparative advantage? The answer is yes. What you need to do to discover your comparative advantage is to find a job in which your *disadvantage* relative to others is smaller. You do not have to be a mathematical genius to figure this out. The market tells you very clearly by offering you the highest income for the job for which you have the smallest disadvantage compared to others. Stated differently, to find your comparative advantage, you simply find which job maximizes your income.

The coaches of sports teams are constantly faced with determining each player's comparative advantage. Babe Ruth was originally one of the best pitchers in professional baseball when he played for the Boston Red Sox. After he was traded to the New York Yankees, the owner and the coach decided to make him an outfielder, even though he was a better pitcher than anyone else on the team roster. They wanted "The Babe" to concentrate on his hitting. Good pitchers do not bring in as many fans as home-run kings. Babe Ruth's comparative advantage was clearly in hitting homers rather than in practicing and developing his pitching game.

Scarcity, Self-Interest, and Specialization

In Chapter 1, you learned about the assumption of rational self-interest. To repeat, for the purposes of our analyses we assume that individuals are rational in that they will do what is in their own self-interest. They will not consciously carry out actions that will make them worse off. In this chapter, you learned that scarcity requires people to make choices. We assume that they make choices based on their self-interest. When they make these choices, they attempt to maximize benefits net of opportunity cost. In so doing, individuals choose their comparative advantage and end up specializing. Ultimately, when people specialize, they increase the money income they make and therefore become richer. When all individuals and businesses specialize simultaneously, the gains are seen in greater material well-being. With any given set of resources, specialization will result in higher output.

THE DIVISION OF LABOR

In any firm that includes specialized human and nonhuman resources, there is a **division of labor** among those resources. The best-known example comes from Adam Smith, who in *The Wealth of Nations* illustrated the benefits of a division of labor in the making of pins, as depicted in the following example:

> One man draws out the wire, another straightens it, a third cuts it, a fourth points it, a fifth grinds it at the top for receiving the head; to make the head requires two or three distinct operations; to put it on is a peculiar business, to whiten the pins is another; it is even a trade by itself to put them into the paper.

Division of labor
The segregation of a resource into different specific tasks; for example, one automobile worker puts on bumpers, another doors, and so on.

Making pins this way allowed 10 workers without very much skill to make almost 48,000 pins "of a middling size" in a day. One worker, toiling alone, could have made perhaps 20 pins a day; therefore, 10 workers could have produced 200. Division of labor allowed for an increase in the daily output of the pin factory from 200 to 48,000! (Smith did not attribute all of the gain to the division of labor according to talent but credited also the use of machinery and the fact that less time was spent shifting from task to task.)

What we are discussing here involves a division of the resource called labor into different uses of labor. The different uses of labor are organized in such a way as to increase the amount of output possible from the fixed resources available. We can therefore talk about an organized division of labor within a firm leading to increased output.

COMPARATIVE ADVANTAGE AND TRADE AMONG NATIONS

Go to www.econtoday.com/chap02 to find out from the World Trade Organization how much international trade takes place. Under "Resources," click on "Trade statistics."

Though most of our analysis of absolute advantage, comparative advantage, and specialization has dealt with individuals, it is equally applicable to nations. First consider the United States. The Plains states have a comparative advantage in the production of grains and other agricultural goods. Relative to the Plains states, the states to the north and east tend to specialize in industrialized production, such as automobiles. Not surprisingly, grains are shipped from the Plains states to the northern states, and automobiles are shipped in the reverse direction. Such specialization and trade allow for higher incomes and standards of living. If both the Plains states and the northern states were separate nations, the same analysis would still hold, but we would call it international trade. Indeed, the European Union (EU) is comparable to the United States in area and population, but instead of one nation, the EU has 25. What U.S. residents call *interstate* trade, Europeans call *international* trade. There is no difference, however, in the economic results—both yield greater economic efficiency and higher average incomes.

Political problems that do not normally arise within a particular nation often do between nations. For example, if California avocado growers develop a cheaper method than growers in southern Florida to produce a tastier avocado, the Florida growers will lose out. They cannot do much about the situation except try to lower their own costs of production or improve their product. If avocado growers in Mexico, however, develop a cheaper method to produce better-tasting avocados, both California and Florida growers can (and likely will) try to raise political barriers that will prevent Mexican avocado growers from freely selling their product in the United States. U.S. avocado growers will use such arguments as "unfair" competition and loss of U.S. jobs. In so doing, they are only partly right: Avocado-growing jobs may decline in the United States, but there is no reason to believe that jobs will decline overall. If the argument of U.S. avocado growers had any validity, every time a region in the United States developed a better way to produce a product manufactured somewhere else in the country, U.S. employment would decline. That has never happened and never will.

When nations specialize where they have a comparative advantage and then trade with the rest of the world, the average standard of living in the world rises. In effect, international trade allows the world to move from inside the global production possibilities curve toward the curve itself, thereby improving worldwide economic efficiency. Thus all countries that engage in trade can benefit from comparative advantage.

Why might companies that assemble products from various components choose to include components manufactured in more than one country?

International EXAMPLE

Multiple Comparative Advantages in Dishwasher Production

Maytag workers assemble dishwashers in Jackson, Tennessee. Thus the dishwashers are officially "made in the U.S.A." International trade is nonetheless a fundamental aspect of Maytag's production of dishwashers.

Chinese workers and firms have a comparative advantage over the residents of most other nations in manufacturing small motors. Hence the motors bolted into the dishwashers are Chinese-made. Mexican producers have a comparative advantage over most countries in making small water pumps, so Mexican-manufactured water pumps are installed in the dishwashers. The workers in Maytag's Tennessee plant have the skills required to assemble dishwasher components more efficiently than workers in other nations. Consequently, the total production cost of a Maytag dishwasher that is *assembled* "in the U.S.A." actually reflects efficiencies arising from comparative advantages in more than one country.

For Critical Analysis
What would happen to the total cost of producing a Maytag dishwasher if the U.S. Congress were to pass a law requiring U.S. dishwasher manufacturers to use only U.S.-manufactured components?

Concepts in Brief

● With a given set of resources, specialization results in higher output; in other words, there are gains to specialization in terms of greater material well-being.

● Individuals and nations specialize in their areas of comparative advantage in order to reap the gains of specialization.

● Comparative advantages are found by determining which activities have the lowest opportunity cost—that is, which activities yield the highest return for the time and resources used.

● A division of labor occurs when different workers are assigned different tasks. Together, the workers produce a desired product.

To test your understanding of the concepts covered in this section, go to the Online Review at www.myeconlab.com/miller.

CASE STUDY: Economics Front and Center

Missing Class but Catching the Lecture

Hernandez attends a university that has an "instructional resources unit" that creates digital videos of all lectures for about 30 courses per semester and places them on the university's internal Web site for students to review if they miss class. She is enrolled in two of these courses.

Today Hernandez is trying to decide whether to attend one or both "live" lectures or view Internet videos tomorrow instead. One class meets in the morning, when Hernandez could be jogging instead. The other is in the afternoon, when she could be attending a lecture by a visiting senator. She has determined that even though she can view the videos at any time, she still will incur opportunity costs if she misses the actual class meeting. One is giving up the opportunity to ask questions of her professor. Another is sacrificing the chance to interact with other class members before, during, and after class. Finally, she will have to give up other activities that she could do instead of watching video lectures on the Web. Even though the availability of class videos has broadened Hernandez's opportunities, she still confronts trade-offs.

Points to Analyze

1. *What is the opportunity cost if Hernandez chooses to miss her morning class?*

2. *What is the opportunity cost if Hernandez attends her afternoon class?*

Concepts Applied
- Scarcity and Choice
- Opportunity Cost
- Law of Increasing Relative Cost

I n the United States, the responsibility for combating criminal activities is shared among local, state, and federal police authorities. The Federal Bureau of Investigation (FBI) is the main crime-fighting force of the federal government. Since its founding early in the twentieth century, the FBI's resources have supplemented those available to local police authorities, sheriff's departments, state police units, and other federal agencies. Together, these U.S. law enforcement agencies seek to catch bank robbers and kidnappers, enforce federal narcotics laws, and break up organized crime.

Altered Crime Enforcement Priorities

The 1993 bombing of the World Trade Center and the 1995 Oklahoma City bombing revealed that U.S. law enforcement officials faced a dangerous new criminal element. Nevertheless, few changes were made in the basic structure of the national law enforcement system. The FBI continued to focus on catching bank robbers, kidnappers, and Mafia kingpins.

Following the 2001 attacks that destroyed the World Trade Center and damaged the Pentagon, however, the FBI decided to attempt to stop terrorist attacks before they occur. The FBI found that pursuing preemptive strikes against domestic and international terrorists required considerable reallocation of its resources. Before 2001, fewer than 1,200 of the FBI's 9,000 agents based in the United States were directly or indirectly involved in antiterrorism activities. Within three years, nearly 2,000 FBI agents had been reassigned to counterterrorism duties.

Choosing a New Point on the Law Enforcement Production Possibilities Curve

The FBI's reassignment of agents suddenly shifted a significant portion of society's crime-fighting resources away from combating traditional lawbreakers. The number of FBI drug investigations fell by more than 50 percent between 2000 and 2004. Many local and state police detectives who had come to rely on the FBI for assistance found themselves thrust into the unfamiliar role of lead investigators in cases involving drugs, kidnapping, and white-collar crimes. At the same time, municipal police agencies found themselves responding to occasional FBI calls for assistance in implementing counterterrorism measures to avert suspected threats to U.S. security.

Local and state law enforcement officials had to perform these new duties using the same amount of resources they had before the FBI's action. The result was predictable for anyone who has studied this chapter. As shown in Figure 2-6, there was a movement along a production possibilities curve relating the provision of antiterrorism services and the production of traditional law enforcement activities such as the depicted movement from point A to point B. Thus the FBI's reallocation of resources to increased counterterrorism activities entailed an opportunity cost. Society as a whole had to sacrifice the production of services aimed at reducing run-of-the-mill crimes in order to increase the production of services designed to prevent terrorist attacks.

Furthermore, because law enforcement resources are not equally suited to every type of policing task, the law of increasing relative cost applied. Each step-up in the production of antiterrorism services entailed an ever-higher opportunity cost in the form of reduced production of traditional law enforcement services. The result was a national law enforcement force better equipped to handle terrorists but less capable of dealing with bank robbers and kidnappers.

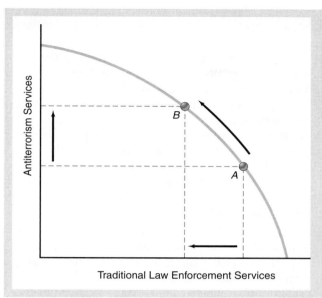

FIGURE 2-6
The Trade-Off Between the Provision of Antiterrorism Services and Traditional Law Enforcement Activities
Given available resources and technology, devoting more resources to producing antiterrorism services entails giving up the production of traditional law enforcement services.

For Critical Analysis

1. Consider a production possibilities curve relating the production of all law enforcement services, including both antiterrorism and traditional policing activities, to the production of *all other* goods and services in the economy. What must happen if society continues to desire to boost counterterrorism efforts while maintaining the same level of traditional law enforcement services?
2. Terrorists seek to destroy both human lives and nonhuman resources and to make existing technology (such as airline passenger jets) less usable. In what sense, therefore, might society regard physical resources directed against terrorism, such as passenger- and baggage-screening devices at airports, as capital goods?

Web Resources

1. To learn more about the FBI resource reallocation that began after the 2001 terrorist attacks, go to www.econtoday.com/chap02.
2. For information about the financial resources the federal government commits to law enforcement efforts, follow the link to the U.S. Justice Department's Management Division available at www.econtoday.com/chap02, and click on the budget summary for the most recent year.

Research Project

Propose a plan of action for how society might shift out the production possibilities curve relating the provision of counterterrorism services to the production of traditional police services without increasing the total number of local, state, and federal law enforcement personnel. (Hint: What other types of resources and what types of technologies might be used instead of people to perform antiterrorism and regular law enforcement tasks?)

SUMMARY DISCUSSION of Learning Objectives

1. **The Problem of Scarcity, Even for the Affluent:** Scarcity is very different from poverty. No one can obtain all one desires from nature without sacrifice. Thus even the richest people face scarcity because they have to make choices among alternatives. Despite their high levels of income or wealth, affluent people, like everyone else, want more than they can have (in terms of goods, power, prestige, and so on).

2. **Why Economists Consider Individuals' Wants but Not Their "Needs":** Goods are all things from which individuals derive satisfaction. Economic goods are those for which the desired quantity exceeds the amount that is directly available from nature at a zero price. To economists, the term *need* is undefinable, whereas humans have unlimited *wants,* which are defined as the goods and services on which we place a positive value.

3. **Why Scarcity Leads People to Evaluate Opportunity Costs:** We measure the opportunity cost of anything by the highest-valued alternative that one must give up to obtain it. The trade-offs that we face as individuals and as a society can be represented by a production possibilities curve (PPC), and moving from one point on a PPC to another entails incurring an opportunity cost. The reason is that along a PPC, all currently available resources and technology are being used, so obtaining more of one good requires shifting resources to production of that good and away from production of another. That is, there is an opportunity cost of allocating scarce resources toward producing one good instead of another good.

4. **Why Obtaining Increasing Increments of a Good Requires Giving Up More and More Units of Other Goods:** Typically, resources are specialized. Thus, when society allocates additional resources to producing more and more of a single good, it must increasingly employ resources that would be better suited for producing other goods. As a result, the law of increasing relative cost holds. Each additional unit of a good can be obtained only by giving up more and more of other goods, which means that the production possibilities curve that society faces is bowed outward.

5. **The Trade-Off Between Consumption Goods and Capital Goods:** If we allocate more resources to producing capital goods today, then, other things being equal, the economy will grow faster than it would have otherwise. Thus the production possibilities curve will shift outward by a larger amount in the future, which means that we can have more consumption goods in the future. The trade-off, however, is that producing more capital goods today entails giving up consumption goods today.

6. **Absolute Advantage versus Comparative Advantage:** A person has an absolute advantage if she can produce more of a specific good than someone else who uses the same amount of resources. Nevertheless, the individual may be better off producing a different good if she has a comparative advantage in producing that good, meaning that she can produce the good at a lower opportunity cost than someone else. By specializing in producing the good for which she has a comparative advantage, she assures herself of reaping gains from specialization in the form of a higher income.

KEY TERMS AND CONCEPTS

absolute advantage (38)

comparative advantage (38)

consumption (36)

division of labor (39)

economic goods (27)

efficiency (34)

entrepreneurship (27)

goods (27)

human capital (27)

inefficient point (34)

labor (27)

land (27)

law of increasing relative cost (35)

opportunity cost (29)

physical capital (27)

production (26)

production possibilities curve (PPC) (30)

scarcity (26)

services (27)

specialization (38)

technology (33)

PROBLEMS

Answers to the odd-numbered problems appear at the back of the book.

2-1. Define opportunity cost. What is your opportunity cost of attending a class at 11:00 A.M.? How does it differ from your opportunity cost of attending a class at 8:00 A.M.?

2-2. If you receive a free ticket to a concert, what, if anything, is your opportunity cost of attending the concert? How does your opportunity cost change if miserable weather on the night of the concert requires you to leave much earlier for the concert hall and greatly extends the time it takes to get home afterward?

2-3. The following table illustrates the points a student can earn on examinations in economics and biology if the student uses all available hours for study.

Economics	Biology
100	40
90	50
80	60
70	70
60	80
50	90
40	100

Plot this student's production possibilities curve. Does the PPC illustrate increasing or decreasing opportunity costs?

2-4. Based on the information provided in Problem 2-3, what is the opportunity cost to this student of allocating enough additional study time on economics to move her grade up from a 90 to a 100?

2-5. Consider the following costs that a student incurs by attending a public university for one semester: $3,000 for tuition, $1,000 for room and board, $500 for books and $3,000 in after-tax wages lost that the student could have earned working. What is the total opportunity cost that the student incurs by attending college for one semester?

2-6. Consider a change in the table in Problem 2-3. The student's set of opportunities is now as follows:

Economics	Biology
100	40
90	60
80	75
70	85
60	93
50	98
40	100

Plot this student's production possibilities curve. Does the PPC illustrate increasing or decreasing opportunity costs? What is the opportunity cost to this student for the additional amount of study time on economics required to move her grade from 60 to 70? From 90 to 100?

2-7. Construct a production possibilities curve for a nation facing increasing opportunity costs for producing food and video games. Show how the PPC changes given the following events.

  a. A new and better fertilizer is invented.
  b. There is a surge in labor, which can be employed in both the agricultural sector and the video game sector.
  c. A new programming language is invented that is less costly to code and is more memory-efficient, enabling the use of smaller game cartridges.
  d. A heat wave and drought result in a 10 percent decrease in usable farmland.

2-8. The president of a university announces to the local media that the university was able to construct its sports complex at a lower cost than it had previously projected. The president argues that the university can now purchase a yacht for the president at no additional cost. Explain why this statement is false by considering opportunity cost.

2-9. You can wash, fold, and iron a basket of laundry in two hours and prepare a meal in one hour. Your roommate can wash, fold, and iron a basket of laundry in three hours and prepare a meal in one hour. Who has the absolute advantage in laundry, and who has an absolute advantage in meal preparation? Who has the comparative advantage in laundry, and who has a comparative advantage in meal preparation?

2-10. Based on the information in Problem 2-9, should you and your roommate specialize in a particular task?

Why? And if so, who should specialize in which task? Show how much labor time you save if you choose to "trade" an appropriate task with your roommate as opposed to doing it yourself.

2-11. On the one hand, Canada goes to considerable lengths to protect its television program and magazine producers from U.S. competitors. The United States, on the other hand, often seeks protection from food imports from Canada. Construct an argument showing that from an economywide viewpoint, these efforts are misguided.

2-12. Using only the concept of comparative advantage, evaluate this statement: "A professor with a Ph.D. in economics should never mow his or her own lawn, because this would fail to take into account the professor's comparative advantage."

2-13. Country A and country B produce the same consumption goods and capital goods and currently have *identical* production possibilities curves. They also have the same resources at present, and they have access to the same technology.

    a. At present, does either country have a comparative advantage in producing capital goods? Consumption goods?

    b. Currently, country A has chosen to produce more consumption goods, compared with country B. Other things being equal, which country will experience the larger outward shift of its PPC during the next year?

    c. Suppose that a year passes with no changes in technology or in factors other than the capital goods and consumption goods choices the countries initially made. In addition, suppose that both countries' PPCs have shifted outward from their initial positions, but not in a parallel fashion. Country B's opportunity cost of producing consumption goods will now be higher than country A's. Does either country have a comparative advantage in producing capital goods? Consumption goods?

Consider the following diagram when answering Problems 2-14, 2-15, and 2-16

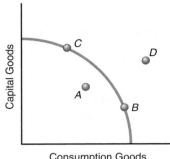

2-14. During a debate on the floor of the U.S. Senate, Senator Creighton makes the statement. "Our nation should not devote so many of its fully employed resources to producing capital goods, become we are already not producing enough consumption goods for our citizens." Compared with the other labled points on the diagram which one could be consistent with the *current* production combination choice that Senator Creighton believes the nation has made?

2-15. In response to Senator Creighton's statement reported in Problem 2-14, Senator Long replies, "We must remain at our current production combination if we want to be able to produce more consumption goods in the future." Of the labled points on the diagram, which one could depict the *future* production combination Senator Long has in mind?

2-16. Senator Borman interjects the following comment after the statements by Senators Creighton and Long reported in Problems 2-14 and 2-15: "In fact, both of my esteemed colleagues are wrong, because an unacceptably large portion of our nation's resources is currently unemployed." Of the labled points on the diagram, which one is consistent with Senator Borman's position?

ECONOMICS ON THE NET

Opportunity Cost and Labor Force Participation Many students choose to forgo full-time employment to concentrate on their studies, thereby incurring a sizable opportunity cost. This application explores the nature of this opportunity cost.

Title: College Enrollment and Work Activity of High School Graduates

Navigation: Go to www.econtoday.com/chap02 to visit the Bureau of Labor Statistics (BLS) home page. Select A–Z Index and then click on *Educational Attainment, Statistics.* Finally, under the heading "Economic News Releases," click on *College Enrollment and Work Activity of High School Graduates.*

Application Read the abbreviated report on college enrollment and work activity of high school graduates. Then answer the following questions.

1. Based on the article, explain who the BLS considers to be in the labor force and who it does not view as part of the labor force.

2. What is the difference in labor force participation rates between high school students entering four-year universities and those entering two-year universities? Using the concept of opportunity cost, explain the difference.

3. What is the difference in labor force participation rates between part-time college students and full-time college students? Using the concept of opportunity cost, explain the difference.

For Group Study and Analysis Read the last paragraph of the article. Then divide the class into two groups. The first group should explain, based on the concept of opportunity cost, the difference in labor force participation rates between youths not in school but with a high school diploma and youths not in school and without a high school diploma. The second half should explain, based on opportunity cost, the difference in labor force participation rates between men and women not in school but with a high school diploma and men and women not in school and without a high school diploma.

Media Resources

If your exam were tomorrow, would you be ready? For each chapter, MyEconLab Practice Tests and Study Plans pinpoint which sections you have mastered and which ones you need to study. That way, you are more efficient with your study time, and you are better prepared for your exams.

In addition to Practice Tests and your personalized Study Plan, you'll find the following media resources in MyEconLab:

1. *Graphs in Motion* animation of Figures 2-1, 2-3, and 2-4.

2. An *Economics in Motion* in-depth animation of the Production Possibilities Curve.

3. Videos featuring the author, Roger LeRoy Miller, on the following subjects:
   ● Scarcity, Resources, and Production
   ● Absolute versus Comparative Advantage

4. Links to the Web sites cited in the marginal Internet Resources, Issues and Applications feature, and Economics on the Net activity.

5. Audio clips of all key terms, additional practice problems, and a PDF version of the material from the print Study Guide.

6. eThemes of the Times, which is a New York Times article to help you understand the real-world applications of what you are learning.

To see how it works, turn to page 16 and then go to www.myeconlab.com/miller.

Get Ahead of the Curve

Demand and Supply

The early 2000s were tough years for many job seekers, including those with a new Ph.D. in economics looking for jobs as college and university instructors. Many of these individuals were seeking positions at the same time that colleges and universities were cutting back on hiring. Their economics training had prepared the applicants to understand the nature of the problem they faced: The *supply* of economics instructors had increased at the same time that the *demand* for economics instructors had declined. As you will learn in this chapter, one outcome could be predicted with certainty: Other things being equal, the wages earned by economics instructors had to fall relative to wages available in other occupations.

Media Resources

Refer to the end of the chapter for a full listing of the multimedia learning materials available in MyEconLab.

LEARNING OBJECTIVES

After reading this chapter, you should be able to:

1. Explain the law of demand
2. Discuss the difference between money prices and relative prices
3. Distinguish between changes in demand and changes in quantity demanded
4. Explain the law of supply
5. Distinguish between changes in supply and changes in quantity supplied
6. Understand how the interaction of the demand for and supply of a commodity determines the market price of the commodity and the equilibrium quantity of the commodity that is produced and consumed

... even though the overall level of prices of goods and services has trended slightly upward during the past several decades, the prices of several consumer products have either held steady or declined? The average of all prices consumers pay for goods and services has risen by more than 30 percent since 1992, but the average price of an item of clothing has remained unchanged. The average price of a desktop personal computer has fallen by more than 50 percent.

Clearly, the prices of various items that consumers purchase can vary considerably *relative* to the prices of other goods and services. If we use the economist's primary set of tools, *demand* and *supply*, we can develop a better understanding of why we observe such variations in relative prices. Demand and supply are two ways of categorizing the influences on the price of goods that you buy and the quantities available. As such, demand and supply characterize virtually all economic analysis of the world around us.

As you will see throughout this text, the operation of the forces of demand and supply takes place in *markets*. A **market** is an abstract concept referring to all the arrangements individuals have for exchanging with one another. Goods and services are sold in markets, such as the automobile market, the health care market, and the compact disc market. Workers offer their services in the labor market. Companies, or firms, buy workers' labor services in the labor market. Firms also buy other inputs in order to produce the goods and services that you buy as a consumer. Firms purchase machines, buildings, and land. These markets are in operation at all times. One of the most important activities in these markets is the setting of the prices of all of the inputs and outputs that are bought and sold in our complicated economy. To understand the determination of prices, you first need to look at the law of demand.

Market
All of the arrangements that individuals have for exchanging with one another. Thus, for example, we can speak of the labor market, the automobile market, and the credit market.

THE LAW OF DEMAND

Demand has a special meaning in economics. It refers to the quantities of specific goods or services that individuals, taken singly or as a group, will purchase at various possible prices, other things being constant. We can therefore talk about the demand for microprocessor chips, french fries, CD players, children, and criminal activities.

Associated with the concept of demand is the **law of demand,** which can be stated as follows:

> *When the price of a good goes up, people buy less of it, other things being equal.*
> *When the price of a good goes down, people buy more of it, other things being equal.*

The law of demand tells us that the quantity demanded of any commodity is inversely related to its price, other things being equal. In an inverse relationship, one variable moves up in value when the other moves down. The law of demand states that a change in price causes a change in the quantity demanded in the *opposite* direction.

Notice that we tacked on to the end of the law of demand the statement "other things being equal." We referred to this in Chapter 1 as the *ceteris paribus* assumption. It means, for example, that when we predict that people will buy fewer DVD players if their price goes up, we are holding constant the price of all other goods in the economy as well as people's incomes. Implicitly, therefore, if we are assuming that no other prices change when we examine the price behavior of DVD players, we are looking at the *relative* price of DVD players.

The law of demand is supported by millions of observations of people's behavior in the marketplace. Theoretically, it can be derived from an economic model based on rational behavior, as was discussed in Chapter 1. Basically, if nothing else changes and the price of

Demand
A schedule of how much of a good or service people will purchase at any price during a specified time period, other things being constant.

Law of demand
The observation that there is a negative, or inverse, relationship between the price of any good or service and the quantity demanded, holding other factors constant.

a good falls, the lower price induces us to buy more over a certain period of time because we can enjoy additional net gains that were unavailable at the higher price. For the most part, if you examine your own behavior, you will see that it generally follows the law of demand.

Relative Prices versus Money Prices

Relative price
The price of one commodity divided by the price of another commodity; the number of units of one commodity that must be sacrificed to purchase one unit of another commodity.

Money price
The price that we observe today, expressed in today's dollars; also called the *absolute* or *nominal price*.

The **relative price** of any commodity is its price in terms of another commodity. The price that you pay in dollars and cents for any good or service at any point in time is called its **money price.** You might hear from your grandparents, "My first new car cost only fifteen hundred dollars." The implication, of course, is that the price of cars today is outrageously high because the average new car might cost $30,000. But that is not an accurate comparison. What was the price of the average house during that same year? Perhaps it was only $12,000. By comparison, then, given that the average price of houses today is close to $200,000, the price of a new car today doesn't sound so far out of line, does it?

The point is that money prices during different time periods don't tell you much. You have to calculate relative prices. Consider an example of the price of prerecorded DVDs versus prerecorded videocassettes from last year and this year. In Table 3-1, we show the money prices of DVDs and videocassettes for two years during which they have both gone up. That means that we have to pay out in today's dollars more for DVDs and more for videocassettes. If we look, though, at the relative prices of DVDs and videocassettes, we find that last year, DVDs were twice as expensive as videocassettes, whereas this year they are only $1\frac{3}{4}$ times as expensive. Conversely, if we compare videocassettes to DVDs, last year the price of videocassettes was half the price of DVDs, but today the price of videocassettes is about 57 percent higher. In the one-year period, though both prices have gone up in money terms, the relative price of DVDs has fallen (and equivalently, the relative price of videocassettes has risen).

When evaluating the effects of price changes, we must always compare *price per constant-quality unit*. Sometimes relative price changes occur because the quality of a product improves, thereby bringing about a decrease in the item's effective price per constant-quality unit.

Even though you are used to buying products that include multiple features, did you know that more and more products are being offered with different features sold separately? Read on.

TABLE 3-1
Money Price versus Relative Price
The money prices of both digital videodiscs (DVDs) and videocassettes have risen. But the relative price of DVDs has fallen (or conversely, the relative price of videocassettes has risen).

	Money Price		Relative Price	
	Price Last Year	Price This Year	Price Last Year	Price This Year
DVDs	$20	$28	$\frac{\$20}{\$10} = 2.0$	$\frac{\$28}{\$16} = 1.75$
Videocassettes	$10	$16	$\frac{\$10}{\$20} = 0.5$	$\frac{\$16}{\$28} = 0.57$

E X A M P L E

What's the Effective Price per Constant-Quality Unit? It Depends on Whether the Product Is "Bundled"

Consumers often pay a single price for products containing more than one feature. For instance, traditionally the price of a hotel room normally covered associated housekeeping services. Consequently, consumers could compare hotel prices per constant-quality unit, which included essential housekeeping services regarded as part of the overall package of amenities that hotels provided. Nowadays, however, a growing number of hotels offer guests a choice: the hotel room will not be cleaned each day unless the guest pays a fee ranging from $2 to $4 per day.

Likewise, in years past, the price of a durable good purchased from a retailer commonly included the privilege of returning the item if the purchaser chose not to keep it. Today many retailers charge customers for handling product returns. Electronics stores, for example, often charge consumers returning video cameras or DVD players restocking fees equal to 10 to 15 percent of the purchase price.

Such separate prices and fees are part of a growing trend toward product *unbundling* in hotel services, retailing, and various other industries. Individual features of products that sellers previously grouped together and sold as a set now are being offered as separately priced items. If this trend continues in these and other industries, consumers may ultimately find it easier to assess the effective price per constant-quality unit of the products. In the meantime, however, consumers seeking the lowest effective price must pay close attention to whether various product features are priced separately or as bundles.

For Critical Analysis
Why might some consumers be willing to pay an office supply store such as Office Depot or Staples a higher price for a pre-assembled desk, rather than paying a significantly lower price for an unassembled desk?

CONCEPTS in Brief

- The law of demand posits an inverse relationship between the quantity demanded of a good and its price, other things being equal.

- The law of demand applies when other things, such as income and the prices of all other goods and services, are held constant.

To test your understanding of the concepts covered in this section, go to the Online Review at www.myeconlab.com/miller.

THE DEMAND SCHEDULE

Let's take a hypothetical demand situation to see how the inverse relationship between the price and the quantity demanded looks (holding other things equal). We will consider the quantity of rewritable CDs demanded *per year*. Without stating the *time dimension*, we could not make sense out of this demand relationship because the numbers would be different if we were talking about the quantity demanded per month or the quantity demanded per decade.

In addition to implicitly or explicitly stating a time dimension for a demand relationship, we are also implicitly referring to *constant-quality units* of the good or service in question. Prices are always expressed in constant-quality units in order to avoid the problem of comparing commodities that are in fact not truly comparable.

In panel (a) of Figure 3-1 on the next page, we see that if the price were $1 apiece, 50 rewritable CDs would be bought each year by our representative individual, but if the price were $5 apiece, only 10 CDs would be bought each year. This reflects the law of demand. Panel (a) is also called simply demand, or a *demand schedule*, because it gives a schedule of alternative quantities demanded per year at different possible prices.

FIGURE 3-1
The Individual Demand Schedule and the Individual Demand Curve

In panel (a), we show combinations A through E of the quantities of rewritable CDs demanded, measured in constant-quality units at prices ranging from $5 down to $1 apiece. These combinations are points on the demand schedule. In panel (b), we plot combinations A through E on a grid. The result is the individual demand curve for rewritable CDs.

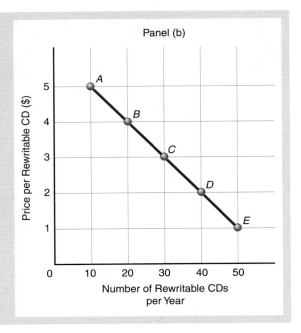

Panel (a)

Combination	Price per Constant-Quality Rewritable CD	Quantity of Constant-Quality Rewritable CDs per Year
A	$5	10
B	4	20
C	3	30
D	2	40
E	1	50

The Demand Curve

Tables expressing relationships between two variables can be represented in graphical terms. To do this, we need only construct a graph that has the price per constant-quality rewritable CD on the vertical axis and the quantity measured in constant-quality rewritable CDs per year on the horizontal axis. All we have to do is take combinations A through E from panel (a) of Figure 3-1 and plot those points in panel (b). Now we connect the points with a smooth line, and *voilà*, we have a **demand curve.**[*] It is downward sloping (from left to right) to indicate the inverse relationship between the price of rewritable CDs and the quantity demanded per year. Our presentation of demand schedules and curves applies equally well to all commodities, including dental floss, bagels, textbooks, credit, and labor. Remember, the demand curve is simply a graphical representation of the law of demand.

Demand curve
A graphical representation of the demand schedule; a negatively sloped line showing the inverse relationship between the price and the quantity demanded (other things being equal).

Individual versus Market Demand Curves

The demand schedule shown in panel (a) of Figure 3-1 and the resulting demand curve shown in panel (b) are both given for an individual. As we shall see, the determination of price in the marketplace depends on, among other things, the **market demand** for a particular commodity. The way in which we measure a market demand schedule and derive a market demand curve for rewritable CDs or any other good or service is by summing (at each price) the individual quantities demanded by all buyers in the market. Suppose that the market demand for rewritable CDs consists of only two buyers: buyer 1, for whom we've already shown the demand schedule, and buyer 2, whose demand schedule is dis-

Market demand
The demand of all consumers in the marketplace for a particular good or service. The summation at each price of the quantity demanded by each individual.

---

[*]Even though we call them "curves," for the purposes of exposition we often draw straight lines. In many real-world situations, demand and supply curves will in fact be lines that do curve. To connect the points in panel (b) with a line, we assume that for all prices in between the ones shown, the quantities demanded will be found along that line.

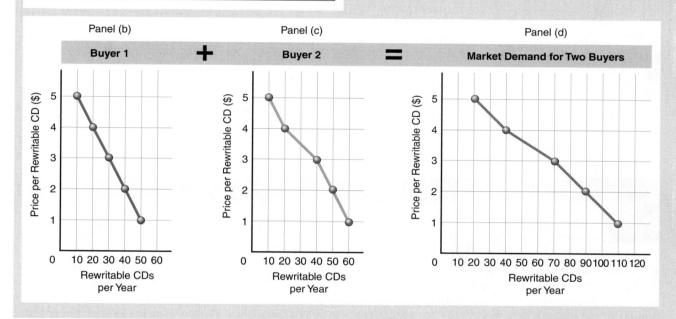

Panel (a)			
(1) Price per Rewritable CD	(2) Buyer 1's Quantity Demanded	(3) Buyer 2's Quantity Demanded	(4) = (2) + (3) Combined Quantity Demanded per Year
$5	10	10	20
4	20	20	40
3	30	40	70
2	40	50	90
1	50	60	110

FIGURE 3-2

The Horizontal Summation of Two Demand Curves

Panel (a) shows how to sum the demand schedule for one buyer with that of another buyer. In column 2 is the quantity demanded by buyer 1, taken from panel (a) of Figure 3-1. Column 4 is the sum of columns 2 and 3. We plot the demand curve for buyer 1 in panel (b) and the demand curve for buyer 2 in panel (c). When we add those two demand curves horizontally, we get the market demand curve for two buyers, shown in panel (d).

played in column 3 of panel (a) of Figure 3-2. Column 1 shows the price, and column 2 shows the quantity demanded by buyer 1 at each price. These data are taken directly from Figure 3-1. In column 3, we show the quantity demanded by buyer 2. Column 4 shows the total quantity demanded at each price, which is obtained by simply adding columns 2 and 3. Graphically, in panel (d) of Figure 3-2, we add the demand curves of buyer 1 [panel (b)] and buyer 2 [panel (c)] to derive the market demand curve.

There are, of course, numerous potential consumers of rewritable CDs. We'll simply assume that the summation of all of the consumers in the market results in a demand schedule, given in panel (a) of Figure 3-3 on the next page, and a demand curve, given in panel (b). The quantity demanded is now measured in millions of units per year. Remember, panel (b) in Figure 3-3 shows the market demand curve for the millions of users of rewritable CDs. The "market" demand curve that we derived in Figure 3-2 was undertaken assuming that there were only two buyers in the entire market. That's why we assume that the "market" demand curve for two buyers in panel (d) of Figure 3-2 is not a smooth line, whereas the true market demand curve in panel (b) of Figure 3-3 is a smooth line with no kinks.

Now that you know about the law of demand, what do you think happened in the last few years in Japan after the government raised the nation's highway tolls?

FIGURE 3-3
The Market Demand Schedule for Rewritable CDs
In panel (a), we add up the existing demand schedules for rewritable CDs. In panel (b), we plot the quantities from panel (a) on a grid; connecting them produces the market demand curve for rewritable CDs.

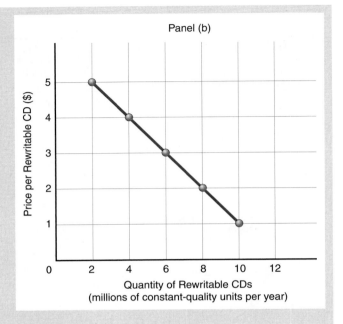

Panel (b)

Panel (a)

Price per Constant-Quality Rewritable CD	Total Quantity Demanded of Constant-Quality Rewritable CDs per Year (millions)
$5	2
4	4
3	6
2	8
1	10

International Policy EXAMPLE

The Japanese Government Discovers How to Prevent Traffic Jams on Expressways

In the United States, many people refer to auto expressways as "freeways." Applying the Japanese word for "free" to expressways would never occur to a resident of Japan, where all 4,350 miles of the nation's expressways are toll roads. The fee to make a two-hour trip on almost any stretch of a Japanese expressway is nearly $50. If the trip includes crossing a bridge, another $50 toll will apply. Someone who wishes to drive the entire length of Japan, a country slightly smaller in size than California, typically must pay at least $325 in tolls.

Since 1997, the average expressway toll in Japan has risen by about 8 percent *per mile*. Based on the law of demand, the result was predictable. Japanese trucking firms have instructed drivers to use expressways when necessary to meet delivery schedules but to keep to regular streets as much as possible to minimize tolls. Local delivery services prohibit their drivers from using expressways at all. Some Tokyo commuters even use global positioning systems in their cars to plot meandering trips on surface streets to avoid using expressways. As a consequence, the number of vehicles driving on Japanese expressways each day has dropped from 3.8 million in 1997 to below 3.6 million today.

For Critical Analysis
Why do you suppose that many Japanese drivers are still willing to pay higher tolls to drive on expressways?

CONCEPTS in Brief

- We measure the demand schedule in terms of a time dimension and in constant-quality units.

- The market demand curve is derived by summing the quantity demanded by individuals at each price. Graphically, we add the individual demand curves horizontally to derive the total, or market, demand curve.

To test your understanding of the concepts covered in this section, go to the Online Review at **www.myeconlab.com/miller**.

SHIFTS IN DEMAND

Assume that the federal government gives every student registered in a college, university, or technical school in the United States a rewritable CD drive (CD-RW drive) to use with personal computers. The demand curve presented in panel (b) of Figure 3-3 would no longer be an accurate representation of total market demand for rewritable CDs. What we have to do is shift the curve outward, or to the right, to represent the rise in demand that would result from this program. There will now be an increase in the number of rewritable CDs demanded at *each and every possible price*. The demand curve shown in Figure 3-4 will shift from D_1 to D_2. Take any price, say, $3 per rewritable CDs. Originally, before the federal government giveaway of CD-RW drives, the amount demanded at $3 was 6 million rewritable CDs per year. After the government giveaway of CD-RW drives, however, the new amount demanded at the $3 price is 10 million rewritable CDs per year. What we have seen is a shift in the demand for rewritable CDs.

Under different circumstances, the shift can also go in the opposite direction. What if colleges uniformly prohibited the use of personal computers by any of their students? Such a regulation would cause a shift inward—to the left—of the demand curve for rewritable CDs. In Figure 3-4, the demand curve would shift to D_3; the quantity demanded would now be less at each and every possible price.

The Other Determinants of Demand

The demand curve in panel (b) of Figure 3-3 is drawn with other things held constant, specifically all of the other factors that determine how much will be bought. There are many such determinants. We refer to these determinants as ***ceteris paribus* conditions,** and they include consumers' income; tastes and preferences; the prices of related goods; expectations regarding future prices, future incomes, and future product availability; and market size (number of buyers). Let's examine each determinant more closely.

Ceteris paribus conditions
Determinants of the relationship between price and quantity that are unchanged along a curve; changes in these factors cause the curve to shift.

Income. For most goods, an increase in income will lead to an increase in demand. The expression *increase in demand* always refers to a comparison between two different demand curves. Thus, for most goods, an increase in income will lead to a rightward shift in the position of the demand curve from, say, D_1 to D_2 in Figure 3-4 on the following page. You can avoid confusion about shifts in curves by always relating a rise in demand to a rightward shift in the demand curve and a fall in demand to a leftward shift in the demand curve. Goods for which the demand rises when consumer income rises are called **normal goods.** Most goods, such as shoes, computers, and DVDs, are "normal goods." For some goods, however, demand *falls* as income rises. These are called **inferior goods.** Beans might be an example. As households get richer, they tend to purchase fewer and fewer beans and purchase more and more meat. (The terms *normal* and *inferior* are merely part of the economist's lexicon; no value judgments are associated with them.)

Remember, a shift to the left in the demand curve represents a decrease in demand, and a shift to the right represents an increase in demand.

Normal goods
Goods for which demand rises as income rises. Most goods are normal goods.

Inferior goods
Goods for which demand falls as income rises.

Tastes and Preferences. A change in consumer tastes in favor of a good can shift its demand curve outward to the right. When Pokémon trading cards became the rage, the demand curve for them shifted outward to the right; when the rage died out, the demand curve shifted inward to the left. Fashions depend to a large extent on people's tastes and preferences. Economists have little to say about the determination of tastes; that is, they don't have any "good" theories of taste determination or why people buy one brand of

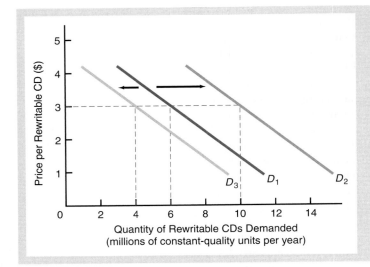

FIGURE 3-4
A Shift in the Demand Curve
If some factor other than price changes, we can show its effect by moving the entire demand curve, say, from D_1 to D_2. We have assumed in our example that this move was precipitated by the government's giving a free CD-RW drive to every registered college student in the United States. Thus, at *all* prices, a larger number of rewritable CDs would be demanded than before. Curve D_3 represents reduced demand compared to curve D_1, caused by a prohibition of personal computers on campus.

product rather than others. Advertisers, however, have various theories that they use to try to make consumers prefer their products over those of competitors.

What do you suppose happened to the demand for grapefruit when people learned that consumption of the fruit could, under certain circumstances, have adverse effects on their health?

EXAMPLE

Why Grapefruit Sales Have Gone Sour

Kids have never been known to like grapefruit, and many busy working people do not like to take the time to eat it. Consequently, grapefruit producers have found that many of their best customers are older, retired individuals.

Elderly people also tend to be the primary consumers of blood pressure and anticholesterol medications. In 1997, medical researchers discovered that grapefruit juice inhibits the production of an intestinal enzyme that breaks down such drugs, thereby amplifying their effects. Thus a person who drinks grapefruit juice while taking these drugs may experience side effects such as headaches and muscle pain. By the early 2000s, most physicians had begun suggesting that individuals taking

blood pressure and anti-cholesterol medications limit their intake of grapefruit juice.

Since the news of this discovery appeared in press reports in 1998, the demand for grapefruit has dropped significantly. In 1997, U.S. residents consumed about 4.6 billion pounds of grapefruit. Now they consume only about 3.4 billion pounds of grapefruit each year.

For Critical Analysis
How do you suppose that the recently publicized discovery that increased grapefruit juice consumption by younger people helps reduce cholesterol is likely to affect the demand for grapefruit?

Prices of Related Goods: Substitutes and Complements. Demand schedules are always drawn with the prices of all other commodities held constant. That is to say, when deriving a given demand curve, we assume that only the price of the good under study changes. For example, when we draw the demand curve for butter, we assume that the price of margarine is held constant. When we draw the demand curve for home cinema speakers, we assume that the price of surround-sound amplifiers is held constant. When we refer to *related goods*, we are talking about goods for which demand is interdependent. If a change in the price of one good shifts the demand for another good, those two goods have interdependent demands. There are two types of demand interdependencies: those in which goods are *substitutes* and those in which goods are *complements*. We can define and distinguish between substitutes and complements in terms of how the change in price of one commodity affects the demand for its related commodity.

Butter and margarine are **substitutes.** Either can be consumed to satisfy the same basic want. Let's assume that both products originally cost $2 per pound. If the price of butter remains the same and the price of margarine falls from $2 per pound to $1 per pound, people will buy more margarine and less butter. The demand curve for butter will shift inward to the left. If, conversely, the price of margarine rises from $2 per pound to $3 per pound, people will buy more butter and less margarine. The demand curve for butter will shift outward to the right. In other words, an increase in the price of margarine will lead to an increase in the demand for butter, and an increase in the price of butter will lead to an increase in the demand for margarine. For substitutes, a change in the price of a substitute will cause a change in demand *in the same direction.*

How do you think food-product manufacturers that can use either flavoring syrups or honey as sweeteners have responded to a recent rise in the price of honey?

Substitutes
Two goods are substitutes when either one can be used for consumption to satisfy a similar want—for example, coffee and tea. The more you buy of one, the less you buy of the other. For substitutes, the change in the price of one causes a shift in demand for the other in the same direction as the price change.

E X A M P L E

Higher Honey Prices Boost the Demand for Flavoring Syrup

The U.S. flavoring syrup industry processes a range of ingredients such as sugar, fruit, corn, and preservatives into concentrated syrups. Various food manufacturers use these flavoring syrups as sweetening ingredients in soft drinks, ice cream, and desserts.

Between 2000 and 2003, the price of honey, a substitute food-sweetening ingredient, increased from $0.60 per pound to just over $1.30 per pound. In 2001 and 2002, food manufacturers responded to the rising price of honey by continuing to buy honey, albeit in somewhat smaller quantities. By 2003, however, a number of food manufacturers had found ways to

alter their recipes so that they could substitute flavoring syrups for honey. These manufacturers then reduced their orders for honey and boosted their orders for flavoring syrups. Thus the rise in the price of a substitute good, honey, caused the demand for flavoring syrups to increase, resulting in a rightward shift in the market demand curve for flavoring syrups.

For Critical Analysis
Why do you suppose that food manufacturers' substitution of flavoring syrups for honey did not occur instantaneously when the price of honey increased so much?

For **complements,** goods typically consumed together, the situation is reversed. Consider desktop computers and printers. We draw the demand curve for printers with the price of desktop computers held constant. If the price per constant-quality unit of computers decreases from, say, $2,000 to $1,000, that will encourage more people to purchase computer peripheral devices. They will now buy more printers, at any given printer price, than before. The demand curve for printers will shift outward to the right. If, by contrast, the price of desktop computers increases from $1,500 to $3,000, fewer people will purchase computer peripheral devices. The demand curve for printers will shift inward to the left. To summarize, a decrease in the price of computers leads to an increase in the demand for printers. An increase in the price of computers leads to a decrease in the demand for printers. Thus, for complements, a change in the price of a product will cause a change in demand *in the opposite direction.*

Complements
Two goods are complements if both are used together for consumption or enjoyment—for example, coffee and cream. The more you buy of one, the more you buy of the other. For complements, a change in the price of one causes an opposite shift in the demand for the other.

Why have higher cement prices induced builders to cut back on hiring construction workers?

E X A M P L E

Reduced Hiring of Construction Workers Is Set in Cement

Cement is an essential ingredient in the construction of building foundations. This is why U.S. builders purchase more than 100 million metric tons of cement every year.

In many parts of the United States, the price of cement has increased significantly in recent years. Builders have responded by redesigning buildings to use less cement and by hiring fewer workers to pour and shape cement. Thus the rise in the price of cement has generated a decrease in the demand for complementary construction workers.

For Critical Analysis
How has the rise in the price of cement likely affected the demand for brick, which is a substitute for cement in certain construction applications?

Expectations. Consumers' expectations regarding future prices, future incomes, and future availability will prompt them to buy more or less of a particular good without a change in its current money price. For example, consumers getting wind of a scheduled 100 percent price increase in rewritable CDs next month will buy more of them today at today's prices. Today's demand curve for rewritable CDs will shift from D_1 to D_2 in Figure 3-4 on page 56. The opposite would occur if a decrease in the price of rewritable CDs were scheduled for next month.

Expectations of a rise in income may cause consumers to want to purchase more of everything today at today's prices. Again, such a change in expectations of higher future income will cause a shift in the demand curve from D_1 to D_2 in Figure 3-4.

Finally, expectations that goods will not be available at any price will induce consumers to stock up now, increasing current demand.

Market Size (Number of Buyers). An increase in the number of buyers (holding buyers' incomes constant) shifts the market demand curve outward. Conversely, a reduction in the number of buyers shifts the market demand curve inward.

Changes in Demand versus Changes in Quantity Demanded

We have made repeated references to demand and to quantity demanded. It is important to realize that there is a difference between a *change in demand* and a *change in quantity demanded*.

Demand refers to a schedule of planned rates of purchase and depends on a great many *ceteris paribus* conditions, such as incomes, expectations, and the prices of substitutes or complements. Whenever there is a change in a *ceteris paribus* condition, there will be a change in demand—a shift in the entire demand curve to the right or to the left.

A quantity demanded is a specific quantity at a specific price, represented by a single point on a demand curve. When price changes, quantity demanded changes according to the law of demand, and there will be a movement from one point to another along the same demand curve. Look at Figure 3-5. At a price of $3 per rewritable CD, 6 million CDs per year are demanded. If the price falls to $1, quantity demanded increases to 10 million per year. This movement occurs because the current market price for the product changes. In Figure 3-5, you can see the arrow pointing down the given demand curve *D*.

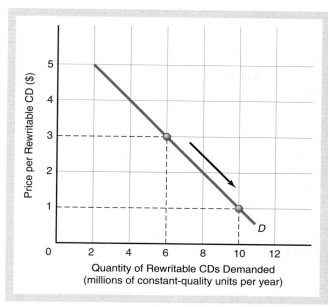

FIGURE 3-5
Movement Along a Given Demand Curve
A change in price changes the quantity of a good demanded. This can be represented as movement along a given demand schedule. If, in our example, the price of rewritable CDs falls from $3 to $1 apiece, the quantity demanded will increase from 6 million to 10 million units per year.

When you think of demand, think of the entire curve. Quantity demanded, in contrast, is represented by a single point on the demand curve.

A change or shift in demand is a movement of the **entire** *curve. The* **only** *thing that can cause the entire curve to move is a change in a determinant* **other than its own price.**

In economic analysis, we cannot emphasize too much the following distinction that must constantly be made:

A change in a good's own price leads to a change in quantity demanded for any given demand curve, other things held constant. This is a movement **on** *the curve.*

A change in any of the **ceteris paribus** *conditions for demand leads to a change in demand. This causes a movement* **of** *the curve.*

CONCEPT in Brief

- Demand curves are drawn with determinants other than the price of the good held constant. These other determinants, called *ceteris paribus* conditions, are (1) income; (2) tastes and preferences; (3) prices of related goods; (4) expectations about future prices, future incomes, and future availability of goods; and (5) market size (the number of buyers in the market). If any one of these determinants changes, the demand schedule will shift to the right or to the left.

- A change in demand comes about only because of a change in the *ceteris paribus* conditions of demand. This change in demand shifts the demand curve to the left or to the right.

- A change in the quantity demanded comes about when there is a change in the price of the good (other things held constant). Such a change in quantity demanded involves a movement along a given demand curve.

To test your understanding of the concepts covered in this section, go to the Online Review at www.myeconlab.com/miller.

THE LAW OF SUPPLY

The other side of the basic model in economics involves the quantities of goods and services that firms will offer for sale to the market. The **supply** of any good or service is the amount that firms will produce and offer for sale under certain conditions during a speci-

Supply
A schedule showing the relationship between price and quantity supplied for a specified period of time, other things being equal.

Law of supply
The observation that the higher the price of a good, the more of that good sellers will make available over a specified time period, other things being equal.

fied time period. The relationship between price and quantity supplied, called the **law of supply,** can be summarized as follows:

> *At higher prices, a larger quantity will generally be supplied than at lower prices, all other things held constant. At lower prices, a smaller quantity will generally be supplied than at higher prices, all other things held constant.*

There is generally a direct relationship between price and quantity supplied. For supply, as the price rises, the quantity supplied rises; as price falls, the quantity supplied also falls. Producers are normally willing to produce and sell more of their product at a higher price than at a lower price, other things being constant. At $5 per rewritable CD, manufacturers would almost certainly be willing to supply a larger quantity than at $1 per disc, assuming, of course, that no other prices in the economy had changed.

As with the law of demand, millions of instances in the real world have given us confidence in the law of supply. On a theoretical level, the law of supply is based on a model in which producers and sellers seek to make the most gain possible from their activities. For example, as a manufacturer of rewritable CDs attempts to produce more and more discs over the same time period, it will eventually have to hire more workers, pay overtime wages (which are higher), and overutilize its machines. Only if offered a higher price per disc will the manufacturer be willing to incur these higher costs. That is why the law of supply implies a direct relationship between price and quantity supplied.

THE SUPPLY SCHEDULE

Just as we were able to construct a demand schedule, we can construct a *supply schedule*, which is a table relating prices to the quantity supplied at each price. A supply schedule can also be referred to simply as *supply*. It is a set of planned production rates that depends on the price of the product. We show the individual supply schedule for a hypothetical producer in panel (a) of Figure 3-6. At $1 per rewritable CD, for example, this producer will supply 20,000 discs per year; at $5, this producer will supply 55,000 discs per year.

The Supply Curve

Supply curve
The graphical representation of the supply schedule; a line (curve) showing the supply schedule, which generally slopes upward (has a positive slope), other things being equal.

We can convert the supply schedule in panel (a) of Figure 3-6 into a **supply curve,** just as we earlier created a demand curve in Figure 3-1. All we do is take the price-quantity combinations from panel (a) of Figure 3-6 and plot them in panel (b). We have labeled these combinations *F* through *J.* Connecting these points, we obtain an upward-sloping curve that shows the typically direct relationship between price and quantity supplied. Again, we have to remember that we are talking about quantity supplied *per year,* measured in constant-quality units.

The Market Supply Curve

Just as we had to sum the individual demand curves to get the market demand curve, we need to sum the individual producers' supply curves to get the market supply curve. Look at Figure 3-7, in which we horizontally sum two typical supply curves for manufacturers of rewritable CDs. Supplier 1's data are taken from Figure 3-6; supplier 2 is added. The numbers are presented in panel (a). The graphical representation of supplier 1 is in panel (b), of supplier 2 in panel (c), and of the summation in panel (d). The result, then, is the supply curve for rewritable CDs for suppliers 1 and 2. We assume that there are more suppliers of rewritable CDs, however. The total market supply schedule and total market supply curve for rewritable CDs are represented in Figure 3-8 on the page 62, with the curve in panel (b) obtained by adding all of the supply curves such as those shown in panels (b)

FIGURE 3-6
The Individual Producer's Supply Schedule and Supply Curve for Rewritable CDs

Panel (a) shows that at higher prices, a hypothetical supplier will be willing to provide a greater quantity of rewritable CDs. We plot the various price-quantity combinations in panel (a) on the grid in panel (b). When we connect these points, we find the individual supply curve for rewritable CDs. It is positively sloped.

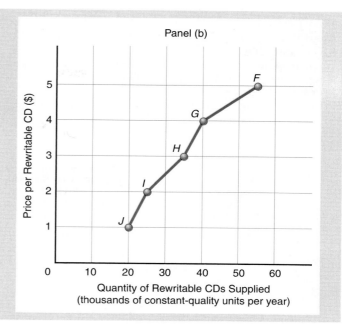

Panel (b)

Combination	Price per Constant-Quality Rewritable CD	Quantity of Rewritable CDs Supplied (thousands of constant-quality units per year)
	Panel (a)	
F	$5	55
G	4	40
H	3	35
I	2	25
J	1	20

FIGURE 3-7
Horizontal Summation of Supply Curves

In panel (a), we show the data for two individual suppliers of rewritable CDs. Adding how much each is willing to supply at different prices, we come up with the combined quantities supplied in column 4. When we plot the values in columns 2 and 3 on grids in panels (b) and (c) and add them horizontally, we obtain the combined supply curve for the two suppliers in question, shown in panel (d).

Panel (a)

(1) Price per Rewritable CD	(2) Supplier 1's Quantity Supplied (thousands)	(3) Supplier 2's Quantity Supplied (thousands)	(4) = (2) + (3) Combined Quantity Supplied per Year (thousands)
$5	55	35	90
4	40	30	70
3	35	20	55
2	25	15	40
1	20	10	30

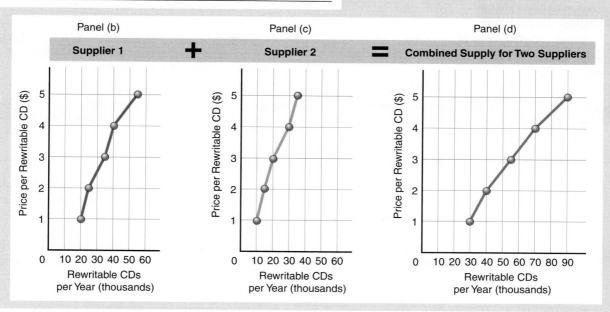

Panel (b) Supplier 1 + Panel (c) Supplier 2 = Panel (d) Combined Supply for Two Suppliers

FIGURE 3-8
The Market Supply Schedule and the Market Supply Curve for Rewritable CDs

In panel (a), we show the summation of all the individual producers' supply schedules; in panel (b), we graph the resulting supply curve. It represents the market supply curve for rewritable CDs and is upward sloping.

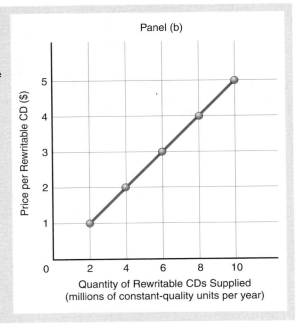

Panel (a)

Price per Constant-Quality Rewritable CD	Quantity of Rewritable CDs Supplied (millions of constant-quality units per year)
$5	10
4	8
3	6
2	4
1	2

and (c) of Figure 3-7 on the previous page. Notice the difference between the market supply curve with only two suppliers in Figure 3-7 and the one with a large number of suppliers—the entire true market—in panel (b) of Figure 3-8. (For simplicity, we assume that the true total market supply curve is a straight line.)

Notice what happens at the market level when price changes. If the price is $3, the quantity supplied is 6 million. If the price goes up to $4, the quantity supplied increases to 8 million per year. If the price falls to $2, the quantity supplied decreases to 4 million per year. Changes in quantity supplied are represented by movements along the supply curve in panel (b) of Figure 3-8.

CONCEPTS in Brief

- There is normally a direct, or positive, relationship between price and quantity of a good supplied, other things held constant.

- The supply curve normally shows a direct relationship between price and quantity supplied. The market supply curve is obtained by horizontally adding individual supply curves in the market.

To test your understanding of the concepts covered in this section, go to the Online Review at www.myeconlab.com/miller.

SHIFTS IN SUPPLY

When we looked at demand, we found out that any change in anything relevant besides the price of the good or service caused the demand curve to shift inward or outward. The same is true for the supply curve. If something besides price changes and alters the willingness of suppliers to produce a good or service, we will see the entire supply curve shift.

Consider an example. There is a new method of manufacturing rewritable CDs that reduces the cost of production by 50 percent. In this situation, producers of rewritable CDs will supply more product at *all* prices because their cost of so doing has fallen dramatically. Competition among manufacturers to produce more at each and every price will shift the supply curve outward to the right from S_1 to S_2 in Figure 3-9. At a price of $3, the quantity supplied was originally 6 million per year, but now the quantity supplied (after the reduction in the costs of production) at $3 per rewritable CD will be 9 million a year. (This is similar to what has happened to the supply curve of personal computers and fax machines in recent years as computer memory chip prices have fallen.)

Consider the opposite case. If the cost of making rewritable CDs doubles, the supply curve in Figure 3-9 will shift from S_1 to S_3. At each and every price, the quantity of rewritable CDs supplied will fall due to the increase in the price of raw materials.

The Other Determinants of Supply

When supply curves are drawn, only the price of the good in question changes, and it is assumed that other things remain constant. The other things assumed constant are the *ceteris paribus* conditions of supply. They include the prices of resources (inputs) used to produce the product, technology and productivity, taxes and subsides, producers' price expectations, and the number of firms in the industry. If *any* of these *ceteris paribus* conditions changes, there will be a shift in the supply curve.

Cost of Inputs Used to Produce the Product. If one or more input prices fall, the supply curve will shift outward to the right; that is, more will be supplied at each and every price. The opposite will be true if one or more inputs become more expensive. For example, when we draw the supply curve of new laptop computers, we are holding the price of microprocessors (and other inputs) constant. When we draw the supply curve of blue jeans, we are holding the cost of cotton fabric fixed.

Technology and Productivity. Supply curves are drawn by assuming a given technology, or "state of the art." When the available production techniques change, the supply curve will shift. For example, when a better production technique for rewritable CDs becomes available, the supply curve will shift to the right. A larger quantity will be forthcoming at each and every price because the cost of production is lower.

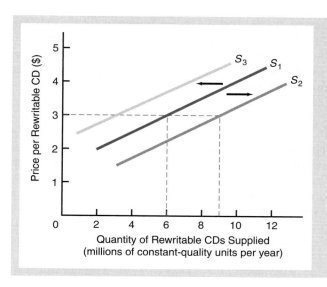

FIGURE 3-9
A Shift in the Supply Curve
If the cost of producing rewritable CDs were to fall dramatically, the supply curve would shift rightward from S_1 to S_2 such that at all prices, a larger quantity would be forthcoming from suppliers. Conversely, if the cost of production rose, the supply curve would shift leftward to S_3.

Subsidy
A negative tax; a payment to a producer from the government, usually in the form of a cash grant per unit.

Taxes and Subsidies. Certain taxes, such as a per-unit tax, are effectively an addition to production costs and therefore reduce the supply. If the supply curve were S_1 in Figure 3-9 on the previous page, a per-unit tax increase would shift it to S_3. A **subsidy** would do the opposite; it would shift the curve to S_2. Every producer would get a "gift" from the government for each unit produced.

How do you think that the supply of new housing in California has been affected by higher costs homebuilders face in meeting environmental regulations, which amount to a tax on each house they construct?

Policy EXAMPLE

Reducing the Supply of New Housing in California

To meet environmental regulations that have been added in recent years, developers and contractors must go through an approval process for new construction that is among the most complicated in the United States. According to some estimates, satisfying the regulations has added about $70,000 to the cost of building each new California home.

Naturally, builders have been willing to construct any given quantity of new houses only if they receive a price that is higher by $70,000 per house. This implies that, other things being equal, the supply curve for new-home construction has shifted upward by $70,000 per house. California's toughened environmental restrictions have, therefore, had the effect of reducing the supply of new houses in that state.

For Critical Analysis
On net, what would happen to the supply of housing if the state of California attempted to boost the production of new homes by granting every builder a $35,000 subsidy for each newly constructed house?

Price Expectations. A change in the expectation of a future relative price of a product can affect a producer's current willingness to supply, just as price expectations affect a consumer's current willingness to purchase. For example, suppliers of rewritable CDs may withhold from the market part of their current supply if they anticipate higher prices in the future. The current quantity supplied at each and every price will decrease.

Number of Firms in the Industry. In the short run, when firms can change only the number of employees they use, we hold the number of firms in the industry constant. In the long run, the number of firms (or the size of some existing firms) may change. If the number of firms increases, the supply curve will shift outward to the right. If the number of firms decreases, it will shift inward to the left.

Changes in Supply versus Changes in Quantity Supplied

We cannot overstress the importance of distinguishing between a movement along the supply curve—which occurs only when the price changes for a given supply curve—and a shift in the supply curve—which occurs only with changes in *ceteris paribus* conditions. A change in the price of the good in quesion always brings about a change in the quantity supplied along a given supply curve. We move to a different point on the existing supply curve. This is specifically called a *change in quantity supplied*. When price changes, quantity supplied changes, and there will be a movement from one point to another along the same supply curve.

When you think of *supply*, think of the entire curve. Quantity supplied is represented by a single point on the supply curve.

*A change or shift in supply is a movement of the entire curve. The **only** thing that can cause the entire curve to move is a change in one of the **ceteris paribus** conditions.*

Consequently,

*A change in the price leads to a change in the quantity supplied, other things being constant. This is a movement **on** the curve.*

*A change in any **ceteris paribus** conditon for supply leads to a change in supply. This causes a movement **of** the curve.*

CONCEPTS in Brief

- If the price changes, we *move along* a curve—there is a change in quantity demanded or supplied. If some other determinant changes, we *shift* a curve—there is a change in demand or supply.

- The supply curve is drawn with other things held constant. If these *ceteris paribus* conditions of supply change, the supply curve will shift. The major *ceteris paribus* conditions are (1) input prices, (2) technology and productivity, (3) taxes and subsidies, (4) expectations of future relative prices, and (5) the number of firms in the industry.

To test your understanding of the concepts covered in this section, go to the Online Review at www.myeconlab.com/miller.

PUTTING DEMAND AND SUPPLY TOGETHER

In the sections on demand and supply, we tried to confine each discussion to demand or supply only. But you have probably already realized that we can't view the world just from the demand side or just from the supply side. There is an interaction between the two. In this section, we will discuss how they interact and how that interaction determines the prices that prevail in our economy. Understanding how demand and supply interact is essential to understanding how prices are determined in our economy and other economies in which the forces of demand and supply are allowed to work.

Let's first combine the demand and supply schedules and then combine the curves.

Go to www.econtoday.com/chap03 to see how the U.S. Department of Agriculture seeks to estimate demand and supply conditions for major agricultural products.

Demand and Supply Schedules Combined

Let's place panel (a) from Figure 3-3 (the market demand schedule) on page 54 and panel (a) from Figure 3-8 (the market supply schedule) on page 62 together in panel (a) of Figure 3-10 on the next page. Column 1 shows the price; column 2, the quantity supplied per year at any given price; and column 3, the quantity demanded. Column 4 is the difference between columns 2 and 3, or the difference between the quantity supplied and the quantity demanded. In column 5, we label those differences as either excess quantity supplied (called a *surplus*, which we shall discuss shortly) or excess quantity demanded (commonly known as a *shortage*, also discussed shortly). For example, at a price of $1, only 2 million rewritable CDs would be supplied, but the quantity demanded would be 10 million. The difference would be −8 million, which we label excess quantity demanded (a shortage). At the other end, a price of $5 would elicit 10 million in quantity supplied, but quantity demanded would drop to 2 million, leaving a difference of +8 million units, which we call excess quantity supplied (a surplus).

Now, do you notice something special about the price of $3? At that price, both the quantity supplied and the quantity demanded per year are 6 million. The difference then is zero. There is neither excess quantity demanded (shortage) nor excess quantity supplied (surplus). Hence the price of $3 is very special. It is called the **market clearing price**—it clears the market of all excess quantities demanded or supplied. There are no willing con-

Market clearing, or equilibrium, price
The price that clears the market, at which quantity demanded equals quantity supplied; the price where the demand curve intersects the supply curve.

FIGURE 3-10
Putting Demand and Supply Together

In panel (a), we see that at the price of $3, the quantity supplied and the quantity demanded are equal, resulting in neither an excess quantity demanded nor an excess quantity supplied. We call this price the equilibrium, or market clearing, price. In panel (b), the intersection of the supply and demand curves is at *E*, at a price of $3 and a quantity of 6 million per year. At point *E*, there is neither an excess quantity demanded nor an excess quantity supplied. At a price of $1, the quantity supplied will be only

2 million per year, but the quantity demanded will be 10 million. The difference is excess quantity demanded at a price of $1. The price will rise, so we will move from point *A* up the supply curve and point *B* up the demand curve to point *E*. At the other extreme, $5 elicits a quantity supplied of 10 million but a quantity demanded of only 2 million. The difference is excess quantity supplied at a price of $5. The price will fall, so we will move down the demand curve and the supply curve to the equilibrium price, $3 per disc.

				Panel (a)
(1)	(2)	(3)	(4) Difference (2) − (3)	(5)
Price per Constant-Quality Rewritable CD	Quantity Supplied (rewritable CDs per year)	Quantity Demanded (rewritable CDs per year)	(rewritable CDs per year)	Condition
$5	10 million	2 million	8 million	Excess quantity supplied (surplus)
4	8 million	4 million	4 million	Excess quantity supplied (surplus)
3	6 million	6 million	0	Market clearing price—equilibrium (no surplus, no shortage)
2	4 million	8 million	−4 million	Excess quantity demanded (shortage)
1	2 million	10 million	−8 million	Excess quantity demanded (shortage)

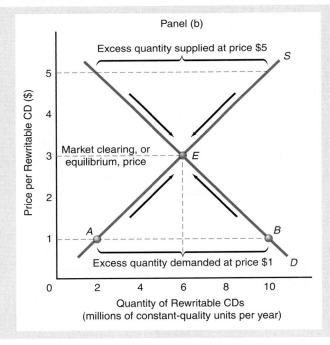

Panel (b)

sumers who want to pay $3 per rewritable CD but are turned away by sellers, and there are no willing suppliers who want to sell rewritable CDs at $3 who cannot sell all they want at that price. Another term for the market clearing price is the **equilibrium price,** the price at which there is no tendency for change. Consumers are able to get all they want at that price, and suppliers are able to sell all they want at that price.

Equilibrium

We can define **equilibrium** in general as a point at which quantity demanded equals quantity supplied at a particular price. There tends to be no movement of the price or the quantity away from this point unless demand or supply changes. Any movement away from this point will set into motion forces that will cause movement back to it. Therefore, equilibrium is a stable point. Any point that is not at equilibrium is unstable and cannot be maintained.

Equilibrium
The situation when quantity supplied equals quantity demanded at a particular price.

The equilibrium point occurs where the supply and demand curves intersect. The equilibrium price is given on the vertical axis directly to the left of where the supply and demand curves cross. The equilibrium quantity is given on the horizontal axis directly underneath the intersection of the demand and supply curves. Equilibrium can change whenever there is a *shock* caused by a change in a *certeris paribus* condition for demand or supply.

A shock to the supply-and-demand system can be represented by a shift in the supply curve, a shift in the demand curve, or a shift in both curves. Any shock to the system will result in a new set of supply-and-demand relationships and a new equilibrium; forces will come into play to move the system from the old price-quantity equilibrium (now a disequilibrium situation) to the new equilibrium, where the new demand and supply curves intersect.

Panel (b) in Figure 3-3 and panel (b) in Figure 3-8 are combined as panel (b) in Figure 3-10. The only difference now is that the horizontal axis measures both the quantity supplied and the quantity demanded per year. Everything else is the same. The demand curve is labeled *D*, the supply curve *S*. We have labeled the intersection of the supply curve with the demand curve as point *E*, for equilibrium. That corresponds to a market clearing price of $3, at which both the quantity supplied and the quantity demanded are 6 million units per year. There is neither excess quantity supplied nor excess quantity demanded. Point *E*, the equilibrium point, always occurs at the intersection of the supply and demand curves. This is the price *toward which* the market price will automatically tend to gravitate.

Shortages

The demand and supply curves depicted in Figure 3-10 represent a situation of equilibrium. But a non-market-clearing, or disequilibrium, price will put into play forces that cause the price to change toward the market clearing price at which equilibrium will again be sustained. Look again at panel (b) in Figure 3-10. Suppose that instead of being at the market clearing price of $3, for some reason the market price is $1. At this price, the quantity demanded of 10 million per year exceeds the quantity supplied of 2 million per year. We have a situation of excess quantity demanded at the price of $1. This is usually called a **shortage.** Consumers of rewritable CDs would find that they could not buy all that they wished at $1 apiece. But forces will cause the price to rise: Competing consumers will bid up the price, and suppliers will increase output in response. (Remember, some buyers would pay $5 or more rather than do without rewritable CDs. They do not want to be left out.) We would move from points *A* and *B* toward point *E*. The process would stop when the price again reached $3 per disc.

Shortage
A situation in which quantity demanded is greater than quantity supplied at a price below the market clearing price.

Economics Front and Center

To consider how a natural disaster can create shortages of services that can only be eliminated speedily by a rapid price change, consider the case study, **The Economics of a Tornado Cleanup Can Hit Close to Home,** on page 70.

At this point, it is important to recall a distinction made in Chapter 2:

Shortages and scarcity are not the same thing.

A shortage is a situation in which the quantity demanded exceeds the quantity supplied at a price *below* the market clearing price. Our definition of scarcity was much more general and all-encompassing: a situation in which the resources available for producing output are insufficient to satisfy all wants. Any choice necessarily costs an opportunity, and the opportunity is lost. Hence we will always live in a world of scarcity because we must constantly make choices, but we do not necessarily have to live in a world of shortages.

Knowing what you do about why prices change, what do you think happened relatively recently when freight trains didn't have enough space to transport all of the grain that farmers wanted to supply?

E X A M P L E

The Price of Rail Transport Responds to a Rail Traffic Logjam

Recently, a big increase in the prices of grains such as wheat and corn, caused by a number of factors, induced farmers to grow more grain. When it came time to ship the grain to market on freight trains, which typically transport more than 40 percent of all U.S. grain, a problem arose. At prevailing rail shipping prices, railroad companies did not wish to provide enough freight cars to transport all the grain that farmers desired to ship. Farmers faced a shortage of rail transport services that led to some of the longest crop-shipping delays in years.

Within weeks, however, the price of rail transport of grain had risen, which induced some farmers to delay their grain shipments and gave railroad companies an incentive to put more freight cars into service. This equalized the quantities of rail freight services demanded and supplied and ended the shortage of grain transport services.

For Critical Analysis
What would have occurred if a government regulation had prevented the price of shipping grain by rail from rising to the equilibrium level?

Surpluses

Surplus
A situation in which quantity supplied is greater than quantity demanded at a price above the market clearing price.

Now let's repeat the experiment with the market price at $5 rather than at the market clearing price of $3. Clearly, the quantity supplied will exceed the quantity demanded at that price. The result will be an excess quantity supplied at $5 per unit. This excess quantity supplied is often called a **surplus.** Given the curves in panel (b) in Figure 3-10 on page 66, however, there will be forces pushing the price back down toward $3 per rewritable CD: Competing suppliers will cut prices and reduce output, and consumers will purchase more at these new lower prices. If the two forces of supply and demand are unrestricted, they will bring the price back to $3 per disc.

Shortages and surpluses are resolved in unfettered markets—markets in which price changes are free to occur. The forces that resolve them are those of competition: In the case of shortages, consumers competing for a limited quantity supplied drive up the price; in the case of surpluses, sellers compete for the limited quantity demanded, thus driving prices down to equilibrium. The equilibrium price is the only stable price, and all (unrestricted) market prices tend to gravitate toward it.

What happens when the price is set below the equilibrium price? Here come the scalpers.

Policy EXAMPLE

Should Shortages in the Ticket Market Be Solved by Scalpers?

If you have ever tried to get tickets to a playoff game in sports, a popular Broadway play, or a superstar's rap concert, you know about "shortages." The standard Super Bowl ticket situation is shown in Figure 3-11. At the face-value price of Super Bowl tickets (P_1), the quantity demanded (Q_2) greatly exceeds the quantity supplied (Q_1). Because shortages last only so long as prices and quantities do not change, markets tend to exhibit a movement out of this disequilibrium toward equilibrium. Obviously, the quantity of Super Bowl tickets cannot change, but the price can go as high as P_2.

Enter the scalper. This colorful term is used because when you purchase a ticket that is being resold at a price higher than face value, the seller is skimming an extra profit off the top ("taking your scalp"). If an event sells out and people who wished to purchase tickets at current prices were unable to do so, ticket prices by definition have been lower than market clearing prices. People without tickets may be willing to buy

high-priced tickets because they place a greater value on the entertainment event than the face value of the ticket. Without scalpers, those individuals would not be able to attend the event. In the case of the Super Bowl, various forms of scalping occur nationwide. Tickets for a seat on the 50-yard line have been sold for more than $2,000 apiece. In front of every Super Bowl arena, you can find ticket scalpers hawking their wares.

In most states, scalping is illegal. In Pennsylvania, convicted scalpers are either fined $5,000 or sentenced to two years behind bars. For an economist, such legislation seems strange. As one New York ticket broker said, "I look at scalping like working as a stockbroker, buying low and selling high. If people are willing to pay me the money, what kind of problem is that?"

For Critical Analysis
What happens to ticket scalpers who are still holding tickets after an event has started?

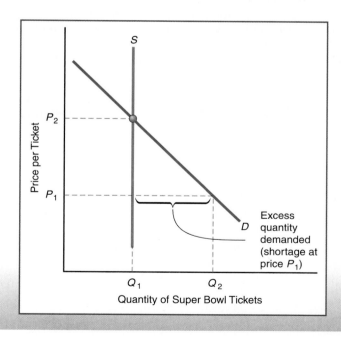

FIGURE 3-11
Shortages of Super Bowl Tickets
The quantity of tickets for any one Super Bowl is fixed at Q_1. At the price per ticket of P_1, the quantity demanded is Q_2, which is greater than Q_1. Consequently, there is an excess quantity demanded at the below–market clearing price. Prices can go as high as P_2 in the scalpers' market.

CONCEPTS in Brief

- The market clearing price occurs at the intersection of the market demand curve and the market supply curve. It is also called the equilibrium price, the price from which there is no tendency to change unless there is a change in demand or supply.

- Whenever the price is greater than the equilibrium price, there is an excess quantity supplied (a surplus).

- Whenever the price is less than the equilibrium price, there is an excess quantity demanded (a shortage).

To test your understanding of the concepts covered in this section, go to the Online Review at www.myeconlab.com/miller.

CASE STUDY: Economics Front and Center

The Economics of a Tornado Cleanup Can Hit Close to Home

An early spring tornado has just rolled through a midwestern town, and more than 500 structures have experienced at least moderate damage. After recovering from the initial shock, one couple, the Richardsons, realize that they are lucky to have only blown-out windows and large holes in their roof, which they quickly cover with plastic sheeting. When they try to find a construction contractor to make permanent repairs, however, they do not feel so lucky any more. Most phone calls to contractors are producing either busy signals or unanswered voice mail messages. The few contractors who respond say that they are overwhelmed with requests for work and cannot possibly begin the Richardsons' repairs for at least a couple of weeks. Meanwhile, temperatures are dropping, and rain is forecast for all of next week.

Finally, two contractors call back and say their companies will do the work, but only at prices that the Richardsons know to be nearly 25 percent higher than the usual prices charged to replace windows and a roof. How can demand and supply analysis explain the situation that the Richardsons are facing?

Points to Analyze

1. *Has the structural damage inflicted on this town by the tornado resulted in changes in the demand for and supply of the services of construction contractors or changes in the quantities demanded and supplied of those services?*

2. *Why are the price quotes the Richardsons have received higher than the "usual" prices charged by local contractors?*

Issues and Applications

Why Your Economics Instructor's Salary May Be Lagging

So far, the 2000s have been tough on young economists interested in teaching students like you at colleges and universities. Jobs have been more difficult to find than in years past. Salaries have been stagnant. The problem that prospective economics instructors face is one they would like to use as an example in an economics course—if only some of them could find teaching positions right away.

Concepts Applied
- Demand and Supply
- Surplus
- Market Clearing Price

A Sudden Spurt in the Supply of New Economists

The level of interest in advanced economics training has ebbed and flowed over the years. In the late 1970s and 1980s, many students became attracted to what is sometimes called the "queen of the social sciences." Enrollments in U.S. economics Ph.D. programs, where many new economics instructors are trained, surged. During the 1990s, enrollments in these programs declined when many people decided to enter the business world instead of becoming economics instructors.

Enrollments at U.S. graduate economics programs changed again in the early 2000s. More students chose careers as economists, which resulted in an increase in the number of individuals trained to teach the subject to college and university students. By 2004, nearly 250 more economics instructors per year were searching for teaching positions at any given price—in this case, a wage rate—than in 2000. Thus there was an increase in the supply of teaching services available from economics instructors.

Fewer Opportunities for New Economics Instructors

Unfortunately for all these budding teachers of economics, the early 2000s were also trying times for colleges and universities. Many publicly supported state institutions experienced funding cutbacks. Private colleges and universities also suffered from drops in stock prices that reduced the value of endowments provided by alumni and other benefactors.

Consequently, there was a fall in the revenues of the colleges and universities that employ economics instructors. These institutions responded to the decline in their revenues by cutting back on the number of job openings for new instructors. By 2004, colleges and universities were searching to fill about 400 fewer economics teaching positions per year than in 2000. That is, at any given wage rate for the services provided by economics instructors, the quantity of services demanded declined. There was a decrease in demand.

Pity Your Economics Instructor

Figure 3-12 on the next page summarizes the combined effects of the increase in the supply of and the decrease in the demand for the services of economics instructors. Following the rightward shift in supply, from S_1 to S_2, and the leftward shift in demand, from D_1 to D_2, there was an excess quantity of teaching services supplied at the initial price of these services, which was the wage rate W_1. Your current economics instructor has taught you how to reason out what had to happen to eliminate the market surplus: The market clearing price of the services economics instructors provided, their wage, had to decline, from W_1 to W_2. On net, the equilibrium quantity of services provided by new economics instructors declined. Hence, as shown in Figure 3-12, the equilibrium quantity fell from Q_1 at point E_1 to Q_2 at point E_2.

FIGURE 3-12

A Simultaneous Increase in the Supply of and Decrease in the Demand for Services of Economics Instructors

During the early 2000s, more individuals offered their services as economics instructors at any given price of their instructional services, or wage rate. At the same time, colleges and universities reduced the quantity of economics instructors' services demanded at each possible wage rate. Consequently, the equilibrium wage rate declined. The net effect was a decrease in the equilibrium quantity of services provided by economics instructors.

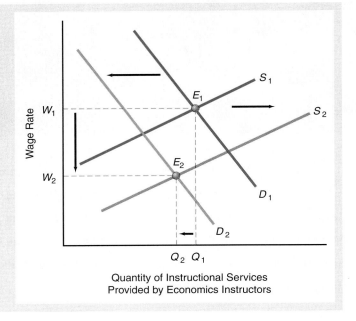

For Critical Analysis

1. How do you suppose that the decline in the relative wages earned by economics instructors during the early 2000s affected the demand for the services of graduate programs that train new economics instructors?
2. What would have happened to the equilibrium quantity of services provided by newly trained economics instructors if the revenues of colleges and universities had *increased* during this period?

Web Resources

1. Track jobs for new economics instructors at the links to academic position openings provided by the American Economic Association's "Job Openings for Economists" site by going to www.econtoday.com/chap03.
2. For the U.S. Department of Labor's outlook on career opportunities in college and university teaching, use the link provided at www.econtoday.com/chap03.

Research Project

Many of today's senior economics instructors are part of the relatively large "baby boom" generation born between the end of World War II and the late 1950s. A number of these individuals are now reaching retirement age. Evaluate what is likely to happen, other things being equal, to the relative wages of younger economics instructors if many of these older instructors retire from their positions during the next few years.

SUMMARY DISCUSSION of Learning Objectives

1. **The Law of Demand:** According to the law of demand, other things being equal, individuals will purchase fewer units of a good at a higher price, and they will purchase more units of a good at a lower price.

2. **Relative Prices versus Money Prices:** When determining the quantity of a good to purchase, people respond to changes in its relative price, the price of the good in terms of other goods, rather than a change in the good's money price expressed in today's dollars. If the price of a CD rises by 50 percent next year while at the same time all other prices, including your wages, also increase by 50 percent, then the relative price of the CD has not

changed. Thus, in a world of generally rising prices, you have to compare the price of one good with the general level of prices of other goods in order to decide whether the relative price of that one good has gone up, gone down, or stayed the same.

3. **A Change in Quantity Demanded versus a Change in Demand:** The demand schedule shows the relationship between various possible prices and respective quantities purchased per unit of time. Graphically, the demand schedule is a downward-sloping demand curve. A change in the price of the good generates a change in the quantity demanded, which is a movement along the demand curve. The determinants of the quantity of a good demanded other than the price of the good are (a) income, (b) tastes and preferences, (c) the prices of related goods, (d) expectations, and (e) market size (the number of buyers). Whenever any of these *ceteris paribus* conditions of demand changes, there is a change in the demand for the good, and the demand curve shifts to a new position.

4. **The Law of Supply:** According to the law of supply, sellers will produce and offer for sale more units of a good at a higher price, and they will produce and offer for sale fewer units of the good at a lower price.

5. **A Change in Quantity Supplied versus a Change in Supply:** The supply schedule shows the relationship between various possible prices and respective quantities produced and sold per unit of time. On a graph, the supply schedule is a supply curve that slopes upward. A change in the price of the good generates a change in the quantity supplied, which is a movement along the supply curve. The determinants of the quantity of a good supplied other than the price of the good are (a) input prices, (b) technology and productivity, (c) taxes and subsidies, (d) price expectations, and (e) the number of sellers. Whenever any of these *ceteris paribus* conditions changes, there is a change in the supply of the good, and the supply curve shifts to a new position

6. **Determining the Market Price and the Equilibrium Quantity:** The market price of a good and the equilibrium quantity of the good that is produced and sold are determined by the intersection of the demand and supply curves. At this intersection point, the quantity demanded by buyers of the good just equals the quantity supplied by sellers. At the market price at this point of intersection, the plans of buyers and sellers mesh exactly. Hence there is neither an excess quantity of the good supplied (surplus) nor an excess quantity of the good demanded (shortage) at this equilibrium point.

KEY TERMS AND CONCEPTS

ceteris paribus conditions (55)

complements (57)

demand (49)

demand curve (52)

equilibrium (67)

inferior goods (55)

law of demand (49)

law of supply (60)

market (49)

market clearing, or equilibrium, price (65)

market demand (52)

money price (50)

normal goods (55)

relative price (50)

shortage (67)

subsidy (64)

substitutes (57)

supply (59)

supply curve (60)

surplus (68)

PROBLEMS

Answers to the odd-numbered problems appear at the back of the book.

3-1. Suppose that in a recent market period, an industry-wide survey determined the following relationship between the price of rap music CDs and the quantity supplied and quantity demanded.

Price	Quantity Demanded	Quantity Supplied
$9	100 million	40 million
$10	90 million	60 million
$11	80 million	80 million
$12	70 million	100 million
$13	60 million	120 million

Illustrate the supply and demand curves for rap CDs given the information in the table. What are the equilibrium price and quantity? If the industry price is $10, is there a shortage or surplus of CDs? How much is the shortage or surplus?

3-2. Suppose that a survey for a later market period indicates that the quantities supplied in the table in Problem 3-1 are unchanged. The quantity demanded, however, has increased by 30 million at each price. Construct the resulting demand curve in the illustration you made for Problem 3-1. Is this an increase or a decrease in demand? What are the new equilibrium quantity and the new market price? Give two examples of changes in *ceteris paribus* conditions in each case that might cause such a change.

3-3. Consider the market for *DSL high-speed* Internet access services, which is a normal good. Explain whether the following events would cause an increase or a decrease in demand or an increase or a decrease in the quantity demanded.

   a. Firms providing cable Internet access services reduce their prices.
   b. Firms providing DSL high-speed Internet access services reduce their prices.
   c. There is a decrease in the incomes earned by consumers of DSL high-speed Internet access services.
   d. Consumers of DSL high-speed Internet access services anticipate a decline in the future price of these services.

3-4. In the market for rap music CDs, explain whether the following events would cause an increase or a decrease in demand or an increase or a decrease in the quantity demanded. Also explain what happens to the equilibrium quantity and the market price.

   a. The price of CD packaging material declines.
   b. The price of CD players declines.
   c. The price of cassette tapes increases dramatically.
   d. A booming economy increases the income of the typical CD buyer.
   e. Many rap fans suddenly develop a fondness for country music.

3-5. Give an example of a complement and a substitute in consumption for each of the following items.

   a. Bacon
   b. Tennis racquets
   c. Coffee
   d. Automobiles

3-6. At the end of the 1990s, the United States imposed high import taxes on a number of European goods due to a trade dispute. One of these goods was Roquefort cheese. Show how this tax affects the market for Roquefort cheese in the United States, shifting the appropriate curve and indicating a new equilibrium quantity and market price.

3-7. Problem 3-6 described a tax imposed on Roquefort cheese. Illustrate the effect of the tax on Roquefort cheese in the market for a similar cheese, such as blue cheese, shifting the appropriate curve and indicating a new equilibrium quantity and market price.

3-8. Consider the market for economics textbooks. Explain whether the following events would cause an increase or a decrease in supply or an increase or a decrease in the quantity supplied.

   a. The market price of paper increases.
   b. The market price of economics textbooks increases.
   c. The number of publishers of economics textbooks increases.
   d. Publishers expect that the market price of economics textbooks will increase next month.

3-9. Consider the market for laptop computers. Explain whether the following events would cause an increase or a decrease in supply or an increase or a decrease in the quantity supplied. Illustrate each, and show what would happen to the equilibrium quantity and the market price.

   a. The price of memory chips used in laptop computers declines.
   b. The price of machinery used to produce laptop computers increases.
   c. The number of manufacturers of laptop computers increases.
   d. There is a decrease in the demand for laptop computers.

3-10. The U.S. government offers significant per-unit subsidy payments to U.S. sugar growers. Describe the effects of the introduction of such subsidies on the market for sugar and the market for artificial sweeteners. Explain whether the demand curve or the supply curve shifts in each market, and if so, in which direction. Also explain what happens to the equilibrium quantity and the market price in each market.

3-11. The supply curve for season tickets for basketball games for your school's team is vertical because there are a fixed number of seats in the school's gymnasium. Before preseason practice sessions begin, your school's administration commits itself to selling season tickets the day before the first basketball game at a predetermined price that happens to equal the current market price. The school will not change that price at any time prior to and including the day tickets go on sale. Illustrate, within a supply and demand framework, the effect of each of the following events on the market for season tickets on the day the school opens ticket sales, and indicate whether a surplus or a shortage would result.

a. The school's star player breaks a leg during preseason practice.

b. During preseason practice, a published newspaper poll of coaches of teams in your school's conference surprises everyone by indicating that your school's team is predicted to win the conference championship.

c. At a preseason practice session that is open to the public, the school president announces that all refreshments served during games will be free of charge throughout the season.

d. Most of your school's basketball fans enjoy an up-tempo, "run and gun" approach to basketball, but after the team's coach quits following the first preseason practice, the school's administration immediately hires a new coach who believes in a deliberate style of play that relies heavily on slow-tempo, four-corners offense.

3-12. Advances in computer technology allow individuals to purchase and download music from the Internet. Buyers may download single songs or complete tracks of songs that are also sold on CDs. Explain the impact of this technological advance on the market for CDs sold in retail stores.

3-13. Ethanol is a motor fuel manufactured from corn, barley, or wheat, and it can be used to power the engines of many autos and trucks. Suppose that the government decides to provide a large per-unit subsidy to ethanol producers. Explain the effects in the markets for the following items:

a. Corn

b. Gasoline

c. Automobiles

3-14. If the price of processor chips used in manufacturing personal computers decreases, what will happen in the market for personal computers? How will the equilibrium price and equilibrium quantity of personal computers change?

3-15. Assume that the cost of aluminum used by soft-drink companies increases. Which of the following correctly describes the resulting effects in the market for canned soft drinks? (More than one statement may be correct.)

a. The demand for soft drinks decreases.

b. The quantity of soft drinks demanded decreases.

c. The supply of soft drinks decreases.

d. The quantity of soft drinks supplied decreases.

ECONOMICS ON THE NET

The U.S. Nursing Shortage For some years media stories have discussed a shortage of qualified nurses in the United States. This application explores some of the factors that have caused the quantity of newly trained nurses demanded to tend to exceed the quantity of newly trained nurses supplied.

Title: Nursing Shortage Resource Web Link

Navigation: Go to the Nursing Shortage Resource Web Link at www.econtoday.com/chap03, and click on *Enrollment Increase Insufficient to Meet the Projected Increase in Demand for New Nurses.*

Application Read the discussion, and answer the following questions.

1. Since 1995, what has happened to the demand for new nurses in the United States? What has happened to the supply of new nurses? Why has the result been a shortage?

2. If there is a free market for the skills of new nurses, what can you predict is likely to happen to the wage rate earned by individuals who have just completed their nursing training?

For Group Study and Analysis Discuss the pros and cons of high schools and colleges trying to factor predictions about future wages into student career counseling. How might this potentially benefit students? What problems might high schools and colleges face in trying to assist students in evaluating the future earnings prospects of various jobs?

If your exam were tomorrow, would you be ready? For each chapter, MyEconLab Practice Tests and Study Plans pinpoint which sections you have mastered and which ones you need to study. That way, you are more efficient with your study time, and you are better prepared for your exams.

In addition to Practice Tests and your personalized Study Plan, you'll find the following media resources in MyEconLab:

1. *Graphs in Motion* animation of Figures 3-2, 3-4, 3-5, 3-6, 3-7, 3-9, and 3-11.

2. An *Economics in Motion* in-depth animation of Demand, Supply, and Equilibrium.

3. Videos featuring the author, Roger LeRoy Miller, on the following subjects:
   - The Difference Between Relative and Absolute Prices and the Importance of Looking at Only Relative Prices
   - The Importance of Distinguishing Between a Shift in a Demand Curve and a Move Along the Demand Curve

   - The Importance of Distinguishing Between a Change in Supply versus a Change in Quantity Supplied

4. Links to the Web sites cited in the marginal Internet Resources, Issues and Applications feature, and Economics on the Net activity.

5. Audio clips of all key terms, additional practice problems, and a PDF version of the material from the print Study Guide.

5. eThemes of the Times, which is a New York Times article to help you understand the real-world applications of what you are learning.

To see how it works, turn to page 16 and then go to www.myeconlab.com/miller.

Get Ahead of the Curve

Chapter 4

Extensions of Demand and Supply Analysis

Charleston (South Carolina), Jacksonville, New Orleans, and Los Angeles all share one common characteristic: they are seaports. Another shared characteristic is that available space for ships to navigate and dock is increasingly scarce in their ports. Indeed, shipping companies have complained in recent years that there has been a "shortage" of available space at many U.S. seaports. In this chapter, you will learn more about shortages and why a shortage eventually should disappear in an unregulated market. You will also learn, however, why the shortage of space at seaports has been a persistent problem in recent years.

LEARNING OBJECTIVES

After reading this chapter, you should be able to:

1. Discuss the essential features of the price system
2. Evaluate the effects of changes in demand and supply on the market price and equilibrium quantity
3. Understand the rationing function of prices
4. Explain the effects of price ceilings
5. Explain the effects of price floors
6. Describe various types of government-imposed quantity restrictions on markets

Media Resources

Refer to the end of the chapter for a full listing of the multimedia learning materials available in MyEconLab.

. . . when there was an unexpected epidemic of a well-known variety of the influenza (or flu) virus in 2003 and 2004, manufacturers of flu vaccines failed to produce as much vaccine as people wanted to purchase? Indeed, on December 5, 2003, makers of flu vaccines announced that they had "run out" of doses and would not be manufacturing any more. People simply had to accept the absence of vaccines and hope that they and their children—who were particularly at risk from the flu—did not contract the virus. What led to this unresolved mismatch between the quantity of flu vaccines demanded and the quantity producers were willing to supply? As you will learn in this chapter, we can use the supply and demand analysis developed in Chapter 3 to answer this question. Similarly, we can use this analysis to examine the "shortage" of apartments in certain cities, the "surplus" of young workers in labor markets, and many other phenomena. All of these examples are part of our economy, which we characterize as a *price system*.

THE PRICE SYSTEM

Price system
An economic system in which relative prices are constantly changing to reflect changes in supply and demand for different commodities. The prices of those commodities are signals to everyone within the system as to what is relatively scarce and what is relatively abundant.

In a **price system,** otherwise known as a *market system,* relative prices are constantly changing to reflect changes in supply and demand for different commodities. The prices of those commodities are the signals to everyone within the system as to what is relatively scarce and what is relatively abundant. Indeed, it is the *signaling* aspect of the price system that provides the information to buyers and sellers about what should be bought and what should be produced. In a price system, there is a clear-cut chain of events in which any changes in demand and supply cause changes in prices that in turn affect the opportunities that businesses and individuals have for profit and personal gain. Such changes influence our use of resources. In this sense, prices provide information.

EXCHANGE AND MARKETS

Voluntary exchange
An act of trading, done on a voluntary basis, in which both parties to the trade are subjectively better off after the exchange.

Terms of exchange
The conditions under which trading takes place. Usually, the terms of exchange are equal to the price at which a good is traded.

The price system features **voluntary exchange,** acts of trading between individuals that make both parties to the trade subjectively better off. The **terms of exchange**—the prices we pay for the desired items—are determined by the interaction of the forces underlying supply and demand. In our economy, the majority of exchanges take place voluntarily in markets. A market encompasses the exchange arrangements of both buyers and sellers that underlie the forces of supply and demand. Indeed, one definition of a market is a low-cost institution for facilitating exchange. A market increases incomes by helping resources move to their highest-valued uses by means of prices.

Transaction Costs

Transaction costs
All of the costs associated with exchanging, including the informational costs of finding out price and quality, service record, and durability of a product, plus the cost of contracting and enforcing that contract.

Individuals turn to markets because markets reduce the cost of exchanges. These costs are sometimes referred to as **transaction costs,** which are broadly defined as the costs associated with finding out exactly what is being transacted as well as the cost of enforcing contracts. If you were Robinson Crusoe and lived alone on an island, you would never incur a transaction cost. For everyone else, transaction costs are just as real as the costs of production. High-speed computers have allowed us to reduce transaction costs by increasing our ability to process information and keep records.

Consider some simple examples of transaction costs. A club warehouse such as Sam's Club or Costco reduce the transaction costs of having to go to numerous specialty stores to obtain the items you desire. Financial institutions, such as commercial banks, have reduced transaction costs of directing funds from savers to borrowers. In general, the more organized the market, the lower the transaction costs. One group of individuals who constantly attempt to lower transaction costs are the much maligned middlemen.

The Role of Middlemen

As long as there are costs of bringing together buyers and sellers, there will be an incentive for intermediaries, normally called middlemen, to lower those costs. This means that middlemen specialize in lowering transaction costs. Whenever producers do not sell their products directly to the final consumer, by definition, one or more middlemen are involved. Farmers typically sell their output to distributors, who are usually called wholesalers, who then sell those products to retailers such as supermarkets.

How do you think that the Internet has changed the way middlemen work?

e - C o m m e r c e E X A M P L E

Shopbots: Middlemen of Choice on the Internet?

Just a few years ago, observers speculated that the Internet would be bad news for middlemen. People would just click their mouse to direct their computer's browser to a Web site where they could deal with a company directly. Nevertheless, software firms have developed *intelligent shopping agents,* sometimes called "shopbots." These are programs that search the Web to help consumers locate items and compare prices. Examples of Internet companies offering shopbots for consumer use are Shopping.com and Price.com, which are part of a shopbot industry that has grown by about 10 percent per year during the past five years.

Many consumers have found that shopbots do a good job of providing price comparisons for identical items. Nevertheless, many critics of shopbots argue that the industry will not continue to grow unless consumers can use shopbots to search for more than just the lowest price of an item. Companies that offer shopbot services have been working frantically to develop new versions that permit consumers to input desired product features in general product categories. In this way, consumers will be able to compare the items offered for sale by different companies based on both the item's price and its quality characteristics.

For Critical Analysis
Why has the massive growth in the number of Web pages broadened the potential market for the services of Internet middlemen such as shopbot companies?

CHANGES IN DEMAND AND SUPPLY

It is in markets that we see the results of changes in demand and supply. In certain situations, it is possible to predict what will happen to equilibrium price and equilibrium quantity when demand or supply changes. Specifically, whenever one curve is stable while the other curve shifts, we can tell what will happen to price and quantity. Consider the possibilities in Figure 4-1 on page 80. In panel (a), the supply curve remains unchanged, but demand increases from D_1 to D_2. Note that the results are an increase in the market clearing price from P_1 to P_2 and an increase in the equilibrium quantity from Q_1 to Q_2.

In panel (b), there is a decrease in demand from D_1 to D_3. This results in a decrease in both the relative price of the good and the equilibrium quantity. Panels (c) and (d) show the effects of a shift in the supply curve while the demand curve is unchanged. In panel (c), the supply curve has shifted rightward. The relative price of the product falls; the equi-

FIGURE 4-1

Shifts in Demand and in Supply: Determinate Results

In panel (a), the supply curve is unchanged at S. The demand curve shifts outward from D_1 to D_2. The equilibrium price and quantity rise from P_1, Q_1 to P_2, Q_2, respectively. In panel (b), again the supply curve is unchanged at S. The demand curve shifts inward to the left, showing a decrease in demand from D_1 to D_3. Both equilibrium price and equilibrium quantity fall. In panel (c), the demand curve now remains unchanged at D. The supply curve shifts from S_1 to S_2. The equilibrium price falls from P_1 to P_2. The equilibrium quantity increases, however, from Q_1 to Q_2. In panel (d), the demand curve is unchanged at D. Supply decreases as shown by a leftward shift of the supply curve from S_1 to S_3. The market clearing price increases from P_1 to P_3. The equilibrium quantity falls from Q_1 to Q_3.

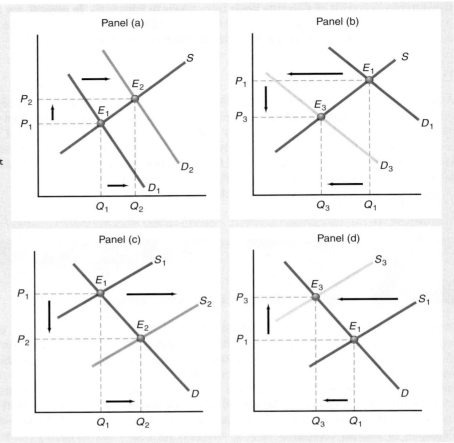

When Both Demand and Supply Shift

The examples in Figure 4-1 show a theoretically determinate outcome of a shift in either the demand curve, holding the supply curve constant, or the supply curve, holding the demand curve constant. When both supply and demand curves change, the outcome is indeterminate for either equilibrium price or equilibrium quantity.

When both demand and supply increase, all we can be certain of is that equilibrium quantity will increase. We do not know what will happen to equilibrium price until we determine whether demand increased relative to supply (equilibrium price will rise) or supply increased relative to demand (equilibrium price will fall). The same analysis applies to decreases in both demand and supply, except that in this case equilibrium quantity falls.

We can be certain that when demand decreases and supply increases at the same time, the equilibrium price will fall, but we do not know what will happen to the equilibrium quantity unless we actually draw the new curves. If supply decreases and demand increases at the same time, we can be sure that equilibrium price will rise, but again we do not know what happens to equilibrium quantity without drawing the curves. In every situ-

librium quantity increases. In panel (d), supply has shifted leftward—there has been a supply decrease. The product's relative price increases; the equilibrium quantity decreases.

ation in which both supply and demand change, you should always draw graphs to determine the resulting change in equilibrium price and quantity.

Why do you suppose that U.S. plywood prices rose considerably between 2001 and 2004, even though plywood production and consumption barely increased?

EXAMPLE

Why Plywood Prices Have Soared

In the mid-2000s, one builder said it was as if "all the galaxies had lined up perfectly" to generate a big increase in the equilibrium price of plywood. Of course, astronomical events had nothing to do with why the market clearing price of a 4-foot-by-8-foot sheet of plywood more than doubled between 2002 and 2004. Two forces were responsible for the big run-up in plywood prices: a simultaneous decrease in supply and an increase in demand.

Lower incomes associated with an economic downturn in 2001 had resulted in a decline in new-home construction from 2001 into 2002, and by 2003 a number of lumber sellers had exited the market. Furthermore, in the summer of 2003, unusually wet weather in forested areas of the United States slowed timber harvesting. By the fall of 2003, therefore, the plywood supply curve had shifted considerably leftward, as illustrated in Figure 4-2.

When U.S. incomes rose once again in 2002 and 2003, the demand for new houses increased, which generated an increase in the demand for plywood. Then, in the early autumn of 2003, the government unexpectedly ordered 766,000 sheets of plywood for the U.S. military. Together these factors caused the plywood demand curve to shift rightward, as shown in Figure 4-2. In the end, the total amount of plywood produced in the United States increased only slightly. The equilibrium price of plywood jumped, however, just as predicted in the figure.

For Critical Analysis
What do you suppose happened to the number of firms in the plywood industry in 2004 and 2005 in response to the large price increase between 2001 and 2004?

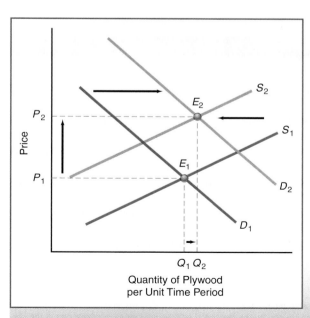

FIGURE 4-2
The Effects of a Simultaneous Decrease in Plywood Supply and Increase in Plywood Demand
In the mid-2000s, various factors contributed to a reduction in the supply of plywood in the United States, depicted by the leftward shift in the plywood supply curve from S_1 to S_2. At the same time, other factors contributed to an increase in the demand for plywood, as shown by the shift in the plywood demand curve from D_1 to D_2. On net, the equilibrium quantity of plywood produced and consumed rose only slightly, from Q_1 at point E_1, to Q_2 at point E_2, but the equilibrium price of plywood increased significantly, from P_1 to P_2.

PRICE FLEXIBILITY AND ADJUSTMENT SPEED

We have used as an illustration for our analysis a market in which prices are quite flexible. Some markets are indeed like that. In others, however, price flexibility may take the form of indirect adjustments such as hidden payments or quality changes. For example, although the published price of bouquets of flowers may stay the same, the freshness of the flowers may change, meaning that the price per constant-quality unit changes. The published price of French bread might stay the same, but the quality could go up or down, thereby changing the price per constant-quality unit. There are many ways to implicitly change prices without actually changing the published price for a *nominal* unit of a product or service.

We must also note that markets do not always return to equilibrium immediately. There may be a significant adjustment time. A shock to the economy in the form of an oil embargo, a drought, or a long strike will not be absorbed overnight. This means that even in unfettered market situations, in which there are no restrictions on changes in prices and quantities, temporary excess quantities supplied or excess quantities demanded may appear. Our analysis simply indicates what the market clearing price and equilibrium quantity ultimately will be, given a demand curve and a supply curve. Nowhere in the analysis is there any indication of the speed with which a market will get to a new equilibrium after a shock. The price may overshoot the equilibrium level. Remember this warning when we examine changes in demand and in supply due to changes in their *ceteris paribus* conditions.

CONCEPTS in Brief

- The terms of exchange in a voluntary exchange are determined by the interaction of the forces underlying demand and supply. These forces take place in markets, which tend to minimize transaction costs.

- When the demand curve shifts outward or inward with an unchanged supply curve, equilibrium price and quantity increase or decrease, respectively. When the supply curve shifts outward or inward given an unchanged demand curve, equilibrium price moves in the direction opposite to equilibrium quantity.

- When there is a shift in demand or supply, the new equilibrium price is not obtained instantaneously. Adjustment takes time.

To test your understanding of the concepts covered in this section, go to the Online Review at **www.myeconlab.com/miller**.

THE RATIONING FUNCTION OF PRICES

A shortage creates forces that cause price to rise toward a market clearing, or equilibrium, level. A surplus brings into play forces that cause price to fall toward its market clearing level. The synchronization of decisions by buyers and sellers that leads to equilibrium is called the *rationing function of prices*. Prices are indicators of relative scarcity. An equilibrium price clears the market. The plans of buyers and sellers, given the price, are not frustrated.[*] It is the free interaction of buyers and sellers that sets the price that eventually clears the market. Price, in effect, rations a good to demanders who are willing and able to pay the highest price. Whenever the rationing function of prices is frustrated by government-enforced price ceilings that set prices below the market clearing level, a prolonged shortage results.

---

*There is a difference between frustration and unhappiness. You may be unhappy because you can't buy a Rolls Royce, but if you had sufficient income, you would not be frustrated in your attempt to purchase one at the current market price. By contrast, you would be frustrated if you went to your local supermarket and could get only two cans of your favorite soft drink when you had wanted to purchase a dozen and had the necessary funds.

Methods of Non-Price Rationing

There are ways other than price to ration goods. *First come, first served* is one method. *Political power* is another. *Physical force* is yet another. Cultural, religious, and physical differences have been and are used as rationing devices throughout the world.

Consider first come, first served as a rationing device. We call this *rationing by queues,* where *queue* means "line." Whoever is willing to wait in line the longest obtains the good that is being sold at less than the market clearing price. All who wait in line are paying a higher *total* price than the money price paid for the good. Personal time has an opportunity cost. To calculate the total price of the good, we must add up the money price plus the opportunity cost of the time spent waiting.

Random assignment is another way to ration goods. You may have been involved in a rationing-by-random-assignment scheme in college if you were assigned a housing unit. Sometimes rationing by random assignment is used to fill slots in popular classes.

Rationing by *coupons* has also been used, particularly during wartime. In the United States during World War II, families were allotted coupons that allowed them to purchase specified quantities of rationed goods, such as meat and gasoline. To purchase such goods, they had to pay a specified price *and* give up a coupon.

Rationing by waiting may occur in situations in which entrepreneurs are free to change prices to equate quantity demanded with quantity supplied but choose not to do so. This results in queues of potential buyers. It may seem to be that the price in the market is being held below equilibrium by some noncompetitive force. That is not true, however.

Such queuing may arise in a free market when the demand for a good is subject to large or unpredictable fluctuations, and the additional costs to firms (and ultimately to consumers) of constantly changing prices or of holding sufficient inventories or providing sufficient excess capacity to cover peak demands are greater than the costs to consumers of waiting for the good. Common examples are waiting in line to purchase a fast-food lunch and queuing to purchase a movie ticket a few minutes before the next show.

Economics Front and Center

When it comes time to allocate tickets for campus sporting events, colleges use a variety of rationing methods; see the case study, **A Full-Court Press for Season Tickets,** on page 92

The Essential Role of Rationing

In a world of scarcity, there is, by definition, competition for what is scarce. After all, any resources that are not scarce can be had by everyone at a zero price in as large a quantity as everyone wants, such as air to burn in internal combustion engines. Once scarcity arises, there has to be some method to ration the available resources, goods, and services. The price system is one form of rationing; the others that we mentioned are alternatives. Economists cannot say which system of rationing is "best." They can, however, say that rationing via the price system leads to the most efficient use of available resources. This means that generally in a freely functioning price system, all of the gains from mutually beneficial trade will be exhausted.

CONCEPTS in Brief

- Prices in a market economy perform a rationing function because they reflect relative scarcity, allowing the market to clear. Other ways to ration goods include first come, first served; political power; physical force; random assignment; and coupons.

- Even when businesspeople can change prices, some rationing by waiting may occur. Such queuing arises when there are large changes in demand coupled with high costs of satisfying those changes immediately.

To test your understanding of the concepts covered in this section, go to the Online Review at **www.myeconlab.com/miller.**

THE POLICY OF GOVERNMENT-IMPOSED PRICE CONTROLS

The rationing function of prices is prevented when governments impose price controls. **Price controls** often involve setting a **price ceiling**—the maximum price that may be allowed in an exchange. The world has had a long history of price ceilings applied to goods, wages, rents, and interest rates, among other things. Occasionally, a government will set a **price floor**—a minimum price below which a good or service may not be sold. These have most often been applied to wages and agricultural products. Let's first consider price ceilings.

Price Ceilings and Black Markets

As long as a price ceiling is below the market clearing price, imposing a price ceiling creates a shortage, as can be seen in Figure 4-3. At any price below the market clearing, or equilibrium, price of P_e, there will always be a larger quantity demanded than quantity supplied—a shortage, as you will recall from Chapter 3. Normally, whenever quantity demanded exceeds quantity supplied—that is, when a shortage exists—there is a tendency for the price to rise to its equilibrium level. But with a price ceiling, this tendency cannot be fully realized because everyone is forbidden to trade at the equilibrium price.

The result is fewer exchanges and **nonprice rationing devices.** In Figure 4-3, at an equilibrium price of P_e, the equilibrium quantity demanded and supplied (or traded) is Q_e. But at the price ceiling of P_1, the equilibrium quantity offered is only Q_s. Because frustrated consumers will be forced to purchase only Q_s units, there is a shortage. The most obvious nonprice rationing device to help clear the market is queuing, or long lines, which we have already discussed. To avoid physical lines, waiting lists may be established.

Typically, an effective price ceiling leads to a **black market.** A black market is a market in which the price-controlled good is sold at an illegally high price through various methods. For example, if the price of gasoline is controlled at lower than the market clearing price, drivers who wish to fill up their cars may offer the gas station attendant a cash

Price controls
Government-mandated minimum or maximum prices that may be charged for goods and services.

Price ceiling
A legal maximum price that may be charged for a particular good or service.

Price floor
A legal minimum price below which a good or service may not be sold. Legal minimum wages are an example.

Nonprice rationing devices
All methods used to ration scarce goods that are price-controlled. Whenever the price system is not allowed to work, nonprice rationing devices will evolve to ration the affected goods and services.

Black market
A market in which goods are traded at prices above their legal maximum prices or in which illegal goods are sold.

FIGURE 4-3
Black Markets
The demand curve is *D*. The supply curve is *S*. The equilibrium price is P_e. The government, however, steps in and imposes a maximum price of P_1 At that lower price, the quantity demanded will be Q_d, but the quantity supplied will be only Q_s. There is a "shortage." The implicit price (including time costs) tends to rise to P_2. If black markets arise, as they generally will, the equilibrium black market price will end up somewhere between P_1 and P_2. The actual quantity transacted will be between Q_s and Q_e.

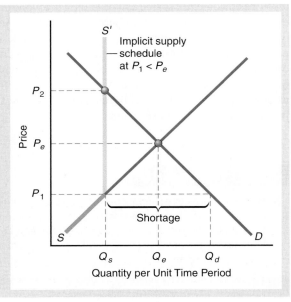

payment on the side (as happened in the 1970s in the United States during price controls on gasoline). If the price of beef is controlled at below its market clearing price, the butcher may allocate otherwise unavailable beef to a customer who offers the butcher good tickets to an upcoming football game. Indeed, the true implicit price of a price-controlled good or service can be increased in an infinite number of ways, limited only by the imagination. (Black markets also occur when goods are made illegal.)

What explains the waiting lists that physicians now establish for access to vaccines intended to prevent illnesses such as whooping cough, diphtheria, chicken pox, and influenza?

EXAMPLE

Why Vaccines Can Sometimes Be So Hard to Obtain

In 1993, Congress established a federal program called Vaccines for Children, which required manufacturers of childhood vaccines to sell one-third of all vaccines to the federal government at a discount of 50 percent. The government then provided vaccines at no charge to children in households without private health insurance.

Later, the government began offering free vaccines to children in low-income families, even if the families had private health insurance. It also began requiring vaccine manufacturers to sell more of their output to the government at the discounted price. Manufacturers responded by cutting back on production. Some private physicians began to experience difficulties keeping vaccines in stock, so they used waiting lists to ration vaccines among children in families covered by private health insurance.

The government reacted to the growing problem of private vaccine shortages by providing vaccines to children in higher-income families deemed to be "underinsured." To provide these additional vaccines, of course, the government began obtaining even more vaccines at half price. Today the government purchases almost 60 percent of all childhood vaccines. Private vaccine shortages are worsening as manufacturers respond to lower prices and profits with further production cutbacks.

For Critical Analysis
What is likely to happen to the length of a typical private physician's vaccine waiting list if the federal government continues to require manufacturers to sell even more half-price vaccines to the Vaccines for Children program?

CONCEPTS in Brief

- Governments sometimes impose price controls in the form of price ceilings and price floors.

- An effective price ceiling is one that sets the legal price below the market clearing price and is enforced. Effective price ceilings lead to nonprice rationing devices and black markets.

To test your understanding of the concepts covered in this section, go to the Online Review at www.myeconlab.com/miller.

THE POLICY OF CONTROLLING RENTS

More than 200 U.S. cities and towns, including Berkeley, California, and New York City, operate under some kind of rent control. **Rent control** is a system under which the local government tells building owners how much they can charge their tenants in rent. In the United States, rent controls date back to at least World War II. The objective of rent control is to keep rents below levels that would be observed in a freely competitive market.

Rent control
The placement of price ceilings on rents in particular cities.

The Functions of Rental Prices

In any housing market, rental prices serve three functions: (1) to promote the efficient maintenance of existing housing and stimulate the construction of new housing, (2) to allocate existing scarce housing among competing claimants, and (3) to ration the use of existing housing by current demanders.

Rent Controls and Construction. Rent controls have discouraged the construction of new rental units. Rents are the most important long-term determinant of profitability, and rent controls have artificially depressed them. Consider some examples. In a recent year in Dallas, Texas, with a 16 percent rental vacancy rate but no rent control laws, 11,000 new rental housing units were built. In the same year in San Francisco, California, only 2,000 units were built, despite a mere 1.6 percent vacancy rate. The major difference? San Francisco has had stringent rent control laws. In New York City, until changes in the law in 1997 and 2003, the only rental units being built were luxury units, which were exempt from controls.

Effects on the Existing Supply of Housing. When rental rates are held below equilibrium levels, property owners cannot recover the cost of maintenance, repairs, and capital improvements through higher rents. Hence they curtail these activities. In the extreme situation, taxes, utilities, and the expenses of basic repairs exceed rental receipts. The result is abandoned buildings. Numerous buildings have been abandoned in New York City. Some owners have resorted to arson, hoping to collect the insurance on their empty buildings before the city claims them for back taxes.

Rationing the Current Use of Housing. Rent controls also affect the current use of housing because they restrict tenant mobility. Consider a family whose children have gone off to college. That family might want to live in a smaller apartment. But in a rent-controlled environment, giving up a rent-controlled unit can entail a substantial cost. In most rent-controlled cities, rents can be adjusted only when a tenant leaves. That means that a move from a long-occupied rent-controlled apartment to a smaller apartment can involve a hefty rent hike. This artificial preservation of the status quo became known in New York as "housing gridlock."

Attempts at Evading Rent Controls

Go to www.econtoday.com/chap04 to learn more about New York City's rent controls from Tenant.net.

The distortions produced by rent controls lead to efforts by both property owners and tenants to evade the rules. This leads to the growth of expensive government bureaucracies whose job it is to make sure that rent controls aren't evaded. In New York City, because rent can be raised only if the tenant leaves, property owners have had an incentive to make life unpleasant for tenants in order to drive them out or to evict them on the slightest pretense. The city has responded by making evictions extremely costly for property owners. Eviction requires a tedious and expensive judicial proceeding. Tenants, for their part, routinely try to sublet all or part of their rent-controlled apartments at fees substantially above the rent they pay to the owner. Both the city and the property owners try to prohibit subletting and typically end up in the city's housing courts—an entire judicial system developed to deal with disputes involving rent-controlled apartments. The overflow and appeals from the city's housing courts are now clogging the rest of New York's judicial system.

Who Gains and Who Loses from Rent Controls?

The big losers from rent controls are clearly property owners. But there is another group of losers—low-income individuals, especially single mothers, trying to find their first apartment. Some observers now believe that rent controls have worsened the problem of home-lessness in such cities as New York.

Often, owners of rent-controlled apartments charge "key money" before a new tenant is allowed to move in. This is a large up-front cash payment, usually illegal but demanded nonetheless—just one aspect of the black market in rent-controlled apartments. Poor individuals cannot afford a hefty key money payment, nor can they assure the owner that their rent will be on time or even paid each month. Because controlled rents are usually below market clearing levels, apartment owners have little incentive to take any risk on low-income individuals as tenants. This is particularly true when a prospective tenant's chief source of income is a welfare check. Indeed, a large number of the litigants in the New York housing courts are welfare mothers who have missed their rent payments due to emergency expenses or delayed welfare checks. Their appeals commonly end in evictions and a new home in a temporary public shelter—or on the streets.

Who benefits from rent control? Ample evidence indicates that upper-income professionals benefit the most. These people can use their mastery of the bureaucracy and their large network of friends and connections to exploit the rent control system. Consider that in New York, actresses Mia Farrow and Cicely Tyson live in rent-controlled apartments, paying well below market rates. So do the director of the Metropolitan Museum of Art, the chairman of Pathmark Stores, and singer and children's book author Carly Simon.

CONCEPTS in Brief

- Rental prices perform three functions: (1) allocating existing scarce housing among competing claimants, (2) promoting efficient maintenance of existing houses and stimulating new housing construction, and (3) rationing the use of existing houses by current demanders.

- Effective rent controls impede the functioning of rental prices. Construction of new rental units is discouraged. Rent controls decrease spending on maintenance of existing ones and also lead to "housing gridlock."

- There are numerous ways to evade rent controls; key money is one.

To test your understanding of the concepts covered in this section, go to the Online Review at www.myeconlab.com/miller.

PRICE FLOORS IN AGRICULTURE

Another way that government can affect markets is by imposing price floors or price supports. In the United States, price supports are most often associated with agricultural products.

Price Supports

During the Great Depression, the federal government swung into action to help farmers. In 1933, it established a system of price supports for many agricultural products. Since then, there have been price supports for wheat, feed grains, cotton, rice, soybeans, sorghum, and dairy products, among other foodstuffs. The nature of the supports is quite simple: The government simply chooses a *support price* for an agricultural product and then acts to ensure that the price of the product never falls below the support level. Figure 4-4 on the following page shows the market demand for and supply of peanuts. Without a price support program, competitive forces would yield an equilibrium price of P_e and an equilibrium quantity of Q_e. Clearly, if the government were to set the support price at P_e or below, the quantity of peanuts demanded would equal the quantity of peanuts supplied at point E, because farmers could sell all they wanted at the market clearing price of P_e.

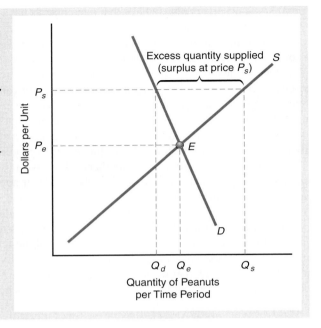

FIGURE 4-4

Agricultural Price Supports
Free market equilibrium occurs at E, with an equilibrium price of P_e and an equilibrium quantity of Q_e. When the government sets a support price at P_s, the quantity demanded is Q_d, and the quantity supplied is Q_s. The difference is the surplus, which the government buys. Note that farmers' total income is from consumers ($P_s \times Q_d$) plus tax-payers [$(Q_s - Q_d) \times P_s$].

But what happens when the government sets the support price *above* P_e, at P_s? At a support price of P_s, the quantity demanded is only Q_d, but the quantity supplied is Q_s. The difference between them is called the *excess quantity supplied,* or *surplus.* As simple as this program seems, its existence creates a fundamental question: How can the government agency charged with administering the price-support program prevent market forces from pushing the actual price down to P_e?

If production exceeds the amount that consumers want to buy at the support price, what happens to the surplus? Quite simply, the government has to buy the surplus—the difference between Q_s and Q_d—if the price support program is to work. As a practical matter, the government acquires the quantity $Q_s - Q_d$ indirectly through a government agency. The government either stores the surplus or sells it to foreign countries at a greatly reduced price (or gives it away free of charge) under the Food for Peace program.

Who Benefits from Agricultural Price Supports?

Although agricultural price supports have traditionally been promoted as a way to guarantee a decent wage for low-income farmers, most of the benefits have in fact gone to the owners of very large farms. Price support payments are made on a per-bushel basis, not on a per-farm basis. Thus, traditionally, the larger the farm, the bigger the benefit from agricultural price supports. In addition, *all* of the benefits from price supports ultimately accrue to *landowners* on whose land price-supported crops could grow.

Back in the early 1990s, Congress indicated an intention to phase out most agricultural subsidies by the early 2000s. What Congress actually *did* throughout the 1990s, however, was to pass a series of "emergency laws" keeping farm subsidies alive. Then, in 2002, the legislative body enacted the Farm Security Act, which now commits the U.S. government to continued price supports for such farm products as wheat, corn, rice, cotton, and soybeans. All told, government payments for these and other products amount to about 20 percent of the annual market value of all U.S. farm production.

Nevertheless, European government price-support payments account for almost twice as much of the total value of European farm output. How do you suppose that the European Union has tried to link agricultural subsidies to governmental efforts to promote environmental protection and food safety?

International Policy EXAMPLE

France Convinces the European Union That Protecting the Environment Requires Agricultural Price Supports

The European Union (EU) allocates about $50 billion per year, or roughly half of its entire budget, to a subsidy program called the Common Agricultural Policy (CAP). In 2003, the French government proposed a new CAP system, which the EU has recently implemented. Under this system, the EU no longer *officially* pays farmers based on what they produce. Instead, the EU formally pays farmers for using agricultural production practices that help protect the environment and promote food safety. Furthermore, the EU has determined that in some cases, the most environmentally sound and safest practices involve no farming at all.

Under the new EU approach, as long as farmers use government-prescribed methods said to help the environment and make foods safer, the CAP program will make payments based on the "value of their production." If the EU determines that protecting the environment or promoting food safety entails not farming at all, then it will pay farmers based on the value of the products they otherwise *would* have grown. These values will be based on "fair prices" as determined by the government, not by the market. In short, the new EU program to promote environmentally friendly and safer agricultural techniques will essentially remain a program of agricultural price supports.

Who will benefit most from implementing this French system of "environmental and food-safety protection"? The answer is French farmers, who already receive about $10 billion per year under CAP, or about 20 percent of the entire EU farm-subsidy budget.

For Critical Analysis
Why will the new EU agricultural subsidy program continue to keep farm prices artificially above market levels?

PRICE FLOORS IN THE LABOR MARKET

The **minimum wage** is the lowest hourly wage rate that firms may legally pay their workers. Proponents want higher minimum wages to ensure low-income workers a "decent" standard of living. Opponents counter that higher minimum wages cause increased unemployment, particularly among unskilled minority teenagers.

The federal minimum wage started in 1938 at 25 cents an hour, about 40 percent of the average manufacturing wage at the time. Typically, its level has stayed at about 40 to 50 percent of average manufacturing wages. It was increased to $5.15 in 1997 and may be higher by the time you read this. Many states and cities have their own minimum wage laws that sometimes exceed the federal minimum.

What happens when the government establishes a floor on wages? The effects can be seen in Figure 4-5 on the following page. We start off in equilibrium with the equilibrium wage rate of W_e and the equilibrium quantity of labor equal to Q_e. A minimum wage, W_m, higher than W_e, is imposed. At W_m, the quantity demanded for labor is reduced to Q_d, and some workers now become unemployed. Note that the reduction in employment from Q_e to Q_d, or the distance from B to A, is less than the excess quantity of labor supplied at wage rate W_m. This excess quantity supplied is the distance between A and C, or the distance between Q_d and Q_s. The reason the reduction in employment is smaller than the excess quantity of labor supplied at the minimum wage is that the excess quantity of labor supplied also includes the *additional* workers who would like to work more hours at the new, higher minimum wage. Some workers may become unemployed as a result of the minimum wage, but others will move to sectors where minimum wage laws do not apply; wages will be pushed down in these uncovered sectors.

Minimum wage
A wage floor, legislated by government, setting the lowest hourly rate that firms may legally pay workers.

Go to www.econtoday.com/chap04 for information from the U.S. Department of Labor concerning recent developments concerning the federal minimum wage.

FIGURE 4-5
The Effect of Minimum Wages

The market clearing wage rate is W_e. The market clearing quantity of employment is Q_e, determined by the intersection of supply and demand at point E. A minimum wage equal to W_m is established. The quantity of labor demanded is reduced to Q_d. The reduction in employment from Q_e to Q_d is equal to the distance between B and A. That distance is smaller than the excess quantity of labor supplied at wage rate W_m. The distance between B and C is the increase in the quantity of labor supplied that results from the higher minimum wage rate.

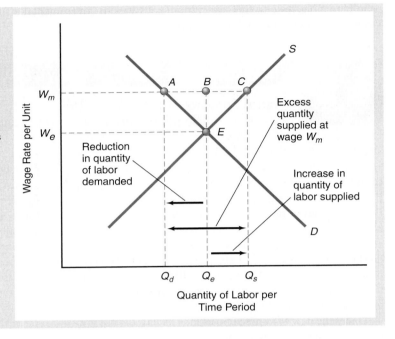

In the long run (a time period that is long enough to allow for full adjustment by workers and firms), some of the reduction in the quantity of labor demanded will result from a reduction in the number of firms, and some will result from changes in the number of workers employed by each firm. Economists estimate that a 10 percent increase in the minimum wage relative to the prices of goods and services decreases total employment of those affected by 1 to 2 percent.[*]

How has the relative minimum wage varied over time?

EXAMPLE

The Relative Minimum Wage Is What Matters

Recall from Chapter 3 that *relative* prices affect decisions. This is also true of wages, the prices of labor inputs. When a person decides whether to offer to work more hours, what matters is what the wage rate is relative to the overall prices of goods and services. If there is inflation over time without changes in the current wage, the *relative* wage rate declines.

Figure 4-6 shows that the money value of the U.S. minimum wage has increased from 25 cents per hour in October 1938 to $5.15 per hour. The inflation-adjusted minimum wage rose between 1938 and the 1960s, although it declined whenever inflation reduced the relative value of the minimum wage. Since the

1960s, the relative minimum wage has tended to decline, except following increases in the money value of the minimum wage. Nevertheless, the relative (or *real,* inflation-adjusted) value of the minimum wage is about 60 percent higher today than in the late 1930s.

For Critical Analysis

How could a government establish a system for keeping the relative value of the minimum wage from changing even in an inflationary environment?

---

[*]Because we are referring to a long-run analysis here, the reduction in the quantity of labor demanded would be demonstrated by an eventual shift inward to the left of the short-run demand curve, *D,* in Figure 4-5 as firms (the consumers of labor) went out of business.

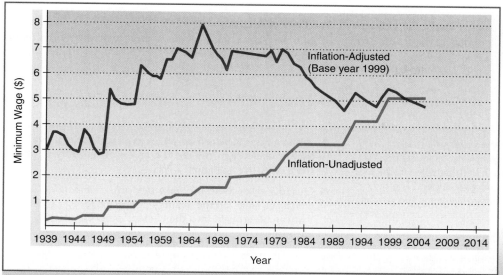

FIGURE 4-6
The Minimum Wage—
Inflation-Adjusted versus
Inflation-Unadjusted
The minimum wage has risen in steps.
The inflation-adjusted value of the
minimum wage has generally trended
downward since the late 1960s, but it
is still 60 percent higher than in 1939.

Source: U.S. Department of Labor.

QUANTITY RESTRICTIONS

Governments can impose quantity restrictions on a market. The most obvious restriction is
an outright ban on the ownership or trading of a good. It is currently illegal to buy and sell
human organs. It is also currently illegal to buy and sell certain psychoactive drugs such as
cocaine, heroin, and marijuana. In some states, it is illegal to start a new hospital without
obtaining a license for a particular number of beds to be offered to patients. This licensing
requirement effectively limits the quantity of hospital beds in some states. From 1933 to
1973, it was illegal for U.S. citizens to own gold except for manufacturing, medicinal, or
jewelry purposes.

Some of the most common quantity restrictions exist in the area of international trade.
The U.S. government, as well as many foreign governments, imposes import quotas on a
variety of goods. An **import quota** is a supply restriction that prohibits the importation of
more than a specified quantity of a particular good in a one-year period. The United States
has had import quotas on tobacco, sugar, and immigrant labor. For many years, there were
import quotas on oil coming into the United States. There are also "voluntary" import quotas on certain goods. Japanese automakers have agreed since 1981 "voluntarily" to restrict
the amount of Japanese cars they send to the United States.

What industry would you guess has the most products subject to U.S. import quotas?

Import quota
A physical supply restriction on imports
of a particular good, such as sugar.
Foreign exporters are unable to sell in
the United States more than the
quantity specified in the import quota.

Policy EXAMPLE

U.S. Textile Quotas Abound

The Office of Textiles and Apparel in the U.S. Department of
Commerce oversees the enforcement of import quotas covering more than 140 categories of textile products. These include fabrics and clothing made of fibers derived from cotton,
wool, silk, and synthetics.

For instance, in any given year imports of pairs of gloves
and mittens from Pakistan cannot exceed 1,281,606 pairs, but
up to 2,364,645 pairs can legally enter the United States from
Cambodia. In addition, as many as 4,575 men's suit jackets can
be imported from the Czech Republic, yet fewer than 3,746

jackets can arrive from the Philippines. Clearly, the U.S. government aims to apply very precise quotas to the textile products of different nations.

For Critical Analysis

Who in the United States stands to gain from restrictions on the quantities of textile imports?

CONCEPTS in Brief

● With a price support system, the government sets a minimum price at which, say, qualifying farm products can be sold. Any farmers who cannot sell at that price in the market can "sell" their surplus to the government. The only way a price support system can survive is for the government or some other entity to buy up the excess quantity supplied at the support price.

● When a floor is placed on wages at a rate that is above market equilibrium, the result is an excess quantity of labor supplied at that minimum wage.

● Quantity restrictions may take the form of import quotas, which are limits on the quantity of specific foreign goods that can be brought into the United States for resale purposes.

To test your understanding of the concepts covered in this section, go to the Online Review at www.myeconlab.com/miller.

CASE STUDY: Economics Front and Center

A Full-Court Press for Season Tickets

Last year, Chris purchased season tickets for her college's home basketball games with ease. When she registered for her classes, she received a ticket order form, which she dropped off at an athletic ticket office with her payment the same day. She received her tickets well in advance of the opening game and attended every game. Her college's team proceeded to surprise every sports prognosticator by winning its conference championship and advancing further than expected in the postseason tournament.

The price of tickets for the coming year's basketball season is the same as last year's price. Chris faces a much different situation than she did last year, however. No season ticket forms are offered when she registers for her classes. Instead, she is told that she must wait in a long line just to sign up to receive a ticket order form. The line moves so slowly that by the time she gets to the sign-up table, she is late for her next class. A college representative then informs her that this year, once she receives and fills out a ticket order, she will have to wait in line again to make payment. In addition, she will be guaranteed tickets to only half of the home games, which the college will distribute to season ticket holders via a random lottery. This will all take time, so students will probably have to wait in more lines to pick up their tickets at the box office the day of the first game. Chris shakes her head and adds her name to the list of students requesting a ticket order form.

Points to Analyze

1. *What rationing method has Chris's college adopted to distribute this season's basketball tickets?*

2. *Is the price of a season ticket at Chris's college really "the same" as last year's price?*

Issues and Applications

Why Ships Face Traffic Jams

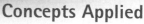

In recent years, the demand for pleasure cruises on passenger ships has increased considerably. Additionally, the number of companies operating cruise ships has increased, so the supply of pleasure cruises has also risen. The result has been a significant increase in the total number of passengers carried by cruise ships. As Figure 4-7 shows, in the early 1980s fewer than 2 million North American passengers traveled on cruise ships each year. Today the annual volume exceeds 8 million.

Concepts Applied
- Changes in Demand and Supply
- Price Ceiling
- Shortage

Government-Determined Prices at U.S. Seaports

To load and unload over 8 million passengers per year, cruise ships must be able to sail into ports and pull alongside docks. Hence the increase in the number of pleasure cruises has generated an increase in the demand for a complementary good—space at U.S. seaports. If there were an unregulated market, we would predict a resulting increase in the prices that ship owners pay to enter and dock at U.S. ports.

In fact, prices charged to use most U.S. port facilities are often regulated, or in some cases even directly set, by government agencies. At some U.S. seaports, such as the Port of Los Angeles, a city department oversees the prices of docking fa-

cilities. In others, such as the Port of Miami, pricing policies are supervised by a county agency. So far, government authorities have been slow to respond to the rising demand for port access by increasing the legally allowed prices for the use of port facilities.

Clogged Bays and Dock Delays

The failure of government agencies to allow the price of seaport usage to rise to the market clearing level has caused the quantity of port space demanded by ship owners to rise above—and to remain above—the quantity of port space

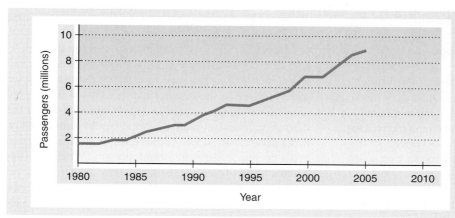

FIGURE 4-7
Annual North American Passenger Volumes on Cruise Ships
The number of North American residents traveling as passengers on cruise ships has more than quadrupled since the early 1980s.

Source: U.S. Department of Commerce.

supplied. The government agencies have effectively placed a ceiling price on port space. The results have been exactly what you might have predicted based on your study of this chapter: There is insufficient space in seaports to handle all the ships whose owners desire to use their facilities. Consequently, as ships near U.S. seaports, they are now required to give at least 24 hours' notice of their arrival so that port authorities can advise them if they need to delay their arrivals in light of space constraints. Even when ships arrive at their scheduled times, they often must wait for several minutes, or in some cases even several hours, before navigating toward their assigned docks.

While the many new cruise ships are moving in and out of harbors, freighters planning to load or unload merchandise at docks are among the ships forced to wait in line to use port facilities. As these freighters wait their turn, the ships' engines continue to burn fuel. In addition, their owners must pay wages to crews for the extra minutes or hours spent waiting in line. For the owner of a typical freighter, these and other costs can add up to considerable sums. According to current estimates, each hour a freighter must wait to arrive or depart entails a cost of nearly $1,000. Thus ship owners ultimately incur higher costs as a result of the shortage of port space at the government-determined prices.

For Critical Analysis

1. What nonprice rationing device are government port authorities using to ration channel passages and docking space?
2. If a cruise ship that requires as much space for safe passage as a freighter is the first to arrive at the point of entry to the only channel to a seaport, which ship's owner effectively "pays a price" for the failure of the government port authority to allow the price of port space to rise to the market clearing price?

Web Resources

1. To learn more about how the Port of Los Angeles establishes prices for the use of space and various port facilities, go to the link at www.econtoday.com/chap04.
2. For a comparative look at the rules governing pricing access to the Port of Miami, go to the link at www.econtoday.com/chap04.

Research Project

Suppose that a U.S. port authority decides to let the market determine the prices that should be charged for the right to enter the port and use its docking facilities. It implements this decision by auctioning rights to port space. All ships that are 48 hours from port must radio in bids for these rights, and the port authority establishes each ship's position in line through the channel to the port and a dock based on the size of its bid. Evaluate the pros and cons of such a system.

S U M M A R Y   D I S C U S S I O N   of Learning Objectives

1. **Essential Features of the Price System:** The price system, otherwise called the market system, allows prices to respond to changes in supply and demand for different commodities. Consumers' and business managers' decisions on resource use depend on what happens to prices. In the price system, exchange takes place in markets. The terms of exchange are communicated by prices in the marketplace, where middlemen reduce transaction costs by bringing buyers and sellers together.

2. **How Changes in Demand and Supply Affect the Market Price and Equilibrium Quantity:** With a given sup-

ply curve, an increase in demand causes a rise in the market price and an increase in the equilibrium quantity, and a decrease in demand induces a fall in the market price and a decline in the equilibrium quantity. With a given demand curve, an increase in supply causes a fall in the market price and an increase in the equilibrium quantity, and a decrease in supply causes a rise in the market price and a decline in the equilibrium quantity. When both demand and supply shift at the same time, indeterminate results may occur. We must know the direction and degree of each shift in order to predict the change in the market price and the equilibrium quantity.

3. **The Rationing Function of Prices:** In the market system, prices perform a rationing function—they ration scarce goods and services. Other ways of rationing include first come, first served; political power; physical force; lotteries; and coupons.

4. **The Effects of Price Ceilings:** Government-imposed price controls that require prices to be no higher than a certain level are price ceilings. If a government sets a price ceiling below the market price, then at the ceiling price the quantity of the good demanded will exceed the quantity supplied. There will be a shortage of the good at the ceiling price. This can lead to nonprice rationing devices and black markets.

5. **The Effects of Price Floors:** Government-mandated price controls that require prices to be no lower than a certain level are price floors. If a government sets a price floor above the market price, then at the floor price the quantity of the good supplied will exceed the quantity demanded. There will be a surplus of the good at the floor price.

6. **Government-Imposed Restrictions on Market Quantities:** Quantity restrictions can take the form of outright government bans on the sale of certain goods, such as human organs or various psychoactive drugs. They can also arise from licensing requirements that limit the number of producers and thereby restrict the amount supplied of a good or service. Another example is an import quota, which limits the number of units of a foreign-produced good that can legally be sold domestically.

KEY TERMS AND CONCEPTS

black market (84)

import quota (91)

minimum wage (89)

nonprice rationing devices (84)

price ceiling (84)

price controls (84)

price floor (84)

price system (78)

rent control (85)

terms of exchange (78)

transaction costs (78)

voluntary exchange (78)

PROBLEMS

Answers to the odd-numbered problems appear at the back of the book.

4-1. Suppose that a rap band called the Raging Pyros has released its first CD with Polyrock Records at a list price of $14.99. Explain how price serves as a purveyor of information to the band, the producer, and the consumer of rap CDs.

4-2. The pharmaceutical industry has benefited from advances in research and development that enable manufacturers to identify potential cures more quickly and therefore at lower cost. At the same time, the aging of our society has increased the demand for new drugs. Construct a supply and demand diagram of the market for pharmaceutical drugs. Illustrate the impact of these developments, and evaluate the effects on the market price and the equilibrium quantity.

4-3. The following table depicts the quantity demanded and quantity supplied of one-bedroom apartments in a small college town.

Monthly Rent	Quantity Demanded	Quantity Supplied
$400	3,000	1,600
$450	2,500	1,800
$500	2,000	2,000
$550	1,500	2,200
$600	1,000	2,400

What are the market price and equilibrium quantity of apartments in this town? If this town imposes a rent control of $450 a month, how many apartments will be rented?

4-4. The U.S. government imposes a price floor that is above the market clearing price. Illustrate the U.S. sugar market with the price floor in place. Discuss the effects of the subsidy on conditions in the market for sugar in the United States.

4-5. The Canadian sugar industry has complained that U.S. sugar manufacturers "dump" sugar surpluses in the Canadian market. U.S. chocolate manufacturers have also complained about the high U.S. price of sugar. Explain how the imposition of a price floor for U.S. sugar, as described in Problem 4-4, affects these two markets. What are the changes in equilibrium quantities and market prices?

4-6. Suppose that the U.S. government places a ceiling on the price of Internet access and a black market for Internet providers arises, with Internet service providers developing hidden connections. Illustrate the black market for Internet access, including the implicit supply schedule, the legal price, the black market supply and demand, and the black market equilibrium price and quantity. Also show why there is a shortage of Internet access at the legal price.

4-7. The table below illustrates the demand and supply schedules for seats on air flights between two cities:

Price	Quantity Demanded	Quantity Supplied
$200	2,000	1,200
$300	1,800	1,400
$400	1,600	1,600
$500	1,400	1,800
$600	1,200	2,000

What are the market price and equilibrium quantity in this market? Now suppose that federal authorities limit the number of flights between the two cities to ensure that no more than 1,200 passengers can be flown. Evaluate the effects of this quota on air flights.

4-8. The consequences of decriminalizing illegal drugs have long been debated. Some claim that legalization will lower the price of these drugs and reduce related crime. Others claim that more people will use these drugs. Suppose that some of these drugs are legalized so that anyone may sell them and use them. Now consider the two claims—that price will fall and quantity demanded will increase. Based on positive economic analysis, are these claims sound?

4-9. Look back at Figure 4-4 on page 88. Suppose that the equilibrium price, P_e, is $1.00 per bushel of peanuts and the support price is $1.25. In addition, suppose that the equilibrium quantity, Q_e, is 5 million bushels and the quantity supplied, Q_s, and quantity demanded, Q_d, with the price support are 8 million and 4 million, respectively. What were farmers' total revenues before the

price support program? What are their total revenues afterward? What is the cost of this program to taxpayers?

4-10. Using the information in Problem 4-9, calculate the total expenditures of peanut consumers before and after the price support program. Explain why these answers make sense.

4-11. Labor is a key input at fast-food restaurants. Suppose that the government boosts the minimum wage above the equilibrium wage of fast-food workers.

  a. How will the quantity of labor employed at restaurants respond to the increase in the minimum wage?

  b. How will the market price and equilibrium quantity of fast-food hamburgers be affected by the increase in the minimum wage?

4-12. Suppose that owners of high-rise office buildings are the main employers of custodial workers in a city. The city has decided to impose rent controls, and it has established a rent ceiling below the previous equilibrium rental rate for offices throughout the city.

  a. How will the quantity of offices the building owners lease change?

  b. How will the market wage and equilibrium quantity of labor services provided by custodial workers be affected by the imposition of rent controls?

4-13. In 2003, the government of a nation established a price support for wheat. The government's support price has been above the equilibrium price each year since, and the government has purchased all wheat over and above the amounts that consumers have bought at the support price. Every year since 2003, there has been an increase in the number of wheat producers in the market. No other factors affecting the market for wheat have changed. Predict what has happened each year since 2003 to each of the following:

  a. Quantity of wheat supplied by wheat producers

  b. Quantity of wheat demanded by wheat consumers

  c. Quantity of wheat purchased by the government

4-14. The government of a large U.S. city recently established a "living wage law" that, beginning January 1 of next year, will require all businesses operating within city limits to pay their workers a wage no lower than $8.50 per hour. The current equilibrium wage for fast-food workers is $7.50 per hour in this city. Predict what will happen to each of the following beginning on January 1 of next year:

  a. The quantity of labor supplied by fast-food workers

  b. The quantity of labor demanded by fast-food producers

  c. The number of unemployed fast-food workers in this city

ECONOMICS ON THE NET

The Floor on Milk Prices At various times, the U.S. government has established price floors for milk. This application gives you an opportunity to apply what you have learned in this chapter to this real-world issue.

Title: Northeast Dairy Compact Commission

Navigation: Go to www.econtoday.com/chap04 to visit the Web site of the Northeast Dairy Compact Commission.

Application Read the contents and answer these questions.

1. Based on the government-set price control concepts discussed in Chapter 4, explain the Northeast Dairy Compact that was once in place in the northeastern United States.

2. Draw a diagram illustrating the supply of and demand for milk in the Northeast Dairy Compact and the supply of and demand for milk outside the Northeast Dairy Compact. Illustrate how the compact affected the quantities demanded and supplied for participants in the compact. In addition, show how this affected the market for milk produced by those producers outside the dairy compact.

3. Economists have found that while the Northeast Dairy Compact functioned, midwestern dairy farmers lost their dominance of milk production and sales. In light of your answer to Question 2, explain how this occurred.

For Group Discussion and Analysis Discuss the impact of congressional failure to reauthorize the compact based on your above answers. Identify which arguments in your debate are based on positive economic analysis and which are normative arguments.

If your exam were tomorrow, would you be ready? For each chapter, MyEconLab Practice Tests and Study Plans pinpoint which sections you have mastered and which ones you need to study. That way, you are more efficient with your study time, and you are better prepared for your exams.

In addition to Practice Tests and your personalized Study Plan, you'll find the following media resources in MyEconLab:

1. *Graphs in Motion* animation of Figures 4-1, 4-3, 4-4, and 4-5.
2. Videos featuring the author, Roger LeRoy Miller, on the following subjects:
   ● Price Flexibility, the Essential Role of Rationing via Price and Alternative Rationing Systems
   ● Minimum Wages

3. Links to the Web sites cited in the marginal Internet Resources, Issues and Applications feature, and Economics on the Net activity.
4. Audio clips of all key terms, additional practice problems, and a PDF version of the material from the print Study Guide.
5. eThemes of the Times, which is a New York Times article to help you understand the real-world applications of what you are learning.

Get Ahead of the Curve

To see how it works, turn to page 16 and then go to www.myeconlab.com/miller.

Chapter 5

The Public Sector and Public Choice

The governments of Japan, South Korea, and China have discussed a plan to promote the development of a new, "Asian" software system for operating personal computers. This proposed operating system would rival the world's main alternatives, the privately produced Microsoft Windows and Linux operating systems. According to some proponents of the governments' plan, computer operating systems are "public goods." Such goods, they contend, require governmental development, production, and distribution on behalf of the citizens of Asian nations. When you have completed this chapter, you will be able to evaluate the merits of this claim.

Media Resources

Refer to the end of the chapter for a full listing of the multimedia learning materials available in MyEconLab.

LEARNING OBJECTIVES

After reading this chapter, you should be able to:

1. Explain how market failures such as externalities might justify economic functions of government
2. Distinguish between private goods and public goods and explain the nature of the free-rider problem
3. Describe political functions of government that entail its involvement in the economy
4. Distinguish between average tax rates and marginal tax rates
5. Explain the structure of the U.S. income tax system
6. Discuss the central elements of the theory of public choice

... since passage of the 1986 tax act, which the Congress of that time indicated would be the last word in U.S. tax legislation for many years to come, more than 80 additional tax laws have been enacted? Just one of these contained 25 sections of tax changes, including 11 that were effective retroactively and 4 that applied within 90 days of the end of that tax year.

Thus Congress devotes considerable time and effort to determining new ways to fund the federal government's operations. The U.S. government collects more than $1 trillion annually in income taxes alone. Local, state, and federal governments additionally raise more than $1 trillion in miscellaneous other taxes, such as sales and excise taxes. Clearly, we cannot ignore the presence of government in our society. One of the reasons the government exists is to take care of the functions that people argue the price system does not do well.

WHAT A PRICE SYSTEM CAN AND CANNOT DO

Throughout the book so far, we have alluded to the benefits of a price system. High on the list is economic efficiency. In its most ideal form, a price system allows resources to move from lower-valued uses to higher-valued uses through voluntary exchange. A situation of economic efficiency arises when all mutually advantageous trades have taken place. In a price system, consumers are sovereign; that is to say, they have the individual freedom to decide what they wish to purchase. Politicians and even business managers do not ultimately decide what is produced; consumers decide. Some proponents of the price system argue that this is its most important characteristic. A market organization of economic activity generally prevents one person from illegally interfering with most of other people's activities. Competition among sellers protects consumers from coercion by one seller, and sellers are protected from coercion by one consumer because other consumers are available.

Sometimes the price system does not generate these results, and too few or too many resources go to specific economic activities. Such situations are called **market failures.** Market failures prevent the price system from attaining economic efficiency and individual freedom. Market failures offer one of the strongest arguments in favor of certain economic functions of government, which we now examine.

Market failure
A situation in which an unrestrained market economy leads to too few or too many resources going to a specific economic activity.

CORRECTING FOR EXTERNALITIES

In a pure market system, competition generates economic efficiency only when individuals know the true opportunity cost of their actions. In some circumstances, the price that someone actually pays for a resource, good, or service is higher or lower than the opportunity cost that all of society pays for that same resource, good, or service.

Consider a hypothetical world in which there is no government regulation against pollution. You are living in a town that until now has had clean air. A steel mill moves into town. It produces steel and has paid for the inputs—land, labor, capital, and entrepreneurship. The price the mill charges for the steel reflects, in this example, only the costs that it incurred. In the course of production, however, the mill gets one input—clean air—by simply taking it. This is indeed an input because in making steel, the furnaces emit smoke. The steel mill doesn't have to pay the cost of using the clean air; rather, it is the people in the community who pay that cost in the form of dirtier clothes, dirtier cars and houses, and more respiratory illnesses. The effect is similar to what would happen if the steel mill

Externality
A consequence of an economic activity that spills over to affect third parties. Pollution is an externality.

Third parties
Parties who are not directly involved in a given activity or transaction.

could take coal or oil or workers' services free. There is an **externality,** an external cost. Some of the costs associated with the production of the steel have "spilled over" to affect **third parties,** parties other than the buyer and the seller of the steel.

External Costs in Graphical Form

Look at panel (a) in Figure 5-1. Here we show the demand curve for steel as D. The supply curve is S_1. The supply curve includes only the costs that the firms have to pay. Equilibrium occurs at point E, with price P_1 and quantity Q_1. Let us take into account the fact that there are externalities—the external costs that you and your neighbors pay in the form of dirtier clothes, cars, and houses and increased respiratory disease due to the air pollution emitted from the steel mill; in this case, suppliers of steel use clean air without having to pay for it. Let's include these external costs in our graph to find out what the full cost of steel production really is. We do this by imagining that steel producers have to pay for the input—clean air—that they previously used at a zero price.

Recall from Chapter 3 that an increase in input prices shifts the supply curve. Thus, in panel (a) of the figure, the supply curve shifts from S_1 to S_2; the external costs equal the vertical distance between A and E_1. If steel firms had to take into account these external costs, the equilibrium quantity would fall to Q_2 and the price would rise to P_2. Equilibrium would shift from E to E_1. If the price of steel does not account for external costs, third parties bear those costs—represented by the distance between A and E_1—in the form of dirtier clothes, houses, and cars and increased respiratory illnesses.

FIGURE 5-1

External Costs and Benefits

In panel (a), we show a situation in which the production of steel generates external costs. If the steel mills ignore pollution, at equilibrium the quantity of steel will be Q_1. If the mills had to pay for the external costs borne by nearby residents that are caused by the steel mills' production, the supply curve would shift the vertical distance A–E_1, to S_2. If consumers of steel were forced to pay a price that reflected the spillover costs, the quantity demanded would fall to Q_2. In panel (b), we show a situation in which inoculations against communicable diseases generate external benefits to those individuals who may not be inoculated but who will benefit because epidemics will not occur. If each individual ignores the external benefit of inoculations, the market clearing quantity will be Q_1. If external benefits are taken into account by purchasers of inoculations, however, the demand curve would shift to D_2. The new equilibrium quantity would be Q_2, and the price would be higher, P_2.

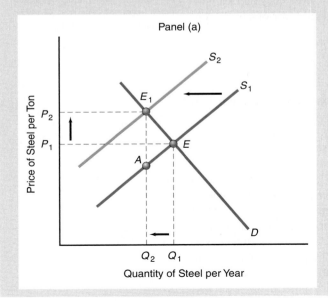

Panel (a)

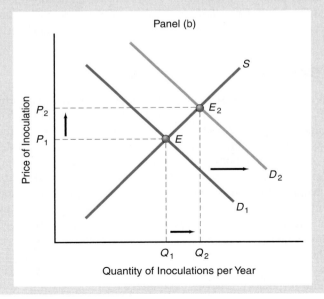

Panel (b)

How do you suppose that a French court sought to correct what it perceived to be a negative externality affecting every auction site on the Internet?

E-Commerce EXAMPLE

A French Court Finds a Way to Regulate the Entire Internet

A few year ago, several groups filed a joint lawsuit in a French court against Yahoo.com. The groups argued that the company's willingness to host Internet auctions of Nazi artifacts violated French laws prohibiting the display of any items that might incite racism. Yahoo had, they argued, illegally "polluted" the Internet by allowing photos and descriptions of Nazi artifacts to appear anywhere on the Internet.

The groups asked for judicial relief in the form of a ban on Yahoo's ability to offer auctions of Nazi artifacts on any Web site that French residents might visit. The judge responded by giving Yahoo an ultimatum: Either find a way to keep French residents from accessing any of its auction sites offering Nazi artifacts for sale, or bar the sale of these items on all of its auction sites around the world. Yahoo decided it would be less costly simply to bar all auctions of Nazi artifacts worldwide. Eventually, eBay and most other Web auction companies adopted similar policies.

For Critical Analysis
Under what circumstances might some collectors of World War II relics have preferred to have paid higher fees at Web auction sites in order to continue buying and selling Nazi artifacts?

External Benefits in Graphical Form

Externalities can also be positive. To demonstrate external benefits in graphical form, we will use the example of inoculations against communicable disease. In panel (b) of Figure 5-1, we show the demand curve as D_1 (without taking account of any external benefits) and the supply curve as S. The equilibrium price is P_1, and the equilibrium quantity is Q_1. We assume, however, that inoculations against communicable diseases generate external benefits to individuals who may not be inoculated but will benefit nevertheless because epidemics will not break out. If such external benefits were taken into account by those who purchase inoculations, the demand curve would shift from D_1 to D_2. The new equilibrium quantity would be Q_2, and the new equilibrium price would be P_2. If people who consider getting inoculations fail to take external benefits into account, this society is not devoting enough resources to inoculations against communicable diseases.

When there are external costs, the market will tend to *overallocate* resources to the production of the good or service in question, for those goods or services will be priced deceptively low. In the steel example, too much will be produced because the steel mill owners and managers are not required to take account of the external cost that steel production is imposing on the rest of society. In essence, the full cost of production is not borne by the owners and managers, so the price they charge the public for steel is lower than it would otherwise be. And, of course, the lower price means that buyers are willing and able to buy more. More steel is produced and consumed than if sellers were to bear external costs.

When there are external benefits, the market *underallocates* resources to the production of that good or service because the good or service is relatively too expensive (because the demand, which fails to reflect the external benefits, is relatively too low). In a market system, too many of the goods that generate external costs are produced, and too few of the goods that generate external benefits are produced.

How the Government Corrects Negative Externalities

The government can in theory correct externalities in a variety of ways in all situations that warrant such action. In the case of negative externalities, at least two avenues are open to the government: special taxes and legislative regulation or prohibition.

Special Taxes. In our example of the steel mill, the externality problem arises because using the air as a waste disposal place is costless to the firm but not to society. The government could make the steel mill pay a tax for dumping its pollutants into the air. The government could attempt to tax the steel mill commensurate with the cost to third parties from smoke in the air. This, in effect, would be a pollution tax or an **effluent fee.** The ultimate effect would be to reduce the supply of steel and raise the price to consumers, ideally making the price equal to the full cost of production to society.

Effluent fee
A charge to a polluter that gives the right to discharge into the air or water a certain amount of pollution; also called a *pollution tax.*

Go to www.econtoday.com/chap05 to learn more about how the Environmental Protection Agency uses regulations to try to protect the environment.

Regulation. Alternatively, to correct a negative externality arising from steel production, the government could specify a maximum allowable rate of pollution. This regulation would require that the steel mill install pollution abatement equipment at its facilities, reduce its rate of output, or some combination of the two. Note that the government's job would not be simple, for it would have to determine the appropriate level of pollution and then measure the pollutants emitted in order to enforce the regulation.

How the Government Corrects Positive Externalities

What can the government do when the production of one good spills *benefits* over to third parties? It has several policy options: financing the production of the good or producing the good itself, subsidies (negative taxes), and regulation.

Government Financing and Production. If the positive externalities seem extremely large, the government has the option of financing the desired additional production facilities so that the "right" amount of the good will be produced. Again consider inoculations against communicable diseases. The government could—and often does—finance campaigns to inoculate the population. It could (and does) even produce and operate inoculation centers where inoculations are given at no charge.

Subsidies. A subsidy is a negative tax; it is a payment made either to a business or to a consumer when the business produces or the consumer buys a good or a service. To generate more inoculations against communicable diseases, the government could subsidize everyone who obtains an inoculation by directly reimbursing those inoculated or by making payments to private firms that provide inoculations. Subsidies reduce the net price to consumers, thereby causing a larger quantity to be demanded.

Regulation. In some cases involving positive externalities, the government can require by law that individuals in the society undertake a certain action. For example, regulations require that all school-age children be inoculated before entering public and private schools. Some people believe that a basic school education itself generates positive externalities. Perhaps as a result of this belief, we have regulations—laws—that require all school-age children to be enrolled in a public or private school.

CONCEPTS in Brief

- External costs lead to an overallocation of resources to the specific economic activity. Two possible ways of correcting these spillovers are taxation and regulation.

- External benefits result in an underallocation of resources to the specific activity. Three possible government corrections are financing the production of the activity, subsidizing private firms or consumers to engage in the activity, and regulation.

To test your understanding of the concepts covered in this section, go to the Online Review at **www.myeconlab.com/miller.**

THE OTHER ECONOMIC FUNCTIONS OF GOVERNMENT

Besides correcting for externalities, the government performs many other economic functions that affect the way exchange is carried out. In contrast, the political functions of government have to do with deciding how income should be redistributed among households and selecting which goods and services have special merits and should therefore be treated differently. The economic and political functions of government can and do overlap.

Let's look at four more economic functions of government.

Providing a Legal System

The courts and the police may not at first seem like economic functions of government. Their activities nonetheless have important consequences for economic activities in any country. You and I enter into contracts constantly, whether they be oral or written, expressed or implied. When we believe that we have been wronged, we seek redress of our grievances through our legal institutions. Moreover, consider the legal system that is necessary for the smooth functioning of our economic system. Our system has defined quite explicitly the legal status of businesses, the rights of private ownership, and a method of enforcing contracts. All relationships among consumers and businesses are governed by the legal rules of the game. In its judicial function, then, the government serves as the referee for settling disputes in the economic arena. In this role, the government often imposes penalties for violations of legal rules.

Much of our legal system is involved with defining and protecting *property rights.* **Property rights** are the rights of an owner to use and to exchange his or her property. One might say that property rights are really the rules of our economic game. When property rights are well defined, owners of property have an incentive to use that property efficiently. Any mistakes in their decisions about the use of property have negative consequences that the owners suffer. Furthermore, when property rights are well defined, owners of property have an incentive to maintain that property so that if they ever desire to sell it, it will fetch a better price.

What populous country still ruled by the Communist Party do you suppose has awakened to the importance of the incentive effects of private property rights?

Property rights
The rights of an owner to use and to exchange property.

International EXAMPLE

Private Property Rights in China

In 1949, China officially became a "people's republic," in which all resources were owned by the government. For almost three decades, the Chinese government made all decisions concerning the production and distribution of goods and services.

Beginning in the 1980s, the Chinese government embarked on a gradual program of business privatization. This policy sparked an increase in economic growth. Nevertheless, government and business leaders eventually recognized that China's economy would be unable to attain its full potential in the absence of a formal declaration of private property rights. A constitutional amendment officially guaranteeing the right to private property was adopted in 2004.

For Critical Analysis
How might the establishment of private property rights have contributed to a burst of Chinese economic growth during the past few years? (Hint: Why might clearer rules about resource ownership make people more willing to start businesses?)

Promoting Competition

Many people believe that the only way to attain economic efficiency is through competition. One of the roles of government is to serve as the protector of a competitive economic system. Congress and the various state governments have passed **antitrust legislation.** Such legislation makes illegal certain (but not all) economic activities that might restrain trade—that is, that might prevent free competition among actual and potential rival firms in the marketplace. The avowed aim of antitrust legislation is to reduce the power of **monopolies**—firms that have great control over the price of the goods they sell. A large number of antitrust laws have been passed that prohibit specific anticompetitive actions. Both the Antitrust Division of the Department of Justice and the Federal Trade Commission attempt to enforce these antitrust laws. Various state judicial agencies also expend efforts at maintaining competition.

Antitrust legislation
Laws that restrict the formation of monopolies and regulate certain anticompetitive business practices.

Monopoly
A firm that has control over the price of a good. In the extreme case, a monopoly is the only seller of a good or service.

Providing Public Goods

The goods used in our examples up to this point have been **private goods**. When I eat a cheeseburger, you cannot eat the same one. So you and I are rivals for that cheeseburger, just as much as rivals for the title of world champion are. When I use a DVD player, you cannot play some other disc at the same time. When I use the services of an auto mechanic, that person cannot work at the same time for you. That is the distinguishing feature of private goods—their use is exclusive to the people who purchase or rent them. The **principle of rival consumption** applies to all private goods by definition. Rival consumption is easy to understand. With private goods, either you use them or I use them.

There is an entire class of goods that are not private goods. These are called **public goods.** The principle of rival consumption does not apply to them. That is, they can be consumed *jointly* by many individuals simultaneously. National defense, police protection, and the legal system, for example, are public goods. If you partake of them, you do not necessarily take away from anyone else's share of those goods.

Private goods
Goods that can be consumed by only one individual at a time. Private goods are subject to the principle of rival consumption.

Principle of rival consumption
The recognition that individuals are rivals in consuming private goods because one person's consumption reduces the amount available for others to consume.

Public goods
Goods for which the principle of rival consumption does not apply; they can be jointly consumed by many individuals simultaneously at no additional cost and with no reduction in quality or quantity. Also no one who fails to help pay for the good can be denied the benefit of the good.

Characteristics of Public Goods. Two fundamental characteristics of public goods set them apart from all other goods.*

1. *Public goods can be used by more and more people at no additional cost and without depriving others of any of the services of the goods.* Once money has been spent on national defense, the defense protection you receive does not reduce the amount of

---

*Sometimes a distinction is made between pure public goods, which have all the characteristics we have described here, and quasi- or near-public goods, which do not. The major feature of near-public goods is that they are jointly consumed, even though nonpaying customers can be, and often are, excluded—for example, movies, football games, and concerts.

protection bestowed on anyone else. The opportunity cost of your receiving national defense once it is in place is zero because once national defense is in place to protect you, it also protects others.

2. *It is difficult to design a collection system for a public good on the basis of how much individuals use it.* It is nearly impossible to determine how much any person uses or values national defense. No one can be denied the benefits of national defense for failing to pay for that public good. This is often called the **exclusion principle.**

One of the problems of public goods is that the private sector has a difficult, if not impossible, time providing them. Individuals in the private sector have little or no incentive to offer public goods. It is difficult for them to make a profit doing so, because nonpayers cannot be excluded. Consequently, true public goods must necessarily be provided by government. Note, though, that economists do not necessarily categorize something as a public good simply because the government provides it.

Free Riders. The nature of public goods leads to the **free-rider problem,** a situation in which some individuals take advantage of the fact that others will assume the burden of paying for public goods such as national defense. Suppose that citizens were taxed directly in proportion to how much they tell an interviewer that they value national defense. Some people will probably tell interviewers that they are unwilling to pay for national defense because they don't want any of it—it is of no value to them. Such people are trying to be free riders. We may all want to be free riders if we believe that someone else will provide the commodity in question that we actually value.

The free-rider problem often arises when it comes to the international burden of defense sharing. A country may choose to belong to a multilateral defense organization, such as the North Atlantic Treaty Organization (NATO), but then consistently attempt to avoid contributing funds to the organization. The nation knows it would be defended by others in NATO if it were attacked but would rather not pay for such defense. In short, it seeks a free ride.

Why do you suppose that in some of the world's poorest regions, the inability of governments to deal with the free-rider problem has provided an opportunity for organizations that promote international terrorism?

Exclusion principle
The principle that no one can be excluded from the benefits of a public good, even if that person has not paid for it.

Free-rider problem
A problem that arises when individuals presume that others will pay for public goods so that, individually, they can escape paying for their portion without causing a reduction in production.

International EXAMPLE

How Solving Free-Rider Problems May Help Combat Terrorism

During the 1990s, the Taliban government took control of Afghanistan and made it a haven for international terrorist organizations, including the Al Qaeda organization that launched attacks on the United States in 2001. A key to the Taliban's success was its ability to collect contributions from all residents—often under the threat of force—to fund a police force. Even though some in Afghanistan did not like the Taliban's strict rules, they appreciated its provision of public safety—a service the previous government had failed to provide. This enabled the Taliban to remain in power until ousted by the U.S. military in 2002.

Likewise, in the Palestinian territories, the government has often been unable to collect revenues from many Palestinians and hence has failed to provide many public services. This situation has fostered the growth of Hamas, an organization that both promotes terrorism against Israel and provides various public services to Palestinians. The ability of Hamas to collect funds from many Palestinian residents in order to coordinate these desirable public service activities has gained the group considerable popular support—plus a source of funds for terrorist operations.

The official Afghani government during the 1990s and the Palestinian government in the 2000s failed to deal with the free-rider problem. Terrorist organizations stepped in to address this government failure by providing public services the governments had been unable to fund. Thus many world leaders contend that establishing forms of government better equipped to tackle the free-rider problem will do much to diminish the strength of terrorist organizations.

For Critical Analysis
How might terrorist organizations themselves experience free-rider problems, and what might the world's governments do to exploit the free-rider problems these groups encounter?

Ensuring Economywide Stability

Our economy sometimes faces the problems of unemployment and rising prices. The government, especially the federal government, has made an attempt to solve these problems by trying to stabilize the economy by smoothing out the ups and downs in overall business activity. The notion that the federal government should undertake actions to stabilize business activity is a relatively new idea in the United States, encouraged by high unemployment rates during the Great Depression of the 1930s and subsequent theories about possible ways that government could reduce unemployment. In 1946, Congress passed the Full-Employment Act, a landmark law concerning government responsibility for economic performance. It established three goals for government stabilization policy: full employment, price stability, and economic growth. These goals have provided the justification for many government economic programs during the post–World War II period.

CONCEPTS in Brief

- The economic activities of government include (1) correcting for externalities, (2) providing a legal system, (3) promoting competition, (4) producing public goods, and (5) ensuring economywide stability.

- Public goods can be consumed jointly. The principle of rival consumption does not apply as it does with private goods.

- Public goods have two characteristics: (1) Once they are produced, there is no opportunity cost when additional consumers use them, because your use of a public good does not deprive others of its simultaneous use; and (2) consumers cannot conveniently be charged on the basis of use.

To test your understanding of the concepts covered in this section, go to the Online Review at www.myeconlab.com/miller.

THE POLITICAL FUNCTIONS OF GOVERNMENT

At least two functions of government are political or normative functions rather than economic ones like those discussed in the first part of this chapter. These two areas are (1) the regulation and provision of merit and demerit goods and (2) income redistribution.

Merit and Demerit Goods

Merit good
A good that has been deemed socially desirable through the political process. Museums are an example.

Certain goods are considered to have special merit. A **merit good** is defined as any good that the political process has deemed socially desirable. (Note that nothing inherent in any particular good makes it a merit good. The designation is entirely subjective.) Some examples of merit goods in our society are sports stadiums, museums, ballets, plays, and concerts. In these areas, the government's role is the provision of merit goods to the people in society who would not otherwise purchase them at market clearing prices or who would not purchase an amount of them judged to be sufficient. This provision may take the form of government production and distribution of merit goods. It can also take the form of reimbursement for payment on merit goods or subsidies to producers or consumers for part of the cost of merit goods. Governments do indeed subsidize such merit goods as professional sports, concerts, ballets, museums, and plays. In most cases, such merit goods would not be so numerous without subsidization.

Demerit goods are the opposite of merit goods. They are goods that, through the political process, are deemed socially undesirable. Heroin, cigarettes, gambling, and cocaine are examples. The government exercises its role in the area of demerit goods by taxing, regulating, or prohibiting their manufacture, sale, and use. Governments justify the relatively high taxes on alcohol and tobacco by declaring them demerit goods. The best-known example of governmental exercise of power in this area is the stance against certain psychoactive drugs. Most psychoactives (except nicotine, caffeine, and alcohol) are either expressly prohibited, as is the case for heroin, cocaine, and opium, or heavily regulated, as in the case of prescription psychoactives.

Income Redistribution

Another relatively recent political function of government has been the explicit redistribution of income. This redistribution uses two systems: the progressive income tax (described later in this chapter) and transfer payments. **Transfer payments** are payments made to individuals for which no services or goods are rendered in return. The three key money transfer payments in our system are welfare, Social Security, and unemployment insurance benefits. Income redistribution also includes a large amount of income **transfers in kind,** as opposed to money transfers. Some income transfers in kind are food stamps, Medicare and Medicaid, government health care services, and subsidized public housing.

The government has also engaged in other activities as a form of redistribution of income. For example, the provision of public education is at least in part an attempt to redistribute income by making sure that the poor have access to education.

Economics Front and Center

To evaluate a situation in which the consumption of publicly provided goods can generate externality effects, consider the real-world problem faced by a college student in **Too Few Opportunities to Play Table Tennis, or Too Many?**, on page 117.

Demerit good
A good that has been deemed socially undesirable through the political process. Heroin is an example.

Transfer payments
Money payments made by governments to individuals for which in return no services or goods are rendered. Examples are welfare, Social Security, and unemployment insurance benefits.

Transfers in kind
Payments that are in the form of actual goods and services, such as food stamps, subsidized public housing, and medical care, and for which in return no goods or services are rendered concurrently.

CONCEPTS in Brief

- Political, or normative, activities of the government include the provision and regulation of merit and demerit goods and income redistribution.

- Merit and demerit goods do not have any inherent characteristics that qualify them as such; rather, collectively, through the political process, we make judgments about

which goods and services are "good" for society and which are "bad."

- Income redistribution can be carried out by a system of progressive taxation, coupled with transfer payments, which can be made in money or in kind, such as food stamps and Medicare.

To test your understanding of the concepts covered in this section, go to the Online Review at www.myeconlab.com/miller.

PAYING FOR THE PUBLIC SECTOR

Jean-Baptiste Colbert, the seventeenth-century French finance minister, said the art of taxation was in "plucking the goose so as to obtain the largest amount of feathers with the least possible amount of hissing." In the United States, governments have designed a variety of methods of plucking the private-sector goose. To analyze any tax system, we must first understand the distinction between marginal tax rates and average tax rates.

Marginal and Average Tax Rates

If somebody says, "I pay 28 percent in taxes," you cannot really tell what that person means unless you know if he or she is referring to average taxes paid or the tax rate on the last dollars earned. The latter concept refers to the **marginal tax rate.***

The marginal tax rate is expressed as follows:

$$\text{Marginal tax rate} = \frac{\text{change in taxes due}}{\text{change in taxable income}}$$

It is important to understand that the marginal tax rate applies only to the income in the highest **tax bracket** reached, where a tax bracket is defined as a specified level of taxable income to which a specific and unique marginal tax rate is applied.

The marginal tax rate is not the same thing as the **average tax rate,** which is defined as follows:

$$\text{Average tax rate} = \frac{\text{total taxes due}}{\text{total taxable income}}$$

Taxation Systems

No matter how governments raise revenues—from income taxes, sales taxes, or other taxes—all of those taxes fit into one of three types of taxation systems: proportional, progressive, or regressive, according to the relationship between the tax rate and income. To determine whether a tax system is proportional, progressive, or regressive, we simply ask, What is the relationship between the average tax rate and the marginal tax rate?

Proportional Taxation. **Proportional taxation** means that regardless of an individual's income, taxes comprise exactly the same proportion. In a proportional taxation system, the marginal tax rate is always equal to the average tax rate. If every dollar is taxed at 20 percent, then the average tax rate is 20 percent, and so is the marginal tax rate.

Under a proportional system of taxation, taxpayers at all income levels end up paying the same *percentage* of their income in taxes. With a proportional tax rate of 20 percent, an individual with an income of $10,000 pays $2,000 in taxes, while an individual making $100,000 pays $20,000. The identical 20 percent rate, therefore, is levied on both taxpayers.

Progressive Taxation. Under **progressive taxation,** as a person's taxable income increases, the percentage of income paid in taxes increases. In a progressive system, the marginal tax rate is above the average tax rate. If you are taxed 5 percent on the first $10,000 you make, 10 percent on the next $10,000 you make, and 30 percent on the last $10,000 you make, you face a progressive income tax system. Your marginal tax rate is always above your average tax rate.

Regressive Taxation. With **regressive taxation,** a smaller percentage of taxable income is taken in taxes as taxable income increases. The marginal rate is *below* the average rate. As income increases, the marginal tax rate falls, and so does the average tax rate. The U.S.

Marginal tax rate
The change in the tax payment divided by the change in income, or the percentage of additional dollars that must be paid in taxes. The marginal tax rate is applied to the highest tax bracket of taxable income reached.

Tax bracket
A specified interval of income to which a specific and unique marginal tax rate is applied.

Average tax rate
The total tax payment divided by total income. It is the proportion of total income paid in taxes.

Proportional taxation
A tax system in which, regardless of an individual's income, the tax bill comprises exactly the same proportion.

Progressive taxation
A tax system in which, as income increases, a higher percentage of the additional income is taxed. The marginal tax rate exceeds the average tax rate as income rises.

Regressive taxation
A tax system in which as more dollars are earned, the percentage of tax paid on them falls. The marginal tax rate is less than the average tax rate as income rises.

---

*The word *marginal* means "incremental" (or "decremental") here.

Social Security tax is regressive. Once the legislative maximum taxable wage base is reached, no further Social Security taxes are paid. Consider a simplified hypothetical example: Suppose that every dollar up to $50,000 is taxed at 10 percent. After $50,000 there is no Social Security tax. Someone making $100,000 still pays only $5,000 in Social Security taxes. That person's average Social Security tax is 5 percent. The person making $50,000, by contrast, effectively pays 10 percent. The person making $1 million faces an average Social Security tax rate of only 0.5 percent in our simplified example.

CONCEPTS in Brief

- Tax rates are applied to tax brackets, defined as spreads of income over which the tax rate is constant.

- Tax systems can be proportional, progressive, or regressive, depending on whether the marginal tax rate is the same as, greater than, or less than the average tax rate as income rises.

To test your understanding of the concepts covered in this section, go to the Online Review at www.myeconlab.com/miller.

THE MOST IMPORTANT FEDERAL TAXES

The federal government imposes income taxes on both individuals and corporations and collects Social Security taxes and a variety of other taxes.

The Federal Personal Income Tax

The most important tax in the U.S. economy is the federal personal income tax, which accounts for about 43 percent of all federal revenues. All American citizens, resident aliens, and most others who earn income in the United States are required to pay federal income taxes on all taxable income. The rates that are paid rise as income increases, as can be seen in Table 5-1 on the next page. Marginal income tax rates at the federal level have varied from as low as 1 percent after the 1913 passage of the Sixteenth Amendment to as high as 94 percent (reached in 1944). There were 14 separate tax brackets prior to the Tax Reform Act of 1986, which reduced the number to three (now six). Advocates of a more progressive income tax system in the United States argue that such a system redistributes income from the rich to the poor, taxes people according to their ability to pay, and taxes people according to the benefits they receive from government. Although there is much controversy over the redistributional nature of our progressive tax system, there is no strong evidence that the tax system has actually ever done much income redistribution in this country. Currently, about 85 percent of all tax-paying U.S. residents pay roughly the same proportion of their total income in federal taxes.

Go to www.econtoday.com/chap05 to learn from the National Center for Policy Analysis about what distinguishes recent flat tax proposals from a truly proportional income tax system. Next, click on "Flat Tax Proposals."

The Treatment of Capital Gains

The difference between the buying and selling price of an asset, such as a share of stock or a plot of land, is called a **capital gain** if it is a profit and a **capital loss** if it is not. The federal government taxes capital gains, and as of 2005, there were several capital gains tax rates.

What appear to be capital gains are not always real gains. If you pay $100,000 for a financial asset in one year and sell it for 50 percent more 10 years later, your nominal capital gain is $50,000. But what if during those 10 years inflation has driven average asset prices up by 50 percent? Your *real* capital gain would be zero, but you would still have to

Capital gain
The positive difference between the purchase price and the sale price of an asset. If a share of stock is bought for $5 and then sold for $15, the capital gain is $10.

Capital loss
The negative difference between the purchase price and the sale price of an asset.

TABLE 5-1
Federal Marginal Income Tax Rates
These rates became effective in 2004. The highest rate includes a 10 percent surcharge on taxable income above $319,101.

Single Persons		Married Couples	
Marginal Tax Bracket	Marginal Tax Rate	Marginal Tax Bracket	Marginal Tax Rate
$0–$7,150	10%	$0–$14,300	10%
$7,151–$29,050	15%	$14,301–$58,100	15%
$29,051–$70,350	25%	$58,101–$117,250	25%
$70,351–$146,750	28%	$117,251–$178,650	28%
$146,751–$319,100	33%	$178,651–$319,100	33%
$319,101 and up	35%	$319,101 and up	35%

Source: U.S. Department of the Treasury.

pay taxes on that $50,000. To counter this problem, many economists have argued that capital gains should be indexed to the rate of inflation. This is exactly what is done with the marginal tax brackets in the federal income tax code. Tax brackets for the purposes of calculating marginal tax rates each year are expanded at the rate of inflation, or the rate at which the average of all prices is rising. So if the rate of inflation is 10 percent, each tax bracket is moved up by 10 percent. The same concept could be applied to capital gains and financial assets. So far, Congress has refused to enact such a measure.

The Corporate Income Tax

Corporate income taxes account for about 11 percent of all federal taxes collected and about 2 percent of all state and local taxes collected. Corporations are generally taxed on the difference between their total revenues (or receipts) and their expenses. The federal corporate income tax structure is given in Table 5-2.

Double Taxation. Because individual stockholders must pay taxes on the dividends they receive, which are paid out of *after-tax* profits by the corporation, corporate profits are taxed twice. If you receive $1,000 in dividends, you have to declare them as income, and

TABLE 5-2
Federal Corporate Income Tax Schedule
These corporate tax rates were in effect through 2005.

Corporate Taxable Income	Corporate Tax Rate
$0–$50,000	15%
$50,001–$75,000	25%
$75,001–$100,000	34%
$100,001–$335,000	39%
$335,001–$10,000,000	34%
$10,000,001–$15,000,000	35%
$15,000,001–$18,333,333	38%
$18,333,334 and up	35%

Source: Internal Revenue Service.

you must pay taxes on them. Before the corporation was able to pay you those dividends, it had to pay taxes on all its profits, including any that it put back into the company or did not distribute in the form of dividends. Eventually, the new investment made possible by those **retained earnings**—profits not given out to stockholders—along with borrowed funds will be reflected in the increased value of the stock in that company. When you sell your stock in that company, you will have to pay taxes on the difference between what you paid for the stock and what you sold it for. In both cases, dividends and retained earnings (corporate profits) are taxed twice. In 2003, Congress reduced the double taxation effect somewhat by enacting legislation that allows most dividends to be taxed at lower rates than are applied to regular income.

Retained earnings
Earnings that a corporation saves, or retains, for investment in other productive activities; earnings that are not distributed to stockholders.

Who Really Pays the Corporate Income Tax? Corporations can exist only as long as consumers buy their products, employees make their goods, stockholders (owners) buy their shares, and bondholders buy their bonds. Corporations per se do not do anything. We must ask, then, who really pays the tax on corporate income? This is a question of **tax incidence.** (The question of tax incidence applies to all taxes, including sales taxes and Social Security taxes.) The incidence of corporate taxation is the subject of considerable debate. Some economists suggest that corporations pass their tax burdens on to consumers by charging higher prices. Other economists argue that it is the stockholders who bear most of the tax. Still others contend that employees pay at least part of the tax by receiving lower wages than they would otherwise. Because the debate is not yet settled, we will not hazard a guess here as to what the correct conclusion may be. Suffice it to say that you should be cautious when you advocate increasing corporation income taxes. *People*— whether owners, consumers, or workers—ultimately end up paying the increase if they own shares in a corporation, buy its products, or work for it.

Tax incidence
The distribution of tax burdens among various groups in society.

CONCEPTS in Brief

- Because corporations must first pay an income tax on most earnings, the personal income tax shareholders pay on dividends received (or realized capital gains) constitutes double taxation.

- The corporate income tax is paid by people in one or more of the following groups: stockholder-owners, consumers of corporate-produced products, and employees of corporations.

To test your understanding of the concepts covered in this section, go to the Online Review at www.myeconlab.com/miller.

Social Security and Unemployment Taxes

Each year, payroll taxes levied on payrolls account for an increasing percentage of federal tax receipts. These taxes, which are distinct from personal income taxes, are for Social Security, retirement, survivors' disability, and old-age medical benefits (Medicare). Today the Social Security tax is imposed on earnings up to roughly $90,000 at a rate of 6.2 percent on employers and 6.2 percent on employees. That is, the employer matches your "contribution" to Social Security. (The employer's contribution is really paid, at least in part, in the form of a reduced wage rate paid to employees.) A Medicare tax is imposed on all wage earnings at a combined rate of 2.9 percent. These taxes and the base on which they are levied are slated to rise in the next decade. Social Security taxes came into existence when the Federal Insurance Contributions Act (FICA) was passed in 1935. The future of Social Security is addressed in Chapter 6.

There is also a federal unemployment tax, which helps pay for unemployment insurance. This tax rate is 0.8 percent on the first $7,000 of annual wages of each employee who earns more than $1,500. Only the employer makes the direct tax payment. This tax covers the costs of the unemployment insurance system and the costs of employment

FIGURE 5-2

Total Government Outlays over Time

Total government outlays (federal, state, and local combined) remained small until the 1930s, except during World War I. Since World War II, government outlays have not fallen back to their historical average.

Sources: *Facts and Figures on Government Finance*, various issues; *Economic Indicators*, various issues.

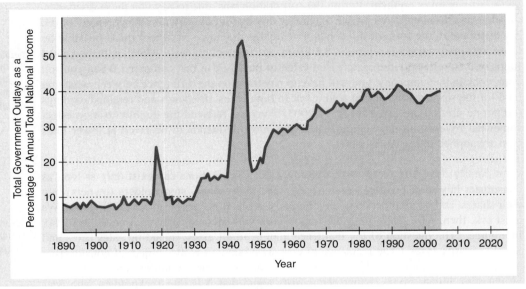

services. In addition to this federal tax, some states with an unemployment system impose their own tax of up to about 3 percent, depending on the past record of the particular employer. An employer who frequently lays off workers will have a slightly higher state unemployment tax rate than an employer who never lays off workers.

SPENDING, GOVERNMENT SIZE, AND TAX RECEIPTS

The size of the public sector can be measured in many different ways. One way is to count the number of public employees. Another is to look at total government outlays. Government outlays include all government expenditures on employees, rent, electricity, and the like. In addition, total government outlays include transfer payments, such as welfare and Social Security. In Figure 5-2, you see that government outlays prior to World War I did not exceed 10 percent of annual national income. There was a spike during World War I, a general increase during the Great Depression, and then a huge spike during World War II. Contrary to previous postwar periods, after World War II government outlays as a percentage of total national income rose steadily before dropping in the 1990s and rising slightly again in the 2000s.

Government Receipts

The main revenue raiser for all levels of government is taxes. We show in the two pie diagrams in Figure 5-3 the percentage of receipts from various taxes obtained by the federal government and by state and local governments.

Federal Government. The largest source of receipts for the federal government is the individual income tax. It accounts for 42.9 percent of all federal revenues. After that come social insurance taxes and contributions (Social Security), which account for 39.0 percent of total revenues. Next come corporate income taxes and then a number of other items, such as taxes on imported goods and excise taxes on such things as gasoline and alcoholic beverages.

State and Local Governments. As can be seen in Figure 5-3, there is quite a bit of difference in the origin of receipts for state and local governments and for the federal govern-

FIGURE 5-3
Sources of Government Tax Receipts

About 82 percent of federal revenues come from income and Social Security taxes (see in panel (a)), whereas state government revenues are spread more evenly across sources (see panel (b)), with less emphasis on taxes based on individual income.

Source: U.S. Department of Commerce, Bureau of Economic Analysis.

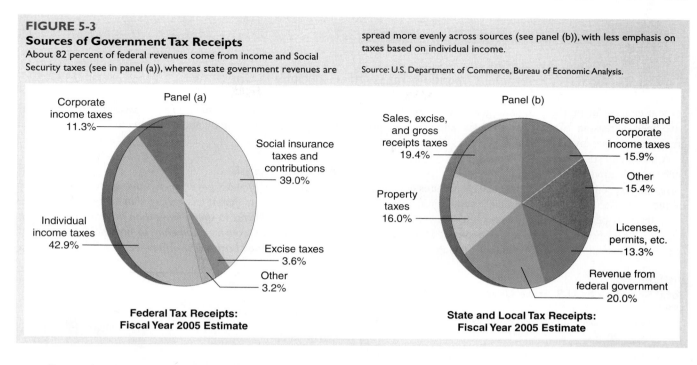

Panel (a)

Corporate income taxes 11.3%

Social insurance taxes and contributions 39.0%

Individual income taxes 42.9%

Excise taxes 3.6%

Other 3.2%

Federal Tax Receipts: Fiscal Year 2005 Estimate

Panel (b)

Sales, excise, and gross receipts taxes 19.4%

Personal and corporate income taxes 15.9%

Other 15.4%

Property taxes 16.0%

Licenses, permits, etc. 13.3%

Revenue from federal government 20.0%

State and Local Tax Receipts: Fiscal Year 2005 Estimate

ment. Personal and corporate income taxes account for only 15.9 percent of total state and local revenues. There are even a few states that collect no personal income tax. The largest sources of state and local receipts (other than from the federal government) are sales taxes, property taxes, and personal and corporate income taxes.

Figure 5-4 shows only the *distribution* of state government spending. How much has spending by state governments *changed* in recent years? See the next page.

Go to www.econtoday.com/ch05 to consider whether Internet sales should be taxed.

FIGURE 5-4
Federal Government Spending Compared to State and Local Spending

The federal government's spending habits are quite different from those of the states and cities. In panel (a), you can see that the categories of most importance in the federal budget are defense, income security, and Social Security, which make up 54.8 percent. In panel (b), the most important category at the state and local level is education, which makes up 34.7 percent. "Other" includes expenditures in such areas as waste treatment, garbage collection, mosquito abatement, and the judicial system.

Sources: *Budget of the United States Government; Government Finances.*

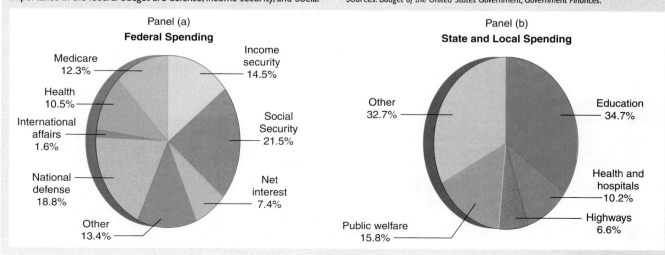

Panel (a)
Federal Spending

Medicare 12.3%

Health 10.5%

International affairs 1.6%

National defense 18.8%

Income security 14.5%

Social Security 21.5%

Net interest 7.4%

Other 13.4%

Panel (b)
State and Local Spending

Other 32.7%

Education 34.7%

Health and hospitals 10.2%

Highways 6.6%

Public welfare 15.8%

Policy EXAMPLE

State Government Spending Takes Off—Especially in One State

As you can see in Figure 5-5, state government expenditures have been increasing. Since 1997, total spending by state governments has risen by more than 39 percent.

Although all states have been spending more funds on items such as education and health care, one state's government in particular has contributed to the rise in expenditures depicted in Figure 5-5. California's government spending increased by more than 36 percent during just the three-year period from 1998 to 2001. For the entire period depicted in Figure 5-5, spending by California's government, which currently ac-

counts for close to 15 percent of total expenditures of all U.S. state governments, rose by about 50 percent.

For Critical Analysis
How could California's government have spent more on average in recent years than it has collected in taxes? (Hint: Unless a person who desires to spend more than the amount earned in a given year can convince someone to provide financial gifts, the individual must borrow the difference.)

FIGURE 5-5
Total Spending by U.S. State Governments Since 1997
State government expenditures have increased by about $150 billion, or more than 39 percent, since 1997.

Source: National Association of State Budget Officers.

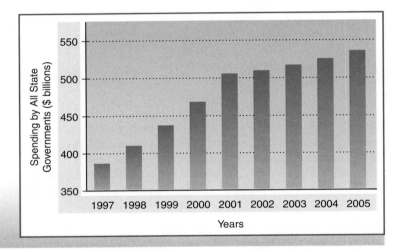

Comparing Federal with State and Local Spending. A typical federal government budget is given in panel (a) of Figure 5-4 on the previous page. The largest three categories are defense, income security, and Social Security, which together constitute 54.8 percent of the total federal budget.

The makeup of state and local expenditures is quite different. As panel (b) shows, education is the biggest category, accounting for 34.7 percent of all expenditures.

CONCEPTS in Brief

- Total government outlays including transfers have continued to grow since World War II and now account for about 38 percent of yearly total national output.

- Government spending at the federal level is different from that at the state and local levels. At the federal level,

defense, income security, and Social Security account for nearly 55 percent of the federal budget. At the state and local levels, education comprises almost 35 percent of all expenditures.

To test your understanding of the concepts covered in this section, go to the Online Review at **www.myeconlab.com/miller**.

COLLECTIVE DECISION MAKING: THE THEORY OF PUBLIC CHOICE

Governments consist of individuals. No government actually thinks and acts; rather, government actions are the result of decision making by individuals in their roles as elected representatives, appointed officials, and salaried bureaucrats. Therefore, to understand how government works, we must examine the incentives of the people in government as well as those who would like to be in government—avowed or would-be candidates for elective or appointed positions—and special-interest lobbyists attempting to get government to do something. At issue is the analysis of **collective decision making.** Collective decision making involves the actions of voters, politicians, political parties, interest groups, and many other groups and individuals. The analysis of collective decision making is usually called the **theory of public choice.** It has been given this name because it involves hypotheses about how choices are made in the public sector, as opposed to the private sector. The foundation of public-choice theory is the assumption that individuals will act within the political process to maximize their *individual* (not collective) well-being. In that sense, the theory is similar to our analysis of the market economy, in which we also assume that individuals are motivated by self-interest.

To understand public-choice theory, it is necessary to point out other similarities between the private market sector and the public, or government, sector; then we will look at the differences.

Collective decision making
How voters, politicians, and other interested parties act and how these actions influence nonmarket decisions.

Theory of public choice
The study of collective decision making.

Similarities in Market and Public-Sector Decision Making

In addition to the assumption of self-interest being the motivating force in both sectors, there are other similarities.

Scarcity. At any given moment, the amount of resources is fixed. This means that for the private and the public sectors combined, there is a scarcity constraint. Everything that is spent by all levels of government plus everything that is spent by the private sector must add up to the total income available at any point in time. Hence every government action has an opportunity cost, just as in the market sector.

Competition. Although we typically think of competition as a private-market phenomenon, it is also present in collective action. Given the scarcity constraint government faces, bureaucrats, appointed officials, and elected representatives will always be in competition for available government funds. Furthermore, the individuals within any government agency or institution will act as individuals do in the private sector: They will try to obtain higher wages, better working conditions, and higher job-level classifications. We assume that they will compete and act in their own interest, not society's.

Similarity of Individuals. Contrary to popular belief, there are not two types of individuals, those who work in the private sector and those who work in the public sector; rather, individuals working in similar positions can be considered similar. The difference, as we shall see, is that the individuals in government face a different **incentive structure** than those in the private sector. For example, the costs and benefits of being efficient or inefficient differ in the private and public sectors.

One approach to predicting government bureaucratic behavior is to ask what incentives bureaucrats face. Take the United States Postal Service (USPS) as an example. The bureaucrats running that government corporation are human beings with IQs not dissimilar to those possessed by workers in similar positions at Microsoft or American Airlines. Yet

Incentive structure
The system of rewards and punishments individuals face with respect to their own actions.

the USPS does not function like either of these companies. The difference can be explained, at least in part, in terms of the incentives provided for managers in the two types of institutions. When the bureaucratic managers and workers at Microsoft make incorrect decisions, work slowly, produce shoddy products, and are generally "inefficient," the profitability of the company declines. The owners—millions of shareholders—express their displeasure by selling some of their shares of company stock. The market value, as tracked on the stock exchange, falls. But what about the USPS? If a manager, a worker, or a bureaucrat in the USPS gives shoddy service, the organization's owners—the taxpayers—have no straightforward mechanism for expressing their dissatisfaction. Despite the postal service's status as a "government corporation," taxpayers as shareholders do not really own shares of stock in the organization that they can sell.

Thus, to understand purported inefficiency in the government bureaucracy, we need to examine incentives and institutional arrangements—not people and personalities.

Differences Between Market and Collective Decision Making

There are probably more dissimilarities between the market sector and the public sector than there are similarities.

Government, or political, goods
Goods (and services) provided by the public sector; they can be either private or public goods.

Government Goods at Zero Price. The majority of goods that governments produce are furnished to the ultimate consumers without payment required. **Government,** or **political, goods** can be either private or public goods. The fact that they are furnished to the ultimate consumer free of charge does *not* mean that the cost to society of those goods is zero, however; it only means that the price *charged* is zero. The full opportunity cost to society is the value of the resources used in the production of goods produced and provided by the government.

For example, none of us pays directly for each unit of consumption of defense or police protection. Rather, we pay for all these things indirectly through the taxes that support our governments—federal, state, and local. This special feature of government can be looked at in a different way. There is no longer a one-to-one relationship between consumption of a government-provided good and payment for that good. Indeed, most taxpayers will find that their tax bill is the same whether or not they consume government-provided goods.

Use of Force. All governments may resort to using force in their regulation of economic affairs. For example, governments can use *expropriation*, which means that if you refuse to pay your taxes, your bank account and other assets may be seized by the Internal Revenue Service. In fact, you have no choice in the matter of paying taxes to governments. Collectively, we decide the total size of government through the political process, but individually, we cannot determine how much service we pay for just for ourselves during any one year.

Majority rule
A collective decision-making system in which group decisions are made on the basis of more than 50 percent of the vote. In other words, whatever more than half of the electorate votes for, the entire electorate has to accept.

Voting versus Spending. In the private market sector, a dollar voting system is in effect. This dollar voting system is not equivalent to the voting system in the public sector. There are at least three differences:

Proportional rule
A decision-making system in which actions are based on the proportion of the "votes" cast and are in proportion to them. In a market system, if 10 percent of the "dollar votes" are cast for blue cars, 10 percent of the output will be blue cars.

1. In a political system, one person gets one vote, whereas in the market system, each dollar one spends counts separately.
2. The political system is run by **majority rule,** whereas the market system is run by **proportional rule.**
3. The spending of dollars can indicate intensity of want, whereas because of the all-or-nothing nature of political voting, a vote cannot.

Ultimately, the main distinction between political votes and dollar votes is that political outcomes may differ from economic outcomes. Remember that economic efficiency is a situation in which, given the prevailing distribution of income, consumers get the economic goods they want. There is no corresponding situation using political voting. Thus we can never assume that a political voting process will lead to the same decisions that a dollar voting process will lead to in the marketplace.

Indeed, consider the dilemma every voter faces. Usually, a voter is not asked to decide on a single issue (although this happens); rather, a voter is asked to choose among candidates who present a large number of issues and state a position on each of them. Just consider the average U.S. senator, who has to vote on several thousand different issues during a six-year term. When you vote for that senator, you are voting for a person who must make thousands of decisions during the next six years.

CONCEPTS in Brief

- The theory of public choice examines how voters, politicians, and other parties collectively reach decisions in the public sector of the economy.

- As in private markets, scarcity and competition have incentive effects that influence public-sector decision making. In contrast to private market situations, however, there is not a one-to-one relationship between consumption of a publicly provided good and the payment for that good.

To test your understanding of the concepts covered in this section, go to the Online Review at www.myeconlab.com/miller.

CASE STUDY: Economics Front and Center

Too Few Opportunities to Play Table Tennis, or Too Many?

In Li's college dormitory, each floor has its own resident organization, which among other things enforces rules regarding student conduct and collects annual dues from each student resident. Each resident organization pools these funds, which are automatically deducted from each student's monthly rent, to purchase items intended to benefit all students who live on the floor. Most of the students who reside on Li's dormitory floor enjoy playing table tennis, but the nearest tables are some distance from the dormitory. Last month, Li and the other residents on his floor voted unanimously to use some of their resident association funds to purchase a ping-pong table. The table was placed in an open lounge area located just outside the entrance to Li's room, and each resident received his own paddle and ball.

Li now has a problem. Since the ping-pong table was purchased, other residents of his floor have been playing table tennis every night, sometimes until as late as 2:00 A.M. Consequently, he has had difficulty concentrating on his studies, and getting a good night's sleep has been even more problematical.

Points to Analyze

1. Is the ping-pong table an example of a public good or a merit good?

2. What is the term for the situation Li faces, and what might he propose that his resident association do to address it?

Can Computer Software Be a Public Good?

Governments around the globe are actively involved in the production of numerous goods and services. All governments provide their citizens with national defense and law enforcement. Most governments today are also heavily involved in providing educational and health care services. Recently, some Asian governments have decided that computer software should join this list.

Concepts Applied

- Principle of Rival Consumption
- Public Goods
- Merit Goods

Governments and Computer Code

At a 2003 Asian economic summit, Japan's government formally proposed the formation of an intergovernmental software production project, to be conducted jointly with the governments of China, South Korea, and potentially other Asian nations. The Japanese government indicated that it would provide an initial amount exceeding 1.5 billion yen (more than $120 million) to fund preliminary work on an Asian-developed, Asian-owned, and Asian-distributed computer operating system.

To explain why Asian governments should become involved in the production of computer software, a Japanese government official described computer operating systems as "public goods." All residents of Japan and other Asian nations, he contended, "need" access to low-cost software to be able to function in today's "high-technology, twenty-first-century economy."

Is Computer Software a Public Good?

To evaluate whether Japanese government officials might be justified in viewing computer operating systems as public goods, let's consider whether such computer software satisfies the two characteristics of public goods. First, can computer operating systems be used by more and more people at no additional cost and without depriving others of any of the

systems' services? In principle, the answer is "yes." At present, a computer operating system such as Microsoft Windows can control flows of input and output commands on a personal computer only if it is installed on the computer's hard drive or some other storage medium. But, if operating systems could be downloaded at no charge from government Web sites, these computer programs truly could be used by additional people at no additional cost and without reducing anyone else's use of the product.

The second characteristic of a public good is that it must satisfy the exclusion principle. Is it difficult to devise a system for funding a computer operating system on the basis of how many individuals use it? The answer to this question is "no." Even if a computer operating system is made easily accessible on the Internet, it would be simple to require a user to pay before downloading the computer code for the system from an Internet site. Numerous private Web-based firms, such as manufacturers of antivirus software, have already proved that they can exclude people from using software if they fail to pay for it.

At best, therefore, computer operating systems might conceivably come close to possessing one of the two features of a public good. Such computer software is not, however, a public good. If Asian governments follow through with their plans to develop, produce, and distribute computer operating systems to their residents, they will actually have chosen to regard this specific form of computer software as a merit good.

1. Once it is posted on a Web site, can a downloadable digital music file, such as an MP3 file, be consumed by additional people without affecting its consumption by anyone else? If so, does this mean that the file is a public good?
2. "If computer operating systems are public goods, then Bill Gates (founder and former top officer of Microsoft) should have had a harder time accumulating a fortune from sales of Microsoft Windows." In light of the exclusion principle, does this statement make a legitimate point?

For Critical Analysis

1. Learn about the development of the Microsoft Windows operating system at www.econtoday.com/chap05.
2. Find out more about the Linux operating system at www.econtoday.com/chap05.

Web Resources

Evaluate the following statement: "Anyone can be excluded from consuming a downloadable digital computer file if she or he fails to pay for it, so no digital file could ever be classified as a public good." Take a stand, and support your answer by reference to real-world examples such as commercial software for digital audio or video files.

Research Project

SUMMARY DISCUSSION of Learning Objectives

1. **How Market Failures Such as Externalities Might Justify Economic Functions of Government:** A market failure is a situation in which an unhindered free market gives rise to too many or too few resources being directed to a specific form of economic activity. A good example of a market failure is an externality, which is a spillover effect on third parties not directly involved in producing or purchasing a good or service. In the case of a negative externality, firms do not pay for the costs arising from spillover effects that their production of a good imposes on others, so they produce too much of the good in question. Government may be able to improve on the situation by restricting production or by imposing fees on producers. In the case of a positive externality, buyers fail to take into account the benefits that their consumption of a good yields to others, so they purchase too little of the good. Government may be able to induce more consumption of the good by regulating the market or subsidizing consumption. It can also provide a legal system to adjudicate disagreements about property rights, conduct antitrust policies to discourage monopoly and promote competition, provide public goods, and engage in policies designed to promote economic stability.

2. **Private Goods versus Public Goods and the Free-Rider Problem:** Private goods are subject to the principle of rival consumption, meaning that one person's consumption of such a good reduces the amount available for another person to consume. This is not so for public goods, which can be consumed by many people simultaneously at no additional cost and with no reduction in the quality or quantity of the good. In addition, public goods are subject to the exclusion principle: No individual can be excluded from the benefits of a public good even if that person fails to help pay for it. This leads to the free-rider problem, which occurs when a person who thinks that others will pay for a public good seeks to avoid contributing to financing production of the good.

3. **Political Functions of Government That Lead to Its Involvement in the Economy:** Through the political process, people may decide that certain goods are merit goods, which they deem socially desirable, or demerit goods, which they feel are socially undesirable. They may call on government to promote the production of merit goods but to restrict or even ban the production and sale of demerit goods. In addition, the political process may determine that income redistribution is socially desirable, and governments may become involved in supervising transfer payments or in-kind transfers in the form of nonmoney payments.

4. **Average Tax Rates versus Marginal Tax Rates:** The average tax rate is the ratio of total tax payments to total income. By contrast, the marginal tax rate is the change

in tax payments induced by a change in total taxable income. Thus the marginal tax rate applies to the last dollar that a person earns.

5. **The U.S. Income Tax System:** The U.S. income tax system assesses taxes against both personal and business income. It is designed to be a progressive tax system, in which the marginal tax rate increases as income rises, so that the marginal tax rate exceeds the average tax rate. This contrasts with a regressive tax system, in which higher-income people pay lower marginal tax rates, resulting in a marginal tax rate that is less than the average tax rate. The marginal tax rate equals the average tax rate only under proportional taxation, in which the marginal tax rate does not vary with income.

6. **Central Elements of the Theory of Public Choice:** The theory of public choice is the study of collective decision making, or the process through which voters, politicians, and other interested parties interact to influence nonmarket choices. Public-choice theory emphasizes the incentive structures, or system of rewards or punishments, that affect the provision of government goods by the public sector of the economy. This theory points out that certain aspects of public-sector decision making, such as scarcity and competition, are similar to those that affect private-sector choices. Others, however, such as legal coercion and majority-rule decision making, differ from those involved in the market system.

KEY TERMS AND CONCEPTS

antitrust legislation (104)

average tax rate (108)

capital gain (109)

capital loss (109)

collective decision making (115)

demerit good (107)

effluent fee (102)

exclusion principle (105)

externality (100)

free-rider problem (105)

government, or political, goods (116)

incentive structure (115)

majority rule (116)

marginal tax rate (108)

market failure (99)

merit good (106)

monopoly (104)

principle of rival consumption (104)

private goods (104)

progressive taxation (108)

property rights (103)

proportional rule (116)

proportional taxation (108)

public goods (104)

regressive taxation (108)

retained earnings (111)

tax bracket (108)

tax incidence (111)

theory of public choice (115)

third parties (100)

transfer payments (107)

transfers in kind (107)

PROBLEMS

Answers to the odd-numbered problems appear at the back of the book.

5-1. Many people who do not smoke cigars are bothered by the odor of cigar smoke. In the absence of any government involvement in the market for cigars, will too many or too few cigars be produced and consumed? From society's point of view, will the market price of cigars be too high or too low?

5-2. Suppose that repeated application of a pesticide used on orange trees causes harmful contamination of groundwater. The pesticide is produced by a large number of chemical manufacturers and is applied annually in orange groves throughout the world. Most orange growers regard the pesticide as a key input in their production of oranges.

  a. Use a diagram of the market for the pesticide to illustrate the implications of a failure of pesticide manufacturers' costs to reflect the social costs of groundwater contamination.

  b. Use your diagram from part (a) to explain a government policy that might be effective in achieving the amount of pesticide production that fully reflects all social costs.

5-3. Now draw a diagram of the market for oranges. Explain how the government policy you discussed in part (b) of Problem 5-2 is likely to affect the market price and equilibrium quantity in the orange market. In what sense do consumers of oranges "pay" for dealing with the spillover costs of pesticide production?

5-4. Suppose that the U.S. government determines that cigarette smoking creates social costs not reflected in the current market price and equilibrium quantity of cigarettes. A study has recommended that the government can correct for the externality effect of cigarette consumption by paying farmers *not* to plant tobacco used to manufacture cigarettes. It also recommends raising the funds to make these payments by increasing taxes on cigarettes. Assuming that the government is correct that cigarette smoking creates external costs, evaluate whether the study's recommended policies might help correct this negative externality.

5-5. The government of a major city in the United States has determined that mass transit, such as bus lines, helps alleviate traffic congestion, thereby benefiting both individual auto commuters and companies that desire to move products and factors of production speedily along streets and highways. Nevertheless, even though several private bus lines are in service, commuters in the city are failing to take the social benefits of the use of mass transit into account.

a. Discuss, in the context of demand-supply analysis, the essential implications of commuters' failure to take into account the social benefits associated with bus ridership.

b. Explain a government policy that might be effective in achieving the socially optimal use of bus services.

5-6. Draw a diagram of the market for automobiles, which are a substitute means of transit. Explain how the government policy you discussed in part (b) of Problem 5-5 is likely to affect the market price and equilibrium quantity in the auto market. How are auto consumers affected by this policy to attain the spillover benefits of bus transit?

5-7. A state government has determined that access to the Internet improves the learning skills of children, which it concluded would have external benefits. It has also concluded that in light of these external benefits, too few of the state's children have Internet access at their homes and in their school classrooms. Assuming that the state's judgments about the benefits of Internet access are correct, propose a policy that could address the situation.

5-8. Does a tennis court provided by a local government agency satisfy both key characteristics of a public good? Why or why not? Based on your answer, is a public tennis court a public good or a merit good?

5-9. To promote increased use of port facilities in a major coastal city, a state government has decided to construct a state-of-the-art lighthouse at a projected cost of $10 million. The state proposes to pay half this cost and asks the city to raise the additional funds. Rather than raise its $5 million in funds via an increase in city taxes and fees, however, the city's government asks major businesses in and near the port area to contribute voluntarily to the project. Discuss key problems that the city is likely to face in raising the funds.

5-10. A senior citizen gets a part-time job at a fast-food restaurant. She earns $8 per hour for each hour she works, and she works exactly 25 hours per week. Thus her total pretax weekly income is $200. Her total income tax assessment each week is $40, but she has determined that she is assessed $3 in taxes for the final hour she works each week.

a. What is this person's average tax rate each week?

b. What is the marginal tax rate for the last hour she works each week?

5-11. For purposes of assessing income taxes, there are three official income levels for workers in a small country: high, medium, and low. For the last hour on the job during a 40-hour workweek, a high-income worker pays a marginal income tax rate of 15 percent, a medium-income worker pays a marginal tax rate of 20 percent, and a low-income worker is assessed a 25 percent marginal income tax rate. Based only on this information, does this nation's income tax system appear to be progressive, proportional, or regressive?

5-12. Governments of country A and country B spend the same amount each year. Spending on functions relating to dealing with market externalities and public goods accounts for 25 percent of government expenditures in country A but makes up 75 percent of government expenditures in country B. Funding to provide merit goods and efforts to restrict the production of demerit goods account for 75 percent of government expenditures in country A but only 25 percent of government expenditures in country B. Which country's government is more heavily involved in the economy through economic functions of government as opposed to political functions? Explain.

5-13. A government agency is contemplating launching an effort to expand the scope of its activities. One rationale for doing so is that another government agency might make the same effort and, if successful, receive larger budget allocations in future years. Another rationale for expanding the agency's activities is that this will make the jobs of its workers more interesting, which may help the agency attract better-qualified employees. Nevertheless, to broaden its legal mandate, the agency will have to convince more than half of the House of Representatives and the Senate to approve a formal proposal to expand its activities. In addition, to expand its activities, the agency must have the authority to force private companies it does not currently regulate to be officially licensed by agency personnel. Identify which aspects of this problem are similar to those faced by firms that operate in private markets and which aspects are specific to the public sector.

ECONOMICS ON THE NET

Putting Tax Dollars to Work In this application, you will learn about how the U.S. government allocates its expenditures. This will enable you to conduct an evaluation of the current functions of the federal government.

Title: Historical Tables: Budget of the United States Government

Navigation: Go to www.econtoday.com/chap05 to visit the home page of the U.S. Government Printing Office. Select the most recent budget available, and then click on *Historical Tables*.

Application After the document downloads, examine Section 3, Federal Government Outlays by Function, and in particular Table 3.1, Outlays by Superfunction and Function. Then answer the following questions:

1. What government functions have been capturing growing shares of government spending in recent years? Which of these do you believe are related to the problem of addressing externalities, providing public goods, or dealing with other market failures? Which appear to be related to political functions instead of economic functions?

2. Which government functions are receiving declining shares of total spending? Are any of these related to the problem of addressing externalities, providing public goods, or dealing with other market failures? Are any related to political functions instead of economic functions?

For Group Study and Analysis Assign groups to the following overall categories of government functions: national defense, health, income security, and Social Security. Have each group prepare a brief report concerning long-term and recent trends in government spending on each category. Each group should take a stand on whether specific spending on items in its category is likely to relate to resolving market failures, public funding of merit goods, regulating the sale of demerit goods, and so on.

If your exam were tomorrow, would you be ready? For each chapter, MyEconLab Practice Tests and Study Plans pinpoint which sections you have mastered and which ones you need to study. That way, you are more efficient with your study time, and you are better prepared for your exams.

In addition to Practice Tests and your personalized Study Plan, you'll find the following media resources in MyEconLab:

1. *Graphs in Motion* animation of Figures 5-1, 5-2, and 5-5.
2. Videos featuring the author, Roger LeRoy Miller, on the following subjects:
   - Private Goods and Public Goods
   - Types of Tax Systems
   - The Corporate Income Tax

3. Links to the Web sites cited in the marginal Internet Resources, Issues and Applications feature, and Economics on the Net activity.
4. Audio clips of all key terms, additional practice problems, and a PDF version of the material from the print Study Guide.
5. eThemes of the Times, which is a New York Times article to help you understand the real-world applications of what you are learning.

To see how it works, turn to page 16 and then go to www.myeconlab.com/miller.

Get Ahead of the Curve

Chapter 6

Taxes, Transfers, and Public Spending

In Lake Oswego, Oregon, the family of a high school student who wants to participate in sports must pay fees as high as $900 per year. In Gurnee, Illinois, every student who wants to play in a middle school band or orchestra must pay a $60 membership fee. Parents or guardians of five-year-olds in Arlington, Massachusetts, must pay $1,500 before the children will be permitted to enroll in kindergarten. All of these fees are being charged by public schools. Yet just a few years ago public school students could participate in school activities at no additional cost to their families. Why are public schools now charging for various services that they once provided at no charge to students and their families? After you have completed your study of this chapter, you will know the answer to this question.

LEARNING OBJECTIVES

After reading this chapter, you should be able to:

1. Understand the key factors influencing the relationship between tax rates and the tax revenues governments collect
2. Explain how the taxes governments levy on purchases of goods and services affect market prices and equilibrium quantities
3. Analyze how Medicare affects the incentives to consume medical services
4. Explain why increases in government spending on public education have not been associated with improvements in measures of student performance
5. Understand how the Social Security system works and explain the nature of the problems it poses for today's students

Media Resources

Refer to the end of the chapter for a full listing of the multimedia learning materials available in MyEconLab.

...the first U.S. public school that provided education beyond the elementary school years was Boston Latin School, which began teaching male students in 1635? Throughout the seventeenth and eighteenth centuries, and well into the nineteenth century, nearly all middle schools and high schools were privately operated. As late as 1860, the United States had a total of only 40 public schools. Most of these were elementary schools, and most U.S. residents' formal education ended there. Students learned to read and to do simple arithmetic before going back to work on a farm or in a shop. Things began to change in the 1870s, when a handful of state supreme courts ruled that state taxes should support public education. State and local governments then began to finance public schools by granting subsidies, typically in the form of a specified dollar amount per enrolled student. Within a few years, public schools had spread throughout the nation, and by 1900 there were more than 6,000 public schools. Now there are about 90,000.

Public education is just one of a number of goods and services currently subsidized by government. Others include police protection, transportation services, and access to health care. To obtain all the funds required to provide these subsidies, state and local governments assess sales taxes, property taxes, income taxes, airline taxes, hotel occupancy taxes, and electricity, gasoline, water, and sewage taxes. At the federal level, there are income taxes, Social Security taxes, Medicare taxes, and so-called excise taxes. When a person dies, state and federal governments also collect estate and inheritance taxes. Clearly, as the subsidization role of governments has broadened, so has their role as tax collectors.

TAXATION FROM THE GOVERNMENT'S POINT OF VIEW

There are three sources of funding available to governments. One source is explicit fees, called user *charges,* for government services. The second and main source of government funding is taxes. Nevertheless, sometimes federal, state, and local governments spend more than they collect in taxes. To do this, they must rely on a third source of financing, which is borrowing. During a specific interval, the **government budget constraint** expresses this basic limitation on public expenditures. It states that the sum of public spending on goods and services and transfer payments during a given period cannot exceed tax revenues plus borrowed funds.

Government budget constraint
The limit on government spending and transfers imposed by the fact that every dollar the government spends, transfers, or uses to repay borrowed funds must ultimately be provided by the taxes it collects.

A government cannot borrow unlimited amounts, however. After all, a government, like an individual or a firm, can convince others to lend it funds only if it can provide evidence that it will repay its debts. A government must ultimately rely on taxation and user charges, the sources of its own current and future revenues, to repay its debts. Over the long run, therefore, taxes and user charges are any government's *fundamental* sources of revenues. This long-term constraint indicates that the total amount that a government plans to spend and transfer today and into the future cannot exceed the total taxes and user charges that it currently earns and can reasonably anticipate collecting in future years. Taxation dwarfs user charges as a source of government resources, so let's begin by looking at taxation from a government's perspective.

Tax Rates and Tax Revenues

In light of the government budget constraint, a major concern of any government is how to collect taxes. Governments commonly face two fundamental issues when they attempt to fund their operations by taxing market activities. One issue is how the tax rates that governments apply relate to the tax revenues they ultimately receive. Another is how the taxes governments impose on market transactions affect market prices and equilibrium quantities.

To collect a tax, a government typically establishes a **tax base,** which is a value of goods, services, incomes, or wealth subject to taxation. As a concrete example, let's consider a sales tax system.

Governments levy **sales taxes** on the prices that consumers pay to purchase each unit of a broad range of goods and services. Sellers collect sales taxes and transmit them to the government. Sales taxes are levied under a system of *ad valorem* **taxation,** which means that the tax is applied "to the value" of the good. Thus a government using a system of *ad valorem* taxation charges a tax rate equal to a fraction of the market price of each unit that a consumer buys. For instance, if the tax rate is 8 percent and the market price of an item is $100, then the amount of the tax on the item is $8.

A sales tax is therefore a proportional tax. The total amount of sales taxes a government collects equals the sales tax rate times the sales tax base, which is the market value of total purchases.

Governments of European nations also tax sales, but they use a form of sales taxation called a *value-added tax.* How have efforts by European governments to require U.S. Internet sellers to collect these taxes from their European customers complicated doing business on the Web?

Tax base
The value of goods, services, incomes, or wealth subject to taxation.

Sales taxes
Taxes assessed on the prices paid on a large set of goods and services.

Ad valorem taxation
Assessing taxes by charging a tax rate equal to a fraction of the market price of each unit purchased.

E-Commerce EXAMPLE

U.S. Web Sellers Find Themselves Collecting Europe's Taxes

Under the value-added tax systems used in most European nations, the total tax assessed on the sale of a particular item depends on tax rates applied at each stage of that item's production. Consider, for instance, the basic stages of bread production: harvesting of grains by farmers, processing of the grains by millers, production of the bread by bakers, and sale of the bread by grocers. Under a system of value-added taxation, the government taxes the final consumer for the market value added at each stage of production by the farmers, millers, bakers, and grocers. Thus the overall tax rate that a consumer pays on the purchase of a loaf of bread ultimately includes tax rates on values added at all stages of production.

Before 2003, U.S. firms selling products to European consumers on the Web treated them just like U.S. consumers. In the United States, a state assesses sales taxes on items sold on the Internet only if the firm from which a person buys an item has a physical presence in the state where the buyer resides. Europeans obviously did not reside in U.S. states, so they did not have to pay sales taxes.

In the summer of 2003, the nations of the European Union (EU) decided that U.S. companies wishing to sell products to European consumers on the Internet had to begin collecting value-added taxes for remittance to EU governments. A U.S. company with an office in a European nation is required to collect value-added taxes based on the specific system used by that nation. A U.S. firm without a European office, however, must figure out how to collect and remit value-added taxes for every nation in the EU. This is a complicated and costly undertaking, because each EU nation has its own tax-remittance procedures. Each country also has its own schedule of value-added tax rates—ranging from as low as 13 percent in Portugal to as high as 25 percent in Sweden.

For Critical Analysis
Why do you suppose that some U.S. firms selling items on the Web have responded to the EU tax change by collecting the required value-added taxes and also by charging additional fees to European consumers?

Static Tax Analysis. There are two approaches to evaluating how changes in tax rates affect government tax collections. **Static tax analysis** assumes that changes in the tax rate have no effect on the tax base. Thus this approach implies that if a state government desires to increase its sales tax collections, it can simply raise the tax rate. Multiplying the higher tax rate by the tax base thereby produces higher tax revenues.

Static tax analysis
Economic evaluation of the effects of tax rate changes under the assumption that there is no effect on the tax base, so that there is an unambiguous positive relationship between tax rates and tax revenues.

Governments often rely on static tax analysis. Sometimes this does not pay off. Consider, for instance, what happened in 1992 when Congress implemented a federal "luxury tax" on purchases of new pleasure boats priced at $100,000 or more. Applying the 10 percent luxury tax rate to the anticipated tax base—sales of new boats during previous years—produced a forecast of hundreds of million of dollars in revenues from the luxury tax. What actually happened, however, was an 80 percent plunge in sales of new luxury boats. People postponed boat purchases or bought used boats instead. Consequently, the tax base all but disappeared, and the federal government collected only a few tens of millions of dollars in taxes on boat sales. Congress repealed the tax a year later.

Dynamic Tax Analysis. The problem with static tax analysis is that it ignores incentive effects created by new taxes or hikes in existing tax rates. According to **dynamic tax analysis,** a likely response to an increase in a tax rate is a decrease in the tax base. When a government pushes up its sales tax rate, for example, consumers have an incentive to cut back on their purchases of goods and services subjected to the higher rate, perhaps by buying them in a locale where there is a lower sales tax rate or perhaps no tax rate at all. As shown in Figure 6-1, the maximum sales tax rate varies considerably from state to state. Someone who lives in a state bordering Oregon, where the sales tax rate can be as high as 8 percent, certainly has a strong incentive to buy higher-priced goods and services in Oregon, where there is no sales tax. Someone who lives in a high-tax county in Alabama has an incentive to buy an item online from an out-of-state firm and also avoid paying sales taxes. Such shifts in expenditures in response to higher relative tax rates can reduce a state's sales tax base and thereby result in lower sales tax collections than the levels predicted by static tax analysis.

Dynamic tax analysis recognizes that increasing the tax rate could actually cause the government's total tax collections to *decline* if a sufficiently large number of consumers react to the higher sales tax rate by cutting back on purchases of goods and services included in the state's tax base. Some residents who live close to other states with lower sales tax rates might, for instance, drive across the state line to do more of their shopping. Other residents might place more orders with catalog companies or online firms located in other legal jurisdictions where this state's sales tax does not apply.

Dynamic tax analysis
Economic evaluation of tax rate changes that recognizes that the tax base eventually declines with ever-higher tax rates, so that tax revenues may eventually decline if the tax rate is raised sufficiently.

FIGURE 6-1
States with the Highest and Lowest Sales Tax Rates
A number of states allow counties and cities to collect their own sales taxes in addition to state sales taxes. This figure shows the maximum sales tax rates for selected states, including county and municipal taxes. Delaware, Montana, New Hampshire, and Oregon have no sales taxes. All other states and the District of Columbia have maximum sales tax rates between the 4 percent rate of Hawaii and the 9.875 percent rate in Arkansas.

Source: U.S. Department of Commerce.

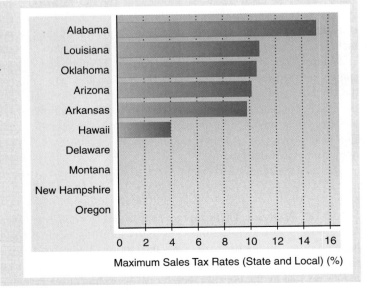

Did you know that even if you do not have to pay sales taxes on out-of-state purchases, your state may have a law requiring you to pay a "use tax" on items shipped to you from outside the state?

Policy EXAMPLE

Some States Make It More Difficult to Avoid Taxes on Out-of-State Purchases

In 18 states and Washington, D.C., state income tax forms now include a line for taxpayers to calculate and include *use taxes*, which apply to items purchased outside the home state but shipped to that state. A few other states also have separate forms that taxpayers are supposed to obtain for reporting and transmitting use taxes. Nevertheless, most states with use taxes currently do not expend sufficient resources to fully enforce these rules. Tax authorities in these locales most often try to collect unpaid use taxes from individuals only when evidence that they have avoided these taxes happens to emerge during investigations of nonpayment of other taxes. Thus many individuals currently fail to pay use taxes even in states that have established this form of taxation.

For Critical Analysis
Why do you suppose that states with use taxes make more effort to collect these taxes from large companies than from individuals? (Hint: Are firms or individuals more likely to purchase large quantities of items from out-of-state producers?)

Maximizing Tax Revenues

Dynamic tax analysis indicates that whether a government's tax revenues ultimately rise or fall in response to a tax rate increase depends on exactly how much the tax base declines in response to the higher tax rate. On the one hand, the tax base may decline by a relatively small amount following an increase in the tax rate, or perhaps even imperceptibly, so that tax revenues rise. For instance, in the situation we imagine a government facing in Figure 6-2, a rise in the tax rate from 5 percent to 6 percent causes tax revenues to increase. In this situation, static tax analysis can provide a good approximation of the revenue effects of an increase in the tax rate. On the other hand, the tax base may decline so

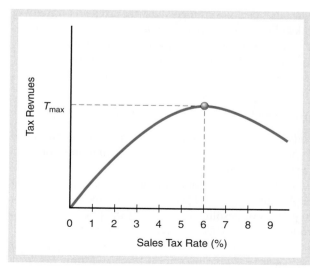

FIGURE 6-2
Maximizing the Government's Sales Tax Revenues
Dynamic tax analysis predicts that ever-higher tax rates bring about declines in the tax base, so that at sufficiently high tax rates the government's tax revenues begin to fall off. This implies that there is a tax rate, 6 percent in this example, at which the government can collect the maximum possible revenues, T_{max}.

much that total tax revenues decrease. In Figure 6-2 on the previous page, for example, increasing the tax rate from 6 percent to 7 percent causes tax revenues to *decline.*

What is most likely is that when the tax rate is already relatively low, increasing the tax rate causes relatively small declines in the tax base. Within a range of relatively low sales tax rates, therefore, increasing the tax rate generates higher sales tax revenues, as illustrated along the upward-sloping portion of the curve depicted in Figure 6-2. If the government continues to push up the tax rate, however, people increasingly have an incentive to find ways to avoid purchasing taxable goods and services. Eventually, the tax base decreases sufficiently that the government's tax collections decline with ever-higher tax rates.

Consequently, governments that wish to maximize their tax revenues should not assess a relatively high tax rate. In the situation illustrated in Figure 6-2, the government maximizes its tax revenues at T_{max} by establishing a sales tax rate of 6 percent. If the government were to raise the rate above 6 percent, it would induce a sufficient decline in the tax base that its tax collections would decline. If the government wishes to collect more than T_{max} in revenues to fund various government programs, it must somehow either expand its sales tax base or develop another tax.

CONCEPTS in Brief

- The static view of the relationship between tax rates and tax revenues implies that higher tax rates generate increased government tax collections.

- According to dynamic tax analysis, higher tax rates cause the tax base to decrease. Tax collections will rise less than predicted by static tax analysis.

- Dynamic tax analysis indicates that there is a tax rate that maximizes the government's tax collections. Setting the tax rate any higher would cause the tax base to fall sufficiently that the government's tax revenues will decline.

To test your understanding of the concepts covered in this section, go to the Online Review at www.myeconlab.com/miller.

TAXATION FROM THE POINT OF VIEW OF PRODUCERS AND CONSUMERS

Both the federal government and state and local governments impose taxes on a variety of market transactions. Take a look back at Figure 5-3 on page 113, and you will see that taxes on the sales of goods and services—sales taxes, gross receipts taxes, and excise taxes—generate almost one-fifth of the total funds available to state and local governments.

These taxes affect market prices and quantities. Let's consider why this is so.

Taxes and the Market Supply Curve

Governments collect taxes on product sales at the source. They require producers to charge these taxes when they sell their output. This means that imposing taxes on final sales of a good or service affects the position of the market supply curve.

Excise tax
A tax levied on purchases of a particular good or service.

Unit tax
A constant tax assessed on each unit of a good that consumers purchase.

To see why, consider panel (a) of Figure 6-3, which shows a gasoline market supply curve S_1 in the absence of taxation. At a price of $1.00 per gallon, gasoline producers are willing and able to supply 180,000 gallons of gasoline per week. If the price increases to $1.10 per gallon, firms increase production to 200,000 gallons of gasoline per week.

Both federal and state governments assess **excise taxes**—taxes on sales of particular commodities—on sales of gasoline. They levy gasoline excise taxes as a **unit tax,** or a

FIGURE 6-3

The Effects of Excise Taxes on the Market Supply and Equilibrium Price and Quantity of Gasoline

Panel (a) shows what happens if the government requires gasoline sellers to collect and transmit a $0.40 unit excise tax on gasoline. To be willing to continue supplying a given quantity, sellers must receive a price that is

$0.40 higher for each gallon they sell, so the market supply curve shifts vertically upward by the amount of the tax. As illustrated in panel (b), this decline in market supply causes a reduction in the equilibrium quantity of gasoline produced and purchased. It also causes a rise in the market price, so that consumers pay part of the tax. Sellers pay the rest in higher costs.

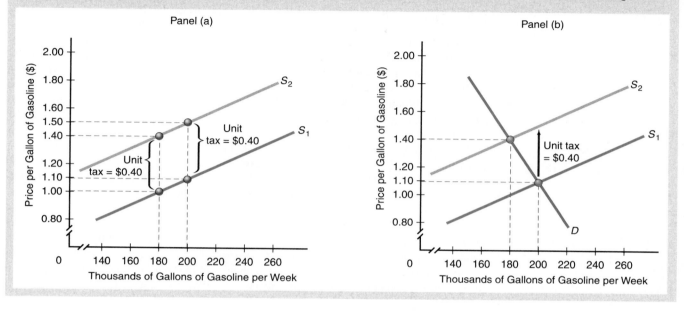

constant tax per unit sold. On average, combined federal and state excise taxes on gasoline are about $0.40 per gallon.

Let's suppose, therefore, that a gasoline producer must transmit a total of $0.40 per gallon to federal and state governments for each gallon sold. Producers must continue to receive a net amount of $1.00 per gallon to induce them to supply 180,000 gallons each week, so they must now receive $1.40 per gallon to supply that weekly quantity. Likewise, gasoline producers now will be willing to supply 200,000 gallons each week only if they receive $0.40 more per gallon, or a total amount of $1.50 per gallon.

As you can see, imposing the combined $0.40 per gallon excise taxes on gasoline shifts the supply curve upward by exactly that amount to S_2. Thus the effect of levying excise taxes on gasoline is to shift the supply curve vertically upward by the total per-unit taxes levied on gasoline sales. Hence there is a decrease in supply. (In the case of an *ad valorem* sales tax, the supply curve would shift upward by a proportionate amount equal to the tax rate.)

How Taxes Affect the Market Price and Equilibrium Quantity

Panel (b) of Figure 6-3 shows how imposing $0.40 per gallon in excise taxes affects the market price of gasoline and the equilibrium quantity of gasoline produced and sold. In the absence of excise taxes, the market supply curve S_1 crosses the demand curve D at a market price of $1.10 per gallon. At this market price, the equilibrium quantity of gasoline is 200,000 gallons of gasoline per week.

The excise tax levy of $0.40 per gallon shifts the supply curve to S_2. At the original $1.10 per gallon price, there is now an excess quantity of gasoline demanded, so the market price of gasoline rises to $1.40 per gallon. At this market price, the equilibrium quantity of gasoline produced and consumed each week is 180,000 gallons.

What factors determine how much the equilibrium quantity of a good or service declines in response to taxation? The answer to this question depends on how responsive quantities demanded and supplied are to changes in price.

Who Pays the Tax?

In our example, imposing excise taxes of $0.40 per gallon of gasoline causes the market price to rise from $1.10 per gallon to $1.40 per gallon. Thus the price that each consumer pays is $0.30 per gallon higher. Consumers pay three-fourths of the excise tax levied on each gallon of gasoline produced and sold.

Gasoline producers must pay the rest of the tax. Their profits decline by $0.10 per gallon because costs have increased by $0.40 per gallon while consumers pay only $0.30 more per gallon.

In the gasoline market, as in other markets for products subject to excise taxes and other taxes on sales, the shapes of the market demand and supply curves determine who pays most of a tax. The reason is that the shapes of these curves reflect the price responsiveness of the quantity demanded by consumers and of the quantity supplied by producers.

In the example illustrated in Figure 6-3, the fact that consumers pay most of the excise taxes levied on gasoline reflects a relatively low responsiveness of quantity demanded by consumers to a change in the price of gasoline. Consumers pay most of the excise taxes on each gallon produced and sold because in this example the amount of gasoline they desire to purchase is relatively unresponsive to a change in the market price induced by excise taxes. We will revisit the issue of who pays excise taxes in Chapter 21.

CONCEPTS in Brief

- When the government levies a tax on sales of a particular product, firms must receive a higher price to continue supplying the same quantity as before, so the supply curve shifts vertically upward. If the tax is a unit excise tax, the supply curve shifts vertically upward by the amount of the tax.

- Imposing a tax on sales of an item reduces the equilibrium quantity produced and consumed and raises the market price.

- When a government assesses a unit excise tax, the market price of the good or service typically rises by an amount less than the per-unit tax. Hence consumers pay a portion of the tax, and firms pay the remainder.

To test your understanding of the concepts covered in this section, go to the Online Review at **www.myeconlab.com/miller.**

PUBLIC SPENDING AND TRANSFER PROGRAMS

Most state governments use sales and excise tax revenues, along with property and other taxes, to fund their spending and transfer programs. Likewise, the federal government uses excise taxes to supplement income tax collections that it uses to finance the bulk of federal purchases and transfers.

Governments use tax revenues to fund spending on public goods, such as the provision of public safety services and national defense. Some government programs subsidize the consumption of merit goods, such as education and health care. Others are pure transfer programs in which governments direct money payments to specific groups, such as when the federal government transfers funds from younger, healthy workers to the elderly and disabled via the Social Security system.

Publicly Subsidized Health Care: Medicare

Not surprisingly, medical expenses are a major concern for many elderly people. Since 1965, that concern has been reflected in the existence of the Medicare program, which pays hospital and physicians' bills for U.S. residents over the age of 65 (and for those younger than 65 in some instances). In return for paying a tax on their earnings while in the workforce (currently set at 2.9 percent of wages and salaries), retirees are ensured that the majority of their hospital and physicians' bills will be paid for with public monies.

Go to www.econtoday.com/chap06 to visit the U.S. government's official Medicare Web site.

The Simple Economics of Medicare. To understand how, in less than 40 years, Medicare became the second-biggest domestic spending program in existence, a bit of economics is in order. Consider Figure 6-4, which shows the demand for and supply of medical care.

The initial equilibrium price is P_0 and equilibrium quantity is Q_0. Perhaps because the government believes that Q_0 is not enough medical care for these consumers, suppose that the government begins paying a subsidy that eventually is set at M for each unit of medical care consumed. This will simultaneously tend to raise the price per unit of care received by providers (physicians, hospitals, and so on) and lower the perceived price per unit that consumers see when they make decisions about how much medical care to consume. As presented in the figure, the price received by providers rises to P_s, while the price paid by consumers falls to P_d. As a result, consumers of medical care want to purchase Q_m units, and suppliers are quite happy to provide it for them.

Medicare Incentives at Work. We can now understand the problems that plague the Medicare system today. First, one of the things that people observed during the 20 years after the founding of Medicare was a huge upsurge in physicians' incomes and medical school applications, the spread of private for-profit hospitals, and the rapid proliferation of

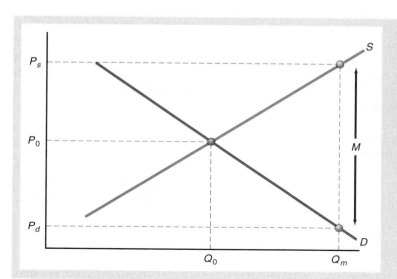

FIGURE 6-4
The Economic Effects of Medicare Subsidies
When the government pays a per-unit subsidy M for medical care, consumers pay the price of services P_d for the quantity of services Q_m. Providers receive the price P_s for supplying this quantity. Originally, the federal government projected its total spending on Medicare to equal an amount such as the area $Q_0 \times (P_0 - P_d)$. Because actual consumption equals Q_m, however, the government's total expenditures actual equal $Q_m \times M$.

new medical tests and procedures. All of this was being encouraged by the rise in the price of medical services from P_0 to P_s, which encouraged entry into this market.

Second, government expenditures on Medicare have routinely turned out to be far in excess of the expenditures forecast at the time the program was put in place or was expanded. The reasons for this are easy to see. Bureaucratic planners often fail to recognize the incentive effects of government programs. On the demand side, they fail to account for the huge increase in consumption (from Q_0 to Q_m) that will result from a subsidy like Medicare. On the supply side, they fail to recognize that the larger amount of services can only be extracted from suppliers at a higher price, P_s. Consequently, original projected spending on Medicare was an area like $Q_0 \times (P_0 - P_d)$, because original plans for the program only allowed for consumption of Q_0 and assumed that the subsidy would have to be only $P_0 - P_d$ per unit. In fact, consumption rises to Q_m, and marginal cost per unit of service rises to P_s, necessitating an increase in the per-unit subsidy to M. Hence actual expenditures turn out to be the far larger number $Q_m \times M$. The introduction of Medicare thus was more expensive than predicted, and every expansion of the program including the 2003 extension of Medicare to cover patients' prescription drug expenses, has followed the same pattern.

Third, total spending on medical services soars, consuming far more income than initially expected. Originally, total spending on medical services was $P_0 \times Q_0$. In the presence of Medicare, spending rises to $P_s \times Q_m$. This helps explain why current health care spending in the United States is about 15 percent of GDP—the largest percentage spent anywhere in the world.

How do you suppose that the prices charged by physicians who refuse to treat Medicare patients and patients covered by other public and private health plans compare with prices charged by physicians who accept such patients?

Economics Front and Center

To think about how government subsidies can sometimes create unintended incentives for producers of medications that doctors prescribe, consider the case study, **To Boost Drug Sales, Is It Time to Raise the Price?**, on page 138.

EXAMPLE

The Doctor Is In, but Insurance Is Out!

Quietly but steadily, a new type of health care clinic has emerged in recent years. What is different about these new clinics is that they will process neither Medicare nor private insurance claims. The clinics accept only cash, check, and credit- and debit-card payments, which they often require patients to tender *before* receiving a physician's care. By avoiding all the costs of handling the paperwork associated with health insurance, many of these clinics can operate with clerical staffs as much as 70 percent lower than clinics that accept Medicare and other forms of health insurance. Their physicians also avoid the headache of trying to convince insurers to reimburse for services already rendered to patients.

Because their costs are lower, physicians at these clinics can charge much lower prices than physicians at clinics that

process health insurance claims. Currently, typical charges at clinics that will not accept payments through government and private health insurance companies are about $35 for an office visit and $20 for a basic blood test. In contrast, typical office-visit fees are $55 or more and blood-test charges start at $100 at clinics that devote considerable resources to handling the red tape associated with claims.

For Critical Analysis
Why might people who are covered by Medicare or private health insurance be willing to pay cash for treatment by physicians who will not accept payments from these insurers?

Economic Issues of Public Education

In the United States, government involvement in health care is a relatively recent phenomenon. In contrast, state and local governments have assumed primary responsibility for public education for many years. Currently, these governments spend well over $500 billion on education—more than 5 percent of total U.S. national income. State and local sales, excise, property, and income taxes finance the bulk of these expenditures. In addition, each year the federal government provides tens of billions of dollars of support for public education through grants and other transfers to state and local governments.

The Now-Familiar Economics of Public Education. State and local governments around the United States have developed a variety of complex mechanisms for funding public education. What all public education programs have in common, however, is the provision of educational services to primary, secondary, and college students at prices well below those that would otherwise prevail in the marketplace for these services.

So how do state and local governments accomplish this? The answer is that they operate public education programs that are very similar to government-subsidized health care programs such as Medicare. Analogously to Figure 6-4 on page 131, public schools provide educational services at a price below the market price. They are willing to produce the quantity of educational services demanded at this below-market price as long as they receive a sufficiently high per-unit subsidy from state and local governments.

For about a century, state and local governments in the United States have used this basic economic mechanism to provide public primary and secondary education. How do you suppose that the more recent involvement of the federal government in subsidizing college and university students has affected tuitions at these institutions?

Policy EXAMPLE

One Reason for College Tuition Hikes: Government Subsidies

Since the 1950s, the federal government has subsidized college and university students through various programs that offer grants, loans, and tax breaks directly to college students. The inflation-adjusted amount of these federal subsidies has increased by about 300 percent since then, partly because more students receive subsidies but also because each subsidized student receives more federal funding. In 1971, the average annual amount of federal aid per subsidized student was, in 2005 dollars, just over $2,600. Today, the average annual amount, in 2005 dollars, received by each federally subsidized student exceeds $5,600. Hence, today's federally subsidized student's willingness to pay for a year of higher education is $3,000

higher than it was in 1971. On top of that, the government transmits this higher average subsidy to many more students. The overall effect of federal support to students, therefore, has been an increase in the market demand for college and university training. This has contributed to the 120 percent increase in the average inflation-adjusted U.S. tuition rate that has taken place since 1971.

For Critical Analysis
What would happen to average tuition rates if federal subsidies were ended?

The Incentive Problems of Public Education. Since the 1960s, various measures of the performances of U.S. primary and secondary students have failed to increase even as public spending on education has risen. Some measures of student performance have even declined.

Many economists argue that the explanation for the failure of student performances to improve relates to the incentive effects that have naturally arisen as government subsidies for public education have increased. A higher per-pupil subsidy creates a difference between the relatively high costs to schools of providing the amount of educational services that parents and students are willing to purchase and the relatively lower valuations of those services by parents and students. As a consequence, schools may have provided services, such as after-school babysitting and various social services, which have contributed relatively little to student learning.

A factor that complicates assessing the effects of education subsidies is that the public school recipients often face little or no competition from unsubsidized providers of educational services. In addition, public schools rarely compete against each other. In most locales, therefore, parents who are unhappy with the quality of services provided at the subsidized price cannot transfer their child to a different public school.

CONCEPTS in Brief

- Medicare subsidizes the consumption of medical care by the elderly, thus increasing the amount of such care consumed. People tend to purchase large amounts of low-value, high-cost services in publicly funded health care programs such as Medicare, because they do not directly bear the full cost of their decisions.

- Basic economic analysis indicates that higher subsidies for public education have widened the differential between parents' and students' relatively low marginal valuations of the educational services of public schools and the higher costs that schools incur in providing those services.

To test your understanding of the concepts covered in this section, go to the Online Review at www.myeconlab.com/miller.

SOCIAL SECURITY

Medicare is one of two major federal transfer programs. The other is Social Security, the federal system that transfers portions of the incomes of working-age people to elderly and disabled individuals. If current laws are maintained, Medicare's share of total national income will double over the next 20 years, as will the number of "very old" people—those over 85 and most in need of care. When Social Security is also taken into account, probably *half* of all federal government spending will go to the elderly by 2025. In a nutshell, senior citizens are the beneficiaries of an expensive and rapidly growing share of all federal spending.

The Ticking Social Security Time Bomb

The federal government finances Social Security contributions with payroll taxes. It currently applies a tax rate of 12.4 percent to a tax base approximately equal to the first roughly $90,000 in wages earned by U.S. workers. If there is no change in the current structure of the Social Security system, the continuing retirements of large numbers of baby boomers, born between the late 1940s and early 1960s, will leave today's college students and their children with a potentially staggering bill to pay. For Social Security and Medicare to be maintained, the payroll (Social Security) tax rate will have to rise to 25 percent. And a payroll tax rate of 40 percent is not unlikely by 2050.

One way to think about the future bill that could face today's college students and their successors in the absence of fundamental changes in Social Security is to consider the number of workers available to support each retiree. In 1946, payroll taxes from 42 workers supported one Social Security recipient. By 1960, just 9 workers funded each retiree's Social Security benefits. Today, roughly 3 workers provide for each retiree's Social Security *and* Medicare benefits. Unless the current system is changed, by 2030 only 2 workers will be available to pay the Social Security and Medicare benefits due each recipient. In that event, a working couple would find themselves responsible for supporting not only themselves and their family, but also someone outside the family who is receiving Social Security and Medicare benefits.

These figures illustrate why efforts to reform these programs have begun to dominate the nation's public agenda. What remains to be seen is how the government will ultimately resolve them.

Good Times for the First Retirees

The Social Security system was founded in 1935, as the United States was recovering from the Great Depression. The decision was made to establish Social Security as a means of guaranteeing a minimum level of pension benefits to all residents. Today, many people regard Social Security as a kind of "social compact"—a national promise to successive generations that they will receive support in their old age.

Big Payoffs for the Earliest Recipients. The first Social Security taxes (called "contributions") were collected in 1937, but it was not until 1940 that retirement benefits were first paid. Ida May Fuller was the first person to receive a regular Social Security pension. She had paid a total of $25 in **Social Security contributions** before she retired. By the time she died in 1975 at age 100, she had received benefits totaling $23,000. Although Fuller did perhaps better than most, for the average retiree of 1940, the Social Security system was still more generous than any private investment plan anyone is likely to devise: After adjusting for inflation, the implicit **rate of return** on their contributions was an astounding 135 percent. (Roughly speaking, every $100 of combined employer and employee contributions yielded $135 *per year* during each and every year of that person's retirement. This is also called the **inflation-adjusted return**.)

Ever since the early days of Social Security, however, the rate of return has decreased. Nonetheless, Social Security was an excellent deal for most retirees during the twentieth century. Figure 6-5 on the next page shows the implicit rate of return for people retiring in different years.

Given that the inflation-adjusted long-term rate of return on the stock market is about 7 to 9 percent, it is clear that for retirees, Social Security was a good deal until at least 1970. In fact, because Social Security benefits are a lot less risky than stocks, Social Security actually remained a pretty good investment for many people until around 1990.

Slowing Membership Growth. Social Security has managed to pay such high returns because at each point in time, current retirees are paid benefits out of the contributions of individuals who are currently working. (The contributions of today's retirees were long ago used to pay the benefits of previous retirees.) As long as Social Security was pulling in growing numbers of workers, either through a burgeoning workforce or by expanding its coverage of individuals in the workforce, the impressive rates of return during the early years of the program were possible.

But as membership growth slowed as the post–World War II baby boom generation began to reach retirement age, the rate of return fell. Moreover, because the early participants received more than they contributed, it follows that if the number of participants stops growing, later participants must receive less—and that ultimately means a *negative* rate of return. And for today's college students—indeed for most people now under the age of 30 or so—that negative rate of return is what lies ahead, unless reforms are implemented.

What Will It Take to Salvage Social Security?

The United States now finds itself with a social compact—the Social Security system— that entails a flow of promised benefits that could exceed the inflow of taxes by about 2010. What, if anything, might be done about this? There are four relevant options to consider.

Social Security contributions
The mandatory taxes paid out of workers' wages and salaries. Although half are supposedly paid by employers, in fact the net wages of employees are lower by the full amount.

Rate of return
The future financial benefit to making a current investment

Inflation-adjusted return
A rate of return that is measured in terms of real goods and services; that is, after the effects of inflation have been factored out.

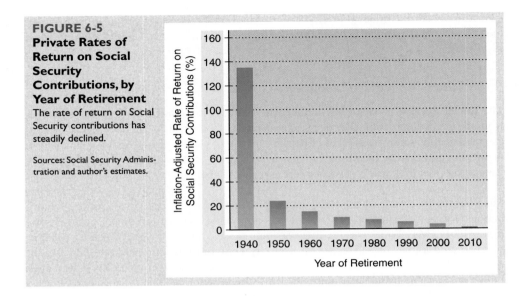

FIGURE 6-5
Private Rates of Return on Social Security Contributions, by Year of Retirement
The rate of return on Social Security contributions has steadily declined.

Sources: Social Security Administration and author's estimates.

Go to www.econtoday.com/chap06 to learn more about Social Security at the official Web site of the Social Security Administration.

1. **Raise Taxes.** The history of Social Security has been one of steadily increasing tax rates applied to an ever-larger portion of workers' wages. In 1935, a Social Security payroll tax rate of 2 percent was applied to the first $3,000 of an individual's earnings (more than $35,000 in today's dollars). Now the Social Security payroll tax rate is 10.4 percentage points higher, and the government applies this tax rate to roughly an additional $55,000 of a worker's wages measured in today's dollars.

   One prominent proposal promises an $80 billion increase in contributions via a 2.2 percentage point hike in the payroll tax rate, to an overall rate of 14.6 percent. Another proposal is to eliminate the current cap on the level of wages to which the payroll tax is applied, which would also generate about $80 billion per year in additional tax revenues. Nevertheless, even a combined policy of eliminating the wage cap and implementing a 2.2 percentage-point tax increase would not, by itself, keep tax collections above benefit payments over the long run.

2. **Reduce Benefit Payouts.** Proposals are on the table to increase the age of full benefit eligibility, perhaps to as high as 70. Another option is to cut benefits to nonworking spouses. A third proposal is to impose "means testing" on some or all Social Security benefits. As things stand now, all individuals covered by the system collect benefits when they retire, regardless of their assets or other sources of retirement income. Under a system of means testing, individuals with substantial amounts of alternative sources of retirement income would receive reduced Social Security benefits.

3. **Reform Immigration Policies.** Many experts believe that significant changes in U.S. immigration laws could offer the best hope of dealing with the tax burdens and workforce shrinkage of the future. Currently, however, more than 90 percent of new immigrants are admitted on the basis of a selection system unchanged since 1952. This system ties immigration rights to family preference. That is why most people admitted to the United States happen to be the spouses, children, or siblings of earlier immigrants. Unless Congress makes skills or training that are highly valued in the U.S. workplace a criterion in the U.S. immigration preference system, new immigrants are unlikely to contribute significant resources to Social Security, because their incomes will remain relatively low. Without reforms, it is unlikely that immigration will relieve much of the pressure building due to our aging population.

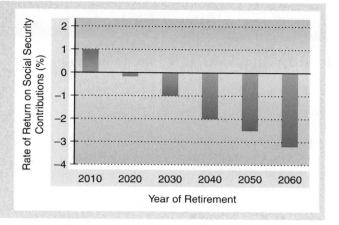

FIGURE 6-6
Projected Social Security Rates of Return for Future Retirees
Whereas workers who paid into Social Security in earlier years got a good deal, those who are now paying in and those who will pay in the future are facing low or negative implicit rates of return.

Source: Social Security Administration; author's estimates.

4. **Find a Way to Increase Social Security's Rate of Return.** As noted earlier, a major current problem for Social Security is a low implicit rate of return. Looking into the future, however, the situation looks even worse. As Figure 6-6 indicates, implicit rates of return for the system will be *negative* by 2020.

   The long-term inflation-adjusted return available in the stock market has been 7 to 9 percent since the 1930s. It is not surprising, therefore, that some observers have advocated that the Social Security system purchase stocks rather than Treasury bonds with the current excess of payroll taxes over current benefit payments. (Because this would necessitate the Treasury's borrowing more from the public, this amounts to having the government borrow money from the public for purposes of investing in the stock market.)

   Although the added returns on stock investments could help stave off tax increases or benefit cuts, there are a few potential problems with this proposal. Despite the stock market's higher long-term returns, the inherent uncertainty of those returns is not entirely consistent with the function of Social Security as a source of *guaranteed* retirement income. Another issue is what stocks would be purchased. Political pressure to invest in companies that happened to be politically popular and to refrain from investing in those that were unpopular, regardless of their returns, would reduce the expected returns from the government's stock portfolio—possibly even below the returns on Treasury bonds.

CONCEPTS in Brief

- Social Security and Medicare payments are using up a large and growing portion of the federal budget. Because of a shrinking number of workers available to support each retiree, the per capita expense for future workers to fund these programs will grow rapidly unless reforms are made.

- During the early years of the Social Security system, taxes were low relative to benefits, resulting in a high rate of return for retirees. As taxes have risen relative to

  benefits, the rate of return on Social Security has fallen steadily.

- There are only four options—or combinations of these four options—for preserving the current social compact: raise taxes, reduce benefit payouts, reform immigration policies, or increase Social Security's rate of return.

CASE STUDY : Economics Front and Center

To Boost Drug Sales, Is It Time to Raise the Price?

Robinson is an executive at a top pharmaceuticals company. She is in charge of determining the prices of medicines used in chemotherapy regimens for cancer patients. It is late in the evening and her subordinates have all gone home, but she is still in her office developing pricing plans for the company's newest chemotherapy drugs. She knows that under government-subsidy programs, reimbursements for chemotherapy treatments go to physicians instead of patients. This, she also knows, gives physicians an incentive to prescribe higher-priced medications. Thus the demand for her companies' drugs is likely to increase if the company raises its price.

Robinson posts a note to herself in an electronic file on her computer: "Tomorrow, find out the highest allowable reimbursement rates physicians can receive for chemotherapy prescriptions under Medicare and Medicaid rules. Then calculate how our drugs should be priced to generate those maximum physician reimbursements."

Points to Analyze

1. *Will the price paid by the Medicare patients receiving a chemotherapy drug produced by Robinson's company be above or below the price that would have prevailed in the absence of the Medicare program?*

2. *Will the price received by the doctors from the government for prescribing the company's chemotherapy drug be above or below the price that would have prevailed in the absence of the Medicare program?*

Issues and Applications

Why Activities Are No Longer "Free" at Many Public Schools

I n a growing number of communities across the United States, public schools are charging hundreds or even thousands of dollars for extracurricular activities, including music, clubs, and sports. Others are charging fees for preschool and kindergarten programs. When parents and guardians refuse to pay fees, school administrators are cutting back on extracurricular activities and offerings of preschool and kindergarten classes. Some schools are even eliminating these programs.

Concepts Applied
- Public Spending
- Public Subsidies

The Economics of School Subsidy Cutbacks

What has driven public schools to charge fees for extracurricular activities that they previously made available to students at no charge? The answer to this question can be inferred from Figure 6-7. As in Figure 6-4 on page 131, the government initially provides a per-unit subsidy, M, to public schools. Given this subsidy, students' families pay the very low price P_d for the quantity of educational services equal to Q_m. Schools receive the total price P_s for supplying this quantity.

In recent years, a number of state and local governments have cut back on the funds they provide for public education. Thus the per-unit subsidy has declined to an amount such as M' in Figure 6-7. At this lower subsidy, schools reduce the quantity of services they are willing to supply to Q'_m, because they receive a lower price, P'_s. Furthermore, families must pay a higher price, P'_d, for students to receive the smaller amount of educational services. Schools charge families the higher price by charging them service fees, such as band or orchestra admittance fees, fees to participate in sports, or fees for a child to attend kindergarten.

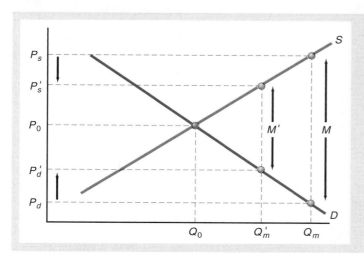

FIGURE 6-7
The Effects of a Reduction in Education Subsidies
A reduction in the per-unit subsidy that the government provides for educational services, from M to M', causes a reduction in the quantity of these services supplied, to Q'_m. In addition, the per-unit price that families must pay for the smaller quantity of services received rises to P'_d.

Paying for Band, Basketball, and Preschool

Why are schools choosing extracurricular activities and pre-school and kindergarten programs for cutbacks? Recall that a higher per-pupil subsidy for public education widens the difference between the relatively high costs to schools of providing all the various services families are willing to purchase and the relatively lower family valuations of those services. As state and local governments have reduced school subsidies, this difference has narrowed. Consequently, schools are cutting back on services with the *lowest* value to families. Most families put higher values on reading, writing, and arithmetic than on band, basketball, and preschool. So these are the first programs that schools typically choose to reduce.

In some locales, proponents of these activities have found alternative ways to fund them. For instance, in some communities, parents, teachers, and administrators have formed groups with names such as "Save Our Sports," which conduct bake sales, car washes, and raffles aimed at raising funds to keep extracurricular programs from dying.

Irrespective of how funds to support extracurricular activities or other school programs are raised, there is no getting around a basic fact. Cutting back on school subsidies causes schools either to stop providing services with relatively low values to most families or to induce the families who place a relatively high value on these services to pay for them directly.

For Critical Analysis

1. In Figure 6-7, what price would families end up paying if state and local governments eliminated all school subsidies?
2. Why do you suppose that a number of high schools that previously offered "free" courses for preparation for college admissions tests are now charging fees for these courses?

Web Resources

1. For recent U.S. Department of Education data on education spending, go to **www.econtoday.com/chap06**.
2. To learn from the National Center for Policy Analysis about how special subsidies for schools providing services to disabled students have affected the number of students classified as "disabled," go to the link available at **www.econtoday.com/chap06**.

Research Project

Each year, the average U.S. public school spends approximately the following amounts per pupil: $4,300 for instructional services, $2,500 for various support services, and $300 for miscellaneous noninstructional expenses. Evaluate why government subsidization of public schools helps explain why they spend an average of $300 per student on items that are unrelated to their primary task of instructing students.

SUMMARY   DISCUSSION   of Learning Objectives

1. **The Relationship Between Tax Rates and Tax Revenues:** Static tax analysis assumes that the tax base does not respond significantly to an increase in the tax rate, so it seems to imply a tax rate hike boosts a government's total tax collections. Dynamic tax analysis reveals, however, increases in tax rates cause the tax base to decline. Thus there is a tax rate that maximizes the government's tax revenues. If the government pushes the tax rate higher, tax collections decline.

2. **How Taxes on Purchases of Goods and Services Affect Market Prices and Quantities:** When a government imposes a per-unit tax on a good or service, a seller is willing to supply any given quantity only if the seller receives a price that is higher by exactly the amount of the tax. Hence the supply curve shifts vertically upward by

the amount of the tax per unit. In a market with typically shaped demand and supply curves, this results in a fall in the equilibrium quantity and an increase in the market price. To the extent that the market price rises, consumers pay a portion of the tax on each unit they buy. Sellers pay the remainder in higher per-unit production costs.

3. **The Effect of Medicare on the Incentives to Consume Medical Services:** Medicare subsidizes the consumption of medical services by the elderly. As a result, the quantity consumed is higher, as is the price sellers receive per unit of those services. As a result, the United States spends a larger portion of national income on medical care for the elderly than any other nation in the world. Medicare also encourages people to consume medical services that are very low in marginal value relative to

the cost of providing them. Medicare thereby places a substantial tax burden on other sectors of the economy.

4. **Why Bigger Subsidies for Public Schools Do Not Necessarily Translate into Improved Student Performance:** When governments subsidize public schools, the last unit of educational services provided by public schools is likely to cost more than its valuation by parents and students. Public schools therefore provide services in excess of those best suited to promoting student learning. This may help explain why measures of overall U.S. student performance have stagnated even as per-pupil subsidies to public schools have increased significantly.

5. **How Social Security Works and Why It Poses Problems for Today's Students:** Since its inception, Social Security benefits have been paid out of taxes. Because of the growing mismatch between elderly and younger citizens, future scheduled benefits vastly exceed future scheduled taxes, so some combination of higher taxes and lower benefits will have to be implemented to maintain the current system. The situation might also be eased a bit if more immigration of skilled workers were permitted and if Social Security contributions were invested in the stock market, where they could earn higher rates of return.

KEY TERMS AND CONCEPTS

ad valorem taxation (125)

dynamic tax analysis (126)

excise tax (128)

government budget constraint (124)

inflation-adjusted return (135)

rate of return (135)

sales taxes (125)

Social Security contributions (135)

static tax analysis (125)

tax base (125)

unit tax (128)

PROBLEMS

Answers to the odd-numbered problems appear at the back of the book.

6-1. Suppose that a state has enacted increases in its sales tax rate every other year since 1997. Assume that during this period, the static tax analysis was fully valid, and the state collected all sales taxes that residents legally owed. The following table summarizes its experience. What were total taxable sales in this state during each year displayed in the table?

Year	Sales Tax Rate	Sales Tax Collections
1997	0.03 (3 percent)	$9.0 million
1999	0.04 (4 percent)	$14.0 million
2001	0.05 (5 percent)	$20.0 million
2003	0.06 (6 percent)	$24.0 million
2005	0.07 (7 percent)	$29.4 million

6-2. The sales tax rate applied to all purchases within a state was 0.04 (4 percent) throughout 2004 but increased to 0.05 (5 percent) during all of 2005. The state government collected all taxes due, but its tax revenues were equal to $40 million each year. What

happened to the sales tax base between 2004 and 2005? What could account for this result?

6-3. A city government imposes a proportional income tax on all people who earn income within its city limits. In 2004, the city's income tax rate was 0.05 (5 percent), and it collected $20 million in income taxes. In 2005, it raised the income tax rate to 0.06 (6.0 percent), and its income tax collections declined to $19.2 million. What happened to the city's income tax base between 2004 and 2005? How could this have occurred?

6-4. The city government of a small town where a large college is located imposes a unit excise tax of $1 on each textbook purchased at local bookstores. If students are always willing to pay whatever price local bookstores charge in order to obtain the textbooks required for their courses, what will be the effect of this tax on the equilibrium textbook price?

6-5. Suppose that the federal government imposes a unit excise tax of $2 per month on the rates that Internet service providers charge for DSL high-speed Internet access in separate markets for the provision of these services to households and businesses.

a. Draw a diagram of normally shaped market demand and supply curves for DSL Internet access services. Use this diagram to make predictions about how the Internet service tax is likely to affect the market price and market quantity.

b. Suppose that in the market for DSL Internet access services provided to households, the market price increases by $2 per month after the unit excise tax is imposed. If the market supply curve slopes upward, what can you say about the shape of the market demand curve over the relevant ranges of prices and quantities? Who pays the excise tax in this market?

c. Suppose that in the market for DSL Internet access services provided to businesses, the market price does not change after the unit excise tax is imposed. If the market supply curve slopes upward, what can you say about the shape of the market demand curve over the relevant ranges of prices and quantities? Who pays the excise tax in this market?

6-6. A government offers to let a number of students at a public school transfer to a private school under two conditions: It will transmit to the private school the same per-pupil subsidy it currently provides the public school, and the private school will be required to admit the students at a below-market tuition rate. Will the economic outcome be the same as the one that would have arisen if the government instead simply provided students with grants to cover the current market tuition rate at the private school?

6-7. After a government implements a voucher program, numerous students in public schools switch to private schools, and parents' and students' valuations of the services provided at both private and public schools adjust to equality with the true market price of educational services. Is anyone likely to lose out nonetheless? If so, who?

6-8. Suppose that your employer is paying you a wage of $10 per hour, and you are working 40 hours per week. Now the government imposes a $2 per hour tax on your employment: $1 is collected from your employer, and $1 is collected from you. The proceeds of the tax are used by the government to buy for you groceries that you value at exactly $80 per week. You are eligible for the grocery program only as long as you continue to work 40 hours per week. Once the plan is in place, what hourly wage will the employer pay you?

6-9. Suppose that the current price of a DVD drive is $100 and that people are buying one million drives per year. In order to improve computer literacy, the government decides to begin subsidizing the purchase of new DVD drives. The government believes that the appropriate price is $60 per drive, so the program offers to send people cash for the difference between $60 and whatever the people pay for each drive they buy.

a. If no one changes his or her drive-buying behavior, how much will this program cost the taxpayers?

b. Will the subsidy cause people to buy more, less, or the same number of drives? Explain.

c. Suppose that people end up buying 1.5 million drives once the program is in place. If the market price of drives does not change, how much will this program cost the taxpayers?

d. Under the assumption that the program causes people to buy 1.5 million drives and also causes the market price of drives to rise to $120, how much will this program cost the taxpayers?

6-10. Scans of internal organs using magnetic resonance imaging (MRI) devices are often covered by subsidized health insurance programs such as Medicare. Consider the following table illustrating hypothetical quantities of individual MRI testing procedures demanded and supplied at various prices, and then answer the questions that follow.

Price	Quantity Demanded	Quantity Supplied
$100	100,000	40,000
$300	90,000	60,000
$500	80,000	80,000
$700	70,000	100,000
$900	60,000	120,000

a. In the absence of a government-subsidized health plan, what is the equilibrium price of MRI tests? What is the amount of society's total expense on MRI tests?

b. Suppose that the government establishes a health plan guaranteeing that all qualified participants can purchase MRI tests at an effective price (that is, out-of-pocket cost) to the individual of $100 per set of tests. How many MRI tests will people consume?

c. What is the per-unit cost incurred by producers to provide the amount of MRI tests demanded at the government-guaranteed price of $100? What is society's total expense on MRI tests?

d. Under the government's coverage of MRI tests, what is the per-unit subsidy it provides? What is the total subsidy that the government pays to support MRI testing at its guaranteed price?

6-11. In the following situations, what is the rate of return on the investment? (Hint: In each case, what is the percentage by which next year's benefit exceeds—or falls short of—this year's cost?)

a. You invest $100 today and receive in return $150 exactly one year from now.

b. You invest $100 today and receive in return $80 exactly one year from now.

6-12. Suppose that the following Social Security reform became law: All current Social Security recipients will continue to receive their benefits, but no increase will be made other than cost-of-living adjustments; U.S.

citizens between age 40 and retirement not yet on Social Security can opt to continue with the current system; those who opt out can place what they would have contributed to Social Security into one or more government-approved mutual funds; and those under 40 must place their contributions into one or more government-approved mutual funds.

Now answer the following questions:

a. Who will be in favor of this reform and why?
b. Who will be against this reform and why?
c. What might happen to stock market indexes?
d. What additional risk is involved for those who end up in the private system?
e. What additional benefits are possible for the people in the private system?
f. Which firms in the mutual fund industry might not be approved by the federal government and why?

ECONOMICS ON THE NET

Social Security Privatization There are many proposals for reforming Social Security, but only one fundamentally alters the nature of the current system: privatization. The purpose of this exercise is to learn more about what would happen if Social Security were privatized.

Title: Social Security Privatization

Navigation: Go to www.econtoday.com/chap06 to learn about Social Security privatization. Click on *FAQ* on *Social Security* in the left-hand column.

Application For each of the three entries noted here, read the entry and answer the question.

1. Click on *How would individual accounts affect women?* According to this article, what are the likely consequences of Social Security privatization for women? Why?

2. Click on *I'm a low-wage worker. How would individual accounts affect me?* What does this article contend are the likely consequences of Social Security privatization for low-wage workers? Why?

3. Click on *I've heard that individual accounts would help minorities. Is that true?* Why does this article argue that

African Americans in particular would benefit from a privatized Social Security system?

For Group Study and Analysis Taking into account the characteristics of your group as a whole, is it likely to be made better off or worse off if Social Security is privatized? Should your decision to support or oppose privatization be based solely on how it affects you personally? Or should your decision take into account how it might affect others in your group?

It will be worthwhile for those not nearing retirement age to examine what the "older" generation thinks about the idea of privatizing the Social Security system in the United States. So create two groups—one for and one against privatization. Each group will examine the following Web site and come up with arguments in favor or against the ideas expressed on it.

Go to www.econtoday.com/chap06 to read a proposal for Social Security reform. Accept or rebut the proposal, depending on the side to which you have been assigned. Be prepared to defend your reasons with more than just your feelings. At a minimum, be prepared to present arguments that are logical, if not entirely backed by facts.

If your exam were tomorrow, would you be ready? For each chapter, MyEconLab Practice Tests and Study Plans pinpoint which sections you have mastered and which ones you need to study. That way, you are more efficient with your study time, and you are better prepared for your exams.

In addition to Practice Tests and your personalized Study Plan, you'll find the following media resources in MyEconLab:

1. *Graphs in Motion* animation of Figures 6-2, 6-3, 6-4, and 6-6.
2. Video featuring the author, Roger LeRoy Miller, on the following subject:
   - Medicare

3. Links to the Web sites cited in the marginal Internet Resources, Issues and Applications feature, and Economics on the Net activity.
4. Audio clips of all key terms, additional practice problems, and a PDF version of the material from the print Study Guide.
5. eThemes of the Times, which is a New York Times article to help you understand the real-world applications of what you are learning.

To see how it works, turn to page 16 and then go to www.myeconlab.com/miller.

Chapter 7

The Macroeconomy: Unemployment, Inflation, and Deflation

The U.S. government knows that it would face a conflict of interest if it had the job of officially announcing the dates of business *contractions* (periods when overall business activity is slowing down) and business *expansions* (intervals during which business activity is increasing). After all, politicians would always want to claim that an expansion is in progress but would never want to admit that a contraction is under way. For this reason, an independent, nonprofit organization called the National Bureau of Economic Research has this responsibility. In this chapter you will learn about the terms that economists use to describe business fluctuations. You will also learn about some interesting changes in patterns of business fluctuations in recent decades.

LEARNING OBJECTIVES

After reading this chapter, you should be able to:

1. Explain how the U.S. government calculates the official unemployment rate
2. Discuss the types of unemployment
3. Describe how price indexes are calculated and define the key types of price indexes
4. Distinguish between nominal and real interest rates
5. Evaluate who loses and who gains from inflation
6. Understand key features of business fluctuations

Media Resources

Refer to the end of the chapter for a full listing of the multimedia learning materials available in MyEconLab.

Did You Know That ... in late 1929 and early 1930, shortly after the infamous U.S. stock market crash that took place in October 1929, most leading U.S. economists failed to predict the Great Depression that followed in the 1930s? For instance, in December 1929, a group of Harvard economists issued the public statement, "The year 1930, as a whole, should prove at least a fairly good year." According to Yale University economist Irving Fisher in January 1930, "it would not be surprising if by next month the worst of the recession will have been felt, and improvement looked for." In fact, the total value of U.S. production fell by more than 50 percent during the three years following October 1929.

Trying to understand and better forecast the overall performance of the national economy is a central objective of macroeconomics. This branch of economics seeks to explain and predict movements in unemployment, the average level of prices, and the total production of goods and services. This chapter introduces you to these key issues of macroeconomics.

UNEMPLOYMENT

Unemployment is normally defined as the number of adults who are actively looking for work but do not have a job. Unemployment creates a cost to the entire economy in terms of lost output. One estimate indicates that at the beginning of the 2000s, when the unemployment rate rose by nearly 2 percentage points and firms were operating below 80 percent of their capacity, the amount of output that the economy lost due to idle resources was roughly 2 percent of the total production throughout the United States. (In other words, we were somewhere inside the production possibilities curve that we talked about in Chapter 2.) That was the equivalent of about $200 billion of schools, houses, restaurant meals, cars, and movies that *could have been* produced. It is no wonder that policymakers closely watch the unemployment figures published by the Department of Labor's Bureau of Labor Statistics.

On a more personal level, the state of being unemployed often results in hardship and failed opportunities as well as a lack of self-respect. Psychological researchers believe that being fired creates at least as much stress as the death of a close friend. The numbers that we present about unemployment can never fully convey its true cost to the people of this or any other nation.

Unemployment
The total number of adults (aged 16 years or older) who are willing and able to work and who are actively looking for work but have not found a job.

Labor force
Individuals aged 16 years or older who either have jobs or who are looking and available for jobs; the number of employed plus the number of unemployed.

Economics Front and Center

For practice thinking about how to classify someone as inside or outside the labor force or as employed or unemployed, take a look at **Are a Self-Employed Dad and a Daughter Who Is Not Working Part of the Labor Force?**, on page 162.

Historical Unemployment Rates

The unemployment rate, defined as the proportion of the measured **labor force** that is unemployed, reached a low of 1.2 percent of the labor force at the end of World War II, after having reached 25 percent during the Great Depression in the 1930s. You can see in Figure 7-1 what happened to unemployment in the United States since 1890. The highest level ever was reached in the Great Depression, but unemployment was also high during the Panic of 1893.

Employment, Unemployment, and the Labor Force

Figure 7-2 presents the population of individuals 16 years of age or older broken into three segments: (1) employed, (2) unemployed, and (3) not in the civilian labor force (a category that includes homemakers, full-time students, military personnel, persons in institutions, and retired persons). The employed and the unemployed, added together, make up the labor force. In 2005, the labor force amounted to 139.5 million + 8.2 million = 147.7 million residents. To calculate the unemployment rate, we simply divide the number

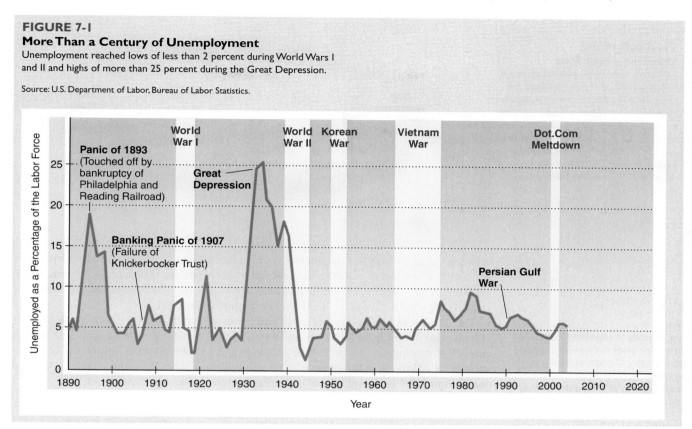

FIGURE 7-1
More Than a Century of Unemployment
Unemployment reached lows of less than 2 percent during World Wars I and II and highs of more than 25 percent during the Great Depression.

Source: U.S. Department of Labor, Bureau of Labor Statistics.

of unemployed by the number of people in the labor force and multiply by 100: 8.2 million/147.7 million × 100 = 5.6 percent.

The Arithmetic Determination of Unemployment

Because there is a transition between employment and unemployment at any point in time—people are leaving jobs and others are finding jobs—there is a simple relationship

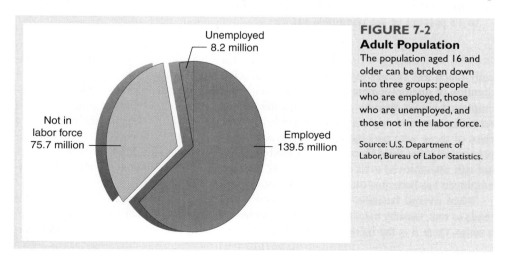

FIGURE 7-2
Adult Population
The population aged 16 and older can be broken down into three groups: people who are employed, those who are unemployed, and those not in the labor force.

Source: U.S. Department of Labor, Bureau of Labor Statistics.

FIGURE 7-3
The Logic of the
Unemployment Rate

Individuals who depart jobs but remain in the labor force are subtracted from the employed and added to the unemployed. When the unemployed acquire jobs, they are subtracted from the unemployed and added to the employed. In an unchanged labor force, if both flows are equal, the unemployment rate is stable. If more people depart jobs than acquire them, the unemployment rate increases, and vice versa.

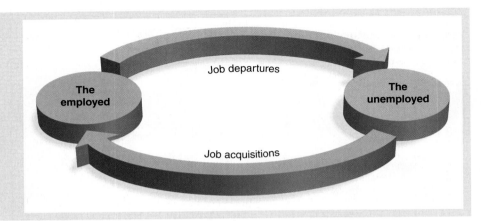

between the employed and the unemployed, as can be seen in Figure 7-3. Job departures are shown at the top of the diagram, and job acquisitions are shown at the bottom. If the numbers of job departures and acquisitions are equal, the unemployment rate stays the same. If departures exceed acquisitions, the unemployment rate rises.

The number of unemployed is some number at any point in time. It is a **stock** of individuals who do not have a job but are actively looking for one. The same is true for the number of employed. The number of people departing jobs, whether voluntarily or involuntarily, is a **flow,** as is the number of people acquiring jobs. Picturing a bathtub like the one in Figure 7-4 is a good way of remembering how stocks and flows work.

Categories of Individuals Who Are Without Work. According to the Bureau of Labor Statistics, an unemployed individual will fall into any of four categories:

1. A **job loser,** whose employment was involuntarily terminated or who was laid off (40 to 60 percent of the unemployed)
2. A **reentrant,** who worked a full-time job before but has been out of the labor force (20 to 30 percent of the unemployed)
3. A **job leaver,** who voluntarily ended employment (less than 10 to around 15 percent of the unemployed)
4. A **new entrant,** who has never worked a full-time job for two weeks or longer (10 to 13 percent of the unemployed)

Duration of Unemployment. If you are out of a job for a week, your situation is typically much less serious than if you are out of a job for, say, 14 weeks. An increase in the duration of unemployment can increase the unemployment rate because workers stay unemployed longer, thereby creating a greater number of them at any given time. The most recent information on duration of unemployment paints the following picture: more than a third of those who become unemployed acquire a new job by the end of one month, approximately one-third more acquire a job by the end of two months, and only about a sixth are still unemployed after six months. The average duration of unemployment for all unemployed has been just over 15 weeks for the past decade.

When overall business activity goes into a downturn, the duration of unemployment tends to rise, thereby causing much of the increase in the estimated unemployment rate. In a sense, then, it is the increase in the *duration* of unemployment during a downturn in na-

Stock
The quantity of something, measured at a given point in time—for example, an inventory of goods or a bank account. Stocks are defined independently of time, although they are assessed at a point in time.

Flow
A quantity measured per unit of time; something that occurs over time, such as the income you make per week or per year or the number of individuals who are fired every month.

Job loser
An individual in the labor force whose employment was involuntarily terminated.

Reentrant
An individual who used to work full time but left the labor force and has now reentered it looking for a job.

Job leaver
An individual in the labor force who quits voluntarily.

New entrant
An individual who has never held a full-time job lasting two weeks or longer but is now seeking employment.

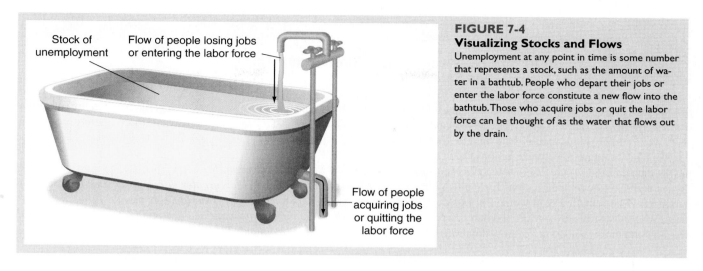

FIGURE 7-4
Visualizing Stocks and Flows
Unemployment at any point in time is some number that represents a stock, such as the amount of water in a bathtub. People who depart their jobs or enter the labor force constitute a new flow into the bathtub. Those who acquire jobs or quit the labor force can be thought of as the water that flows out by the drain.

tional economic activity that generates the bad news that concerns policymakers in Washington, D.C. Furthermore, the individuals who stay unemployed longer than six months are the ones who create the pressure on Congress to "do something." What Congress does, typically, is extend and supplement unemployment benefits.

The Discouraged Worker Phenomenon. Critics of the published unemployment rate calculated by the federal government believe that it fails to reflect the true numbers of **discouraged workers** and "hidden unemployed." Though there is no exact definition or way to measure discouraged workers, the Department of Labor defines them as people who have dropped out of the labor force and are no longer looking for a job because they believe that the job market has little to offer them. To what extent do we want to include in the measured labor force individuals who voluntarily choose not to look for work or those who take only a few minutes a day to scan the want ads and then decide that there are no jobs?

Some economists argue that people who work part-time but are willing to work full-time should be classified as "semihidden" unemployed. Estimates range as high as 6 million workers at any one time. Offsetting this factor, though, is *overemployment*. An individual working 50 or 60 hours a week is still counted as only one full-time worker.

Discouraged workers
Individuals who have stopped looking for a job because they are convinced that they will not find a suitable one.

Labor Force Participation. The way in which we define unemployment and membership in the labor force will affect what is known as the **labor force participation rate.** It is defined as the proportion of noninstitutionalized working-age individuals who are employed or seeking employment.

The U.S. labor force participation rate has risen somewhat over time, from 60 percent in 1950 to about 67 percent today. The gender composition of the U.S. labor force has changed considerably during this time. In 1950, more than 83 percent of men and fewer than 35 percent of women participated in the U.S. labor force. Today, fewer than 75 percent of men and more than 60 percent of women are U.S. labor force participants. How does the U.S. female labor participation rate compare with rates of labor force participation in other nations?

Labor force participation rate
The percentage of noninstitutionalized working-age individuals who are employed or seeking employment.

At 60 Percent, U.S. Women Outdo Most Female Labor Force Participation Rates

Figure 7-5 displays estimated labor force participation rates for several nations around the world. It indicates that the female labor force participation rate in the United States is higher than in some developed nations, such as France, but lower than in others, such as Sweden. Women in the United States and other developed nations have much higher rates of labor force participation than women in less developed countries, where most of the world's women reside. Some of the reasons that more women in developed nations enter the labor force are that these women have greater access to education and training and face fewer barriers to competing with men for jobs.

For Critical Analysis

Is it more likely that greater labor force participation by women contributes to a nation's economic development or that it simply happens to accompany greater development of a country's economy?

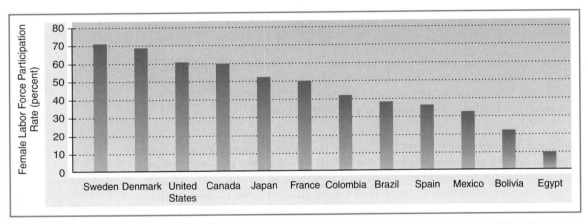

FIGURE 7-5
Female Labor Force Participation Rates in Selected Nations
Female labor force participation rates in the United States and other developed nations tend to be much higher than the rates of labor force participation by women who live in less developed countries.

Source: World Bank.

<hr />

CONCEPTS in Brief

- Unemployed persons are adults who are willing and able to work and are actively looking for a job but have not found one. The unemployment rate is computed by dividing the number of unemployed by the total labor force, which is equal to those who are employed plus those who are unemployed.

- The unemployed are job losers, reentrants, job leavers, and new entrants to the labor force. The flow of people departing jobs and people acquiring jobs determines the stock of unemployed as well as the stock of employed.

- The duration of unemployment affects the unemployment rate. The number of unemployed workers can remain the same, but if the duration of unemployment increases, the measured unemployment rate will go up.

- Whereas overall labor force participation has risen only modestly since World War II, there has been a major increase in female labor force participation.

To test your understanding of the concepts covered in this section, go to the Online Review at **www.myeconlab.com/miller**.

The Major Types of Unemployment

Unemployment has been categorized into four basic types: frictional, structural, cyclical, and seasonal.

Frictional Unemployment.

Of the more than 147 million people in the labor force, more than 14 million will have either changed jobs or taken new jobs during the year; every single month, about one worker in 20 will have quit, been laid off (told to expect to be rehired later), or been permanently fired; another 6 percent will have gone to new jobs or returned to old ones. In the process, more than 21 million persons will have reported themselves unemployed at one time or another. This continuous flow of individuals from job to job and in and out of employment is called **frictional unemployment.** There will always be some frictional unemployment as resources are redirected in the market, because job-hunting costs are never zero, and workers never have full information about available jobs. To eliminate frictional unemployment, we would have to prevent workers from leaving their present jobs until they had already lined up other jobs at which they would start working immediately. And we would have to guarantee first-time job seekers a job *before* they started looking.

Frictional unemployment
Unemployment due to the fact that workers must search for appropriate job offers. This takes time, and so they remain temporarily unemployed.

Structural Unemployment.

Structural changes in our economy cause some workers to become unemployed permanently or for very long periods of time because they cannot find jobs that use their particular skills. This is called **structural unemployment.** Structural unemployment is not caused by general business fluctuations, although business fluctuations may affect it. And unlike frictional unemployment, structural unemployment is not related to the movement of workers from low-paying to high-paying jobs.

At one time, economists thought about structural unemployment only from the perspective of workers. The concept applied to workers who did not have the ability, training, and skills necessary to obtain available jobs. Today, it still encompasses these workers. In addition, however, economists increasingly look at structural unemployment from the viewpoint of employers, many of whom face government mandates to provide funds for social insurance programs for their employees, to announce plant closings months or even years in advance, and so on. There is now considerable evidence that government labor market policies influence how many positions businesses wish to create, thereby affecting structural unemployment. In the United States, many businesses appear to have adjusted to these policies by hiring more "temporary workers" or establishing short-term contracts with "private consultants," which may have reduced the extent of U.S. structural unemployment in recent years.

Structural unemployment
Unemployment resulting from a poor match of workers' abilities and skills with current requirements of employers.

Cyclical Unemployment.

Cyclical unemployment is related to business fluctuations. It is defined as unemployment associated with changes in business conditions—primarily recessions and depressions. The way to lessen cyclical unemployment would be to reduce the intensity, duration, and frequency of ups and downs of business activity. Economic policymakers attempt, through their policies, to reduce cyclical unemployment by keeping business activity on an even keel.

Cyclical unemployment
Unemployment resulting from business recessions that occur when aggregate (total) demand is insufficient to create full employment.

Seasonal Unemployment.

Seasonal unemployment comes and goes with seasons of the year in which the demand for particular jobs rises and falls. In northern states, construction workers can often work only during the warmer months; they are seasonally unemployed during the winter. Summer resort workers can usually get jobs in resorts only during the summer season. They, too, become seasonally unemployed during the winter; the opposite is true for ski resort workers.

Seasonal unemployment
Unemployment resulting from the seasonal pattern of work in specific industries. It is usually due to seasonal fluctuations in demand or to changing weather conditions, rendering work difficult, if not impossible, as in the agriculture, construction, and tourist industries.

The unemployment rate that the Bureau of Labor Statistics releases each month is "seasonally adjusted." This means that the reported unemployment rate has been adjusted to remove the effects of variations in seasonal unemployment. Thus the unemployment rate that the media dutifully announce reflects only the sum of frictional unemployment, structural unemployment, and cyclical unemployment.

Why do you suppose that the word *unemployment* did not appear in many dictionaries until after the 1870s?

Policy EXAMPLE

How the Word *Unemployment* Found Its Meaning

Until the late nineteenth century, people in the United States were unacquainted with the word *unemployment*. The failure of able-bodied people to work in a largely agricultural country with so much plentiful land was generally regarded as an indication of laziness, not misfortune. Thus people without gainful employment commonly were objects of scorn, not of pity.

During the booming industrialization of the latter half of the nineteenth century, about half of the native-born population and nearly all immigrants landed jobs in manufacturing and transportation industries. Then a financial panic in 1873 generated thousands of business failures, and many tens of thousands of workers found themselves suddenly without gainful employment.

Statisticians conducting the 1878 census in particularly hard-hit Massachusetts decided that they had to come up with a category for all these people who had become jobless so abruptly. They decided to use the term *unemployment*, which the state census previously had applied to anyone without an occupation, including children under the age of 10. Henceforth, the Massachusetts government decided, those classified as unemployed would be working-age individuals "out of work and seeking it." This, of course, came to be the definition we apply today.

For Critical Analysis
Would unemployment exist if everyone was self-employed?

Full Employment

Does full employment mean that everybody has a job? Certainly not, for not everyone is looking for a job—full-time students and full-time homemakers, for example, are not. Is it possible for everyone who is looking for a job always to find one? No, because transaction costs in the labor market are not zero. Transaction costs are those associated with any activity whose goal is to enter into, carry out, or terminate contracts. In the labor market, these costs involve time spent looking for a job, being interviewed, negotiating the terms of employment, and so on.

We will always have some frictional unemployment as individuals move in and out of the labor force, seek higher-paying jobs, and move to different parts of the country. **Full employment** is therefore a concept implying some sort of balance or equilibrium in an ever-shifting labor market. Of course, this general notion of full employment must somehow be put into numbers so that economists and others can determine whether the economy has reached the full-employment point.

Economists do this by estimating the **natural rate of unemployment,** the rate that is expected to prevail in the long run once all workers and employers have fully adjusted to any changes in the economy. If correctly estimated, the natural rate of unemployment should not reflect cyclical unemployment. When seasonally adjusted, the natural unemployment rate should take into account only frictional and structural unemployment.

A long-standing difficulty, however, has been a lack of agreement about how to estimate the natural unemployment rate. From the mid-1980s to the early 1990s, the

Full employment
An arbitrary level of unemployment that corresponds to "normal" friction in the labor market. In 1986, a 6.5 percent rate of unemployment was considered full employment. Today, it is assumed to be around 5 percent.

Natural rate of unemployment
The rate of unemployment that is estimated to prevail in long-run macroeconomic equilibrium, when all workers and employers have fully adjusted to any changes in the economy.

President's Council of Economic Advisers (CEA) consistently estimated that the natural unemployment rate in the United States was about 6.5 percent. Even into the 2000s, the approach to estimating the natural rate of unemployment that Federal Reserve staff economists have employed—which was intended to improve on the CEA's traditional method—yielded a natural rate just over 6 percent. When the measured unemployment rate fell to 4 percent in 2000, however, economists began to rethink their approach to estimating the natural unemployment rate. This led some to alter their estimation methods to take into account such factors as greater rivalry among domestic businesses and increased international competition, which led to an estimated natural rate of unemployment of roughly 5 percent. We shall return to the concept of the natural unemployment rate in Chapter 10.

CONCEPTS in Brief

- Frictional unemployment occurs because of transaction costs in the labor market. For example, workers do not have full information about vacancies and must search for jobs. Structural unemployment occurs when there is a poor match of workers' skills and abilities with available jobs, perhaps because workers lack appropriate training or government labor rules reduce firms' willingness to hire.

- The levels of frictional and structural unemployment are used in part to determine our (somewhat arbitrary) measurement of full employment.

To test your understanding of the concepts covered in this section, go to the Online Review at www.myeconlab.com/miller.

INFLATION AND DEFLATION

During World War II, you could buy bread for 8 to 10 cents a loaf and have milk delivered fresh to your door for about 25 cents a half gallon. The average price of a new car was less than $700, and the average house cost less than $3,000. Today bread, milk, cars, and houses all cost more—a lot more. Prices are more than 12 times what they were in 1940. Clearly, this country has experienced quite a bit of *inflation* since then. We define **inflation** as an upward movement in the average level of prices. The opposite of inflation is **deflation,** defined as a downward movement in the average level of prices. Notice that these definitions depend on the *average* level of prices. This means that even during a period of inflation, some prices can be falling if other prices are rising at a faster rate. The prices of electronic equipment have dropped dramatically since the 1960s, even though there has been general inflation.

To discuss what has happened to prices here and in other countries, we have to know how to measure inflation.

Inflation
A sustained increase in the average of all prices of goods and services in an economy.

Deflation
A sustained decrease in the average of all prices of goods and services in an economy.

Inflation and the Purchasing Power of Money

The value of a dollar does not stay constant when there is inflation. The value of money is usually talked about in terms of **purchasing power.** A dollar's purchasing power is the real goods and services that it can buy. Consequently, another way of defining inflation is as a decline in the purchasing power of money. The faster the rate of inflation, the greater the rate of decline in the purchasing power of money.

One way to think about inflation and the purchasing power of money is to discuss dollar values in terms of *nominal* versus *real* values. The nominal value of anything is simply its price expressed in today's dollars. In contrast, the real value of anything is its value expressed in purchasing power, which varies with the overall price level. Let's say that you received a $100 bill from your grandparents this year. One year from now, the nominal

Purchasing power
The value of money for buying goods and services. If your money income stays the same but the price of one good that you are buying goes up, your effective purchasing power falls, and vice versa.

value of that bill will still be $100. The real value will depend on what the purchasing power of money is after one year's worth of inflation. Obviously, if there is inflation during the year, the real value of that $100 bill will have diminished.

How much do you suppose that inflation has reduced the purchasing power of a dollar bill during the past hundred years?

EXAMPLE

A Dollar Really Doesn't Buy Much Any More

Between 1900 and the 1930s, the purchasing power of the U.S. dollar fluctuated considerably. By 1918 a dollar was only able to buy what 40 cents could have purchased in 1900. Then a decrease in the overall price level during the next two decades caused the purchasing power of the dollar to increase somewhat. By the late 1930s, a person could use a dollar to buy the amount of goods and services that could have been obtained for about 60 cents in 1900.

Since the late 1930s, however, persistent inflation has been a fact of life in the United States. Today's one-dollar bill can purchase 5 percent of the goods and services that someone living in 1900 could have bought with a dollar. Thus a dollar now has the same purchasing power that a nickel possessed in 1900.

For Critical Analysis
Would society necessarily benefit if the government announced that 20 units of "old dollars" must be traded for each unit of "new dollars" on a particular date, thereby raising the purchasing power of each "new dollar" to the 1900 level?

Measuring the Rate of Inflation

How can we measure the rate of inflation? This is a thorny problem for government statisticians. It is easy to determine how much the price of an individual commodity has risen: If last year a light bulb cost 50 cents and this year it costs 75 cents, there has been a 50 percent rise in the price of that light bulb over a one-year period. We can express the change in the individual light bulb price in one of several ways: The price has gone up 25 cents; the price is one and a half (1.5) times as high; the price has risen by 50 percent. An *index number* of this price rise is simply the second way (1.5) multiplied by 100, meaning that the index today would stand at 150. We multiply by 100 to eliminate decimals because it is easier to think in terms of percentage changes using integers. This is the standard convention adopted for convenience in dealing with index numbers or price levels.

Computing a Price Index. The measurement problem becomes more complicated when it involves a large number of goods, especially if some prices have risen faster than others and some have even fallen. What we have to do is pick a representative bundle, a so-called market basket, of goods and compare the cost of that market basket of goods over time. When we do this, we obtain a **price index,** which is defined as the cost of a market basket of goods today, expressed as a percentage of the cost of that identical market basket of goods in some starting year, known as the **base year.**

Price index
The cost of today's market basket of goods expressed as a percentage of the cost of the same market basket during a base year.

Base year
The year that is chosen as the point of reference for comparison of prices in other years.

$$\text{Price index} = \frac{\text{cost today of market basket}}{\text{cost of market basket in base year}} \times 100$$

In the base year, the price index will always be 100, because the year in the numerator and in the denominator of the fraction is the same; therefore, the fraction equals 1, and when we multiply it by 100, we get 100. A simple numerical example is given in Table 7-1. In

TABLE 7-1

Calculating a Price Index for a Two-Good Market Basket
In this simplified example, there are only two goods—corn and computers. The quantities and base-year prices are given in columns 2 and 3. The cost of the 1997 market basket, calculated in column 4, comes to $1,400. The 2007 prices are given in column 5. The cost of the market basket in 2007, calculated in column 6, is $1,650. The price index for 2007 compared with 1997 is 117.86.

(1) Commodity	(2) Martket Basket Quantity	(3) 1997 Price per Unit	(4) Cost of Market Basket in 1997	(5) 2007 Price per Unit	(6) Cost of Market Basket in 2007
Corn	100 bushels	$ 4	$ 400	$ 8	$ 800
Computers	2	500	1,000	425	850
Totals			$1,400		$1,650

$$\text{Price index} = \frac{\text{cost of market basket in 2007}}{\text{cost of market basket in base year 1997}} \times 100 = \frac{\$1,650}{\$1,400} \times 100 = 117.86$$

the table, there are only two goods in the market basket—corn and computers. The *quantities* in the basket are the same in the base year, 1997, and the current year, 2007; only the *prices* change. Such a *fixed-quantity* price index is the easiest to compute because the statistician need only look at prices of goods and services sold every year rather than actually observing how much of these goods and services consumers actually purchase each year.

Real-World Price Indexes. Government statisticians calculate a number of price indexes. The most often quoted are the **Consumer Price Index (CPI)**, the **Producer Price Index (PPI)**, and the **GDP deflator.** The CPI attempts to measure changes only in the level of prices of goods and services purchased by wage earners. The PPI attempts to show what has happened to the average price of goods and services produced and sold by a typical firm. (There are also *wholesale price indexes* that track the price level for commodities that firms purchase from other firms.) The GDP deflator attempts to show changes in the level of prices of all new goods and services produced in the economy. The most general indicator of inflation is the GDP deflator because it measures the changes in the prices of everything produced in the economy.

Consumer Price Index (CPI)
A statistical measure of a weighted average of prices of a specified set of goods and services purchased by typical consumers in urban areas.

Producer Price Index (PPI)
A statistical measure of a weighted average of prices of goods and services that firms produce and sell.

GDP deflator
A price index measuring the changes in prices of all new goods and services produced in the economy.

The CPI. The Bureau of Labor Statistics (BLS) has the task of identifying a market basket of goods and services of the typical consumer. Today, the BLS uses the time period 1982–1984 as its base of market prices. It intends to change the base to 1993–1995 but has yet to do so. It has, though, updated the expenditure weights for its market basket of goods to reflect consumer spending patterns in 1993–1995. All CPI numbers since February 1998 reflect the new expenditure weights.

Economists have known for years that the way the BLS measures changes in the Consumer Price Index is flawed. Specifically, the BLS has been unable to account for the way consumers substitute less expensive items for higher-priced items. The reason is that the CPI is a fixed-quantity price index, meaning that the BLS implicitly ignores changes in consumption patterns that occur between years in which it revises the index. Until recently, the BLS has been unable to take quality changes into account as they occur. Now, though, it is subtracting from certain list prices estimated effects of qualitative improvements and adding to other list prices to account for deteriorations in quality. An additional flaw is that the CPI usually ignores successful new products until long after they have been introduced.

The PPI. There are a number of Producer Price Indexes, including one for foodstuffs, another for intermediate goods (goods used in the production of other goods), and one for finished goods. Most of the producer prices included are in mining, manufacturing, and agriculture. The PPIs can be considered general-purpose indexes for nonretail markets.

Although in the long run the various PPIs and the CPI generally show the same rate of inflation, such is not the case in the short run. Most often the PPIs increase before the CPI because it takes time for producer price increases to show up in the prices that consumers pay for final products. Often changes in the PPIs are watched closely as a hint that inflation is going to increase or decrease.

Go to www.econtoday.com/chap07 to obtain information about inflation and unemployment in other countries from the International Monetary Fund. Click on "World Economic Outlook Databases."

The GDP Deflator. The broadest price index reported in the United States is the GDP deflator, where GDP stands for gross domestic product, or annual total national income. Unlike the CPI and the PPIs, the GDP deflator is *not* based on a fixed market basket of goods and services. The basket is allowed to change with people's consumption and investment patterns. In this sense, the changes in the GDP deflator reflect both price changes and the public's market responses to those price changes. Why? Because new expenditure patterns are allowed to show up in the GDP deflator as people respond to changing prices.

Personal Consumption Expenditure (PCE) Index.
A statistical measure of average price using annually updated weights based on surveys of consumer spending.

The PCE Index. Another price index that takes into account changing expenditure patterns is the **Personal Consumption Expenditure (PCE) Index.** The Bureau of Economic Analysis, an agency of the U.S. Department of Commerce, uses continuously updated annual surveys of consumer purchases to construct the weights for the PCE Index. Thus an advantage of the PCE Index is that weights in the index are updated every year. The Federal Reserve has used the rate of change in the PCE Index as its primary inflation indicator because Fed officials believe that the updated weights in the PCE Index make it more accurate than the CPI as a measure of consumer price changes. Nevertheless, the CPI remains the most widely reported price index, and the U.S. government continues to use the CPI to adjust the value of Social Security benefits to account for inflation.

Historical Changes in the CPI. Until the mid-1990s, the Consumer Price Index showed a fairly dramatic trend upward since about World War II. Figure 7-6 shows the annual rate of change in the CPI since 1860. Prior to World War II, there were numerous periods of deflation along with periods of inflation. Persistent year-in and year-out inflation seems to be a post–World War II phenomenon, at least in this country. As far back as before the American Revolution, prices used to rise during war periods but then would fall back toward prewar levels afterward. This occurred after the Revolutionary War, the War of 1812, the Civil War, and to a lesser extent World War I. Consequently, the overall price level in 1940 wasn't much different from 150 years earlier.

CONCEPTS in Brief

- Once we pick a market basket of goods, we can construct a price index that compares the cost of that market basket today with the cost of the same market basket in a base year.

- The Consumer Price Index (CPI) is the most often used price index in the United States. The Producer Price Index (PPI) is also widely mentioned.

- The GDP deflator measures what is happening to the average price level of *all* new, domestically produced final goods and services in our economy.

- The Personal Consumption Expenditure (PCE) Index uses annually updated weights from consumer spending surveys to measure average prices faced by consumers.

To test your understanding of the concepts covered in this section, go to the Online Review at www.myeconlab.com/miller.

FIGURE 7-6
Inflation and Deflation in U.S. History

Since the Civil War, the United States has experienced alternating inflation and deflation. Here we show them as reflected by changes in the Consumer Price Index. Since World War II, the periods of inflation have not been followed by periods of deflation; that is, even during peacetime, the price index has continued to rise. The yellow areas represent wartime.

Source: U.S. Department of Labor, Bureau of Labor Statistics.

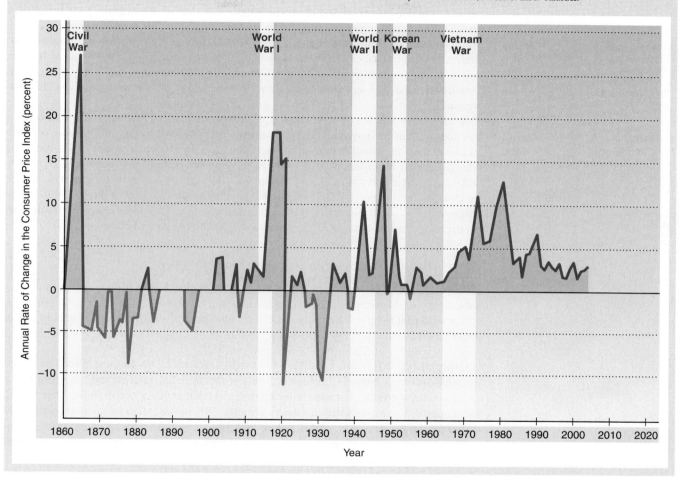

Anticipated versus Unanticipated Inflation

To determine who is hurt by inflation and what the effects of inflation are in general, we have to distinguish between anticipated and unanticipated inflation. We will see that the effects on individuals and the economy are vastly different, depending on which type of inflation exists.

Anticipated inflation is the rate of inflation that most individuals believe will occur. If the rate of inflation this year turns out to be 10 percent, and that's about what most people thought it was going to be, we are in a situation of fully anticipated inflation.

Unanticipated inflation is inflation that comes as a surprise to individuals in the economy. For example, if the inflation rate in a particular year turns out to be 10 percent when on average people thought it was going to be 5 percent, there will have been unanticipated inflation—inflation greater than anticipated.

Some of the problems caused by inflation arise when it is unanticipated, for when it is anticipated, many people are able to protect themselves from its ravages. Keeping the

Anticipated inflation
The inflation rate that we believe will occur; when it does, we are in a situation of fully anticipated inflation.

Unanticipated inflation
Inflation at a rate that comes as a surprise, either higher or lower than the rate anticipated.

distinction between anticipated and unanticipated inflation in mind, we can easily see the relationship between inflation and interest rates.

Inflation and Interest Rates

Nominal rate of interest
The market rate of interest expressed in today's dollars.

Let's start in a hypothetical world in which there is no inflation and anticipated inflation is zero. In that world, you may be able to borrow funds—to buy a computer or a car, for example—at a **nominal rate of interest** of, say, 6 percent. If you borrow the funds to purchase a computer or a car and your anticipation of inflation turns out to be accurate, neither you nor the lender will have been fooled. The dollars you pay back in the years to come will be just as valuable in terms of purchasing power as the dollars that you borrowed.

Real rate of interest
The nominal rate of interest minus the anticipated rate of inflation.

What you ordinarily want to know when you borrow money is the *real* rate of interest that you will have to pay. The **real rate of interest** is defined as the nominal rate of interest minus the anticipated rate of inflation. If you are able to borrow money at 6 percent and you anticipated an inflation rate of 6 percent, your real rate of interest would be zero—lucky you, particularly if the actual rate of inflation turned out to be 6 percent. In effect, we can say that the nominal rate of interest is equal to the real rate of interest plus an *inflationary premium* to take account of anticipated inflation. That inflationary premium covers depreciation in the purchasing power of the dollars repaid by borrowers.[*]

Does Inflation Necessarily Hurt Everyone?

Most people think that inflation is bad. After all, inflation means higher prices, and when we have to pay higher prices, are we not necessarily worse off? The truth is that inflation affects different people differently. Its effects also depend on whether it is anticipated or unanticipated.

Unanticipated Inflation: Creditors Lose and Debtors Gain. In most situations, unanticipated inflation benefits borrowers because the nominal interest rate they are being charged does not fully compensate for the inflation that actually occurred. In other words, the lender did not anticipate inflation correctly. Whenever inflation rates are underestimated for the life of a loan, creditors lose and debtors gain. Periods of considerable unanticipated (higher than anticipated) inflation occurred in the late 1960s, the early 1970s, and the late 1970s. During those years, creditors lost and debtors gained.

Cost-of-living adjustments (COLAs)
Clauses in contracts that allow for increases in specified nominal values to take account of changes in the cost of living.

Protecting Against Inflation. Banks attempt to protect themselves against inflation by raising nominal interest rates to reflect anticipated inflation. Adjustable-rate mortgages in fact do just that: The interest rate varies according to what happens to interest rates in the economy. Workers can protect themselves by **cost-of-living adjustments (COLAs),** which are automatic increases in wage rates to take account of increases in the price level.

To the extent that you hold non-interest-bearing cash, you will lose because of inflation. If you have put $100 in a mattress and the inflation rate is 10 percent for the year, you will have lost 10 percent of the purchasing power of that $100. If you have your funds in a non-interest-bearing checking account, you will suffer the same fate. Individuals attempt to reduce the cost of holding cash by putting it into interest-bearing accounts, a wide variety of which often pay nominal rates of interest that reflect anticipated inflation.

---

[*]Whenever there are relatively high rates of anticipated inflation, we must add an additional factor to the inflationary premium—the product of the real rate of interest times the anticipated rate of inflation. Usually, this last term is omitted because the anticipated rate of inflation is not high enough to make much of a difference.

The Resource Cost of Inflation. Some economists believe that the main cost of inflation is the opportunity cost of resources used to protect against inflation and the distortions introduced as firms attempt to plan for the long run. Individuals have to spend time and resources to figure out ways to adjust their behavior in case inflation is different from what it has been in the past. That may mean spending a longer time working out more complicated contracts for employment, for purchases of goods in the future, and for purchases of raw materials.

Inflation requires that price lists be changed. This is called the **repricing, or menu, cost of inflation.** The higher the rate of inflation, the higher the repricing cost of inflation.

> **Repricing, or menu, cost of inflation**
> The cost associated with recalculating prices and printing new price lists when there is inflation.

Another major problem with inflation is that usually it does not proceed perfectly evenly. Consequently, the rate of inflation is not exactly what people anticipate. When this is so, the purchasing power of money changes in unanticipated ways. Because money is what we use as the measuring rod of the value of transactions we undertake, we have a more difficult time figuring out what we have really paid for things. As a result, resources tend to be misallocated in such situations because people have not really valued them accurately.

Think of any period during which you have to pay a higher price for something that was cheaper before. You are annoyed. But every time you pay a higher price, that represents the receipt of higher income for someone else. Therefore, it is impossible for all of us to be worse off because of rising prices. (Of course, we all become poorer if great variations in the rate of inflation cause us to incur the cost of resource misallocations.) There are numerous costs to inflation, but they aren't the ones commonly associated with inflation in the popular press. One way to think of inflation is that it is simply a *change in the accounting system.* One year the price of fast-food hamburgers averages $1; 10 years later the price of fast-food hamburgers averages $2. Clearly, $1 doesn't mean the same thing 10 years later. If we changed the name of our unit of accounting each year so that one year we paid $1 for fast-food hamburgers and 10 years later we paid, say, 1 peso, this lesson would be driven home.

CONCEPTS in Brief

- Whenever inflation is greater than anticipated, creditors lose and debtors gain. Whenever the rate of inflation is less than anticipated, creditors gain and debtors lose.

- Holders of cash lose during periods of inflation because the purchasing power of their cash depreciates at the rate of inflation.

- Households and businesses spend resources in attempting to protect themselves against the prospect of inflation, thus imposing a resource cost on the economy.

To test your understanding of the concepts covered in this section, go to the Online Review at **www.myeconlab.com/miller.**

CHANGING INFLATION AND UNEMPLOYMENT: BUSINESS FLUCTUATIONS

Some years unemployment goes up, and some years it goes down. Some years there is a lot of inflation, and other years there isn't. We have fluctuations in all aspects of our macroeconomy. The ups and downs in economywide economic activity are sometimes called **business fluctuations.** When business fluctuations are positive, they are called **expansions**—speedups in the pace of national economic activity. The opposite of an expansion is a **contraction,** which is a slowdown in the pace of national economic activity. The top of an expansion is usually called its *peak,* and the bottom of a contraction is usually called its *trough.* Business fluctuations used to be called *business cycles,* but that term

> **Business fluctuations**
> The ups and downs in business activity throughout the economy.
>
> **Expansion**
> A business fluctuation in which the pace of national economic activity is speeding up.
>
> **Contraction**
> A business fluctuation during which the pace of national economic activity is slowing down.

no longer seems appropriate because *cycle* implies regular or automatic recurrence, and we have never had automatic recurrent fluctuations in general business and economic activity. What we have had are contractions and expansions that vary greatly in length. For example, the ten post–World War II expansions have averaged 57 months, but three of those exceeded 90 months, and two lasted less than 25 months.

If the contractionary phase of business fluctuations becomes severe enough, we call it a **recession.** An extremely severe recession is called a **depression.** Typically, at the beginning of a recession, interest rates rise, and as the recession gets worse, they fall. At the same time, people's income starts to fall and the duration of unemployment increases so that the unemployment rate increases. In times of expansion, the opposite occurs.

In Figure 7-7, you see that typical business fluctuations occur around a growth trend in overall national business activity shown as a straight upward-sloping line. Starting out at a peak, the economy goes into a contraction (recession). Then an expansion starts that moves up to its peak, higher than the last one, and the sequence starts over again.

The official dating of business recessions is done by the National Bureau of Economic Research (NBER). What recession do you suppose that this organization has had some trouble dating?

Recession
A period of time during which the rate of growth of business activity is consistently less than its long-term trend or is negative.

Depression
An extremely severe recession.

EXAMPLE

The National Bureau of Economic Research Complicates the Presidential Blame Game

In late 2001, the National Bureau of Economic Research declared that a recession had begun in March of that year, or about two months after Republican President George W. Bush took office. Following a long U.S. political tradition, Democratic opponents were quick to condemn the new president's economic policies for contributing to, or perhaps even bringing about, the downturn.

More than two years later, however, economists at the NBER, who had by then determined that the recession had ended in November 2001, began to second-guess their earlier decision about when it started. Further analysis of U.S. economic data, they indicated, showed that the recession probably began in November 2000, before Bush had become president. Of course, Republican defenders of President Bush quickly responded by blaming the economic downturn on Bill Clinton, the Democratic president who had been in office at that time.

For Critical Analysis
Why do you suppose that it can be difficult to precisely date the beginning or end of an expansion or a recession?

A Historical Picture of Business Activity in the United States

Go to www.econtoday.com/chap07 to learn about how economists at the National Bureau of Economic Research formally determine when a recession is under way.

Figure 7-8 traces changes in U.S. business activity from 1880 to the present. Note that the long-term trend line is shown as horizontal, so all changes in business activity focus around that trend line. Major changes in business activity in the United States occurred during the Great Depression and World War II. Note that none of the actual business fluctuations that you see in Figure 7-8 exactly mirror the idealized course of a business fluctuation shown in Figure 7-7.

Explaining Business Fluctuations: External Shocks

As you might imagine, because changes in national business activity affect everyone, economists for decades have attempted to understand and explain business fluctuations. For years, one of the most obvious explanations has been external events that tend to dis-

FIGURE 7-7
The Idealized Course of Business Fluctuations
A hypothetical business cycle would go from peak to trough and back again in a regular cycle.

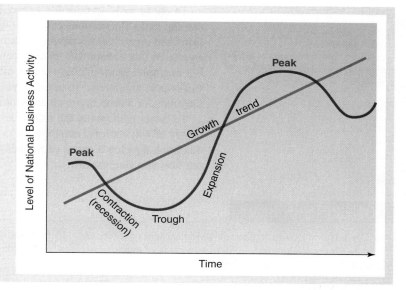

rupt the economy. In many of the graphs in this chapter, you have seen that World War II was a critical point in this nation's economic history. A war is certainly an external shock—something that originates outside our economy.

FIGURE 7-8
National Business Activity, 1880 to the Present
Variations around the trend of U.S. business activity have been frequent since 1880.

Sources: *American Business Activity from 1790 to Today,* 67th ed., AmeriTrust Co., January 1996, plus author's projections.

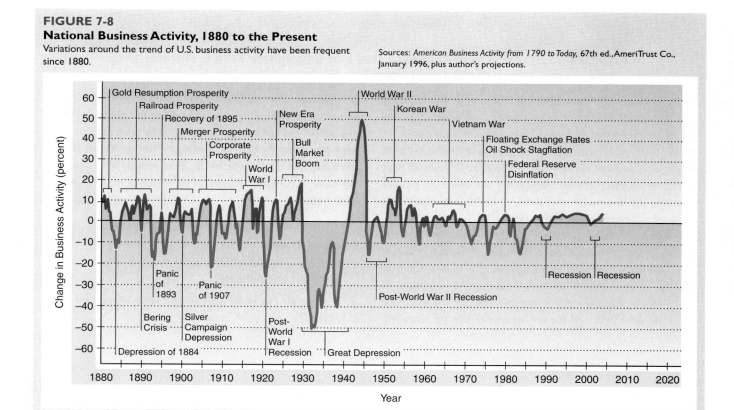

Leading indicators
Events that have been found to exhibit changes before changes in business activity.

To try to help account for external shocks that may induce business fluctuations and thereby make fluctuations easier to predict, the U.S. Department of Commerce and private firms and organizations tabulate indexes (weighted averages) of **leading indicators.** These are events that economists have noticed typically occur *before* changes in business activity. For example, economic downturns often follow such events as a reduction in the average workweek, an increase in unemployment insurance claims, a decrease in the prices of raw materials, or a drop in the quantity of money in circulation.

To better understand the roll of shocks in influencing business fluctuations, we need a theory of why national economic activity changes. The remainder of the macro chapters in this book develop a series of models that will help you understand the ups and downs of our business fluctuations.

CONCEPTS in Brief

- The ups and downs in economywide business activity are called business fluctuations, which consist of expansions and contractions in overall business activity.

- The lowest point of a contraction is called the trough; the highest point of an expansion is called the peak.

- A recession is a downturn in business activity for some length of time.

- One possible explanation for business fluctuations relates to external shocks, such as wars, dramatic increases in the prices of raw materials, and earthquakes, floods, and droughts.

To test your understanding of the concepts covered in this section, go to the Online Review at www.myeconlab.com/miller.

CASE STUDY: Economics Front and Center

Are a Self-Employed Dad and a Daughter Who Is Not Working Part of the Labor Force?

Johnson is a self-employed painter. On most days he paints room interiors alone. From time to time, however, he has taken on exterior house-painting jobs, which pay higher implicit hourly rates. Whenever he has tackled home exteriors, he has usually hired his daughter, who will be 18 years old next week, to help after school. Johnson has not landed an exterior painting job in a couple of months, so he has not required his daughter's assistance during that time.

Johnson is hoping to expand his thriving painting business into a larger operation. To learn more about how to function in the business world, he is taking courses at a local community college in the evenings. Currently, he is enrolled in a course in principles of macroeconomics, and his class has just discussed how the labor force and the unemployment rate are measured.

Now Johnson is wondering whether his daughter is technically part of the labor force but unemployed. She just graduated from high school and had been actively looking for a job until about a week ago, when she gave up looking any further. In fact, Johnson is not even certain whether *he*, as an actively self-employed individual, is currently included as an employed member of the labor force.

Points to Analyze

1. *Is Johnson's daughter currently part of the labor force but unemployed?*

2. *Is Johnson currently part of the labor force and employed?*

Issues and Applications

The Shortening of Business Contractions, and the Lengthening of Business Expansions

The National Bureau of Economic Research (NBER), based in Cambridge, Massachusetts, has developed official dates of U.S. contractions and expansions going back to December 1854. Average durations of these are displayed in Table 7-2. This table also shows average lengths of two measures of overall business *cycles*, which are complete periods between the two most recent lowest points of business activity (the "Trough from Previous Trough" column) or between the two most recent highest points (the "Peak from Previous Peak" column).

Concepts Applied
- Business Fluctuations
- Contractions
- Expansions

Shorter Contractions, Longer Expansions

Scan down the "Contraction" and "Expansion" columns, and you will notice that contractions have tended to be shorter since 1945, and expansions have tended to be longer.

The average length of a U.S. business contraction before 1945 was close to 22 months, and the average length of a business expansion was nearly 27 months. Since 1945, the average contraction has lasted only a little over 10 months, and the average expansion has lasted 57 months.

Longer Business Cycles

The overall *business cycle* can be measured either as the total time from one trough, or low point, in business activity to the next (the "Trough from Previous Trough" column in the table) or from one peak, or high point, in business activity to the next (the "Peak from Previous Peak" column). Before 1945, the average business cycle, measured either way, was almost 48 months. Since then, the average length of a business cycle has been more than 67 months.

Thus the cycle of business fluctuations has become longer because business expansions have lengthened considerably. At the same time, the U.S. economy has tended to spend less time contracting. Naturally, this changing pattern of business fluctuations has been good news for the U.S. economy.

TABLE 7-2
Business Cycle Expansions and Contractions
These are average durations of U.S. business cycles, as established by the National Bureau of Economic Research.
Source: NBER.

Time Interval for Average of Cycles	Duration in Months			
	Contraction Peak to Trough	**Expansion** Previous Trough to This Peak	**Cycle** Trough from Previous Trough	Peak from Previous Peak
1854–1919 (16 cycles)	22	27	48	49
1919–1945 (6 cycles)	18	35	53	53
1945–2001 (10 cycles)	10	57	67	67

For Critical Analysis

1. How many months shorter, on average, have 1945–2001 contractions been than 1854–1919 contractions?
2. How many months longer, on average, have 1945–2001 expansions been than 1854–1919 expansions?

Web Resources

1. Learn about the functions of the National Bureau of Economic Research at www.econtoday.com/chap07.
2. Find out more about the role of the Council of Economic Advisers in the U.S. executive branch of government at www.econtoday.com/chap07.

Research Project

In 1946, the U.S. Congress enacted the Employment Act, which committed the federal government to trying to maintain full employment of the nation's working population. In addition, since the 1950s and 1960s businesses have developed better ways of managing inventories of goods in response to variations in total expenditures, thereby smoothing swings in total production. Consider why these two developments might complicate evaluating whether shortened contractions and lengthened expansions should be credited to governmental economic policymaking.

SUMMARY DISCUSSION of Learning Objectives

1. **How the U.S. Government Calculates the Official Unemployment Rate:** The total number of workers who are officially unemployed are noninstitutionalized people aged 16 or older who are willing and able to work and who are actively looking for work but have not found a job. To calculate the unemployment rate, the government determines what percentage this quantity is of the labor force, which consists of all noninstitutionalized people aged 16 years or older who either have jobs or are available for and actively seeking employment. Thus the official unemployment rate does not include discouraged workers who have stopped looking for work because they are convinced that they will not find suitable employment; these individuals are not included in the labor force.

2. **The Types of Unemployment:** Workers who are temporarily unemployed because they are searching for appropriate job offers are frictionally unemployed. The structurally unemployed lack the skills currently required by prospective employers. People unemployed due to business contractions are said to be cyclically unemployed. And certain workers can find themselves seasonally unemployed because of the seasonal patterns of occupations within specific industries. The natural unemployment rate is the seasonally adjusted rate of unemployment including only those who are frictionally and structurally unemployed during a given interval..

3. **How Price Indexes Are Calculated and Key Price Indexes:** To calculate any price index, economists multiply 100 times the ratio of the cost of a market basket of goods and services in the current year to the cost of the same market basket in a base year. The market basket used to compute the Consumer Price Index (CPI) is a weighted set of goods and services purchased by a typical consumer in urban areas. The Producer Price Index (PPI) is a weighted average of prices of goods sold by a typical firm. The GDP deflator measures changes in the overall level of prices of all goods produced in the economy during a given interval.

4. **Nominal Interest Rate versus Real Interest Rate:** The nominal interest rate is the market rate of interest applying to contracts expressed in current dollars. The real interest rate is net of inflation that borrowers and lenders anticipate will erode the value of nominal interest payments during the period that a loan is repaid. Hence the real interest rate equals the nominal interest rate minus the expected inflation rate.

5. **Losers and Gainers from Inflation:** Creditors lose as a result of unanticipated inflation, or inflation that comes as a surprise after they have made a loan, because the real value of the interest payments they receive will turn out to be lower than they had expected. Borrowers gain when unanticipated inflation occurs, because the real value of their interest payments declines. Key costs of inflation

are the expenses that individuals and businesses incur to protect themselves against inflation, costs of altering business plans because of unexpected changes in prices, and menu costs arising from expenses incurred in repricing goods and services.

6. **Key Features of Business Fluctuations:** Business fluctuations are increases and decreases in business activity.

A positive fluctuation is an expansion, which is an upward movement in business activity from a trough, or low point, to a peak, or high point. A negative fluctuation is a contraction, which is a drop in the pace of business activity from a previous peak to a new trough.

KEY TERMS AND CONCEPTS

anticipated inflation (157)

base year (154)

business fluctuations (159)

Consumer Price Index (CPI) (155)

contraction (159)

cost-of-living adjustments (COLAs) (158)

cyclical unemployment (151)

deflation (153)

depression (160)

discouraged workers (149)

expansion (159)

flow (148)

frictional unemployment (151)

full employment (152)

GDP deflator (155)

inflation (153)

job leaver (148)

job loser (148)

labor force (146)

labor force participation rate (149)

leading indicators (162)

natural rate of unemployment (152)

new entrant (148)

nominal rate of interest (158)

Personal Consumption Expenditure (PCE) Index (156)

price index (154)

Producer Price Index (PPI) (155)

purchasing power (153)

real rate of interest (158)

recession (160)

reentrant (148)

repricing, or menu, cost of inflation (159)

seasonal unemployment (151)

stock (148)

structural unemployment (151)

unanticipated inflation (157)

unemployment (146)

PROBLEMS

Answers to the odd-numbered problems appear at the back of the book.

7-1. Suppose that you receive two offers to begin employment after you complete your studies, which will be one year from now. You wish to take one of the two positions. You are indifferent between the jobs and their locations, however, and both job offers include the same benefits package. Job A will entail an annual salary of $24,000 beginning a year from now, and job B will pay an annual salary of $25,000. Neither salary will be adjusted until you complete a year of employment. After you study the regions where the firms are located, you determine that there is likely to be no inflation over the two years where employer A is located. By way of contrast, employer B is in an area where the annual inflation rate over the next two

years is likely to be 5 percent. Which job should you accept?

7-2. Suppose that an elderly woman is retired, but she has become bored with retirement and is considering going back to work. She receives $1,000 in Social Security payments each month, and this is her only source of income. If she accepts other employment, her Social Security payment drops by $1 for every $2 in pretax earnings from that source of employment. She has been offered a job as an assistant manager of a fast-food restaurant at a pretax salary of $1,500 per month. Out of these earnings, she would have to pay a 7 percent Social Security tax and a 15 percent income tax. What would be her effective monthly earnings from working at the fast-food job, taking into account both the resulting change in her Social Security payment and the taxes that she would have to pay on her earned income?

7-3. If the U.S. adult population is 200 million, the number employed is 152 million, and the number unemployed is 8 million, what is the unemployment rate?

7-4. In Problem 7-3, there is a difference of 40 million between the adult population and the combined total of people who are employed and unemployed. How do we classify these 40 million people? Based on these figures, what is the U.S. labor force participation rate?

7-5. During the course of a year, the labor force consists of the same 1,000 people. Of these, 20 lack skills that employers desire and hence remain unemployed throughout the year. At the same time, every month during the year, 30 different people become unemployed, and 30 other different people who were unemployed find jobs. There is no seasonal employment.
   a. What is the frictional unemployment rate?
   b. What is the unemployment rate?
   c. Suppose that a system of unemployment compensation is established. Each month, 30 new people (not including the 20 lacking required skills) continue to become unemployed, but each monthly group of newly unemployed now takes two months to find a job. After this change, what is the frictional unemployment rate?
   d. After the change discussed in part (c), what is the unemployment rate?

7-6. Suppose that a nation has a labor force of 100 people. In January, Amy, Barbara, Carine, and Denise are unemployed; in February, those four find jobs, but Evan, Francesco, George, and Horatio become unemployed. Suppose further that every month, the previous four who were unemployed find jobs and four different people become unemployed. Throughout the year, however, the same three people—Ito, Jack, and Kelley—continually remain unemployed because they lack sufficient skills to obtain jobs.
   a. What is this nation's frictional unemployment rate?
   b. What is its structural unemployment rate?
   c. What is its unemployment rate?

7-7. In a country with a labor force of 200, a different group of 10 people becomes unemployed each month, but becomes employed once again a month later. No others outside these groups are unemployed.
   a. What is this country's unemployment rate?

   b. What is the average duration of unemployment?
   c. Suppose that establishment of a system of unemployment compensation increases to two months the interval that it takes each group of job losers to become employed each month. Nevertheless, a different group of 10 people still becomes unemployed each month. Now what is the average duration of unemployment?
   d. Following the change discussed in part (c), what is the country's unemployment rate?

7-8. A nation's frictional unemployment rate is 1 percent. Seasonal unemployment does not exist in this country. Its cyclical rate of unemployment is 3 percent, and its structural unemployment rate is 4 percent. What is this nation's overall rate of unemployment? What is its natural rate of unemployment?

7-9. In 2004, the cost of a market basket of goods was $2,000. In 2006, the cost of the same market basket of goods was $2,100. Use the price index formula to calculate the price index for 2006 if 2004 is the base year.

7-10. Consider the following price indexes: 90 in 2005, 100 in 2006, 110 in 2007, 121 in 2008, and 150 in 2009. Answer the following questions.
   a. What is the base year?
   b. What is the inflation rate from 2006 and 2007?
   c. What is the inflation rate from 2007 and 2008?
   d. If the cost of a market basket in 2006 is $2,000, what is the cost of the same basket of goods and services in 2005? In 2009?

7-11. The real interest rate is 4 percent, and the nominal interest rate is 6 percent. What is the anticipated rate of inflation?

7-12. Currently, the price index used to calculate the inflation rate is equal to 90. The general expectation throughout the economy is that next year its value will be 99. The current nominal interest rate is 12 percent. What is the real interest rate?

7-13. At present, the nominal interest rate is 7 percent, and the expected inflation rate is 5 percent. The current year is the base year for the price index used to calculate inflation.
   a. What is the real interest rate?
   b. What is the anticipated value of the price index next year?

7-14. Suppose that in 2009 there is a sudden, unanticipated burst of inflation. Consider the situations faced by the following individuals. Who gains and who loses?

a. A homeowner whose wages will keep pace with inflation in 2009 but whose monthly mortgage interest payments to a savings bank will remain fixed

b. An apartment landlord who has guaranteed to his tenants that their monthly rent payments during 2009 will be the same as they were during 2008

c. A banker who made an auto loan that the auto buyer will repay at a fixed rate of interest during 2009

d. A retired individual who earns a pension with fixed monthly payments from her past employer during 2009

ECONOMICS ON THE NET

Looking at the Unemployment and Inflation Data This chapter reviewed key concepts relating to unemployment and inflation. In this application, you get a chance to examine U.S. unemployment and inflation data on your own.

Title: Bureau of Labor Statistics: Employment and Unemployment

Navigation: Use the link at www.econtoday.com/chap07 to visit the "Employment & Unemployment" page of the Bureau of Labor Statistics (BLS). Click on "Labor Force Statistics from the Current Population Survey.

Application Perform the indicated operations, and answer the following questions:

1. Click checkmarks in the boxes for Civilian Labor Force, Employment Level, and Unemployment Level. Retrieve

the data. Can you identify periods of sharp cyclical swings? Do they show up in data for the labor force, employment, or unemployment?

2. Are cyclical factors important?

For Group Study and Analysis Divide the class into groups, and assign a price index to each group. Ask each group to take a look at the index for All Years at the link to the BLS statistics on inflation at www.econtoday.com/chap07. Have each group identify periods during which their index accelerated or decelerated (or even fell). Do the indexes ever provide opposing implications about inflation and deflation?

If your exam were tomorrow, would you be ready? For each chapter, MyEconLab Practice Tests and Study Plans pinpoint which sections you have mastered and which ones you need to study. That way, you are more efficient with your study time, and you are better prepared for your exams.

In addition to Practice Tests and your personalized Study Plan, you'll find the following media resources in MyEconLab:

1. *Graphs in Motion* animation of Figures 7-3, 7-4, 7-6, and 7-8.
2. Videos featuring the author, Roger LeRoy Miller, on the following subjects:
   - Major Types of Unemployment
   - Measuring the Rate of Inflation
   - Inflation and Interest Rates

3. Links to the Web sites cited in the marginal Internet Resources, Issues and Applications feature, and Economics on the Net activity.
4. Audio clips of all key terms, additional practice problems, and a PDF version of the material from the print Study Guide.
5. eThemes of the Times, which is a New York Times article to help you understand the real-world applications of what you are learning.

Get Ahead of the Curve

To see how it works, turn to page 16 and then go to www.myeconlab.com/miller.

Chapter 8

Measuring the Economy's Performance

"Taken all together, how would you say things are these days—would you say you're very happy, pretty happy, or not too happy?" This is one of the questions asked in the United States General Social Survey. Researchers in sociology, political science, and other social sciences often use answers that people give to this and similar questions in random surveys to try to track the average life satisfaction of people in different income groups. They also ask people in high-, medium-, and low-income nations these kinds of questions to try to determine whether the average life satisfaction of a nation's residents varies with the nation's overall economic performance. The measure of national economic performance they typically use is *gross domestic product,* which you will learn about in this chapter.

Media Resources

Refer to the end of the chapter for a full listing of the multimedia learning materials available in MyEconLab.

LEARNING OBJECTIVES

After reading this chapter, you should be able to:

1. Describe the circular flow of income and output
2. Define gross domestic product (GDP)
3. Understand the limitations of using GDP as a measure of national welfare
4. Explain the expenditure approach to tabulating GDP
5. Explain the income approach to computing GDP
6. Distinguish between nominal GDP and real GDP

... before the 2000s, the Bureau of Economic Analysis (BEA), the unit of the Department of Commerce charged with measuring the overall performance of the U.S. economy, treated business expenses on computer software as "purchased inputs"? This meant that the BEA regarded business spending on software solely as an expense item, much like paper is an expense for newspaper publishers. Thus software was not explicitly included in *gross domestic product,* the government's key measure of overall economic activity.

Today the BEA treats business spending on software as a final purchase that is part of national output. To make it possible to compare today's national output to the levels of years past, the BEA revised its measures of gross domestic product for the 1980s and 1990s. It found that including business software as part of total national output made the recession of 1990–1991 appear much milder. When it had excluded business software expenditures, the reported decline in gross domestic product during that recession was 2.7 percent. After it included business spending on software and recalculated, the BEA found that there was a much smaller 1.8 percent decline in gross domestic product.

Clearly, it matters how the government conducts what has become known as **national income accounting** in an effort to measure the nation's overall economic performance. How this is done is the main focus of this chapter. But first we need to look at the flow of income within an economy, for it is the flow of goods and services from businesses to consumers and of payments from consumers to businesses that constitutes economic activity.

National income accounting
A measurement system used to estimate national income and its components; one approach to measuring an economy's aggregate performance.

THE SIMPLE CIRCULAR FLOW

The concept of a circular flow of income (ignoring taxes) involves two principles:

1. In every economic exchange, the seller receives exactly the same amount that the buyer spends.
2. Goods and services flow in one direction and money payments flow in the other.

In the simple economy shown in Figure 8-1 on the following page, there are only businesses and households. It is assumed that businesses sell their *entire* output *immediately* to households and that households spend their *entire* income *immediately* on consumer products. Households receive their income by selling the use of whatever factors of production they own, such as labor services.

Profits Explained

We have indicated in Figure 8-1 that profit is a cost of production. You might be under the impression that profits are not part of the cost of producing goods and services, but profits are indeed a part of this cost because entrepreneurs must be rewarded for providing their services or they won't provide them. Their reward, if any, is profit. The reward—the profit—is included in the cost of the factors of production. If there were no expectations of profit, entrepreneurs would not incur the risk associated with the organization of productive activities. That is why we consider profits a cost of doing business.

Total Income or Total Output

The arrow that goes from businesses to households at the bottom of Figure 8-1 is labeled "Total income." What would be a good definition of **total income?** If you answered "the total of all individuals' income," you would be right. But all income is actually a payment for something, whether it be wages paid for labor services, rent paid for the use of land, in-

Total income
The yearly amount earned by the nation's resources (factors of production). Total income therefore includes wages, rent, interest payments, and profits that are received by workers, landowners, capital owners, and entrepreneurs, respectively.

FIGURE 8-1
The Circular Flow of Income and Product

Businesses provide final goods and services to households (upper clockwise loop), who in turn pay for them (upper counterclockwise loop). Payments flow in a counterclockwise direction and can be thought of as a circular flow. The dollar value of output is identical to total income because profits are defined as being equal to total business receipts minus business outlays for wages, rents, and interest. Households provide factor services to businesses and receive income (lower loops).

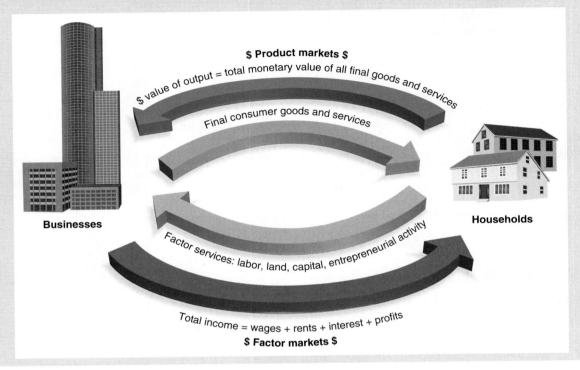

$ Product markets $

$ value of output = total monetary value of all final goods and services

Final consumer goods and services

Businesses

Households

Factor services: labor, land, capital, entrepreneurial activity

Total income = wages + rents + interest + profits

$ Factor markets $

Final goods and services
Goods and services that are at their final stage of production and will not be transformed into yet other goods or services. For example, wheat is not ordinarily considered a final good because it is usually used to make a final good, bread.

terest paid for the use of capital, or profits paid to entrepreneurs. It is the amount paid to the resource suppliers. Therefore, total income is also defined as the annual *cost* of producing the entire output of **final goods and services.**

The arrow going from households to businesses at the top of the figure represents the dollar value of output in the economy. This is equal to the total monetary value of all final goods and services for this simple economy. In essence, it represents the total business receipts from the sale of all final goods and services produced by businesses and consumed by households. Business receipts are the opposite side of household expenditures. When households purchase goods and services, those payments become a *business receipt.* Every transaction, therefore, simultaneously involves an expenditure and a receipt.

Product Markets. Transactions in which households buy goods take place in the product markets—that's where households are the buyers and businesses are the sellers of consumer goods. *Product market* transactions are represented in the upper loops in Figure 8-1. Note that consumer goods and services flow to household demanders, while money flows in the opposite direction to business suppliers.

Factor Markets. *Factor market* transactions are represented by the lower loops in Figure 8-1. In the factor market, households are the sellers; they sell resources such as labor, land, capital, and entrepreneurial ability. Businesses are the buyers in factor markets; business expenditures represent receipts or, more simply, income for households. Also, in the lower loops of Figure 8-1, factor services flow from households to businesses, while the money paid for these services flows in the opposite direction from businesses to households. Observe also the flow of money (counterclockwise) from households to businesses and back again from businesses to households: It is an endless circular flow.

Why the Dollar Value of Total Output Must Equal Total Income

Total income represents the income received by households in payment for the production of goods and services. Why must total income be identical to the dollar value of total output? First, as Figure 8-1 shows, spending by one group is income to another. Second, it is a matter of simple accounting and the economic definition of profit as a cost of production. Profit is defined as what is *left over* from total business receipts after all other costs—wages, rents, interest—have been paid. If the dollar value of total output is $1,000 and the total of wages, rent, and interest for producing that output is $900, profit is $100. Profit is always the *residual* item that makes total income equal to the dollar value of total output.

CONCEPTS in Brief

- In the circular flow model of income and output, households sell factor services to businesses that pay for those factor services. The receipt of payments is total income. Businesses sell goods and services to households that pay for them.

- The dollar value of total output is equal to the total monetary value of all final goods and services produced.

- The dollar value of final output must always equal total income; the variable that adjusts to make this so is known as profit.

To test your understanding of the concepts covered in this section, go to the Online Review at www.myeconlab.com/miller.

NATIONAL INCOME ACCOUNTING

We have already mentioned that policymakers need information about the state of the national economy. Historical statistical records on the performance of the national economy aid economists in testing their theories about how the economy really works. National income accounting is therefore important. Let's start with the most commonly presented statistic on the national economy.

Gross Domestic Product (GDP)

Gross domestic product (GDP) represents the total market value of the nation's annual final product, or output, produced per year by factors of production located within national borders. We therefore formally define GDP as the total market value of all final goods and services produced in an economy during a year. We are referring here to the value of a *flow of production*. A nation produces at a certain rate, just as you receive income at a certain rate. Your income flow might be at a rate of $5,000 per year or $50,000 per year. Suppose you are told that someone earns $500. Would you consider this a good salary? There is no way to answer that question unless you know whether the person is earning $500 per month or per week or per day. Thus you have to specify a time period for all flows. Income received is a flow. You must contrast this with, for example, your total accumulated savings, which are a stock measured at a point in time, not over time. Implicit in just about everything we deal with in this chapter is a time period—usually one year. All the measures of domestic product and income are specified as *rates* measured in dollars per year.

Gross domestic product (GDP)
The total market value of all final goods and services produced by factors of production located within a nation's borders.

Stress on Final Output

Intermediate goods
Goods used up entirely in the production of final goods.

GDP does not count **intermediate goods** (goods used up entirely in the production of final goods) because to do so would be to count them twice. For example, even though grain that a farmer produces may be that farmer's final product, it is not the final product for the nation. It is sold to make bread. Bread is the final product.

We can use a numerical example to clarify this point further. Our example will involve determining the value added at each stage of production. **Value added** is the amount of dollar value contributed to a product at each stage of its production. In Table 8-1, we see the difference between total value of all sales and value added in the production of a donut. We also see that the sum of the values added is equal to the sale price to the final consumer. It is the 45 cents that is used to measure GDP, not the 96 cents. If we used the 96 cents, we would be double-counting from stages 2 through 5, for each intermediate good would be counted at least twice—once when it was produced and again when the good it was used in making was sold. Such double counting would grossly exaggerate GDP.

Value added
The dollar value of an industry's sales minus the value of intermediate goods (for example, raw materials and parts) used in production.

TABLE 8-1
Sales Value and Value Added at Each Stage of Donut Production

(1) Stage of Production	(2) Dollar Value of Sales	(3) Value Added
Stage 1: Fertilizer and seed	$.03	$.03
Stage 2: Growing	.06	.03
Stage 3: Milling	.12	.06
Stage 4: Baking	.30	.18
Stage 5: Retailing	.45	.15
Total dollar value of all sales	$.96	Total value added $.45

Stage 1: A farmer purchases 3 cents' worth of fertilizer and seed, which are used as factors of production in growing wheat.

Stage 2: The farmer grows the wheat, harvests it, and sells it to a miller for 6 cents. Thus we see that the farmer has added 3 cents' worth of value. Those 3 cents represent income over and above expenses incurred by the farmer.

Stage 3: The miller purchases the wheat for 6 cents and adds 6 cents as the value added; that is, there is 6 cents for the miller as income. The miller sells the ground wheat flour to a donut-baking company.

Stage 4: The donut-baking company buys the flour for 12 cents and adds 18 cents as the value added. It then sells the donut to the final retailer.

Stage 5: The donut retailer sells fresh hot donuts at 45 cents apiece, thus creating an additional value of 15 cents.

We see that the total value of transactions involved in the production of one donut was 96 cents, but the total value added was 45 cents, which is exactly equal to the retail price. The total value added is equal to the sum of all income payments.

Exclusion of Financial Transactions, Transfer Payments, and Secondhand Goods

Remember that GDP is the measure of the dollar value of all final goods and services produced in one year. Many more transactions occur that have nothing to do with final goods and services produced. There are financial transactions, transfers of the ownership of pre-existing goods, and other transactions that should not and do not get included in our measure of GDP.

Financial Transactions. There are three general categories of purely financial transactions: (1) the buying and selling of securities, (2) government transfer payments, and (3) private transfer payments.

Securities. When you purchase a share of existing stock in Microsoft Corporation, someone else has sold it to you. In essence, there was merely a *transfer* of ownership rights. You paid $100 to obtain the stock certificate. Someone else received the $100 and gave up the stock certificate. No producing activity was consummated at that time, unless a broker received a fee for performing the transaction, in which case only the fee is part of GDP. The $100 transaction is not included when we measure GDP.

Government Transfer Payments. Transfer payments are payments for which no productive services are concurrently provided in exchange. The most obvious government transfer payments are Social Security benefits, veterans' payments, and unemployment compensation. The recipients make no contribution to current production in return for such transfer payments (although they may have made contributions in the past to be eligible to receive them). Government transfer payments are not included in GDP.

Go to www.econtoday.com/chap08 for the most up-to-date U.S. economic data at the Web site of the Bureau of Economic Analysis.

Private Transfer Payments. Are you receiving funds from your parents in order to attend school? Has a wealthy relative ever given you a gift of cash? If so, you have been the recipient of a private transfer payment. This is merely a transfer of funds from one individual to another. As such, it does not constitute productive activity and is not included in GDP.

Transfer of Secondhand Goods. If I sell you my two-year-old laptop computer, no current production is involved. I transfer to you the ownership of a computer that was produced years ago; in exchange, you transfer to me $350. The original purchase price of the computer was included in GDP in the year I purchased it. To include it again when I sell it to you would be counting the value of the computer a second time.

Other Excluded Transactions. Many other transactions are not included in GDP for practical reasons:

- Household production—house cleaning, child care, and other tasks performed by people in their *own* households and for which they are not paid through the marketplace
- Otherwise legal underground transactions—those that are legal but not reported and hence not taxed, such as paying housekeepers in cash that is not declared as income
- Illegal underground activities—these include prostitution, illegal gambling, and the sale of illicit drugs

Did you know that if illegal transactions were included in official measures of GDP, many nations would report much higher levels of GDP than they do at present?

E X A M P L E

The Underground Economy

The portion of a nation's total economic activity devoted to hidden, income-generating pursuits not included in the country's official gross domestic product is called its *underground economy*. Many of these activities keep a number of people gainfully employed, thereby adding to their incomes and permitting them to consume more than they would otherwise. Most of these underground endeavors constitute illegal tax evasion. Some involve illegal products, too.

Figure 8-2 displays estimates of the size of the underground economy as a percentage of officially reported GDP in the United States and a dozen other nations. As you can see, the underground economy probably amounts to a little less than 10 percent of U.S. GDP and slightly larger shares of GDP in Germany and Japan. In other, less developed nations, however, the underground economy is a much larger share of GDP.

For Critical Analysis
Why do you suppose that the underground economy tends to be relatively larger in nations with both higher taxes and complicated rules for establishing and operating private businesses?

FIGURE 8-2
Relative Size of the Underground Economy in Selected Nations
Unrecorded economic activity is a significant fraction of GDP in many of the world's nations.

Source: World Bank.

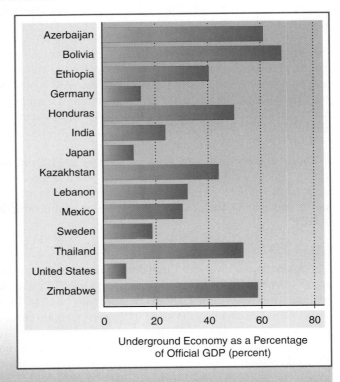

Underground Economy as a Percentage of Official GDP (percent)

Recognizing the Limitations of GDP

Like any statistical measure, gross domestic product is a concept that can be both well used and misused. Economists find it especially valuable as an overall indicator of a nation's economic performance. But it is important to realize that GDP has significant weaknesses. Because it includes only the value of goods and services traded in markets, it excludes *nonmarket* production, such as the household services of homemakers discussed earlier. This can cause some problems in comparing the GDP of an industrialized country with the GDP of a highly agrarian nation in which nonmarket production is relatively more important. It also causes problems if nations have different definitions of legal versus illegal activities. For instance, a nation with legalized gambling will count the value of gambling services, which has a reported market value as a legal activity. But in a country where gambling is illegal, individuals who provide such services will not report the market value of gambling activities, and so they will not be counted in that country's GDP. This can complicate comparing GDP in the nation where gambling is legal with GDP in the country that prohibits gambling.

Furthermore, although GDP is often used as a benchmark measure for standard-of-living calculations, it is not necessarily a good measure of the well-being of a nation. No measured figure of total national annual income can take account of changes in the degree of labor market discrimination, declines or improvements in personal safety, or the quantity or quality of leisure time. Measured GDP also says little about our environmental quality of life. As the now-defunct Soviet Union illustrated to the world, the large-scale production of such items as minerals, electricity, and irrigation for farming can have negative effects on the environment: deforestation from strip mining, air and soil pollution from particulate emissions or nuclear accidents at power plants, and erosion of the natural balance between water and salt in bodies of water such as the Aral Sea. Hence it is important to recognize the following point:

GDP is a measure of the value of production in terms of market prices and an indicator of economic activity. It is not a measure of a nation's overall welfare.

Nonetheless, GDP is a relatively accurate and useful measure to map *changes* in the economy's domestic economic performance. Understanding GDP is thus important for recognizing changes in economic performance over time.

CONCEPTS in Brief

- GDP is the total market value of final goods and services produced in an economy during a one-year period by factors of production within the nation's borders. It represents the dollar value of the flow of production over a one-year period.

- To avoid double counting, we look only at final goods and services produced or, equivalently, at value added.

- In measuring GDP, we must exclude (1) purely financial transactions, such as the buying and selling of securities; (2) government transfer payments and private transfer payments; and (3) the transfer of secondhand goods.

- Many other transactions are excluded from measured GDP, among them household services rendered by homemakers, underground economy transactions, and illegal economic activities, even though many of these result in the production of final goods and services.

- GDP is a useful measure for tracking changes in the market value of overall economic activity over time, but it is not a measure of the well-being of a nation's residents because it fails to account for nonmarket transactions, the amount and quality of leisure time, environmental or safety issues, discrimination, and other factors that influence general welfare.

To test your understanding of the concepts covered in this section, go to the Online Review at **www.myeconlab.com/miller.**

TWO MAIN METHODS OF MEASURING GDP

The definition of GDP is the total value of all final goods and services produced during a year. How, exactly, do we go about actually computing this number?

The circular flow diagram presented in Figure 8-1 on page 170 gave us a shortcut method for calculating GDP. We can look at the *flow of expenditures,* which consists of consumption, investment, government purchases of goods and services, and net expenditures in the foreign sector (net exports). This is called the **expenditure approach** to meas-

Expenditure approach
Computing GDP by adding up the dollar value at current market prices of all final goods and services.

Income approach
Measuring GDP by adding up all components of national income, including wages, interest, rent, and profits.

Durable consumer goods
Consumer goods that have a life span of more than three years.

Nondurable consumer goods
Consumer goods that are used up within three years.

Services
Mental or physical labor or help purchased by consumers. Examples are the assistance of physicians, lawyers, dentists, repair personnel, housecleaners, educators, retailers, and wholesalers; things purchased or used by consumers that do not have physical characteristics.

Gross private domestic investment
The creation of capital goods, such as factories and machines, that can yield production and hence consumption in the future. Also included in this definition are changes in business inventories and repairs made to machines or buildings.

Investment
Any use of today's resources to expand tomorrow's production or consumption.

Producer durables, or capital goods
Durable goods having an expected service life of more than three years that are used by businesses to produce other goods and services.

Fixed investment
Purchases by businesses of newly produced producer durables, or capital goods, such as production machinery and office equipment.

Inventory investment
Changes in the stocks of finished goods and goods in process, as well as changes in the raw materials that businesses keep on hand. Whenever inventories are decreasing, inventory investment is negative; whenever they are increasing, inventory investment is positive.

uring GDP, in which we add the dollar value of all final goods and services. We could also use the *flow of income,* looking at the income received by everybody producing goods and services. This is called the **income approach,** in which we add the income received by all factors of production.

Deriving GDP by the Expenditure Approach

To derive GDP using the expenditure approach, we must look at each of the separate components of expenditures and then add them together. These components are consumption expenditures, investment, government expenditures, and net exports.

Consumption Expenditures. How do we spend our income? As households or as individuals, we spend our income through consumption expenditure (C), which falls into three categories: **durable consumer goods, nondurable consumer goods,** and **services.** Durable goods are *arbitrarily* defined as items that last more than three years; they include automobiles, furniture, and household appliances. Nondurable goods are all the rest, such as food and gasoline. Services are intangible commodities: medical care, education, and the like.

Housing expenditures constitute a major proportion of anybody's annual expenditures. Rental payments on apartments are automatically included in consumption expenditure estimates. People who own their homes, however, do not make rental payments. Consequently, government statisticians estimate what is called the *implicit rental value* of existing owner-occupied homes. It is roughly equal to the amount of rent you would have to pay if you did not own the home but were renting it from someone else.

Gross Private Domestic Investment. We now turn our attention to **gross private domestic investment** (I) undertaken by businesses. When economists refer to investment, they are referring to additions to productive capacity. **Investment** may be thought of as an activity that uses resources today in such a way that they allow for greater production in the future and hence greater consumption in the future. When a business buys new equipment or puts up a new factory, it is investing; it is increasing its capacity to produce in the future.

In estimating gross private domestic investment, government statisticians also add consumer expenditures on *new* residential structures because new housing represents an addition to our future productive capacity in the sense that a new house can generate housing services in the future.

The layperson's notion of investment often relates to the purchase of stocks and bonds. For our purposes, such transactions simply represent the *transfer of ownership* of assets called stocks and bonds. Thus you must keep in mind the fact that in economics, investment refers *only* to *additions* to productive capacity, not to transfers of assets.

Fixed versus Inventory Investment. In our analysis, we will consider the basic components of investment. We have already mentioned the first one, which involves a firm's buying equipment or putting up a new factory. These are called **producer durables,** or **capital goods.** A producer durable, or a capital good, is simply a good that is purchased not to be consumed in its current form but to be used to make other goods and services. The purchase of equipment and factories—capital goods—is called **fixed investment.**

The other type of investment has to do with the change in inventories of raw materials and finished goods. Firms do not immediately sell off all their products to consumers. Some of this final product is usually held in inventory waiting to be sold. Firms hold inventories to meet future expected orders for their products. When a firm increases its inventories of finished products, it is engaging in **inventory investment.** Inventories consist of all finished goods on hand, goods in process, and raw materials.

The reason that we can think of a change in inventories as being a type of investment is that an increase in such inventories provides for future increased consumption possibilities. When inventory investment is zero, the firm is neither adding to nor subtracting from the total stock of goods or raw materials on hand. Thus, if the firm keeps the same amount of inventories throughout the year, inventory *investment* has been zero.

How do you suppose that greater use of the Internet by businesses has helped them reduce their inventories?

E - Commerce E X A M P L E

How the Internet Has Contributed to Lower U.S. Inventory Investment

A fundamental development in U.S. business during the 1990s was the widespread implementation of *just-in-time inventory techniques*, which are procedures that companies use to keep inventories from either running out or building up beyond desirable levels. The Internet has facilitated the implementation of many just-in-time inventory techniques. When a company that supplies basic components used in a variety of electronic products experiences an inventory buildup, it has several options for reducing its inventory via the Internet. The company can, for instance, offer some of its inventory for sale on organized business-to-business exchanges that currently handle total transactions exceeding $1 trillion per year. In addition, it can use computer programs offered by software developers such as Ariba and Commerce One to operate its own Internet auctions and sell some of its excess inventory to the highest bidders. Alternatively, the

company can purchase the Web auction services of eBay or other firms to assist in selling off some of its inventory buildup.

There is considerable evidence that the use of Internet-based just-in-time inventory techniques has contributed to the noticeable decline in the ratio of inventories to sales in U.S. manufacturing that is depicted in Figure 8-3. In 1990, the value of this ratio was about 1.75, which means in that year U.S. companies had about 75 percent more items in their inventories than they sold. Since then, this ratio has fallen below 1.35, which could happen only if businesses have just about enough items on hand to match their sales.

For Critical Analysis
What would it mean if the inventory-sales ratio depicted in Figure 8-3 fell below 1.0?

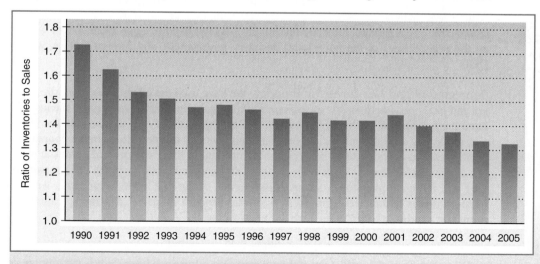

FIGURE 8-3
The Ratio of Inventories to Sales in the United States Since 1990
The ratio of business inventories to sales has dropped considerably in recent years.

Source: U.S. Census Bureau.

Government Expenditures. In addition to personal consumption expenditures, there are government purchases of goods and services (*G*). The government buys goods and services from private firms and pays wages and salaries to government employees. Generally, we value goods and services at the prices at which they are sold. But many government goods and services are not sold in the market. Therefore, we cannot use their market value when computing GDP. The value of these goods is considered equal to their *cost*. For example, the value of a newly built road is considered equal to its construction cost and is included in the GDP for the year it was built.

Net Exports (Foreign Expenditures). To get an accurate representation of gross domestic product, we must include the foreign sector. As U.S. residents, we purchase foreign goods called *imports*. The goods that foreigners purchase from us are our *exports*. To determine the *net* expenditures from the foreign sector, we subtract the value of imports from the value of exports to get net exports (*X*) for a year:

$$\text{Net exports }(X) = \text{total exports} - \text{total imports}$$

To understand why we subtract imports rather than ignoring them altogether, recall that we want to estimate *domestic* output, so we have to subtract U.S. expenditures on the goods produced in other nations.

Presenting the Expenditure Approach

We have just defined the components of GDP using the expenditure approach. When we add them all together, we get a definition for GDP, which is as follows:

$$\text{GDP} = C + I + G + X$$

where

$$C = \text{consumption expenditures}$$

$$I = \text{investment expenditures}$$

$$G = \text{government expenditures}$$

$$X = \text{net exports}$$

The Historical Picture. To get an idea of the relationship among *C*, *I*, *G*, and *X*, look at Figure 8-4, which shows GDP, personal consumption expenditures, government purchases, and gross private domestic investment plus net exports since 1929. When we add up the expenditures of the household, business, government, and foreign sectors, we get GDP.

Depreciation and Net Domestic Product. We have used the terms *gross domestic product* and *gross private domestic investment* without really indicating what *gross* means. The dictionary defines it as "without deductions," the opposite of *net*. Deductions for what? you might ask. The deductions are for something we call **depreciation.** In the course of a year, machines and structures wear out or are used up in the production of domestic product. For example, houses deteriorate as they are occupied, and machines need repairs or they will fall apart and stop working. Most capital, or durable, goods depreciate. An estimate of this is subtracted from gross domestic product to arrive at a figure called **net domestic product (NDP),** which we define as follows:

$$\text{NDP} = \text{GDP} - \text{depreciation}$$

Depreciation is also called **capital consumption allowance** because it is the amount of the capital stock that has been consumed over a one-year period. In essence, it equals the amount a business would have to put aside to repair and replace deteriorating machines. Because we know that

$$\text{GDP} = C + I + G + X$$

Depreciation
Reduction in the value of capital goods over a one-year period due to physical wear and tear and also to obsolescence; also called *capital consumption allowance.*

Net domestic product (NDP)
GDP minus depreciation.

Capital consumption allowance
Another name for depreciation, the amount that businesses would have to save in order to take care of the deterioration of machines and other equipment.

FIGURE 8-4
GDP and Its Components

Here we see a display of gross domestic product, personal consumption expenditures, government purchases, and gross private domestic invest- ment plus net exports for the years since 1929. Actually, during the Great Depression of the 1930s, gross private domestic investment *plus* net exports was negative because we were investing very little at that time.

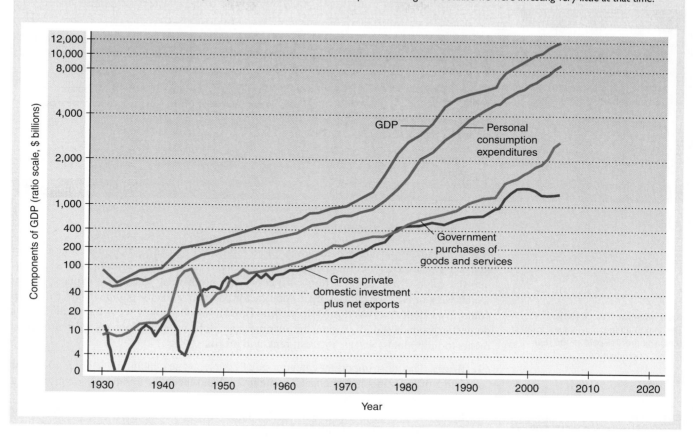

we know that the formula for NDP is

$$\text{NDP} = C + I + G + X - \text{depreciation}$$

Alternatively, because net $I = I -$ depreciation,

$$\text{NDP} = C + \text{net } I + G + X$$

Net investment measures *changes* in our capital stock over time and is positive nearly every year. Because depreciation does not vary greatly from year to year as a percentage of GDP, we get a similar picture of what is happening to our national economy by looking at either NDP or GDP data.

Net investment is an important variable to observe over time nonetheless. If everything else remains the same in an economy, changes in net investment can have dramatic conse- quences for future economic growth (a topic we cover in more detail in Chapter 9). Posi- tive net investment by definition expands the productive capacity of our economy. This means that there is increased capital, which will generate even more income in the future. When net investment is zero, we are investing just enough to take account of depreciation. Our economy's productive capacity remains unchanged. Finally, when net investment is

Net investment
Gross private domestic investment minus an estimate of the wear and tear on the existing capital stock. Net investment therefore measures the change in capital stock over a one-year period.

negative, we can expect negative economic growth prospects in the future. Negative net investment means that our productive capacity is actually declining—we are disinvesting. This actually occurred during the Great Depression.

CONCEPTS in Brief

- The expenditure approach to measuring GDP requires that we add up consumption expenditures, gross private investment, government purchases, and net exports. Consumption expenditures include consumer durables, consumer nondurables, and services.

- Gross private domestic investment *excludes* transfers of asset ownership. It includes only additions to the productive capacity of a nation, repairs on existing capital goods, and changes in business inventories.

- We value government expenditures at their cost because we usually do not have market prices at which to value government goods and services.

- To obtain net domestic product (NDP), we subtract from GDP the year's depreciation of the existing capital stock.

To test your understanding of the concepts covered in this section, go to the Online Review at **www.myeconlab.com/miller.**

Deriving GDP by the Income Approach

Gross domestic income (GDI)
The sum of all income—wages, interest, rent, and profits—paid to the four factors of production.

If you go back to the circular flow diagram in Figure 8-1 on page 170, you see that product markets are at the top of the diagram and factor markets are at the bottom. We can calculate the value of the circular flow of income and product by looking at expenditures—which we just did—or by looking at total factor payments. Factor payments are called income. We calculate **gross domestic income (GDI),** which we will see is identical to gross domestic product (GDP). Using the income approach, we have four categories of payments to individuals: wages, interest, rent, and profits.

Go to www.econtoday.com/chap08 to examine recent trends in U.S. GDP and its components.

1. *Wages.* The most important category is, of course, wages, including salaries and other forms of labor income, such as income in kind and incentive payments. We also count Social Security taxes (both the employees' and the employers' contributions).
2. *Interest.* Here interest payments do not equal the sum of all payments for the use of funds in a year. Instead, interest is expressed in *net* rather than in gross terms. The interest component of total income is only net interest received by households plus net interest paid to us by foreigners. Net interest received by households is the difference between the interest they receive (from savings accounts, certificates of deposit, and the like) and the interest they pay (to banks for mortgages, credit cards, and other loans).
3. *Rent.* Rent is all income earned by individuals for the use of their real (nonmonetary) assets, such as farms, houses, and stores. As stated previously, we have to include here the implicit rental value of owner-occupied houses. Also included in this category are royalties received from copyrights, patents, and assets such as oil wells.
4. *Profits.* Our last category includes total gross corporate profits plus *proprietors' income.* Proprietors' income is income earned from the operation of unincorporated businesses, which include sole proprietorships, partnerships, and producers' cooperatives. It is unincorporated business profit.

Indirect business taxes
All business taxes except the tax on corporate profits. Indirect business taxes include sales and business property taxes.

All of the payments listed are *actual* factor payments made to owners of the factors of production. When we add them together, though, we do not yet have gross domestic income. We have to take account of two other components: **indirect business taxes,** such as sales and business property taxes, and depreciation, which we have already discussed.

Indirect Business Taxes. Indirect taxes are the (nonincome) taxes paid by consumers when they buy goods and services. When you buy a book, you pay the price of the book plus any state and local sales tax. The business is actually acting as the government's agent in collecting the sales tax, which it in turn passes on to the government. Such taxes therefore represent a business expense and are included in gross domestic income.

Depreciation. Just as we had to deduct depreciation to get from GDP to NDP, so we must *add* depreciation to go from net domestic income to gross domestic income. Depreciation can be thought of as the portion of the current year's GDP that is used to replace physical capital consumed in the process of production. Because somebody has paid for the replacement, depreciation must be added as a component of gross domestic income.

The last two components of GDP—indirect business taxes and depreciation—are called **nonincome expense items.**

Figure 8-5 on the following page shows a comparison between gross domestic product and gross domestic income for 2005. Whether you decide to use the expenditure approach or the income approach, you will come out with the same number. There are sometimes statistical discrepancies, but they are usually relatively small.

Nonincome expense items
The total of indirect business taxes and depreciation.

CONCEPTS in Brief

- To derive GDP using the income approach, we add up all factor payments, including wages, interest, rent, and profits.
- To get an accurate estimate of GDP with this method, we must also add indirect business taxes and depreciation to those total factor payments.

To test your understanding of the concepts covered in this section, go to the Online Review at www.myeconlab.com/miller.

OTHER COMPONENTS OF NATIONAL INCOME ACCOUNTING

Gross domestic income or product does not really tell how much income people have access to for spending purposes. To get to those kinds of data, we must make some adjustments, which we now do.

National Income (NI)

We know that net domestic product (NDP) is the total market value of goods and services available to consume and to add to the capital stock. NDP however, fails to include business transfers, which should count as part of income earned by U.S. factors of production, but does not include indirect business taxes, which should not. We therefore add to NDP business transfers net of indirect business taxes and other related adjustments. We also add net U.S. income earned abroad. The result is what we define as **national income (NI)**— income earned by all factors of production in the United States.

National income (NI)
The total of all factor payments to resource owners. It can be obtained from net domestic product (NDP) by subtracting indirect business taxes and transfers and adding net U.S. income earned abroad and other business income adjustments.

Personal Income (PI)

National income does not actually represent what is available to individuals to spend because some people obtain income for which they have provided no concurrent good or service and others earn income but do not receive it. In the former category are mainly recipients of transfer payments from the government, such as Social Security, welfare, and

FIGURE 8-5
Gross Domestic Product and Gross Domestic Income, 2005 (in billions of 2005 dollars per year)
By using the two different methods of computing the output of the economy, we come up with gross domestic product and gross domestic income, which are by definition equal. One approach focuses on expenditures, or the flow of product; the other approach concentrates on income, or the flow of costs.

Source: U.S. Department of Commerce. Author's estimates.

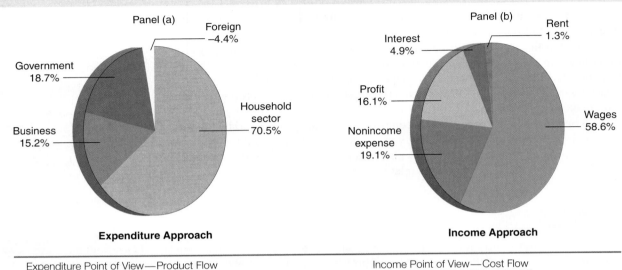

Expenditure Point of View—Product Flow Expenditures by Different Sectors:		Income Point of View—Cost Flow Domestic Income (at Factor Cost):	
Household sector		*Wages*	
Personal consumption expenses	$8,644.4	All wages, salaries, and	
		supplemental employee compensation	$7,176.2
Government sector		*Rent*	
Purchase of goods and services	2,290.3	All rental income of individuals plus implicit	
		rent on owner-occupied dwellings	159.2
Business sector		*Interest*	
Gross private domestic investment		Net interest paid by business	600.1
(including depreciation)	1,861.9		
		Profit	
Foreign sector		Proprietorial income	894.0
Net exports of goods and services	−550.5	Corporate profits before taxes deducted	1,077.7
		Nonincome expense items	
		Indirect business taxes	921.6
		Depreciation	1,539.7
		Statistical discrepancy	−122.4
Gross domestic product	$12,246.1	Gross domestic income	$12,246.1

food stamps. These payments represent shifts of funds within the economy by way of the government, where no good or service is concurrently rendered in exchange. For the other category, income earned but not received, the most obvious examples are corporate retained earnings that are plowed back into the business, contributions to social insurance,

	Billions of Dollars
Gross domestic product (GDP)	12,246.1
Minus depreciation	−1,539.7
Net domestic product (NDP)	10,706.4
Minus indirect business taxes and transfers	−998.3
Plus other business income adjustments	1,035.6
Plus net U.S. income earned abroad	22.6
National income (NI)	10,766.3
Minus corporate taxes, Social Security contributions, corporate retained earnings	−1,341.0
Plus government transfer payments	+775.9
Personal income (PI)	10,201.2
Minus personal income tax and nontax payments	−1,289.3
Disposable personal income (DPI)	8,911.9

TABLE 8-2
Going from GDP to Disposable Income, 2005

Source: U.S. Department of Commerce, and author's estimates

and corporate income taxes. When transfer payments are added and when income earned but not received is subtracted, we end up with **personal income (PI)**—income *received* by the factors of production prior to the payment of personal income taxes.

Disposable Personal Income (DPI)

Everybody knows that you do not get to take home all your salary. To get **disposable personal income (DPI),** we subtract all personal income taxes from personal income. This is the income that individuals have left for consumption and saving.

Deriving the Components of GDP

Table 8-2 shows how to derive the various components of GDP. It explains how to go from gross domestic product to net domestic product to national income to personal income and then to disposable personal income. On the frontpapers of your book, you can see the historical record for GDP, NDP, NI, PI, and DPI for selected years since 1929.

We have completed our rundown of the different ways that GDP can be computed and of the different variants of national income and product. What we have not yet touched on is the difference between national income measured in this year's dollars and national income representing real goods and services.

Personal income (PI)
The amount of income that households actually receive before they pay personal income taxes.

Disposable personal income (DPI)
Personal income after personal income taxes have been paid.

CONCEPTS in Brief

- To obtain national income, we subtract indirect business taxes from net domestic product. National income gives us a measure of all factor payments to resource owners.

- To obtain personal income, we must add government transfer payments, such as Social Security benefits and food stamps. We must subtract income earned but not received by factor owners, such as corporate retained earnings, Social Security contributions, and corporate income taxes.

- To obtain disposable personal income, we subtract all personal income taxes from personal income. Disposable personal income is income that individuals actually have for consumption or saving.

To test your understanding of the concepts covered in this section, go to the Online Review at www.myeconlab.com/miller.

DISTINGUISHING BETWEEN NOMINAL AND REAL VALUES

Nominal values
The values of variables such as GDP and investment expressed in current dollars, also called *money values;* measurement in terms of the actual market prices at which goods and services are sold.

Real values
Measurement of economic values after adjustments have been made for changes in the average of prices between years.

So far, we have shown how to measure *nominal* income and product. When we say "nominal," we are referring to income and product expressed in the current "face value" of today's dollar. Given the existence of inflation or deflation in the economy, we must also be able to distinguish between the **nominal values** that we will be looking at and the **real values** underlying them. Nominal values are expressed in current dollars. Real income involves our command over goods and services—purchasing power—and therefore depends on money income and a set of prices. Thus real income refers to nominal income corrected for changes in the weighted average of all prices. In other words, we must make an adjustment for changes in the price level. Consider an example. Nominal income *per person* in 1960 was only about $2,900 per year. In 2005, nominal income per person was about $42,000. Were people really that bad off in 1960? No, for nominal income in 1960 is expressed in 1960 prices, not in the prices of today. In today's dollars, the per-person income of 1960 would be closer to $14,000, or about 33 percent of today's income per person. This is a meaningful comparison between income in 1960 and income today. Next we will show how we can translate nominal measures of income into real measures by using an appropriate price index, such as the CPI or the GDP deflator discussed in Chapter 7.

Correcting GDP for Price Changes

Constant dollars
Dollars expressed in terms of real purchasing power using a particular year as the base or standard of comparison, in contrast to current dollars.

If a digital videodisc (DVD) costs $20 this year, 10 DVDs will have a market value of $200. If next year they cost $25 each, the same 10 DVDs will have a market value of $250. In this case, there is no increase in the total quantity of DVDs, but the market value will have increased by one-fourth. Apply this to every single good and service produced and sold in the United States, and you realize that changes in GDP, measured in *current* dollars, may not be a very useful indication of economic activity. If we are really interested in variations in the *real* output of the economy, we must correct GDP (and just about everything else we look at) for changes in the average of overall prices from year to year. Basically, we need to generate an index that approximates the changes in average prices and then divide that estimate into the value of output in current dollars to adjust the value of output to what is called **constant dollars,** or dollars corrected for general price level changes. This price-corrected GDP is called *real GDP.*

How much has correcting for price changes caused real GDP to differ from nominal GDP during the past few years?

E X A M P L E

Correcting GDP for Price Index Changes, 1995–2005

Let's take a numerical example to see how we can adjust GDP for changes in the price index. We must pick an appropriate price index in order to adjust for these price level changes. We mentioned the Consumer Price Index, the Producer Price Index, and the GDP deflator in Chapter 7. Let's use the GDP deflator to adjust our figures. Table 8-3 gives 11 years of GDP figures. Nominal GDP figures are shown in column 2. The price index (GDP deflator) is in column 3, with

base year of 2000 when the GDP deflator equals 100. Column 4 shows real (inflation-adjusted) GDP in 2000 dollars.

The formula for real GDP is

$$\text{Real GDP} = \frac{\text{nominal GDP}}{\text{price index}} \times 100$$

The step-by-step derivation of real (constant-dollar) GDP is as follows: The base year is 2000, so the price index for that year must equal 100. In 2000, nominal GDP was $9,817.0 billion, and so was real GDP expressed in 2000 dollars. In 2001, the price index increased to 102.374. Thus, to correct 2001's nominal GDP for inflation, we divide the price index, 102.374, into the nominal GDP figure of $10,100.8 billion and then multiply it by 100. The rounded result is $9,866.6 billion, which is 2001 GDP expressed in terms of the purchasing power of dollars in 2000. What about a situation when the price index is lower than in 2000? Look at 1995. Here the price index shown in column 3 is only 92.106. That means that in 1995, the average of all prices was about 92 percent of

prices in 2000. To obtain 1995 GDP expressed in terms of 2000 purchasing power, we divide nominal GDP, $7,397.7 billion, by 92.106 and then multiply by 100. The rounded result is a larger number—$8,031.7 billion. Column 4 in Table 8-3 is a better measure of how the economy has performed than column 2, which shows nominal GDP changes.

For Critical Analysis

A few years ago, the base year for the GDP deflator was 1996. What does a change in the base year for the price index affect?

(1)	(2) Nominal GDP (billions of dollars	(3) Price Index (base year	(4) = [(2) ÷ (3)] × 100 Real GDP (billions of dollars per year,
Year	per year)	2000 = 100)	in constant 2000 dollars)
1995	7,397.7	92.106	8,031.7
1996	7,816.9	93.852	8,328.9
1997	8,304.3	95.413	8,703.5
1998	8,747.0	96.472	9,066.9
1999	9,268.4	97.868	9,470.3
2000	9,817.0	100.000	9,817.0
2001	10,100.8	102.374	9,866.6
2002	10,480.8	103.945	10,083.0
2003	10,987.9	105.673	10,398.0
2004	11,602.3	108.737	10,670.1
2005	12,246.1	111.348	10,998.0

TABLE 8-3

Correcting GDP for Price Index Changes

To correct GDP for price index changes, we first have to pick a price index (the GDP deflator) with a specific year as its base. In our example, the base level is 2000 prices; the price index for that year is 100. To obtain 2000 constant-dollar GDP, we divide the price index into nominal GDP and multiply by 100. In other words, we divide column 3 into column 2 and multiply by 100. This gives us column 4, which (taking into account rounding of the deflator) is a measure of real GDP expressed in 2000 purchasing power.

Source: U.S. Department of Commerce, Bureau of Economic Analysis, author's estimates.

Plotting Nominal and Real GDP

Nominal GDP and real GDP since 1970 are plotted in Figure 8-6 on the following page. Notice that there is quite a big gap between the two GDP figures, reflecting the amount of inflation that has occurred. Note, further, that the choice of a base year is arbitrary. We have chosen 2000 as the base year in our example. This happens to be the base year that is currently used by the government.

Per Capita GDP

Looking at changes in real GDP may be deceiving, particularly if the population size has changed significantly. If real GDP over a 10-year period went up 100 percent, you might jump to the conclusion that the real income of a typical person in the economy had increased by that amount. But what if during the same period population increased by 200 percent? Then what would you say? Certainly, the amount of real GDP per person, or *per*

Economics Front and Center

To contemplate a situation in which it would be important to make a clear distinction between nominal GDP and real GDP, consider **Failing to Distinguish Between Nominal GDP and Real GDP,** on page 189.

FIGURE 8-6
Nominal and Real GDP
Here we plot both nominal and real GDP. Real GDP is expressed in the

purchasing power of 2000 dollars. The gap between the two represents price level changes.

Source: U.S. Department of Commerce.

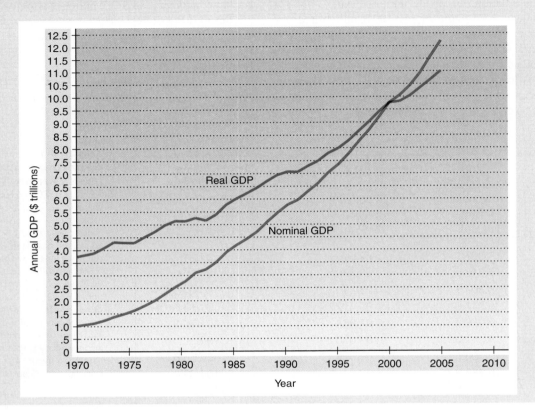

capita real GDP, would have fallen, even though *total* real GDP had risen. What we must do to account not only for price changes but also for population changes is first deflate GDP and then divide by the total population, doing this for each year. If we were to look at certain less developed countries, we would find that in many cases, even though real GDP has risen over the past several decades, per capita real GDP has remained constant or fallen because the population has grown just as rapidly or even faster.

The Chain-Weighted Measure of the Growth in Real GDP

In December 1995, the Commerce Department's Bureau of Economic Analysis (BEA) made a fundamental change in the way it computes real GDP. Remember that real GDP consists of consumer spending, business investment, government expenditures on goods and services, and net foreign trade. To calculate real GDP, the BEA had used a weighted sum of 1,100 components of these four categories. Until 1996, these 1,100 components were fixed in weight, and their relative importance changed only periodically. For example, the last revision was made in 1987. Otherwise stated, the BEA had been using a *fixed-weight* measure of changes in real GDP.

Now the BEA changes the weights of the different components of real GDP to reflect changes in their relative prices and in their relative shares in the overall economy's output. This measure is called *chain-weighted real GDP*. To calculate a year's *change* in chain-weight real GDP, it is necessary to compare one year's chain-weighted real GDP with the previous year's value. The BEA publishes data on chain-weighted real GDP, and you can find chain-weighted real GDP statistics on the front-papers of this book, which show our national income accounts.

Why do you suppose that real GDP has literally been getting less heavy with each passing year?

EXAMPLE

Real GDP Really Lightens Up

Apparently, the U.S. economy is worth its weight in Pentium chips. At least, that is how some observers have summed up the latest trend in U.S. economic performance. The real value of total output of goods and services is about five times what it was about 50 years ago. But the *physical weight* of U.S. gross domestic product is only slightly higher today than it was 50 or even 100 years ago. Only a small portion of the growth of real GDP stems from increases in the tonnage of physical products in their final forms. The remaining portion represents new insights into how to rearrange those physical materials into new forms, many of which are lighter than the old ones.

Consider that a traditional heavyweight good produced in the U.S. economy, a ton (2,000 pounds) of rolled steel, has an inflation-adjusted price of about $370. At this price, produc-

tion of rolled steel contributes only 19 cents per pound to real GDP. By way of contrast, a microprocessor with an inflation-adjusted price of $500 weighs about 0.02 pound, which implies a $25,000-per-pound contribution to real GDP. A Viagra tablet that weighs about 0.0007 pound has an inflation-adjusted price of about $8, so it contributes more than $11,000 per pound to total real GDP. A downloadable antivirus program that sells for an inflation-adjusted price of $50 does not weigh anything, and this pushes the average weight of real GDP even further downward.

For Critical Analysis
Does a reduction in the average weight of a nation's output necessarily increase the nation's real GDP?

CONCEPTS in Brief

- To correct nominal GDP for price changes, we first use a base year for our price index and assign it the number 100. Then we construct an index based on how a weighted average of prices has changed relative to that base year. For example, if in the next year a weighted average of the prices indicates that prices have increased by 10 percent, we would assign it the number 110. We then divide each year's price index, so constructed, into its respective nominal GDP figure (and multiply by 100).

- We can divide the population into real GDP to obtain per capita real GDP.

To test your understanding of the concepts covered in this section, go to the Online Review at www.myeconlab.com/miller.

COMPARING GDP THROUGHOUT THE WORLD

It is relatively easy to compare the standard of living of a family in Los Angeles with that of one living in Boston. Both families get paid in dollars and can buy the same goods and services at Wal-Mart, McDonald's, and Costco. It is not so easy, however, to make a similar comparison between a family living in the United States and one in, say, India. The first problem concerns money. Indians get paid in rupees, their national currency, and buy goods and services with those rupees. How do we compare the average standard of living measured in rupees with that measured in dollars?

Foreign Exchange Rates

Foreign exchange rate
The price of one currency in terms of another.

In earlier chapters, you have encountered international examples that involved local currencies, but the dollar equivalent has always been given. The dollar equivalent is calculated by looking up the **foreign exchange rate** that is published daily in major newspapers throughout the world. If you know that you can exchange $1.25 per euro, the exchange rate is 1.25 to 1 (or otherwise stated, a dollar is worth 0.80 euros). So, if French incomes per capita are, say, 23,168.80 euros, that translates, at an exchange rate of $1.25 per euro, to $28,961. For years, statisticians calculated relative GDP by simply adding up each country's GDP in its local currency and dividing by the respective dollar exchange rate.

True Purchasing Power

The problem with simply using foreign exchange rates to convert other countries' GDP and per capita GDP into dollars is that not all goods and services are bought and sold in a world market. Restaurant food, housecleaning services, and home repairs do not get exchanged across countries. In countries that have very low wages, those kinds of services are much cheaper than foreign exchange rate computations would imply. Government statistics claiming that per capita income in some poor country is only $300 a year seem shocking. But such a statistic does not tell you the true standard of living of people in that country. Only by looking at what is called **purchasing power parity** can you determine other countries' true standards of living compared to ours.

Purchasing power parity
Adjustment in exchange rate conversions that takes into account differences in the true cost of living across countries.

Given that nations use different currencies, how can we compare nations' levels of real GDP per capita?

International EXAMPLE

Purchasing Power Parity Comparisons of World Incomes

A few years ago, the International Monetary Fund accepted the purchasing power parity approach as the correct one. It started presenting international statistics on each country's GDP relative to every other's based on purchasing power parity. The results were surprising. As you can see from Table 8-4, China's per capita GDP is higher based on purchasing power parity than when measured at market foreign exchange rates.

For Critical Analysis
What is the percentage increase in China's per capita GDP when one switches from foreign exchange rates to purchasing power parity?

**TABLE 8-4
Comparing GDP
Internationally**

Source: World Bank.

Country	Annual GDP Based on Purchasing Power Parity (billions of U.S. dollars)	Per Capita GDP Based on Purchasing Power Parity (U.S. dollars)	Per Capita GDP Based on Foreign Exchange Rates (U.S. dollars)
United States	10,413.3	36,110	35,400
Japan	3,481.4	27,380	34,010
China	5,791.9	4,520	960

(continued)

Country	Annual GDP Based on Purchasing Power Parity (billions of U.S. dollars)	Per Capita GDP Based on Purchasing Power Parity (U.S. dollars)	Per Capita GDP Based on Foreign Exchange Rates (U.S. dollars)
Germany	2,226.0	26,980	22,740
France	1,608.8	27,040	22,240
Russia	1,165.1	8,080	2,130
India	2,778.0	2,650	470
Italy	1,510.0	26,170	19,080
United Kingdom	1,594.2	26,580	25,510
Brazil	1,299.8	7,450	2,830

Table 8-4 *(continued)*

CONCEPTS in Brief

- The foreign exchange rate is the price of one currency in terms of another.

- Statisticians often calculate relative GDP by adding up each country's GDP in its local currency and dividing by the dollar exchange rate.

- Because not all goods and services are bought and sold in the world market, we must correct exchange rate conversions of other countries' GDP figures to take into account differences in the true cost of living across countries.

To test your understanding of the concepts covered in this section, go to the Online Review at **www.myeconlab.com/miller.**

CASE STUDY: Economics Front and Center

Failing to Distinguish Between Nominal GDP and Real GDP

Rodriguez heads up the international acquisitions unit of a U.S.-based firm. She has just received a proposal from a business in Ecuador that has expressed an interest in selling its operations to her firm. As part of its sales pitch, the company that has put itself up for sale touts Ecuador as a nation in which gross domestic product has experienced positive growth for more than four decades. This is proof, the company claims in its proposal, that Ecuador has an excellent business climate.

Rodriguez knows that Ecuador's price level fluctuated considerably throughout the 1990s and into the 2000s. Indeed, a quick look at some statistical sources indicates to Rodriguez that Ecuador's price level rose very rapidly in the early 1990s, declined in the late 1990s, and increased once more in the early

2000s. She wonders if the company offering to sell its operations has bothered to adjust its GDP figures for these wide changes in the level of prices. She finds herself becoming somewhat skeptical of the entire proposal.

Points to Analyze

1. *Why is it possible that real GDP in Ecuador might have declined during certain years in the early 1990s even if the nation's nominal GDP increased every year?*

2. *If Ecuador's nominal GDP rose during the late 1990s when average prices were falling, what unambiguously happened to the nation's real GDP?*

Does More GDP Make People Happier?

Concepts Applied
- Gross Domestic Product
- Limitations of GDP as a Measure of Economic Activity

Each year, a group of social scientists canvasses a random sample of 15,000 Europeans, asking questions such as, "On the whole, are you very satisfied, fairly satisfied, not very satisfied, or not at all satisfied with the life you lead?" Since 1975, about 27 percent of Europeans have indicated that they are very satisfied with the lives they lead, about 5 percent have answered that they are not at all satisfied, and the remainder have fallen between the two extremes. Researchers have asked similar questions in other surveys conducted in nations around the world. By assigning numerical "scores" to answers, such as "very satisfied equals 4" and "not at all satisfied equals 1," these researchers have developed "quantitative" measurements of "life satisfaction." Then they have sought to uncover the main determinants of an average person's level of happiness.

Can Happiness Be Measured?

Typically, economists have more confidence in results based on how people in an economy *actually* behave than in people's answers to questions about how they *say* they behave or how they *feel* about the choices they make. Most economists have doubts about whether answers to survey questions are reliable objective measures of "happiness."

Certainly, economists recognize that individuals can rate whether their satisfaction from consuming one item is greater than their satisfaction from consuming another. They also acknowledge that individuals can judge whether their overall satisfaction this week is higher than it was last week. Many economists question, however, whether one person's satisfaction from consuming an item can be legitimately compared with another's. They also question whether one person's overall level of happiness at any point in time can be ranked against the happiness of someone else. Indeed, most economists long ago gave up on the idea of developing any objective measures of individual satisfaction.

An Undeniable Fact: Measured Life Satisfaction Is Related to Gross Domestic Product

Nevertheless, a few economists have sought to defend the usefulness of real GDP as a general indicator of the overall well-being of a nation's residents. In answer to various claims that overall global welfare has fallen dramatically even in the face of considerable advances in world real GDP, these economists have studied the relationship between survey measures of life satisfaction and real GDP per person.

They point out that study after study shows that survey measures of life satisfaction are related to real GDP per person. Figure 8-7, for instance, displays average values of an index of life satisfaction for groups of nations with high, medium, and low values of real GDP per person. As you can see, countries with higher average real GDP per person have higher reported levels of life satisfaction. This positive relationship between real GDP and survey measures of happiness appears to hold true even after taking into account other factors likely to influence people's reported life satisfaction, such as a happy marriage, good health, or spiritual contentment. Thus, if—and this is a *big* if—one can place any value on life satisfaction surveys, real GDP per person appears to be one significant factor affecting reported relative levels of happiness.

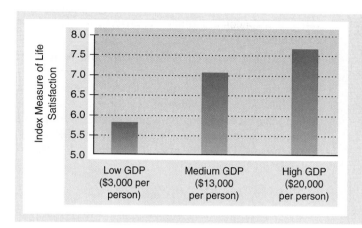

FIGURE 8-7

An Index Measure of Reported Life Satisfaction and Average Real GDP per Person

An index measure of overall life satisfaction gleaned from survey questions rises as average real GDP per person increases.

Source: Michael Hagerty and Ruut Veenhoven, "Wealth and Happiness Revisited: Growing Wealth of Nations *Does* Go with Greater Happiness," University of California at Davis and Erasmus University, December 2000.

For Critical Analysis

1. How can real GDP per person be higher in one country than in another country even if the first country has lower aggregate real GDP than the second?
2. Under what circumstance might a significant rise in *nominal* GDP per person lead to a widespread *reduction* in overall life satisfaction, after taking into account marital happiness, good health, and other factors likely to affect life satisfaction?

Web Resources

1. To read a discussion of reasons why rising incomes do not necessarily make people happier, use the link available at www.econtoday.com/chap08.
2. For an examination of the pros and cons of GDP and other possible measures of a nation's average standard of living, go to www.econtoday.com/chap08.

Research Project

What are some of the key arguments favoring using real GDP per person as an indicator of average life satisfaction within a nation? What are important arguments against using real GDP per person as a measure of the happiness of a typical resident of a nation?

SUMMARY DISCUSSION of Learning Objectives

1. **The Circular Flow of Income and Output:** The circular flow of income and output captures two fundamental principles: (a) In every economic transaction, the seller receives exactly the same amount that the buyer spends; and (b) goods and services flow in one direction, and money payments flow in the other direction. In the circular flow, households ultimately purchase the nation's total output of final goods and services. They make these purchases using income—wages, rents, interest, and profits—earned from selling labor, land, capital, and entrepreneurial services. Hence the values of total income and total output must be the same in the circular flow.

2. **Gross Domestic Product (GDP):** A nation's gross domestic product is the total market value of its final output of goods and services produced within a given year using factors of production located within the nation's borders. Because GDP measures the value of a flow of production during a year in terms of market prices, it is not a measure of a nation's wealth.

3. **The Limitations of Using GDP as a Measure of National Welfare:** Gross domestic product is a useful measure for tracking year-to-year changes in the value of a nation's overall economic activity in terms of market prices. But it excludes nonmarket transactions that may

contribute to or detract from general welfare. It also fails to account for factors such as labor market discrimination, personal safety, environmental quality, and the amount of and quality of leisure time available to a nation's residents. That is why GDP is not an accurate measure of national well-being.

4. **The Expenditure Approach to Tabulating GDP:** To calculate GDP using the expenditure approach, we sum consumption spending, investment expenditures, government spending, and net export expenditures. Thus we add up the total amount spent on newly produced goods and services during the year to obtain the dollar value of the output produced and purchased during the year.

5. **The Income Approach to Computing GDP:** To tabulate GDP using the income approach, we add total wages and salaries, rental income, interest income, profits, and nonincome expense items—indirect business taxes and depreciation—to obtain gross domestic income, which is equivalent to gross domestic product. Thus the total value of all income earnings (equivalent to total factor costs) equals GDP.

6. **Distinguishing Between Nominal GDP and Real GDP:** Nominal GDP is the value of newly produced output during the current year measured at current market prices. Real GDP adjusts the value of current output into constant dollars by correcting for changes in the overall level of prices from year to year. To calculate real GDP, we divide nominal GDP by the price index (the GDP deflator) and multiply by 100.

KEY TERMS AND CONCEPTS

capital consumption allowance (178)

constant dollars (184)

depreciation (178)

disposable personal income (DPI) (183)

durable consumer goods (176)

expenditure approach (175)

final goods and services (170)

fixed investment (176)

foreign exchange rate (188)

gross domestic income (GDI) (180)

gross domestic product (GDP) (171)

gross private domestic investment (176)

income approach (176)

indirect business taxes (180)

intermediate goods (172)

inventory investment (176)

investment (176)

national income (NI) (181)

national income accounting (169)

net domestic product (NDP) (178)

net investment (179)

nominal values (184)

nondurable consumer goods (176)

nonincome expense items (182)

personal income (PI) (183)

producer durables, or capital goods (176)

purchasing power parity (188)

real values (184)

services (176)

total income (169)

value added (172)

PROBLEMS

Answers to the odd-numbered problems appear at the back of the book.

8-1. Suppose that at the end of this year a parent decides to leave income-earning employment and remove a two-year-old child from private day care. Next year, the parent will stay home to care for the child. How will the fact that this individual will not work in the marketplace next year affect measured GDP?

8-2. In Problem 8-1, how will measured GDP be affected by the fact that this individual, instead of the private day-care center, will be providing child care?

8-3. Consider the following hypothetical data for the U.S. economy in 2010 (all amounts are in trillions of dollars).

Consumption	11.0
Indirect business taxes	.8
Depreciation	1.3
Government spending	1.8
Imports	1.7
Gross private domestic investment	2.0
Exports	1.5

a. Based on the data, what is GDP? NDP? NI?

b. Suppose that in 2011, exports fall to $1.3 trillion, imports rise to $1.85 trillion, and gross private domestic investment falls to $1.25 trillion. What will GDP be in 2011, assuming that other values do not change between 2010 and 2011?

c. Note that according to the fictitious data in (b), depreciation (capital consumption allowance) exceeds gross private domestic investment in 2011. How would this affect future U.S. productivity, particularly if it were to continue beyond 2011?

8-4. Look back at Table 8-3 on page 185, which explains how to calculate real GDP in terms of 2000 constant dollars. Change the base year to 2004. Recalculate the price index, and then recalculate real GDP—that is, express column 4 of Table 8-3 in terms of 2004 dollars instead of 2000 dollars.

8-5. Consider the following hypothetical data for the U.S. economy in 2010 (in trillions of dollars), and assume that there are no statistical discrepancies or other adjustments.

Profit	2.8
Indirect business taxes	.8
Rent	.7
Interest	.8
Wages	8.2
Depreciation	1.3
Consumption	11.0
Exports	1.5
Government and business transfer payments	2.0
Personal income taxes and nontax payments	1.7
Imports	1.7
Corporate taxes and retained earnings	.5
Social Security contributions	2.0
Government spending	1.8

a. What is gross domestic income? GDP?

b. What is gross private domestic investment?

c. What is personal income? Personal disposable income?

8-6. Which of the following are production activities that are included in GDP? Which are not?

a. Mr. King paints his own house.

b. Mr. King paints houses for a living.

c. Mrs. King earns income by taking baby photos in her home photography studio.

d. Mrs. King takes photos of planets and stars as part of her astronomy hobby.

e. E*Trade charges fees to process Internet orders for stock trades.

f. Mr. Ho purchases 300 shares of stock via an Internet trade order.

g. Mrs. Ho receives a Social Security payment.

h. Ms. Chavez makes a $300 payment for an Internet-based course on stock trading.

i. Mr. Langham sells a used laptop computer to his neighbor.

8-7. Explain what happens to contributions to GDP in each of the following situations.

a. A woman who makes a living charging for investment advice on her Internet Web site marries one of her clients, to whom she now provides advice at no charge.

b. A tennis player who won two top professional tournaments earlier this year as an unpaid amateur turns professional and continues his streak by winning two more before the year is out.

c. A company that had been selling used firearms illegally finally gets around to obtaining an operating license and performing background checks as specified by law prior to each gun sale.

8-8. Explain what happens to the official measure of GDP in each of the following situations.

a. Air quality improves significantly throughout the United States, but there are no effects on aggregate production or on market prices of final goods and services.

b. The U.S. government spends considerably less on antipollution efforts this year than it did in recent years.

c. The quality of cancer treatments increases, so patients undergo fewer treatments, which hospitals continue to provide at the same price as before.

8-9. Which of the following activities of a computer manufacturer during the current year are included in this year's measure of GDP?

a. The manufacturer purchases a chip in June, uses it as a component in a computer in August, and sells the computer to a customer in November.

b. A retail outlet of the company sells a computer manufactured during the current year.

c. A marketing arm of the company receives fee income during the current year when a buyer of one of its computers elects to use the computer manufacturer as her Internet service provider.

8-10. Consider the following table for the economy of a nation whose residents produce five final goods.

Good	2005 Price	2005 Quantity	2009 Price	2009 Quantity
Shampoo	$ 2	15	$ 4	20
DVD drives	200	10	250	10
Books	40	5	50	4
Milk	3	10	4	3
Candy	1	40	2	20

Assuming a 2005 base year:

a. What is nominal GDP for 2005 and 2009?

b. What is real GDP for 2005 and 2009?

8-11. In the table for Problem 8-10, if 2005 is the base year, what is the price index for 2005? For 2009? (Round decimal fractions to the nearest tenth.)

8-12. Consider the following table for the economy of a nation whose residents produce four final goods.

Good	2007 Price	2007 Quantity	2008 Price	2008 Quantity
Computers	$1,000	10	$800	15
Bananas	6	3,000	11	1,000
Televisions	100	500	150	300
Cookies	1	10,000	2	10,000

Assuming a 2008 base year:

a. What is nominal GDP for 2007 and 2008?

b. What is real GDP for 2007 and 2008?

8-13. In the table for Problem 8-12, if 2008 is the base year, what is the price index for 2007? (Round decimal fractions to the nearest tenth.)

8-14. Suppose that early in a year, a hurricane hits a town in Florida and destroys a substantial number of homes. A portion of this stock of housing, which had a market value of $100 million (not including the market value of the land), was uninsured. The owners of the residences spent a total of $5 million during the rest of the year to pay salvage companies to help them save remaining belongings. A small percentage of uninsured owners had sufficient resources to spend a total of $15 million during the year to pay construction companies to rebuild their homes. Some were able to devote their own time, the opportunity cost of which was valued at $3 million, to work on rebuilding their homes. The remaining people, however, chose to sell their land at its market value and abandon the remains of their houses. What was the combined effect of these transactions on GDP for this year? (Hint: Which transactions took place in the markets for final goods and services?) In what ways, if any, does the effect on GDP reflect a loss in welfare for these individuals?

8-15. Suppose that in 2009, geologists discover large reserves of oil under the tundra in Alaska. These reserves have a market value estimated at $50 billion at current oil prices. Oil companies spend $1 billion to hire workers and move and position equipment to begin exploratory pumping during that same year. In the process of loading some of the oil onto tankers at a port, one company accidentally spills some of the oil into a bay and ultimately pays more than $1 billion to other companies to clean it up. The oil spill kills thousands of birds, seals, and other wildlife. What was the combined effect of these events on GDP for this year? (Hint: Which transactions took place in the markets for final goods and services?) In what ways, if any, does the effect on GDP reflect a loss in national welfare?

ECONOMICS ON THE NET

Tracking the Components of Gross Domestic Product One way to keep tabs on the components of GDP is via the FRED database at the Web site of the Federal Reserve Bank of St. Louis.

Title: Gross Domestic Product and Components

Navigation: Use the link at www.econtoday.com/chap08 to visit the home page of the Federal Reserve Bank of St. Louis. Click on *FRED*. Then click on *Gross Domestic Product and Components.*

Application

1. Click on *Gross Domestic Product.* Write down nominal GDP data for the past 10 quarters.

2. Back up to *Real Gross Domestic Product in Fixed 2000 Dollars.* Write down the amounts for the past 10 quarters. Use the formula on page 184 to calculate the price level for each quarter. Has the price level decreased or increased in recent quarters?

For Group Study and Analysis Divide the class into "consumption," "investment," "government sector," and "foreign sector" groups. Have each group evaluate the contribution of each category of spending to GDP and to its quarter-to-quarter volatility. Reconvene the class, and discuss the factors that appear to create the most variability in GDP.

If your exam were tomorrow, would you be ready? For each chapter, MyEconLab Practice Tests and Study Plans pinpoint which sections you have mastered and which ones you need to study. That way, you are more efficient with your study time, and you are better prepared for your exams.

In addition to Practice Tests and your personalized Study Plan, you'll find the following media resources in MyEconLab:

1. *Graphs in Motion* animation of Figures 8-1, 8-4, and 8-6.
2. Videos featuring the author, Roger LeRoy Miller, on the following subjects:
   ● What GDP Excludes
   ● Investment and GDP
   ● Comparing GDP Throughout the World

3. Links to the Web sites cited in the marginal Internet Resources, Issues and Applications feature, and Economics on the Net activity.
4. Audio clips of all key terms, additional practice problems, and a PDF version of the material from the print Study Guide.
5. eThemes of the Times, which is a New York Times article to help you understand the real-world applications of what you are learning.

To see how it works, turn to page 16 and then go to www.myeconlab.com/miller.

Get Ahead of the Curve

Chapter 9

Global Economic Growth and Development

Businesspeople typically wish to market their products in nations with strong growth prospects. To assess a country's outlook for growth, they often examine its stock prices. They reason that stock prices should depend on firms' anticipated future earnings, because if investors anticipate that firms will earn more in the future, they are more likely to buy the firms' stocks today. In turn, firms' earnings should be positively related to *productivity*, or the ability to produce goods and services with given quantities of labor and capital. Thus higher stock prices should reflect a favorable outlook for productivity and, in turn, for economic growth.

What is economic growth, how do we measure it, and what are its effects? These are the questions this chapter considers.

Media Resources

Refer to the end of the chapter for a full listing of the multimedia learning materials available in MyEconLab.

LEARNING OBJECTIVES

After reading this chapter, you should be able to:

1. Define economic growth
2. Recognize the importance of economic growth rates
3. Describe the fundamental determinants of economic growth
4. Explain why productivity increases are crucial for maintaining economic growth
5. Understand the basis of new growth theory
6. Discuss the fundamental factors that contribute to a nation's economic development

... FedEx (formerly Federal Express) recently equipped all of its drivers with handheld package-tracking devices possessing wireless capabilities that have helped reduce the average time of a package pickup by 10 seconds? Across the world, drivers pick up millions of packages every day, so this single change in the way the company did things saved hundreds of thousands of hours of drivers' time. This permitted FedEx to ship even more packages using the same number of drivers and other company resources. The investment in new equipment expanded the company's productive capabilities. Now it is time to consider increases in the productive capabilities of a nation as a whole, or *economic growth*.

Did You Know That

HOW DO WE DEFINE ECONOMIC GROWTH?

Recall from Chapter 2 that we can show economic growth graphically as an outward shift of a production possibilities curve, as is seen in Figure 9-1. If there is economic growth between 2007 and 2035, the production possibilities curve will shift outward toward the red curve. The distance that it shifts represents the amount of economic growth, defined as the increase in the productive capacity of a nation. Although it is possible to come up with a measure of a nation's increased productive capacity, it would not be easy. Therefore, we turn to a more readily obtainable definition of economic growth.

Most people have a general idea of what economic growth means. When a nation grows economically, its citizens must be better off in at least some ways, usually in terms of their material well-being. Typically, though, we do not measure the well-being of any nation solely in terms of its total output of real goods and services or in terms of real GDP without making some adjustments. After all, India has a real GDP more than 15 times as large as that of Denmark. The population in India, though, is about 200 times greater than that of Denmark. Consequently, we view India as a relatively poor country and Denmark as a relatively rich country. Thus, when we measure economic growth, we must adjust for population growth. Our formal definition becomes this: **Economic growth** occurs when there are increases in *per capita* real GDP, measured by the rate of change in per capita real GDP per year. Figure 9-2 on the following page presents the historical record of real GDP per person in the United States.

Economic growth
Increases in per capita real GDP measured by its rate of change per year.

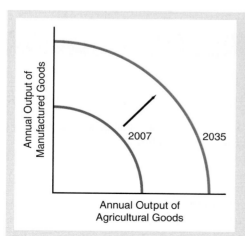

FIGURE 9-1
Economic Growth
If there is growth between 2007 and 2035, the production possibilities curve for the entire economy will shift outward from the blue line labeled 2007 to the red line labeled 2035. The distance that it shifts represents an increase in the productive capacity of the nation.

FIGURE 9-2
The Historical Record of U.S. Economic Growth
The graph traces per capita real GDP in the United States since 1900. Data are given in 2000 dollars.

Source: U.S. Department of Commerce.

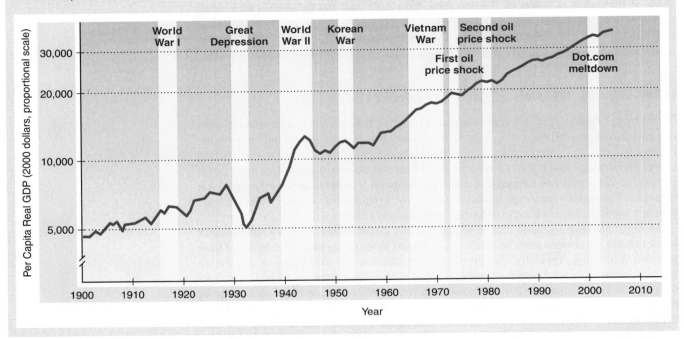

Problems in Definition

Our definition of economic growth says nothing about the *distribution* of output and income. A nation might grow very rapidly in terms of increases in per capita real output, while its poor people remain poor or become even poorer. Therefore, in assessing the economic growth record of any nation, we must be careful to pinpoint which income groups have benefited the most from such growth. How much does economic growth differ across countries?

International EXAMPLE

Growth Rates Around the World

Table 9-1 shows the average annual rate of growth of real GDP per person in selected countries. Notice that during the time period under study the United States is positioned about midway in the pack. Even though we are one of the world's richest countries, our rate of economic growth in recent decades has not been particularly high. The reason that U.S. per capita real GDP has remained higher than per capita real GDP in most other nations is that the United States has been able to sustain growth over many decades. This is something that most other countries have so far been unable to accomplish.

For Critical Analysis
"The largest change is from zero to one." Does this statement have anything to do with relative growth rates in poorer versus richer countries?

Country	Average Annual Rate of Growth of Real GDP Per Capita, 1980–2005 (%)
Brazil	1.0
France	1.7
Sweden	1.8
Germany	1.9
Canada	2.0
United States	2.3
Spain	2.5
Japan	2.9
Turkey	3.0
Indonesia	3.5
Malaysia	3.7
India	3.9
China	6.6

TABLE 9-1
Per Capita Real GDP Growth Rates in Various Countries

Sources: World Bank; International Monetary Fund.

Real standards of living can go up without any positive economic growth. This can occur if individuals are, on average, enjoying more leisure by working fewer hours but producing as much as they did before. For example, if per capita real GDP in the United States remained at $40,000 a year for a decade, we could not automatically jump to the conclusion that U.S. residents were, on average, no better off. What if, during that same 10-year period, average hours worked fell from 37 per week to 33 per week? That would mean that during the 10 years under study, individuals in the labor force were "earning" 4 more hours of leisure a week. Actually, nothing so extreme has occurred in this country, but something similar has. Average hours worked per week fell steadily until the 1960s, when they leveled off. That means that during much of the history of this country, the increase in per capita real GDP *understated* the actual economic growth that we were experiencing because we were enjoying more and more leisure as time passed.

Go to www.econtoday.com/chap09 to get the latest figures and estimates on economic growth throughout the world.

Is Economic Growth Bad?

Some commentators on our current economic situation believe that the definition of economic growth ignores its negative effects. Some psychologists even contend that economic growth makes us worse off. They say that the more we grow, the more "needs" are created so that we feel worse off as we become richer. Our expectations are rising faster than reality, so we presumably always suffer from a sense of disappointment. Also, the economist's measurement of economic growth does not take into account the spiritual and cultural aspects of the good life. As with all activities, both costs and benefits are associated with growth. You can see some of those listed in Table 9-2 on the next page.

Any measure of economic growth that we use will be imperfect. Nonetheless, the measures that we do have allow us to make comparisons across countries and over time and, if used judiciously, can enable us to gain important insights. Per capita real GDP, used so often, is not always an accurate measure of economic well-being, but it is a serviceable measure of productive activity.

TABLE 9-2
Costs and Benefits of Economic Growth

Benefits	Costs
Reduction in illiteracy	Environmental pollution
Reduction in poverty	Breakdown of the family
Improved health	Isolation and alienation
Longer lives	Urban congestion
Political stability	

The Importance of Growth Rates

Notice back in Table 9-1 on page 199 that the growth rates in real per capita income for most countries differ very little—generally by only a few percentage points. You might want to know why such small differences in growth rates are important. What would it matter if we grew at 3 percent rather than at 4 percent per year?

It matters a lot—not for next year or the year after but for the more distant future. The power of *compounding* is impressive. Let's see what happens with three different annual rates of growth: 3 percent, 4 percent, and 5 percent. We start with $1 trillion per year of gross domestic product of the United States at some time in the past. We then compound this $1 trillion, or allow it to grow at these three different growth rates. The difference is huge. In 50 years, $1 trillion per year becomes $4.38 trillion per year if compounded at 3 percent per year. Just one percentage point more in the growth rate, 4 percent, results in a real GDP of $7.11 trillion per year in 50 years, almost double the previous amount. Two percentage points difference in the growth rate—5 percent per year—results in a real GDP of $11.5 trillion per year in 50 years, or nearly three times as much. Obviously, very small differences in annual growth rates result in great differences in economic growth. That is why nations are concerned if the growth rate falls even a little in absolute percentage terms.

Thus, when we talk about growth rates, we are talking about compounding. In Table 9-3, we show how $1 compounded annually grows at different interest rates. We see in the 3 percent column that $1 in 50 years grows to $4.38. We merely multiplied $1 trillion times 4.38 to get the growth figure in our earlier example. In the 5 percent column, $1 grows to $11.50 after 50 years. Again, we multiplied $1 trillion times 11.50 to get the growth figure for 5 percent in the preceding example.

If the rates of economic growth in China and India continue at the same pace these nations have experienced during the past decade, when will GDP per capita in those nations begin to get closer to the U.S. level?

International EXAMPLE

Economic Growth in China and India Accelerates

China and India have per capita GDP levels well below those of the United States. Chinese per capita GDP is only slightly above one-eighth of U.S. per capita GDP. Indian per capita GDP is less than one-twentieth of the U.S. level. Since the 1970s, however, aggregate real GDP in India has risen at an annual rate nearly *twice* as high as total U.S. real GDP growth. China's real GDP has grown nearly *three* times faster than U.S. real GDP.

It is unlikely that China and India will maintain these high rates of aggregate real GDP growth, which have been fueled in part by transfers of new technologies from developed nations. Nevertheless, even if the two nations' average real GDP growth rates were to drop to just 2 to 3 percentage points higher than the U.S. growth rate, real growth compounding implies that real GDP in both countries will eventually surpass U.S. real GDP. By the middle of this century, China's real GDP is likely to be about 75 percent larger than U.S. real GDP, and India's real GDP probably will be just about equal to U.S. real GDP.

The rate of population growth is diminishing in both China and India, so continued growth in real GDP will translate into considerable growth in real GDP per capita. By mid-century China's per capita real GDP will be about one-half the U.S. level, or four times higher relative to U.S. per capita real GDP

than it is today. India's per capita real GDP will be roughly one-fourth the U.S. level, or about five times higher relative to U.S. per capita real GDP than it is at present.

The compounding effects of economic growth clearly take time to accumulate. Nevertheless, higher relative rates of economic growth in China, India, or any other nation ultimately must yield per capita incomes closer to the U.S. level.

For Critical Analysis

If the above scenario plays out, so that the U.S. share of world GDP falls from about one-fifth to one-tenth, will U.S. residents have a lower standard of living?

TABLE 9-3
One Dollar Compounded Annually at Different Interest Rates
Here we show the value of a dollar at the end of a specified period during which it has been compounded annually at a specified interest rate. For example, if you took $1 today and invested it at 5 percent per year, it would yield $1.05 at the end of one year. At the end of 10 years, it would equal $1.63, and at the end of 50 years, it would equal $11.50.

Number of Years	3%	4%	5%	6%	8%	10%	20%
1	1.03	1.04	1.05	1.06	1.08	1.10	1.20
2	1.06	1.08	1.10	1.12	1.17	1.21	1.44
3	1.09	1.12	1.16	1.19	1.26	1.33	1.73
4	1.13	1.17	1.22	1.26	1.36	1.46	2.07
5	1.16	1.22	1.28	1.34	1.47	1.61	2.49
6	1.19	1.27	1.34	1.41	1.59	1.77	2.99
7	1.23	1.32	1.41	1.50	1.71	1.94	3.58
8	1.27	1.37	1.48	1.59	1.85	2.14	4.30
9	1.30	1.42	1.55	1.68	2.00	2.35	5.16
10	1.34	1.48	1.63	1.79	2.16	2.59	6.19
20	1.81	2.19	2.65	3.20	4.66	6.72	38.30
30	2.43	3.24	4.32	5.74	10.00	17.40	237.00
40	3.26	4.80	7.04	10.30	21.70	45.30	1,470.00
50	4.38	7.11	11.50	18.40	46.90	117.00	9,100.00

CONCEPTS in Brief

- Economic growth can be defined as the increase in real per capita real GDP measured by its rate of change per year.
- The benefits of economic growth are reductions in illiteracy, poverty, and illness and increases in life spans and political stability. The costs of economic growth may include environmental pollution, alienation, and urban congestion.
- Small percentage-point differences in growth rates lead to large differences in real GDP over time. These differences can be seen by examining a compound interest table such as the one in Table 9-3.

To test your understanding of the concepts covered in this section, go to the Online Review at www.myeconlab.com/miller.

PRODUCTIVITY INCREASES: THE HEART OF ECONOMIC GROWTH

Let's say that you are required to type 10 term papers and homework assignments a year. You have a computer, but you do not know how to touch-type. You end up spending an average of two hours per typing job. The next summer, you buy a touch-typing tutorial to use on your computer and spend a few minutes a day improving your speed. The following term, you spend only one hour per typing assignment, thereby saving 10 hours a semester. You have become more productive. This concept of productivity summarizes your ability (and everyone else's) to produce the same output with fewer imputs. Thus **labor productivity** is normally measured by dividing the total real domestic output (real GDP) by the number of workers or the number of labor hours. Labor productivity increases whenever average output produced per worker during a specified time period increases.

Labor productivity
Total real domestic output (real GDP) divided by the number of workers (output per worker).

Which U.S. businesses do you think have experienced the greatest productivity improvements during the past few decades?

E X A M P L E

The Labor Productivity Boom in U.S. Manufacturing

Among U.S. industries that specialize in manufacturing physical goods, labor productivity has increased steadily over the years. In many manufacturing industries, production tasks that once took two weeks and a dozen workers to finish now require only two people and a few hours to complete. Since the 1950s, therefore, labor productivity in U.S. manufacturing has grown at a pace nearly three times faster than the rate of growth of productivity in the rest of the economy. Annual U.S. manufacturing output is five times higher than in the 1950s, even though total employment in manufacturing—about 16 million people—is the same today as it was back then.

For Critical Analysis
U.S. employment has more than doubled since the 1950s, so what has happened to the percentage of workers employed in manufacturing jobs?

Clearly, there is a relationship between economic growth and increases in labor productivity. If you divide all resources into just capital and labor, economic growth can be defined simply as the cumulative contribution to per capita GDP growth of three components: the rate of growth of capital, the rate of growth of labor, and the rate of growth of capital and labor productivity. If everything else remains constant, improvements in labor productivity ultimately lead to economic growth and higher living standards.

Go to www.econtoday.com/chap09 for information about the latest trends in U.S. labor productivity.

Figure 9-3 displays estimates of the relative contributions of growth of labor and capital and growth of labor and capital productivity to economic growth in the United States, nations in South Asia, and Latin American countries. The contribution of the growth of labor resources to total output has accounted for at least half of economic growth in all three regions. Total capital is the sum of physical capital, such as tools and machines, and human capital, which is the amount of knowledge acquired from research and education. Figure 9-3 shows the separate contributions of the growth of these forms of capital, which together have accounted for roughly a third of the growth rate of per capita incomes in the United States, South Asia, and Latin America. In these three parts of the world, growth in overall capital and labor productivity has contributed the remaining 7 to 18 percent.

SAVING: A FUNDAMENTAL DETERMINANT OF ECONOMIC GROWTH

Economic growth does not occur in a vacuum. It is not some predetermined fate of a nation. Rather, economic growth depends on certain fundamental factors. One of the most

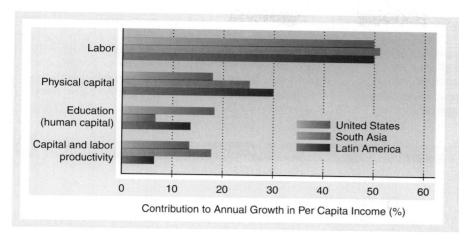

FIGURE 9-3
Factors Accounting for Economic Growth in Selected Regions
In the United States, South Asia, and Latin America, growth in labor resources is the main contributor to economic growth.

Source: International Monetary Fund.

important factors that affects the rate of economic growth and hence long-term living standards is the rate of saving.

A basic proposition in economics is that if you want more tomorrow, you have to consume less today.

> *To have more consumption in the future, you have to consume less today and save the difference between your consumption and your income.*

On a national basis, this implies that higher saving rates eventually mean higher living standards in the long run, all other things held constant. Concern has been growing in the United States that we are not saving enough. Saving is important for economic growth because without saving, we cannot have investment. If there is no investment in our capital stock, there could be little hope of much economic growth.

The relationship between the rate of saving and per capita real GDP is shown in Figure 9-4. Among the nations with the highest rates of saving are Singapore, Japan, and Germany.

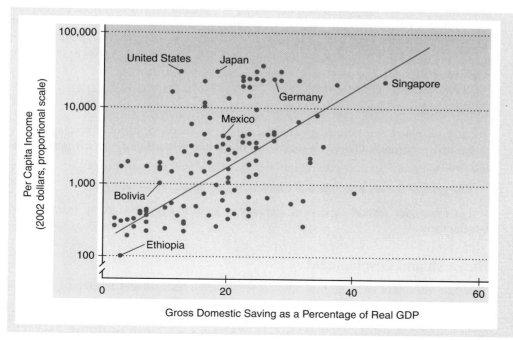

FIGURE 9-4
Relationship Between Rate of Saving and Per Capita Real GDP
This diagram shows the relationship between per capita real GDP and the rate of saving expressed as the average share of annual real GDP saved.

Source: World Bank.

CONCEPTS in Brief

- Economic growth is numerically equal to the rate of growth of capital plus the rate of growth of labor plus the rate of growth in the productivity of capital and of labor. Improvements in labor productivity, all other things being equal, lead to greater economic growth and higher living standards.

- One fundamental determinant of the rate of growth is the rate of saving. To have more consumption in the future, we have to save rather than consume. In general, countries that have had higher rates of saving have had higher rates of growth in real GDP.

To test your understanding of the concepts covered in this section, go to the Online Review at www.myeconlab.com/miller.

NEW GROWTH THEORY AND THE DETERMINANTS OF GROWTH

A simple arithmetic definition of economic growth has already been given. The growth rates of capital and labor plus the growth rate of their productivity constitute the rate of economic growth. Economists have had good data on the growth of the physical capital stock in the United States as well as on the labor force. But when you add those two growth rates together, you still do not get the total economic growth rate in the United States. The difference has to be due to improvements in productivity. Economists typically labeled this "improvements in technology," and that was that. More recently, proponents of what is now called **new growth theory** argue that technology cannot simply be looked at as an outside factor without explanation. Technology must be understood in terms of what drives it. What are the forces that make productivity grow in the United States and elsewhere?

New growth theory
A theory of economic growth that examines the factors that determine why technology, research, innovation, and the like are undertaken and how they interact.

Growth in Technology

Consider some startling statistics about the growth in technology. Microprocessor speeds may increase from 4,000 megahertz to 10,000 megahertz by the year 2015. By that same year, the size of the thinnest circuit line within a transistor may decrease by 90 percent. The typical memory capacity (RAM) of computers will jump from 512 megabytes, or about eight times the equivalent text in the *Encyclopaedia Britannica,* to 128 gigabytes—a 250-fold increase. Predictions are that computers may become as powerful as the human brain by 2020.

Technology: A Separate Factor of Production

We now recognize that technology must be viewed as a separate factor of production that is sensitive to rewards. Otherwise stated, one of the major foundations of new growth theory is this:

> *The greater the rewards, the more technological advances we will get.*

Let's consider several aspects of technology here, the first one being research and development.

Research and Development

A certain amount of technological advance results from research and development (R&D) activities that have as their goal the development of specific new materials, new products, and new machines. How much spending a nation devotes to R&D can have an impact on its long-term economic growth. Part of how much a nation spends depends on what businesses decide is worth spending. That in turn depends on their expected rewards from successful R&D. If your company develops a new way to produce computer memory chips, how much will it be rewarded? The answer depends on whether others can freely copy the new technique.

Patents. To protect new techniques developed through R&D, we have a system of **patents,** in which the federal government gives the patent holder the exclusive right to make, use, and sell an invention for a period of 20 years. One can argue that this special position given to owners of patents increases expenditures on R&D and therefore adds to long-term economic growth. Figure 9-5 shows that U.S. patent grants fell during the 1970s, increased steadily after 1982, and then surged following 1995 until 2001.

Patent
A government protection that gives an inventor the exclusive right to make, use, or sell an invention for a limited period of time (currently, 20 years).

Positive Externalities and R&D. As we discussed in Chapter 5, positive externalities are benefits from an activity that are not enjoyed by the instigator of the activity. In the case of R&D spending, a certain amount of the benefits go to other companies that do not have to pay for them. In particular, according to economists David Coe of the International Monetary Fund and Elhanan Helpman of Tel Aviv University, about a quarter of the global productivity gains of R&D investment in the top seven industrialized countries goes to foreigners. For every 1 percent rise in the stock of R&D in the United States alone, for example, productivity in the rest of the world increases by about 0.25 percent. One country's R&D expenditures benefit foreigners because they are able to import goods from technologically advanced countries and then use them as inputs in making their own industries more efficient. In addition, countries that import high-tech goods are able to imitate the technology.

The Open Economy and Economic Growth

People who study economic growth today emphasize the importance of the openness of the economy. Free trade encourages a more rapid spread of technology and industrial ideas. Moreover, open economies may experience higher rates of economic growth because their own industries have access to a bigger market. When trade barriers are erected in the form of tariffs and the like, domestic industries become isolated from global technological progress. This occurred for many years in former communist countries and in

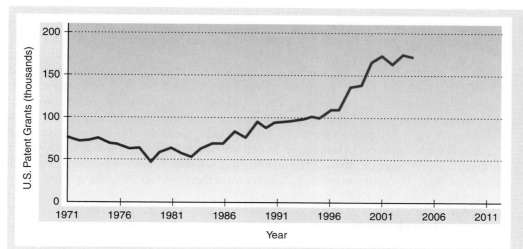

FIGURE 9-5
U.S. Patent Grants
The U.S. Patent and Trademark Office gradually began awarding more patent grants between the early 1980s and the mid-1990s. Since then, there was a significant increase in the number of patents it has granted each year until 2001.

Source: U.S. Patent and Trademark Office.

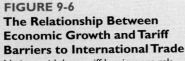

FIGURE 9-6
The Relationship Between Economic Growth and Tariff Barriers to International Trade
Nations with low tariff barriers are relatively open to international trade and have tended to have higher average annual rates of real GDP per capita growth since 1965.

Source: World Bank.

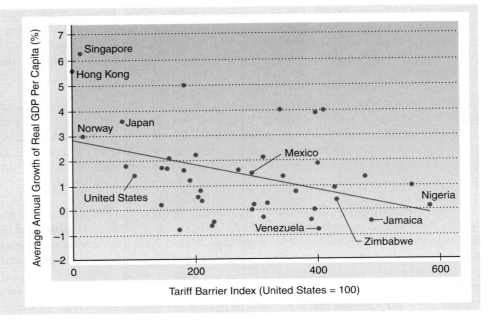

many developing countries in Africa, Latin America, and elsewhere. Figure 9-6 shows the relationship between economic growth and openness as measured by the level of tariff barriers.

Innovation and Knowledge

We tend to think of technological progress as, say, the invention of the transistor. But invention means nothing by itself; **innovation** is required. Innovation involves the transformation of something new, such as an invention, into something that benefits the economy either by lowering production costs or by providing new goods and services. Indeed, the new growth theorists believe that real wealth creation comes from innovation and that invention is but a facet of innovation.

Innovation
Transforming an invention into something that is useful to humans.

Historically, technologies have moved relatively slowly from invention to innovation to widespread use, and the dispersion of new technology remains for the most part slow and uncertain. The inventor of the transistor thought it might be used to make better hearing aids. At the time it was invented, the *New York Times*'s sole reference to it was in a small weekly column called "News of Radio." When the laser was invented, no one really knew what it could be used for. It was initially used to help in navigation, measurement, and chemical research. Today, it is used in the reproduction of music, printing, surgery, telecommunications, and optical data transmittal and storage. Tomorrow, who knows?

Figure 9-7 shows the process by which raw ideas turn into written ideas that are submitted for study in typical research and development laboratories. Businesses select a few of these for initial study and choose fewer still to evaluate in large research projects. Out of these full-scale research efforts, a few significant developments emerge and are launched as new products. If businesses are lucky, one or two of these product launches may ultimately pay off.

Why have inventors of the process of sending telephone transmissions as packets of digital information on the Internet discovered that their efforts have paid off differently than they originally anticipated?

E-Commerce EXAMPLE

VoIP Finally Comes into Its Own

A general concept known as Voice over Internet Protocol (VoIP) has been around since the early 1990s. At that time, the inventors of VoIP realized that any signal that could be converted into packets of digital information, including telephone signals, could be transmitted on the Internet. The concept was straightforward, but implementing it in the marketplace turned out to be a challenge. When VoIP inventors tried selling their own VoIP services to individual consumers, they ran into a fundamental problem. To succeed, the inventors had to convince many people simultaneously to switch from regular telephone service to the Internet-based VoIP service. After all, unless numerous consumers converted to VoIP phone service, there would not be enough people to talk to on the other end of an Internet connection. By the late 1990s, it was apparent that most of the initial efforts to establish consumer-to-consumer VoIP were going nowhere fast.

By the early 2000s, however, two events had altered the prospects of VoIP. First, by that time many companies were employing new technologies that permitted them to route in-coming phone calls to computers. These companies found that they could operate their *internal* telephone systems more cost-effectively by using VoIP to convert regular phone calls to digital information within their own phone networks. Second, providers of telephone services, such as Verizon and SBC, implemented VoIP technologies within their own networks for routing traditional phone calls. By the mid-2000s, therefore, market forces had created a situation in which VoIP was in wide use everywhere *except* inside people's homes. Thus the first place many inventors of VoIP systems attempted to introduce the technology turned out to be the last place it had a chance of succeeding as an innovation.

For Critical Analysis
How might the trends toward greater use of cell phones and increased integration of wireless computer technology in cell phones improve the chances that VoIP may ultimately emerge as a true innovation in consumer-to-consumer telecommunications?

FIGURE 9-7
The Winnowing Process of Research and Development
Only a portion of new ideas are actually submitted for formal study, and just a fraction of these become subjects of research projects. Very few ideas actually lead to the development of new products.

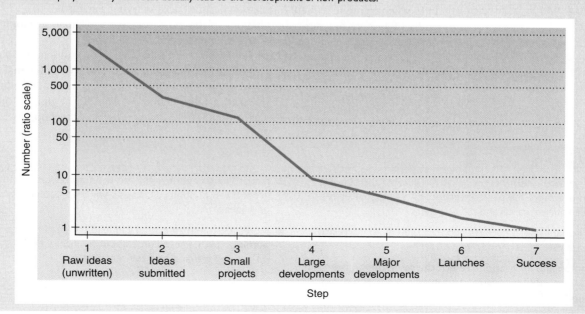

The Importance of Ideas and Knowledge

Economist Paul Romer has added at least one important factor that determines the rate of economic growth. He contends that production and manufacturing knowledge is just as important as the other determinants and perhaps even more so. He considers knowledge a factor of production that, like capital, has to be paid for by forgoing current consumption. Economies must therefore invest in knowledge just as they invest in machines. Because past investment in capital may make it more profitable to acquire more knowledge, there may be an investment-knowledge cycle in which investment spurs knowledge and knowledge spurs investment. A once-and-for-all increase in a country's rate of investment may permanently raise that country's growth rate. (According to traditional theory, a once-and-for-all increase in the rate of saving and therefore in the rate of investment simply leads to a new steady-state standard of living, not one that continues to increase.)

Another way of looking at knowledge is that it is a store of ideas. According to Romer, ideas are what drive economic growth. We have become, in fact, an idea economy. Consider Microsoft Corporation. A relatively small percentage of that company's labor force is involved in actually building products. Rather, a majority of Microsoft employees are attempting to discover new ideas that can be translated into computer code that can then be turned into products. The major conclusion that Romer and other new growth theorists draw is this:

Economic growth can continue as long as we keep coming up with new ideas.

The Importance of Human Capital

Knowledge, ideas, and productivity are all tied together. One of the threads is the quality of the labor force. Increases in the productivity of the labor force are a function of increases in human capital, the fourth factor of production discussed in Chapter 2. Recall that human capital consists of the knowledge and skills that people in the workforce acquire through education, on-the-job training, and self-teaching. To increase your own human capital, you have to invest by forgoing income-earning activities while you attend school. Society also has to invest in the form of libraries and teachers. According to the new growth theorists, human capital is at least as important as physical capital, particularly when trying to explain international differences in living standards.

It is therefore not surprising that one of the most effective ways that developing countries can become developed is by investing in secondary schooling.

One can argue that policy changes that increase human capital will lead to more technological improvements. One of the reasons that concerned citizens, policymakers, and politicians are looking for a change in the U.S. schooling system is that our educational system seems to be falling behind that of other countries. This lag is greatest in science and mathematics—precisely the areas required for developing better technology.

CONCEPTS in Brief

- New growth theory argues that the greater the rewards, the more rapid the pace of technology. And greater rewards spur research and development.

- The openness of a nation's economy seems to correlate with its rate of economic growth.

- Invention and innovation are not the same thing. Inventions are useless until innovation transforms them into things that people find valuable.

- According to the new growth economists, economic growth can continue as long as we keep coming up with new ideas.

- Increases in human capital can lead to greater rates of economic growth. These come about by increased education, on-the-job training, and self-teaching.

To test your understanding of the concepts covered in this section, go to the Online Review at www.myeconlab.com/miller.

POPULATION AND IMMIGRATION AS THEY AFFECT ECONOMIC GROWTH

There are several ways to view population growth as it affects economic growth. On the one hand, population growth means an increase in the amount of labor, which is one major component of economic growth. On the other hand, population growth can be seen as a drain on the economy because for any given amount of GDP, more population means lower per capita GDP. According to MIT economist Michael Kremer, the first view is historically correct. His conclusion is that population growth drives technological progress, which then increases economic growth. The theory is simple: If there are 50 percent more people in the United States, there will be 50 percent more geniuses. And with 50 percent more people, the rewards for creativity are commensurately greater. Otherwise stated, the larger the potential market, the greater the incentive to become ingenious.

A larger market also provides an incentive for well-trained people to immigrate, which undoubtedly helps explain why the United States attracts a disproportionate number of top scientists from around the globe.

Does immigration help spur economic growth? Yes, according to the late economist Julian Simon, who pointed out that "every time our system allows in one more immigrant, on average, the economic welfare of American citizens goes up. . . . Additional immigrants, both the legal and the illegal, raise the standard of living of U.S. natives and have little or no negative impact on any occupational or income class." He further argued that immigrants do not displace natives from jobs but rather create jobs through their purchases and by starting new businesses. Immigrants' earning and spending simply expand the economy.

Not all researchers agree with Simon, and few studies have tested the theories advanced here. The area is currently the focus of much research.

Economics Front and Center

Immigration can potentially contribute to economic growth by enlarging the nation's stock of human capital; see **The Senator Doesn't Like Opening the Borders to Immigrants, but Some Immigrants Have a Lot to Offer,** on page 214.

PROPERTY RIGHTS AND ENTREPRENEURSHIP

If you were in a country where bank accounts and businesses were periodically expropriated by the government, how willing would you be to leave your financial assets in a savings account or to invest in a business? Certainly, you would be less willing than if such things never occurred. In general, the more certain private property rights are, the more capital accumulation there will be. People will be willing to invest their savings in endeavors that will increase their wealth in future years. This requires that property rights in their wealth be sanctioned and enforced by the government. In fact, some economic historians have attempted to show that it was the development of well-defined private property rights and legal structures that allowed Western Europe to increase its growth rate after many centuries of stagnation. The ability and certainty with which they can reap the gains from investing also determine the extent to which business owners in other countries will invest capital in developing countries. The threat of nationalization that hangs over some developing nations probably stands in the way of foreign investments that would allow these nations to develop more rapidly.

The legal structure of a nation is closely tied to the degree with which its citizens use their own entrepreneurial skills. In Chapter 2, we identified entrepreneurship as the fifth factor of production. Entrepreneurs are the risk takers who seek out new ways to do things and create new products. To the extent that entrepreneurs are allowed to capture the rewards from their entrepreneurial activities, they will seek to engage in those activities. In countries where such rewards cannot be captured because of a lack of property rights, there will be less entrepreneurship. Typically, this results in fewer investments and a lower rate of growth. We shall examine the implications this has for policymakers in Chapter 18.

ECONOMIC DEVELOPMENT

Development economics
The study of factors that contribute to the economic development of a country.

How did developed countries travel paths of growth from extreme poverty to relative riches? That is the essential issue of **development economics,** which is the study of why some countries grow and develop and others do not and of policies that might help developing economies get richer. It is not enough simply to say that people in different countries are different and that is why some countries are rich and some countries are poor. Economists do not deny that different cultures have different work ethics, but they are unwilling to accept such a pat and fatalistic answer.

Look at any world map. About four-fifths of the countries you will see on the map are considered relatively poor. The goal of economists who study development is to help the more than 4 billion people today with low living standards join the more than 2 billion people who have at least moderately high living standards.

Putting World Poverty into Perspective

Most U.S. residents cannot even begin to understand the reality of poverty in the world today. At least one-half, if not two-thirds, of the world's population lives at subsistence level, with just enough to eat for survival. Indeed, the World Bank estimates that nearly 30 percent of the world's people live on less than $1 per day. The official poverty line in the United States is set above the average income of at least half the human beings on the planet. This is not to say that we should ignore domestic problems with the poor and homeless simply because they are living better than many people elsewhere in the world. Rather, it is necessary for us to maintain an appropriate perspective on what are considered problems for this country relative to what are considered problems elsewhere.

The Relationship Between Population Growth and Economic Development

World population is growing at the rate of just over 2.4 people a second. That amounts to 210,500 a day or 76.9 million a year. Today, there are nearly 7 billion people on earth. By 2050, according to the United Nations, the world's population will be close to leveling off at around 9.3 billion. Panel (a) of Figure 9-8 shows which countries are growing the most. Panel (b) emphasizes an implication of panel (a), which is that virtually all the growth in population is occurring in developing nations. Many developed countries are expected to lose population over the next several decades.

Ever since the Reverend Thomas Robert Malthus wrote *An Essay on the Principle of Population* in 1798, excessive population growth has been a concern. Modern-day Malthusians are able to generate great enthusiasm for the concept that population growth is bad. Over and over, media pundits and a number of scientists tell us that rapid population growth threatens economic development and the quality of life.

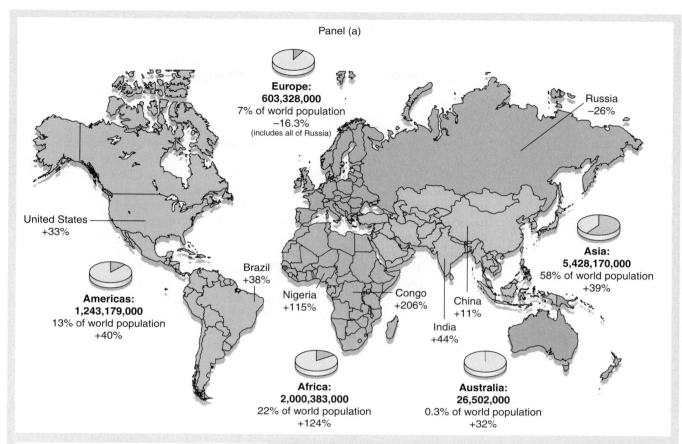

Panel (a)

Europe:
603,328,000
7% of world population
−16.3%
(includes all of Russia)

Russia
−26%

United States
+33%

Brazil
+38%

Americas:
1,243,179,000
13% of world population
+40%

Nigeria
+115%

Congo
+206%

China
+11%

India
+44%

Asia:
5,428,170,000
58% of world population
+39%

Africa:
2,000,383,000
22% of world population
+124%

Australia:
26,502,000
0.3% of world population
+32%

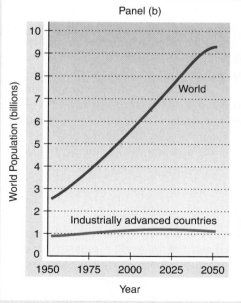

Panel (b)

FIGURE 9-8
Expected Growth in World Population by 2050
Panel (a) shows that Asia and Africa are expected to gain the most in population by the year 2050. Panel (b) indicates that population will increase in developing countries before beginning to level off around 2050, while industrially advanced nations will grow very little in population in the first half of this century.

Source: United Nations.

Malthus Was Proved Wrong. Malthus predicted that population would outstrip food supplies. This prediction has never been supported by the facts, according to economist Nicholas Eberstadt of the Harvard Center for Population Studies. As the world's population has grown, so has the world's food supply, measured by calories per person. Furthermore, the price of food, corrected for inflation, has been falling steadily for more than a century. That means that the supply of food has been expanding faster than the rise in demand caused by increased population.

Growth Leads to Smaller Families. Furthermore, economists have found that as nations become richer, average family size declines. Otherwise stated, the more economic development occurs, the slower the population growth rate becomes. This has certainly been true in Western Europe and in the former Soviet Union, where populations in some countries are actually declining. Predictions of birthrates in developing countries have often turned out to be overstated if those countries experience rapid economic growth. This was the case in Hong Kong, Mexico, Taiwan, and Colombia. Recent research on population and economic development has revealed that social and economic modernization has been accompanied by what might be called a fertility revolution—the spread of deliberate limitations on family size within marriage and a decline in childbearing. Modernization reduces infant mortality, which in turn reduces the incentive for couples to have many children to make sure that a certain number survive to adulthood. Modernization also lowers the demand for children for a variety of reasons, not the least being that couples in more developed countries do not need to rely on their children to take care of them in old age.

The Stages of Development: Agriculture to Industry to Services

If we analyze the development of modern rich nations, we find that they went through three stages. First is the agricultural stage, when most of the population is involved in agriculture. Then comes the manufacturing stage, when much of the population becomes involved in the industrialized sector of the economy. And finally there is a shift toward services. That is exactly what happened in the United States: The so-called tertiary, or service, sector of the economy continues to grow, whereas the manufacturing sector (and its share of employment) is declining in relative importance.

Of particular significance, however, is the requirement for early specialization in a nation's comparative advantage (see Chapter 2). The doctrine of comparative advantage is particularly appropriate for the developing countries of the world. If trading is allowed among nations, a country is normally best off if it produces what it has a comparative advantage in producing and imports the rest (for more details, see Chapter 33). This means that many developing countries should continue to specialize in agricultural production or in labor-intensive manufactured goods.

Keys to Economic Development

Go to www.econtoday.com/chap09 to contemplate whether there may be a relationship between inequality and a nation's growth and to visit the home page of the World Bank's Thematic Group on Inequality, Poverty, and Socioeconomic Performance.

One theory of development states that for a country to develop, it must have a large natural resource base. This theory goes on to assert that much of the world is running out of natural resources, thereby limiting economic growth and development. Only the narrowest definition of a natural resource, however, could lead to such an opinion. In broader terms, a natural resource is something occurring in nature that we can use for our own purposes. As emphasized by new growth theory, natural resources therefore include knowledge of the use of something. The natural resources that we could define several hundred years ago did not, for example, include hydroelectric power—no one knew that such a natural resource existed or how to bring it into existence.

Natural resources by themselves are not a prerequisite for or a guarantee of economic development, as demonstrated by Japan's extensive development despite a lack of domestic oil resources and by Brazil's slow pace of development in spite of a vast array of natural resources. Resources must be transformed into something usable for either investment or consumption.

Economists have found that four factors seem to be highly related to the pace of economic development:

1. *An educated population.* Both theoretically and empirically, we know that a more educated workforce aids economic development because it allows individuals to build on the ideas of others. According to economists David Gould and Roy Ruffin, increasing the rate of enrollment in secondary schools in less developed nations by only 2 percentage points, from 8 percent to 10 percent, raises the average rate of economic growth by half a percent per year. Thus we must conclude that developing countries can advance more rapidly if they invest more heavily in secondary education. Or, stated in the negative, economic development cannot be sustained if a nation allows a sizable portion of its population to remain uneducated. Education allows young people who grow up poor to acquire skills that enable them to avoid poverty as adults.

2. *Establishing a system of property rights.* As noted earlier, if you were in a country where bank accounts and businesses were periodically expropriated by the government, you would be reluctant to leave your money in a savings account or to invest in a business. Expropriation of private property rarely takes place in developed countries. It has occurred in numerous developing countries, however. For example, private property was once nationalized in Chile and still is for the most part in Cuba. Economists have found that other things being equal, the more certain private property rights are, the more private capital accumulation and economic growth there will be.

3. *Letting "creative destruction" run its course.* The twentieth-century economist Joseph Schumpeter championed the concept of "creative destruction," through which new businesses ultimately create new jobs and economic growth after first destroying old jobs, old companies, and old industries. Such change is painful and costly, but it is necessary for economic advancement. Nowhere is this more important than in developing countries, where the principle is often ignored. Many developing nations have had a history of supporting current companies and industries by discouraging new technologies and new companies from entering the marketplace. The process of creative destruction has not been allowed to work its magic in these countries.

4. *Limiting protectionism.* Open economies experience faster economic development than economies closed to international trade. Trade encourages individuals and businesses to discover ways to specialize so that they can become more productive and earn higher incomes. Increased productivity and subsequent increases in economic growth are the results. Thus the less government protects the domestic economy by imposing trade barriers, the faster that economy will experience economic development. According to a study by economists Nouriel Roubini and Xavier Sala-i-Martin, when a country goes from being relatively open to relatively closed via government-enacted trade barriers, it will have a 2.5-percentage-point decrease in its annual rate of economic growth.

Go to www.econtoday.com/chap09 to link to a World Trade Organization explanation of how free trade promotes greater economic growth and higher employment.

CONCEPTS in Brief

- Although many people believe that population growth hinders economic development, there is little evidence to support that notion. What is clear is that economic development tends to lead to a reduction in the rate of population growth.

- Historically, there are three stages of economic development: the agricultural stage, the manufacturing stage, and the service-sector stage, when a large part of the workforce is employed in providing services.

- Although one theory of economic development holds that a sizable natural resource base is the key to a nation's development, this fails to account for the importance of the human element: The labor force must be capable of using a country's natural resources.

- Fundamental factors contributing to the pace of economic development are training and education, a well-defined system of property rights, allowing new generations of companies and industries to replace older generations, and promoting an open economy by allowing international trade.

To test your understanding of the concepts covered in this section, go to the Online Review at **www.myeconlab.com/miller.**

CASE STUDY: Economics Front and Center

The Senator Doesn't Like Opening the Borders to Immigrants, but Some Immigrants Have a Lot to Offer

Peterson has just graduated from college and is now a junior member of the staff of a U.S. senator. He has been asked to draft a statement detailing the senator's position on the economic growth implications of immigration. His research on the topic has uncovered the following facts. First, more than a fifth of scientists actively involved in research at U.S. universities are immigrants. Second, foreign-born scientists residing in the United States write about 60 percent of published research studies in the physical sciences and about 30 percent of research publications in the life sciences. Third, nearly a fourth of the founders or chief executives of U.S. biotechnology firms that have become public companies since the early 1990s were born abroad.

Peterson knows that in the past the senator who employs him has generally been opposed to permitting unhindered immi-

gration. Nevertheless, the senator also strongly favors policies that promote economic growth. Peterson's task, given what he has learned, is to compose a draft statement reconciling the senator's two positions.

Points to Analyze

1. *Why might unhindered immigration have uncertain effects on U.S. per capita GDP even though immigrant scientists contribute so much to the nation's stock of knowledge and expertise?*

2. *How might Peterson draw on the insights of new growth theory to draft a position statement ruling out unhindered immigration but proposing greater openness to "targeted immigrants"?*

Concepts Applied
- Productivity
- Economic Growth

As you learned in this chapter, increased productivity of labor and capital contributes to greater economic growth. Therefore, if businesspeople could predict changes in overall business productivity, they would be better able to gauge the prospects for future economic growth. This would help them determine if they should build new manufacturing facilities or open more retail outlets in anticipation of increased sales to people earning higher incomes.

The Relationship Between Productivity and Stock Prices

Analyzing changing trends in stock prices may offer one way to predict future productivity. Companies' current and future earnings are related to productivity, so investors have good reason to keep close tabs on productivity trends when deciding how much they are willing to pay for shares of stock. Thus, when investors are convinced that productivity is on an upswing, stock prices should increase, other things being equal. If investors have good reason to anticipate a drop-off in business productivity, then they will tend to bid lower amounts for shares of stock, and market share prices should fall.

Investors have strong incentives to forecast business productivity and act on their forecasts in ways that influence stock prices. Consequently, it is arguable that movements in stock price indexes might prove to be useful signals of future business productivity.

Using Stock Prices to Forecast Business Productivity

To evaluate whether it is possible to use stock prices to forecast future productivity growth, Evan Koenig of the Federal Reserve Bank of Dallas studied whether the ratio of stock prices to firms' earnings and dividends in a current quarter helps to predict U.S. productivity growth in subsequent quarters. His evaluation considered the period from the early 1980s to the early 2000s and took into consideration other factors likely to influence stock prices, such as movements in interest rates, inflation expectations, and trends in employment.

As you can see in Figure 9-9, movements in the ratio of stock prices to earnings and dividends yielded relatively accurate predictions of future productivity growth during this period. Hence, there is some evidence that variations in stock prices really can assist in forecasting future changes in business productivity that ultimately matter so much for economic growth.

Support for an Investor's Rule of Thumb

For years, businesspeople seeking to assess growth prospects in many of the world's less developed countries have struggled with the relatively small amounts of productivity data available for these nations. In the absence of other information, businesspeople considering investing in these countries have often relied on a rule of thumb that trends in stock prices might indicate future economic growth trends. The relationship provided in Figure 9-9 indicates that this rule of thumb could actually be a useful approach to assessing nations' growth prospects.

FIGURE 9-9
Actual and Predicted Productivity Growth
Predictions of productivity growth using stock prices closely match actual growth in business productivity.

Source: Evan Koenig, "Productivity, the Stock Market, and Monetary Policy in the New Economy," *Southwest Economy*, Federal Reserve Bank of Dallas, January/February 2000, 6–12.

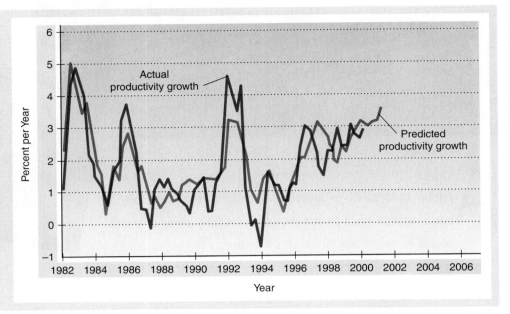

For Critical Analysis

1. Even if a general rise in stock prices correctly indicates a future boost in business productivity, is it still possible that the rate of economic growth could remain unchanged or even decline? (Hint: Is productivity the only factor that affects economic growth?)
2. If a nation's stock prices trend upward over a period of several years, and productivity and the rate of growth of real GDP subsequently increase, yet real GDP per capita declines, what might have happened during this interval?

Web Resources

1. To learn more about the broader economic implications of the relationship between the stock market and productivity, go to the link to the home page of the Federal Reserve Bank of Dallas at www.econtoday.com/chap09. Click on "Economic and Financial Data" and then on "Southwest Economy," scan down to "January/February 2000," and download that issue to read Evan Koenig's paper entitled "Productivity, the Stock Market, and Monetary Policy in the New Economy."
2. To track the latest trends in U.S. business productivity, go to the link to the home page of the Bureau of Labor Statistics at www.econtoday.com/chap09. and click on "Productivity and Costs."

Research Project

Why might a business have an interest in trying to forecast future movements in productivity for the economy as a whole? Provide a list of potential reasons, and then explain how successful predictions about overall productivity growth could help an individual company improve its own current and future profitability.

S U M M A R Y   D I S C U S S I O N   of Learning Objectives

1. **Economic Growth:** The rate of economic growth is the annual rate of change in per capita real GDP. This measure of the growth of a nation's economy takes into account both its growth in overall production of goods and services and the growth of its population. It is an average measure that does not account for possible changes in the

distribution of income or various welfare costs or benefits that may accompany growth of the economy.

2. **Why Economic Growth Rates Are Important:** Over long intervals, relatively small differences in the rate of economic growth can accumulate to produce large disparities in per capita incomes. The reason is that like accumulations of interest, economic growth compounds over time. Thus, if a nation's per capita real GDP growth rises by 3 percentage points per year, it has a level of per capita real GDP that is more than four times higher after 50 years, but a country with a per capita real GDP growth rate 4 percentage points higher per year ends up with per capita real GDP more than seven times higher.

3. **The Key Determinants of Economic Growth:** The fundamental factors contributing to economic growth are growth in a nation's pool of labor, growth of its capital stock, and growth in the productivity of its capital and labor. A key determinant of capital accumulation is a nation's saving rate. Higher saving rates contribute to greater investment and hence increased capital accumulation and economic growth.

4. **Why Productivity Increases Are Crucial for Maintaining Economic Growth:** For a nation with a rela-tively stable population and a steady rate of capital accumulation, productivity growth emerges as a fundamental factor influencing near-term changes in economic growth. Higher productivity growth unambiguously contributes to greater annual increases in a nation's per capita real GDP.

5. **New Growth Theory:** This is a relatively recent theory that examines why individuals and businesses conduct research into inventing and developing new technologies and how this process interacts with the rate of economic growth. This theory emphasizes how rewards to techno-logical innovation contribute to higher economic growth rates. A key implication of the theory is that ideas and knowledge are crucial elements of the growth process.

6. **Fundamental Factors That Contribute to a Nation's Economic Development:** The key characteristics shared by nations that succeed in attaining higher levels of eco-nomic development are significant opportunities for their residents to obtain training and education, protection of property rights, policies that permit new companies and industries to replace older ones, and the avoidance of protectionist barriers that hinder international trade.

KEY TERMS AND CONCEPTS

development economics (210)	innovation (206)	new growth theory (204)
economic growth (197)	labor productivity (202)	patent (205)

PROBLEMS

Answers to the odd-numbered problems appear at the back of the book.

9-1. The graph shows a production possibilities curve for 2008 and two potential production possibilities curves for 2009, denoted 2009$_A$ and 2009$_B$.

   a. Which of the labeled points corresponds to maxi-mum feasible 2008 production that is more likely to be associated with the curve denoted 2009$_A$?

   b. Which of the labeled points corresponds to maxi-mum feasible 2008 production that is more likely to be associated with the curve denoted 2009$_B$?

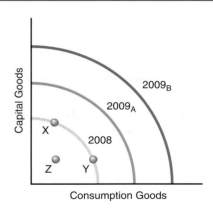

9-2. A nation's capital goods wear out over time, so a portion of its capital goods become unusable every year. Last year, its residents decided to produce no capital goods. It has experienced no growth in its population or in the amounts of other productive resources during the past year. In addition, the nation's technology and resource productivity have remained unchanged during the past year. Will the nation's economic growth rate for the current year be negative, zero, or positive?

9-3. In the situation described in Problem 9-2, suppose that educational improvements during the past year enable the people of this nation to repair all capital goods so that they continue to function as well as new. All other factors are unchanged, however. In light of this single change to the conditions faced in this nation, will the nation's economic growth rate for the current year be negative, zero, or positive?

9-4. Consider the following data. What is the per capita real GDP in each of these countries?

Country	Population (millions)	Real GDP ($ billions)
A	10	55
B	20	60
C	5	70

9-5. Suppose that during the next 10 years, real GDP triples and population doubles in each of the nations in Problem 9-4. What will per capita real GDP be in each country after 10 years have passed?

9-6. Consider the following table displaying annual growth rates for nations X, Y, and Z, each of which entered 2005 with real per capita GDP equal to $20,000:

Country	Annual Growth Rate (%)			
	2005	2006	2007	2008
X	7	1	3	4
Y	4	5	7	9
Z	5	4	3	2

a. Which nation was most likely to have suffered a sizable earthquake in early 2006 that destroyed a significant portion of its stock of capital goods?

What is this nation's per capita real GDP at the end of 2008, rounded to the nearest dollar?

b. Which nation was most likely to have adopted policies in 2005 that encouraged a *gradual* shift in production from capital goods to consumption goods? What is this nation's per capita real GDP at the end of 2008, rounded to the nearest dollar?

c. Which nation was most likely to have adopted policies in 2005 that encouraged a *gradual* shift in production from consumption goods to capital goods? What is this nation's per capita real GDP at the end of 2008, rounded to the nearest dollar?

9-7. Per capita real GDP grows at a rate of 3 percent in country F and at a rate of 6 percent in country G. Both begin with equal levels of per capita real GDP. Use Table 9-3 on page 201 to determine how much higher per capita real GDP will be in country G after 20 years. How much higher will real GDP be in country G after 40 years?

9-8. Per capita real GDP in country L is three times as high as in country M. The economic growth rate in country M, however, is 8 percent, while country L's economy grows at a rate of 5 percent. Use Table 9-3 on page 201 to determine approximately how many years it will be before per capita real GDP in country M surpasses per capita real GDP in country L.

9-9. Per capita real GDP in country S is only half as great as per capita real GDP in country T. Country T's rate of economic growth is 4 percent. The government of country S, however, enacts policies that achieve a growth rate of 20 percent. Use Table 9-3 on page 201 to determine how long country S must maintain this growth rate before its per capita real GDP surpasses that of country T.

9-10. In 2006, a nation's population was 10 million. Its nominal GDP was $40 billion, and its price index was 100. In 2007, its population had increased to 12 million, its nominal GDP had risen to $57.6 billion, and its price index had increased to 120. What was this nation's economic growth rate during the year?

9-11. Between the start of 2006 and the start of 2007, a country's economic growth rate was 4 percent. Its population did not change during the year, nor did its price level. What was the rate of increase of the country's nominal GDP during this one-year interval?

ECONOMICS ON THE NET

Multifactor Productivity and Its Growth Growth in productivity is a key factor determining a nation's overall economic growth.

Title: Bureau of Labor Statistics: Multifactor Productivity Trends

Navigation: Use the link at www.econtoday.com/chap09 to visit the multifactor productivity home page of the Bureau of Labor Statistics.

Application Read the summary, and answer the following questions.

1. What does multifactor productivity measure? Based on your reading of this chapter, how does multifactor productivity relate to the determination of economic growth?

2. Click on *Manufacturing Industries: Multifactor Productivity Trends*. According to these data, which industries have exhibited the greatest productivity growth in recent years?

For Group Study and Analysis Divide the class into three groups to examine multifactor productivity data for the private business sector, the private nonfarm business sector, and the manufacturing sector. Have each group identify periods when multifactor productivity growth was particularly fast or slow. Then compare notes. Does it appear to make a big difference which sector one looks at when evaluating periods of greatest and least growth in multifactor productivity?

If your exam were tomorrow, would you be ready? For each chapter, MyEconLab Practice Tests and Study Plans pinpoint which sections you have mastered and which ones you need to study. That way, you are more efficient with your study time, and you are better prepared for your exams.

In addition to Practice Tests and your personalized Study Plan, you'll find the following media resources in MyEconLab:

1. *Graphs in Motion* animation of Figures 9-1, 9-2, 9-5, 9-6, and 9-8.
2. Videos featuring the author, Roger LeRoy Miller, on the following subjects:
   - Growth Rates and Compound Interest
   - Saving and Economic Growth
   - The Importance of Human Capital

3. Links to the Web sites cited in the marginal Internet Resources, Issues and Applications feature, and Economics on the Net activity.
4. Audio clips of all key terms, additional practice problems, and a PDF version of the material from the print Study Guide.
5. eThemes of the Times, which is a New York Times article to help you understand the real-world applications of what you are learning.

To see how it works, turn to page 16 and then go to www.myeconlab.com/miller.

Get Ahead of the Curve

Chapter 10
Real GDP and the Price Level in the Long Run

The Economist magazine tracks something it calls the "*D*-word Index." This is the number of media mentions of deflation, or a decline in the price level over time. The magazine found that between late 2001 and 2004, the *D*-word Index increased by more than 400 percent. It seems unlikely that deflation will occur any time soon in the United States, but Japan and China have experienced deflation off and on for several years, and other parts of East Asia have also witnessed price level dips. Nevertheless, throughout much of the rest of the world, inflation remains the norm. In this chapter you will learn about the factors that determine whether a nation experiences long-term deflation or inflation.

Refer to the end of the chapter for a full listing of the multimedia learning materials available in MyEconLab.

LEARNING OBJECTIVES

After reading this chapter, you should be able to:

1. Understand the concept of long-run aggregate supply
2. Describe the effect of economic growth on the long-run aggregate supply curve
3. Explain why the aggregate demand curve slopes downward and list key factors that cause this curve to shift
4. Discuss the meaning of long-run equilibrium for the economy as a whole
5. Evaluate why economic growth can cause deflation
6. Evaluate likely reasons for persistent inflation in recent decades

...the children's classic *The Wonderful Wizard of Oz*, written in 1900 by L. Frank Baum, was also an allegory about how a nation should achieve long-run price stability? According to economist Hugh Rockoff of Rutgers University, Baum's book was intended to support the populist political movement that arose in the 1890s. The economic issue of central concern to the populists was widespread *deflation*. The U.S. price level had generally declined since the end of the Civil War, and from time to time unexpected drops in prices greatly disrupted the lives of farmers, shopkeepers, and workers in the Midwest and West. According to Rockoff, the small-minded Munchkins that Dorothy meets after a tornado transports her to the Land of Oz probably symbolize inhabitants of eastern states whom Baum perceived as insensitive to the plight of informally educated but commonsensical western farmers (symbolized by the Scarecrow) and urban workers in danger of losing their hearts and souls (symbolized by the Tin Man). The city inhabited by the Wizard of Oz, the Emerald City (symbolic of Washington, D.C.), is green—the color of money. The same is true of the Wizard's home, the Emerald Palace (representing the White House). Before Dorothy and her friends enter the Emerald City, however, they must put on green-colored glasses held together with gold buckles, symbolizing the U.S. government's policy of forcing westerners to use money supported only by gold. The populists believed that the way to halt the nation's persistent and variable deflation was to expand the quantity of money in circulation by basing money's value on silver as well as gold. For this reason, in Baum's book the slippers that help Dorothy get back to Kansas are made of silver (the writers of the 1939 movie version of the book changed them to ruby slippers). Rockoff speculates that the Cowardly Lion represents William Jennings Bryan, the "roaring orator" and presidential candidate who decried gold but then retreated—in a way that Baum evidently found cowardly—for political reasons. Oz, of course, is the abbreviation for ounces, in which gold is measured, and the yellow brick road is paved with bars of gold.

Why did the United States experience persistent deflation during the latter part of the nineteenth century? Did the populists and their literary supporter, L. Frank Baum, have a legitimate point in arguing that the United States ought to expand the quantity of money in circulation to halt deflation? To answer these questions, you must learn about the factors that influence the long-run stability of the price level.

OUTPUT GROWTH AND THE LONG-RUN AGGREGATE SUPPLY CURVE

In Chapter 2, we showed the derivation of the production possibilities curve. At any point in time, the economy can be inside or on the PPC but never outside it. Along the PPC, a country's resources are fully employed in the production of goods and services, and the sum total of the inflation-adjusted value of all final goods and services produced is the nation's real GDP. Economists refer to the total of all planned production for the entire economy as the **aggregate supply** of real output.

Aggregate supply
The total of all planned production for the economy.

The Long-Run Aggregate Supply Curve

Put yourself in a world in which nothing has been changing, year in and year out. The price level has not changed. Technology has not changed. The prices of inputs that firms must purchase have not changed. Labor productivity has not changed. All resources are fully employed, so the economy operates on its production possibilities curve, such as the one depicted in panel (a) of Figure 10-1 on the following page. This is a world that is fully adjusted and in which people have all the information they are ever going to get about that

FIGURE 10-1

The Production Possibilities and the Economy's Long-Run Aggregate Supply Curve

At a point in time, a nation's base of resources and its technological capabilities define the position of its production possibilities curve, as shown in panel (a). This defines the real GDP that the nation can produce when resources are fully employed, which determines the position of the long-run aggregate supply curve (*LRAS*) displayed in panel (b). Because people have complete information and input prices adjust fully in the long run, the *LRAS* is vertical.

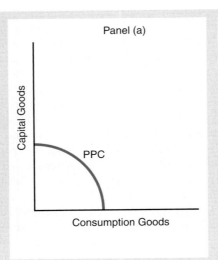

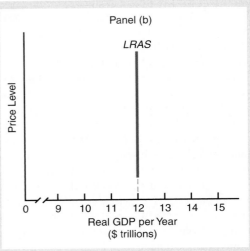

Long-run aggregate supply curve
A vertical line representing the real output of goods and services after full adjustment has occurred. It can also be viewed as representing the real GDP of the economy under conditions of full employment—the full-employment level of real GDP.

Endowments
The various resources in an economy, including both physical resources and such human resources as ingenuity and management skills.

Go to www.econtoday.com/chap10 to find out how fast wages are adjusting. Then click on "Employment Cost Index."

world. The **long-run aggregate supply curve** (*LRAS*) in this world is some amount of real GDP—say, $12 trillion of real GDP. We can represent long-run aggregate supply by a vertical line at $12 trillion of real GDP. This is what you see in panel (b) of the figure. That curve, labeled *LRAS*, is a vertical line determined by technology and **endowments,** or resources that exist in our economy. It is the full-information and full-adjustment level of real output of goods and services. It is the level of real GDP that will continue being produced year after year, forever, if nothing changes.

Another way of viewing the *LRAS* is to think of it as the full-employment level of real GDP. When the economy reaches full employment along its production possibilities curve, no further adjustments will occur unless a change occurs in the other variables that we are assuming constant and stable. Some economists like to think of the *LRAS* as occurring at the level of real GDP consistent with the natural rate of unemployment, the unemployment rate that occurs in an economy with full adjustment in the long run. As we discussed in Chapter 7, many economists like to think of the natural rate of unemployment as consisting of frictional and structural unemployment.

To understand why the long-run aggregate supply curve is vertical, think about the long run, which is a sufficiently long period that all factors of production and prices, including wages and other input prices, can change. A change in the level of prices of goods and services has no effect on real GDP per year in the long run, because higher prices will be accompanied by comparable changes in input prices. Suppliers will therefore have no incentive to increase or decrease their production of goods and services. Remember that in the long run, everybody has full information, and there is full adjustment to price level changes.

Economic Growth and Long-Run Aggregate Supply

In Chapter 9, you learned about the factors that determine growth in per capita real GDP: the annual growth rate of labor, the rate of year-to-year capital accumulation, and the rate of growth of the productivity of labor and capital. As time goes by, population gradually increases, and labor force participation rates may even rise. The capital stock typically grows as businesses add such capital equipment as new information technology hardware. Furthermore, technology improves. Thus the economy's production possibilities increase, and the production possibilities curve shifts outward, as shown in panel (a) of Figure 10-2.

The result is economic growth: Aggregate real GDP and per capita real GDP increase. This means that at least in a growing economy such as ours, the *LRAS* will shift outward to

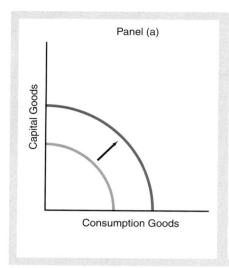

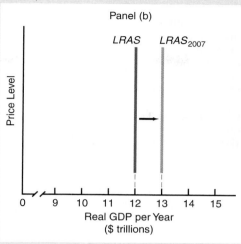

FIGURE 10-2
The Long-Run Aggregate Supply Curve and Shifts in It
In panel (a), we repeat a diagram that we used in Chapter 2 to show the meaning of economic growth. Over time, the production possibilities curve shifts outward. In panel (b), we demonstrate the same principle by showing the long-run aggregate supply curve as initially a vertical line at $12 trillion of real GDP per year. As our productive abilities increase, the *LRAS* moves outward to *LRAS*$_{2007}$.

the right, as in panel (b). We have drawn the *LRAS* for the year 2007 to the right of our original *LRAS* of $12 trillion of real GDP. The number we have attached to *LRAS*$_{2007}$ is $13 trillion of real GDP, but that is only a guess. The point is that it is to the right of today's *LRAS* curve.

We may conclude that in a growing economy, the *LRAS* shifts ever farther to the right over time. If the *LRAS* happened to shift rightward at a constant pace, real GDP would increase at a steady annual rate. As shown in Figure 10-3 on the next page, this means that real GDP would increase along a long-run, or *trend,* path that is an upward-sloping line. Thus, if the *LRAS* shifts rightward from $12 trillion to $13 trillion between now and 2007 and then increases at a steady pace of $500 billion per year every year thereafter, in 2009 long-run real GDP will equal $14 trillion, in 2011 it will equal $15 trillion, and so on.

How do you think that the growth of government regulation of the economy has affected the trend path for U.S. real GDP?

Policy E X A M P L E

Regulation and Economic Growth

If the extent of federal government regulation of activities in U.S. product and labor markets can be measured by the sheer volume of published regulations, then the scope of regulation has increased by more than 500 percent since 1950. To satisfy health and safety, environmental, labor, and various other regulations, companies must shift resources away from producing goods and services. Consequently, the regulation of economic activities entails an opportunity cost for society: forgone production of real GDP.

John Dawson of Appalachian State University and John Seater of North Carolina State University have estimated the degree to which federal regulations have reduced U.S. real GDP growth. They have calculated that the trend rate of annual growth of real GDP is almost one percentage point lower due to regulatory growth. Thus, if there had been no increase in federal regulations since the early 1950s, the economy's long-run aggregate supply curve would have shifted much farther to the right over the past five decades. Dawson and Seater estimate that in the absence of increased government regulation, U.S. real GDP would be at least 40 percent higher today.

For Critical Analysis
How do the various activities involved in satisfying federal regulations get counted in real GDP? (Hint: Income payments must be made to owners of resources directed toward meeting regulatory requirements.)

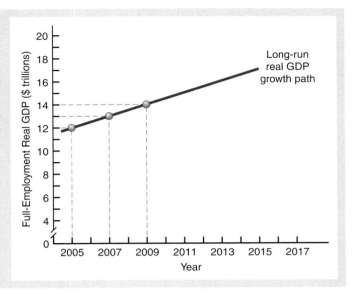

FIGURE 10-3
A Sample Long-Run Growth Path for Real GDP

Year-to-year shifts in the long-run aggregate supply curve yield a long-run trend path for real GDP growth. In this example, real GDP grows by a steady amount of $500 billion each year.

CONCEPTS in Brief

- The long-run aggregate supply curve, *LRAS*, is a vertical line determined by amounts of available resources such as labor and capital and by technology and resource productivity. The position of the *LRAS* gives the full-information and full-adjustment level of real GDP.

- The natural rate of unemployment occurs at the long-run level of real GDP given by the position of the *LRAS*.

- If labor or capital increases from year to year or if the productivity of either of these resources rises from one year to the next, the *LRAS* shifts rightward. In a growing economy, therefore, real GDP and per capita real GDP gradually rise over time.

To test your understanding of the concepts covered in this section, go to the Online Review at www.myeconlab.com/miller.

SPENDING AND TOTAL EXPENDITURES

In equilibrium, individuals, businesses, and governments purchase all the goods and services produced, valued in trillions of real dollars. As explained in Chapters 7 and 8, GDP is the dollar value of total expenditures on domestically produced final goods and services. Because all expenditures are made by individuals, firms, or governments, the total value of these expenditures must be what each of these market participants decides it shall be.

The decisions of individuals, managers of firms, and government officials determine the annual dollar value of total expenditures. You can certainly see this in your role as an individual. You decide what the total dollar amount of your expenditures will be in a year. You decide how much you want to spend and how much you want to save. Thus, if we want to know what determines the total value of GDP, the answer is clear: the spending decisions of individuals like you; firms; and local, state, and national governments. In an open economy, we must also include foreign individuals, firms, and governments (foreigners, for short) that decide to spend their money income in the United States.

Simply stating that the dollar value of total expenditures in this country depends on what individuals, firms, governments, and foreigners decide to do really doesn't tell us much, though. Two important issues remain:

1. What determines the total amount that individuals, firms, governments, and foreigners want to spend?
2. What determines the equilibrium price level and the rate of inflation (or deflation)?

The *LRAS* tells us only about the economy's long-run real GDP. To answer these additional questions, we must consider another important concept. This is **aggregate demand,** which is the total of all *planned* real expenditures in the economy.

Aggregate demand
The total of all planned expenditures in the entire economy.

AGGREGATE DEMAND

The **aggregate demand curve,** *AD*, gives the various quantities of all final commodities demanded at various price levels, all other things held constant. Recall the components of GDP that you studied in Chapter 8: consumption spending, investment expenditures, government purchases, and net foreign demand for domestic production. They are all components of aggregate demand. Throughout this chapter and the next, whenever you see the aggregate demand curve, realize that it is a shorthand way of talking about the components of GDP that are measured by government statisticians when they calculate total economic activity each year. In Chapter 12, you will look more closely at the relationship between these components and, in particular, at how consumption spending depends on income.

Aggregate demand curve
A curve showing planned purchase rates for all final goods and services in the economy at various price levels, all other things held constant.

The Aggregate Demand Curve

The aggregate demand curve gives the total value, in base-year dollars, of *real* domestic final goods and services that will be purchased at each price level—everything produced for final use by households, businesses, the government, and foreign residents. It includes stereos, socks, shoes, medical and legal services, computers, and millions of other goods and services that people buy each year.

A graphical representation of the aggregate demand curve is seen in Figure 10-4. On the horizontal axis is measured real GDP. For our measure of the price level, we use the GDP price deflator on the vertical axis. The aggregate demand curve is labeled *AD*. If the GDP deflator is 120, aggregate quantity demanded is $12 trillion per year (point *A*). At the price level 140, it is $11 trillion per year (point *B*). At the price level 160, it is $10 trillion per year (point *C*). The higher the price level, the lower the total real value of final goods and services demanded in the economy, everything else remaining constant, as shown by the arrow along *AD* in Figure 10-4. Conversely, the lower the price level, the higher the total real GDP demanded by the economy, everything else staying constant.

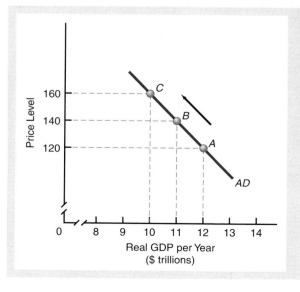

FIGURE 10-4
The Aggregate Demand Curve

The aggregate demand curve, *AD*, slopes downward. If the price level is 120, we will be at point *A* with $12 trillion of real GDP demanded per year. As the price level increases to 140 and to 160, we move up the aggregate demand curve to points *B* and *C*.

Let's take the year 2005. Estimates based on U.S. Department of Commerce preliminary statistics reveals the following information:

- Nominal GDP was estimated to be $12,246.1 billion.
- The price level as measured by the GDP deflator was about 111.3 (base year is 2000, for which the index equals 100).
- Real GDP (output) was approximately $10,998.0 billion in 2000 dollars.

What can we say about 2005? Given the dollar cost of buying goods and services and all of the other factors that go into spending decisions by individuals, firms, governments, and foreigners, the total amount of planned spending on final goods and services by firms, individuals, governments, and foreign residents was $10,998.0 billion in 2005 (in terms of 2000 dollars).

What Happens When the Price Level Rises?

What if the price level in the economy rose to 160 tomorrow? What would happen to the amount of real goods and services that individuals, firms, governments, and foreigners wish to purchase in the United States? We know from Chapter 3 that when the price of one good or service rises, the quantity of it demanded will fall. But here we are talking about the *price level*—the average price of *all* goods and services in the economy. The answer is still that the total quantities of real goods and services demanded would fall, but the reasons are different. When the price of one good or service goes up, the consumer substitutes other goods and services. For the entire economy, when the price level goes up, the consumer doesn't simply substitute one good for another, for now we are dealing with the demand for *all* goods and services in the nation. There are *economywide* reasons that cause the aggregate demand curve to slope downward. They involve at least three distinct forces: the *real-balance effect,* the *interest rate effect,* and the *open economy effect.*

Real-balance effect
The change in expenditures resulting from a change in the real value of money balances when the price level changes, all other things held constant; also called the *wealth effect.*

The Real–Balance Effect. A rise in the price level will have an effect on spending. Individuals, firms, governments, and foreigners carry out transactions using money, a portion of which consists of currency and coins that you have in your pocket (or stashed away) right now. Because people use money to purchase goods and services, the amount of money that people have influences the amount of goods and services they want to buy. For example, if you find a $10 bill on the sidewalk, the amount of money you have will rise. Given your now greater level of money balances—currency in this case—you will almost surely increase your spending on goods and services. Similarly, if while on a trip downtown you had your pocket picked, your desired spending would be affected. For example, if your wallet had $70 in it when it was stolen, the reduction in your cash balances—in this case currency—would no doubt cause you to reduce your planned expenditures. You would ultimately buy fewer goods and services.

This response is sometimes called the **real-balance effect** (or *wealth effect*) because it relates to the real value of your cash balances. While your *nominal* cash balances may remain the same, any change in the price level will cause a change in the *real* value of those cash balances—hence the real-balance effect on total planned expenditures.

When you think of the real-balance effect, just think of what happens to your real wealth if you have, say, a $100 bill hidden under your mattress. If the price level increases by 10 percent, the purchasing power of that $100 bill drops by 10 percent, so you have become less wealthy. That will reduce your spending on all goods and services by some small amount.

Economics Front and Center

To think through a case study of how the real-balance, interest rate, and open economy effects can affect an individual's planned spending, see **Responding to a Rise in the Price Level,** on page 234.

The Interest Rate Effect. There is a more subtle but equally important effect on your desire to spend. As the price level rises, interest rates increase. This raises borrowing costs for consumers and businesses. They will borrow less and consequently spend less. The fact that a higher price level pushes up interest rates and thereby reduces borrowing and spending is known as the **interest rate effect.**

Higher interest rates make it more costly for people to finance purchases of houses and cars. Higher interest rates also make it less profitable for firms to install new equipment and to erect new office buildings. Whether we are talking about individuals or firms, a rise in the price level will cause higher interest rates, which in turn reduce the amount of goods and services that people are willing to purchase. Therefore, an increase in the price level will tend to reduce total planned expenditures. (The opposite occurs if the price level declines.)

The Open Economy Effect: The Substitution of Foreign Goods. Recall from Chapter 8 that GDP includes net exports—the difference between exports and imports. In an open economy, we buy imports from other countries and ultimately pay for them through the foreign exchange market. The same is true for foreign residents who purchase our goods (exports). Given any set of exchange rates between the U.S. dollar and other currencies, an increase in the price level in the United States makes U.S. goods more expensive relative to foreign goods. Foreigners have downward-sloping demand curves for U.S. goods. When the relative price of U.S. goods goes up, foreign residents buy fewer U.S. goods and more of their own. At home, relatively cheaper prices for foreign goods cause U.S. residents to want to buy more foreign goods instead of domestically produced goods. The result is a fall in exports and a rise in imports when the domestic price level rises. That means that a price level increase tends to reduce net exports, thereby reducing the amount of real goods and services purchased in the United States. This is known as the **open economy effect.**

What Happens When the Price Level Falls?

What about the reverse? Suppose now that the GDP deflator falls to 100 from an initial level of 120. You should be able to trace the three effects on desired purchases of goods and services. Specifically, how do the real-balance, interest rate, and open economy effects cause people to want to buy more? You should come to the conclusion that the lower the price level, the greater the total planned spending on goods and services.

The aggregate demand curve, *AD*, shows the quantity of aggregate output that will be demanded at alternative price levels. It is downward sloping, just like the demand curve for individual goods. The higher the price level, the lower the amount of total planned expenditures, and vice versa.

Demand for All Goods and Services versus Demand for a Single Good or Service

Even though the aggregate demand curve, *AD*, in Figure 10-4 on page 225 looks similar to the one for individual demand, *D*, for a single good or service that you encountered in Chapters 3 and 4, the two are not the same. When we derive the aggregate demand curve, we are looking at the entire economic system. The aggregate demand curve, *AD*, differs from an individual demand curve, *D*, because we are looking at total planned expenditures on *all* goods and services when we construct *AD*.

SHIFTS IN THE AGGREGATE DEMAND CURVE

In Chapter 3, you learned that any time a nonprice determinant of demand changes, the demand curve will shift inward to the left or outward to the right. The same analysis holds for the aggregate demand curve, except we are now talking about the non-price-level determinants of aggregate demand. So when we ask the question, "What determines the position of the aggregate demand curve?" the fundamental proposition is as follows:

Interest rate effect
One of the reasons that the aggregate demand curve slopes downward: Higher price levels increase the interest rate, which in turn causes businesses and consumers to reduce desired spending due to the higher cost of borrowing.

Open economy effect
One of the reasons that the aggregate demand curve slopes downward: Higher price levels result in foreign residents desiring to buy fewer U.S.-made goods, while U.S. residents now desire more foreign-made goods, thereby reducing net exports. This is equivalent to a reduction in the amount of real goods and services purchased in the United States.

TABLE 10-1 **Determinants of Aggregate Demand** Aggregate demand consists of the demand for domestically produced consumption goods, investment goods, government purchases, and net exports. Consequently, any change in total planned spending on any one of these components of real GDP will cause a change in aggregate demand. Some possibilities are listed here.	Changes That Cause an Increase in Aggregate Demand	Changes That Cause a Decrease in Aggregate Demand
	A drop in the foreign exchange value of the dollar	A rise in the foreign exchange value of the dollar
	Increased security about jobs and future income	Decreased security about jobs and future income
	Improvements in economic conditions in other countries	Declines in economic conditions in other countries
	A reduction in real interest rates (nominal interest rates corrected for inflation) not due to price level changes	A rise in real interest rates (nominal interest rates corrected for inflation) not due to price level changes
	Tax decreases	Tax increases
	An increase in the amount of money in circulation	A decrease in the amount of money in circulation

Any non-price-level change that increases aggregate spending (on domestic goods) shifts **AD** *to the right. Any non-price-level change that decreases aggregate spending (on domestic goods) shifts* **AD** *to the left.*

The list of potential determinants of the position of the aggregate demand curve is long. Some of the most important "curve shifters" for aggregate demand are presented in Table 10-1.

CONCEPTS in Brief

- Aggregate demand is the total of all planned expenditures in the economy, and aggregate supply is the total of all planned production in the economy. The aggregate demand curve shows the various quantities of total planned spending on final goods and services at various price levels; it is downward sloping.

- There are three reasons why the aggregate demand curve is downward sloping: the real-balance effect, the interest rate effect, and the open economy effect.

- The real-balance effect occurs because price level changes alter the real value of cash balances, thereby causing people

  to desire to spend more or less, depending on whether the price level decreases or increases.

- The interest rate effect is caused by interest rate changes that mimic price level changes. At higher interest rates, people seek to buy fewer houses and cars, and at lower interest rates, they seek to buy more.

- The open economy effect occurs because of a shift away from expenditures on domestic goods and a shift towards expenditures on foreign goods when the domestic price level increases.

To test your understanding of the concepts covered in this section, go to the Online Review at www.myeconlab.com/miller.

LONG-RUN EQUILIBRIUM AND THE PRICE LEVEL

As noted in Chapter 3, equilibrium occurs where the demand and supply curves intersect. The same is true for the economy as a whole, as shown in Figure 10-5: The equilibrium price level occurs at the point where the aggregate demand curve *(AD)* crosses the long-run aggregate supply curve *(LRAS)*. At this equilibrium price level of 120, the total of all planned real expenditures for the entire economy is equal to actual real GDP produced by

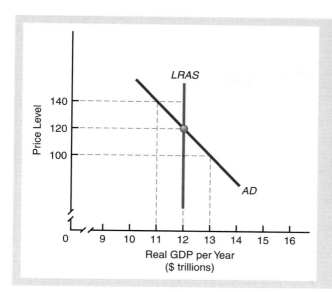

FIGURE 10-5
Long-Run Economywide
Equilibrium
For the economy as a whole, long-run equilibrium occurs at the price level where the aggregate demand curve crosses the long-run aggregate supply curve. At this long-run equilibrium price level, which is 120 in the diagram, total planned real expenditures equal real GDP at full employment, which in our example is a real GDP of $12 trillion.

firms after all adjustments have taken place. Thus the equilibrium depicted in Figure 10-5 is the economy's *long-run equilibrium.*

Note that if the price level were to increase to 140, actual real GDP would exceed total planned real expenditures. Inventories of unsold goods would begin to accumulate, and firms would stand ready to offer more services than people wish to purchase. As a result, the price level would tend to fall. If the price level were 100, then total planned real expenditures by individuals, businesses, and the government would exceed actual real GDP, and the price level would move toward 120.

THE EFFECTS OF ECONOMIC GROWTH ON THE PRICE LEVEL

We now have a basic theory of how real GDP and the price level are determined in the long run when all of a nation's resources can change over time and all input prices can adjust fully to changes in the overall level of prices of goods and services that firms produce. Let's begin by evaluating the effects of economic growth on the nation's price level.

Take a look at panel (a) of Figure 10-6 on the following page, which shows what happens, other things being equal, when the *LRAS* shifts rightward over time. If the economy were to grow steadily during, say, a 10-year interval, the long-run aggregate supply schedule would shift to the right, from $LRAS_1$ to $LRAS_2$. In panel (a), this results in a downward movement along the aggregate demand schedule. The equilibrium price level falls, from 120 to 60. Thus, if all factors that affect total planned real expenditures are unchanged, so that the aggregate demand curve does not noticeably move during the 10-year period of real GDP growth, the growing economy in the example would experience deflation. This is known as **secular deflation,** or a persistently declining price level resulting from economic growth in the presence of relatively unchanged aggregate demand.

Secular deflation
A persistent decline in prices resulting from economic growth in the presence of stable aggregate demand.

The Wizard of Oz Revisited

L. Frank Baum and his contemporaries experienced secular deflation during the two decades preceding the publication of *The Wonderful Wizard of Oz.* Between 1872 and 1894, the price of bricks fell by 50 percent, the price of sugar by 67 percent, the price of wheat by 69 percent, the price of nails by 70 percent, and the price of copper by nearly 75

FIGURE 10-6

Secular Deflation versus Long-Run Price Stability in a Growing Economy

Panel (a) illustrates what happens when economic growth occurs without a corresponding increase in aggregate demand. The result is a decline in the price level over time, known as *secular deflation*. Panel (b) shows that in principle, secular deflation can be avoided if the aggregate demand curve shifts rightward at the same pace that the long-run aggregate supply curve shifts to the right.

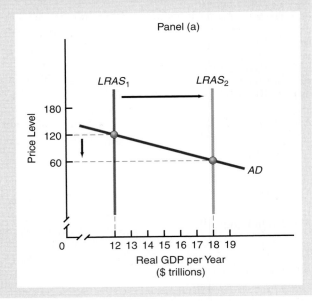

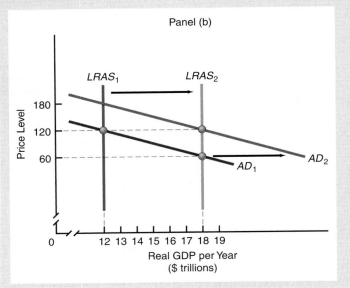

Go to www.econtoday.com/chap10 to learn about how the price level has changed during recent years. Then click on "Gross Domestic Product and Components" (for GDP deflators) or "Consumer Price Indexes."

percent. Baum and other populists offered a proposal for ending deflation: They wanted the government to issue new money backed by silver. As noted in Table 10-1 on page 228, an increase in the quantity of money in circulation causes the aggregate demand curve to shift to the right. It is clear from panel (b) of Figure 10-6 that the increase in the quantity of money would indeed have pushed the price level back upward.

Bad Timing for Silver Money

In 1890, Congress passed the Treasury Note Act, otherwise known as the Silver Purchase Act, which required the U.S. Treasury to purchase silver and issue currency known as silver certificates. This effort to expand the quantity of money barely got off the ground, however, before stock market panics hit in the spring and summer of 1893. People began to hoard gold, and the price of silver, a substitute, fell. To limit the government's losses on its silver holdings, Congress, at the urging of President Grover Cleveland, repealed the Silver Purchase Act. William Jennings Bryan sought the Democratic presidential nomination to oppose Republican William McKinley in 1896, and in an emotional speech, he decried the repeal of the Silver Purchase Act, saying, "You shall not press down upon the brow of labor this crown of thorns, you shall not crucify mankind upon a cross of gold." Although Bryan's speechmaking abilities made him a public sensation, he nonetheless lost the election, which sounded the death knell for the populist effort to increase the quantity of money in circulation via silver certificates. According to Rutgers University economist Hugh Rockoff, Baum represented the twin enemies of silver, Presidents Cleveland (of New York) and McKinley (of Ohio), as the Wicked Witch of the East and the Wicked Witch of the West.

At the time Baum wrote, the steam engine powered the industrial growth that generated secular deflation. How do you suppose that the flow of information among computers within company networks and across the Internet is influencing economic growth today?

E-Commerce EXAMPLE

Information Technologies and Long-Run Aggregate Supply

The use of computers to communicate has enhanced and extended the relationships among companies and individuals. The creation of computer networks within companies and the expansion of software and hardware that link businesses to households via the Internet have fueled economic growth in two ways. First, adoption of these information technologies has added to the world's stock of capital resources that can be used to design and produce goods and services in future years. Second, the new information technologies have promoted the development of entrepreneurial talent in people whose creativity has been enhanced by the Web, thereby contributing to growth in overall productivity. Both of these factors have contributed to rightward shifts in the long-run aggregate supply curve.

How much has the adoption of information technologies contributed to economic growth in the world's developed nations? Consensus estimates by various economists indicate

that since 1995, the contribution of information technologies to growth in both capital resources and overall productivity has accounted for at least one-third of real GDP growth in the United States, Canada, and the United Kingdom. In France and Germany, where adoption of information technologies has proceeded at a slower pace, their contribution to real GDP growth has been only about 10 percent. This is probably a key reason why real GDP in these and other European nations grew at only about half the pace of U.S., Canadian, and U.K. real GDP during the first half of the 2000s.

For Critical Analysis
How do you think that an upsurge in information technology adoption in France, Germany, and other European nations during recent years will affect their rates of economic growth during the years to come?

CAUSES OF INFLATION

Of course, so far during your lifetime, deflation has not been a problem in the United States. Figure 10-7 shows annual U.S. inflation rates for the past few decades. Clearly, inflation rates have been variable. The other obvious fact, however, is that inflation rates have been consistently *positive*. The price level in the United States has *risen* almost every year. For today's United States, secular deflation has not been a big political issue. If anything, it is secular *inflation* that has plagued the nation.

FIGURE 10-7
Inflation Rates in the United States

U.S. inflation rates rose considerably during the 1970s but declined to lower levels since the 1980s. Nevertheless, the United States has experienced inflation every year since 1959.

Sources: *Economic Report of the President; Economic Indicators*, various issues.

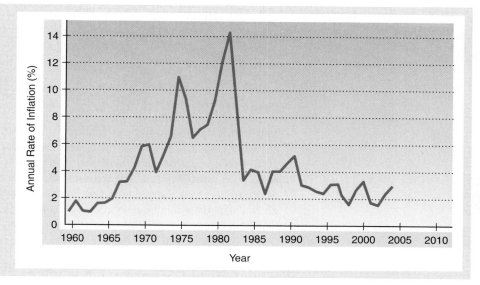

Supply-Side Inflation?

What causes such persistent inflation? The model of aggregate demand and long-run aggregate supply provides two possible explanations for inflation. One potential rationale is depicted in panel (a) of Figure 10-8. This panel shows a rise in the price level caused by a *decline in long-run aggregate supply.* Hence one possible reason for persistent inflation would be continual reductions in economywide production.

Recall now the factors that would cause the aggregate supply schedule to shift leftward. One might be reductions in labor force participation, higher marginal tax rates on wages, or the provision of government benefits that give households incentives *not* to supply labor services to firms. Although tax rates and government benefits have increased during recent decades, so has the U.S. population. Nevertheless, the significant overall rise in real GDP that has taken place during the past few decades tells us that population growth and productivity gains have dominated other factors. In fact, the aggregate supply schedule has actually shifted *rightward,* not leftward, over time. Consequently, this supply-side explanation for persistent inflation *cannot* be the correct explanation.

Why do you suppose that the European Central Bank has concluded that sharp increases in marginal tax rates in European nations have contributed to higher inflation?

International EXAMPLE

The Inflationary Effects of Increasing Marginal Tax Rates in Europe

Since the early 1990s, European nations, like the United States, have experienced positive growth in real GDP. The governments of most European countries, however, impose much higher marginal tax rates on wages, incomes, and sales of goods and services. Taking all these taxes into account, the overall marginal tax rate for the typical European resident has been rising steadily since the early 1990s and currently exceeds 45 percent. In contrast, the overall marginal tax rate faced by the average U.S. resident has remained at about 28 percent for several years.

The higher marginal tax rates have had the effect of slowing the rate at which the long-run aggregate supply curve shifts rightward in European nations. As a consequence, the price level is higher each year than it would have been otherwise. The European Central Bank estimates that by the mid-2000s, increases in marginal tax rates had added about one-half of a percentage point to the average annual rate of inflation across Europe. During 2004, for instance, the average annual European inflation rate could have been as low as 1.7 percent, but because of higher marginal tax rates, the actual inflation rate was about 2.2 percent.

For Critical Analysis
How have higher marginal tax rates affected the average annual rate of growth in real GDP in European nations?

Demand-Side Inflation

This leaves only one other explanation for the persistent inflation that the United States has experienced in recent decades. This explanation is depicted in panel (b) of Figure 10-8. If aggregate demand increases for a given level of long-run aggregate supply, the price level must increase. The reason is that at an initial price level such as 120, people desire to purchase more goods and services than firms are willing and able to produce given currently available resources and technology. As a result, the rise in aggregate demand leads only to a general rise in the price level, such as the increase to a value of 140 depicted in the figure.

FIGURE 10-8

Explaining Persistent Inflation

As shown in panel (a), it is possible for a decline in long-run aggregate supply to cause a rise in the price level. Long-run aggregate supply *increases*, however, in a growing economy, so this cannot explain the observation of persistent U.S. inflation. Panel (b) provides the actual explana-tion of persistent inflation in the United States and most other nations today, which is that increases in aggregate demand push up the long-run equilibrium price level. Thus it is possible to explain persistent inflation in a growing economy if the aggregate demand curve shifts rightward at a faster pace than the long-run aggregate supply curve.

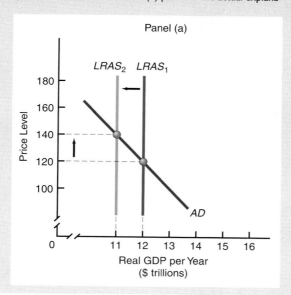

Panel (a)

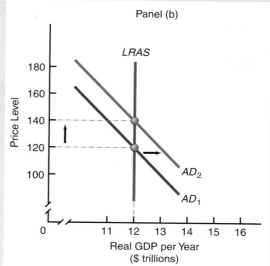

Panel (b)

From a long-run perspective, we are left with only one possibility: Persistent inflation in a growing economy is possible only if the aggregate demand curve shifts rightward over time at a faster pace than the rightward progression of the long-run aggregate supply curve. Thus, in contrast to the experience of people who lived in the latter portion of the nineteenth century, when aggregate demand grew too slowly relative to aggregate supply to maintain price stability, your grandparents, parents, and you have lived in times when aggregate demand has grown too *speedily*. The result has been a continual upward drift in the price level, or long-term inflation.

Figure 10-9 on page 234 shows that real GDP has grown in most years since 1970. Nevertheless, this growth has been accompanied by higher prices every single year.

CONCEPTS in Brief

- When the economy is in long-run equilibrium, the price level adjusts to equate total planned real expenditures by individuals, businesses, and the government with total planned production by firms.

- Economic growth causes the long-run aggregate supply schedule to shift rightward over time. If the position of the aggregate demand curve does not change, the long-run equilibrium price level tends to decline, and there is secular deflation.

- Because the U.S. economy has grown in recent decades, the persistent inflation during those years has been caused by the aggregate demand curve shifting rightward at a faster pace than the long-run aggregate supply curve.

To test your understanding of the concepts covered in this section, go to the Online Review at www.myeconlab.com/miller.

FIGURE 10-9

Economic Growth and Inflation in the United States, 1970 to the Present

This figure shows the points where aggregate demand and aggregate supply have intersected each year from 1970 to the present. The United States has experienced economic growth over this period, but not without inflation.

Sources: *Economic Report of the President; Economic Indicators,* various issues; author's estimates.

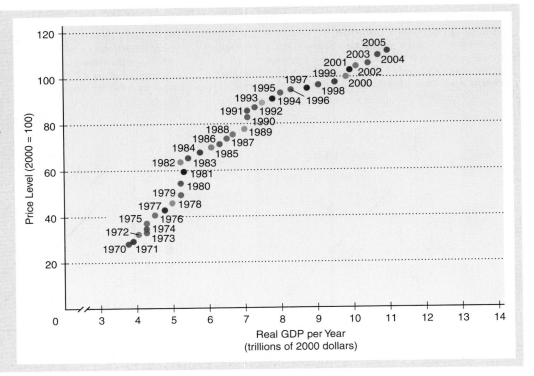

CASE STUDY: Economics Front and Center

Responding to a Rise in the Price Level

Taylor recently graduated from college. She has landed a job providing an income that will fund many of the purchases she had postponed while she was in school. Taylor has a long list of planned expenditures she has determined she can just "afford" to make, given her annual salary. These include acquiring a new set of fashionable business clothes, replacing her foreign-manufactured compact car with a sporty, U.S.-manufactured sedan, and moving from her rental apartment to a more conveniently located condominium.

Some recent events have complicated her careful planning, however. The inflation rate, which had averaged no more than 2 percent throughout her college years, has suddenly jumped to 3.5 percent. U.S. automobile prices are rising even faster than the overall inflation rate. Furthermore, interest rates on mortgage loans for condominium purchases are rising with each

passing week. Taylor now realizes that because her next salary increase likely will not occur for several months, she will have to give up something on her list of planned expenditures.

Points to Analyze

1. *How has the jump in the rate of growth in the overall U.S. price level caused Taylor to confront all three effects accounting for the downward slope of the aggregate demand curve?*

2. *If Taylor decides to postpone taking out a mortgage loan to purchase a condominium until at least next year, which of the three effects accounts for her own reduction in planned expenditures in response to the jump in the price level?*

Distinguishing Between Different Sources of Deflation

Several nations have experienced deflation in recent years. A number of media commentators have suggested that deflation must be a sign of serious troubles in these nations' economies. Policymakers in these countries, they argue, should do everything in their power to prevent deflation. Societies are better off, according to the media commentators, experiencing periodic bouts of inflation than even a hint of deflation.

Concepts Applied
- Deflation
- Long-Run Aggregate Supply
- Aggregate Demand
- Long-Run Equilibrium

U.S. Deflation in the Early 1930s

Many of the media commentators who are so worried about deflation attempt to draw parallels between current deflations and the deflationary experience of much of the world during the Great Depression of the 1930s. As you can see in panel (a) of Table 10-2 on the following page, the U.S. price level fell every year between 1930 and 1933. In addition, U.S. real GDP declined during each of these years.

Let's think about how this could have occurred in the context of the aggregate demand–aggregate supply framework developed in this chapter. A decline in equilibrium real GDP over a period of several years can be caused by a persistent fall in long-run aggregate supply. This will cause a sustained leftward movement along the aggregate demand curve and raise the equilibrium price level. In fact, the opposite occured—the price level fell year after year during the early 1930s, which implies that aggregate demand must also have declined significantly during this period. Thus the deflation of the 1930s can best be explained by simultaneous decreases in *both* long-run aggregate supply *and* aggregate demand.

Japanese and Chinese Deflation in the 2000s

Now take a look at panels (b) and (c) of Table 10-2, which display annual rates of growth of real GDP and rates of deflation for Japan and China. Both nations experienced moderate decreases in their price levels during the early 2000s. At the same time, however, real GDP rose in both countries. In contrast to the U.S. experience of the 1930s, therefore, deflation accompanied *increases* in real GDP in Japan and China.

The increases in real GDP during this period imply that long-run aggregate supply rose in both nations. As you learned in this chapter, if aggregate demand remains unchanged, the result of a rightward shift in the *LRAS* curve is a decline in the equilibrium price level. This indicates that the deflationary experiences of Japan and China in the 2000s were very different from the U.S. bout with deflation in the 1930s. In the 2000s, a rise in long-run aggregate supply has boosted real GDP and reduced the price level in Japan and China. In contrast, in the 1930s a temporary fall in long-run aggregate supply caused U.S. real GDP to fall at the same time that lower aggregate demand pushed down the U.S. price level. Media commentators have been misguided in trying to draw direct parallels between the deflations of the 1930s and the 2000s.

TABLE 10-2
Deflationary Episodes in the United States, Japan, and China
U.S. deflation during the early 1930s accompanied declines in real GDP. In contrast, deflation in Japan and China during the early 2000s took place while real GDP was increasing.

(a) United States, 1930–1933				
	1930	1931	1932	1933
Real GDP growth	−13.1	−12.1	−17.5	−4.8
Rate of deflation	−0.9	−9.2	−10.2	−2.5

(b) Japan, 2001–2004				
	2001	2002	2003	2004
Real GDP growth	+1.0	+0.5	+2.0	+1.4
Rate of deflation	−1.6	−1.7	−2.5	−2.0

(c) China, 2001–2004				
	2001	2002	2003	2004
Real GDP growth	+7.5	+8.0	+7.5	+7.5
Rate of deflation	−0.8	−1.3	−0.8	+0.7

Sources: Federal Reserve Bank of Cleveland, 2002 Annual Report; International Monetary Fund.

For Critical Analysis:

1. Does deflation necessarily accompany a lower standard of living?
2. How can the aggregate demand–aggregate supply framework explain why real GDP and the price level both rose in the United States between 2001 and 2004?

Web Resources

1. To read a Federal Reserve Bank of Cleveland survey of issues associated with deflation, go to the link at **www.econtoday.com/chap10**. and click on "2002 Annual Report."
2. For a look at the Japanese and Chinese experiences with deflation from Japan's perspective, go to **www.econtoday.com/chap10**.

Research Project

As you learned in Chapter 7, unanticipated deflation redistributes resources from debtors to creditors. If policymakers in China and Japan wish to prevent such redistributions from occurring, what types of policies might they enact to maintain long-run price stability in the face of increased long-run aggregate supply?

SUMMARY DISCUSSION of Learning Objectives

1. **Long-Run Aggregate Supply:** The long-run aggregate supply curve is vertical at the amount of real GDP that firms plan to produce when they have full information and when complete adjustment of input prices to any changes in output prices has taken place. This is the full-employment level of real GDP, or the economywide output level at which the natural rate of unemployment—the sum of frictional and structural unemployment as a percentage of the labor force—occurs.

2. **Economic Growth and the Long-Run Aggregate Supply Curve:** Economic growth is an expansion of a country's production possibilities. Thus the production possibilities curve shifts rightward when the economy grows, and so does the nation's long-run aggregate supply curve. In a growing economy, the changes in full-employment real GDP defined by the shifting long-run aggregate supply curve define the nation's long-run, or trend, growth path.

3. **Why the Aggregate Demand Curve Slopes Downward and Factors That Cause It to Shift:** A rise in the price level reduces the real value of cash balances in the hands of the public, which induces people to cut back on planned spending. This is the real-balance effect. In addition, higher interest rates typically accompany increases in the price level, and this interest rate effect induces people to cut back on borrowing and, consequently, spending. Finally, a rise in the price level at home causes domestic goods to be more expensive relative to foreign goods, so that there is a fall in exports and a rise in imports, both of which cause domestic planned expenditures to fall. These three factors together account for the downward slope of the aggregate demand curve. A shift in the aggregate demand curve results from a change in total planned real expenditures at any given price level and may be caused by a number of factors, including changes in security about jobs and future income, tax changes, variations in the quantity of money in circulation, changes in real interest rates, movements in exchange rates, and changes in economic conditions in other countries.

4. **Long-Run Equilibrium for the Economy:** In a long-run economywide equilibrium, the price level adjusts until total planned real expenditures equal actual real GDP. Thus the long-run equilibrium price level is determined at the point where the aggregate demand curve intersects the long-run aggregate supply curve. If the price level is below its long-run equilibrium value, total planned real expenditures exceed actual real GDP, and the level of prices of goods and services will rise back toward the long-run equilibrium price level. In contrast, if the price level is above its long-run equilibrium value, actual real GDP is greater than total planned real expenditures, and the price level declines in the direction of the long-run equilibrium price level.

5. **Why Economic Growth Can Cause Deflation:** If the aggregate demand curve is stationary during a period of economic growth, the long-run aggregate supply curve shifts rightward along the aggregate demand curve. The long-run equilibrium price level falls, so there is deflation. Historically, economic growth has in this way generated secular deflation, or relatively long periods of declining prices.

6. **Likely Reasons for Recent Persistent Inflation:** One event that can induce inflation is a decline in long-run aggregate supply, because this causes the long-run aggregate supply curve to shift leftward. In a growing economy, however, the long-run aggregate supply curve generally shifts rightward. This indicates that a much more likely cause of persistent inflation is a pace of aggregate demand growth that exceeds the pace at which long-run aggregate supply increases.

KEY TERMS AND CONCEPTS

aggregate demand (225)

aggregate demand curve (225)

aggregate supply (221)

endowments (222)

interest rate effect (227)

long-run aggregate supply curve (222)

open economy effect (227)

real-balance effect (226)

secular deflation (229)

PROBLEMS

Answers to the odd-numbered problems appear at the back of the book.

10-1. Many economists view the natural rate of unemployment as the level observed when real GDP is given by the position of the long-run aggregate supply curve. How can there be positive unemployment in this situation?

10-2. Suppose that the long-run aggregate supply curve is positioned at a real GDP level of $12 trillion, and the long-run equilibrium price level (in index number form) is 115. What is the full-employment level of *nominal* GDP?

10-3. Continuing from Problem 10-2, suppose that the full-employment level of *nominal* GDP in the following year rises to $14.2 trillion. The long-run equilibrium price level, however, remains unchanged. By how much (in real dollars) has the long-run aggregate supply curve shifted to the right in the following year?

10-4. Suppose that the position of a nation's long-run aggregate supply curve has not changed, but its long-run equilibrium price level has increased. Which of the following factors might account for this event?

a. A rise in the value of the domestic currency relative to other world currencies

b. An increase in the quantity of money in circulation

c. An increase in the labor force participation rate

d. A decrease in taxes

e. A rise in real incomes of countries that are key trading partners of this nation

f. Increased long-run economic growth

10-5. Suppose that during a given year, the quantity of U.S. real GDP that can be produced in the long run rises from $11.9 trillion to $12.0 trillion with no change in the various factors that influence aggregate demand. What will happen to the U.S. long-run equilibrium price level during this particular year?

10-6. Assume that the position of a nation's aggregate demand curve has not changed, but the long-run equilibrium price level has declined. Other things being equal, which of the following factors might account for this event?

a. An increase in labor productivity

b. A decrease in the capital stock

c. A decrease in the quantity of money in circulation

d. The discovery of new mineral resources used to produce various goods

e. A technological improvement

10-7. Suppose that there is a sudden rise in the price level. What will happen to economywide planned spending on purchases of goods and services? Why?

10-8. Assume that the economy is in long-run equilibrium with complete information and that input prices adjust rapidly to changes in the prices of goods and services. If there is a sudden rise in the price level, what happens to real GDP?

10-9. Consider the accompanying diagram when answering the questions that follow.

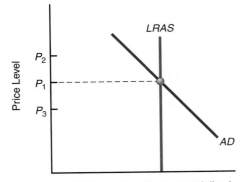

Real GDP per Year (base year dollars)

a. Suppose that the current price level is P_2. Explain why the price level will decline toward P_1.

b. Suppose that the current price level is P_3. Explain why the price level will rise toward P_1.

10-10. A country's long-run equilibrium price level has increased, but the position of its aggregate demand schedule has not changed. What has happened? What specific factors might have accounted for this event?

10-11. In this chapter you learned that if aggregate demand is unchanged, we can predict that deflation sometimes accompanies economic growth. Based on what you learned in Chapter 7 about the effects of expected and unexpected inflation, is predictable deflation necessarily undesirable? Support your position.

10-12. This year, a nation's long-run equilibrium real GDP and price level both increased. Which of the following combinations of factors might simultaneously account for *both* occurrences?

a. An isolated earthquake at the beginning of the year destroyed part of the nation's capital stock, and the nation's government significantly reduced its purchases of goods and services.

b. There was a minor technological improvement at the end of the previous year, and the quantity of money in circulation rose significantly during the year.

c. Labor productivity increased somewhat throughout the year, and consumers significantly increased their total planned purchases of goods and services.

d. The capital stock increased somewhat during the year, and the quantity of money in circulation declined considerably.

10-13. Explain how, if at all, each of the following events would affect equilibrium real GDP and the long-run equilibrium price level.

a. A reduction in the quantity of money in circulation

b. An income tax rebate from the government to households, which they can apply only to purchases of goods and services

c. A technological improvement

d. A decrease in the value of the home currency in terms of the currencies of other nations

ECONOMICS ON THE NET

Wages, Productivity, and Aggregate Supply How much firms pay their employees and the productivity of those employees influence firms' total planned production, so changes in these factors affect the position of the aggregate supply curve. This application gives you the opportunity to examine recent trends in measures of the overall wages and productivity of workers.

Title: Bureau of Labor Statistics: Economy at a Glance

Navigation: Use the link at www.econtoday.com/chap10 to visit the Bureau of Labor Statistics Web site.

Application Perform the indicated operations, and answer the following questions.

1. Click on *Employment Costs,* and then click on *Employee Cost Index.* What are the recent trends in wages and salaries and in benefits? In the long run, how should these trends be related to movements in the overall price level?

2. Back up to the home page, and click on *Productivity and Costs* and then *PDF* next to "Economic News Releases: Productivity and Costs." How has labor productivity be-

haved recently? What does this imply for the long-run aggregate supply curve?

3. Back up to U.S. Economy at a Glance, and now click on *National Employment,* and then *PDF* next to "Economic News Releases: Employment Situation Summary." Does it appear that the U.S. economy is currently in a long-run growth equilibrium?

For Group Study and Analysis

1. Divide the class into aggregate demand and long-run aggregate supply groups. Have each group search the Internet for data on factors that influence its assigned curve. For which factors do data appear to be most readily available? For which factors are data more sparse or more subject to measurement problems?

2. The BLS home page displays a map of the United States. Assign regions of the nation to different groups, and have each group develop a short report about current and future prospects for economic growth within its assigned region. What similarities exist across regions? What regional differences are there?

Media Resources

If your exam were tomorrow, would you be ready? For each chapter, MyEconLab Practice Tests and Study Plans pinpoint which sections you have mastered and which ones you need to study. That way, you are more efficient with your study time, and you are better prepared for your exams.

In addition to Practice Tests and your personalized Study Plan, you'll find the following media resources in MyEconLab:

1. *Graphs in Motion* animation of Figures 10-1, 10-2, 10-3, 10-4, 10-5, 10-6, 10-7, and 10-8.
2. Videos featuring the author, Roger LeRoy Miller, on the following subjects:
   - The Long-Run Aggregate Supply Curve
   - The Aggregate Demand Curve and What Happens When the Price Level Rises
   - Shifts in the Aggregate Demand Curve

3. Links to the Web sites cited in the marginal Internet Resources, Issues and Applications feature, and Economics on the Net activity.
4. Audio clips of all key terms, additional practice problems, and a PDF version of the material from the print Study Guide.
5. eThemes of the Times, which is a New York Times article to help you understand the real-world applications of what you are learning.

Get Ahead of the Curve

To see how it works, turn to page 16 and then go to www.myeconlab.com/miller.

Chapter 11

Classical and Keynesian Macro Analyses

Cargo ships transport nearly 8 million containers to the United States each year. Getting a single container from one foreign location to a U.S. port can involve as many as 25 different parties and 35 to 40 separate shipping documents. Thus a typical cargo ship's load generates as many as 100,000 legal documents. Nevertheless, due to heightened terrorism concerns, between 2002 and 2005 the U.S. government added a completely new layer of bureaucracy for shippers. It began requiring detailed reports on the contents of every single container at least 24 hours before it is scheduled to arrive at a U.S. port. This new regulation caused U.S. shipping costs to rise by billions of dollars per year. In this chapter, you will learn why this rise in regulatory costs tended to reduce the rate of growth in real GDP.

Media Resources

Refer to the end of the chapter for a full listing of the multimedia learning materials available in MyEconLab.

LEARNING OBJECTIVES

After reading this chapter, you should be able to:

1. Discuss the central assumptions of the classical model
2. Describe the short-run determination of equilibrium real GDP and the price level in the classical model
3. Explain circumstances under which the short-run aggregate supply curve may be either horizontal or upward sloping
4. Understand what factors cause shifts in the short-run and long-run aggregate supply curves
5. Evaluate the effects of aggregate demand and supply shocks on equilibrium real GDP in the short run
6. Determine the causes of short-run variations in the inflation rate

... the price of a bottle containing 6.5 ounces of Coca-Cola remained unchanged at 5 cents from 1886 to 1959? The prices of many other goods and services changed at least slightly during that 73-year period, and since then the prices of most items, including Coca-Cola, have generally moved in an upward direction. Nevertheless, prices of final goods and services have not always adjusted immediately in response to changes in the input prices. Consequently, one approach to understanding the determination of real GDP and the price level emphasizes *incomplete* adjustment in the prices of many goods and services. The simplest version of this approach was first developed by a twentieth-century economist named John Maynard Keynes (pronounced like *canes*). It assumes that in the short run, prices of most goods and services are nearly as rigid as the price of Coca-Cola from 1886 to 1959. Although the modern version of the Keynesian approach allows for greater flexibility of prices in the short run, incomplete price adjustment still remains a key feature of the modern Keynesian approach.

*Did You Know **That***

The Keynesian approach does not retain the long-run assumption, which you encountered in Chapter 10, of fully adjusting prices. Economists who preceded Keynes employed this assumption in creating an approach to understanding variations in real GDP and the price level that Keynes called the *classical model*. Like Keynes, we shall begin our study of variations in real GDP and the price level by considering the earlier, classical approach.

THE CLASSICAL MODEL

The classical model, which traces its origins to the 1770s, was the first systematic attempt to explain the determinants of the price level and the national levels of output, income, employment, consumption, saving, and investment. Classical economists—Adam Smith, J. B. Say, David Ricardo, John Stuart Mill, Thomas Malthus, A. C. Pigou, and others—wrote from the 1770s to the 1930s. They assumed, among other things, that all wages and prices were flexible and that competitive markets existed throughout the economy.

Say's Law

Every time you produce something for which you receive income, you generate the income necessary to make expenditures on other goods and services. That means that an economy producing $12 trillion of GDP (final goods and services) simultaneously produces the income with which these goods and services can be purchased. As an accounting identity, *actual* aggregate output always equals *actual* aggregate income. Classical economists took this accounting identity one step further by arguing that total national supply creates its own national demand. They asserted what has become known as **Say's law:**

> **Supply creates its own demand; hence it follows that** desired *expenditures will equal* **actual** *expenditures.*

What does Say's law really mean? It states that the very process of producing specific goods (supply) is proof that other goods are desired (demand). People produce more goods than they want for their own use only if they seek to trade them for other goods. Someone offers to supply something only because he or she has a demand for something else. The implication of this, according to Say, is that no general glut, or overproduction, is possible in a market economy. From this reasoning, it seems to follow that full employment of labor and other resources would be the normal state of affairs in such an economy.

Say acknowledged that an oversupply of some goods might occur in particular markets. He argued that such surpluses would simply cause prices to fall, thereby decreasing

Say's law
A dictum of economist J. B. Say that supply creates its own demand; producing goods and services generates the means and the willingness to purchase other goods and services.

FIGURE 11-1
Say's Law and the Circular Flow
Here we show the circular flow of income and output. The very act of supplying a certain level of goods and services necessarily equals the level of goods and services demanded, in Say's simplified world.

production as the economy adjusted. The opposite would occur in markets in which shortages temporarily appeared.

All this seems reasonable enough in a simple barter economy in which households produce most of the goods they want and trade for the rest. This is shown in Figure 11-1, where there is a simple circular flow. But what about a more sophisticated economy in which people work for others and money is used instead of barter? Can these complications create the possibility of unemployment? And does the fact that laborers receive money income, some of which can be saved, lead to unemployment? No, said the classical economists to these last two questions. They based their reasoning on a number of key assumptions.

Assumptions of the Classical Model

The classical model makes four major assumptions:

1. *Pure competition exists.* No single buyer or seller of a commodity or an input can affect its price.
2. *Wages and prices are flexible.* The assumption of pure competition leads to the notion that prices, wages, interest rates, and the like are free to move to whatever level supply and demand dictate (as the economy adjusts). Although no *individual* buyer can set a price, the community of buyers or sellers can cause prices to rise or to fall to an equilibrium level.
3. *People are motivated by self-interest.* Businesses want to maximize their profits, and households want to maximize their economic well-being.
4. *People cannot be fooled by money illusion.* Buyers and sellers react to changes in relative prices. That is to say, they do not suffer from **money illusion.** For example, workers will not be fooled into thinking that a doubling of wages makes them better off if the price level has also doubled during the same time period.

Money illusion
Reacting to changes in money prices rather than relative prices. If a worker whose wages double when the price level also doubles thinks he or she is better off, that worker is suffering from money illusion.

The classical economists concluded, after taking account of the four major assumptions, that the role of government in the economy should be minimal. If all prices and wages are flexible, any problems in the macroeconomy will be temporary. The market will correct itself.

Equilibrium in the Credit Market

When income is saved, it is not reflected in product demand. It is a type of *leakage* from the circular flow of income and output because saving withdraws funds from the income stream. Therefore, total planned consumption spending *can* fall short of total current real GDP. In such a situation, it does not appear that supply necessarily creates its own demand.

The classical economists did not believe that the complicating factor of saving in the circular flow model of income and output was a problem. They contended that each dollar saved would be invested by businesses so that the leakage of saving would be matched by the injection of business investment. *Investment* here refers only to additions to the nation's capital stock. The classical economists believed that businesses as a group would intend to invest as much as households wanted to save.

Equilibrium between the saving plans of consumers and the investment plans of businesses comes about, in the classical economists' model, through the working of the credit market. In the credit market, the *price* of credit is the interest rate. At equilibrium, the price of credit—the interest rate—ensures that the amount of credit demanded equals the amount of credit supplied. Planned investment just equals planned saving, so there is no reason to be concerned about the leakage of saving. This is illustrated graphically in Figure 11-2.

In the figure, the vertical axis measures the rate of interest in percentage terms; on the horizontal axis are the amounts of desired saving and desired investment per unit time period. The desired saving curve is really a supply curve of saving. It shows that people wish to save more at higher interest rates than at lower interest rates.

By contrast, the higher the rate of interest, the less profitable it is to invest and the lower is the level of desired investment. Thus the desired investment curve slopes downward. In this simplified model, the equilibrium rate of interest is 5 percent, and the equilibrium quantity of saving and investment is $1.6 trillion per year.

As the rate at which U.S. households save out of their after-tax income has declined to historically low levels, where are U.S. businesses obtaining funds to invest?

Go to www.econtoday.com/chap11 to link to Federal Reserve data on U.S. interest rates.

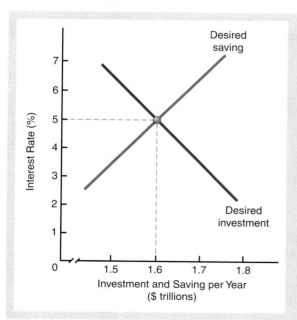

FIGURE 11-2

Equating Desired Saving and Investment in the Classical Model

The schedule showing planned investment is labeled "Desired investment." The supply of resources used for investment occurs when individuals do not consume but save instead. The desired saving curve is shown as an upward-sloping supply curve of saving. The equilibrating force here is, of course, the interest rate. At higher interest rates, people desire to save more. But at higher interest rates, businesses wish to engage in less investment because it is less profitable to invest. In this model, at an interest rate of 5 percent, planned investment just equals planned saving, which is $1.6 trillion per year.

EXAMPLE

Will the Drop in the Private Saving Rate Choke Off Gross Private Domestic Investment?

Many media stories have discussed the sharp decline in the personal saving rate, which equals *net* household saving—net of borrowing—as a percentage of gross domestic product. Since 1992, the personal saving rate has fallen from 9 percent to about 0.8 percent of GDP. According to some media commentators, this means that funds for business investment necessarily are dwindling to a trickle.

Nevertheless, during recent years, gross private domestic investment in the U.S. economy has amounted to 13 to 14 percent of GDP. Clearly, net household saving funds only a small portion of gross private domestic investment. Firms also obtain investment funds by retaining and reinvesting some of their earnings. A third source is other countries. Foreign residents have poured hundreds of billions of dollars per

year of their savings into the United States. Thus it is *gross* private saving including these additional sources, *not* just net household saving, that is equivalent to gross private domestic investment in equilibrium. Indeed, measured U.S. gross private saving has averaged 13 to 14 percent of GDP in recent years. If not for statistical discrepancies arising from the government's difficulties in accurately measuring saving, gross private saving would exactly equal gross private domestic investment, as shown in Figure 11-2 on page 243.

For Critical Analysis
What would happen to equilibrium U.S. investment if foreign residents suddenly decided that they no longer wished to save in the United States?

Go to www.econtoday.com/chap11 to find out the latest U.S. saving rate from the Bureau of Economic Analysis. Select "Personal saving as a percentage of disposable personal income."

Economics Front and Center

To see how changes in the condition of the labor market can affect the choices confronting an individual job seeker, see the case study, **Holding Out for a Better Salary Offer in an Improved Job Climate,** on page 258.

Equilibrium in the Labor Market

Now consider the labor market. If an excess quantity of labor is supplied at a particular wage level, the wage level must be above equilibrium. By accepting lower wages, unemployed workers will quickly be put back to work. We show equilibrium in the labor market in Figure 11-3.

Assume that equilibrium exists at $16 per hour and 150 million workers employed. If the wage rate were $18 per hour, there would be unemployment—160 million workers would want to work, but businesses would want to hire only 140 million. In the classical model, this unemployment is eliminated rather rapidly by wage rates dropping back to $16 per hour.

The Relationship Between Employment and Real GDP. Employment is not to be regarded simply as some isolated figure that government statisticians estimate. Rather, the level of employment in an economy determines its real GDP (output), other things held constant. A hypothetical relationship between input (number of employees) and the value of output (rate of real GDP per year) is shown in Table 11-1. The row that has 150 million workers per year as the labor input is highlighted. That might be considered a hypothetical level of full employment, and it is related to a rate of real GDP of $12 trillion per year.

Classical Theory, Vertical Aggregate Supply, and the Price Level

In the classical model, long-term unemployment is impossible. Say's law, coupled with flexible interest rates, prices, and wages, would always tend to keep workers fully employed so that the aggregate supply curve, as shown in Figure 11-4 on page 246, is vertical at Y_0. We have labeled the supply curve *LRAS*, consistent with the long-run aggregate supply curve introduced in Chapter 10. It was defined there as the quantity of output that would be produced in an economy with full information and full adjustment of wages and prices year in and year out. *LRAS* is therefore at the long-run, full (natural) rate of

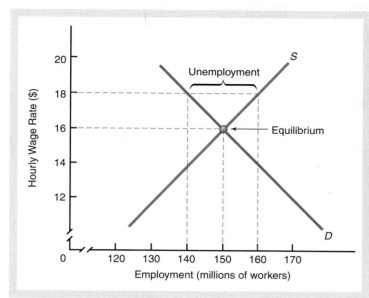

FIGURE 11-3
Equilibrium in the Labor Market
The demand for labor is downward sloping; at higher wage rates, firms will employ fewer workers. The supply of labor is upward sloping; at higher wage rates, more workers will work longer, and more people will be willing to work. The equilibrium wage rate is $16 with an equilibrium employment per year of 150 million workers.

TABLE 11-1
The Relationship Between Employment and Real GDP
Other things being equal, an increase in the quantity of labor input increases real GDP. In this example, if 150 million workers are employed, real GDP is $12 trillion in base year dollars.

Labor Input per Year (millions of workers)	Real GDP per Year ($ trillions)
140	9
144	10
148	11
150	12
154	13
156	14

unemployment. In the classical model, this happens to be the *only* aggregate supply curve that exists. The classical economists made little distinction between the long run and the short run. Prices adjust so fast that the economy is essentially always on or quickly moving toward *LRAS*. Furthermore, because the labor market adjusts rapidly, Y_0 is always at, or soon to be at, full employment. Full employment does not mean zero unemployment because there is always some frictional and structural unemployment (discussed in Chapter 7), even in the classical world. This is the natural rate of unemployment.

Effect of an Increase in Aggregate Demand in the Classical Model. In this model, any change in aggregate demand will quickly cause a change in the price level. Consider starting at E_1, at price level 120. If aggregate demand shifts to AD_2, the economy will tend toward point A, but because this is beyond full employment, prices will rise, and the economy will find itself back on the vertical *LRAS* at point E_2 at a higher price level, 130. The price level will increase as a result of the increase in AD because employers will end up bidding up wages for workers, as well as bidding up the prices of other inputs.

FIGURE 11-4

Classical Theory and Increases in Aggregate Demand

The classical theorists believed that Say's law, flexible interest rates, prices, and wages would always lead to full employment at Y_0 along the vertical aggregate supply curve, *LRAS*. With aggregate demand AD_1 the price level is 120. An increase in aggregate demand shifts AD_1, to AD_2. At price level 120, the quantity of real GDP demanded per year is at point A on AD_2, or Y_1. But this is greater than at full employment. Prices rise, and the economy quickly moves from E_1, to E_2, at the higher price level of 130.

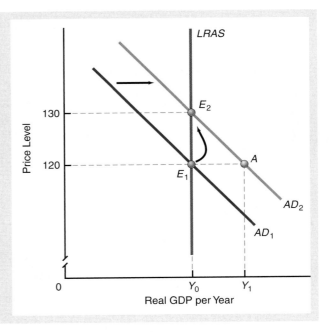

The level of real GDP per year clearly does not depend on the level of aggregate demand. Hence we say that in the classical model, the equilibrium level of real GDP per year is completely *supply-determined*. Changes in aggregate demand affect only the price level, not real GDP.

Effect of a Decrease in Aggregate Demand in the Classical Model. The effect of a decrease in aggregate demand in the classical model is the converse of the analysis just presented for an increase in aggregate demand. You can simply reverse AD_2 and AD_1 in Figure 11-4. To help you see how this analysis works, consider the flowchart in Figure 11-5.

FIGURE 11-5

Effect of a Decrease in Aggregate Demand in the Classical Model

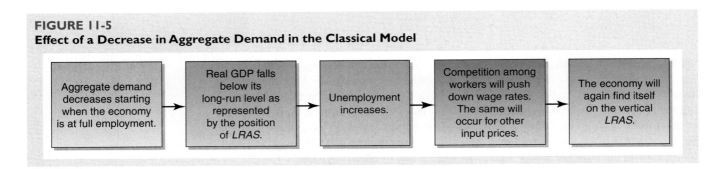

CONCEPTS in Brief

- Say's law states that supply creates its own demand and therefore *desired* expenditures will equal *actual* expenditures.

- The classical model assumes that (1) pure competition exists, (2) wages and prices are completely flexible, (3) individuals are motivated by self-interest, and (4) they cannot be fooled by money illusion.

- When saving is introduced into the model, equilibrium occurs in the credit market through changes in the interest rate such that desired saving equals desired investment at the equilibrium rate of interest.

- In the labor market, full employment occurs at a wage rate at which quantity demanded equals quantity supplied. That

particular level of employment is associated with a full-employment value of real GDP per year.

- In the classical model, because LRAS is vertical, the equilibrium level of real GDP is supply-determined. Any changes in aggregate demand simply change the price level.

To test your understanding of the concepts covered in this section, go to the Online Review at www.myeconlab.com/miller.

KEYNESIAN ECONOMICS AND THE KEYNESIAN SHORT-RUN AGGREGATE SUPPLY CURVE

The classical economists' world was one of fully utilized resources. There would be no unused capacity and no unemployment. But then in the 1930s Europe entered a period of economic decline that could not be explained by the classical model. John Maynard Keynes developed an explanation that has since become known as the Keynesian model. Keynes and his followers argued that prices, especially the price of labor (wages), were inflexible downward due to the existence of unions and long-term contracts between businesses and workers. That meant that prices were "sticky." Keynes argued that in such a world, which has large amounts of excess capacity and unemployment, an increase in aggregate demand will not raise the price level, and a decrease in aggregate demand will not cause firms to lower prices.

This situation is depicted in Figure 11-6. For simplicity, Figure 11-6 does not show the point where the economy reaches capacity, and that is why *SRAS* never starts to slope upward. Moreover, we don't show *LRAS* in Figure 11-6 either. It would be a vertical line at the level of real GDP per year that is consistent with full employment. The short-run aggregate supply curve is labeled as the horizontal line *SRAS*. If we start out in equilibrium with aggregate demand at AD_1, the equilibrium level of real GDP per year is Y_1 at point E_1, and the equilibrium price level is P_0. If there is a rise in aggregate demand, so that the aggregate demand curve shifts outward to the right to AD_2, the equilibrium price level at

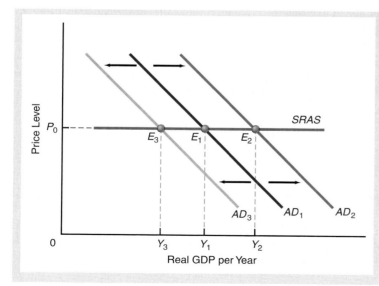

FIGURE 11-6
Demand-Determined Equilibrium Real GDP at Less Than Full Employment

Keynes assumed that prices will not fall when aggregate demand falls and that there is excess capacity, so prices will not rise when aggregate demand increases. Thus the short-run aggregate supply curve is simply a horizontal line at the given price level, P_0, represented by *SRAS*. An aggregate demand shock that increases aggregate demand to AD_2 will increase the equilibrium level of real GDP per year to Y_2. An aggregate demand shock that decreases aggregate demand to AD_3 will decrease the equilibrium level of real GDP to Y_3. The equilibrium price level will not change.

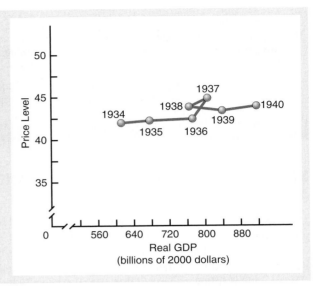

FIGURE 11-7
Real GDP and the Price Level, 1934–1940
Keynes suggested that in a depressed economy, increased aggregate spending can increase output without raising prices. The data for the United States' recovery from the Great Depression seem to bear this out. In such circumstances, real GDP is demand-determined.

point E_2 will not change; only the equilibrium level of real GDP per year will increase, to Y_2. Conversely, if there is a fall in demand that shifts the aggregate demand curve to AD_3, the equilibrium price level will again remain at P_0 at point E_3, but the equilibrium level of real GDP per year will fall to Y_3.

Under such circumstances, the equilibrium level of real GDP per year is completely *demand-determined*.

The horizontal short-run aggregate supply curve represented in Figure 11-6 is often called the **Keynesian short-run aggregate supply curve.** According to Keynes, unions and long-term contracts are real-world factors that explain the inflexibility of *nominal* wage rates. Such stickiness of wages makes *involuntary* unemployment of labor a distinct possibility. The classical assumption of everlasting full employment no longer holds.

A good example of a horizontal short-run aggregate supply curve can be seen by examining data from the 1930s. Look at Figure 11-7, where you see real GDP in billions of 2000 dollars on the horizontal axis and the price level index on the vertical axis. From the early days of recovery from the Great Depression to the outbreak of World War II, real GDP increased without much rise in the price level. During this period, the economy experienced neither supply constraints nor any dramatic changes in the price level. The most simplified Keynesian model in which prices do not change is essentially an immediate post-Depression model that fits the data very well during this period.

Keynesian short-run aggregate supply curve
The horizontal portion of the aggregate supply curve in which there is excessive unemployment and unused capacity in the economy.

OUTPUT DETERMINATION USING AGGREGATE DEMAND AND AGGREGATE SUPPLY: FIXED VERSUS CHANGING PRICE LEVELS IN THE SHORT RUN

The underlying assumption of the simplified Keynesian model is that the relevant range of the short-run aggregate supply schedule (*SRAS*) is horizontal, as depicted in panel (a) of Figure 11-8. There you see that short-run aggregate supply is fixed at price level 120. If aggregate demand is AD_1 then the equilibrium level of real GDP is $12 trillion per year. If aggregate demand increases to AD_2 then the equilibrium level of real GDP increases to $13 trillion per year.

FIGURE 11-8

Real GDP Determination with Fixed versus Flexible Prices

In panel (a), the price level index is fixed at 120. An increase in aggregate demand from AD_1 to AD_2 moves the equilibrium level of real GDP from $12 trillion per year to $13 trillion per year in base year dollars. In panel (b), *SRAS* is upward sloping. The same shift in aggregate demand yields an equilibrium level of real GDP of only $12.5 trillion per year and a higher price level index at 130.

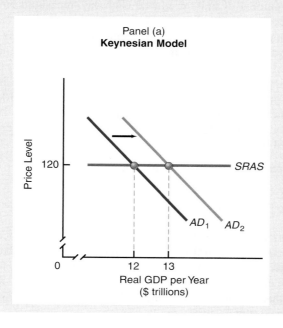

Panel (a)
Keynesian Model

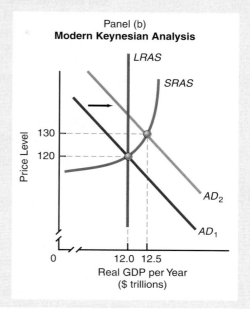

Panel (b)
Modern Keynesian Analysis

As discussed in Chapter 10, the price level has drifted upward during recent decades. Hence the assumption of totally sticky prices is an oversimplification. Modern Keynesian analysis recognizes that *some*—but not complete—price adjustment takes place in the short run. Panel (b) of Figure 11-8 displays a more general **short-run aggregate supply curve** (*SRAS*). This curve represents the relationship between the price level and real GDP with incomplete price adjustment and in the absence of complete information in the short run. Allowing for partial price adjustment implies that *SRAS* slopes upward, and its slope is steeper after it crosses long-run aggregate supply, *LRAS*. This is because higher and higher prices are required to induce firms to raise their production of goods and services to levels that temporarily exceed full-employment real GDP.

With gradual price adjustment in the short run, if aggregate demand is AD_1 then the equilibrium level of real GDP in panel (b) is also $12 trillion per year, also at a price level of 120. An increase in aggregate demand to AD_2 such as occurred in panel (a) produces a different equilibrium, however. Equilibrium real GDP increases to $12.5 trillion per year, which is less than in panel (a) because an increase in the price level to 130 causes real GDP to decline.

In the modern Keynesian short run, when the price level rises gradually, real GDP can be expanded beyond the level consistent with its long-run growth path, discussed in Chapter 10, for a variety of reasons:

1. In the short run, most labor contracts implicitly or explicitly call for flexibility in hours of work at the given wage rate. Therefore, firms can use existing workers more intensively in a variety of ways: They can get workers to work harder, to work more hours per day, and to work more days per week. Workers can also be

Short-run aggregate supply curve
The relationship between total planned economywide production and the price level in the short run, all other things held constant. If prices adjust incompletely in the short run, the curve is positively sloped.

switched from *uncounted* production, such as maintenance, to *counted* production, which generates counted production of goods and services. The distinction between counted and uncounted is simply what is measured in the marketplace, particularly by government statisticians and accountants. If a worker cleans a machine, there is no measured output. But if that worker is put on the production line and helps increase the number of units produced each day, measured output will go up. That worker's production has then been counted.

2. Existing capital equipment can be used more intensively. Machines can be worked more hours per day. Some can be made to operate faster. Maintenance can be delayed.

3. Finally, if wage rates are held constant, a higher price level leads to increased profits from additional production, which induces firms to hire more workers. The duration of unemployment falls, and thus the unemployment rate falls. And people who were previously not in the labor force (homemakers and younger or older workers) can be induced to enter.

All these adjustments cause real GDP to rise as the price level increases.

SHIFTS IN THE AGGREGATE SUPPLY CURVE

Just as non-price-level factors can cause a shift in the aggregate demand curve, there are non-price-level factors that can cause a shift in the aggregate supply curve. The analysis here is more complicated than the analysis for the non-price-level determinants for aggregate demand, for here we are dealing with both the short run and the long run—*SRAS* and *LRAS*. Still, anything other than the price level that affects the production of final goods and services will shift aggregate supply curves.

Shifts in Both Short- and Long–Run Aggregate Supply

There is a core class of events that cause a shift in both the short-run aggregate supply curve and the long-run aggregate supply curve. These include any change in our endowments of the factors of production.* Any change in a factor influencing economic growth—labor, capital, or technology—will shift *SRAS* and *LRAS*. Look at Figure 11-9. Initially, the two curves are $SRAS_1$ and $LRAS_1$. Now consider a major discovery of mineral deposits in Idaho, in an area where no one thought deposits of mineral inputs existed. This shifts $LRAS_1$ to $LRAS_2$ at $12.5 trillion of real GDP. $SRAS_1$ also shifts outward horizontally to $SRAS_2$.

Shifts in *SRAS* Only

Some events, particularly those that are short-lived, will temporarily shift *SRAS* but not *LRAS*. One of the most obvious is a change in input prices, particularly those caused by external events that are not expected to last forever. Consider the possibility of an announced 90-day embargo of oil from the Middle East to the United States. Oil is an impor-

---

*There is a complication here. A big enough increase in natural resources not only shifts aggregate supply outward but also affects aggregate demand. Aggregate demand is a function of people's wealth, among other things. A big domestic oil discovery, for example, will make enough people richer that desired total spending will increase. For the sake of simplicity, we ignore this complication.

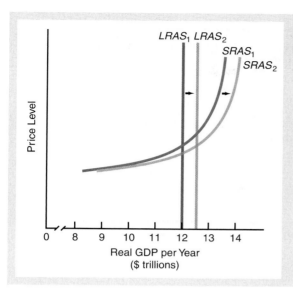

FIGURE 11-9

Shifts in Both Short- and Long-Run Aggregate Supply

Initially, the two supply curves are $SRAS_1$ and $LRAS_1$. Now consider a discovery of mineral deposits in Idaho in an area where no one thought such productive inputs existed. This shifts $LRAS_1$ to $LRAS_2$ at $12.5 trillion of real GDP. $SRAS_1$ also shifts outward horizontally to $SRAS_2$.

tant input in many production activities. The 90-day oil embargo will cause at least a temporary increase in the price of this input. You can see what happens in Figure 11-10. *LRAS* remains fixed, but $SRAS_1$ shifts to $SRAS_2$, reflecting the increase in input prices—the higher price of oil. This is because the rise in the costs of production at each level of real GDP per year requires a higher price level to cover those increased costs.

We summarize the possible determinants of aggregate supply in Table 11-2 on the next page. These determinants will cause a shift in the short-run or the long-run aggregate supply curve or both, depending on whether they are temporary or permanent.

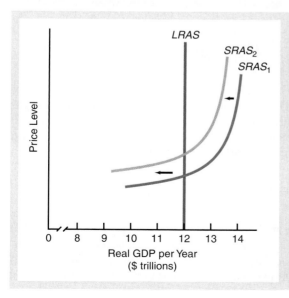

FIGURE 11-10

Shifts in *SRAS* Only

A temporary increase in an input price will shift the short-run aggregate supply curve from $SRAS_1$ to $SRAS_2$.

TABLE 11-2
Determinants of Aggregate Supply
The determinants listed here can affect short-run or long-run aggregate supply (or both), depending on whether they are temporary or permanent.

Changes That Cause an Increase in Aggregate Supply	Changes That Cause a Decrease in Aggregate Supply
Discoveries of new raw materials	Depletion of raw materials
Increased competition	Decreased competition
A reduction in international trade barriers	An increase in international trade barriers
Fewer regulatory impediments to business	More regulatory impediments to business
An increase in the supply of labor	A decrease in labor supplied
Increased training and education	Decreased training and education
A decrease in marginal tax rates	An increase in marginal tax rates
A reduction in input prices	An increase in input prices

CONCEPTS in Brief

- If we assume that we are operating on a horizontal short-run aggregate supply curve, the equilibrium level of real GDP per year is completely demand-determined.

- The horizontal short-run aggregate supply curve has been called the Keynesian short-run aggregate supply curve because Keynes believed that many prices, especially wages, would not be reduced even when aggregate demand decreased.

- In modern Keynesian theory, the short-run aggregate supply curve, *SRAS*, shows the relationship between the price level and real GDP without full adjustment or full informa-

tion. It is upward sloping because it allows for only partial price adjustment in the short run.

- Real GDP can be expanded in the short run because firms can use existing workers and capital equipment more intensively. Also, in the short run, when input prices are fixed, a higher price level means higher profits, which induces firms to hire more workers.

- Any change in factors influencing long-run output, such as labor, capital, or technology, will shift both *SRAS* and *LRAS*. A temporary shift in input prices, however, will shift only *SRAS*.

To test your understanding of the concepts covered in this section, go to the Online Review at www.myeconlab.com/miller.

CONSEQUENCES OF CHANGES IN AGGREGATE SHORT-RUN DEMAND

We now have a basic model to apply when evaluating short-run adjustments of the equilibrium price level and equilibrium real GDP when there are shocks to the economy. Whenever there is a shift in the aggregate demand or supply curves, the equilibrium price level or real GDP level (or both) may change. These shifts are called **aggregate demand shocks** on the demand side and **aggregate supply shocks** on the supply side.

Aggregate demand shock
Any event that causes the aggregate demand curve to shift inward or outward.

Aggregate supply shock
Any event that causes the aggregate supply curve to shift inward or outward.

Effects When Aggregate Demand Falls While Aggregate Supply Is Stable

Now we can show what happens in the short run when aggregate supply remains stable but aggregate demand falls. The short-run outcome may be a recession and a rise in the unemployment rate. In Figure 11-11, you see that with AD_1, both long-run and short-run equilibrium are at $12 trillion of real GDP per year (because *SRAS* and *LRAS* also intersect

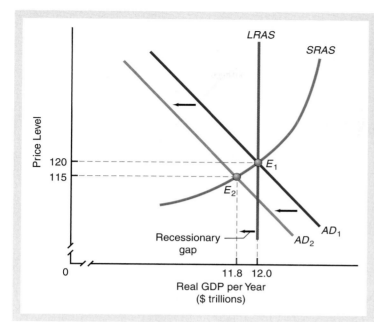

FIGURE 11-11
The Short-Run Effects of Stable Aggregate Supply and a Decrease in Aggregate Demand: The Recessionary Gap
If the economy is at equilibrium at E_1, with price level 120 and real GDP per year of $12 trillion, a shift inward of the aggregate demand curve to AD_2 will lead to a new short-run equilibrium at E_2. The equilibrium price level will fall to 115, and the short-run equilibrium level of real GDP per year will fall to $11.8 trillion. There will be a recessionary gap of $200 billion.

AD_1 at that level of real GDP). The long-run equilibrium price level is 120. A reduction in aggregate demand shifts the aggregate demand curve to AD_2. The new intersection with *SRAS* is at $11.8 trillion per year, which is less than the long-run equilibrium level of real GDP. The difference between $12 trillion and $11.8 trillion is called a **recessionary gap,** defined as the difference between the short-run equilibrium level of real GDP and real GDP if the economy were operating at full employment on its *LRAS*.

In effect, at E_2, the economy is in short-run equilibrium at less than full employment. With too many unemployed inputs, input prices will begin to fall. Eventually, *SRAS* will have to shift down. Where will it intersect AD_2?

Recessionary gap
The gap that exists whenever equilibrium real GDP per year is less than full-employment real GDP as shown by the position of the long-run aggregate supply curve.

Short-Run Effects When Aggregate Demand Increases

We can reverse the situation and have aggregate demand increase to AD_2, as is shown in Figure 11-12 on the next page. The initial equilibrium conditions are exactly the same as in Figure 11-11. The move to AD_2 increases the short-run equilibrium from E_1 to E_2 such that the economy is operating at $12.2 trillion of real GDP per year, which exceeds *LRAS*. This is a condition of an overheated economy, typically called an **inflationary gap.**

At E_2 in Figure 11-12, the economy is at a short-run equilibrium that is beyond full employment. In the short run, more can be squeezed out of the economy than occurs in the long-run, full-information, full-adjustment situation. Firms will be operating beyond long-run capacity. Inputs will be working too hard. Input prices will begin to rise. That will eventually cause *SRAS* to shift upward. At what point on AD_2 in Figure 11-12 will the new *SRAS* stop shifting?

How do you suppose the price level in China responded to a sudden rise in aggregate demand in 2003?

Inflationary gap
The gap that exists whenever equilibrium real GDP per year is greater than full-employment real GDP as shown by the position of the long-run aggregate supply curve.

FIGURE 11-12
The Effects of Stable Aggregate Supply with an Increase in Aggregate Demand: The Inflationary Gap

The economy is at equilibrium at E_1. An increase in aggregate demand of AD_2 leads to a new short-run equilibrium at E_2 with the price level rising from 120 to 125 and equilibrium real GDP per year rising from $12 trillion to $12.2 trillion. The difference, $200 billion, is called the inflationary gap.

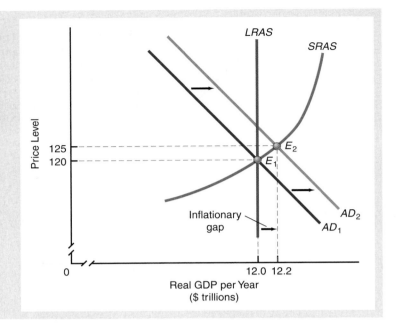

International EXAMPLE

Aggregate Demand Takes Off in China, and So Does Inflation

During 2003, Chinese firms increased their planned investment expenditures by more than 15 percent. In addition, the quantity of money—which in China is called the *yuan*—suddenly rose by more than 20 percent. Together, these factors brought about a significant increase in total planned expenditures at any given price level.

To examine how the rise in planned investment spending and the money supply affected the Chinese economy, consider Figure 11-13. The rise in total planned expenditures at any given price level caused the aggregate demand curve to shift to the right, from AD_1 to AD_2. This caused the short-run

FIGURE 11-13
The Effects of Increased Planned Investment and a Higher Money Supply in China

When planned business investment and the money supply both increased simultaneously in China, total planned expenditures increased at any given price level. Consequently, the aggregate demand curve shifted rightward, and equilibrium temporarily moved from E_1 to E_2.

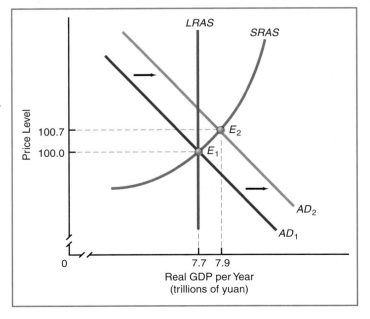

equilibrium to move from E_1 to E_2. Real GDP rose above its long-run level of about 7.7 trillion yuan per year to about 7.9 trillion. The GDP deflator rose from 100, using 2002 as the base year, to about 100.7. Thus China experienced an inflation rate of 0.7 percent in 2003. This might not seem like much, but it was a shock to many residents of China, who had experienced steady *deflation* since 1997.

For Critical Analysis
What do you suppose happened in China during 2004 when planned investment and the money supply continued to increase? (How did these events affect aggregate demand in 2004?)

EXPLAINING SHORT-RUN VARIATIONS IN INFLATION: DEMAND-PULL OR COST-PUSH?

In Chapter 10, we noted that in a growing economy, the explanation for persistent inflation is that aggregate demand rises over time at a faster pace than the full-employment level of real GDP. Short-run variations in inflation, however, can arise as a result of both demand *and* supply factors. Figure 11-12 presents a demand-side theory explaining a short-run jump in prices, sometimes called *demand-pull inflation.* Whenever the general level of prices rises in the short run because of increases in aggregate demand, we say that the economy is experiencing **demand-pull inflation**—inflation caused by increases in aggregate demand.

An alternative explanation for increases in the price level comes from the supply side. Look at Figure 11-14. The initial equilibrium conditions are the same as in Figure 11-12. Now, however, there is a decrease in the aggregate supply curve, from $SRAS_1$ to $SRAS_2$. Equilibrium shifts from E_1 to E_2. The price level increases from 120 to 125, while the equilibrium level of real GDP per year decreases from $12 trillion to $11.8 trillion. Such a decrease in aggregate supply causes what is called **cost-push inflation.**

As the example of cost-push inflation shows, if the economy is initially in equilibrium on its *LRAS,* a decrease in *SRAS* will lead to a rise in the price level. Thus any abrupt change in one of the factors that determine aggregate supply will alter the equilibrium level of real GDP and the equilibrium price level. If the economy is for some reason operating to the left of its *LRAS,* an increase in *SRAS* will lead to a simultaneous *increase* in the equilibrium level of real GDP per year and a *decrease* in the price level. You should be able to show this in a graph similar to Figure 11-14.

Demand-pull inflation
Inflation caused by increases in aggregate demand not matched by increases in aggregate supply.

Cost-push inflation
Inflation caused by decreases in short-run aggregate supply.

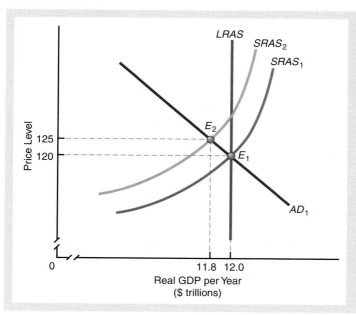

FIGURE 11-14
Cost-Push Inflation
If aggregate demand remains stable but $SRAS_1$ shifts to $SRAS_2$, equilibrium changes from E_1 to E_2. The price level rises from 120 to 125. If there are continual decreases in aggregate supply of this nature, the situation is called cost-push inflation.

How do you think the damage that a 2003 typhoon inflicted on productive resources in South Korea affected real GDP and the price level in that Asian nation?

International EXAMPLE

Cost-Push Inflation Blows into South Korea

In September 2003, Typhoon Maemi slammed into South Korea's coast. The storm, which was the worst typhoon in Korean history, ravaged the nation's largest port in the city of Busan. Winds damaged 775 roads, 27 bridges, and hundreds of manufacturing facilities; toppled gigantic cranes at shipping docks; and forced the temporary shutdown of two nuclear power plants.

For several weeks following the typhoon, South Korean firms had fewer resources available to produce and distribute goods and services at any given price level. The result, as shown in Figure 11-15, was a shift in the nation's short-run aggregate supply curve. The equilibrium temporarily shifted from E_1, at 136.0 billion *won* (South Korea's currency) of real GDP per year and a price level of 115.1, to E_2, with equilibrium real GDP of 133.7 billion won and a price level of 115.8.

For Critical Analysis
What do you think happened to the equilibrium situation in South Korea by the end of 2003, when nearly all roads, bridges, factories, cranes, and docks had been repaired?

FIGURE 11-15
The Effects of a Typhoon on the South Korean Economy
The worst typhoon in South Korean history in 2003 temporarily reduced the amount of resources available to produce goods and services at any given price level. This resulted in a leftward shift of the nation's short-run aggregate supply curve, from $SRAS_1$ to $SRAS_2$. The equilibrium went from E_1 to E_2, with a higher price level and a lower equilibrium real GDP per year.

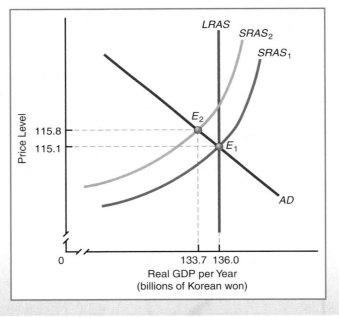

AGGREGATE DEMAND AND SUPPLY IN AN OPEN ECONOMY

In many of the international examples in the early chapters of this book, we had to translate foreign currencies into dollars when the open economy was discussed. We used the exchange rate, or the dollar price of other currencies. In Chapter 10, you also learned that the open economy effect was one of the reasons why the aggregate demand curve slopes downward. When the domestic price level rises, U.S. residents want to buy cheaper-priced foreign goods. The opposite occurs when the U.S. domestic price level falls. Currently, the foreign sector of the U.S. economy constitutes over 14 percent of all economic activities.

How a Weaker Dollar Affects Aggregate Supply

Assume that the dollar becomes weaker in international foreign exchange markets. If last week the dollar could buy 0.87 euro but this week it now buys only 0.80 euro, the dollar has become weaker. To the extent that U.S. companies import raw and partially processed goods from abroad, a weaker dollar can lead to higher input prices. This will lead to a shift inward to the left in the short-run aggregate supply curve as shown in panel (a) of Figure 11-16. In that simplified model, equilibrium real GDP would fall, and the price level would rise. Employment would also tend to decrease.

Go to www.econtoday.com/chap11 for Federal Reserve Bank of New York data showing how the dollar's value is changing relative to other currencies.

How a Weaker Dollar Affects Aggregate Demand

A weaker dollar also has another effect that we must consider. Foreign residents will find that U.S.-made goods are now less expensive, expressed in their own currency. After all, before the dollar weakened, a $10 compact disc cost a French person 8.7 euros when the exchange rate was 0.87 euro per $1. After the dollar became weaker and the exchange rate changed to 0.80 euro per $1, that same $10 CD would cost 8 euros. Conversely, U.S. residents will find that the weaker dollar makes imported goods more expensive. The result for U.S. residents is more exports and fewer imports, or higher net exports (exports minus imports). If net exports rise, employment in export industries will rise: This is represented in panel (b) of Figure 11-16. After the dollar becomes weaker, the aggregate demand curve shifts outward from AD_1 to AD_2. The result is a tendency for equilibrium real GDP and the price level to rise and for unemployment to decrease.

FIGURE 11-16
The Two Effects of a Weaker Dollar
When the dollar decreases in value in the international currency market, there are two effects. The first is higher prices for imported inputs, causing a shift inward to the left in the short-run aggregate supply schedule from $SRAS_1$ to $SRAS_2$ in panel (a). Equilibrium tends to move from E_1 to E_2 at a higher price level and a lower equilibrium real GDP per year. Second, a weaker dollar can also affect the aggregate demand curve because it will lead to more net exports and cause AD_1 to rise to AD_2 in panel (b). Due to this effect, equilibrium would move from E_1 to E_2, at a higher price level and a higher equilibrium real GDP per year. On balance, the price level rises, but real GDP may rise or fall.

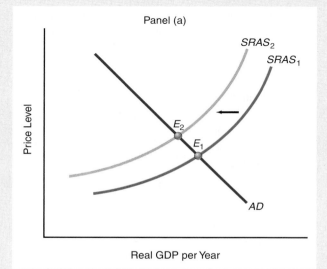

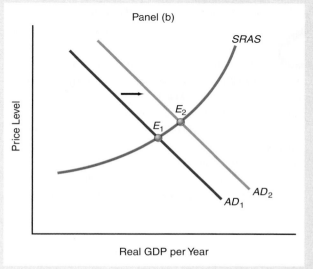

The Net Effect

We have learned, then, that a weaker dollar *simultaneously* leads to a decrease in *SRAS* and an increase in *AD*. In such situations, the effect on real output depends on which curve shifts more. If the aggregate demand curve shifts more than the short-run aggregate supply curve, equilibrium real GDP will rise. Conversely, if the aggregate supply curve shifts more than the aggregate demand curve, equilibrium real GDP will fall.

You should be able to redo this entire analysis for a stronger dollar.

CONCEPTS in Brief

- Short-run equilibrium occurs at the intersection of the aggregate demand curve, *AD*, and the short-run aggregate supply curve, *SRAS*. Long-run equilibrium occurs at the intersection of *AD* and the long-run aggregate supply curve, *LRAS*. Any unanticipated shifts in aggregate demand or supply are called aggregate demand shocks or aggregate supply shocks.

- When aggregate demand shifts while aggregate supply is stable, a recessionary gap can occur, defined as the difference between the equilibrium level of real GDP and how much the economy could be producing if it were operating on its *LRAS*. The reverse situation leads to an inflationary gap.

- With stable aggregate supply, an abrupt shift in *AD* may lead to what is called demand-pull inflation. With a stable aggre-

gate demand, an abrupt shift inward in *SRAS* may lead to what is called cost-push inflation.

- A change in the international value of the dollar can affect both the *SRAS* and aggregate demand. A weaker dollar will raise the cost of imported inputs, thereby causing *SRAS* to shift inward to the left, leading to a higher price level and a lower equilibrium real GDP per year, given no change in aggregate demand. At the same time, a weaker dollar will also lead to higher net exports, causing the aggregate demand curve to shift outward, leading to a higher price level and a higher equilibrium real GDP per year. The net effect depends on which shift is larger. The opposite analysis applies to a strengthening dollar in international currency markets.

To test your understanding of the concepts covered in this section, go to the Online Review at **www.myeconlab.com/miller.**

CASE STUDY: Economics Front and Center

Holding Out for a Better Salary Offer in an Improved Job Climate

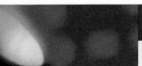

Shannon will be graduating at the end of the current academic year. At the beginning of the fall semester, his college's career center had warned that with economic activity lagging, fewer recruiters would be holding interviews on campus. Thus he had felt lucky to land two interviews in October. It is now March, and one of the firms that interviewed him last fall has made a job offer, but at a lower salary than he had hoped to receive. The firm has given him until the end of April to make a decision.

Since October, annualized U.S. real GDP growth has been near record levels. Many job recruiters who had canceled visits to campus in the fall have rescheduled to conduct interviews

this semester. Shannon has managed to schedule interviews with several firms during the next two weeks. He is now hoping that he can convince one or two more companies to offer him a position before the end of April, and at a higher starting salary.

Points to Analyze

1. *Based on the situation confronting Shannon, has the spring labor market been experiencing an excess quantity of labor supplied or an excess quantity of labor demanded?*

2. *Why might Shannon reasonably anticipate a rise in starting salaries for new college graduates?*

I n August 2002, President George W. Bush signed the Trade Act, which among other things created a new set of transportation-security rules aimed at reducing the likelihood that terrorists would smuggle weapons or bombs into the United States. The legislation requires all transportation companies to send fax or e-mail messages informing the Bureau of Customs and Border Protection of the contents of all cargoes and the intended recipients. This "automated notification" requirement is designed to give officials time to identify suspicious shipments so that they can swiftly intercept and inspect them for contraband.

Concepts Applied

- Short-Run Aggregate Supply Curve
- Aggregate Supply Shock

One Regulation with Very Widespread Effects

The new rules imposed under the 2002 Trade Act apply to every mode of transportation: trucks, trains, ships, and planes. The advance notice required differs depending on the type of transportation, ranging from at least 30 minutes for trucks to 24 hours for ships.

Many large trucking firms were already using electronic systems to direct deliveries, so it was relatively straightforward, albeit costly, for them to alter their systems to transmit automatic messages to government officials. Costs were greater for smaller trucking firms, which were forced to make rapid transitions to electronic systems or, at a minimum, purchase fax machines and incur much higher long-distance telephone bills. In response to the two-hour notification requirement for international air cargoes mandated by the law, parcel delivery companies such as FedEx and UPS had to restructure aspects of their overnight delivery systems. Freight train operators and owners of cargo ships also had to make expensive changes in their record-keeping procedures.

An Aggregate Supply Shock

Ultimately, the higher costs faced by international transport firms led to higher shipping prices for U.S. companies using imported components to produce goods and services. The result was an aggregate supply shock. Over time, as transportation companies recalibrated their shipping procedures to account for the Trade Act's notification requirements, the effects of the requirements on shipping costs and prices diminished. In addition, U.S. companies using foreign-produced components adjusted their inventory-management systems to take into account regulation-induced shipment delays. Thus the Trade Act's main impact was a reduction in short-run aggregate supply. By 2004, the legislation's effect on long-run aggregate supply was more muted.

Nevertheless, the 2002 Trade Act is an important element that economists factor into their efforts to explain the relatively sluggish economic recovery during the two years following the 2001 recession. Even as other factors were causing aggregate demand and aggregate supply to increase and generate a business recovery, the supply shock generated by the Trade Act's shipping regulations tended to have a depressing effect on equilibrium real GDP.

For Critical Analysis

1. Many shipment delays occurred during the weeks following the implementation of the Trade Act's notification requirements. How might these delays have contributed to a short-run reduction in aggregate supply, even if the shipping prices that U.S. firms paid did not change? (Hint: Think about opportunity costs.)

2. Suppose that other factors had not led to net increases in aggregate demand and aggregate supply in the United States between 2002 and 2004. If so, what effects would the aggregate supply shock created by the Trade Act's notification requirements have had on the U.S. price level and U.S. real GDP between 2002 and 2004?

Web Resources

1. To learn more about the U.S. government's border regulations, go to the home page of the Bureau of Customs and Border Protection via www.econtoday.com/chap11.

2. For a summary of the notification requirements for international shipments established by the Trade Act of 2002, read the document available from Hogan & Hartson LLP at the link at www.econtoday.com/chap11.

Research Project

Consider the list of factors in Table 11-2 that can cause a decrease in aggregate supply. Discuss conditions under which each factor is likely to bring about a reduction in long-run aggregate supply as well as a decrease in short-run aggregate supply. Evaluate the short- and longer-term effects on the U.S. price level and U.S. real GDP following such an event.

SUMMARY DISCUSSION of Learning Objectives

1. **Central Assumptions of the Classical Model:** There are four fundamental assumptions of the classical model: (a) pure competition prevails, so no individual buyer or seller of a good or service or of a factor of production can affect its price; (b) wages and prices are completely flexible; (c) people are motivated by self-interest; and (d) buyers and sellers do not experience money illusion, meaning that they respond only to changes in relative prices.

2. **Short-Run Determination of Equilibrium Real GDP and the Price Level in the Classical Model:** Under the four assumptions of the classical model, the short-run aggregate supply curve is vertical at full-employment real GDP and thus corresponds to the long-run aggregate supply curve. So, even in the short run, real GDP cannot increase in the absence of changes in factors, such as labor, capital, and technology, which induce longer-term economic growth. Given the position of the classical aggregate supply curve, movements in the equilibrium price level are generated by variations in the position of the aggregate demand curve.

3. **Circumstances Under Which the Short-Run Aggregate Supply Curve May Be Horizontal or Upward Sloping:** If product prices and wages and other input prices are "sticky," perhaps because of labor and other contracts,

the short-run aggregate supply schedule can be horizontal over much of its range. This is the Keynesian short-run aggregate supply curve. More generally, however, to the extent that there is incomplete adjustment of prices in the short run, the short-run aggregate supply curve slopes upward.

4. **Factors That Induce Shifts in the Short-Run and Long-Run Aggregate Supply Curves:** The long-run aggregate supply curve shifts in response to changes in the availability of labor or capital or to changes in technology and productivity, and changes in these factors also cause the short-run aggregate supply curve to shift. Because output prices may adjust only partially to changing input prices in the short run, however, a widespread change in the prices of factors of production, such as an economywide change in wages, can cause a shift in the short-run aggregate supply curve without affecting the long-run aggregate supply curve.

5. **Effects of Aggregate Demand and Supply Shocks on Equilibrium Real GDP in the Short Run:** An aggregate demand shock that causes the aggregate demand curve to shift leftward pushes equilibrium real GDP below full-employment real GDP in the short run, so there is a recessionary gap. An aggregate demand shock that induces a rightward shift in the aggregate demand curve results in

an inflationary gap in which short-run equilibrium real GDP exceeds full-employment real GDP.

6. **Causes of Short-Run Variations in the Inflation Rate:** In the short run, an upward movement in the price level can occur in the form of demand-pull inflation when the aggregate demand curve shifts rightward along an upward-sloping short-run aggregate supply curve. Cost-push inflation can arise in the short run when the short-run aggregate supply curve shifts leftward along the aggregate demand curve.

KEY TERMS AND CONCEPTS

aggregate demand shock (252)

aggregate supply shock (252)

cost-push inflation (255)

demand-pull inflation (255)

inflationary gap (253)

Keynesian short-run aggregate supply curve (248)

money illusion (242)

recessionary gap (253)

Say's law (241)

short-run aggregate supply curve (249)

PROBLEMS

Answers to the odd-numbered problems appear at the back of the book.

11-1. Consider a country whose economic structure matches the assumptions of the classical model. After reading a recent best-seller documenting a growing population of low-income elderly people who were ill-prepared for retirement, most residents of this country decide to increase their saving at any given interest rate. Explain whether or how this could affect the following:

a. The current equilibrium interest rate
b. Current equilibrium real GDP
c. Current equilibrium employment
d. Current equilibrium investment
e. Future equilibrium real GDP

11-2. Consider a country with an economic structure consistent with the assumptions of the classical model. Suppose that businesses in this nation suddenly anticipate higher future profitability from investments they undertake today. Explain whether or how this could affect the following:

a. The current equilibrium interest rate
b. Current equilibrium real GDP
c. Current equilibrium employment
d. Current equilibrium saving
e. Future equilibrium real GDP

11-3. "There is *absolutely no distinction* between the classical model and the model of long-run equilibrium discussed in Chapter 10." Is this statement true or false? Support your answer.

11-4. A nation in which the classical model applies experiences a decline in the quantity of money in circulation. Use an appropriate aggregate demand and aggregate supply diagram to explain what happens to equilibrium real GDP and to the equilibrium price level.

11-5. Suppose that the classical model is appropriate for a country that has suddenly experienced an influx of immigrants who possess a wide variety of employable skills and who have reputations for saving relatively large portions of their incomes, compared with native-born residents, at any given interest rate. Evaluate the effects of this event on the following:

a. Current equilibrium employment
b. Current equilibrium real GDP
c. The current equilibrium interest rate
d. Current equilibrium investment
e. Future equilibrium real GDP

11-6. Suppose that the Keynesian short-run aggregate supply curve is applicable for a nation's economy. Use appropriate diagrams to assist in answering the following questions:

a. What are two factors that can cause the nation's real GDP to increase in the short run?
b. What are two factors that can cause the nation's real GDP to increase in the long run?

11-7. What determines how much real GDP responds to changes in the price level along the short-run aggregate supply curve?

11-8. At a point along the short-run aggregate supply curve that is to the right of the point where it crosses the long-run aggregate supply curve, what must be true of the unemployment rate relative to the long-run, full-employment rate of unemployment? Why?

11-9. Suppose that the stock market crashes in an economy with an upward-sloping short-run aggregate supply curve, and consumer and business confidence plummets. What are the short-run effects on equilibrium real GDP and the equilibrium price level?

11-10. Consider an open economy in which the aggregate supply curve slopes upward in the short run. Firms in this nation do not import raw materials or any other productive inputs from abroad, but foreign residents purchase many of the nation's goods and services. What is the most likely short-run effect on this nation's economy if there is a significant downturn in economic activity in other nations around the world?

ECONOMICS ON THE NET

Money, the Price Level, and Real GDP The classical and Keynesian theories have differing predictions about how changes in the money supply should affect the price level and real GDP. Here you get to look at data on growth in the money supply, the price level, and real GDP.

Title: Federal Reserve Bank of St. Louis Monetary Trends

Navigation: Use the link at www.econtoday.com/chap11 to visit the Federal Reserve Bank of St. Louis. Click on *Gross Domestic Product and M2*.

Application Read the article; then answer these questions.

1. Classical theory indicates that *ceteris paribus,* changes in the price level should be closely related to changes in aggregate demand induced by variations in the quantity of money. Click on *Gross Domestic Product and M2,* and take a look at the charts labeled "Gross Domestic Prod-

uct Price Index" and "M2." Are annual percentage changes in these variables closely related?

2. Keynesian theory predicts that *ceteris paribus,* changes in GDP and the quantity of money should be directly related. Take a look at the charts labeled "Real Gross Domestic Product" and "M2." Are annual percentage changes in these variables closely related?

For Group Study and Analysis Both classical and Keynesian theories of relationships among real GDP, the price level, and the quantity of money hinge on specific assumptions. Have class groups search through the FRED database (accessible at www.econtoday.com/chap11) to evaluate factors that provide support for either theory's predictions. Which approach appears to receive greater support from recent data? Does this necessarily imply that this is the "true theory"? Why or why not?

If your exam were tomorrow, would you be ready? For each chapter, MyEconLab Practice Tests and Study Plans pinpoint which sections you have mastered and which ones you need to study. That way, you are more efficient with your study time, and you are better prepared for your exams.

In addition to Practice Tests and your personalized Study Plan, you'll find the following media resources in MyEconLab:

1. *Graphs in Motion* animation of Figures 11-2, 11-3, 11-4, 11-5, 11-6, 11-8, 11-9, 11-10, 11-11, 11-12, 11-14, and 11-15.
2. An *Economics in Motion* in-depth animation of Aggregate Demand and Aggregate Supply.
3. Videos featuring the author, Roger LeRoy Miller, on the following subjects:
   ● Say's Law

   ● The Short-Run Aggregate Supply Curve
   ● Shifts in the Short-Run Aggregate Supply Curve
4. Links to the Web sites cited in the marginal Internet Resources, Issues and Applications feature, and Economics on the Net activity.
5. Audio clips of all key terms, additional practice problems, and a PDF version of the material from the print Study Guide.
6. eThemes of the Times, which is a New York Times article to help you understand the real-world applications of what you are learning.

To see how it works, turn to page 16 and then go to www.myeconlab.com/miller.

Get Ahead of the Curve

Chapter 12

Consumption, Real GDP, and the Multiplier

I n the late 1990s, media attention was lavished on economic prognosticators who proclaimed that the United States had witnessed the dawning of a "new economy" of unparalleled stability and growth. In the brave new twenty-first-century world they sketched out to rapt audiences, investments in new information technologies would propel the U.S. economy to never-before-seen heights. What happened was not quite what the prognosticators predicted. Between 2000 and 2001, the annual growth of business spending on computers, software, and other information technology products plunged from more than 11 percent per year to *negative* 10 percent per year. In this chapter, you will learn how to analyze the economic consequences of a significant shrinkage in business investment expenditures.

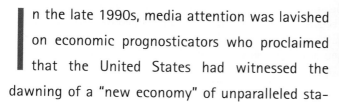

LEARNING OBJECTIVES

After reading this chapter, you should be able to:

1. Distinguish between saving and savings and explain how saving and consumption are related
2. Explain the key determinants of consumption and saving in the Keynesian model
3. Identify the primary determinants of planned investment
4. Describe how equilibrium real GDP is established in the Keynesian model
5. Evaluate why autonomous changes in total planned expenditures have a multiplier effect on equilibrium real GDP
6. Understand the relationship between total planned expenditures and the aggregate demand curve

Media Resources

Refer to the end of the chapter for a full listing of the multimedia learning materials available in MyEconLab.

Did You Know That . . . one of the main contributors to stable U.S. real GDP growth during much of the 1990s was the unremitting and significant growth of business investment? Between 1993 and 2000, real gross private domestic investment grew steadily at an average rate of almost 9 percent per year. It wasn't long before many U.S. residents forgot that investment spending had previously been the most volatile component of total planned expenditures. In 2001, however, they got a rude reminder of the fickleness of investment spending when the smooth uphill climb of U.S. investment turned sharply downward.

John Maynard Keynes focused much of his research on how unanticipated changes in investment spending affect a nation's aggregate spending and real GDP. The key to determining the broader economic effects of investment fluctuations, Keynes reasoned, was to understand the relationship between how much people earn and their willingness to engage in personal consumption spending. Thus Keynes argued that a prerequisite to understanding how investment affects a nation's economy is to understand the determinants of household consumption. In this chapter, you will learn how an understanding of household consumption expenditures can assist you in evaluating the GDP effects of variations in business investment.

SOME SIMPLIFYING ASSUMPTIONS IN A KEYNESIAN MODEL

Continuing in the Keynesian tradition, we will assume that the short-run aggregate supply curve within the current range of real GDP is horizontal. That is, we assume that it is similar to Figure 11-6 on page 247, meaning that the equilibrium level of real GDP is demand-determined. This is why Keynes wished to examine the elements of desired aggregate expenditures. Because of the Keynesian assumption of inflexible prices, inflation is not a concern. Hence real values are identical to nominal values.

To simplify the income determination model that follows, a number of assumptions are made:

1. Businesses pay no indirect taxes (for example, sales taxes).
2. Businesses distribute all of their profits to shareholders.
3. There is no depreciation (capital consumption allowance), so gross private domestic investment equals net investment.
4. The economy is closed—that is, there is no foreign trade.

Given all these simplifying assumptions, real disposable income will be equal to real GDP minus taxes.*

Another Look at Definitions and Relationships

You can do only two things with a dollar of disposable income: consume it or save it. If you consume it, it is gone forever. If you save the entire dollar, however, you will be able to consume it (and perhaps more if it earns interest) at some future time. That is the distinction between **consumption** and **saving.** Consumption is the act of using income for the purchase of consumption goods. **Consumption goods** are goods purchased by households for

Consumption
Spending on new goods and services out of a household's current income. Whatever is not consumed is saved. Consumption includes such things as buying food and going to a concert.

Saving
The act of not consuming all of one's current income. Whatever is not consumed out of spendable income is, by definition, saved. *Saving* is an action measured over time (a flow), whereas *savings* are a stock, an accumulation resulting from the act of saving in the past.

Consumption goods
Goods bought by households to use up, such as food and movies.

---

*Strictly speaking, we are referring here to net taxes—the difference between taxes paid and transfer payments received. If taxes are $1 trillion but individuals receive transfer payments—Social Security, unemployment benefits, and so forth—of $300 billion, net taxes are equal to $700 billion.

immediate satisfaction. Consumption goods are such things as food and movies. By definition, whatever you do not consume you save and can consume at some time in the future.

Stocks and Flows: The Difference Between Saving and Savings. It is important to distinguish between *saving* and *savings*. *Saving* is an action that occurs at a particular rate—for example, $10 per week or $520 per year. This rate is a flow. It is expressed per unit of time, usually a year. Implicitly, then, when we talk about saving, we talk about a *flow* or rate of saving. *Savings*, by contrast, is a *stock* concept, measured at a certain point or instant in time. Your current *savings* are the result of past *saving*. You may currently have *savings* of $2,000 that are the result of four years' *saving* at a rate of $500 per year. Consumption is also a flow concept. You consume from after-tax income at a certain rate per week, per month, or per year.

Relating Income to Saving and Consumption. Obviously, a dollar of take-home income can be either consumed or not consumed. Realizing this, we can see the relationship among saving, consumption, and disposable income:

$$\text{Consumption} + \text{saving} \equiv \text{disposable income}$$

This is called an *accounting identity*. It has to hold true at every moment in time. From it we can derive the definition of saving:

$$\text{Saving} \equiv \text{disposable income} - \text{consumption}$$

Recall that disposable income is what you actually have left to spend after you pay taxes.

Investment

Investment is also a flow concept. As noted in Chapter 8, *investment* as used in economics differs from the common use of the term. In common speech, it is often used to describe putting funds into the stock market or real estate. In economic analysis, investment is defined to include expenditures by firms on new machines and buildings—**capital goods**—that are expected to yield a future stream of income. This is called *fixed investment*. We also include changes in business inventories in our definition. This we call *inventory investment*.

Investment
Spending by businesses on things such as machines and buildings, which can be used to produce goods and services in the future. The investment part of real GDP is the portion that will be used in the process of producing goods in the future.

Capital goods
Producer durables; nonconsumable goods that firms use to make other goods.

CONCEPTS in Brief

- If we assume that we are operating on a horizontal short-run aggregate supply curve, the equilibrium level of real GDP per year is completely demand-determined.

- *Saving* is a flow, something that occurs over time. It equals disposable income minus consumption. *Savings* are a stock. They are the accumulation resulting from saving.

- Investment is also a flow. It includes expenditures on new machines, buildings, and equipment and changes in business inventories.

To test your understanding of the concepts covered in this section, go to the Online Review at www.myeconlab.com/miller.

DETERMINANTS OF PLANNED CONSUMPTION AND PLANNED SAVING

In the classical model, the supply of saving was determined by the rate of interest: The higher the rate of interest, the more people wanted to save and therefore the less people wanted to consume. In contrast, according to Keynes, the interest rate is *not* the most important determinant of an individual's real saving and consumption decisions.

TABLE 12-1

Real Consumption and Saving Schedules: A Hypothetical Case

Column 1 presents real disposable income from zero up to $60,000 per year; column 2 indicates planned consumption per year; column 3 presents planned saving per year. At levels of disposable income below $30,000, planned saving is negative. In column 4, we see the aver- age propensity to consume, which is merely planned consumption divided by disposable income. Column 5 lists average propensity to save, which is planned saving divided by disposable income. Column 6 is the marginal propensity to consume, which shows the proportion of *additional* income that will be consumed. Finally, column 7 shows the proportion of *additional* income that will be saved, or the marginal propensity to save.

Combination	(1) Real Disposable Income per Year (Y_d)	(2) Planned Real Consumption per Year (C)	(3) Planned Real Saving per Year ($S \equiv Y_d - C$) (1) − (2)	(4) Average Propensity to Consume ($APC \equiv C/Y_d$) (2) ÷ (1)	(5) Average Propensity to Save ($APS \equiv S/Y_d$) (3) ÷ (1)	(6) Marginal Propensity to Consume ($MPC \equiv \Delta C/\Delta Y_d$)	(7) Marginal Propensity to Save ($MPS \equiv \Delta S/\Delta Y_d$)
A	$ 0	$ 6,000	$−6,000	—	—	—	—
B	6,000	10,800	−4,800	1.8	−.8	.8	.2
C	12,000	15,600	−3,600	1.3	−.3	.8	.2
D	18,000	20,400	−2,400	1.133	−.133	.8	.2
E	24,000	25,200	−1,200	1.05	−.05	.8	.2
F	30,000	30,000	0	1.0	.0	.8	.2
G	36,000	34,800	1,200	.967	.033	.8	.2
H	42,000	39,600	2,400	.943	.057	.8	.2
I	48,000	44,400	3,600	.925	.075	.8	.2
J	54,000	49,200	4,800	.911	.089	.8	.2
K	60,000	54,000	6,000	.9	.1	.8	.2

Keynes argued that real saving and consumption decisions depend primarily on a household's current real disposable income.

Consumption function
The relationship between amount consumed and disposable income. A consumption function tells us how much people plan to consume at various levels of disposable income.

The relationship between planned real consumption expenditures of households and their current level of real disposable income has been called the **consumption function.** It shows how much all households plan to consume per year at each level of real disposable income per year. The first two columns of Table 12-1 illustrate a consumption function for a hypothetical household.

We see from Table 12-1 that as real disposable income rises, planned consumption also rises, but by a smaller amount, as Keynes suggested. Planned saving also increases with disposable income. Notice, however, that below an income of $30,000, the planned saving of this hypothetical household is actually negative. The further that income drops below that level, the more the household engages in **dissaving,** either by going into debt or by using up some of its existing wealth.

Dissaving
Negative saving; a situation in which spending exceeds income. Dissaving can occur when a household is able to borrow or use up existing assets.

Graphing the Numbers

We now graph the consumption and saving relationships presented in Table 12-1. In the upper part of Figure 12-1, the vertical axis measures the level of planned real consumption per year, and the horizontal axis measures the level of real disposable income per year. In the lower part of the figure, the horizontal axis is again real disposable income per year, but now the vertical axis is planned real saving per year. All of these are on a dollars-per-year basis, which emphasizes the point that we are measuring flows, not stocks.

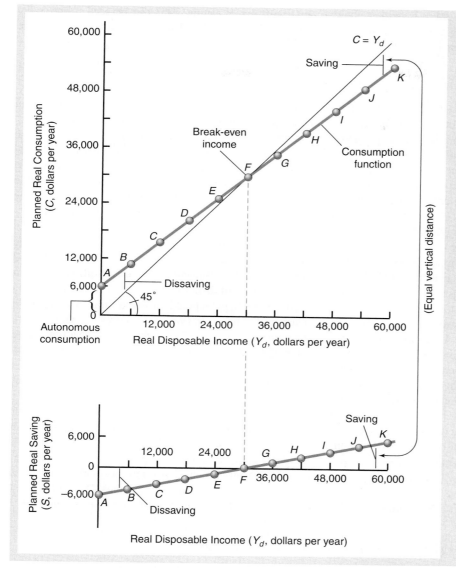

FIGURE 12-1
The Consumption and Saving Functions
If we plot the combinations of real disposable income and planned real consumption from columns 1 and 2 in Table 12-1, we get the consumption function. At every point on the 45-degree line, a vertical line drawn to the income axis is the same distance from the origin as a horizontal line drawn to the consumption axis. Where the consumption function crosses the 45-degree line at F, we know that planned real consumption equals real disposable income and there is zero saving. The vertical distance between the 45-degree line and the consumption function measures the rate of real saving or dissaving at any given income level. If we plot the relationship between column 1, real disposable income, and column 3, planned real saving, from Table 12-1, we arrive at the saving function shown in the lower part of this diagram. It is the complement of the consumption function presented above it.

As you can see, we have taken income-consumption and income-saving combinations *A* through *K* and plotted them. In the upper part of Figure 12-1, the result is called the *consumption function.* In the lower part, the result is called the *saving function.* Mathematically, the saving function is the *complement* of the consumption function because consumption plus saving always equals disposable income. What is not consumed is, by definition, saved. The difference between actual disposable income and the planned rate of consumption per year *must* be the planned rate of saving per year.

How can we find the rate of saving or dissaving in the upper part of Figure 12-1? We draw a line that is equidistant from both the horizontal and the vertical axes. This line is 45 degrees from either axis and is often called the **45-degree reference line.** At every point on the 45-degree reference line, a vertical line drawn to the income axis is the same distance from the origin as a horizontal line drawn to the consumption axis. Thus, at point *F,* where the consumption function intersects the 45-degree line, real disposable income equals planned real consumption. Point *F* is sometimes called the *break-even income point*

45-degree reference line
The line along which planned real expenditures equal real GDP per year.

because there is neither positive nor negative real saving. This can be seen in the lower part of Figure 12-1 as well. The planned annual rate of real saving at a real disposable income level of $30,000 is indeed zero.

Dissaving and Autonomous Consumption

To the left of point *F* in either part of Figure 12-1 on the previous page, this hypothetical family engages in dissaving, either by going into debt or by consuming existing assets, including savings. The rate of real saving or dissaving in the upper part of the figure can be found by measuring the vertical distance between the 45-degree line and the consumption function. This simply tells us that if our hypothetical household starts with more than $30,000 of real disposable income per year and then temporarily finds its real disposable income below $30,000, it will not cut back its real consumption by the full amount of the reduction. It will instead go into debt or consume existing assets in some way to compensate for part of the loss.

Now look at the point on the diagram where real disposable income is zero but planned consumption is $6,000. This amount of real planned consumption, which does not depend at all on actual real disposable income, is called **autonomous consumption.** The autonomous consumption of $6,000 is *independent* of disposable income. That means that no matter how low the level of real income of our hypothetical household falls, the household will always attempt to consume at least $6,000 per year. (We are, of course, assuming here that the household's real disposable income does not equal zero year in and year out. There is certainly a limit to how long our hypothetical household could finance autonomous consumption without any income.) That $6,000 of yearly consumption is determined by things other than the level of income. We don't need to specify what determines autonomous consumption; we merely state that it exists and that in our example it is $6,000 per year.

Just remember that the word *autonomous* means "existing independently." In our model, autonomous consumption exists independently of the hypothetical household's level of real disposable income. (Later we will review some of the non-real-disposable-income determinants of consumption.) There are many possible types of autonomous expenditures. Hypothetically, we can consider that investment is autonomous—independent of income. We can assume that government expenditures are autonomous. We will do just that at various times in our discussions to simplify our analysis of income determination.

Average Propensity to Consume and to Save

Let's now go back to Table 12-1 on page 266, and this time let's look at columns 4 and 5: **average propensity to consume (APC)** and **average propensity to save (APS).** They are defined as follows:

$$\text{APC} \equiv \frac{\text{real consumption}}{\text{real disposable income}}$$

$$\text{APS} \equiv \frac{\text{real saving}}{\text{real disposable income}}$$

Notice from column 4 in Table 12-1 that for this hypothetical household, the average propensity to consume decreases as real disposable income increases. This decrease simply means that the fraction of the household's real disposable income going to consumption falls as income rises. The same fact can be found in column 5. The average propensity to save, which at first is negative, finally hits zero at an income level of $30,000 and then

Autonomous consumption
The part of consumption that is independent of (does not depend on) the level of disposable income. Changes in autonomous consumption shift the consumption function.

Average propensity to consume (APC)
Real consumption divided by real disposable income; for any given level of real income, the proportion of total real disposable income that is consumed.

Average propensity to save (APS)
Real saving divided by real disposable income; for any given level of real income, the proportion of total real disposable income that is saved.

becomes positive. In this example, the APS reaches a value of 0.1 at income level $60,000. This means that the household saves 10 percent of a $60,000 income.

It's quite easy for you to figure out your own average propensity to consume or to save. Just divide what you consumed by your total real disposable income for the year, and the result will be your personal APC at your current level of income. Also, divide your real saving during the year by your real disposable income to calculate your own APS.

Marginal Propensity to Consume and to Save

Now we go to the last two columns in Table 12-1: **marginal propensity to consume (MPC)** and **marginal propensity to save (MPS).** The term *marginal* refers to a small incremental or decremental change (represented by the Greek letter delta, Δ, in Table 12-1). The marginal propensity to consume, then, is defined as

$$MPC \equiv \frac{\text{change in real consumption}}{\text{change in real disposable income}}$$

The marginal propensity to save is defined similarly as

$$MPS \equiv \frac{\text{change in real saving}}{\text{change in real disposable income}}$$

What do MPC and MPS tell you? They tell you what percentage of a given increase or decrease in real income will go toward consumption and saving, respectively. The emphasis here is on the word *change.* The marginal propensity to consume indicates how much you will change your planned real consumption if there is a change in your real disposable income. If your marginal propensity to consume is 0.8, that does not mean that you consume 80 percent of *all* disposable income. The percentage of your total real disposable income that you consume is given by the average propensity to consume, or APC. As Table 12-1 indicates, the APC is not equal to 0.8. In contrast, an MPC of 0.8 means that you will consume 80 percent of any *increase* in your disposable income. Hence the MPC cannot be less than zero or greater than one. It follows that households increase their planned real consumption by more than zero and less than 100 percent of any increase in real disposable income that they receive.

Consider a simple example in which we show the difference between the average propensity to consume and the marginal propensity to consume. Assume that your consumption behavior is exactly the same as our hypothetical household's behavior depicted in Table 12-1. You have an annual real disposable income of $54,000. Your planned consumption rate, then, from column 2 of Table 12-1 is $49,200. So your average propensity to consume is $49,200/$54,000 = 0.911. Now suppose that at the end of the year, your boss gives you an after-tax bonus of $6,000. What would you do with that additional $6,000 in real disposable income? According to the table, you would consume $4,800 of it and save $1,200. In that case, your *marginal* propensity to consume would be $4,800/$6,000 = 0.8 and your marginal propensity to save would be $1,200/$6,000 = 0.2. What would happen to your *average* propensity to consume? To find out, we add $4,800 to $49,200 of planned consumption, which gives us a new consumption rate of $54,000. The average propensity to consume is then $54,000 divided by the new higher salary of $60,000. Your APC drops from 0.911 to 0.9.

In contrast, your MPC remains, in our simplified example, 0.8 all the time. Look at column 6 in Table 12-1. The MPC is 0.8 at every level of income. (Therefore, the MPS is always equal to 0.2 at every level of income.) Underlying the constancy of MPC is the assumption that the amount that you are willing to consume out of additional income will remain the same in percentage terms no matter what level of real disposable income is your starting point.

Marginal propensity to consume (MPC)
The ratio of the change in consumption to the change in disposable income. A marginal propensity to consume of 0.8 tells us that an additional $100 in take-home pay will lead to an additional $80 consumed.

Marginal propensity to save (MPS)
The ratio of the change in saving to the change in disposable income. A marginal propensity to save of 0.2 indicates that out of an additional $100 in take-home pay, $20 will be saved. Whatever is not saved is consumed. The marginal propensity to save plus the marginal propensity to consume must always equal 1, by definition.

Economics Front and Center

To think through the common-sense implications of the consumption and saving functions, consider the case study, **An Individual Confronts Theory with Some Facts**, on page 284.

Some Relationships

Consumption plus saving must equal income. Both your total real disposable income and the change in total real disposable income are either consumed or saved. The proportions of either measure must equal 1, or 100 percent. This allows us to make the following statements:

$$APC + APS = 1 (= 100 \text{ percent of total income})$$

$$MPC + MPS = 1 (= 100 \text{ percent of the } change \text{ in income})$$

The average propensities as well as the marginal propensities to consume and save must total 1, or 100 percent. Check the two statements by adding the figures in columns 4 and 5 for each level of real disposable income in Table 12-1. Do the same for columns 6 and 7.

Causes of Shifts in the Consumption Function

A change in any other relevant economic variable besides real disposable income will cause the consumption function to shift. The number of such nonincome determinants of the position of the consumption function is virtually unlimited. Real household **wealth** is one determinant of the position of the consumption function. An increase in the real wealth of the average household will cause the consumption function to shift upward. A decrease in real wealth will cause it to shift downward. So far we have been talking about the consumption function of an individual or a household. Now let's move on to the national economy. We'll consider the consumption function for the entire nation.

Wealth
The stock of assets owned by a person, household, firm, or nation. For a household, wealth can consist of a house, cars, personal belongings, stocks, bonds, bank accounts, and cash.

CONCEPTS in Brief

- The consumption function shows the relationship between planned rates of real consumption and real disposable income per year. The saving function is the complement of the consumption function because real saving plus real consumption must equal real disposable income.

- The average propensity to consume (APC) is equal to real consumption divided by real disposable income. The average propensity to save (APS) is equal to real saving divided by real disposable income.

- The marginal propensity to consume (MPC) is equal to the change in planned real consumption divided by the change in real disposable income. The marginal propensity to save (MPS) is equal to the change in planned real saving divided by the change in real disposable income.

- Any change in real disposable income will cause the planned rate of consumption to change; this is represented by a movement along the consumption function. Any change in a nonincome determinant of consumption will shift the consumption function.

To test your understanding of the concepts covered in this section, go to the Online Review at www.myeconlab.com/miller.

DETERMINANTS OF INVESTMENT

Investment, you will remember, consists of expenditures on new buildings and equipment and changes in business inventories. Historically, real gross private domestic investment in the United States has been extremely volatile over the years relative to real consumption. If we were to look at net private domestic investment (investment after depreciation has been deducted), we would see that in the depths of the Great Depression and at the peak of the World War II effort, the figure was negative. In other words, we were eating away at our capital stock—we weren't even maintaining it by completely replacing depreciated equipment.

If we compare real investment expenditures historically with real consumption expenditures, we find that the latter are less variable over time than the former. Why is this so? One possible reason is that the real investment decisions of businesses are based on highly variable, subjective estimates of how the economic future looks.

The Planned Investment Function

Consider that at all times, businesses perceive an array of investment opportunities. These investment opportunities have rates of return ranging from zero to very high, with the number (or dollar value) of all such projects inversely related to the rate of return. Because a project is profitable only if its rate of return exceeds the opportunity cost of the investment—the rate of interest—it follows that as the interest rate falls, planned investment spending increases, and vice versa. Even if firms use retained earnings (internal financing) to fund an investment, the lower the market rate of interest, the smaller the *opportunity cost* of using those retained earnings. Thus it does not matter in our analysis whether the firm must seek financing from external sources or can obtain such financing by using retained earnings. Whatever the method of financing, as the interest rate falls, more investment opportunities will be profitable, and planned investment will be higher.

It should be no surprise, therefore, that the investment function is represented as an inverse relationship between the rate of interest and the value of planned real investment. A hypothetical investment schedule is given in panel (a) of Figure 12-2 and plotted in panel (b). We see from this schedule that if, for example, the rate of interest is 5 percent, the dollar value of planned investment will be $1.6 trillion per year. Notice, by the way, that planned investment is also given on a per-year basis, showing that it represents a flow, not a stock. (The stock counterpart of investment is the stock of capital in the economy measured in dollars at a point in time.)

FIGURE 12-2
Planned Real Investment
As shown in the hypothetical planned investment schedule in panel (a), the rate of planned real investment is inversely related to the rate of interest. If we plot the data pairs from panel (a), we obtain the investment function, *I*, in panel (b). It is negatively sloped.

Panel (a)

Annual Rate of Interest (%)	Planned Real Investment per Year ($ trillions)
10	1.1
9	1.2
8	1.3
7	1.4
6	1.5
5	1.6
4	1.7
3	1.8
2	1.9
1	2.0

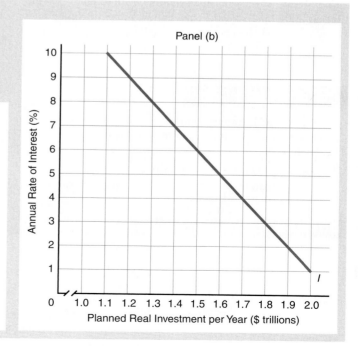

What Causes the Investment Function to Shift?

Go to the link to economic data provided by the Federal Reserve Bank of St. Louis via the link at www.econtoday.com/chap12 to see how U.S. real private investment has varied in recent years.

Because planned real investment is assumed to be a function of the rate of interest, any non-interest-rate variable that changes can have the potential of shifting the investment function. One of those variables is the expectations of businesses. If higher future sales are expected, more machines and bigger plants will be planned for the future. More investment will be undertaken because of the expectation of higher future profits. In this case, the investment schedule, I, would shift outward to the right, meaning that more investment would be desired at all rates of interest. Any change in productive technology can potentially shift the investment function. A positive change in productive technology would stimulate demand for additional capital goods and shift I outward to the right. Changes in business taxes can also shift the investment schedule. If they increase, we predict a leftward shift in the planned investment function because higher taxes imply a lower (after-tax) rate of return.

How would you surmise that an improved economic outlook has influenced planned investment in Japan?

International EXAMPLE

Japanese Businesses Go on a Shopping Spree

Throughout most of the 1990s and early 2000s, even as market interest rates hovered close to zero, Japanese companies engaged in less investment spending than they had during the 1980s when the Japanese economy was booming. Expectations of weak future sales in the stagnant economy that developed after the early 1990s discouraged firms from purchasing new equipment and factories.

Economic activity in Japan finally began to recover beginning in 2002, and so did firms' anticipations of future sales. Many companies began replacing facilities they had installed back in the 1980s. Others went further and bought additional capital equipment that would permit them to expand their productive capabilities. In 2003 alone, Japanese investment in new equipment and facilities increased by almost $1 billion, or close to 25 percent.

For Critical Analysis
What happened to the planned investment schedule in Japan during 2003?

CONCEPTS in Brief

- The planned investment schedule shows the relationship between real investment and the rate of interest; it slopes downward.

- The non-interest-rate determinants of planned investment are expectations, innovation and technological changes, and business taxes.

- Any change in the non-interest-rate determinants of planned investment will cause the planned investment function to shift so that at each and every rate of interest a different amount of planned investment will be made.

To test your understanding of the concepts covered in this section, go to the Online Review at www.myeconlab.com/miller.

CONSUMPTION AS A FUNCTION OF REAL GDP

We are interested in determining the equilibrium level of real GDP per year. But when we examined the consumption function earlier in this chapter, it related planned real consumption expenditures to the level of real disposable income per year. We have already

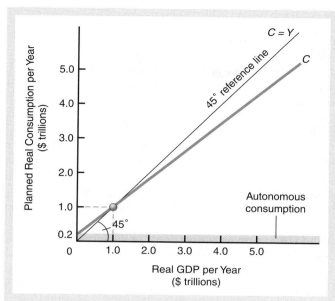

FIGURE 12-3

Consumption as a Function of Real GDP

This consumption function shows the rate of planned expenditures for each level of real GDP per year. In this example, there is an autonomous component of consumption equal to $0.2 trillion. Along the 45-degree reference line, planned real consumption expenditures per year, C, are identical to real GDP per year, Y. The consumption curve intersects the 45-degree reference line at a value of $1 trillion per year in base year dollars.

shown where adjustments must be made to GDP in order to get real disposable income (see Table 8-2 on page 183). Real disposable income turns out to be less than real GDP because real net taxes (real taxes minus real government transfer payments) are usually about 11 to 18 percent of GDP. A representative average is about 15 percent, so disposable income, on average, has in recent years been around 85 percent of GDP.

To simplify our model, assume that real disposable income, Y_d, differs from real GDP by the same absolute amount every year. Therefore, we can relatively easily substitute real GDP for real disposable income in the consumption function.

We can now plot any consumption function on a diagram in which the horizontal axis is no longer real disposable income but rather real GDP, as in Figure 12-3. Notice that there is an autonomous part of real consumption that is so labeled. The difference between this graph and the graphs presented earlier in this chapter is the change in the horizontal axis from real disposable income to real GDP per year. For the rest of this chapter, assume that this calculation has been made, and the result is that the MPC out of real GDP equals 0.8, suggesting that 20 percent of changes in real disposable income is saved: In other words, of an additional after-tax $100 earned, an additional $80 will be consumed.

The 45-Degree Reference Line

Like the earlier graphs, Figure 12-3 shows a 45-degree reference line. The 45-degree line bisects the quadrant into two equal spaces. Thus, along the 45-degree reference line, planned real consumption expenditures, C, equal real GDP per year, Y. One can see, then, that at any point where the consumption function intersects the 45-degree reference line, planned real consumption expenditures will be exactly equal to real GDP per year, or C = Y. Note that in this graph, because we are looking only at planned real consumption on the vertical axis, the 45-degree reference line is where planned real consumption, C, is always equal to real GDP per year, Y. Later, when we add real investment, government spending, and net exports to the graph, the 45-degree reference line with respect to *all* planned real expenditures will be labeled as such on the vertical axis. In any event, consumption and real GDP are equal at $1 trillion per year. That is where the consumption curve, C, intersects the 45-degree reference line. At that GDP level, all real GDP is consumed.

Adding the Investment Function

Another component of private aggregate demand is, of course, investment spending, *I*. We have already looked at the planned investment function, which related real investment to the rate of interest. You see that as the downward-sloping curve in panel (a) of Figure 12-4. Recall from Figure 11-2 (on page 243) that the equilibrium rate of interest is determined at the intersection of the desired savings schedule, which is labeled *S* and is upward sloping. The equilibrium rate of interest is 5 percent, and the equilibrium rate of real investment is $1.6 trillion per year. The $1.6 trillion of real investment per year is *autonomous* with respect to real GDP—that is, it is independent of real GDP. In other words, given that we have a determinant investment level of $1.6 trillion at a 5 percent rate of interest, we can treat this level of real investment as constant, regardless of the level of GDP. This is shown in panel (b) of Figure 12-4. The vertical distance of real investment spending is $1.6 trillion. Businesses plan on investing a particular amount—$1.6 trillion per year—and will do so no matter what the level of real GDP.

How do we add this amount of real investment spending to our consumption function? We simply add a line above the *C* line that we drew in Figure 12-3 that is higher by the vertical distance equal to $1.6 trillion of autonomous real investment spending. This is shown by the arrow in panel (c) of Figure 12-4. Our new line, now labeled *C + I* is called the *consumption plus investment line*. In our simple economy without real government expenditures and net exports, the *C + I* curve represents total planned real expenditures as they relate to different levels of real GDP per year. Because the 45-degree reference line shows all the points where planned real expenditures (now *C + I*) equal real GDP, we label it *C + I = Y*. Equilibrium *Y* equals $9 trillion per year. Equilibrium occurs when total planned real expenditures equal real GDP (given that any amount of production of goods and services in this model in the short run can occur without a change in the price level).

FIGURE 12-4
Combining Consumption and Investment

In panel (a), we show the determination of real investment in trillions of dollars per year. It occurs where the investment schedule intersects the saving schedule at an interest rate of 5 percent and is equal to $1.6 trillion per year. In panel (b), investment is a constant $1.6 trillion per year.

When we add this amount to the consumption line, we obtain in panel (c) the *C + I* line, which is vertically higher than the *C* line by exactly $1.6 trillion. Real GDP is equal to *C + I* at $9 trillion per year where total planned real expenditure, *C + I*, is equal to actual real GDP, for this is where the *C + I* line intersects the 45-degree reference line, on which *C + I* is equal to *Y* at every point.

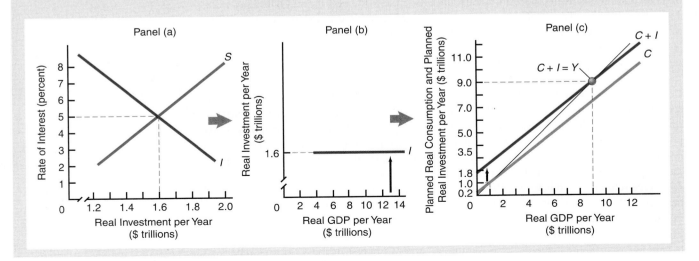

SAVING AND INVESTMENT: PLANNED VERSUS ACTUAL

Figure 12-5 shows the planned investment curve as a horizontal line at $1.6 trillion per year in base year dollars. Real investment is completely autonomous in this simplified model—it does not depend on real GDP.

The planned saving curve is represented by S. Because in our model whatever is not consumed is, by definition, saved, the planned saving schedule is the complement of the planned consumption schedule, represented by the C line in Figure 12-3 (on page 273). For better exposition, we look at only a part of the saving and investment schedules—annual levels of real GDP between $7 and $11 trillion.

Why does equilibrium have to occur at the intersection of the planned saving and planned investment schedules? If we are at E in Figure 12-5, planned saving equals planned investment. All anticipations are validated by reality. There is no tendency for businesses to alter the rate of production or the level of employment because they are neither increasing nor decreasing their inventories in an unplanned way.

If real GDP is $11 trillion instead of $9 trillion, planned investment, as usual, is $1.6 trillion per year, but it is exceeded by planned saving, which is $2 trillion per year. This means that consumers will purchase fewer goods and services than businesses had anticipated. Unplanned business inventories will now rise at the rate of $400 billion per year, bringing actual investment into line with actual saving because the $400 billion increase in inventories is included in actual investment. But this cannot continue for long. Businesses will respond to the unplanned increase in inventories by cutting back production of goods and services and reducing employment, and we will move toward a lower level of real GDP.

Conversely, if real GDP is $7 trillion per year, planned investment continues annually at $1.6 trillion, but planned saving is only $1.2 trillion. This means that households and businesses are purchasing more goods and services than businesses had planned. Businesses will find that they must draw down their inventories below the planned level by $400 billion (business inventories will fall now at the unplanned rate of $400 billion per year), bringing actual investment into equality with actual saving because the $400 billion decline in inventories is included in actual investment (thereby decreasing it). But this

FIGURE 12-5

Planned and Actual Rates of Saving and Investment
Only at the equilibrium level of real GDP of $9 trillion per year will   planned saving equal actual saving, planned investment equal actual investment, and hence planned saving equal planned investment.

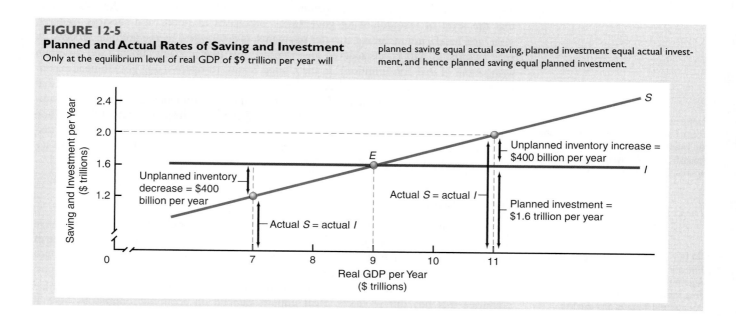

situation cannot last forever either. In their attempt to increase inventories to the desired previous level, businesses will increase production of goods and services and increase employment, and real GDP will rise toward its equilibrium value of $9 trillion per year. Figure 12-5 demonstrates the necessary equality between actual saving and actual investment. Inventories adjust so that saving and investment, after the fact, are *always* equal in this simplified model. (Remember that changes in inventories count as part of investment.)

Every time the saving rate planned by households differs from the investment rate planned by businesses, there will be a shrinkage or an expansion in the circular flow of income and output (introduced in Chapter 8) in the form of unplanned inventory changes. Real GDP and employment will change until unplanned inventory changes are again zero—that is, until we have attained the equilibrium level of real GDP.

CONCEPTS in Brief

- We assume that the consumption function has an autonomous part that is independent of the level of real GDP per year. It is labeled "autonomous consumption."

- For simplicity, we assume that real investment is autonomous with respect to real GDP and therefore unaffected by the level of real GDP per year.

- The equilibrium level of real GDP can be found where planned saving equals planned investment.

- Whenever planned saving exceeds planned investment, there will be unplanned inventory accumulation, and real GDP will fall as producers cut production of goods and services. Whenever planned saving is less than planned investment, there will be unplanned inventory depletion, and real GDP will rise as producers increase production of goods and services.

To test your understanding of the concepts covered in this section, go to the Online Review at www.myeconlab.com/miller.

KEYNESIAN EQUILIBRIUM WITH GOVERNMENT AND THE FOREIGN SECTOR ADDED

Government

We have to add real government spending, G, to our macroeconomic model. We assume that the level of resource-using government purchases of goods and services (federal, state, and local), *not* including transfer payments, is determined by the political process. In other words, G will be considered autonomous, just like real investment (and a certain component of real consumption). In the United States, resource-using government expenditures are around 20 percent of real GDP. The other side of the coin, of course, is that there are real taxes, which are used to pay for much of government spending. We will simplify our model greatly by assuming that there is a constant **lump-sum tax** of $1.5 trillion a year to finance $1.5 trillion of government spending. This lump-sum tax will reduce disposable income by the same amount. We show this in Table 12-2 (column 2), where we give the numbers for a complete model.

Lump-sum tax
A tax that does not depend on income. An example is a $1,000 tax that every household must pay, irrespective of its economic situation.

The Foreign Sector

For years, the media have focused attention on the nation's foreign trade deficit. We have been buying merchandise and services from foreign residents—real imports—the value of which exceeds the value of the real exports we have been selling to them. The difference between real exports and real imports is *real net exports,* which we label X in our graphs. The level of real exports depends on international economic conditions, especially in the countries that buy our products. Real imports depend on economic conditions here at

Go to www.econtoday.com/chap12 to find out from the U.S. Department of Agriculture how the North American Free Trade Agreement has affected U.S. agricultural imports and exports.

TABLE 12-2
The Determination of Equilibrium Real GDP with
Government and Net Exports Added
Figures are trillions of dollars.

(1)	(2)	(3)	(4)	(5)	(6)	(7)	(8)	(9)	(10)	(11)
Real GDP	Real Taxes	Real Disposable Income	Planned Real Consumption	Planned Real Saving	Planned Real Investment	Real Government Spending	Real Net Exports (exports minus imports)	Total Planned Real Expenditures (4) + (6) + (7) + (8)	Unplanned Inventory Changes	Direction of Change in Real GDP
6.0	1.5	4.5	4.3	.2	1.6	1.5	−.2	7.2	−1.2	Increase
7.0	1.5	5.5	5.1	.4	1.6	1.5	−.2	8.0	−1.0	Increase
8.0	1.5	6.5	5.9	.6	1.6	1.5	−.2	8.8	−.8	Increase
9.0	1.5	7.5	6.7	.8	1.6	1.5	−.2	9.6	−.6	Increase
10.0	1.5	8.5	7.5	1.0	1.6	1.5	−.2	10.4	−.4	Increase
11.0	1.5	9.5	8.3	1.2	1.6	1.5	−.2	11.2	−.2	Increase
12.0	1.5	10.5	9.1	1.4	1.6	1.5	−.2	12.0	0	Neither (equilibrium)
13.0	1.5	11.5	9.9	1.6	1.6	1.5	−.2	12.8	+.2	Decrease
14.0	1.5	12.5	10.7	1.8	1.6	1.5	−.2	13.6	+.4	Decrease

home. For simplicity, let us assume that real imports exceed real exports (real net exports, X, is negative) and furthermore that the level of real net exports is autonomous—independent of real national income. Assume a level of X of −$0.2 trillion per year, as shown in column 8 of Table 12-2.

Determining the Equilibrium Level of GDP per Year

We are now in a position to determine the equilibrium level of real GDP per year under the continuing assumptions that the price level is unchanging; that investment, government, and the foreign sector are autonomous; and that planned consumption expenditures are determined by the level of real GDP. As can be seen in Table 12-2, total planned real expenditures of $12 trillion per year equal real GDP of $12 trillion per year, and this is where we reach equilibrium.

Remember that equilibrium *always* occurs when total planned real expenditures equal real GDP (given that any amount of production of goods and services in this model in the short run can occur without a change in the price level).

Now look at Figure 12-6 on page 278, which shows the equilibrium level of real GDP. There are two curves, one showing the consumption function, which is the exact duplicate of the one shown in Figure 12-3, and the other being the $C + I + G + X$ curve, which intersects the 45-degree reference line (representing equilibrium) at $12 trillion per year.

Whenever total planned real expenditures differ from real GDP, there are unplanned inventory changes. When total planned real expenditures are greater than real GDP, inventory levels drop in an unplanned manner. To get inventories back up, firms seek to expand their production of goods and services, which increases real GDP. Real GDP rises toward its equilibrium level. Whenever total planned real expenditures are less than real GDP, the op-

FIGURE 12-6
The Equilibrium Level of Real GDP
The consumption function, with no government and thus no taxes, is shown as *C*. When we add autonomous investment, government spending, and net exports, we obtain *C + I + G + X*. We move from E_1 to E_2. Equilibrium real GDP is $12 trillion per year.

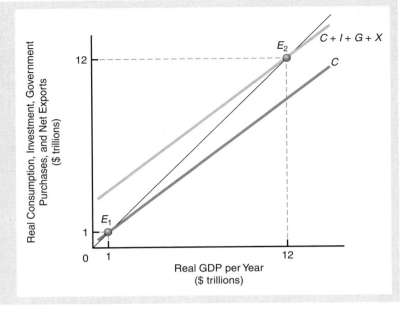

posite occurs. There are unplanned inventory increases, causing firms to cut back on their production of goods and services. The result is a drop in real GDP toward the equilibrium level.

CONCEPTS in Brief

- When we add autonomous investment, *I*, and autonomous government spending, *G*, to the consumption function, we obtain the *C + I + G* curve, which represents total planned expenditures for a closed economy. In an open economy, we add the foreign sector, which consists of exports minus imports, or net exports, *X*. Total planned expenditures are thus represented by the *C + I + G + X* curve.

- Equilibrium real GDP can be found by locating the intersection of the total planned real expenditures curve with the 45-degree reference line. At that level of real GDP per

year, planned real consumption plus planned real investment plus real government expenditures plus real net exports will equal real GDP.

- Whenever total planned real expenditures exceed real GDP, there will be unplanned decreases in inventories; production of goods and services will increase, and a higher level of equilibrium real GDP will prevail. Whenever total planned real expenditures are less than real GDP, there will be unplanned increases in inventories; production of goods and services will decrease, and equilibrium real GDP will decrease.

To test your understanding of the concepts covered in this section, go to the Online Review at www.myeconlab.com/miller.

THE MULTIPLIER

Look again at panel (c) of Figure 12-4 on page 274. Assume for the moment that the only real expenditures included in real GDP are real consumption expenditures. Where would the equilibrium level of real GDP be in this case? It would be where the consumption function (*C*) intersects the 45-degree reference line, which is at $1 trillion per year. Now we add the autonomous amount of planned real investment, $1.6 trillion, and then determine what the new equilibrium level of real GDP will be. It turns out to be $9 trillion per year. Adding $1.6 trillion per year of investment spending increased equilibrium real GDP by *five* times that amount, or by $8 trillion per year.

What is operating here is the multiplier effect of changes in autonomous spending. The **multiplier** is the number by which a permanent change in autonomous real investment or autonomous real consumption is multiplied to get the change in the equilibrium level of real GDP. Any permanent increases in autonomous real investment or in any autonomous component of consumption will cause an even larger increase in real GDP. Any permanent decreases in autonomous real spending will cause even larger decreases in real GDP per year. To understand why this multiple expansion (or contraction) in equilibrium real GDP occurs, let's look at a simple numerical example.

We'll use the same figures we used for the marginal propensity to consume and to save. MPC will equal 0.8, or $\frac{4}{5}$ and MPS will equal 0.2, or $\frac{1}{5}$. Now let's run an experiment and say that businesses decide to increase planned real investment permanently by $100 billion a year. We see in Table 12-3 that during what we'll call the first round in column 1, investment is increased by $100 billion; this also means an increase in real GDP of $100 billion, because the spending by one group represents income for another, shown in column 2. Column 3 gives the resultant increase in consumption by households that received this additional $100 billion in income. This is found by multiplying the MPC by the increase in real GDP. Because the MPC equals 0.8, real consumption expenditures during the first round will increase by $80 billion.

But that's not the end of the story. This additional household consumption is also spending, and it will provide $80 billion of additional income for other individuals. Thus, during the second round, we see an increase in real GDP of $80 billion. Now, out of this increased real GDP, what will be the resultant increase in consumption expenditures? It will be 0.8 times $80 billion, or $64 billion. We continue these induced expenditure rounds and find that an initial increase in autonomous investment expenditures of $100 billion, will eventually cause the equilibrium level of real GDP to increase by $500 billion. A permanent $100 billion increase in autonomous real investment spending has induced an

Multiplier
The ratio of the change in the equilibrium level of real GDP to the change in autonomous real expenditures; the number by which a change in autonomous real investment or autonomous real consumption, for example, is multiplied to get the change in equilibrium real GDP.

TABLE 12-3
The Multiplier Process
We trace the effects of a permanent $100 billion increase in autonomous real investment spending on real GDP. If we assume a marginal propensity to consume of 0.8, such an increase will eventually elicit a $500 billion increase in equilibrium real GDP per year.

	Assumption: MPC = 0.8, or $\frac{4}{5}$		
(1)	(2) Annual Increase in Real GDP ($ billions)	(3) Annual Increase in Planned Real Consumption ($ billions)	(4) Annual Increase in Planned Real Saving ($ billions)
Round			
1 ($100 billion per year increase in *I*)	100.00	80.000	20.000
2	80.00	64.000	16.000
3	64.00	51.200	12.800
4	51.20	40.960	10.240
5	40.96	32.768	8.192
.	.	.	.
.	.	.	.
.	.	.	.
All later rounds	163.84	131.072	32.768
Totals (*C* + *I* + *G*)	500.00	400.000	100.000

additional $400 billion increase in real consumption spending, for a total increase in real GDP of $500 billion. In other words, equilibrium real GDP will change by an amount equal to five times the change in real investment.

The Multiplier Formula

It turns out that the autonomous spending multiplier is equal to the reciprocal of the marginal propensity to save. In our example, the MPC was $\frac{4}{5}$; therefore, because MPC + MPS = 1, the MPS was equal to $\frac{1}{5}$. The reciprocal is 5. That was our multiplier. A $100 billion increase in planned investment led to a $500 billion increase in the equilibrium level of real GDP. Our multiplier will always be the following:

$$\text{Multiplier} \equiv \frac{1}{1 - \text{MPC}} \equiv \frac{1}{\text{MPS}}$$

You can always figure out the multiplier if you know either the MPC or the MPS. Let's consider an example. If MPS $= \frac{1}{4}$,

$$\text{Multiplier} = \frac{1}{\frac{1}{4}} = 4$$

Because MPC + MPS = 1, it follows that MPS = 1 − MPC. Hence we can always figure out the multiplier if we are given the marginal propensity to consume. In this example, if the marginal propensity to consume is given as $\frac{3}{4}$,

$$\text{Multiplier} = \frac{1}{1 - \frac{3}{4}} = \frac{1}{\frac{1}{4}} = 4$$

By taking a few numerical examples, you can demonstrate to yourself an important property of the multiplier:

The smaller the marginal propensity to save, the larger the multiplier.

Otherwise stated:

The larger the marginal propensity to consume, the larger the multiplier.

Demonstrate this to yourself by computing the multiplier when the marginal propensity to save equals $\frac{3}{4}$, $\frac{1}{2}$, and $\frac{1}{4}$. What happens to the multiplier as the MPS gets smaller?

When you have the multiplier, the following formula will then give you the change in equilibrium real GDP due to a permanent change in autonomous spending:

$$\text{Multiplier} \times \text{change in autonomous spending} = \text{change in equilibrium real GDP}$$

The multiplier, as noted earlier, works for a permanent increase or a permanent decrease in autonomous spending. In our earlier example, if the autonomous component of consumption had fallen permanently by $100 billion, the reduction in equilibrium real GDP would have been $500 billion per year.

Significance of the Multiplier

Depending on the size of the multiplier, it is possible that a relatively small change in planned investment or autonomous consumption can trigger a much larger change in equilibrium real GDP per year. In essence, the multiplier magnifies the fluctuations in equilibrium real GDP initiated by changes in autonomous spending.

As was just stated, the larger the marginal propensity to consume, the larger the multiplier. If the marginal propensity to consume is $\frac{1}{2}$, the multiplier is 2. In that case, a $1 billion decrease in (autonomous) real investment will elicit a $2 billion decrease in equilibrium real GDP per year. Conversely, if the marginal propensity to consume is $\frac{9}{10}$, the multiplier will be 10. That same $1 billion decrease in planned real investment expenditures with a multiplier of 10 will lead to a $10 billion decrease in equilibrium real GDP per year.

How do you suppose that a simultaneous increase in two forms of autonomous expenditures affected equilibrium U.S. real GDP in 2003?

E X A M P L E

How a Double-Whammy Multiplier Effect Unexpectedly Benefited the U.S. Economy

During the year following the 2001 recession, U.S. real GDP increased by only 2.2 percent. The 2002 rate of increase in real GDP was at least one percentage point lower than the real GDP growth the U.S. economy had experienced immediately after most previous recessions. Many economic forecasters decided that they had been overly optimistic in predicting that annual real GDP growth for 2003 might be as high as 3.5 percent. Most reduced their 2002 forecasts of 2003 real GDP growth closer to 2.5 percent.

Then two things happened during the second half of 2003: business investment spending and net exports both suddenly increased. The combined effect of these two events was a significant rise in autonomous spending, which had a predictable multiplier effect on real GDP. For the last six months of 2003, real GDP growth exceeded 6 percent. This sudden burst

pushed the rate of growth of real GDP for 2003 above 4 percent. Instead of having been too optimistic, economic forecasters turned out to have been much too pessimistic. This was because they failed to predict the increases in autonomous spending and the resulting multiplier effects generated by higher investment and net exports.

For Critical Analysis
Why is the multiplier effect of each additional dollar of autonomous investment spending the same as the multiplier effect of an additional dollar of autonomous net export spending? (Hint: Does an additional dollar of investment spending shift the C + I + G + X curve upward by any more than an additional dollar of net export spending?)

THE MULTIPLIER EFFECT WHEN THE PRICE LEVEL CAN CHANGE

Clearly, the multiplier effect on equilibrium overall *real* GDP will not be as great if part of the increase in *nominal* GDP occurs because of increases in the price level. We show this in Figure 12-7 on page 282. The intersection of AD_1 and *SRAS* is at a price level of 120 with equilibrium real GDP of $12 trillion per year. An increase in autonomous spending shifts the aggregate demand curve outward to the right to AD_2. If price level remained at 120, the short-run equilibrium level of real GDP would increase to $12.5 trillion per year because, for the $100 billion increase in autonomous spending, the multiplier would be 5, as it was in Table 12-3. But the price level does not stay fixed because ordinarily the *SRAS* curve is positively sloped. In this diagram, the new short-run equilibrium level of real GDP is hypothetically $12.3 trillion. Instead of the multiplier being 5, it is only 3. The multiplier is smaller because part of the additional income is used to pay higher prices; not all is spent on additional goods and services, as is the case when the price level is fixed.

FIGURE 12-7
Multiplier Effect on Equilibrium Real GDP
A $100 billion increase in autonomous spending (investment, government, or net exports), which moves AD_1 to AD_2, will yield a full multiplier effect only if prices are constant. If the price index increases from 120 to 125, the multiplier effect is less, and equilibrium real GDP goes up only to, say, $12.3 trillion per year instead of $12.5 trillion per year.

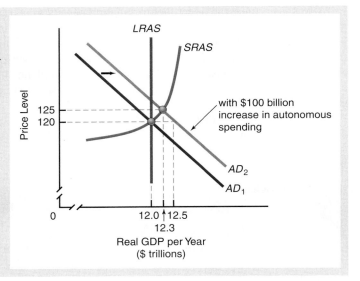

If the economy is at an equilibrium level of real GDP that is greater than *LRAS,* the implications for the multiplier are even more severe. Look again at Figure 12-7. The *SRAS* curve starts to slope upward more dramatically after $12 trillion of real GDP per year. Therefore, any increase in aggregate demand will lead to a proportionally greater increase in the price level and a smaller increase in equilibrium real GDP per year. The multiplier effect of any increase in autonomous spending will be relatively small because most of the changes will be in the price level. Moreover, any increase in the short-run equilibrium level of real GDP will tend to be temporary because the economy is temporarily above *LRAS*—the strain on its productive capacity will raise the price level.

THE RELATIONSHIP BETWEEN AGGREGATE DEMAND AND THE $C + I + G + X$ CURVE

There is clearly a relationship between the aggregate demand curves that you studied in Chapters 10 and 11 and the $C + I + G + X$ curve developed in this chapter. After all, aggregate demand consists of consumption, investment, and government purchases, plus the foreign sector of our economy. There is a major difference, however, between the aggregate demand curve, *AD,* and the $C + I + G + X$ curve: The latter is drawn with the price level held constant, whereas the former is drawn, by definition, with the price level changing. To derive the aggregate demand curve from the $C + I + G + X$ curve, we must now allow the price level to change. Look at the upper part of Figure 12-8. Here we see the $C + I + G + X$ curve at a price level equal to 100, and at $12 trillion of real GDP per year, planned real expenditures exactly equal real GDP. This gives us point *A* in the lower graph, for it shows what real GDP would be at a price level of 100.

Now let's assume that in the upper graph, the price level increases to 125. What are the effects?

1. A higher price level can decrease the purchasing power of any cash that people hold (the real-balance effect). This is a decrease in real wealth, and it causes consumption expenditures, *C,* to fall, thereby putting downward pressure on the $C + I + G + X$ curve.

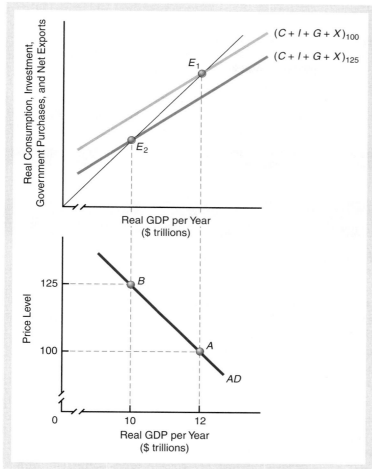

FIGURE 12-8
The Relationship Between *AD* and the *C* + *I* + *G* + *X* Curve

In the upper graph, the $C + I + G + X$ curve at a price level equal to 100 intersects the 45-degree reference line at E_1 or $12 trillion of real GDP per year. That gives us point A (price level = 100; real GDP = $12 trillion) in the lower graph. When the price level increases to 125, the $C + I + G + X$ curve shifts downward, and the new level of real GDP at which planned real expenditures equal real GDP is at E_2 at $10 trillion per year. This gives us point B in the lower graph. Connecting points A and B, we obtain the aggregate demand curve.

2. Because individuals attempt to borrow more to replenish their real cash balances, interest rates will rise, which will make it more costly for people to buy houses and cars (the interest rate effect). Higher interest rates make it less profitable, for example, to install new equipment and to erect new buildings. Therefore, the rise in the price level indirectly causes a reduction in total planned spending on goods and services.

3. In an open economy, our higher price level causes foreign spending on our goods to fall (the open economy effect). Simultaneously, it increases our demand for others' goods. If the foreign exchange price of the dollar stays constant for a while, there will be an increase in imports and a decrease in exports, thereby reducing the size of *X*, again putting downward pressure on the $C + I + G + X$ curve.

The result is that a new $C + I + G + X$ curve at a price level equal to 125 generates an equilibrium at E_2 at $10 trillion of real GDP per year. This gives us point *B* in the lower part of Figure 12-8. When we connect points *A* and *B*, we obtain the aggregate demand curve, *AD*.

CONCEPTS in Brief

- Any change in autonomous spending shifts the expenditure curve and causes a multiplier effect on equilibrium real GDP per year.

- The multiplier is equal to the reciprocal of the marginal propensity to save.

- The smaller the marginal propensity to save, the larger the multiplier. Otherwise stated, the larger the marginal propensity to consume, the larger the multiplier.

- The $C + I + G + X$ curve is drawn with the price level held constant, whereas the AD curve allows the price level to change. Each different price level generates a new $C + I + G + X$ curve.

To test your understanding of the concepts covered in this section, go to the Online Review at www.myeconlab.com/miller.

CASE STUDY: Economics Front and Center

An Individual Confronts Theory with Some Facts

Chen graduated from college last December and has completed a full year of post-college, full-time employment. As part of the process of filling out her tax forms for the latest year, she is reviewing her financial records for the past five years. During the four years she was in college, assistance from her parents and scholarships covered her tuition and room and board, but she was responsible for all of her other consumption spending. The first year she was in college, she consumed almost exactly $5,000 in other goods and services, which she fully funded by drawing on savings she had accumulated before college. During each of the next three years that she was in college, she earned about $3,000 in after-tax income from part-time jobs, and in each of those years her consumption spending was about $7,500.

This year, her first year of post-college, full-time employment with no outside income sources, she earned just over $42,000, or

about 14 times more than she did during each of her last three years in college. After determining her total taxes for her first year of employment, Chen calculates that she spent about 87 percent of her after-tax income for that year on goods and services. She is pleased that she was able to apply the remaining 13 percent of her after-tax income toward replenishing the savings she drew upon while in college.

Points to Analyze

1. *In what ways were Chen's consumption and saving behavior during her college years consistent with the theories you learned about in this chapter?*

2. *Why does it make sense that during the most recent year, Chen's consumption spending fell as a percentage of her after-tax income?*

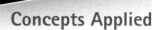

D uring the 1990s, "new economy" proponents contended that business investments in advanced communications systems, high-powered computers, and sophisticated software would aid the U.S. economy in two ways. First, information technology (IT) investments would promote more rapid innovation that would increase the rate of productivity growth and thereby generate greater long-term economic growth. Second, a steady upswing in investments in IT would stimulate a stable stream of planned investment expenditures, thereby keeping the U.S. economy on an even keel for the foreseeable future.

Concepts Applied
- Total Planned Expenditures
- Equilibrium Real GDP
- Multiplier Effect

Investment Instability in the New Economy

There is growing evidence that advocates of the new economy idea may well have been correct about the longer-term growth implications of IT investments. In retrospect, however, it appears that they were wrong in suggesting that IT-driven investment spending would make the U.S. economy more stable.

As you can see in Figure 12-9, the rate of growth in business investment in IT products actually dropped like a rock at the beginning of the 2000s. Double-digit annual growth in IT investment through 2000 turned into a double-digit shrinkage in 2001.

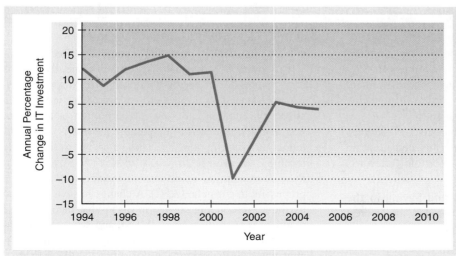

FIGURE 12-9

Annual Rates of Growth in U.S. Information Technology Investment

U.S. business investment in IT products grew at a rapid pace during the late 1990s before experiencing negative rates of growth in 2001 and 2002.

Sources: Bureau of Economic Analysis, *Economic Indicators* (various issues), and author's estimates.

The Multiplier Matters in the New Economy, Too

In light of Figure 12-9 and given what you learned in this chapter, it should be no surprise that a recession took place in 2001. The rapid shrinkage in IT investment resulted in a sudden drop in total planned investment. This, in turn, caused a decrease in U.S. total planned expenditures, which had a multiplier effect that reduced growth in equilibrium U.S. real GDP.

Since the 2001 recession, many economists have speculated that investment spending on advanced IT may continue to be unstable in years to come. They worry that as new types of IT are developed, investment-spending booms may be followed by investment-spending busts in repeat performances of the late 1990s and early 2000s. If so, higher rates of economic growth in the new economy may be accompanied by somewhat less economic stability.

For Critical Analysis

1. What effect did the fall in IT investment have on the position of the $C + I + G + X$ curve?
2. If autonomous consumption increased in 2001, as some economists believe happened, how might that have made the 2001 recession less severe than it otherwise could have been?

Web Resources

1. For access to Bureau of Economic Analysis data on components of U.S. business investment spending, including investment in equipment and software, use the link at www.econtoday.com/chap12.
2. At the economic data site provided by the Federal Reserve Bank of St. Louis, track the largest component of total investment expenditures, fixed private investment, using the link available at www.econtoday.com/chap12.

Research Project

Make a list of the various ways that you can envision firms engaging in investment spending, arranged in order of stability with forms of spending likely to be most stable at the top and those likely to be least stable at the bottom. (Remember that inventory investment should be someplace in your list.) Consider how the adoption of new information technologies could induce firms to increase the share of investment spending for certain items on your list while reducing the share of investment spending for other items, and make a prediction about whether overall investment is likely to be more or less stable as a result.

SUMMARY DISCUSSION of Learning Objectives

1. **The Difference Between Saving and Savings and the Relationship Between Saving and Consumption:** Saving is a flow over time, whereas savings is a stock of resources at a point in time. Thus the portion of your disposable income you do not consume during a week, a month, or a year is an addition to your stock of savings. By definition, saving during a year plus consumption during that year must equal total disposable (after-tax) income earned that year.

2. **Key Determinants of Consumption and Saving in the Keynesian Model:** In the classical model, the interest rate is the fundamental determinant of saving, but in the Keynesian model, the primary determinant is disposable income. The reason is that as real disposable income in-

creases, so do real consumption expenditures. Because consumption and saving equal disposable income, this means that saving must also vary with changes in disposable income. Of course, factors other than disposable income can affect consumption and saving. The portion of consumption that is not related to disposable income is called autonomous consumption. The ratio of saving to disposable income is the average propensity to save (APS), and the ratio of consumption to disposable income is the average propensity to consume (APC). A change in saving divided by the corresponding change in disposable income is the marginal propensity to save (MPS), and a change in consumption divided by the corresponding change in disposable income is the marginal propensity to consume (MPC).

3. **The Primary Determinants of Planned Investment:** An increase in the interest rate reduces the profitability of investment, so planned investment varies inversely with the interest rate. Hence the investment schedule slopes downward. Other factors that influence planned investment, such as business expectations, productive technology, or business taxes, can cause the investment schedule to shift. In the basic Keynesian model, changes in real GDP do not affect planned investment, meaning that investment is autonomous with respect to real GDP.

4. **How Equilibrium Real GDP Is Established in the Keynesian Model:** In equilibrium, total planned real consumption, investment, government, and net export expenditures equal real GDP, so $C + I + G + X = Y$. This occurs at the point where the $C + I + G + X$ curve crosses the 45-degree reference line. In a world without government spending and taxes, equilibrium also occurs when planned saving is equal to planned investment. Furthermore, at equilibrium real GDP, there is no tendency for business inventories to expand or contract.

5. **Why Autonomous Changes in Total Planned Real Expenditures Have a Multiplier Effect on Equilibrium Real GDP:** Any increase in autonomous expenditures, such as an increase in investment caused by a rise in business confidence, causes a direct rise in real GDP. The resulting increase in disposable income in turn stimulates increased consumption, and the amount of this increase is the marginal propensity to consume multiplied by the rise in disposable income that results. As consumption increases, however, so does real GDP, which induces a further increase in consumption spending. The ultimate expansion of real GDP is equal to the multiplier, $1/(1 - MPC)$, times the increase in autonomous expenditures. Because $MPS \equiv 1 - MPC$, the multiplier can also be written as $1/MPS$.

6. **The Relationship Between Total Planned Expenditures and the Aggregate Demand Curve:** An increase in the price level decreases the purchasing power of money holdings, which induces households and businesses to cut back on expenditures. In addition, as individuals and firms seek to borrow to replenish their cash balances, the interest rate tends to rise, which further discourages spending. Furthermore, a higher price level reduces exports as foreign residents cut back on purchases of domestically produced goods. These combined effects shift the $C + I + G + X$ curve downward following a rise in the price level, so that equilibrium real GDP falls. This yields the downward-sloping aggregate demand curve.

KEY TERMS AND CONCEPTS

autonomous consumption (268)

average propensity to consume (APC) (268)

average propensity to save (APS) (268)

capital goods (265)

consumption (264)

consumption function (266)

consumption goods (264)

dissaving (266)

45-degree reference line (267)

investment (265)

lump-sum tax (276)

marginal propensity to consume (MPC) (269)

marginal propensity to save (MPS) (269)

multiplier (279)

saving (264)

wealth (270)

PROBLEMS

Answers to the odd-numbered problems appear at the back of the book.

12-1. Examine the accompanying table.

Disposable Income	Saving	Consumption
$ 200	−$ 40	_____
400	0	_____
600	40	_____
800	80	_____
1,000	120	_____
1,200	160	_____

a. Complete the table on the previous page.

b. Add two columns to the right of the table. Calculate the average propensity to save and the average propensity to consume at each level of disposable income. (Round to the nearest hundredth.)

c. Determine the marginal propensity to save and the marginal propensity to consume.

12-2. Classify each of the following as either a stock or a flow.

a. Myung Park earns $850 per week.

b. Time Warner purchases $100 million in new computer equipment this month.

c. Sally Schmidt has $1,000 in a savings account at a credit union.

d. XYZ, Inc., produces 200 units of output per week.

e. Giorgio Giannelli owns three private jets.

f. DaimlerChrysler's inventories decline by 750 autos per month.

g. Russia owes $25 billion to the International Monetary Fund.

12-3. An Internet service provider (ISP) is contemplating an investment of $50,000 in new computer servers and related hardware. The ISP projects an annual rate of return on this investment of 6 percent.

a. The current market interest rate is 5 percent per year. Will the ISP undertake the investment?

b. Suddenly there is an economic downturn. Although the market interest rate does not change, the ISP anticipates that the projected rate of return on the investment will be only 4 percent per year. Will the ISP now undertake the investment?

12-4. Consider the table at the end of this problem when answering the following questions. For this hypothetical economy, the marginal propensity to save is constant at all levels of real GDP, and investment spending is autonomous. There is no government.

a. Complete the table. What is the marginal propensity to save? What is the marginal propensity to consume?

b. Draw a graph of the consumption function. Then add the investment function to obtain $C + I$.

c. Under the graph of $C + I$, draw another graph showing the saving and investment curves. Note that the $C + I$ curve crosses the 45-degree reference line in the upper graph at the same level of real GDP where the saving and investment curves cross in the lower graph. (If not, redraw your graphs.) What is this level of real GDP?

d. What is the numerical value of the multiplier?

e. What is equilibrium real GDP without investment? What is the multiplier effect from the inclusion of investment?

f. What is the average propensity to consume at equilibrium real GDP?

g. If autonomous investment declines from $400 to $200, what happens to equilibrium real GDP?

Real GDP	Consumption	Saving	Investment
$ 2,000	$2,200	$____	$400
4,000	4,000	____	____
6,000	____	____	____
8,000	____	____	____
10,000	____	____	____
12,000	____	____	____

12-5. Consider the table below when answering the following questions. For this hypothetical economy, the marginal propensity to consume is constant at all levels of real GDP, and investment spending is autonomous. Equilibrium real GDP is equal to $8,000. There is no government.

Real GDP	Consumption	Saving	Investment
$ 2,000	$ 2,000	____	____
4,000	3,600	____	____
6,000	5,200	____	____
8,000	6,800	____	____
10,000	8,400	____	____
12,000	10,000	____	____

a. Complete the table. What is the marginal propensity to consume? What is the marginal propensity to save?

b. Draw a graph of the consumption function. Then add the investment function to obtain $C + I$.

c. Under the graph of $C + I$, draw another graph showing the saving and investment curves. Does the $C + I$ curve cross the 45-degree reference line in the upper graph at the same level of real GDP where the saving and investment curves cross in the lower graph, at the equilibrium real GDP of $8,000? (If not, redraw your graphs.)

d. What is the average propensity to save at equilibrium real GDP?

e. If autonomous consumption were to rise by $100, what would happen to equilibrium real GDP?

12-6. Calculate the multiplier for the following cases.

    a. MPS = 0.25
    b. MPC = $\frac{5}{6}$
    c. MPS = 0.125
    d. MPC = $\frac{6}{7}$
    e. $C = \$200 + 0.85Y$

12-7. A nation's consumption function (expressed in millions of inflation-adjusted dollars) is $C = \$800 + 0.80Y$. There are no taxes in this nation.

    a. What is the value of autonomous saving?
    b. What is the marginal propensity to save in this economy?
    c. What is the value of the multiplier?

12-8. Based on the information in Problem 12-7, complete the following table. (Round all decimal fractions to the nearest hundredth.)

Real GDP (Y)	Average Propensity to Consume (APC)	Average Propensity to Save (APS)
$10,000	_____	_____
11,000	_____	_____
12,000	_____	_____
13,000	_____	_____
14,000	_____	_____
15,000	_____	_____

12-9. Assume that the multiplier in a country is equal to 4 and that autonomous real consumption spending is $1 trillion. If current real GDP is $12 trillion, what is the current value of real consumption spending?

12-10. The multiplier in a country is equal to 5, and households pay no taxes. At the current equilibrium real GDP of $14 trillion, total real consumption spending by households is $12 trillion. What is real autonomous consumption in this country?

12-11. At an initial point on the aggregate demand curve, the price level is 125, and real GDP is $10 trillion. When the price level falls to a value of 120, total autonomous expenditures increase by $250 billion. The marginal propensity to consume is 0.75. What is the level of real GDP at the new point on the aggregate demand curve?

12-12. At an initial point on the aggregate demand curve, the price level is 100, and real GDP is $12 trillion. After the price level rises to 110, however, there is an upward movement along the aggregate demand curve, and real GDP declines to $11 trillion. If total autonomous spending declined by $200 billion in response to the increase in the price level, what is the marginal propensity to consume in this economy?

12-13. In an economy in which the multiplier has a value of 3, the price level has decreased from 115 to 110. As a consequence, there has been a movement along the aggregate demand curve from $12 trillion in real GDP to $12.9 trillion in real GDP.

    a. What is the marginal propensity to save?
    b. What was the amount of the change in autonomous expenditures generated by the decline in the price level?

ECONOMICS ON THE NET

The Relationship Between Consumption and Real GDP According to the basic consumption function we considered in this chapter, consumption rises at a fixed rate when both disposable income and real GDP increase. Your task here is to evaluate how reasonable this assumption is and to determine the relative extent to which variations in consumption appear to be related to variations in real GDP.

Title: Gross Domestic Product and Components

Navigation: Use the link at www.econtoday.com/chap12 to visit the Federal Reserve Bank of St. Louis's Web page on Gross Domestic Product and Components.

Application

1. Scan down the alphabetical list, and click on *Personal Consumption Expenditure (Bil. of $; Q)*. Then click on "Download Data," Write down consumption expenditures for the past eight quarters. Now back up to *Gross Domestic Product and Components*, click on *Gross Domestic Product, 1 Decimal (Bil. $; Q)*, click on "Download Data," and write down GDP for the past eight quarters. Use these data to calculate implied values for the marginal propensity to consume, assuming that taxes do not vary with income. Is there any problem with this assumption?

2. Back up to *Gross Domestic Product and Components*. Now click on *Gross Domestic Product: Implicit Price*

Deflator. Scan through the data since the mid-1960s. In what years did the largest variations in GDP take place? What component or components of GDP appear to have accounted for these large movements?

For Group Study and Analysis Assign groups to use the FRED database to try to determine the best measure of aggregate U.S. disposable income for the past eight quarters. Reconvene as a class, and discuss each group's approach to this issue.

Media Resources

If your exam were tomorrow, would you be ready? For each chapter, MyEconLab Practice Tests and Study Plans pinpoint which sections you have mastered and which ones you need to study. That way, you are more efficient with your study time, and you are better prepared for your exams.

In addition to Practice Tests and your personalized Study Plan, you'll find the following media resources in MyEconLab:

1. *Graphs in Motion* animation of Table 12-3 and Figures 12-1, 12-5, 12-6, 12-7, and 12-8.
2. Videos featuring the author, Roger LeRoy Miller, on the following subjects:
   ● The Marginal Propensity to Consume
   ● The Determinants of Investment
   ● The Multiplier

3. Links to the Web sites cited in the marginal Internet Resources, Issues and Applications feature, and Economics on the Net activity.
4. Audio clips of all key terms, additional practice problems, and a PDF version of the material from the print Study Guide.
5. eThemes of the Times, which is a New York Times article to help you understand the real-world applications of what you are learning.

Get Ahead of the Curve

To see how it works, turn to page 16 and then go to www.myeconlab.com/miller.

The Keynesian Cross and the Multiplier

We can see the multiplier effect more clearly if we look at Figure B-1, in which we see only a small section of the graphs that we used in Chapter 12. We start with equilibrium real GDP of $11.5 trillion per year. This equilibrium occurs with total planned real expenditures represented by $C + I + G + X$. The $C + I + G + X$ curve intersects the 45-degree reference line at $11.5 trillion per year. Now we increase real investment, I, by $100 billion. This increase in investment shifts the entire $C + I + G + X$ curve vertically to $C + I' + G + X$. The vertical shift represents that $100 billion increase in autonomous investment. With the higher level of planned expenditures per year, we are no longer in equilibrium at E. Inventories are falling. Production of goods and services will increase as firms try to replenish their inventories. Eventually, real GDP will catch up with total planned expenditures. The new equilibrium level of real GDP is established at E' at the intersection of the new $C + I' + G + X$ curve and the 45-degree reference line, along which $C + I + G + X = Y$ (total planned expenditures equal real GDP). The new equilibrium level of real GDP is $12 trillion per year. Thus the increase in equilibrium real GDP is equal to five times the permanent increase in planned investment spending.

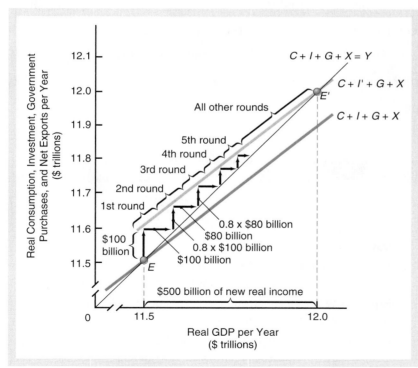

FIGURE B-1
Graphing the Multiplier
We can translate Table 12-3 on page 279 into graphic form by looking at each successive round of additional spending induced by an autonomous increase in planned investment of $100 billion. The total planned expenditures curve shifts from $C + I + G + X$, with its associated equilibrium level of real GDP of $11.5 trillion, to a new curve labeled $C + I' + G + X$. The new equilibrium level of real GDP is $12 trillion. Equilibrium is again established.

The European Monetary Union (EMU), the group of nations that use the euro as a common currency, was created in 1999. Each country in the EMU has agreed to abide by the "Growth and Stability Pact." One part of this agreement is intended to ensure that each member nation's government keeps its expenditures closely aligned with its total tax collections. An EMU national government that violates the agreement is supposed to pay a fine and be required to reduce its expenditures or raise its taxes. Nevertheless, the governments of two of the nations that pushed hardest for adoption of this rule, France and Germany, have turned out to be the biggest violators. In this chapter you will learn why they chose to break the agreement they previously championed.

Refer to the end of the chapter for a full listing of the multimedia learning materials available in MyEconLab.

LEARNING OBJECTIVES

After reading this chapter, you should be able to:

1. Use traditional Keynesian analysis to evaluate the effects of discretionary fiscal policies
2. Discuss ways in which indirect crowding out and direct expenditure offsets can reduce the effectiveness of fiscal policy actions
3. Explain why the Ricardian equivalence theorem calls into question the usefulness of tax changes
4. List and define fiscal policy time lags and explain why they complicate efforts to engage in fiscal "fine-tuning"
5. Describe how certain aspects of fiscal policy function as automatic stabilizers for the economy

...between 2002 and 2004, U.S. government expenditures rose 8.2 percent per year, which was the largest rate of increase in half a century? A portion of this increase in federal government spending was used to step up U.S. antiterrorism defenses. The biggest increases, however, were in discretionary, nondefense expenditures, which rose by more than 20 percent. Included were funding for such items as the Rock and Roll Hall of Fame in Cleveland, Ohio; an indoor rain forest in Coralville, Iowa; the National Cowgirl Museum and Hall of Fame in Ft. Worth, Texas; and a golf awareness program in St. Augustine, Florida. In this chapter you will learn about the consequences of higher government spending for equilibrium real GDP and the price level. You will also consider the macroeconomic effects of changes in the tax revenues used to help fund public spending.

DISCRETIONARY FISCAL POLICY

The making of deliberate, discretionary changes in government expenditures or taxes (or both) to achieve certain national economic goals is the realm of **fiscal policy.** Some national goals are high employment (low unemployment), price stability, economic growth, and improvement in the nation's international payments balance. Fiscal policy can be thought of as a deliberate attempt to cause the economy to move to full employment and price stability more quickly than it otherwise might.

Fiscal policy has typically been associated with the economic theories of John Maynard Keynes and what is now called *traditional* Keynesian analysis. Recall from Chapter 11 that Keynes's explanation of the Great Depression was that there was insufficient aggregate demand. Because he believed that wages and prices were "sticky downward," he argued that the classical economists' picture of an economy moving automatically and quickly toward full employment was inaccurate. To Keynes and his followers, government had to step in to increase aggregate demand. In other words, expansionary fiscal policy initiated by the federal government was the way to ward off recessions and depressions.

Fiscal policy
The discretionary changing of government expenditures or taxes to achieve national economic goals, such as high employment with price stability.

Changes in Government Spending

In Chapter 11, we looked at the recessionary gap and the inflationary gap (see Figures 11-11 and 11-12 on pages 253 and 254). The recessionary gap was defined as the amount by which the current level of real GDP fell short of the economy's potential production if it were operating on its *LRAS* curve. The inflationary gap was defined as the amount by which the short-run equilibrium level of real GDP exceeds the long-run equilibrium level as given by *LRAS*. Let us examine fiscal policy first in the context of a recessionary gap.

When There Is a Recessionary Gap.
The government, along with firms, individuals, and foreign residents, is one of the spending agents in the economy. When the government decides to spend more, all other things held constant, the dollar value of total spending must rise. Look at panel (a) of Figure 13-1 on the following page. We start at short-run equilibrium with AD_1 intersecting *SRAS* at $11.5 trillion of real GDP per year. There is a recessionary gap of $500 billion of real GDP per year—the difference between *LRAS* (the economy's long-run potential) and the short-run equilibrium level of real GDP per year. When the government decides to spend more (expansionary fiscal policy), the

FIGURE 13-1

Expansionary and Contractionary Fiscal Policy:
Changes in Government Spending

If there is a recessionary gap and short-run equilibrium is at E_1 in panel (a), fiscal policy can presumably increase aggregate demand to AD_2. The new equilibrium is at E_2 at higher real GDP per year and a higher price level. In panel (b), the economy is at short-run equilibrium at E_1, which is at a higher real GDP than the *LRAS*. To reduce this inflationary gap, fiscal policy can be used to decrease aggregate demand from AD_1 to AD_2. Eventually, equilibrium will fall to E_2, which is on the *LRAS*.

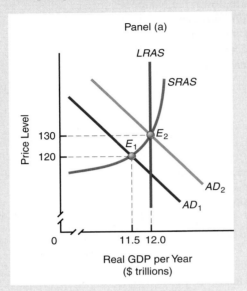

Panel (a)

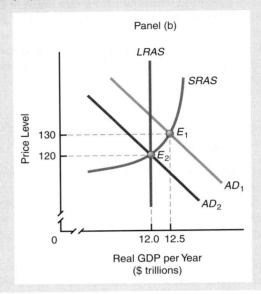

Panel (b)

aggregate demand curve shifts to the right to AD_2. Here we assume that the government knows exactly how much more to spend so that AD_2 intersects *SRAS* at $12 trillion, or at *LRAS*. Because of the upward-sloping *SRAS*, the price level rises from 120 to 130 as real GDP goes to $12 trillion per year.

When There Is an Inflationary Gap. The entire process shown in panel (a) of Figure 13-1 can be reversed, as shown in panel (b). An inflationary gap occurs at the intersection of *SRAS* and AD_1, at point E_1. Real GDP cannot be sustained at $12.5 trillion indefinitely, because this exceeds long-run aggregate supply, which in real terms is $12 trillion. If the government recognizes this and reduces its spending (pursues a contractionary fiscal policy), this action reduces aggregate demand from AD_1 to AD_2. Equilibrium will fall to E_2 on the *LRAS*, where real GDP per year is $12 trillion. The price level will fall from 130 to 120.

Changes in Taxes

The spending decisions of firms, individuals, and foreign residents depend on the taxes levied on them. Individuals in their role as consumers look to their disposable (after-tax) income when determining their desired rates of consumption. Firms look at their after-tax profits when deciding on the levels of investment to undertake. Foreign residents look at the tax-inclusive cost of goods when deciding whether to buy in the United States or elsewhere. Therefore, holding all other things constant, a rise in taxes causes a reduction in aggregate demand because it reduces consumption, investment, or net exports. What actually happens depends, of course, on the parties on whom the taxes are levied.

Compared with other developed countries, do you think that the percentage of GDP that goes to taxes in the United States is relatively high or relatively low?

International Policy EXAMPLE

To Pay the Highest Taxes, Live in Sweden

Figure 13-2 displays total government tax revenues as a share of GDP in the world's most developed nations. The nation in which the highest portion of GDP goes to government tax collections is Sweden. *More than half* of Sweden's GDP is taxed away from households and firms for government use.

The United States and Japan have the lowest total government tax collections as percentages of GDP. Among the world's most developed nations, they are the only ones where

less than 30 percent of GDP is transformed into government tax revenues.

For Critical Analysis
In which countries listed in Figure 13-2 would you anticipate that government spending as a percentage of GDP would be the highest?

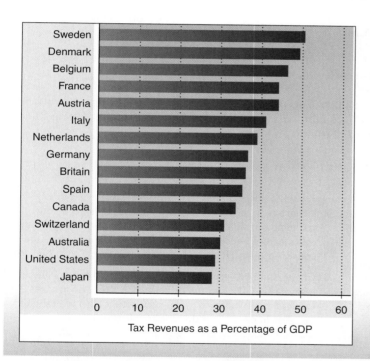

FIGURE 13-2
Government Tax Revenues as a Percentage of GDP in Developed Nations
Among the world's most developed nations, the government of Sweden collects the highest portion of GDP as taxes, and taxes as a share of GDP are lowest in Japan and the United States.

Source: Organization for Economic Cooperation and Development.

When the Current Short-Run Equilibrium Is Greater Than *LRAS*. Assume that aggregate demand is AD_1 in panel (a) of Figure 13-3 on page 296. It intersects *SRAS* at E_1, which yields real GDP greater than *LRAS*. In this situation, an increase in taxes shifts the aggregate demand curve inward to the left. For argument's sake, assume that it intersects *SRAS* at E_2, or exactly where *LRAS* intersects AD_2. In this situation, the level of real GDP falls from $12.5 trillion per year to $12 trillion per year. The price level falls from 120 to 100.

When the Current Short-Run Equilibrium Is Less Than *LRAS*. Look at panel (b) in Figure 13-3. AD_1 intersects *SRAS* at E_1, with real GDP at $11.5 trillion, less than the *LRAS*

FIGURE 13-3
Contractionary and Expansionary Fiscal Policy: Changes in Taxes

In panel (a), the economy is initially at E_1, where real GDP exceeds long-run equilibrium real GDP. Contractionary fiscal policy can move aggregate demand to AD_2 so that the new equilibrium is at E_2 at a lower price level, and real GDP is now consistent with *LRAS*. In panel (b), with a recessionary gap (in this case of $500 billion), taxes are cut. AD_1 moves to AD_2. The economy moves from E_1 to E_2, and real GDP is now at $12 trillion per year, the long-run equilibrium level.

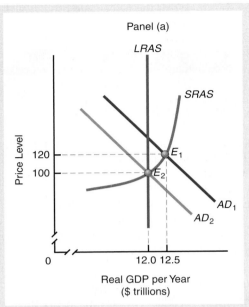

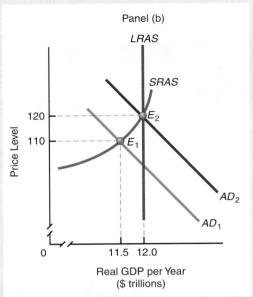

of $12 trillion. In this situation, a decrease in taxes shifts the aggregate demand curve outward to the right. At AD_2, equilibrium is established at E_2, with the price level at 120 and equilibrium real GDP at $12 trillion per year.

CONCEPTS in Brief

- Fiscal policy is defined as making discretionary changes in government expenditures or taxes to achieve such national goals as high employment or reduced inflation.

- If there is a recessionary gap and the economy is operating at less than long-run aggregate supply (*LRAS*), an increase in government spending can shift the aggregate demand curve to the right and perhaps lead to a higher equilibrium level of real GDP per year.

- If there is an inflationary gap, a decrease in government spending can shift the aggregate demand curve to the left, reducing the equilibrium level of real GDP per year to be consistent with *LRAS*.

- Changes in taxes can have similar effects on the equilibrium rate of real GDP and the price level. A decrease in taxes can lead to an increase in the equilibrium level of real GDP per year. In contrast, if there is an inflationary gap, an increase in taxes can decrease equilibrium real GDP.

To test your understanding of the concepts covered in this section, go to the Online Review at www.myeconlab.com/miller.

POSSIBLE OFFSETS TO FISCAL POLICY

Fiscal policy does not operate in a vacuum. Important questions have to be answered: If government expenditures increase, how are those expenditures financed, and by whom? If taxes are increased, what does the government do with the taxes? What will happen if individuals worry about increases in *future* taxes because the government is spending more today without raising current taxes? All of these questions involve *offsets* to the effects of fiscal policy. We will look at each of them and others in detail.

Indirect Crowding Out

Let's take the first example of fiscal policy in this chapter—an increase in government expenditures. If government expenditures rise and taxes are held constant, something has to give. Our government does not simply take goods and services when it wants them. It has to pay for them. When it pays for them and does not simultaneously collect the same amount in taxes, it must borrow. That means that an increase in government spending without raising taxes creates additional government borrowing from the private sector (or from foreign residents).

Induced Interest Rate Changes. Holding everything else constant, if the government attempts to borrow more from the private sector to pay for its increased budget deficit, it is not going to have an easy time selling its bonds. If the bond market is in equilibrium, when the government tries to sell more bonds, it is going to have to offer a better deal in order to get rid of them. A better deal means offering a higher interest rate. This is the interest rate effect of expansionary fiscal policy financed by borrowing from the public. Consequently, when the federal government finances increased spending by additional borrowing, it will push interest rates up. When interest rates go up, it is less profitable for firms to finance new construction, equipment, and inventories. It is also more expensive for individuals to finance purchases of cars and homes.

Thus a rise in government spending, holding taxes constant (that is, deficit spending), tends to crowd out private spending, dampening the positive effect of increased government spending on aggregate demand. This is called the **crowding-out effect.** In the extreme case, the crowding out may be complete, with the increased government spending having no net effect on aggregate demand. The final result is simply more government spending and less private investment and consumption. Figure 13-4 shows how the crowding-out effect occurs.

The Firm's Investment Decision. To understand the interest rate effect better, consider a firm that is contemplating borrowing $100,000 to expand its business. Suppose that the interest rate is 5 percent. The interest payments on the debt will be 5 percent times $100,000, or $5,000 per year ($417 per month). A rise in the interest rate to 8 percent will push the payments to 8 percent of $100,000, or $8,000 per year ($667 per month). The extra $250 per month in interest expenses will discourage some firms from making the investment. Consumers face similar decisions when they purchase houses and cars. An increase in the interest rate causes their monthly payments to go up, thereby discouraging some of them from purchasing cars and houses.

Crowding-out effect
The tendency of expansionary fiscal policy to cause a decrease in planned investment or planned consumption in the private sector; this decrease normally results from the rise in interest rates.

FIGURE 13-4
The Crowding-Out Effect, Step by Step

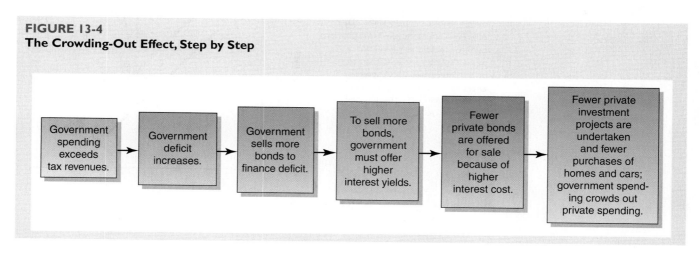

Graphical Analysis. You see in Figure 13-5 that the initial equilibrium, E_1, is below *LRAS*. But suppose that government expansionary fiscal policy in the form of increased government spending (without increasing current taxes) shifts aggregate demand from AD_1 to AD_2. In the absence of the crowding-out effect, real GDP would increase to $12 trillion per year, and the price level would rise to 140 (point E_2). With the (partial) crowding-out effect, however, as investment and consumption decline, partly offsetting the rise in government spending, the aggregate demand curve shifts inward to the left to AD_3. The new equilibrium is now at E_3, with real GDP of $11.75 trillion per year at a price level of 135. In other words, crowding out dilutes the effect of expansionary fiscal policy, and a recessionary gap remains.

Planning for the Future: The Ricardian Equivalence Theorem

Economists have often implicitly assumed that people look at changes in taxes or changes in government spending only in the present. What if people actually think about the size of *future* tax payments? Does this have an effect on how they react to an increase in government spending with no current tax increases? Some economists believe that the answer is yes. What if people's horizons extend beyond this year? Don't we then have to take into account the effects of today's government policies on the future?

Consider an example. The government wants to reduce taxes by $100 billion today. Assume that government spending remains constant. Assume further that the government initially has a balanced budget. Thus the only way for the government to pay for this $100 billion tax cut is to borrow $100 billion today. The public will owe $100 billion plus interest later. Realizing that a $100 billion tax cut today is mathematically equivalent to $100 billion plus interest later, people may wish to save the tax cut to meet future tax liabilities—payment of interest and repayment of debt.

Consequently, a tax cut may not affect total planned expenditures. A reduction in taxes without a reduction in government spending may therefore have no impact on aggregate demand.

Similarly, increased government spending without an increase in taxes will not necessarily have a large impact on aggregate demand. In terms of Figure 13-5, the aggregate de-

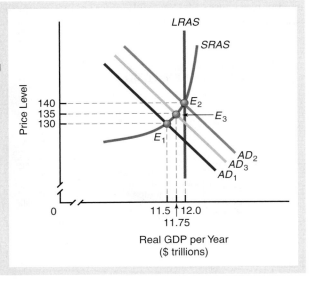

FIGURE 13-5
The Crowding-Out Effect
Expansionary fiscal policy that causes deficit financing initially shifts AD_1 to AD_2. Equilibrium initially moves toward E_2. But expansionary fiscal policy pushes up interest rates, thereby reducing interest-sensitive spending. This effect causes the aggregate demand curve to shift inward to AD_3, and the new short-run equilibrium is at E_3.

mand curve will shift inward from AD_2 to AD_3. In the extreme case, if consumers fully compensate for a higher future tax liability by saving more, the aggregate demand curve shifts all the way back to AD_1 in Figure 13-5. This is the case of individuals fully discounting their increased tax liabilities. The result is that an increased budget deficit created entirely by a current tax cut has literally no effect on the economy. This is known as the **Ricardian equivalence theorem,** after the nineteenth-century economist David Ricardo, who first developed the argument publicly.

For economists who believe in the Ricardian equivalence theorem, it does not matter how government expenditures are financed—by taxes or by issuing debt. Is the theorem correct? Research indicates that Ricardian equivalence effects may exist but has not provided much compelling evidence about their magnitudes.

Ricardian equivalence theorem
The proposition that an increase in the government budget deficit has no effect on aggregate demand.

Direct Expenditure Offsets

Government has a distinct comparative advantage over the private sector in certain activities such as diplomacy and national defense. Otherwise stated, certain resource-using activities in which the government engages do not compete with the private sector. In contrast, some of what government does competes directly with the private sector, such as education. When government competes with the private sector, **direct expenditure offsets** to fiscal policy may occur. For example, if the government starts providing milk at no charge to students who are already purchasing milk, there is a direct expenditure offset. Households spend less directly on milk, but government spends more.

Normally, the impact of an increase in government spending on aggregate demand is analyzed by implicitly assuming that government spending is *not* a substitute for private spending. This is clearly the case for a cruise missile. Whenever government spending is a substitute for private spending, however, a rise in government spending causes a direct reduction in private spending to offset it.

Direct expenditure offsets
Actions on the part of the private sector in spending income that offset government fiscal policy actions. Any increase in government spending in an area that competes with the private sector will have some direct expenditure offset.

The Extreme Case.
In the extreme case, the direct expenditure offset is dollar for dollar, so we merely end up with a relabeling of spending from private to public. Assume that you have decided to spend $100 on groceries. Upon your arrival at the checkout counter, you find a U.S. Department of Agriculture official. She announces that she will pay for your groceries—but only the ones in the cart. Here increased government spending is $100. You leave the store in bliss. But just as you are deciding how to spend the $100, an Internal Revenue Service agent appears. He announces that as a result of the current budgetary crisis, your taxes are going to rise by $100. You have to pay right now. Increases in taxes have now been $100. We have a balanced-budget increase in government spending. In this scenario, *total* spending does not change. We simply end up with higher government spending, which directly offsets exactly an equal reduction in consumption. Aggregate demand and GDP are unchanged. Otherwise stated, if there is a full direct expenditure offset, the government spending multiplier is zero.

The Less Extreme Case.
Much government spending has a private-sector substitute. When government expenditures increase, private spending tends to decline somewhat (but generally not dollar for dollar), thereby mitigating the upward impact on total aggregate demand. To the extent that there are some direct expenditure offsets to expansionary fiscal policy, predicted changes in aggregate demand will be lessened. Consequently, real GDP and the price level will be less affected.

Why do you suppose that a portion of U.S. government spending on research and development does not necessarily generate a rise in aggregate demand?

Policy EXAMPLE

The Direct Offset of Government Grants

Private companies fund a considerable amount of scientific and engineering research. So does the government. Although some of this research is conducted by people employed directly by government agencies, the government also helps fund research by providing grants to researchers. Many such grants provide dollar payments directly to researchers to fund part or all of their salaries and those of their assistants. In addition, the government often helps pay for special equipment required for various research activities.

Since 2000, the number of full-time researchers using funds provided by government grants has risen by 9 percent. Total federal outlays for research and development have in-

creased by more than 45 percent, from just over $69 billion to over $100 billion.

In the absence of government grants, a portion of this growth in research funding would have been provided by the private sector. This helps explain why the government's share of total national spending on research and development has risen from 25 percent in 2000 to almost 35 percent today.

For Critical Analysis
How might increased government spending on research and development that simply replaces private spending dollar for dollar affect aggregate demand?

The Supply-Side Effects of Changes in Taxes

We have talked about changing taxes and changing government spending, the traditional tools of fiscal policy. We have not really talked about the possibility of changing *marginal* tax rates. Recall from Chapter 5 that the marginal tax rate is the rate applied to the last bracket of taxable income. In our federal tax system, higher marginal tax rates are applied as income rises. In that sense, the United States has a progressive federal individual income tax system. Expansionary fiscal policy might involve reducing marginal tax rates. Advocates of such changes argue that lower tax rates will lead to an increase in productivity because individuals will work harder and longer, save more, and invest more and that increased productivity will lead to more economic growth, which will lead to higher real GDP. The government, by applying lower marginal tax rates, will not necessarily lose tax revenues, for the lower marginal tax rates will be applied to a growing tax base because of economic growth—after all, tax revenues are the product of a tax rate times a tax base.

This relationship, which you may recall from the discussion of sales taxes in Chapter 6, is sometimes called the *Laffer curve,* named after economist Arthur Laffer, who explained the relationship to some journalists and politicians in 1974. It is reproduced in Figure 13-6 on the following page. On the vertical axis are tax revenues, and on the horizontal axis is the marginal tax rate. As you can see, total tax revenues initially rise but then eventually fall as the tax rate continues to increase after reaching some unspecified tax-revenue-maximizing rate at the top of the curve.

People who support the notion that reducing taxes does not necessarily lead to reduced tax revenues are called supply-side economists. **Supply-side economics** involves changing the tax structure to create incentives to increase productivity. Due to a shift in the aggregate supply curve to the right, there can be greater real GDP without upward pressure on the price level.

Consider the supply-side effects of changes in marginal tax rates on labor. An increase in tax rates reduces the opportunity cost of leisure, thereby inducing individuals (at least

Supply-side economics
The suggestion that creating incentives for individuals and firms to increase productivity will cause the aggregate supply curve to shift outward.

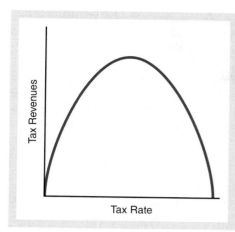

FIGURE 13-6
Laffer Curve
The Laffer curve indicates that tax revenues initially rise with a higher tax rate. Eventually, however, tax revenues decline as the tax rate increases.

on the margin) to reduce their work effort and to consume more leisure. But an increase in tax rates will also reduce spendable income, thereby shifting the demand curve for leisure inward to the left, which tends to increase work effort. The outcome of these two effects on the choice of leisure (and thus work) depends on which of them is stronger. Supply-side economists argue that at various times in years past, the first effect dominated: Increases in marginal tax rates caused workers to work less, and decreases in marginal tax rates caused workers to work more.

CONCEPTS in Brief

- Indirect crowding out occurs because of an interest rate effect in which the government's efforts to finance its deficit spending cause interest rates to rise, thereby crowding out private investment and spending, particularly on cars and houses. This is called the crowding-out effect.

- Direct expenditure offsets occur when government spending competes with the private sector and is increased. A direct crowding-out effect may occur.

- A number of economists believe in the Ricardian equivalence theorem, which holds that an increase in the government budget deficit has no effect on aggregate demand because individuals anticipate that their future taxes will increase and therefore save more today to pay for them.

- Changes in marginal tax rates may cause supply-side effects if a reduction in marginal tax rates induces enough additional work, saving, and investing. Government tax receipts can actually increase. This is called supply-side economics.

To test your understanding of the concepts covered in this section, go to the Online Review at www.myeconlab.com/miller.

DISCRETIONARY FISCAL POLICY IN PRACTICE: COPING WITH TIME LAGS

We can discuss fiscal policy in a relatively precise way. We draw graphs with aggregate demand and supply curves to show what we are doing. We could even in principle estimate the offsets that we just discussed. Even if we were able to measure all of these offsets exactly, however, would-be fiscal policymakers still face a problem: The conduct of fiscal policy involves a variety of time lags.

Recognition time lag
The time required to gather information about the current state of the economy.

Action time lag
The time between recognizing an economic problem and implementing policy to solve it. The action time lag is quite long for fiscal policy, which requires congressional approval.

Effect time lag
The time that elapses between the implementation of a policy and the results of that policy.

Economics Front and Center

To examine various factors that can complicate fiscal fine-tuning, consider the case study, **So Much Spending, So Little Accomplished,** on page 305.

Automatic, or built-in, stabilizers
Special provisions of certain federal programs that cause changes in desired aggregate expenditures without the action of Congress and the president. Examples are the federal progressive tax system and unemployment compensation.

Policymakers must be concerned with time lags. Quite apart from the fact that it is difficult to measure economic variables, it takes time to collect and assimilate such data. Thus policymakers must contend with the **recognition time lag,** the months that may elapse before national economic problems can be identified.[*]

After an economic problem is recognized, a solution must be formulated; thus there will be an **action time lag** between the recognition of a problem and the implementation of policy to solve it. For fiscal policy, the action time lag is particularly long. Such policy must be approved by Congress and is subject to political wrangling and infighting. The action time lag can easily last a year or two. Then it takes time to put the policy into effect. After Congress enacts fiscal policy legislation, it takes time to decide such matters as who gets new federal construction contracts.

Finally, there is the **effect time lag:** After fiscal policy is enacted, it takes time for the policy to affect the economy. To demonstrate the effects, economists need only shift curves on a chalkboard, but in real time, such effects take quite a while to work their way through the economy.

Because the various fiscal policy time lags are long, a policy designed to combat a recession might not produce results until the economy is already out of that recession and perhaps experiencing inflation, in which case the fiscal policy would worsen the situation. Or a fiscal policy designed to eliminate inflation might not produce effects until the economy is in a recession; in that case, too, fiscal policy would make the economic problem worse rather than better.

Furthermore, because fiscal policy time lags tend to be *variable* (by anywhere from one to three years), policymakers have a difficult time fine-tuning the economy. Clearly, fiscal policy is more an art than a science.

AUTOMATIC STABILIZERS

Not all changes in taxes (or in tax rates) or in government spending (including government transfers) constitute discretionary fiscal policy. There are several types of automatic (or nondiscretionary) fiscal policies. Such policies do not require new legislation on the part of Congress. Specific automatic fiscal policies—called **automatic,** or **built-in, stabilizers**—include the tax system itself and the government transfer system; the latter includes unemployment compensation and welfare spending.

The Tax System as an Automatic Stabilizer

You know that if you work less, you are paid less, and therefore you pay fewer taxes. The amount of taxes that our government collects falls automatically during a recession. Basically, incomes and profits fall when business activity slows down, and the government's take drops too. Some economists consider this an automatic tax cut, which therefore stimulates aggregate demand. It reduces the extent of any negative economic fluctuation.

The progressive nature of the federal personal and corporate income tax systems magnifies any automatic stabilization effect that might exist. If your hours of work are reduced because of a recession, you still pay some federal personal income taxes. But because of our progressive system, you may drop into a lower tax bracket, thereby paying a lower marginal tax rate. As a result, your disposable income falls by a smaller percentage than your before-tax income falls.

---

[*]For example, final annual data for GDP, after various revisions, are not available until three to six months after the year's end.

Why do you suppose that rising employee contributions to employer-provided health care plans have made it harder for the federal government to predict its tax collections?

Policy EXAMPLE

The U.S. Government Finds an Unexpected Leak in Its Stream of Tax Revenues

Most federal tax revenues come from income taxes. Therefore, to predict its tax collections accurately, the U.S. government has to accurately forecast real GDP. The government has never performed this task very well, however, so its tax revenue projections are notoriously inaccurate.

Another problem has emerged in the 2000s to bedevil the government's revenue forecasts and cause it to persistently overpredict its income tax collections. Under U.S. tax laws, workers pay taxes on the income they receive via paychecks or direct deposits to their bank accounts. Workers do not, however, owe income taxes on any portion of their incomes that is withheld to pay their contributions to employer-provided health plans. Before 2002, workers' incomes and health-benefit contributions typically increased at nearly the same pace from year to year. During 2003 and 2004, this pattern changed.

Many workers agreed to accept lower wage and salary increases in exchange for enhanced health benefits. Nontaxable worker contributions to health care plans rose by almost 7 percent per year, but taxable incomes rose by less than 3 percent per year. The result was a smaller increase in total taxable earnings than the government had anticipated. This caused the government to overestimate, month after month, the amount of income tax revenues that would be available for it to spend.

For Critical Analysis

How would aggregate demand respond if Congress enacted a law removing the tax exemption from workers' contributions to health care plans? (Hint: What would happen to total taxes on overall incomes if such a change were made?)

Unemployment Compensation and Welfare Payments

Like our tax system, unemployment compensation payments stabilize aggregate demand. Throughout the business cycle, unemployment compensation reduces *changes* in people's disposable income. When business activity drops, most laid-off workers automatically become eligible for unemployment compensation from their state governments. Their disposable income therefore remains positive, although at a lower level than when they were employed. During boom periods, there is less unemployment, and consequently fewer unemployment payments are made to the labor force. Less purchasing power is being added to the economy because fewer unemployment checks are paid out. Historically, the relationship between the unemployment rate and unemployment compensation payments has been strongly positive.

Welfare payments act similarly as an automatic stabilizer. When a recession occurs, more people become eligible for welfare payments. Therefore, those people do not experience so dramatic a drop in disposable income as they would have otherwise.

Stabilizing Impact

The key stabilizing impact of our tax system, unemployment compensation, and welfare payments is their ability to mitigate changes in disposable income, consumption, and the equilibrium level of real GDP. If disposable income is prevented from falling as much as it otherwise would during a recession, the downturn will be moderated. In contrast, if disposable income is prevented from rising as rapidly as it otherwise would during a boom, the boom is less likely to get out of hand. The progressive income tax and unemployment

FIGURE 13-7
Automatic Stabilizers
Here we assume that as real GDP rises, tax revenues rise and government transfers fall, other things remaining constant. Thus, as the economy expands from Y_f to Y_1, a budget surplus automatically arises; as the economy contracts from Y_f to Y_2, a budget deficit automatically arises. Such automatic changes tend to drive the economy back toward its full-employment real GDP.

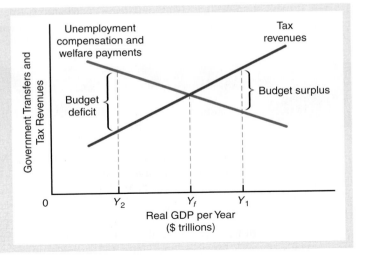

compensation thus provide automatic stabilization to the economy. We present the argument graphically in Figure 13-7.

WHAT DO WE REALLY KNOW ABOUT FISCAL POLICY?

There are two ways of looking at fiscal policy. One prevails during normal times and the other during abnormal times.

Fiscal Policy During Normal Times

Go to www.econtoday.com/chap13 to learn about the current outlook for the budget of the U.S. government.

During normal times (without "excessive" unemployment, inflation, or problems in the national economy), we know that due to the recognition time lag and the modest size of any fiscal policy action that Congress will actually take, discretionary fiscal policy is probably not very effective. Congress ends up doing too little too late to help in a minor recession. Moreover, fiscal policy that generates repeated tax changes (as has happened) creates uncertainty, which may do more harm than good. To the extent that fiscal policy has any effect during normal times, it probably achieves this by way of automatic stabilizers rather than by way of discretionary policy.

Fiscal Policy During Abnormal Times

During abnormal times, fiscal policy may be effective. Consider some classic examples: the Great Depression and war periods.

The Great Depression. When there is a catastrophic drop in real GDP, as there was during the Great Depression, fiscal policy may be able to stimulate aggregate demand. Because so many people are income-constrained during such periods, government spending is a way to get income into their hands—income that they are likely to spend immediately.

Wartime. Wars are in fact reserved for governments. War expenditures are not good substitutes for private expenditures—they have little or no direct expenditure offsets. Consequently, war spending as part of expansionary fiscal policy usually has noteworthy effects, such as occurred while we were waging World War II, when real GDP increased dramatically.

The "Soothing" Effect of Keynesian Fiscal Policy

One view of traditional Keynesian fiscal policy does not relate to its being used on a regular basis. As you have learned in this chapter, many problems are associated with attempting to use fiscal policy. But if we should encounter a severe downturn, fiscal policy is available. Knowing this may reassure consumers and investors. After all, the ability of the federal government to prevent another Great Depression—given what we know about how to use fiscal policy today—may take some of the large risk out of consumers' and investors' calculations. This may induce more buoyant and stable expectations of the future, thereby smoothing investment spending.

CONCEPTS in Brief

- Time lags of various sorts reduce the effectiveness of fiscal policy. These include the recognition time lag, the action time lag, and the effect time lag.

- Two automatic, or built-in, stabilizers are the progressive income tax and unemployment compensation.

- Built-in stabilizers automatically tend to moderate changes in disposable income resulting from changes in overall business activity.

- Although discretionary fiscal policy may not necessarily be a useful policy tool in normal times because of time lags, it may work well during abnormal times, such as depressions and wartimes. In addition, the existence of fiscal policy may have a soothing effect on consumers and investors.

To test your understanding of the concepts covered in this section, go to the Online Review at www.myeconlab.com/miller.

CASE STUDY: Economics Front and Center

So Much Spending, So Little Accomplished

Lassiter was elected to the U.S. Senate three years ago. His first legislative triumph occurred during his initial six months in office. He was instrumental in the passage of a law establishing numerous federal government research centers throughout the country, including in several cities in his home state. The federal government spent tens of billions of dollars constructing the centers. It is now spending billions more operating the centers, which employ thousands of people.

Senator Lassiter is examining a report prepared by members of his staff on the overall economic impact of the research centers during their first full year of operation. The report indicates that so far, the net effect on employment has been slight. Indeed, the centers in Lassiter's home state have mainly absorbed researchers who lost existing jobs with private research companies. Most of these firms closed after the new government research centers landed contracts that previously had gone to the private

firms. The report does find, however, that construction of the research centers generated a short-term boost in aggregate demand. It concludes that various time lags in the effects of government spending on aggregate demand make the timing of the effects of the research centers uncertain. Senator Lassiter closes the report and begins drafting a new bill aimed at authorizing a major expansion of the original network of research centers.

Points to Analyze

1. *What immediate factors have reduced the aggregate demand effects of the government expenditures championed by Senator Lassiter?*

2. *What types of time lags could have delayed real GDP and employment effects that these expenditures may yet generate?*

France and Germany Discover That Tax Cuts Can Pay Off

Concepts Applied
- Fiscal Policy
- Supply-Side Economics

Prior to the 1999 formation of the European Monetary Union (EMU), participating nations agreed to abide by a "Growth and Stability Pact." Among other things, this agreement established formal limits on the extent to which governments of member nations could permit mismatches between their expenditures and tax revenues. Within a short time, however, France and Germany discovered that abiding by the agreement actually seemed to be delivering low growth and instability. By 2001, rates of GDP growth in both nations had slipped to the negative range, and unemployment rates were rising rapidly, to more than 10 percent of each nation's labor force.

Tax Cuts to the Rescue

With the European Central Bank determining monetary policy for the whole EMU, the governments of both France and Germany decided it was time to look after their national interests via fiscal policy. Rates of French and German government spending were already very high, so the governments chose to cut taxes.

Neither government used the term *supply-side economics* to describe its tax-cutting policies. Nevertheless, both reduced taxes in an effort to induce a rise in aggregate demand. They also cut marginal tax rates to boost productivity and generate a rise in aggregate supply. Within months after various tax cuts had been enacted, French and German real GDP growth rates increased, and rates of unemployment began to decline for a time.

A Rule Made to Be Broken?

The immediate effects of the French and German tax cuts were declines in government tax revenues. Because neither government reduced its rate of spending, the result was predictable: government spending rose well above tax collections.

During this period, governments of all other EMU nations abided by the Growth and Stability Pact's fiscal policy limitations. Some EMU nations called for the two countries to pay fines specified for violations of the pact's fiscal limits. For France, this would have amounted to about 0.5 percent of French GDP. Ultimately, however, the two countries' governments only had to promise to try to realign their spending and taxes. The fiscal rules of the Growth and Stability Pact turned out at best to be rough guidelines instead of enforceable limitations on EMU fiscal policies.

For Critical Analysis

1. Other things being equal, what were the likely effects of the French and German fiscal policies on the EMU price level? (Hint: The effects of French and German government spending and taxation on total planned expenditures for the EMU as a whole are very much like the effects of California and New York state government spending on total planned expenditures in the United States.)
2. According to supply-side economics, what would have been the long-term effects on French and German real GDP and on the EMU price level if the governments had enacted temporary tax rebates but had left marginal tax rates unchanged?

1. For more information about the legalities of the Growth and Stability Pact, go to www.econtoday.com/chap13.

2. To learn more about the economic intent of the Growth and Stability Pact, follow the link to the European Commission's discussion at www.econtoday.com/chap13.

Why might the EMU nations have decided that raising taxes in equal measure with increases in government spending would help promote stability of EMU-wide real GDP and of the EMU price level? Could the French and German governments make any arguments that their fiscal policies may have helped promote economic growth, even if they were not necessarily consistent with the stability aims of the Growth and Stability Pact?

SUMMARY DISCUSSION of Learning Objectives

1. **The Effects of Discretionary Fiscal Policies Using Traditional Keynesian Analysis:** In the Keynesian short-run framework of analysis, a deliberate increase in government spending or a reduction in taxes can raise aggregate demand. Thus these fiscal policy actions can shift the aggregate demand curve outward along the short-run aggregate supply curve and thereby close a recessionary gap in which current real GDP is less than the long-run level of real GDP. Likewise, an intentional reduction in government spending or a tax increase will reduce aggregate demand. These fiscal policy actions shift the aggregate demand curve inward along the short-run aggregate supply curve and close an inflationary gap in which current real GDP exceeds the long-run level of real GDP.

2. **How Indirect Crowding Out and Direct Expenditure Offsets Can Reduce the Effectiveness of Fiscal Policy Actions:** Indirect crowding out occurs when the government engages in expansionary fiscal policy by increasing government spending or reducing taxes. When government spending exceeds tax revenues, the government must borrow by issuing bonds that compete with private bonds and thereby drive up market interest rates. This reduces, or crowds out, interest-sensitive private spending, thereby reducing the net effect of the fiscal expansion on aggregate demand. As a result, the aggregate demand curve shifts by a smaller amount than it would have in the absence of the crowding-out effect, and fiscal policy has a somewhat lessened net effect on equilibrium real GDP. Increased government spending may also substitute directly for private expenditures, and the resulting decline in private spending directly offsets the increase in total planned expenditures that the government had intended to bring about. This also mutes the net change in aggregate demand brought about by a fiscal policy action.

3. **The Ricardian Equivalence Theorem:** According to this proposition, when the government cuts taxes and borrows to finance the tax reduction, people realize that eventually the government will have to repay the loan. Thus they anticipate that taxes will have to increase in the future. This induces them to save the proceeds of the tax cut to meet their future tax liabilities. Consequently, a tax cut fails to induce an increase in aggregate consumption spending. On net, therefore, if the Ricardian equivalence theorem is valid, a tax cut has no effect on total planned expenditures and aggregate demand.

4. **Fiscal Policy Time Lags and the Effectiveness of Fiscal "Fine-Tuning":** Efforts to engage in fiscal policy actions intended to bring about carefully planned changes in aggregate demand are often complicated by policy time lags. One of these is the recognition time lag, which is the time required to collect information about the economy's current situation. Another is the action time lag, the period between recognition of a problem and implementation of a policy intended to address it. Finally, there is the effect time lag, which is the interval between policy implementation and its having an effect on the economy. For fiscal policy, all of these lags can be lengthy and variable, often lasting one to three years. Hence fiscal "fine-tuning" may be a misnomer.

5. **Automatic Stabilizers:** In our tax system, income taxes diminish automatically when economic activity drops, and unemployment compensation and welfare payments increase. Thus, when there is a decline in real GDP, the automatic reduction in income tax collections and increases in unemployment compensation and welfare payments tend to mute the reduction in total planned expenditures that would otherwise have resulted. The existence of these government programs thereby tends to stabilize the economy automatically in the face of variations in autonomous expenditures that induce fluctuations in economic activity.

KEY TERMS AND CONCEPTS

action time lag (302)

automatic, or built-in, stabilizers (302)

crowding-out effect (297)

direct expenditure offsets (299)

effect time lag (302)

fiscal policy (293)

recognition time lag (302)

Ricardian equivalence theorem (299)

supply-side economics (300)

PROBLEMS

Answers to the odd-numbered problems appear at the back of the book.

13-1. Suppose that Congress and the president decide that economic performance is weakening and that the government should "do something" about the situation. They make no tax changes but do enact new laws increasing government spending on a variety of programs.

  a. Prior to the congressional and presidential action, careful studies by government economists indicated that the direct multiplier effect of a rise in government expenditures on equilibrium real GDP is equal to 6. In the 12 months since the increase in government spending, however, it has become clear that the actual ultimate multiplier effect on real GDP will be unlikely to exceed half of that amount. What factors might account for this?

  b. Another year and a half elapses following passage of the government-spending boost. The government has undertaken no additional policy actions, nor have there been any other events of significance. Nevertheless, by the end of the second year, real GDP has returned to its original level, and the price level has increased sharply. Provide a possible explanation for this outcome.

13-2. Suppose that Congress enacts a significant tax cut with the expectation that this action will stimulate aggregate demand and push up real GDP in the short run. In fact, however, neither real GDP nor the price level changes significantly following the tax cut. What might account for this outcome?

13-3. Explain how time lags in discretionary fiscal policymaking could thwart the efforts of Congress and the president to stabilize real GDP in the face of an economic downturn. Is it possible that these time lags could actually cause discretionary fiscal policy to *destabilize* real GDP?

13-4. Determine whether each of the following is an example of a direct expenditure offset to fiscal policy.

  a. In an effort to help rejuvenate the nation's railroad system, a new government agency buys unused track, locomotives, and passenger and freight cars, many of which private companies would otherwise have purchased and put into regular use.

  b. The government increases its expenditures without raising taxes; to cover the resulting budget deficit, it issues more bonds, thereby pushing up the market interest rate and discouraging private planned investment spending.

  c. The government finances the construction of a classical music museum that otherwise would never have received private funding.

13-5. Determine whether each of the following is an example of indirect crowding out resulting from an expansionary fiscal policy action.

  a. The government provides a subsidy to help keep an existing firm operating, even though a group of investors would otherwise have provided a cash infusion that would have kept the company in business.

  b. The government reduces its taxes without decreasing its expenditures; to cover the resulting budget deficit, it issues more bonds, thereby pushing up the market interest rate and discouraging private planned investment spending.

  c. Government expenditures fund construction of a high-rise office building on a plot of land where a private company would otherwise have constructed an essentially identical building.

13-6. Under what circumstance might a tax reduction cause a long-run increase in real GDP and a long-run reduction in the price level?

13-7. Determine whether each of the following is an example of a discretionary fiscal policy action.

  a. A recession occurs, and government-funded unemployment compensation is paid out to laid-off workers.

  b. Congress votes to fund a new jobs program designed to put unemployed workers to work.

  c. The Federal Reserve decides to reduce the quantity of money in circulation in an effort to slow inflation.

  d. Under powers authorized by an act of Congress, the president decides to authorize an emergency release of funds for spending programs intended to head off economic crises.

13-8. Determine whether each of the following is an example of an automatic fiscal stabilizer.

  a. A government agency arranges to make loans to businesses automatically whenever an economic downturn begins.

  b. As the economy heats up, the resulting increase in equilibrium real GDP immediately results in higher income tax payments, which dampen consumption spending somewhat.

  c. As the economy starts to recover from a recession and more people go back to work, government-funded unemployment compensation payments begin to decline.

  d. To stem an overheated economy, the president, using special powers granted by Congress, authorizes emergency impoundment of funds that Congress had previously authorized for spending on government programs.

13-9. Suppose that there is an inflationary gap. Discuss one discretionary fiscal policy action that might eliminate this gap.

13-10. Suppose that there is a recessionary gap. Discuss one discretionary fiscal policy action that might eliminate this gap.

13-11. Currently, a government's budget is balanced. The marginal propensity to consume is 0.80. The government has determined that each additional $10 billion in new government debt it issues to finance a budget deficit pushes up the market interest rate by 0.1 percentage point. It has also determined that every 0.1 percentage point change in the market interest rate generates a change in planned investment expenditures equal to $2 billion. Finally, the government knows that to close a recessionary gap and take into account the resulting change in the price level, it must generate a net rightward shift in the aggregate demand curve equal to $200 billion. Assuming that there are no direct expenditure offsets to fiscal policy, how much should the government increase its expenditures?

13-12. A government is currently operating with an annual budget deficit of $40 billion. The government has determined that every $10 billion reduction in the amount of bonds it issues each year would reduce the market interest rate by 0.1 percentage point. Furthermore, it has determined that every 0.1 percentage point change in the market interest rate generates a change in planned investment expenditures in the opposite direction equal to $5 billion. The marginal propensity to consume is 0.75. Finally, the government knows that to eliminate an inflationary gap and take into account the resulting change in the price level, it must generate a net leftward shift in the aggregate demand curve equal to $40 billion. Assuming that there are no direct expenditure offsets to fiscal policy, how much should the government increase taxes?

13-13. If the Ricardian equivalence theorem is not relevant, then an income-tax-rate cut should affect short-run equilibrium real GDP. Explain why.

13-14. Suppose that Congress enacts a lump-sum tax cut of $750 billion. The marginal propensity to consume is equal to 0.75. If Ricardian equivalence holds true, what is the effect on equilibrium real GDP? On saving?

ECONOMICS ON THE NET

Federal Government Spending and Taxation A quick way to keep up with the federal government's spending and taxation is by examining federal budget data at the White House Internet address.

Title: Historical Tables: Budget of the United States Government

Navigation: Use the link at www.econtoday.com/chap13 to visit the Office of Management and Budget. Select the most recent budget. Then click on *Historical Tables*.

Application After the document downloads, perform the indicated operations and answer the questions.

1. Go to section 2, "Composition of Federal Government Receipts." Take a look at Table 2.2, "Percentage Composition of Receipts by Source." Before World War II, what was the key source of revenues of the federal government? What has been the key revenue source since World War II?

2. Now scan down the document to Table 2.3, "Receipts by Source as Percentages of GDP." Have any government revenue sources declined as a percentage of GDP? Which ones have noticeably risen in recent years?

For Group Study and Analysis Split into four groups, and have each group examine section 3, "Federal Government Outlays by Function," and in particular Table 3.1, "Outlays by Superfunction and Function." Assign groups to the following functions: national defense, health, income security, and Social Security. Have each group prepare a brief report concerning long-term and recent trends in government spending on each function. Which functions are capturing growing shares of government spending in recent years? Which are receiving declining shares of total spending?

Media Resources

If your exam were tomorrow, would you be ready? For each chapter, MyEconLab Practice Tests and Study Plans pinpoint which sections you have mastered and which ones you need to study. That way, you are more efficient with your study time, and you are better prepared for your exams.

In addition to Practice Tests and your personalized Study Plan, you'll find the following media resources in MyEconLab:

1. *Graphs in Motion* animation of Figures 13-1, 13-3, 13-4, 13-5, 13-6, 13-7, and C-2.
2. Videos featuring the author, Roger LeRoy Miller, on the following subjects:
   ● The Crowding-Out Effect
   ● Time Lags

3. Links to the Web sites cited in the marginal Internet Resources, Issues and Applications feature, and Economics on the Net activity.
4. Audio clips of all key terms, additional practice problems, and a PDF version of the material from the print Study Guide.
5. eThemes of the Times, which is a New York Times article to help you understand the real-world applications of what you are learning.

Get Ahead of the Curve

To see how it works, turn to page 16 and then go to www.myeconlab.com/miller.

Fiscal Policy: A Keynesian Perspective

The traditional Keynesian approach to fiscal policy differs in three ways from that presented in Chapter 13. First, it emphasizes the underpinnings of the components of aggregate demand. Second, it assumes that government expenditures are not substitutes for private expenditures and that current taxes are the only taxes taken into account by consumers and firms. Third, the traditional Keynesian approach focuses on the short run and so assumes that as a first approximation, the price level is constant.

CHANGES IN GOVERNMENT SPENDING

Figure C-1 measures real GDP along the horizontal axis and total planned real expenditures (aggregate demand) along the vertical axis. The components of aggregate demand are real consumption (C), investment (I), government spending (G), and net exports (X). The height of the schedule labeled $C + I + G + X$ shows total planned real expenditures (aggregate demand) as a function of real GDP. This schedule slopes upward because consumption depends positively on real GDP. Everywhere along the 45-degree reference line, planned real spending equals real GDP. At the point Y^*, where the $C + I + G + X$ line intersects the 45-degree line, planned real spending is consistent with real GDP per year. At any income less than Y^*, spending exceeds real GDP, and so real GDP and thus real spending will tend to rise. At any level of real GDP greater than Y^*, planned spending is less than real GDP, and so real GDP and thus spending will tend to decline. Given the determinants of C, I, G, and X, total real spending (aggregate demand) will be Y^*.

The Keynesian approach assumes that changes in government spending cause no direct offsets in either consumption or investment spending because G is not a substitute for C, I, or X. Hence a rise in government spending from G to G' causes the $C + I + G + X$ line

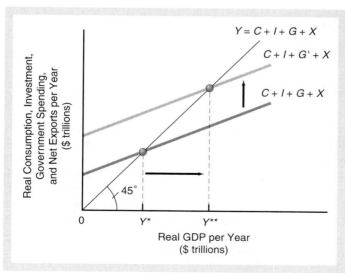

FIGURE C-1

The Impact of Higher Government Spending on Aggregate Demand

Government spending increases, causing $C + I + G + X$ to move to $C + I + G' + X$. Equilibrium real GDP per year increases to Y^{**}.

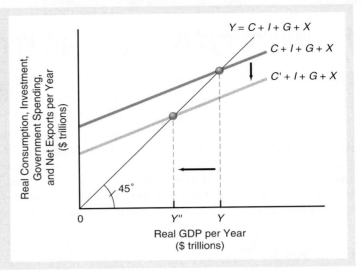

FIGURE C-2
The Impact of Higher Taxes on Aggregate Demand
Higher taxes cause consumption to fall to C'. Equilibrium real GDP per year decreases to Y''.

to shift upward by the full amount of the rise in government spending, yielding the line $C + I + G' + X$. The rise in real government spending causes real GDP to rise, which in turn causes consumption spending to rise, which further increases real GDP. Ultimately, aggregate demand rises to Y^{**}, where spending again equals real GDP. A key conclusion of the Keynesian analysis is that total spending rises by *more* than the original rise in government spending because consumption spending depends positively on real GDP.

CHANGES IN TAXES

According to the Keynesian approach, changes in current taxes affect aggregate demand by changing the amount of real disposable (after-tax) income available to consumers. A rise in taxes reduces disposable income and thus reduces real consumption; conversely, a tax cut raises disposable income and thus causes a rise in consumption spending. The effects of a tax increase are shown in Figure C-2. Higher taxes cause consumption spending to decline from C to C', causing total spending to shift downward to $C' + I + G + X$. In general, the decline in consumption will be less than the increase in taxes because people will also reduce their saving to help pay the higher taxes.

THE BALANCED-BUDGET MULTIPLIER

One interesting implication of the Keynesian approach concerns the impact of a balanced-budget change in government real spending. Suppose that the government increases spending by $1 billion and pays for it by raising current taxes by $1 billion. Such a policy is called a *balanced-budget increase in real spending.* Because the higher spending tends to push aggregate demand *up* by *more* than $1 billion while the higher taxes tend to push aggregate demand *down* by *less* than $1 billion, a most remarkable thing happens: A balanced-budget increase in G causes total spending to rise by *exactly* the amount of the rise in G—in this case, $1 billion. We say that the *balanced-budget multiplier* is equal to 1. Similarly, a balanced-budget reduction in government spending will cause total spending to fall by exactly the amount of the government spending cut.

THE FIXED PRICE LEVEL ASSUMPTION

The final key feature of the Keynesian approach is that it typically assumes that as a first approximation, the price level is fixed. Recall that nominal GDP equals the price level multiplied by real GDP. If the price level is fixed, an increase in government spending that causes nominal GDP to rise will show up exclusively as a rise in *real* GDP. This will in turn be accompanied by a decline in the unemployment rate because the additional real GDP can be produced only if additional factors of production, such as labor, are utilized.

PROBLEMS

Answers to the odd-numbered problems appear at the back of the book.

C-1. Assume that equilibrium real GDP is $12.2 trillion and full-employment equilibrium (*FE*) is $12.55 trillion. The marginal propensity to save is $\frac{1}{7}$. Answer the questions using the data in the following graph.

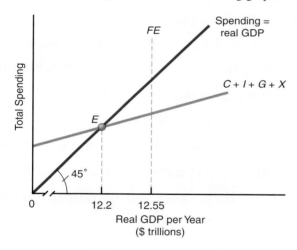

a. What is the marginal propensity to consume?
b. By how much must new investment or government spending increase to bring the economy up to full employment?

c. By how much must government cut personal taxes to stimulate the economy to the full-employment equilibrium?

C-2. Assume that MPC $= \frac{4}{5}$ when answering the following questions.

a. If government expenditures rise by $2 billion, by how much will the aggregate expenditure curve shift upward? By how much will equilibrium real GDP per year change?
b. If taxes increase by $2 billion, by how much will the aggregate expenditure curve shift downward? By how much will equilibrium real GDP per year change?

C-3. Assume that MPC $= \frac{4}{5}$ when answering the following questions.

a. If government expenditures rise by $1 billion, by how much will the aggregate expenditure curve shift upward?
b. If taxes rise by $1 billion, by how much will the aggregate expenditure curve shift downward?
c. If both taxes and government expenditures rise by $1 billion, by how much will the aggregate expenditure curve shift? What will happen to the equilibrium level of real GDP?
d. How does your response to the second question in part (c) change if MPC $= \frac{3}{4}$? If MPC $= \frac{1}{2}$?

2005 Defense Budget

Chapter 14

Deficit Spending and the Public Debt

From the 1980s until the mid-1990s, the U.S. government spent more funds than it collected. So did the governments of many other nations, including Canada, France, Germany, and the United Kingdom. Then, during the late 1990s, the gap between government spending and receipts narrowed in these nations. By 2000, the U.S., Canadian, German, and U.K. governments were collecting more funds than they were spending; among these countries, only in France did spending still exceed receipts. Since the early 2000s, however, government spending in all these countries except Canada has once again outpaced tax collections. To understand why many nations' government budgets often move together, you must learn more about the difference between government spending and receipts, called the government's budget *deficit*.

Media Resources

Refer to the end of the chapter for a full listing of the multimedia learning materials available in MyEconLab.

LEARNING OBJECTIVES

After reading this chapter, you should be able to:

1. Explain how federal government budget deficits occur
2. Define the public debt and understand alternative measures of the public debt
3. Evaluate circumstances under which the public debt could be a burden to future generations
4. Discuss why the federal budget deficit might be measured incorrectly
5. Analyze the macroeconomic effects of government budget deficits
6. Describe possible ways to reduce the government budget deficit

...in 2000, the U.S. government projected that it would spend less on goods and services than it would collect in taxes—that is, that it would operate with a *budget surplus*—every year until at least 2015? In fact, these projections turned out to be wide of the mark. Since 2001, the U.S. government has actually spent more than it has collected in taxes every year, and it *now* projects annual *budget deficits*—government expenditures in excess of tax revenues—until at least 2012.

Should you be worried that the federal government anticipates spending more than it receives during the coming decade? The answer, as you will see in this chapter, is both yes and no. First, let's examine what the government actually does when it spends more than it receives.

PUBLIC DEFICITS AND DEBTS: FLOWS VERSUS STOCKS

A **government budget deficit** exists if the government spends more than it receives in taxes during a given period of time. The government has to finance this shortfall somehow. Barring any resort to money creation (the subject matter of Chapters 15, 16, and 17), the U.S. Treasury sells IOUs on behalf of the U.S. government, in the form of securities that are normally called bonds. In effect, the federal government asks U.S. and foreign households, businesses, and governments to lend funds to the government to cover its deficit. For example, if the federal government spends $100 billion more than it receives in revenues, the Treasury will raise that $100 billion by selling $100 billion of new Treasury bonds. Those who buy the Treasury bonds (lend funds to the U.S. government) will receive interest payments over the life of the bond. In return, the U.S. Treasury receives immediate purchasing power. In the process, it also adds to its indebtedness to bondholders.

Government budget deficit
An excess of government spending over government revenues during a given period of time.

Distinguishing Between Deficits and Debts

You have already learned about flows. Gross domestic product (GDP), for instance, is a flow because it is a dollar measure of the total amount of final goods and services produced within a given period of time, such as a year.

The federal deficit is also a flow. Suppose that the current federal deficit is $400 billion. This means that the federal government is currently spending at a rate of $400 billion *per year* more than it is collecting in taxes and other revenues.

Of course, governments do not always spend more each year than the revenues they receive. If a government spends an amount exactly equal to the revenues it collects during a given period, then during this interval the government operates with a **balanced budget.** If a government spends less than the revenues it receives during a given period, then during this interval it experiences a **government budget surplus.**

Balanced budget
A situation in which the government's spending is exactly equal to the total taxes and other revenues it collects during a given period of time.

Government budget surplus
An excess of government revenues over government spending during a given period of time.

The Public Debt

You have also learned about stocks, which are measured at a point in time. Stocks change between points in time as a result of flows. The amount of unemployment, for example, is a stock. It is the total number of people who wish to find work but are unable to do so at a given point in time. Suppose that the stock of unemployed workers at the beginning of the month is 7.9 million and that at the end of the month the stock of unemployed workers has increased to 8.1 million. This means during the month, assuming an unchanged labor force there was a net flow of 0.2 million individuals away from the state of being employed to the state of being out of work but seeking employment.

Public debt
The total value of all outstanding federal government securities.

Go to www.econtoday.com/chap14 to learn more about the activities of the Congressional Budget Office, which reports to the legislative branch of the U.S. government about the current state of the federal government's spending and receipts.

Likewise, the total accumulated **public debt** is a stock measured at a given point in time, and it changes from one time to another as a result of government budget deficits or surpluses. For instance, on December 31, 2003, one measure of the public debt was $3.9 trillion. During 2004, the federal government operated at a deficit of nearly $0.45 trillion. As a consequence, on December 31, 2004, this measure of the public debt had increased to about $4.4 trillion.

GOVERNMENT FINANCE: SPENDING MORE THAN TAX COLLECTIONS

Following four consecutive years—1998 through 2001—of official budget surpluses, the federal government began to experience budget deficits once more beginning in 2002. Since then, government spending has increased considerably, and tax revenues have failed to keep pace. Consequently, the federal government has operated with a deficit each year since 2002, and most observers anticipate a steady flow of government red ink for the foreseeable future.

The Historical Record of Federal Budget Deficits

Figure 14-1 charts inflation-adjusted expenditures and revenues of the federal government since 1940. The *real* annual budget deficit is the arithmetic difference between real expenditures and real revenues during years in which the government's spending has exceeded its revenues. As you can see, there is nothing out of the ordinary about federal budget deficits. Indeed, the annual budget surpluses of the late 1990s and early 2000s were somewhat out of the ordinary. The 1998 budget surplus was the first since 1968 when the government briefly operated with a surplus. Before the 1998–2001 budget surpluses, the U.S. government had not experienced back-to-back annual surpluses since the 1950s.

FIGURE 14-1
Federal Budget Deficits and Surpluses Since 1940
Federal budget deficits (expenditures in excess of receipts, in red) have been much more common than federal budget surpluses (receipts in excess of expenditures, in green).

Source: Office of Management and Budget.

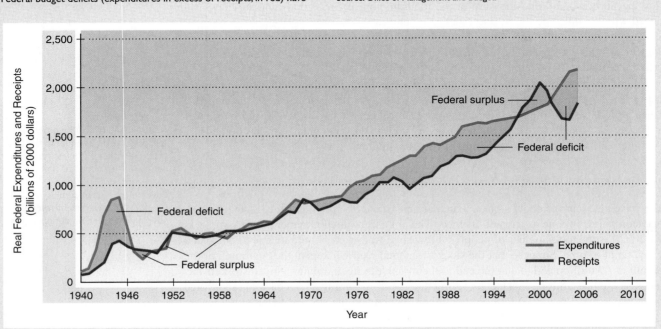

Indeed, since 1940 the U.S. government has operated with an annual budget surplus for a total of only 13 years. In all other years, it has collected insufficient taxes and other revenues to fund its spending. Every year this has occurred, the federal government has borrowed to finance its additional expenditures.

Even though Figure 14-1 accounts for inflation, it does not give a clear picture of the size of the federal government's deficits or surpluses in relation to overall economic activity in the United States. Figure 14-2 provides a clearer view of the size of government deficits or surpluses relative to the size of the U.S. economy by expressing them as percentages of GDP. As you can see, the federal budget deficit reached a peak of nearly 6 percent of GDP in the early 1980s. It then fell back, increased once again during the late 1980s and early 1990s, and then declined steadily into the budget surplus years of 1998–2001. Since 2001, the government budget deficit has risen to about 4 percent of GDP.

The Resurgence of Federal Government Deficits

Why has the government's budget slipped from a surplus equal to nearly 2.5 percent of GDP into a deficit of at least 4 percent of GDP? The simple answer is that since 2001 the government has spent more than it has collected in revenues. As noted in Chapter 13, government spending increased at a faster pace between 2002 and 2004 than in any other period of the same length since the end of World War II.

The more complex answer also considers government revenues. In 2001, Congress and the executive branch slightly reduced income tax rates and also cut federal capital gains taxes and estate taxes. Because tax rates were reduced toward the end of a recession when real income growth was relatively low, government tax revenues were stagnant for a time. When economic activity began to expand sharply in 2003, tax revenues started rising at a

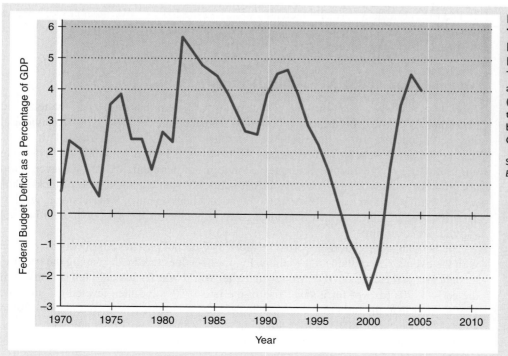

FIGURE 14-2
The Federal Budget Deficit Expressed as a Percentage of GDP
The federal budget deficit has generally been rising as a share of GDP. (Note that the negative values for the 1998–2001 period designate budget surpluses as a percentage of GDP during those years.)

Sources: *Economic Report of the President; Economic Indicators*, various issues.

pace closer to the rapid rate of growth of government spending. Nevertheless, annual federal expenditures are continuing to exceed annual tax collections. As long as this situation persists, the U.S. government will operate with a budget deficit, just as it did so often during the previous six decades.

CONCEPTS in Brief

- Whenever the federal government spends more than it receives during a given year, it operates with a budget deficit. If federal government spending exactly equals government revenues, then the government experiences a balanced budget. If the federal government collects more revenues than it spends, then it operates with a budget surplus.

- The federal budget deficit is a flow, whereas accumulated budget deficits represent a stock, called the public debt.

- The federal budget deficit expressed as a percentage of GDP hit its most recent peak of around 6 percent in the early 1980s. Between 1998 and 2001, the federal government experienced a budget surplus, but since then its budget has once more been in deficit. Currently, the deficit amounts to about 4 percent of GDP.

To test your understanding of the concepts covered in this section, go to the Online Review at **www.myeconlab.com/miller.**

EVALUATING THE RISING PUBLIC DEBT

Gross public debt
All federal government debt irrespective of who owns it.

Net public debt
Gross public debt minus all government interagency borrowing.

All federal public debt, taken together, is called the **gross public debt.** We arrive at the **net public debt** when we subtract from the gross public debt the portion that is held by government agencies (in essence, what the federal government owes to itself). For instance, if the Social Security Administration holds U.S. Treasury bonds, the U.S. Treasury makes debt payments to another agency of the government. On net, therefore, the U.S. government owes these payments to itself.

The net public debt normally increases whenever the federal government experiences a budget deficit. That is, the net public debt increases when government outlays are greater than total government receipts.

Accumulation of the Net Public Debt

Table 14-1 displays for various years since 1940 the federal budget deficit, the total and per capita net public debt (the amount owed on the net public debt by a typical individual), and the net interest cost of the public debt in total and as a percentage of GDP. It shows that the net public debt grew continuously for many years before declining slightly during the 1998–2001 budget surpluses. Expressed in terms of per capita figures, however, it did not grow particularly rapidly. Nor did the net public debt per capita drop very quickly during the late 1990s and early 2000s when the government operated with a budget surplus. Thus the amount that a typical individual owes to holders of the net public debt has not varied much over time.

The net public debt levels reported in Table 14-1 do not provide a basis of comparison with the overall size of the U.S. economy. Figure 14-3 does this by displaying the net public debt as a percentage of GDP. We see that after World War II, this ratio fell steadily until the early 1970s (except for a small rise in the late 1950s) and then leveled off until the 1980s. After that, the ratio of the net public debt to GDP more or less continued to rise to around 50 percent of GDP, before dropping slightly in the late 1990s and early 2000s. With the reappearance of budget deficits since 2001, the ratio has begun to rise once again.

(1) Year	(2) Federal Budget Deficit (billions of current dollars)	(3) Net Public Debt (billions of current dollars)	(4) Per Capita Net Public Debt (current dollars)	(5) Net Interest Costs (billions of current dollars)	(6) Net Interest as a Percentage of GDP
1940	3.9	42.7	323.2	.9	.90
1945	53.9	235.2	1,681.2	3.1	1.45
1950	3.1	219.0	1,438.0	4.8	1.68
1955	3.0	226.6	1,365.9	4.9	1.23
1960	.3	237.2	1,312.7	6.9	1.37
1965	1.6	261.6	1,346.4	8.6	1.26
1970	2.8	284.9	1,389.1	14.4	1.47
1975	45.1	396.9	1,837.5	23.3	1.52
1980	73.8	709.3	3,140.5	52.5	1.92
1985	212.3	1,499.4	6,322.9	129.4	3.22
1990	221.4	2,410.4	9,641.6	175.6	3.23
1995	164.0	3,604.4	13,519.9	232.1	3.24
2000	−236.4	3,409.8	12,074.4	223.0	2.34
2001	−127.4	3,319.6	11,627.3	201.5	2.08
2002	157.8	3,540.4	12,267.5	164.1	1.57
2003	375.3	3,913.6	13,448.8	144.6	1.34
2004	438.8	4,320.6	15,002.4	145.7	1.33
2005	371.1	4,659.8	16,209.0	163.9	1.46

Sources: U.S. Department of the Treasury; Office of Management and Budget. Note: Data for 2005 are estimates.

TABLE 14-1
The Federal Deficit, Our Public Debt, and the Interest We Pay on It
Net public debt in column 3 is defined as total federal debt *excluding* all loans between federal government agencies. Per capita net public debt is obtained by dividing the net public debt by the population.

FIGURE 14-3
Net U.S. Public Debt as a Percentage of GDP
During World War II, the net public debt grew dramatically. After the war, it fell until the 1970s, started rising in the 1980s, declined once more in the 1990s, and recently has begun increasing again.

Source: U.S. Department of the Treasury.

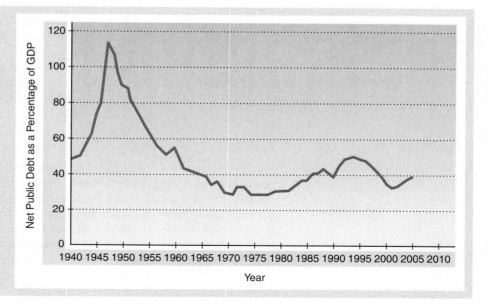

Annual Interest Payments on the Public Debt

Columns 5 and 6 of Table 14-1 on the previous page show an important consequence of the net public debt. This is the interest that the government must pay to those who hold the bonds it has issued to finance past budget deficits. Those interest payments started rising dramatically around 1975 and then declined in the 1990s and early 2000s. Expressed as a percentage of GDP, interest payments on the net public debt today are about 16 percent higher than they were a half century ago. Government deficits are once again on the up-swing, and market interest rates could rise in the future. Thus interest payments expressed as a percentage of GDP are likely to rise in the years to come.

If U.S. residents were the sole owners of the government's debts, the interest payments on the net public debt would go only to U.S. residents. In this situation, we would owe the debt to ourselves, with most people being taxed so that the government could pay interest to others (or to ourselves). During the 1970s, however, the share of the net public debt owned by foreign individuals, businesses, and governments started to rise, reaching 20 percent in 1978. From there it declined until the late 1980s, when it began to rise rapidly. Today, foreign residents, businesses, and governments hold more than 40 percent of the net public debt. Thus we do not owe the debt just to ourselves.

Burdens of the Public Debt

Do current budget deficits and the accumulating public debt create social burdens? One perspective on this question considers possible burdens on future generations. Another focuses on transfers from U.S. residents to residents of other nations.

How Today's Budget Deficits Might Burden Future Generations.
If the federal government wishes to purchase goods and services valued at $100 billion, it can finance this expenditure either by raising taxes by $100 billion or by selling $100 billion in bonds. Many economists maintain that the second option, deficit spending, would lead to a higher level of national consumption and a lower level of national saving than the first option.

The reason, say these economists, is that if people are taxed, they will have to forgo private consumption now as society substitutes government goods for private goods. If the government does not raise taxes but instead sells bonds to finance the $100 billion in expenditures, the public's disposable income remains the same. Members of the public have merely shifted their allocations of assets to include $100 billion in additional government bonds. There are then two possibilities. One is that people will fail to realize that their liabilities (in the form of future taxes due to an increased public debt that must eventually be paid off) have *also* increased by $100 billion. Another is that people will believe that they can consume the governmentally provided goods without forgoing any private consumption because the bill for the government goods will be paid by *future* taxpayers.

The Crowding-Out Effect.
But if full employment exists, and society raises its present consumption by adding consumption of publicly provided goods to the same quantity of privately provided goods, then something must be *crowded out*. In a closed economy, investment expenditures on capital goods must decline. As you learned in Chapter 13, the mechanism by which investment is crowded out is an increase in the interest rate. Deficit spending increases the total demand for credit but leaves the total supply of credit unaltered. The rise in interest rates causes a reduction in the growth of investment and capital formation, which in turn slows the growth of productivity and improvement in society's living standard.

This perspective suggests that deficit spending can impose a burden on future generations in two ways. First, unless the deficit spending is allocated to purchases that lead to long-term increases in real GDP, future generations will have to be taxed at a higher rate. That is, it is only by imposing higher taxes on future generations that the government will be able to retire the higher public debt resulting from the present generation's consumption of governmentally provided goods. Second, the increased level of consumption by the present generation crowds out investment and reduces the growth of capital goods, leaving future generations with a smaller capital stock and thereby reducing their wealth.

Do you think that the recent debate among U.S. policymakers about the advisability of operating with deficits that add to a potentially burdensome public debt is really "new"?

Policy EXAMPLE

Public Debt: Jefferson's Burden or Hamilton's Blessing?

When Thomas Jefferson contemplated the nation's public debt, he concluded that his generation of citizens "should consider ourselves unauthorized to saddle our posterity with our debts, and morally bound to pay them ourselves." Thus Jefferson promoted issuing no government bonds with maturities longer than 19 years, which he estimated to be the length of each generation. Better yet, he argued, the government should always balance its budget, thereby avoiding the accumulation of burdensome debts.

The first Treasury secretary, Alexander Hamilton, offered a completely contrary viewpoint. "A national debt, if not excessive, will be to us as a national blessing," he contended, "and will be a powerful cement of our union." By maintaining a regular state of indebtedness upon which it made steady payments, he felt, the government would establish a strong reputa-

tion for creditworthiness, upon which future generations could draw in times of economic crisis.

Little wonder that President George Washington lamented the "dissensions" between his two key economic advisers on the advisability of accumulating a public debt. The disagreements, he worried, were "tearing our vitals."

For Critical Analysis

Why do you suppose that James Madison, who shared Jefferson's views on the public debt, nonetheless proposed temporary deficit spending while serving as the nation's fourth president during the War of 1812? (Hint: How might Madison have planned to alter postwar government spending and taxes to prevent the public debt from accumulating in future years?)

Paying Off the Public Debt in the Future. Suppose that after 50 years of running deficits, the public debt becomes so large that each adult person's implicit share of the net public debt liability is $50,000. Suppose further that the government chooses (or is forced) to pay off the debt at that time. Will that generation be burdened with our government's overspending? A large portion of the debt is, after all, owed to ourselves. It is true that every adult will have to come up with $50,000 in taxes to pay off the debt, but then the government will use these funds to pay off the bondholders. In many, but not all, cases, the bondholders and taxpayers will be the same people. Thus *some* people will be burdened because they owe $50,000 and own less than $50,000 in government bonds. Others, however, will receive more than $50,000 for the bonds they own. Nevertheless, as a generation within society, they will pay and receive about the same amount of funds.

Of course, there could be a burden on some low-income adults who will find it difficult or impossible to obtain $50,000 to pay off the tax liability. Still, nothing says that taxes to pay off the debt must be assessed equally. Indeed, it seems likely that a special tax would be levied, based on the ability to pay.

Our Debt to Foreign Residents. So far we have been assuming that we owe all of the public debt to ourselves. But, as we saw earlier, that is not the case. What about the 40 percent owned by foreign residents?

It is true that if foreign residents buy U.S. government bonds, we do not owe that debt to ourselves. Thus, when debts held by foreign residents come due, future U.S. residents will be taxed to repay these debts plus accumulated interest. Portions of the incomes of future U.S. residents will then be transferred abroad. In this way, a potential burden on future generations may result.

But this transfer will not necessarily be a burden. Foreign residents will buy our government's debt if the real rate of return on the bonds it issues exceeds the real rate of return that investors can earn in another country. If they buy U.S. bonds voluntarily, they perceive a benefit in doing so.

It is important to realize that not all government expenditures can be viewed as consumption. Government expenditures on such things as highways, bridges, dams, research and development, and education might properly be viewed as investments. If the rate of return on such investments exceeds the interest rate paid to foreign residents, both foreign residents and future U.S. residents will be better off. If funds obtained by selling bonds to foreign residents are expended on wasteful projects, however, a burden may well be placed on future generations.

We can apply the same reasoning to the problem of current investment and capital creation being crowded out by current deficits. If deficits lead to slower growth rates, future generations will be poorer. But if the government expenditures are really investments, and if the rate of return on such public investments exceeds the interest rate paid on the bonds, both present and future generations will be economically better off.

CONCEPTS in Brief

- When we subtract the funds that government agencies borrow from each other from the gross public debt, we obtain the net public debt.

- The public debt may impose a burden on future generations if they have to be taxed at higher rates to pay for the current generation's increased consumption of governmentally provided goods. In addition, there may be a burden if the debt leads to crowding out of current investment,

resulting in less capital formation and hence a lower economic growth rate.

- If foreign residents hold a significant part of our public debt, then we no longer "owe it to ourselves." If the rate of return on the borrowed funds is higher than the interest to be paid to foreign residents, future generations can be made better off by government borrowing. Future generations will be worse off, however, if the opposite is true.

To test your understanding of the concepts covered in this section, go to the Online Review at www.myeconlab.com/miller.

FEDERAL BUDGET DEFICITS IN AN OPEN ECONOMY

Many economists believe that it is no accident that foreign residents hold such a large portion of the U.S. public debt. Their reasoning suggests that a U.S. trade deficit—a situation in which the value of U.S. imports of goods and services exceeds the value of its exports—will often accompany a government budget deficit.

Trade Deficits and Government Budget Deficits

Figure 14-4 shows U.S. trade deficits and surpluses compared to federal budget deficits and surpluses. In 1983, imports began to consistently exceed exports on an annual basis in the United States. At the same time, the federal budget deficit rose dramatically. When the

FIGURE 14-4
The Related U.S. Deficits

The United States exported more than it imported until 1983. Then it started experiencing large trade deficits, as shown in this diagram. The federal budget has been in deficit most years since the 1960s. The question is, has the federal budget deficit created the trade deficit?

Sources: *Economic Report of the President; Economic Indicators*, various issues.

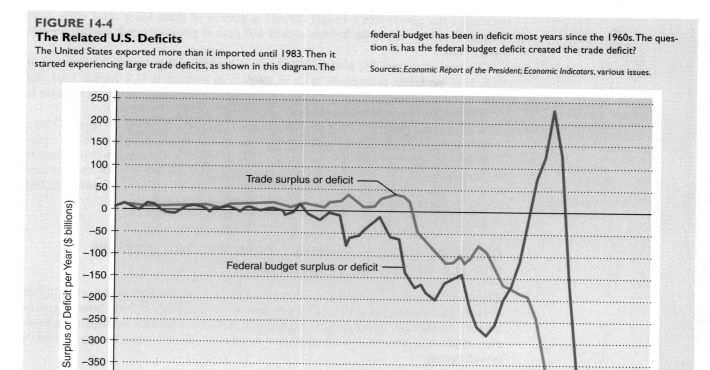

federal budget officially moved into the surplus territory between 1998 and 2001, the U.S. trade deficit briefly eased very slightly. Since the early 2000s, however, both deficits have been increasing once more.

Thus it appears that there is a relationship between trade deficits and government budget deficits: Larger trade deficits tend to accompany larger government budget deficits.

Why the Two Deficits Are Related

Intuitively, there is a reason why we would expect federal budget deficits to be associated with trade deficits. You might call this the unpleasant arithmetic of trade and budget deficits.

Suppose that, initially, the government's budget is balanced; government expenditures are matched by an equal amount of tax collections and other government revenues. Now assume that the federal government begins to experience a budget deficit; it increases its spending, collects fewer taxes, or both. Assume further that domestic consumption and domestic investment do not decrease relative to GDP. Where, then, do the funds come from to finance the government's budget deficit? A portion of these funds must come from abroad. That is to say, dollar holders abroad will have to purchase newly created government bonds.

Of course, foreign dollar holders will choose to hold the new government bonds only if there is an economic inducement to do so, such as an increase in U.S. interest rates. All other things held constant, interest rates will indeed rise whenever there is an increase in deficits financed by increased borrowing.

When foreign dollar holders purchase the new U.S. government bonds, they will have fewer dollars to spend on our goods, that is, U.S. exports. Hence, when our nation's government operates with a budget deficit, we should expect to see foreign dollar holders spending more on U.S. government bonds and less on U.S.-produced goods and services. As a consequence of the U.S. government deficit, therefore, we should anticipate a decline in U.S. exports relative to U.S. imports, or a higher U.S. trade deficit.

GROWING U.S. GOVERNMENT DEFICITS: IMPLICATIONS FOR U.S. ECONOMIC PERFORMANCE

We have seen that one consequence of higher U.S. government budget deficits is higher international trade deficits. Higher budget deficits are also likely to have broader consequences for the economy. Reaching a consensus about these broader consequences, however, requires agreement about exactly how to measure deficits within the government's overall budget.

Which Government Deficit Is the "True" Deficit?

Assessing the implications of higher government deficits is complicated by the fact that the government may report distorted measures of its own budget. One problem is that the U.S. government has never adopted a particularly business-like approach to tracking its expenditures and receipts. Another is that even within its own accounting system, the government persists in choosing "official" measures that yield the lowest reported deficits and highest reported surpluses.

Capital Budgeting Theory. The federal government has only one budget to guide its spending and taxing each fiscal year. It does not distinguish between current spending for upkeep of the grounds of the U.S. Capitol building, for example, and spending for a new aircraft carrier that will last for many years to come. In contrast, businesses, as well as state and local governments, have two budgets. One, called the *operating budget*, includes expenditures for current operations, such as salaries and interest payments. The other, called a *capital budget*, includes expenditures on investment items, such as machines, buildings, roads, and dams. Municipal governments, for example, may pay for items on the capital budget by long-term borrowing.

If the federal government used a capital budgeting system, we would see that a large portion of the more than $400 billion deficit estimated for fiscal year 2005 was being used to finance activities or assets yielding long-term returns. According to Office of Management and Budget (OMB) estimates for that year, investment-type outlays such as payments for military equipment and loans for research and development exceeded $175 billion.

For years, many economists have recommended that Congress create a capital budget and remove investment outlays from its operating budget. Opponents of such a change point out that it would allow the government to grow even faster than currently. After all, many new expenditures could be placed in the capital budget, thereby cutting the size of the operating budget deficit and reducing pressure on Congress to curtail the growth of federal government spending.

Pick a Deficit, Any Deficit. Even using standard accounting techniques, the "official" U.S. government budget deficit can vary drastically, depending on what the government chooses to include or not include. Every year, the OMB makes predictions about the federal budget deficit. So does the Congressional Budget Office. The two budget agencies each produce several deficit estimates for each fiscal year. They give them names such as the "baseline deficit," the "policy deficit," or the "on-budget deficit."

There is also a deficit that is reduced by the amount of the Social Security surplus—for 2003 and 2004 combined a reduction on the order of $500 billion—even though Congress supposedly regards the Social Security surplus as a pool of funds set aside for future disbursement rather than a source of funds for current spending. We could go on, but the point is not to know the details of these various measures of "the government deficit," but rather to understand that no one number gives a complete picture of the total amount of the government budget deficit.

Public discourse might be simplified if everyone could agree on a single measure of the deficit, but the government's accounting system does not make it easy to determine which deficit figure is clearly "best." Thus we should probably anticipate that for years to come, politicians and government officials will continue to bandy about whatever deficit figures best advance their own particular causes.

For more information about the role of the Office of Management and Budget in the government's budgeting process, go to www.econtoday.com/chap14.

The Macroeconomic Consequences of Budget Deficits

No matter how we choose to measure the federal government's deficit, everyone can agree that it has been rising in recent years. Let's consider, therefore, the broader effects of higher government budget deficits on the U.S. economy. When evaluating additional macroeconomic effects of government deficits, two important points must be kept well in mind. First, given the level of government expenditures, the main alternative to the deficit is higher taxes. Therefore, the effects of a deficit should be compared to the effects of higher taxes, not to zero. Second, it is important to distinguish between the effects of deficits when full employment exists and the effects when substantial unemployment exists.

Short-Run Macroeconomic Effects of Higher Budget Deficits. How do increased government budget deficits affect the economy in the short run? The answer depends on the initial state of the economy. Recall from Chapter 13 that higher government spending and lower taxes that generate budget deficits typically add to total planned expenditures, even after taking into account direct and indirect expenditure offsets. When there is a recessionary gap, the increase in aggregate demand can eliminate the recessionary gap and push the economy toward its full-employment real GDP level. In the presence of a short-run recessionary gap, therefore, government deficit spending can stabilize both real GDP and employment.

If the economy is at the full-employment level of real GDP, however, increased total planned expenditures and higher aggregate demand generated by a larger government budget deficit create an inflationary gap. Although greater deficit spending temporarily raises equilibrium real GDP above the full-employment level, the price level also increases.

Long-Run Macroeconomic Effects of Higher Budget Deficits. In a long-run macroeconomic equilibrium, the economy has fully adjusted to changes in all factors. These factors include changes in government spending and taxes and, consequently, the government budget deficit. Although increasing the government budget deficit raises aggregate demand, in the long run equilibrium real GDP remains at its full-employment level. Further increases in the government deficit via higher government expenditures or tax cuts can only be inflationary. They have no effect on equilibrium real GDP, which remains at the full-employment level in the long run.

The fact that long-run equilibrium real GDP is unaffected in the face of increased government deficits has an important implication:

> *In the long run, higher government budget deficits have no effect on equilibrium real GDP. Ultimately, therefore, government spending in excess of government receipts simply redistributes a larger share of real GDP to government-provided goods and services.*

Thus, if the government operates with higher deficits over an extended period, the ultimate result is a shrinkage in the share of privately provided goods and services. By continually spending more than it collects in taxes and other revenue sources, the government takes up a larger portion of economic activity.

CONCEPTS in Brief

- Given constant shares of domestic consumption and domestic investment relative to GDP, funds to finance higher government budget deficits must come from abroad. To obtain the dollars required to purchase newly issued government bonds, foreign residents must sell more goods and services in the United States than U.S. residents sell abroad; thus U.S. imports must exceed U.S. exports. For this reason, the federal budget deficit and the international trade deficit tend to be related.

- Some people argue that the federal budget deficit is measured incorrectly because it lumps together spending on capital and spending on consumption. Establishing separate operating and capital budgets might, according to this view, promote more accurate measurement of federal finances.

- Higher government deficits arise from increased government spending or tax cuts, which raise aggregate demand. Thus larger government budget deficits can raise real GDP in a recessionary-gap situation. If the economy is already at the full-employment level of real GDP, however, higher government deficits can only temporarily push equilibrium real GDP above the full-employment level.

- In the long run, higher government budget deficits cause the equilibrium price level to rise but fail to raise equilibrium real GDP above the full-employment level. Thus the long-run effect of increased government deficits is simply a redistribution of real GDP from privately provided goods and services to government-provided goods and services.

To test your understanding of the concepts covered in this section, go to the Online Review at www.myeconlab.com/miller.

How Could the Government Reduce All Its Red Ink?

There have been many suggestions about how to reduce the government deficit. One way to reduce the deficit is to increase tax collections.

Increasing Taxes for Everyone. From an arithmetic point of view, a federal budget deficit can be wiped out by simply increasing the amount of taxes collected. Let's see what this would require. The data for 2004 are instructive. The Office of Management and Budget estimated the 2004 federal budget deficit at about $521 billion. To have prevented this deficit from occurring by raising taxes, in 2004 the government would have had to collect $3,750 more in taxes from *every worker* in the United States. Needless to say, reality is such that we will never see annual federal budget deficits wiped out by simple tax increases.

Why do you think that operating with deficits encourages a number of state governments to consider imposing taxes on activities that currently are untaxed?

E-Commerce EXAMPLE

Would Taxing Internet Sales Wipe Out States' Deficits?

Since 2002, state governments across the United States have faced shortfalls in their state budgets amounting collectively to about $15 billion per year. As various state governments have searched for new sources of revenue to reduce their budget deficits, applying state sales taxes to Internet purchases has emerged as one possibility.

At present, a large portion of the market transactions that take place on the Web are not subject to state sales taxes. How much revenue would taxing Internet sales generate for state governments? Most estimates indicate that the total sales tax "take" from fully applying sales taxes to e-commerce would range somewhere between $300 million and $3.8 billion. Thus subjecting all Web purchases to state sales taxes would raise sufficient funds to cover only 2 to 25 percent of the states' collective budgetary shortfall.

For Critical Analysis
How must governments of states with constitutions permitting deficit spending always *finance their deficits? (Hint: Only the federal government currently has the power to create money to buy bonds.)*

Taxing the Rich. Some people suggest that the way to eliminate the deficit is to raise taxes on the rich. Data from the Internal Revenue Service (IRS) indicate that more than 84 percent of all federal income taxes are already being paid by the 25 percent of families earning the highest incomes in the United States. The entire lower 50 percent of families (those earning less than $60,000 per year) pay only slightly less than 4 percent of federal income taxes. At present, families whose incomes are in the top 5 percent pay nearly 57 percent of all federal income taxes each year. The richest 1 percent pay about 37 percent of all income taxes.

What does it mean to tax the rich more? If you talk about taxing "millionaires," you are referring to those who pay taxes on more than $1 million in income per year. There are fewer than 60,000 of them. Even if you were to double the taxes they currently pay, the reduction in the deficit would be relatively trivial. Changing marginal tax rates at the upper end will produce similarly unimpressive results. The IRS has determined that an increase in the top marginal tax rate from 35 percent to 45 percent will raise, at best, only about $30 billion in additional taxes. (This assumes that people do not figure out a way to avoid the higher tax rate.) Extra revenues of $30 billion per year represent only about 8 percent of the estimated 2005 federal budget deficit.

The reality is that the data do not support the notion that tax increases can reduce deficits. Although reducing a deficit in this way is possible arithmetically, politically just the opposite has occurred.

> *Since World War II, for every dollar increase in taxes legislated, federal government spending has increased about $1.60.*

Clearly, when more tax revenues have been collected, Congress has usually responded by increasing government spending.

Reducing Expenditures. Reducing expenditures is another way to decrease the federal budget deficit. Figure 14-5 on the following page shows various components of government spending as a percentage of total expenditures. There you see that military spending as a share of total federal expenditures has risen slightly in recent years but it remains much lower than in most previous years.

FIGURE 14-5

Components of Federal Expenditures as Percentages of Total Federal Spending

Although military spending as a percentage of total federal spending has risen and fallen with changing national defense concerns, national defense expenditures as a percentage of total spending have generally trended downward since the mid-1950s. Social Security and other income security programs and Medicare and other health programs now account for larger shares of total federal spending than any other programs.

Source: Office of Management and Budget.

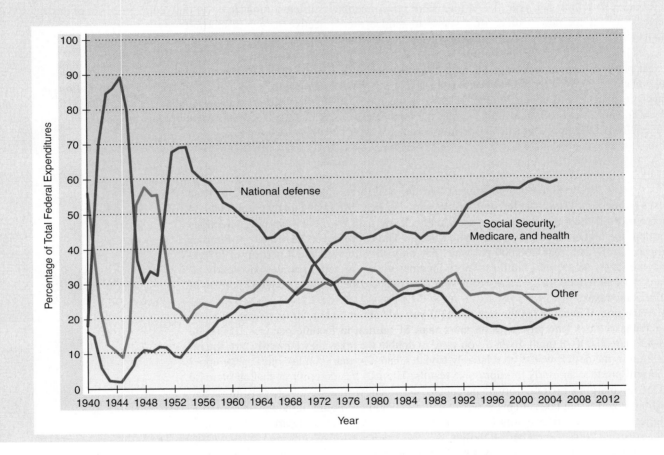

Entitlements
Guaranteed benefits under a government program such as Social Security, Medicare, or Medicaid.

Noncontrollable expenditures
Government spending that changes automatically without action by Congress.

During the Cold War that stretched from the conclusion of World War II until 1992, military spending was the most important aspect of the federal budget. Figure 14-5 shows that it no longer is, even taking into account the war on terrorism that began in late 2001. **Entitlements,** which are legislated federal government payments that anyone who qualifies is entitled to receive, are now the most important component of the federal budget. These include payments for Social Security and other income security programs and for Medicare and other health programs such as Medicaid. Entitlements are consequently often called **noncontrollable expenditures,** or nondiscretionary expenditures unrelated to national defense that automatically change without any direct action by Congress.

Why do you suppose that some economists contend that the growth of entitlements causes the current public debt to dramatically understate the true amount of the government's future financial obligations?

International Policy EXAMPLE

Unrealized Public Debts, Especially in Canada

As you have learned, the net public debt is the best available hard-and-fast measure of the total amount of actual borrowings that a government has to repay. Nevertheless, this explicit measure of a government's obligations may seriously understate the true weight of debts faced by governments that issue entitlement guarantees.

Peter Heller of the International Monetary Fund has developed a measure of public indebtedness that adds to the official net public debt an estimate of all other *implicit* future indebtedness arising from entitlements currently unfunded by taxes. According to this broader estimate of the public debt, Heller concludes that total U.S. public indebtedness is actually more than *250 percent* of GDP, instead of 40 percent of GDP as implied by the official measure of the net public debt.

Heller's implicit indebtedness measures indicate that in Belgium, where the net public debt is already equal to GDP,

adding in currently unfunded guarantees pushes total government indebtedness to more than 300 percent of GDP. In Spain, the figure is more than 350 percent. The country with the highest level of implied indebtedness arising from unfunded entitlement programs, however, is Canada. Even though Canada's official net public debt is less than 50 percent of its GDP, there are so many unfunded Canadian entitlement guarantees that total implied government indebtedness is about 420 percent of GDP.

For Critical Analysis

If governments with large entitlement programs fail to cut the programs and are unable to collect sufficient taxes to fund the programs, what other options will they have for raising funds to cover guaranteed outlays?

Is It Time to Begin Whittling Away at Entitlements? In 1960, spending on entitlements represented about 10 percent of the total federal budget. Today entitlement expenditures make up more than half of total federal spending. Consider Social Security, Medicare, and Medicaid. In constant 2000 dollars, in 2004 Social Security, Medicare, and Medicaid represented about $1,010 billion of federal expenditures, compared to almost $700 billion of other spending by the federal government. (These exclude military and international payments and interest on the government debt.)

Entitlement payments for Social Security, Medicare, and Medicaid now exceed all other domestic spending. Entitlements are growing faster than any other part of the federal government budget. During the past two decades, real spending on entitlements (adjusted for inflation) grew between 7 and 8 percent per year, while the economy grew less than 3 percent per year. Social Security payments are growing in real terms at about 6 percent per year, but Medicare and Medicaid are growing at double-digit rates. The passage of Medicare prescription drug benefits in 2003 simply added to the already rapid growth of these health care entitlements.

Many people believe that entitlement programs are "necessary" federal expenditures. Interest on the public debt must be paid, but Congress can change just about every other federal expenditure labeled "necessary." The federal budget deficit is not expected to drop in the near future because entitlement programs are not likely to be eliminated. Governments have trouble cutting government benefit programs once they are established. This means that containing federal budget deficits is likely to prove to be a difficult task.

Economics Front and Center

To contemplate the complications that entitlement spending poses for deficit-cutting efforts, consider the case study, **Congress Is Less Fun When There Is Less Discretion,** on page 330.

CONCEPTS in Brief

- One way to reduce federal budget deficits is to increase taxes. Proposals to reduce deficits by raising taxes on the highest-income individuals will not appreciably reduce budget deficits, however.

- Another way to decrease federal budget deficits is to cut back on government spending, particularly on entitlements, defined as benefits guaranteed under government programs such as Social Security and Medicare.

To test your understanding of the concepts covered in this section, go to the Online Review at www.myeconlab.com/miller.

CASE STUDY : Economics Front and Center

Congress Is Less Fun When There Is Less Discretion

Congresswoman French (D, Illinois) is a member of a House budget subcommittee. In the past, her position has been a plum assignment because committee members have been able to use the political leverage of their positions to obtain discretionary funds for their home districts. They are finding that times are changing, however. A new president just campaigned on the promise to veto any bill that either raises taxes or raises the federal budget deficit. Now the congresswoman and her committee colleagues face the task of developing an initial proposal for the government's budget for the coming fiscal year.

As Congresswoman French looks over the documents on her desk, she faces the facts. Entitlement spending was more than $1.3 trillion in 2005. If the Congressional Budget Office's estimates are correct, guaranteed entitlement spending will rise above $1.5 trillion next year. She also faces another fact: during her own campaign, she made two promises—to fight any cuts in entitlement programs and to direct more discretionary spending to her constituents back home. This year, she realizes, will probably prove to be her toughest year in politics.

Points to Analyze

1. *Why does automatic growth in entitlement spending complicate efforts to reduce federal government deficits?*

2. *Why might people naturally disagree about whether growth in the net public debt, which is generated by deficits that in turn result from higher entitlement expenditures, is "burdensome" to society?*

Issues and Applications

International Cycles in Government Budget Deficits and Surpluses

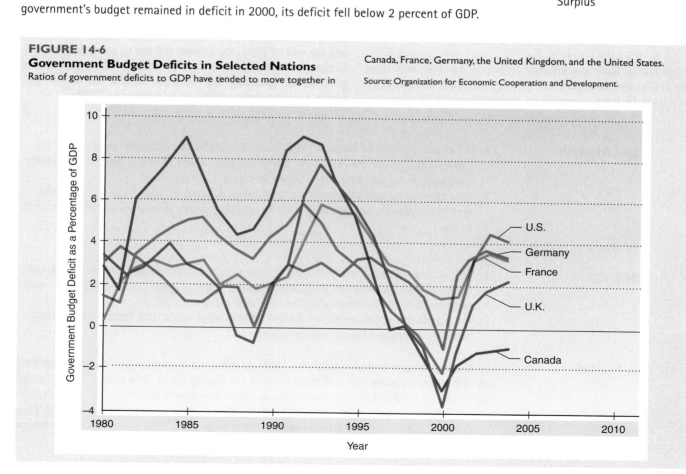

Figure 14-6 plots national government deficits as percentages of GDP for Canada, France, Germany, the United Kingdom, and the United States. It shows that in these countries, deficits as shares of GDP increased during the first half of the 1980s, dropped somewhat in the late 1980s, rose again into the early 1990s, and then fell throughout the remainder of the 1990s. By 2000, the governments of all but France were operating with a budget surplus (the negative deficit-GDP ratios shown in Figure 14-6). Although the French government's budget remained in deficit in 2000, its deficit fell below 2 percent of GDP.

Concepts Applied

- Government Budget Deficit
- Government Budget Surplus

FIGURE 14-6

Government Budget Deficits in Selected Nations

Ratios of government deficits to GDP have tended to move together in Canada, France, Germany, the United Kingdom, and the United States.

Source: Organization for Economic Cooperation and Development.

By the end of 2001, German, U.K., and U.S. government spending once more began to exceed receipts. The Canadian government's surplus began to narrow, and the French government's deficit began to widen. Consequently, as shown in Figure 14-6, deficit-GDP ratios have been rising during the 2000s.

Deficits as Reflections of Common Business Cycles

Why have government deficits tended to move together in these and many other nations of the world? Many of the world's nations have had more open economies since the 1970s, so their business cycles have tended to be more closely aligned. Most national governments rely on income taxes and other taxes that vary with GDP. Their tax revenues rise with increases in GDP and fall with decreases in GDP. The nations depicted in the figure all experienced business-cycle contractions in the early 1980s, early 1990s, and early 2000s. Tax revenues fell during each contraction, which contributed to higher deficits.

Other Common Factors Affecting Budget Deficits

Other factors have also affected deficits in the same way since the 1980s. Before the 1990s, military spending was a significant part of total government expenditures in Western nations, such as those displayed in Figure 14-6. After the fall of the Soviet Union, all these nations' governments were able to slash military expenditures, which helped them reduce their deficits. Likewise, at least in part, the common increase in deficit-GDP ratios in these countries after 2000 also reflects increases in government defense expenditures on combating terrorism.

Shared stock market trends have also contributed to common deficit-GDP movements across nations in the 1990s and 2000s. The governments of most countries tax capital gains on shares of stock. When world stock markets were booming during the 1990s, governments' collections of capital gains taxes increased. This contributed further to the decreasing deficit-GDP ratios during the 1990s displayed in Figure 14-6. Then, when world stock markets dropped between late 2000 and the end of 2001, the bottom fell out of governments' collections of capital gains taxes. This added to the gaps between government spending and receipts around the world and, hence, to rising deficit-GDP ratios during the 2000s.

For Critical Analysis

1. If Canada, the United Kingdom, and the United States were to experience economic expansions through the rest of the 2000s but France and Germany were to experience contractions, would the pattern shown in Figure 14-6 continue?
2. How can capital gains taxes, like income taxes, function as automatic fiscal stabilizers? (Hint: When a nation's GDP is on an upswing, prices in its stock markets also tend to rise.)

Web Resources

1. To examine the most recent U.S. government budget documents, go to the link to the Office of Management and Budget provided at www.econtoday.com/chap14, and click on "Budget Documents" in the left-hand margin.
2. For access to the Congressional Budget Office's most recent U.S. federal deficit projections, go to www.econtoday.com/chap14.

Research Project

List the key factors that you think are likely to influence a nation's government spending and tax revenues. How many of these factors are also likely to vary as the country's real GDP rises or falls? What can you conclude about the extent to which any nation's government deficit will tend to be influenced by changing business-cycle conditions? Why does this greatly complicate governments' efforts to develop deficit projections for future years?

SUMMARY DISCUSSION of Learning Objectives

1. **Federal Government Budget Deficits:** Whenever the flow of government expenditures exceeds the flow of government revenues during a period of time, a budget deficit occurs. If government expenditures are less than government revenues during a given interval, a budget surplus occurs. The government operates with a balanced budget during a specific period if its expenditures are equal to its revenues. The federal budget deficit expressed as a percentage of GDP most recently hit a peak of around 6 percent in the early 1980s. The federal government operated with a surplus between 1998 and 2001. The government budget went into deficit once more starting in 2002. The amount of the deficit is currently about 4 percent of GDP.

2. **The Public Debt:** The federal budget deficit is a flow, whereas accumulated budget deficits are a stock, called the public debt. The gross public debt is the stock of total government bonds, and the net public debt is the difference between the gross public debt and the amount of government agencies' holdings of government bonds. The net public debt as a share of GDP reached its peak right after World War II. In recent years, it has been running at more than 35 percent of GDP.

3. **How the Public Debt Might Prove a Burden to Future Generations:** If people are taxed, they must forgo private consumption as society substitutes government goods for private goods. Thus, if future generations must be taxed at higher rates to pay for the current generation's increased consumption of governmentally provided goods, future generations may experience a burden from the public debt. Also contributing to this potential burden is any current crowding out of investment as a consequence

of additional debt accumulation, which can reduce capital formation and future economic growth. Furthermore, if capital invested by foreign residents who purchase some of the U.S. public debt has not been productively used, future generations will be worse off. If this capital is productive investment, however, future generations will be better off.

4. **Why the Federal Budget Deficit Might Be Incorrectly Measured:** Some people contend that the federal budget deficit is measured incorrectly because it combines government capital and consumption expenditures. They argue that the federal government should have an operating budget and a capital budget.

5. **The Macroeconomic Effects of Government Budget Deficits:** Because higher government deficits are caused by increased government spending or tax cuts, they contribute to a rise in total planned expenditures and aggregate demand. If there is a short-run recessionary gap, higher government deficits can thereby push equilibrium real GDP toward the full-employment level. If the economy is already at the full-employment level of real GDP, however, then a higher deficit creates a short-run inflationary gap. In the long run, increased deficits only redistribute real GDP from privately provided goods and services to government-provided goods and services.

6. **Possible Ways to Reduce the Government Budget Deficit:** Suggested ways to reduce the deficit are to increase taxes, particularly on the rich, and to reduce expenditures, particularly on entitlements, defined as guaranteed benefits under government programs such as Social Security and Medicare.

KEY TERMS AND CONCEPTS

balanced budget (315)

entitlements (328)

government budget deficit (315)

government budget surplus (315)

gross public debt (318)

net public debt (318)

noncontrollable expenditures (328)

public debt (316)

PROBLEMS

Answers to the odd-numbered problems appear at the back of the book.

14-1. In 2007, government spending is $2.2 trillion, and taxes collected are $1.8 trillion. What is the federal government deficit in that year?

14-2. Suppose that the Office of Management and Budget provides the following estimates of federal budget receipts, federal budget spending, and GDP, all expressed in billions of dollars. Calculate the implied estimates of the federal budget deficit as a percentage of GDP for each year.

Year	Federal Budget Receipts	Federal Budget Spending	GDP
2007	2,198.2	2,553.3	13,143.1
2008	2,264.2	2,619.7	13,826.5
2009	2,329.8	2,682.6	14,573.2
2010	2,392.4	2,741.6	15,316.0

14-3. It may be argued that the effects of a higher public debt are the same as the effects of a higher deficit. Why?

14-4. What happens to the net public debt if the federal government operates next year with a:
  a. budget deficit?
  b. balanced budget?
  c. budget surplus?

14-5. What is the relationship between the gross public debt and the net public debt?

14-6. Suppose that another government agency uses funds received from the central treasury department of its nation's government to buy government bonds from the central treasury department. The treasury increases its tax collections to fund the government agency's bond purchases. What happens to the gross public debt? What happens to the net public debt?

14-7. Suppose that the government agency in Problem 14-6 purchases previously issued government bonds from private individuals and companies instead of from the government treasury department. What happens to the gross public debt? What happens to the net public debt?

14-8. Explain in your own words why there is likely to be a relationship between federal budget deficits and U.S. international trade deficits.

14-9. Suppose that the share of U.S. GDP going to domestic consumption remains constant. Initially, the federal government was operating with a balanced budget, but this year it has increased its spending well above its collections of taxes and other sources of revenues. To fund its deficit spending, the government has issued bonds. So far, very few foreign residents have shown any interest in purchasing the bonds.
  a. What must happen to induce foreign residents to buy the bonds?
  b. If foreign residents desire to purchase the bonds, what is the most important source of dollars to buy them?

14-10. The Social Security surplus is a net sum of funds that Congress claims to "set aside" to help cover future payments of Social Security benefits. Why does including the Social Security surplus in a calculation of the government budget deficit reduce the reported size of the deficit?

14-11. Proponents of federal capital budgeting argue that whenever the government invests in capital expenditures, such as spending on roads and dams, such spending should be recorded in a separate budget called the capital budget. In doing so, the federal government's budget deficit would be reduced by the amount of government capital spending. Would this alteration in the approach to measuring the government deficit actually change anything? Explain.

14-12. Suppose that the economy is experiencing a recessionary gap. Use an appropriate diagram to assist in explaining how an increase in the government budget deficit could help close this gap, other things being equal. In addition, discuss why, given that many taxes and government benefits vary with real GDP, we might expect to see the deficit automatically shrink as this gap begins to close.

14-13. Suppose that the economy is currently at full employment. Explain how an increase in the government budget deficit affects the equilibrium price level and equilibrium real GDP in the short run, other things being equal.

14-14. To reduce the size of the deficit (and reduce the growth of the net public debt), a politician suggests that "we should tax the rich." The politician makes a simple arithmetic calculation in which he applies the higher tax rate to the total income reported by "the rich" in a previous year. He says that this is how much the government could receive from increasing taxes

on "the rich." What is the major fallacy in such calculations?

ECONOMICS ON THE NET

The Public Debt Examining the federal government's budget data enables its current estimates of the public debt to be determined.

Title: Historical Tables: Budget of the United States Government

Navigation: Use the link at www.econontoday.com/chap14 to visit the Office of Management and Budget. Select the most recent budget. Then click on *Historical Tables*.

Application After the document downloads, perform the indicated operations and answer the questions.

1. In the Table of Contents in the left-hand margin of the Historical Tables, click on Table 7.1, "Federal Debt at the End of the Year, 1940-2009." In light of the discussion in this chapter, which column shows the net public debt?

What is the conceptual difference between the gross public debt and the net public debt? Last year, what was the dollar difference between these two amounts?

2. Table 7.1 includes estimates of the gross and net public debt over the next several years. Suppose that these estimates turn out to be accurate. Calculate how much the net public debt would increase on average each year. What are possible ways that the government could prevent these predicted increases from occurring?

For Group Study and Analysis Divide into two groups, and have each group take one side in answering the question, "Is the public debt a burden or a blessing?" Have each group develop rationales for supporting its position. Then reconvene the entire class, and discuss the relative merits of the alternative positions and rationales.

If your exam were tomorrow, would you be ready? For each chapter, MyEconLab Practice Tests and Study Plans pinpoint which sections you have mastered and which ones you need to study. That way, you are more efficient with your study time, and you are better prepared for your exams.

In addition to Practice Tests and your personalized Study Plan, you'll find the following media resources in MyEconLab:
1. *Graphs in Motion* animation of Figures 14-1, 14-4, and 14-5.
2. Links to the Web sites cited in the marginal Internet Resources, Issues and Applications feature, and Economics on the Net activity.

3. Audio clips of all key terms, additional practice problems, and a PDF version of the material from the print Study Guide.
4. eThemes of the Times, which is a New York Times article to help you understand the real-world applications of what you are learning.

To see how it works, turn to page 16 and then go to www.myeconlab.com/miller.

Get Ahead of the Curve

Chapter 15

Money, Banking, and Central Banking

Each year, the U.S. government produces roughly 70 new coins for every U.S. resident, or approximately 20 billion new coins. About half of all the new coins produced are pennies. Thus, if we add up the dollar value of all coins—pennies, nickels, dimes, quarters, and golden dollars—introduced into circulation each year, the total sum is only a few billion dollars. This is a tiny fraction of the $400 billion average annual increase in one measure of the U.S. money supply over the past six years. The quantity of paper currency also increases each year, but currency growth explains only a portion of the annual growth in the U.S. money supply. In this chapter you will learn about other contributors to U.S. money growth, such as increases in certain deposit account balances at banks, savings institutions, and credit unions.

Media Resources

Refer to the end of the chapter for a full listing of the multimedia learning materials available in MyEconLab.

LEARNING OBJECTIVES

After reading this chapter, you should be able to:

1. Define the fundamental functions of money
2. Identify key properties that any good that functions as money must possess
3. Explain official definitions of the quantity of money in circulation
4. Understand why financial intermediaries such as banks exist
5. Describe the basic structure of the Federal Reserve System
6. Discuss the major functions of the Federal Reserve

...each large coin—quarters and the occasional dollar coin—produced by the U.S. Mint and introduced into circulation by the Federal Reserve costs about 12 cents to produce? The resulting profits of 13 to 88 cents from producing and distributing these coins go straight to the U.S. Treasury. All told, the U.S. Mint's profits from coin production increase the U.S. government's revenues by at least $1 billion every year.

Coins, paper currency, and bank accounts on which people write checks are all included in the Federal Reserve's measure of the total amount of *money* that we can use to purchase goods and services. Money has been important to society for thousands of years. In the fourth century B.C., Aristotle claimed that everything had to "be accessed in money, for this enables men always to exchange their services, and so makes society possible." Money is indeed a part of our everyday existence. Nevertheless, we have to be careful when we talk about money. Often we hear a person say, "I wish I had more money," instead of "I wish I had more wealth," thereby confusing the concepts of money and wealth. Economists use the term **money** to mean anything that people generally accept in exchange for goods and services. Table 15-1 provides a list of some items that various civilizations have used as money. The best way to understand how these items served this purpose is to examine the functions of money.

Money
Any medium that is universally accepted in an economy both by sellers of goods and services as payment for those goods and services and by creditors as payment for debts.

THE FUNCTIONS OF MONEY

Money traditionally has four functions. The one that most people are familiar with is money's function as a *medium of exchange*. Money also serves as a *unit of accounting*, a *store of value* or *purchasing power*, and a *standard of deferred payment*. Anything that serves these four functions is money. Anything that could serve these four functions could be considered money.

TABLE 15-1
Types of Money
This is a partial list of things that have been used as money. Native Americans used *wampum*, beads made from shells. Fijians used whale teeth. The early colonists in North America used tobacco. And cigarettes were used in post–World War II Germany and in Poland during the breakdown of Communist rule in the late 1980s.

Iron	Boar tusk	Playing cards
Copper	Red woodpecker scalps	Leather
Brass	Feathers	Gold
Wine	Glass	Silver
Corn	Polished beads (wampum)	Knives
Salt	Rum	Pots
Horses	Molasses	Boats
Sheep	Tobacco	Pitch
Goats	Agricultural implements	Rice
Tortoise shells	Round stones with centers removed	Cows
Porpoise teeth	Crystal salt bars	Paper
Whale teeth	Snail shells	Cigarettes

Source: Roger LeRoy Miller and David D. VanHoose, *Money, Banking, and Financial Markets*, 2nd ed. (Cincinnati: South Western, 2004), p. 6.

Money as a Medium of Exchange

Medium of exchange
Any asset that sellers will accept as payment.

When we say that money serves as a **medium of exchange,** we mean that sellers will accept it as payment in market transactions. Without some generally accepted medium of exchange, we would have to resort to *barter.* In fact, before money was used, transactions took place by means of barter. **Barter** is simply a direct exchange. In a barter economy, the shoemaker who wants to obtain a dozen water glasses must seek out a glassmaker who at exactly the same time is interested in obtaining a pair of shoes. For this to occur, there has to be a *double coincidence of wants* for each specific item to be exchanged. If there isn't, the shoemaker must go through several trades in order to obtain the desired dozen glasses—perhaps first trading shoes for jewelry, then jewelry for some pots and pans, and then the pots and pans for the desired glasses.

Barter
The direct exchange of goods and services for other goods and services without the use of money.

Money facilitates exchange by reducing the transaction costs associated with means-of-payment uncertainty. That is, with regard to goods that the partners in any exchange are willing to accept, the existence of money means that individuals no longer have to hold a diverse collection of goods as an exchange inventory. As a medium of exchange, money allows individuals to specialize in any area in which they have a comparative advantage and to receive money payments for their labor. Money payments can then be exchanged for the fruits of other people's labor. The use of money as a medium of exchange permits more specialization and the inherent economic efficiencies that come with it (and hence greater economic growth).

Money as a Unit of Accounting

Unit of accounting
A measure by which prices are expressed; the common denominator of the price system; a central property of money.

A **unit of accounting** is a way of placing a specific price on economic goods and services. It is the common denominator, the commonly recognized measure of value. The dollar is the unit of accounting in the United States. It is the yardstick that allows individuals easily to compare the relative value of goods and services. Accountants at the U.S. Department of Commerce use dollar prices to measure national income and domestic product, a business uses dollar prices to calculate profits and losses, and a typical household budgets regularly anticipated expenses using dollar prices as its unit of accounting.

Another way of describing money as a unit of accounting is to say that it serves as a *standard of value* that allows economic actors to compare the relative worth of various goods and services. This allows for comparison shopping, for example.

Money as a Store of Value

Store of value
The ability to hold value over time; a necessary property of money.

One of the most important functions of money is that it serves as a **store of value** or purchasing power. The money you have today can be set aside to purchase things later on. In the meantime, money retains its nominal value, which you can apply to those future purchases. If you have $1,000 in your checking account, you can choose to spend it today on goods and services, spend it tomorrow, or spend it a month from now. In this way, money provides a way to transfer value (wealth) into the future.

Money as a Standard of Deferred Payment

Standard of deferred payment
A property of an asset that makes it desirable for use as a means of settling debts maturing in the future; an essential property of money.

The fourth function of the monetary unit is as a **standard of deferred payment.** This function involves the use of money both as a medium of exchange and as a unit of accounting. Debts are typically stated in terms of a unit of accounting; they are paid with a monetary medium of exchange. That is to say, a debt is specified in a dollar amount and paid in currency (or by check). A corporate bond, for example, has a face value—the dollar value stated on it, which is to be paid upon maturity. The periodic interest payments on that corporate bond are specified and paid in dollars, and when the bond comes due (at maturity), the corporation pays the face value in dollars to the holder of the bond.

LIQUIDITY

Money is an asset—something of value—that accounts for part of personal wealth. Wealth in the form of money can be exchanged later for other assets, goods, or services. Although it is not the only form of wealth that can be exchanged for goods and services, it is the most widely and most readily accepted one. This attribute of money is called **liquidity.** We say that an asset is *liquid* when it can easily be acquired or disposed of without high transaction costs and with relative certainty as to its value. Money is by definition the most liquid asset. Compare it, for example, with a share of stock listed on the New York Stock Exchange. To sell that stock, you may call a stockbroker, who will place the sell order for you. This generally must be done during normal business hours. You have to pay a commission to the broker. Moreover, there is a distinct probability that you will get more or less for the stock than you originally paid for it. This is not the case with money. People can easily convert money to other asset forms. Therefore, most individuals hold at least a part of their wealth in the form of the most liquid of assets, money. You can see how assets rank in liquidity relative to one another in Figure 15-1.

When we hold money, however, we pay a price for this advantage of liquidity. Because cash in your pocket and many checking or debit account balances do not earn interest, that price is the interest yield that could have been obtained had the asset been held in another form—for example, in the form of stocks and bonds.

> *The cost of holding money (its opportunity cost) is measured by the alternative interest yield obtainable by holding some other asset.*

MONETARY STANDARDS, OR WHAT BACKS MONEY

In the past, many different monetary standards have existed. For example, commodity money, which is a physical good that may be valued for other uses it provides, has been used (see Table 15-1 on page 337). The main forms of commodity money were gold and silver. Today, though, most people throughout the world accept coins, paper currency, and balances in **transactions accounts** (checking accounts with banks and other financial institutions; also called **checkable deposits**) in exchange for items sold, including labor services. The question

Liquidity
The degree to which an asset can be acquired or disposed of without much danger of any intervening loss in *nominal* value and with small transaction costs. Money is the most liquid asset.

Transactions accounts
Checking account balances in commercial banks and other types of financial institutions, such as credit unions and mutual savings banks; any accounts in financial institutions on which you can easily write checks without many restrictions.

Checkable deposits
Any deposits in a thrift institution or a commercial bank on which a check may be written; for all intents and purposes, a transactions account.

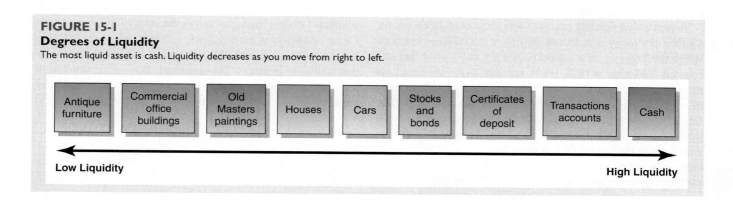

FIGURE 15-1
Degrees of Liquidity
The most liquid asset is cash. Liquidity decreases as you move from right to left.

Fiduciary monetary system
A system in which money is issued by the government and its value is based uniquely on the public's faith that the currency represents command over goods and services.

remains, why are we willing to accept as payment something that has no intrinsic value? After all, you could not sell checks to anybody for use as a raw material in manufacturing. The reason is that payments in the modern world arise from a **fiduciary monetary system.** This means that the value of the payments rests on the public's confidence that such payments can be exchanged for goods and services. *Fiduciary* comes from the Latin *fiducia,* which means "trust" or "confidence." In our fiduciary monetary system, money, in the form of currency or transactions accounts, is not convertible to a fixed quantity of gold, silver, or some other precious commodity. The bills are just pieces of paper. Coins have a value stamped on them that today is much greater than the market value of the metal in them. Nevertheless, currency and transactions accounts are money because of their acceptability and predictability of value.

Acceptability

Transactions accounts and currency are money because they are accepted in exchange for goods and services. They are accepted because people have confidence that these items can later be exchanged for other goods and services. This confidence is based on the knowledge that such exchanges have occurred in the past without problems. Even during a period of inflation, we might still be inclined to accept money in exchange for goods and services because it is so useful. Barter is a costly and time-consuming alternative.

Realize that money is always socially defined. Acceptability is not something that you can necessarily predict. For example, the U.S. government has tried to circulate types of money, such as the $2 bill, that turned out to be socially unacceptable. How many $2 bills have you seen lately? The answer is probably none. No one wanted to make room for $2 bills in register tills or billfolds.

Why do you suppose that it is now just as important for machines to accept a unit of currency as it is for people to find it acceptable?

EXAMPLE

What Happens When People Will Accept Currency, but Machines Will Not?

On October 9, 2003, the U.S. Treasury Department's Bureau of Engraving and Printing introduced the first colorful new $20 bills, which it had designed to hinder counterfeiting. In a ceremonial introduction of the redesigned currency, Treasury officials put the first bill into circulation by using it to purchase stamps from a vending machine at a Washington, D.C. post office.

A post office vending machine was not a random choice for a public ceremony introducing the first of the replacement bills. When the Treasury first started producing redesigned, but less colorful, $20 bills in 1998, many vending machines could not recognize the currency. People who commonly used currency in vending machines, therefore, shunned the new $20 bills. Consequently, as part of its planning for the more colorful 2003 improvement on the 1998 redesign, the Treasury Department worked with the vending machine industry, as well as the gambling industry and mass-transit authorities, to make sure cash-exchanging machines would accept the colorful $20 bills.

By October 11, 2003, however, Treasury officials were swamped with calls complaining about the more colorful bills they had just introduced. Most of the calls came from owners of grocery stores. When designing the latest $20 bills, the Treasury Department had forgotten to consult with makers of the automated payment machines used in groceries' self-service checkout counters. Grocery managers across the country had to post signs asking customers to exchange new $20 bills, which the machines could not recognize, for old ones before using the machines to purchase their groceries. The managers then rushed to place orders for software and hardware upgrades for their automated payment machines, often at a cost as high as $40 per machine.

For Critical Analysis
Why do you think that the Treasury's Bureau of Engraving and Printing introduces new currency gradually, rather than all at once?

Predictability of Value

The purchasing power of the dollar (its real value) varies inversely with the price level. The more rapid the rate of increase of some price level index, such as the Consumer Price Index, the more rapid the decrease in the real value, or purchasing power, of a dollar. Money retains its usefulness even if its purchasing power is declining year in and year out, as in periods of inflation, if it still retains the characteristic of predictability of value. If you anticipate that the inflation rate is going to be around 3 percent during the next year, you know that any dollar you receive a year from now will have a purchasing power equal to 3 percent less than that same dollar today. Thus you will not necessarily refuse to accept money in exchange simply because you know that its value will decline by the rate of inflation during the next year. You may, however, wish to be compensated for that expected decline in money's real value.

CONCEPTS in Brief

- Money is defined by its functions, which are as a medium of exchange, a unit of accounting or standard of value, a store of value or purchasing power, and a standard of deferred payment.

- Money is a highly liquid asset because it can be disposed of with low transaction costs and with relative certainty as to its value.

- Modern nations have fiduciary monetary systems—national currencies are not convertible into a fixed quantity of a commodity such as gold or silver.

- Money is accepted in exchange for goods and services because people have confidence that it can later be exchanged for other goods and services. In other words, money has predictable value.

To test your understanding of the concepts covered in this section, go to the Online Review at www.myeconlab.com/miller.

DEFINING MONEY

Money is important. Changes in the total **money supply**—the amount of money in circulation—and changes in the rate at which the money supply increases or decreases affect important economic variables (at least in the short run), such as the rate of inflation, interest rates, employment, and the level of real GDP. Although there is widespread agreement among economists that money is indeed important, they have struggled to reach agreement about how to define and measure it. There are two basic approaches: the **transactions approach,** which stresses the role of money as a medium of exchange, and the **liquidity approach,** which stresses the role of money as a temporary store of value.

The Transactions Approach to Measuring Money: M1

Using the transactions approach to measuring money, the money supply consists of currency, checkable deposits, and traveler's checks. The official designation of the money supply, including currency, checkable deposits, and traveler's checks not issued by banks, is **M1.** The various elements of M1 for a typical year are presented in panel (a) of Figure 15-2 on the following page.

Currency. In the United States, currency includes coins minted by the U.S. Treasury and paper currency in the form of Federal Reserve notes issued by the Federal Reserve banks (to be discussed shortly). In other nations, currency also consists of coins and paper bills.

Money supply
The amount of money in circulation.

Transactions approach
A method of measuring the money supply by looking at money as a medium of exchange.

Liquidity approach
A method of measuring the money supply by looking at money as a temporary store of value.

M1
The money supply, taken as the total value of currency plus checkable deposits plus traveler's checks not issued by banks.

FIGURE 15-2
Composition of the U.S. M1 and M2 Money Supply, 2005
Panel (a) shows estimates of the M1 money supply, of which the largest component (over 50 percent) is currency. M2 consists of M1 plus three other components, the most important of which is savings deposits at all depository institutions.

Sources: *Federal Reserve Bulletin, Economic Indicators*, various issues; author's estimates.

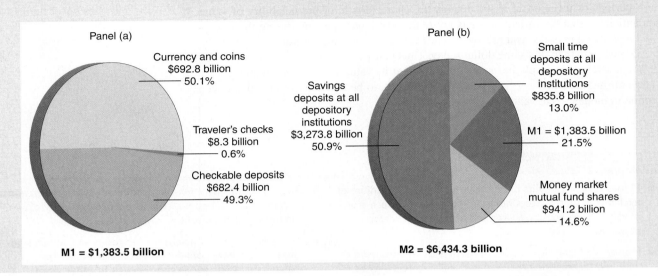

Panel (a)
Currency and coins
$692.8 billion
50.1%
Traveler's checks
$8.3 billion
0.6%
Checkable deposits
$682.4 billion
49.3%
M1 = $1,383.5 billion

Panel (b)
Small time deposits at all depository institutions
$835.8 billion
13.0%
Savings deposits at all depository institutions
$3,273.8 billion
50.9%
M1 = $1,383.5 billion
21.5%
Money market mutual fund shares
$941.2 billion
14.6%
M2 = $6,434.3 billion

The typical resident of another nation uses currency denominated in local money terms, but in many countries the U.S. dollar is the preferred currency for many transactions. For this reason, the bulk of U.S. currency "in circulation" actually does not circulate within the borders of the United States. Figure 15-3 displays the estimated value of U.S. currency in circulation elsewhere in the world. In any given year, at least two-thirds of the U.S. currency in existence circulates outside the United States!

The United States is one of only a few nations that continues to issue a very small-denomination unit of currency—the dollar—in paper form. The norm in most other nations is to issue small denominations as coins instead of paper currency. For instance, when new European euro notes went into circulation in 2002, the smallest-denomination paper currency note was 5 euros, which was then worth roughly $5. The reason that most countries issue small currency denominations in the form of coins is that in the long run, coins are less costly than paper money to keep in circulation. A normal dollar bill wears out in about 18 months, but a typical coin lasts about 30 years. So, even though a dollar coin costs about 12 cents to produce, or more than three times the cost of producing a dollar bill, maintaining dollar coins in circulation over many years would be much less costly. Nevertheless, so far U.S. efforts to introduce dollar coins have not succeeded.

Checkable Deposits. Individuals conduct most of their larger transactions with checks and debit cards. The convenience and safety of using checks and debit cards have made checkable deposit accounts the most important component of the money supply. Checking and debit transactions are a means of transferring the ownership of deposits in financial institutions. Hence, checking deposits are normally acceptable as a medium of exchange. The financial institutions that offer checkable deposits are numerous and include commercial banks and virtually all **thrift institutions**—savings banks, savings and loan associations (S&Ls), and credit unions.

Thrift institutions
Financial institutions that receive most of their funds from the savings of the public; they include mutual savings banks, savings and loan associations, and credit unions.

FIGURE 15-3
The Value of U.S. Currency in Circulation Outside the United States
The amount of U.S. dollars circulating beyond U.S. borders has grown steadily in recent years.

Sources: Board of Governors of the Federal Reserve System and author's estimates.

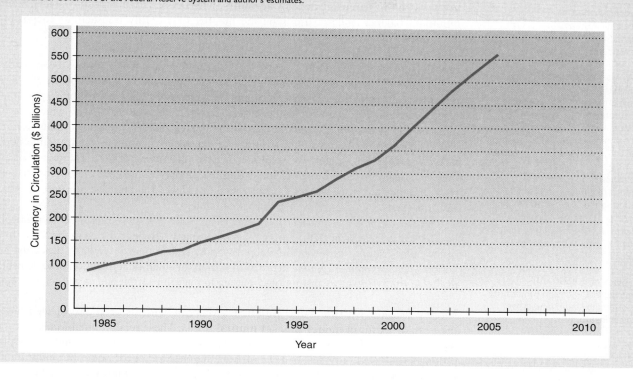

Traveler's Checks. Traveler's checks are paid for by the purchaser at the time of transfer. The total quantity of traveler's checks outstanding issued by institutions other than banks is part of the M1 money supply.* American Express, Citibank, Cook's, and other institutions issue traveler's checks.

The Liquidity Approach to Measuring Money: M2

The liquidity approach to defining and measuring the U.S. money supply involves taking into account not only the most liquid assets that people use as money, which are already included in the definition of M1, but also other assets that are highly liquid—that is, that can be converted into money quickly without loss of nominal dollar value and without much cost. Any (non-M1) assets that come under this definition have been called **near moneys.** Thus the liquidity approach to the definition of the money supply views money as a temporary store of value and so includes all of M1 *plus* all near moneys. Panel (b) of Figure 15-2 on the previous page shows the components of **M2**—money as a temporary store of value. We examine each of these components in turn.

Traveler's checks
Financial instruments purchased from a bank or a nonbanking organization and signed during purchase that can be used as cash upon a second signature by the purchaser.

Near moneys
Assets that are almost money. They have a high degree of liquidity and thus can be easily converted into money without loss in value. Time deposits and short-term U.S. government securities are examples.

M2
M1 plus (1) savings and small-denomination time deposits at all depository institutions, (2) balances in retail money market mutual funds, and (3) money market deposit accounts (MMDAs).

*Banks place the funds that are to be used to redeem traveler's checks in a special deposit account, and they are therefore already counted as checkable accounts. Nonbank issuers, however, do not place these funds in checkable accounts. Improvements in data collection have made it possible to estimate the total amount of nonbank traveler's checks, and since June 1981 they have been included in M1.

Savings Deposits. Total **savings deposits** in all **depository institutions** (such as commercial banks, savings banks, savings and loan associations, and credit unions) are part of the M2 money supply. A savings deposit has no set maturity.

Since 1982, banks and thrift institutions have offered a popular form of savings deposit known as **money market deposit accounts (MMDAs).** These deposits usually require a minimum balance and set limits on the number of monthly transactions (deposits and withdrawals by check).

Small-Denomination Time Deposits. A basic distinction has always been made between a checkable deposit, which is a checking account, and a **time deposit,** which theoretically requires notice of withdrawal and on which the financial institution pays the depositor interest. The name indicates that there is an agreed period during which the funds must be left in the financial institution. If the deposit holder withdraws funds before the end of that period, the institution issuing the deposit may apply a penalty. Time deposits include savings certificates and small **certificates of deposit (CDs).** The owner of a savings certificate is given a receipt indicating the amount deposited, the interest rate to be paid, and the maturity date. A CD is an actual certificate that indicates the date of issue, its maturity date, and other relevant contractual matters.

The distinction between checkable deposits and time deposits has blurred over time, but it is still used in the official definition of the money supply. To be included in the M2 definition of the money supply, however, time deposits must be less than $100,000—hence the designation *small-denomination time deposits.* A variety of small-denomination time deposits are available from depository institutions, ranging in maturities from one month to 10 years.

Money Market Mutual Fund Balances. Many individuals keep part of their assets in the form of shares in **money market mutual funds.** These retail mutual funds invest only in short-term credit instruments. The majority of these money market funds allow check-writing privileges, provided that the size of the check exceeds some minimum amount, usually $100. All money market mutual fund balances except those held by large institutions (which typically use them more like large time deposits) are included in M2.

M2 and Other Money Supply Definitions. When all of these assets are added together, the result is M2. The composition of M2 is given in panel (b) of Figure 15-2 (p. 342).

Economists and researchers have come up with additional definitions of money. Some are simply broader than M2.* Assets are added to or subtracted from the definition. Just remember that there is no best definition of the money supply. For different purposes and under varying institutional circumstances, different definitions are appropriate. The definition that seems to correlate best with economic activity on an economywide basis for most countries is probably M2 although some businesspeople and policymakers prefer a monetary aggregate known as *MZM.* The MZM aggregate is the so-called money-at-zero-maturity money stock. Obtaining MZM entails adding to M1 the same deposits without set maturities, such as savings deposits, that are included in M2. MZM includes *all* money market funds, however, and it excludes all deposits with fixed maturities, such as small-denomination time deposits.

---

*They include M3, which is equal to M2 plus large-denomination time deposits and repurchase agreements, which are agreements to sell securities for repurchase at a later date issued by commercial banks and thrift institutions; Eurodollars (dollar-denominated deposits) held by U.S. residents and foreign branches of U.S. banks worldwide and all banking offices in the United Kingdom and Canada; and balances in both taxable and tax-exempt institution-only money market mutual funds. An even broader definition is called L, for *liquidity.* It is defined as M3 plus nonbank public holdings of U.S. savings bonds, Treasury bills, and other short-term securities.

CONCEPTS in Brief

- The money supply can be defined in a variety of ways, depending on whether we use the transactions approach or the liquidity approach. Using the transactions approach, the money supply consists of currency, checkable deposits, and traveler's checks. This is called M1.

- Checkable deposits (transactions accounts) are any deposits in financial institutions on which the deposit owner can write checks.

- When we add savings deposits, small-denomination time deposits (certificates of deposit), money market deposit accounts, and retail money market mutual fund balances to M1, we obtain the measure known as M2.

To test your understanding of the concepts covered in this section, go to the Online Review at www.myeconlab.com/miller.

FINANCIAL INTERMEDIATION AND BANKS

Most nations, including the United States, have a banking system that encompasses two types of institutions. One type consists of private banking institutions. These include commercial banks, which are privately owned profit-seeking institutions, and thrift institutions, such as savings banks, savings and loan associations, and credit unions. Thrift institutions may be profit-seeking institutions, or they may be *mutual* institutions that are owned by their depositors. The other type of institution is a **central bank,** which typically serves as a banker's bank and as a bank for the national treasury or finance ministry.

Central bank
A banker's bank, usually an official institution that also serves as a country's treasury's bank. Central banks normally regulate commercial banks.

Direct versus Indirect Financing

When individuals choose to hold some of their savings in new bonds issued by a corporation, their purchases of the bonds are in effect direct loans to the business. This is an example of *direct finance,* in which people lend funds directly to a business. Business financing is not always direct. Individuals might choose instead to hold a time deposit at a bank. The bank may then lend to the same company. In this way, the same people can provide *indirect finance* to a business. The bank makes this possible by *intermediating* the financing of the company.

Financial Intermediation

Banks and other financial institutions are all in the same business—transferring funds from savers to investors. This process is known as **financial intermediation,** and its participants, such as banks and savings institutions, are **financial intermediaries.** The process of financial intermediation is illustrated in Figure 15-4 on the next page.

Asymmetric Information, Adverse Selection, and Moral Hazard. Why might people wish to direct their funds through a bank instead of lending them directly to a business? One important reason is **asymmetric information**—the fact that the business may have better knowledge of its own current and future prospects than potential lenders do. For instance, the business may know that it intends to use borrowed funds for projects with a high risk of failure that would make repaying the loan difficult. This potential for borrowers to use the borrowed funds in unworthy projects is known as **adverse selection.** Alternatively, a business that had intended to undertake low-risk projects may change manage-

Financial intermediation
The process by which financial institutions accept savings from businesses, households, and governments and lend the savings to other businesses, households, and governments.

Financial intermediaries
Institutions that transfer funds between ultimate lenders (savers) and ultimate borrowers.

Asymmetric information
Information possessed by one party in a financial transaction but not by the other party.

Adverse selection
The likelihood that individuals who seek to borrow money may use the funds that they receive for unworthy, high-risk projects.

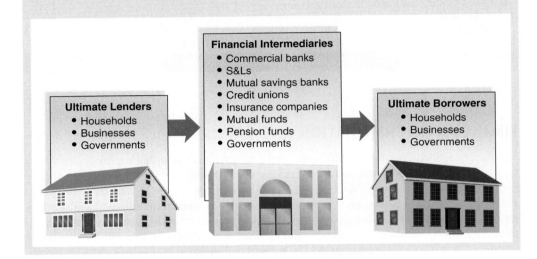

FIGURE 15-4
The Process of Financial Intermediation
The process of financial intermediation is depicted here. Note that ultimate lenders and ultimate borrowers are the same economic units—households, businesses, and governments—but not necessarily the same individuals. Whereas individual households can be net lenders or borrowers, households as an economic unit are net lenders. Specific businesses or governments similarly can be net lenders or borrowers; as economic units, both are net borrowers.

Ultimate Lenders
• Households
• Businesses
• Governments

Financial Intermediaries
• Commercial banks
• S&Ls
• Mutual savings banks
• Credit unions
• Insurance companies
• Mutual funds
• Pension funds
• Governments

Ultimate Borrowers
• Households
• Businesses
• Governments

ment after receiving a loan, and the new managers may use the borrowed funds in riskier ways. The possibility that a borrower might engage in behavior that increases risk after borrowing funds is called **moral hazard.**

Moral hazard
The possibility that a borrower might engage in riskier behavior after a loan has been obtained.

To minimize the possibility that a business might fail to repay a loan, people thinking about lending funds directly to the business must study the business carefully before making the loan, and they must continue to monitor its performance afterward. Alternatively, they can choose to avoid the trouble by holding deposits with financial intermediaries, which then specialize in evaluating the creditworthiness of business borrowers and in keeping tabs on their progress until loans are repaid. Thus adverse selection and moral hazard both help explain why people use financial intermediaries.

Larger Scale and Lower Management Costs. Another important reason that financial intermediaries exist is that they make it possible for many people to pool their funds, thereby increasing the size, or *scale,* of the total amount of savings managed by an intermediary. This centralization of management reduces costs and risks below the levels savers would incur if all were to manage their savings alone. *Pension fund companies,* which are institutions that specialize in managing funds that individuals save for retirement, owe their existence largely to their abilities to provide such cost savings to individual savers. Likewise, *investment companies,* which are institutions that manage portfolios of financial instruments called mutual funds on behalf of shareholders, also exist largely because of cost savings from their greater scale of operations.

How do you suppose that highly creditworthy, multinational companies are often able to borrow billions of dollars more than any single financial intermediary is willing to lend?

Economics Front and Center

To think about how some companies avoid using the intermediation services of insurance companies, consider the case study, **Insurers Face Facts as Customers Self-Insure More of Their Risks**, on page 356.

E X A M P L E

To Coordinate Syndicated Loans, Banks Need Not Apply

It is not unusual for very large, multinational companies to wish to borrow tens of billions of dollars to finance individual projects. No single bank has the resources to lend such an amount all at once. Consequently, it is common for groups of banks known as "syndicates" to provide the funds jointly. Nevertheless, someone must take responsibility for coordinating these so-called *syndicated loans.*

Traditionally, a company wishing to arrange a syndicate loan has paid a lead bank to round up other banks to join a syndicate and to coordinate the lending arrangements. As a charge for providing these services, the lead bank assesses the borrowing company a slightly higher loan interest rate and various fees. The lead bank also profits from charging other banks joining the syndicate a fee of 0.1 to 0.2 percent of the total value of the loan.

Since the early 2000s, however, a growing number of large companies have been organizing syndicated loans on their own, thereby avoiding paying millions of dollars in additional interest and fees. In 2000, such self-organized syndicated loans accounted for fewer than 5 percent of worldwide syndicated lending. Today, nearly 30 percent of all syndicated loans are arranged by the borrower instead of a lead bank.

For Critical Analysis
In what way have borrowers that self-arrange syndicated loans engaged in financial dis*intermediation?*

Financial Institution Liabilities and Assets. Every financial intermediary has its own sources of funds, which are **liabilities** of that institution. When you deposit $100 in your checking account in a bank, the bank creates a liability—it owes you $100—in exchange for the funds deposited. A commercial bank gets its funds from checking and savings accounts; an insurance company gets its funds from insurance policy premiums.

Each financial intermediary has a different primary use of its **assets.** For example, a credit union usually makes small consumer loans, whereas a savings bank makes mainly mortgage loans. Table 15-2 on the following page lists the assets and liabilities of typical financial intermediaries. Be aware, though, that the distinctions between different types of financial institutions are becoming more and more blurred. As laws and regulations change, there will be less need to make any distinction. All may ultimately be treated simply as financial intermediaries.

Liabilities
Amounts owed; the legal claims against a business or household by nonowners.

Assets
Amounts owned; all items to which a business or household holds legal claim.

Financial Intermediation Across National Boundaries

Some countries' governments restrict the financial intermediation process to within their national boundaries. They do so by imposing legal restraints called **capital controls** that bar certain flows of funds across their borders. Nevertheless, today many nations have reduced or even eliminated capital controls. This permits their residents to strive for **international financial diversification** by engaging in the direct or indirect financing of companies located in various nations.

Because business conditions may be good in one country, as they were in the United States in the mid-2000s, at the same time that they are poor in another, such as Germany during the mid-2000s, people can limit their overall lending risks through international financial diversification. One way to do this is to hold a portion of one's savings with an investment company that offers a **world index fund.** This is a carefully designed set of globally issued bonds yielding returns that historically tend to move in offsetting directions. By holding world index funds, individuals can earn the average return on bonds from a number of nations while keeping overall risk of loss to a minimum.

Capital controls
Legal restrictions on the ability of a nation's residents to hold and trade assets denominated in foreign currencies.

International financial diversification
Financing investment projects in more than one country.

World index fund
A portfolio of bonds issued in various nations whose individual yields generally move in offsetting directions, thereby reducing the overall risk of losses.

TABLE 15-2
Financial Intermediaries and Their Assets and Liabilities

Financial Intermediary	Assets	Liabilities
Commercial banks	Car loans and other consumer debt, business loans, government securities, home mortgages	Checkable deposits, savings deposits, various other time deposits, money market deposit accounts
Savings and loan associations and savings banks	Home mortgages, some consumer and business debt	Savings and loan shares, checkable deposits, various time deposits, money market deposit accounts
Credit unions	Consumer debt, long-term mortgage loans	Credit union shares, checkable deposits
Insurance companies	Mortgages, stocks, bonds, real estate	Insurance contracts, annuities, pension plans
Pension and retirement funds	Stocks, bonds, mortgages, time deposits	Pension plans
Money market mutual funds	Short-term credit instruments such as large-bank CDs, Treasury bills, and high-grade commercial paper	Fund shares with limited checking privileges

Holding shares in a world index fund is an example of indirect finance across national borders through financial intermediaries. Banks located in various countries take part in the process of international financial intermediation by using some of the funds of depositors in their home nations to finance loans to companies based in other nations. Today, bank financing of U.S. business activities increasingly stems from loans by non-U.S. banks.

Indeed, as Table 15-3 indicates, the world's largest banks are not based in the United States. Today, most of the largest banking institutions, sometimes called *megabanks,* are based in Europe and Japan. These megabanks typically take in deposits and lend throughout the world. Although they report their profits and pay taxes in their home nations, these megabanks are in all other ways international banking institutions.

BANKING STRUCTURES THROUGHOUT THE WORLD

Multinational businesses have relationships with megabanks based in many nations. Individuals and companies increasingly retain the services of banks based outside their home countries. The business of banking varies from nation to nation, however. Each country has its own distinctive banking history, and this fact helps explain unique features of the world's banking systems. Countries' banking systems differ in a number of ways. In some nations, banks are the crucial component of the financial intermediation process, but in others, banking is only part of a varied financial system. In addition, some countries have only a few large banks, while others, such as the United States, have relatively large num-

Bank	Country	Assets ($ billions)
Mizuho Financial Group	Japan	1,285
Citigroup	United States	1,264
UBS AG	Switzerland	1,121
Credit Agricole Groupe	France	1,105
HSBC Holdings	United Kingdom	1,034
Deutsche Bank	Germany	1,015
BNP Paribas	France	989
Mitsubishi Tokyo Financial Group	Japan	975
Sumitomo Mitsui Financial Group	Japan	950
Royal Bank of Scotland	United Kingdom	806

Source: *The Banker,* July, 2004.

TABLE 15-3
The World's Largest Banks
Historically, there usually are few U.S. banks among the world's top 10.

bers of banks of various sizes. The legal environments regulating bank dealings with individual and business customers also differ considerably across nations.

A World of National Banking Structures

The extent to which banks are the predominant means by which businesses finance their operations is a key way that national banking systems differ. For instance, in Britain, nearly 70 percent of funds raised by businesses typically stem from bank borrowings, and the proportions for Germany and Japan are on the order of 50 percent and 65 percent, respectively. By contrast, U.S. businesses normally raise less than 30 percent of their funds through bank loans.

The relative sizes of banks also differ from one country to another. The five largest banks in Belgium, Denmark, France, Italy, Luxembourg, Portugal, Spain, and the United Kingdom have over 30 percent of the deposits of their nations' residents. In Greece and the Netherlands, this figure is over 80 percent. In contrast, the top five U.S. banks account for less than 25 percent of the deposit holdings of U.S. residents. In Germany, Japan, and Britain, about two-thirds of total bank assets are held by the largest 10 banks. In the United States, this figure is less than one-third.

Traditionally, another feature that has distinguished national banking systems has been the extent to which they have permitted **universal banking.** Under this form of banking, there are few, if any, limits on the ability of banks to offer a full range of financial services and to own shares of corporate stock. In Germany, Britain, and other European nations, banks have had the right to sell insurance and to own stock for many years. Japanese banks face greater restrictions on their activities than European banks, but many Japanese banks have long had the authority to buy stocks. Until very recently, U.S. banks could not hold *any* shares of stock, even for brief periods, and were subject to limitations on their ability to offer insurance policies to their customers. This state of affairs changed, however, with passage of the Gramm-Leach-Bliley Act of 1999. This legislation authorized U.S. commercial banks to market insurance and to own stock. Consequently, national differences in banking powers are much narrower than they were just a few years ago.

How do you suppose that European banks are continuing to earn high fees from sending funds from one nation to another, even though European governments commonly claim that banking is now "borderless" within the European Union?

To learn more from the Bank for International Settlements about worldwide banking developments, go to www.econtoday.com/chap15. Select "BIS Annual Report."

Universal banking
An environment in which banks face few or no restrictions on their powers to offer a full range of financial services and to own shares of stock in corporations.

International EXAMPLE

European Union Banks Continue to Earn High Fees from Cross-Border Payments

When the European Union (EU), which now consists of 25 nations, was first established in 1990, one goal was to create a "single banking market," in which banks in all the EU member nations would operate as if no national borders existed. In January 2004, this goal finally became a reality, at least on paper. At that time, a new EU regulation went into effect requiring all EU banks to charge the same amount to process cross-border payments as they charge for funds transfers within their home countries.

There was a catch, however. Only someone making a "qualifying" cross-border payment can obtain service from a bank on the same terms as those requesting domestic funds transfers. To "qualify," the individual or firm requesting the cross-border payment must provide the bank with a number of precise details, including, among other things, the bank identification number and international bank identification code of the European bank that will receive the cross-border

payment. EU banks themselves have ready access to such information, but most require the customer to provide it before a cross-border payment will qualify for equal treatment with domestic funds transfers.

So far, only about 1 percent of customers who have requested cross-border payments have provided banks with sufficient information to meet these requirements. Thus European banks have been able to continue charging their customers fees as high as 17 percent of each payment amount to transfer funds to banks located in other EU nations.

For Critical Analysis
Why do you suppose that 99 percent of European residents who request cross-border payments to other EU banks have been willing to pay significant fees rather than collecting sufficient information to avoid the fees?

CONCEPTS in Brief

- Financial intermediaries transfer funds from ultimate lenders (savers) to ultimate borrowers. This process of financial intermediation is undertaken by depository institutions such as commercial banks, savings and loan associations, savings banks, and credit unions, as well as by insurance companies, mutual funds, pension funds, and governments.

- Financial intermediaries specialize in tackling problems of asymmetric information. They address the adverse selection problem by carefully reviewing the creditworthiness of loan applicants, and they deal with the moral hazard prob-

lem by monitoring borrowers after they receive loans. Many financial intermediaries also take advantage of cost reductions arising from the centralized management of funds pooled from the savings of many individuals.

- In the absence of capital controls that inhibit flows of funds across national borders, many financial intermediaries also take advantage of overall risk reductions made possible by international financial diversification. This has led to the development of megabanks, which operate in many countries.

To test your understanding of the concepts covered in this section, go to the Online Review at www.myeconlab.com/miller.

Central Banks and Their Roles

The first central bank, which began operations in 1668, was Sweden's Sveriges Riksbank (called the Risens Standers Bank until 1867). In 1694, the English Parliament established the most historically famous of central banks, the Bank of England. It authorized the Bank of England to issue currency notes redeemable in silver, and initially the Bank of England's notes circulated alongside currency notes issued by the government and private finance companies. Until 1800, the Riksbank and the Bank of England were the only central banks. The number of central banks worldwide was less than 10 as late as 1873. The number expanded considerably toward the end of the nineteenth century and again during the second half of the twentieth century, as shown in Figure 15-5.

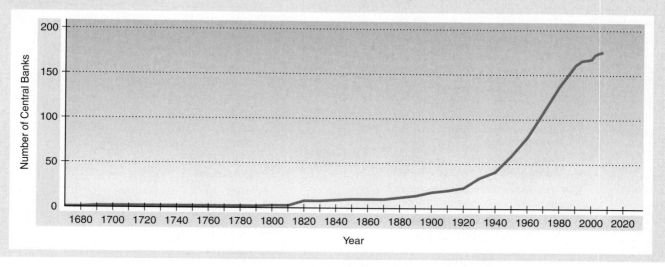

FIGURE 15-5
The Number of Central Banking Institutions, 1670 to the Present
The twentieth century witnessed considerable growth in the number of central banks.

Sources: Data from Forrest Capie, Charles Goodhart, and Norbert Schnadt, "The Development of Central Banking," in Forrest Capie et al., *The Future of Central Banking: The Tercentenary Symposium of the Bank of England* (Cambridge: Cambridge University Press, 1994), and author's estimates.

The duties of central banks fall into three broad categories:

1. They perform banking functions for their nations' governments.
2. They provide financial services for private banks.
3. They conduct their nations' monetary policies.

The third is the area of central banking that receives the most media attention, even though most central banks devote the bulk of their resources to the other two tasks.

THE FEDERAL RESERVE SYSTEM

The Federal Reserve System, also known simply as **the Fed,** is the most important regulatory agency in the United States' monetary system and is usually considered the monetary authority. The Fed was established by the Federal Reserve Act, signed on December 13, 1913, by President Woodrow Wilson. The act was the outgrowth of recommendations from the National Monetary Commission, which had been authorized by the Aldridge-Vreeland Act of 1908. Basically, the commission had attempted to find a way to counter the periodic financial panics that had occurred in our country. Based on the commission's recommendations, which were developed after considerable study of the Bank of England and other central banks, Congress established the Federal Reserve System to aid and supervise banks and also to provide banking services for the U.S. Treasury.

The Fed
The Federal Reserve System; the central bank of the United States.

Organization of the Federal Reserve System

Figure 15-6 on the following page shows how the Federal Reserve System is organized. It is managed by the Board of Governors, composed of seven full-time members appointed by the U.S. president with the approval of the Senate. The 12 Federal Reserve district banks have a total of 25 branches. The boundaries of the 12 Federal Reserve districts and

FIGURE 15-6
Organization of the Federal Reserve System

The 12 Federal Reserve district banks are headed by 12 separate presidents. The main authority of the Fed resides with the Board of Governors of the Federal Reserve System, whose seven members are appointed for 14-year terms by the president of the United States and confirmed by the Senate. Open market operations are carried out through the Federal Open Market Committee (FOMC), consisting of the seven members of the Board of Governors plus five presidents of the district banks (always including the president of the New York bank, with the others rotating).

Source: Board of Governors of the Federal Reserve System, *The Federal Reserve System: Purposes and Functions*, 7th ed. (Washington, D.C., 1984), p. 5.

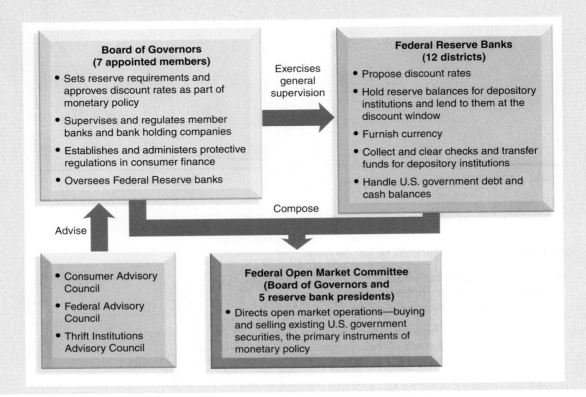

the cities in which Federal Reserve banks are located are shown in Figure 15-7. The Federal Open Market Committee (FOMC) determines the future growth of the money supply and other important variables. This committee is composed of the members of the Board of Governors, the president of the New York Federal Reserve Bank, and presidents of four other Federal Reserve banks, rotated periodically.

Depository Institutions

Depository institutions—all financial institutions that accept deposits—that comprise our monetary system consist of about 8,000 commercial banks, 1,500 savings and loan associations and savings banks, and 12,000 credit unions. All depository institutions may purchase services from the Federal Reserve System on an equal basis. Also, almost all depository institutions are required to keep a certain percentage of their deposits in reserve at the Federal Reserve district banks or as vault cash. This percentage depends on the bank's volume of business. (For further discussion, see Chapter 16.)

FIGURE 15-7
The Federal Reserve System
The Federal Reserve System is divided into 12 districts, each served by one of the Federal Reserve district banks, located in the cities indicated. The Board of Governors meets in Washington, D.C.

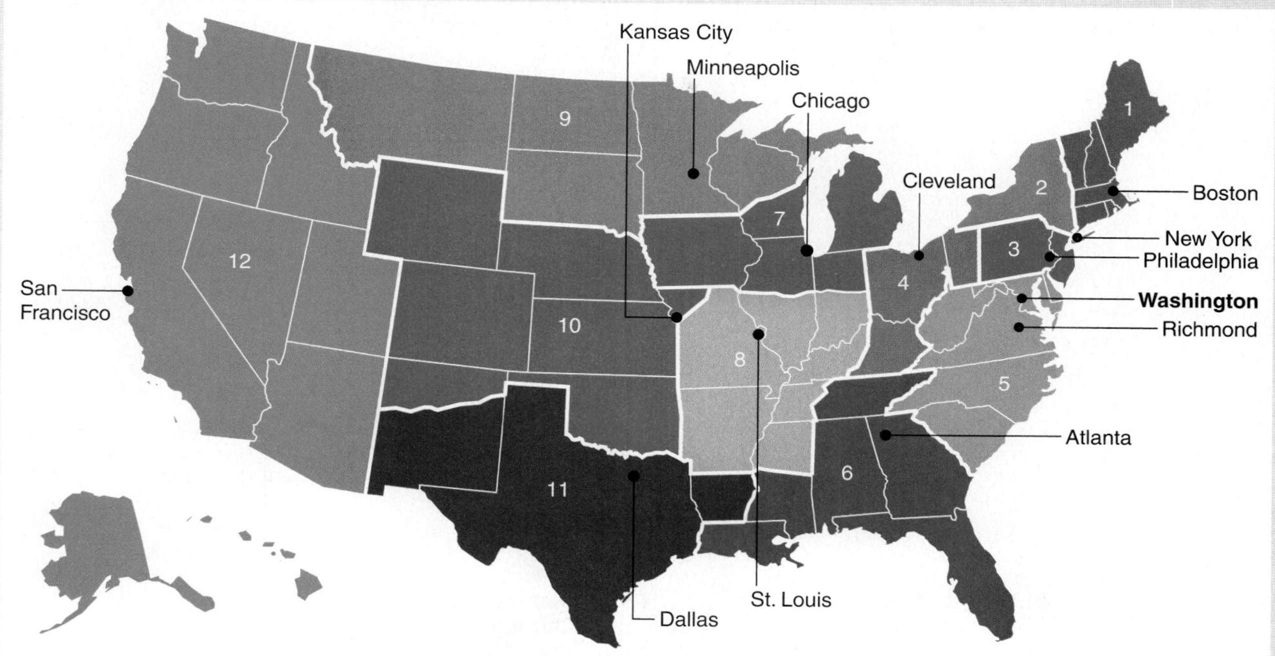

Functions of the Federal Reserve System

Here we will present in detail what the Federal Reserve does.

1. *The Fed supplies the economy with fiduciary currency.* The Federal Reserve banks supply the economy with paper currency called Federal Reserve notes. For example, during holiday seasons, when very large numbers of currency transactions take place, more paper currency is desired. Commercial banks respond to the increased number and dollar amounts of depositors' currency withdrawals by turning to the Federal Reserve banks to replenish vault cash. Hence the Federal Reserve banks must have on hand a sufficient amount of cash to accommodate the demands for paper currency at different times of the year. Note that even though all Federal Reserve notes are printed at the Bureau of Printing and Engraving in Washington, D.C., each note is assigned a code indicating from which of the 12 Federal Reserve banks it "originated." Moreover, each of these notes is an obligation (liability) of the Federal Reserve System, *not* the U.S. Treasury.

2. *The Fed provides a system for check collection and clearing.* The Federal Reserve System has established a clearing mechanism for checks. Suppose that John Smith in Chicago writes a check to Jill Jones, who lives in San Francisco. When Jill receives the check in the mail, she deposits it at her commercial bank. Her bank then deposits the check in the Federal Reserve Bank of San Francisco. In

FIGURE 15-8
How a Check Clears

The check-clearing process for an out-of-town check normally involves four steps, including two with Federal Reserve district banks.

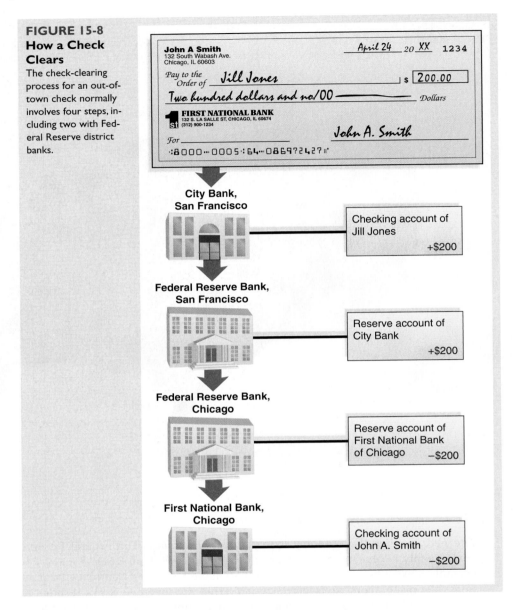

turn, the Federal Reserve Bank of San Francisco sends the check to the Federal Reserve Bank of Chicago. The Chicago Fed then sends the check to John Smith's commercial bank, where the amount of the check is deducted from John's account. The schematic diagram in Figure 15-8 illustrates this check-clearing process.

The Fed's check collection and clearing operations compete with private clearinghouses. Since the Fed began charging for these services, a considerable volume of this business has shifted back to the private sector. At present, the Federal Reserve processes about one-third of all checks in the United States.

Why do you think that the Federal Reserve has been promoting replacing physical check transfers with Internet-based "check image transmission"?

E-Commerce EXAMPLE

Check Out *Check 21* for Twenty-First-Century Check Clearing

During the 1990s, the Federal Reserve decided to transfer most of its check-clearing operations to the Federal Reserve Bank of Atlanta. Since then, the Fed's fleet of Lear jets has been flying boxes of checks from the cities of the various Fed district banks to one of the world's busiest airports. There, the boxes of checks are loaded onto trucks and driven through some of the busiest city traffic in the nation to a downtown sorting facility. After the checks are sorted and reboxed, they are driven back through traffic to the Atlanta airport to be flown to their final destinations for clearing.

Since early 2004, the volume of checks physically circulating through Atlanta has begun to decline. At the same time, the average speed of Fed check clearing has been rising. As authorized by the Check Clearing for the Twenty-First Century ("Check 21") Act of 2003, both the Fed and private check-clearing services

have been using the Internet to clear a steadily increasing volume of checks. Employees of Fed district banks use special machines that conduct high-speed scans to create digital images of checks. Then they transmit these images to other Fed district banks and depository institutions via the Web. The physical checks cleared in this manner require no further transportation beyond the warehouses where they are stored before being destroyed.

For Critical Analysis
How is the speedier check clearing made possible by the Check 21 Act likely to affect the willingness of individuals and firms to continue writing checks, rather than switching to debit cards and other alternative means of payment?

3. ***The Fed holds depository institutions' reserves.*** The 12 Federal Reserve district banks hold the reserves (other than vault cash) of depository institutions. As you will see in Chapter 16, depository institutions are required by law to keep a certain percentage of their deposits as reserves. Even if they weren't required to do so by law, they would still wish to keep some reserves. Depository institutions act just like other businesses. A firm would not try to operate with a zero balance in its checking account. It would keep a positive balance on hand from which it could draw for expected and unexpected transactions. So, too, a depository institution desires to have reserves in its banker's bank (the Federal Reserve) on which it can draw funds as needed for expected and unexpected transactions.

4. ***The Fed acts as the government's fiscal agent.*** The Federal Reserve is the banker and fiscal agent for the federal government. The government, as we are all aware, collects large sums of funds through taxation. The government also spends and distributes equally large sums. Consequently, the U.S. Treasury has a checking account with the Federal Reserve. Thus the Fed acts as the government's banker, along with commercial banks that hold government deposits. The Fed also helps the government collect certain tax revenues and aids in the purchase and sale of government securities.

5. ***The Fed supervises depository institutions.*** The Fed (along with the comptroller of the currency, the Federal Deposit Insurance Corporation, the Office of Thrift Supervision in the Treasury Department, and the National Credit Union Administration) is a supervisor and regulator of depository institutions. The Fed and other regulators periodically and without warning examine depository institutions to see what kinds of loans have been made, what has been used as security for the loans, and who has received them. Whenever such an examination indicates that a bank is not conforming to current banking rules and standards, the Fed can exert pressure on the bank to alter its banking practices.

6. ***The Fed acts as the "lender of last resort."*** As a central bank, the Fed stands ready to assist, temporarily, any part of the banking system that is in trouble. In this sense, it acts as a lender of last resort to depository institutions that it has decided should not be allowed to fail.

7. ***The Fed regulates the money supply.*** Perhaps the Fed's most important task is its ability to regulate the nation's money supply. To understand how the Fed manages the money supply, we must examine more closely its reserve-holding function and the way in which depository institutions aid in expansion and contraction of the money supply. We will do this in Chapter 16.

8. ***The Fed intervenes in foreign currency markets.*** Sometimes the Fed attempts to keep the value of the dollar from changing. It does this by buying and selling U.S. dollars in foreign exchange markets. You will read more about this important topic in Chapter 34.

CONCEPTS in Brief

- A central bank is a banker's bank that typically acts as the fiscal agent for its nation's government as well. The central bank in the United States is the Federal Reserve System, which was established on December 13, 1913.

- There are 12 Federal Reserve district banks, with 25 branches. The Federal Reserve is managed by the Board of Governors in Washington, D.C. The Fed interacts with virtually all depository institutions in the United States, most of which must keep a certain percentage of deposits on reserve with the Fed. The Fed serves as the chief regulatory agency for all depository institutions that have Federal Reserve System membership.

- The functions of the Federal Reserve System are to supply fiduciary currency, provide for check collection and clearing, hold depository institution reserves, act as the government's fiscal agent, supervise depository institutions, act as the lender of last resort, regulate the supply of money, and intervene in foreign currency markets.

To test your understanding of the concepts covered in this section, go to the Online Review at www.myeconlab.com/miller.

CASE STUDY: Economics Front and Center

Insurers Face Facts as Customers Self-Insure More of Their Risks

Hartwell, a young employee at American Risk Assurance Company, has been asked to serve on a task force that is considering a major challenge faced by the insurer. Several of the company's large customers are developing ways to "manage" their risks instead of insuring them. Applying portfolio-management techniques and using sophisticated financial contracts, an increasing number of companies have begun regarding their risks of potentially insurable losses as a "risk portfolio." For example, one former American Risk Assurance client developed an internal computer model for examining different types of risk. Managers use this model to determine what portion of the firm's potential losses should be absorbed by shareholders and what portion should be transferred to insurers. After implementing its new approach to risk management, the former client decided to terminate its policy with American Risk Assurance.

Other companies have adopted similar systems. As a consequence, American Risk Assurance has been losing numerous corporate customers. Hartwell listens as one member of the task force points out that some insurance companies have responded to this trend by offering "portfolio insurance." Instead of insuring individual risks, such as the risk of fire or fraud, these insurers now insure the net risk of a *basket* of exposures that companies confront. Another member suggests that American Risk Assurance might market its insurance expertise to customers that implement self-insurance programs. The company could, this committee member argues, earn steady fee income by coordinating companies' efforts, which it could do at relatively low cost if it is able to develop a large pool of self-insuring clients. Hartwell contemplates which of these two suggestions might prove more advantageous for the company.

Points to Analyze

1. *Which of the factors accounting for financial intermediation do you think best explain the existence of insurance companies such as American Risk Assurance?*

2. *Which of the two proposals that Hartwell has heard relies in part on the idea that American Risk Assurance might benefit from providing financial services on a large scale?*

Issues and Applications

Determining How Many Coins to Circulate

A s the U.S. monetary authority, the Federal Reserve's main job is to control the overall money supply. As a central bank, however, the Fed also has the job of distributing currency, which it obtains from the U.S. Bureau of Engraving and Printing, and coins, which it obtains from the U.S. Mint.

The Federal Reserve distributes coins through 37 distribution offices, including coin offices located at the 12 Federal Reserve banks and their branches, and more than 100 additional coin terminals operated by armored carriers such as Brinks and Loomis-Fargo. The Federal Reserve pays these private armored carriers to transport coins to and from financial institutions, including commercial banks, savings institutions, and credit unions.

Concepts Applied
- Money Supply
- Currency
- Coins

Determining the Amount of Coins to Circulate

The U.S. Mint produces coins according to orders from the Federal Reserve System and sells them to the Fed at their face value. The coins typically cost much less than their face value to produce, so the Mint earns profits from coin production that it turns over to the U.S. Treasury.

To determine how many coins to order from the Mint, the Federal Reserve must forecast how many coins banks will request in order to satisfy anticipated coin demands of their customers. Thus the actual quantity of coins demanded depends on how many coins people and businesses desire to hold in relation to paper currency and deposit account balances at banks and other depository institutions.

Adjusting to the Public's Desired Coin Holdings

The public's demand for coins as a part of their total money holdings exhibits considerable seasonal fluctuations. People typically use more coins in the summer months for parking meters at the beach and for use in soft-drink machines. They also use more coins around the holidays at the end of the year, even though the demand for coins otherwise is much lower during winter months.

The Fed has learned to anticipate seasonal fluctuations in the public's desired coin holdings. It has also adjusted to a slight downward trend in the use of the penny that has been accompanied by upward trends in holdings of nickels, dimes, and quarters.

What Happens When the Fed Gets It Wrong?

Every once in a while, however, events take place that can considerably complicate the Fed's task of supplying the quantity of coins the public wishes to hold. One of these events was a law passed by Congress requiring the Mint to produce commemorative quarters honoring individual U.S. states. Beginning in 1999, these quarters are being distributed in the same chronological sequence as the states entered the Union. The Fed failed to realize how many children would begin collecting these quarters on poster board maps of the United States. Instead, it continued distributing quarters based on its usual assumptions about coin demand.

In 2000, banks in certain parts of the country began reporting shortages of quarters. The Fed hurriedly transmitted orders for more quarters to the Mint, which worked overtime to produce additional quarters that were then rushed, at considerable expense to the Fed, to regions experiencing a lack of quarters.

357

For the Federal Reserve, therefore, the overall level of the U.S. money supply is not the only issue of concern. The *composition* of the money supply can also sometimes present a problem that must be addressed by Fed policymakers.

For Critical Analysis

1. If the public's demand for coins were to decline unexpectedly, what could the Fed do to keep the overall money supply from changing?
2. Why do you suppose that the Fed has found that the public's demand for coins does not appear to be affected by the overall state of the economy? (Hint: Do you suppose that coins are used mostly for making purchases or simply for making change?)

Web Resources

1. Learn more about the U.S. Mint by going to its home page via the link at www.econtoday.com/chap15.
2. To learn about the printing of currency in the United States, go to the home page of the Bureau of Engraving and Printing via the link at www.econtoday.com/chap15.

Research Project

The profits that the U.S. Mint earns from selling coins to the Fed at their face value, even though they are much cheaper to manufacture, are part of the government's total profits from producing money, known as *seigniorage* (pronounced "seen-yur-ij"). The U.S. Bureau of Engraving and Printing analogously earns profits from printing currency and selling it to the Fed. The Fed distributes the currency to banks, which then provide currency to depositors when they make cash withdrawals. The Fed pays no interest on currency even though currency is the largest liability on the Fed's balance sheet. In addition, the Fed rarely pays interest on funds that private depository institutions hold on reserve at Federal Reserve banks. Discuss how the Fed earns seigniorage from its activities as a central bank, and speculate about why the U.S. Congress has always raised objections when the Fed has proposed paying banks interest on their reserve deposits at Federal Reserve banks. (Hint: Most of the Fed's assets are U.S. Treasury securities, on which it earns considerable interest income. It keeps some of this income to fund its operations and passes the remainder on to the U.S. Treasury.)

SUMMARY DISCUSSION of Learning Objectives

1. **The Key Functions of Money:** Money has four functions. It is a medium of exchange, which means that people use money to make payments for goods, services, and financial assets. It is also a unit of accounting, meaning that prices are quoted in terms of money values. In addition, money is a store of value, so people can hold money for future use in exchange. Furthermore, money is a standard of deferred payment, enabling lenders to make loans and buyers to repay those loans with money.

2. **Important Properties of Goods That Serve as Money:** A good will successfully function as money only if people are widely willing to accept the good in exchange for other goods and services. People must have confidence that others will be willing to trade their goods and services for the good used as money. In addition, though people may continue to use money even if inflation erodes its real purchasing power, they will do so only if the value of money is relatively predictable.

3. **Official Definitions of the Quantity of Money in Circulation:** The narrow definition of the quantity of money in circulation, called M1, focuses on money's role as a medium of exchange. It includes only currency, checkable deposits, and traveler's checks. A broader definition, called M2, stresses money's role as a temporary store of value. M2 is equal to M1 plus near-money assets such as savings deposits, small-denomination time deposits, money market deposit accounts, and noninstitutional holdings of money market mutual fund balances.

4. **Why Financial Intermediaries Such as Banks Exist:** Financial intermediaries help reduce problems stemming from the existence of asymmetric information in financial transactions. Asymmetric information can lead to adverse selection, in which uncreditworthy individuals and firms seek loans, and moral hazard problems, in which an individual or business that has been granted credit begins to engage in riskier practices. Financial intermedi-

aries may also permit savers to benefit from economies of scale, which is the ability to reduce the costs and risks of managing funds by pooling funds and spreading costs and risks across many savers.

5. **The Basic Structure of the Federal Reserve System:** The central bank of the United States is the Federal Reserve System, which consists of 12 district banks with 25 branches. The governing body of the Federal Reserve System is the Board of Governors, which is based in Washington, D.C. Decisions about the quantity of money in circulation are made by the Federal Open Market Committee, which is composed of the Board of Governors and five Federal Reserve bank presidents.

6. **Major Functions of the Federal Reserve:** The main functions of the Federal Reserve System are supplying the economy with fiduciary currency, providing a system for check collection and clearing, holding depository institutions' reserves, acting as the government's fiscal agent, supervising banks, acting as a lender of last resort, regulating the money supply, and intervening in foreign exchange markets.

KEY TERMS AND CONCEPTS

adverse selection (345)

assets (347)

asymmetric information (345)

barter (338)

capital controls (347)

central bank (345)

certificates of deposit (CDs) (344)

checkable deposits (339)

depository institutions (344)

the Fed (351)

fiduciary monetary system (340)

financial intermediaries (345)

financial intermediation (345)

international financial diversification (347)

liabilities (347)

liquidity (339)

liquidity approach (341)

M1 (341)

M2 (343)

medium of exchange (338)

money (337)

money market deposit accounts (MMDAs) (344)

money market mutual funds (344)

money supply (341)

moral hazard (346)

near moneys (343)

savings deposits (344)

standard of deferred payment (338)

store of value (338)

thrift institutions (342)

time deposit (344)

transactions accounts (339)

transactions approach (341)

traveler's checks (343)

unit of accounting (338)

universal banking (349)

world index fund (347)

PROBLEMS

Answers to the odd-numbered problems appear at the back of the book.

15-1. Until 1946 residents of the island of Yap used large doughnut-shaped stones as financial assets. Although prices of goods and services were not quoted in terms of the stones, the stones were often used in exchange for particularly large purchases, such as payments for livestock. To make the transaction, several individuals would place a large stick through a stone's center and carry it to its new owner. A stone was difficult for any one person to steal, so an owner typically would lean it against the side of his or her home as a sign to others of accumulated purchasing power that would hold value for later use in exchange. Loans would often be repaid using the stones. In what ways did these stones function as money?

15-2. During the late 1970s, prices quoted in terms of the Israeli currency, the shekel, rose so fast that grocery stores listed their prices in terms of the U.S. dollar and provided customers with dollar-shekel conversion tables that they updated daily. Although people continued to buy goods and services and make loans using shekels, many Israeli citizens converted shekels to dollars to avoid a reduction in their wealth due to inflation. In what way did the U.S. dollar function as money in Israel during this period?

15-3. During the 1945–1946 Hungarian hyperinflation, when the rate of inflation reached 41.9 *quadrillion* percent per month, the Hungarian government discovered that the real value of its tax receipts was falling dramatically. To keep real tax revenues more stable, it created a good called a "tax pengö," in which all bank deposits were denominated for purposes of taxation. Nevertheless, payments for goods and services were made only in terms of the regular Hungarian currency, whose value tended to fall rapidly even though the value of a tax pengö remained stable. Prices were also quoted only in terms of the regular currency. Lenders, however, began denominating loan payments in terms of tax pengös. In what ways did the tax pengö function as money in Hungary in 1945 and 1946?

15-4. Considering the following data (expressed in billions of U.S. dollars), calculate M1 and M2.

Currency	650
Savings deposits and money market deposit accounts	3,000
Small-denomination time deposits	1,000
Traveler's checks outside banks and thrifts	10
Total money market mutual funds	1,000
Institution-only money market mutual funds	200
Demand deposits	450
Other checkable deposits	490

15-5. Considering the following data (expressed in billions of U.S. dollars), calculate M1 and M2.

Demand deposits and other checkable deposits	625
Savings deposits	400
Small-denomination time deposits	950
Money market deposit accounts	850
Noninstitution money market mutual funds	400
Traveler's checks outside banks and thrifts	25
Currency	600
Institution-only money market mutual funds	250

15-6. Identify whether each of the following items is counted in M1 only, M2 only, both M1 and M2, or neither:

a. A $1,000 balance in a checking account at a mutual savings bank

b. A $100,000 certificate of deposit issued by a New York bank

c. A $10,000 time deposit an elderly widow holds at her credit union

d. A $50 traveler's check

e. A $50,000 money market deposit account balance

15-7. Identify whether each of the following amounts is counted in M1 only, M2 only, both M1 and M2, or neither:

a. $50 billion in U.S. Treasury bills

b. $15 billion in small-denomination time deposits

c. $5 billion in traveler's checks

d. $20 billion in money market deposit accounts

15-8. Indicate which of the following items are counted in M2 but not in M1.

a. A $20 Federal Reserve note

b. A $500 time deposit

c. A $50 traveler's check

d. A $25,000 money market deposit account

15-9. Match each of the rationales for financial intermediation listed below with one of the following financial intermediaries: insurance company, pension fund, savings bank. Explain your choices.

a. Adverse selection

b. Moral hazard

c. Lower management costs generated by larger scale

15-10. Match each of the rationales for financial intermediation listed below with one of the following financial intermediaries: commercial bank, money market mutual fund, stockbroker. Explain your choices.

a. Adverse selection

b. Moral hazard

c. Lower management costs generated by larger scale

15-11. In the early 1990s, many pension funds and mutual funds began offering U.S. savers special portfolios composed only of financial instruments issued by companies and governments of other nations. In 1997 and 1998, many savers who held these portfolios earned very low returns. By contrast, most people who allocated 100 percent of their savings only to U.S. financial instruments earned higher returns. Does this experience mean that international financial diversification is a mistake? Explain your reasoning.

15-12. A few years ago, a Florida county commissioner and her husband, a Washington lobbyist, were indicted for securities laws violations. Allegedly, they sought to improve the terms under which the county could issue new municipal bonds. Suppose this information had not come to light and had made the municipal bonds more risky than they otherwise might have seemed to potential buyers. Would this have been an example of adverse selection or of moral hazard? Explain your reasoning.

15-13. In what sense is currency a liability of the Federal Reserve System?

15-14. In what respects is the Fed like a private banking institution? In what respects is it more like a government agency?

15-15. Take a look at the map of the locations of the Federal Reserve districts and their headquarters in Figure 15-7 on page 353. Today, the U.S. population is centered just west of the Mississippi River—that is, about half of the population is either to the west or the east of a line running roughly just west of this river. Can you reconcile the current locations of Fed districts and banks with this fact? Why do you suppose the Fed has its current geographic structure?

ECONOMICS ON THE NET

What's Happened to the Money Supply? Deposits at banks and other financial institutions make up a portion of the U.S. money supply. This exercise gives you the chance to see how changes in these deposits influence the Fed's measures of money.

Title: FRED (Federal Reserve Economic Data)

Navigation: Go to www.econtoday.com/chap15 to visit the Web page of the Federal Reserve Bank of St. Louis.

Application

1. Select the data series for Demand Deposits at Commercial Banks (Bil. of $; M), either seasonally adjusted or not. Scan through the data. Do you notice any recent trend? (Hint: Compare the growth in the figures before 1993 with their growth after 1993.) In addition, take a look at the data series for currency and for other checkable deposits. Do you observe similar recent trends in these series?

2. Back up, and click on M1 Money Stock (Bil. of $; M), again, either seasonally adjusted or not. Does it show any change in pattern beginning around 1993?

For Group Study and Analysis FRED contains considerable financial data series. Assign individual members or groups of the class the task of examining data on assets included in M1, M2, and MZM. Have each student or group look for big swings in the data. Then ask the groups to report to the class as a whole. When did clear changes occur in various categories of the monetary aggregates? Were there times that people appeared to shift funds from one aggregate to another? Are there any other noticeable patterns that may have had something to do with economic events during various periods?

Media Resources

If your exam were tomorrow, would you be ready? For each chapter, MyEconLab Practice Tests and Study Plans pinpoint which sections you have mastered and which ones you need to study. That way, you are more efficient with your study time, and you are better prepared for your exams.

In addition to Practice Tests and your personalized Study Plan, you'll find the following media resources in MyEconLab:

1. *Graphs in Motion* animation of Figures 15-1, 15-3, 15-4, and 15-8.

2. An *Economics in Motion* in-depth animation of the Federal Reserve system.

3. Videos featuring the author, Roger LeRoy Miller, on the following subjects:
   - The Functions of Money
   - Monetary Standards, or What Backs Money
   - The Federal Reserve system

4. Links to the Web sites cited in the marginal Internet Resources, Issues and Applications feature, and Economics on the Net activity.

5. Audio clips of all key terms, additional practice problems, and a PDF version of the material from the print Study Guide.

6. eThemes of the Times, which is a New York Times article to help you understand the real-world applications of what you are learning.

To see how it works, turn to page 16 and then go to www.myeconlab.com/miller.

Get Ahead of the Curve

Money Creation and Deposit Insurance

O n August 14, 2003, cascading power-plant outages caused by a power-line failure in Ohio turned out lights from southern Michigan to parts of New York, including most of New York City. The collapse of the electricity grid also shut off power to thousands of bank branches, automated teller machines, and payment systems. Suddenly, financial institutions throughout the northeastern United States were unable to settle obligations. Deposit accounts that were part of the U.S. money supply were technically still flush with cash, but institutions were unable to access or transmit electronic account information. In this chapter, you will learn about the tools the Federal Reserve put to use for the U.S. financial system in this hour of need.

Media Resources

Refer to the end of the chapter for a full listing of the multimedia learning materials available in MyEconLab.

LEARNING OBJECTIVES

After reading this chapter, you should be able to:

1. Describe how the Federal Reserve assesses reserve requirements on banks and other depository institutions
2. Understand why the money supply is unaffected when someone deposits in a depository institution a check drawn on another depository institution
3. Explain why the money supply changes when someone deposits in a depository institution a check drawn on the Federal Reserve System
4. Determine the maximum potential extent to which the money supply will change following a Federal Reserve purchase or sale of government securities
5. Discuss the ways in which the Federal Reserve conducts monetary policy
6. Explain the essential features of federal deposit insurance

...the U.S. government now provides federal deposit insurance, which originally covered checking and savings deposits at banks, savings institutions, and credit unions, to a unit of Toyota Motor Company? The world's second-largest automaker operates a Nevada-based "industrial loan company" that offers loans and other financial services to Toyota car dealers. The federal government's insurance program now protects the first $100,000 of each checking and savings account held at this Toyota banking unit, just as it does for deposits at more traditional banking institutions. The program also insures "money market sweep accounts" issued by stockbrokers Merrill Lynch & Co. and Salomon Smith Barney, which shift funds from clients' uninsured money market funds to federally insured checking and savings accounts at banks affiliated with the brokers.

Why does the government insure checking and savings deposits issued by banks but choose not to protect money market funds? The answer has to do with the fact that many deposit funds at banks are in transactions accounts from which people can order funds to be transferred via checks and debit cards. The widespread failure of banks would have a significant effect on the nation's money supply, thereby reducing total liquidity in the economy. A key objective of deposit insurance is to prevent such an event from occurring.

If you were to attend a luncheon of local bankers and ask the question, "Do you as bankers create money?" you would get a uniformly negative response. Bankers are certain that they do not create money. Indeed, *by itself*, no individual bank can create money. But through actions initiated by a central bank such as the Federal Reserve, depository institutions *together* do create money; they determine the total deposits outstanding. In this chapter, we shall examine the money multiplier process, which explains how an injection of new money into the banking system leads to an eventual multiple expansion in the total money supply. We shall also consider an important institutional change that has had important effects on the U.S. money supply. Then we shall examine federal deposit insurance and its role in the U.S. monetary and financial system.

LINKS BETWEEN CHANGES IN THE MONEY SUPPLY AND OTHER ECONOMIC VARIABLES

How fast the money supply grows or does not grow is important because no matter what model of the economy is used, theories link the money supply growth rate to economic growth or to business fluctuations. There is in fact a long-standing relationship between changes in the money supply and changes in GDP. Some economists use this historical evidence to argue that money is an important determinant of the level of economic activity in the economy.

Another key economic variable in our economy is the price level. As you learned in Chapter 10, both the quantity of money and the price level have risen since the 1950s, and one theory attributes changes in the rate of inflation to changes in the growth rate of money in circulation. Figure 16-1 on page 364 shows the relationship between the rate of growth of the money supply and the inflation rate. There seems to be a loose, long-run, direct relationship between growth in the money supply and changes in the rate of inflation. Increases in the money supply growth rate seem to lead to increases in the inflation rate, after a time lag.

THE ORIGINS OF FRACTIONAL RESERVE BANKING

As early as 1000 B.C., uncoined gold and silver were being used as money in Mesopotamia. Goldsmiths weighed and assessed the purity of those metals; later they started issuing paper notes indicating that the bearers held gold or silver of given weights

FIGURE 16-1
Money Supply Growth versus the Inflation Rate
These data plots indicate a loose correspondence between money supply growth and the inflation rate. Actually, closer inspection reveals a direct relationship between changes in the growth rate of money and changes in

the inflation rate *in a later period.* This relationship seemed to hold well into the 1990s, when it became less strong.

Sources: *Economic Report of the President; Federal Reserve Bulletin; Economic Indicators,* various issues; author's estimates.

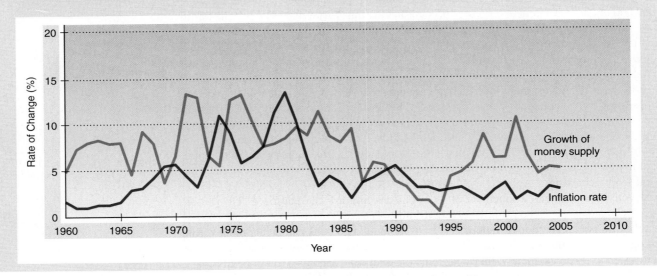

and purity on deposit with the goldsmith. These notes could be transferred in exchange for goods and became the first paper currency. The gold and silver on deposit with the goldsmiths were the first bank deposits. Eventually, goldsmiths realized that inflows of gold and silver on deposit always exceeded the average amount of gold and silver withdrawn at any given time—often by a predictable ratio. These goldsmiths started making loans by issuing to borrowers paper notes that exceeded in value the amount of gold and silver they actually kept on hand. They charged interest on these loans. This constituted the earliest form of what is now called **fractional reserve banking.** We know that goldsmiths operated this way in Delphi, Didyma, and Olympia in Greece as early as the seventh century B.C. In Athens, fractional reserve banking was well developed by the sixth century B.C.

Fractional reserve banking
A system in which depository institutions hold reserves that are less than the amount of total deposits.

DEPOSITORY INSTITUTION RESERVES

In a fractional reserve banking system, banks do not keep sufficient reserves on hand to cover 100 percent of their depositors' accounts. And the reserves that are held by depository institutions in the United States are not kept in gold and silver, as they were with the early goldsmiths, but rather in the form of deposits on reserve with Federal Reserve district banks and in vault cash. Depository institutions are required by the Fed to maintain a specified percentage of certain customer deposits as **reserves.** There are three distinguishable types of reserves: legal, required, and excess.

Reserves
In the U.S. Federal Reserve System, deposits held by Federal Reserve district banks for depository institutions, plus depository institutions' vault cash.

Legal Reserves

For depository institutions, **legal reserves** constitute anything that the law permits them to claim as reserves. Today that consists only of deposits held at the Federal Reserve district bank plus vault cash. Government securities, for example, are not legal reserves, even

Legal reserves
Reserves that depository institutions are allowed by law to claim as reserves—for example, deposits held at Federal Reserve district banks and vault cash.

though the owners and managers of the depository institutions may consider them such because they can easily be turned into cash, should the need arise, to meet unusually large net withdrawals by customers. Economists refer to all legal reserves that banks hold with the Federal Reserve or keep in their vaults as their *total reserves*.

Required Reserves

Required reserves are the minimum amount of legal reserves that a depository institution must have to "back" checkable deposits. They are expressed as a ratio of required reserves to total checkable deposits (banks need hold no reserves on noncheckable deposits). The **required reserve ratio** for almost all checkable deposits is 10 percent (except for roughly the first $50 million in deposits at any depository institution, which is subject to only a 3 percent requirement). The general formula is

Required reserves = checkable deposits * required reserve ratio

Take a hypothetical example. If the required level of reserves is 10 percent and the bank* has $1 billion in customer checkable deposits, it must hold at least $100 million as reserves. As we shall discuss later in this chapter, during the 1990s, banks discovered a novel way to reduce the amounts of reserves that they are required to hold.

Required reserves
The value of reserves that a depository institution must hold in the form of vault cash or deposits with the Fed.

Required reserve ratio
The percentage of total deposits that the Fed requires depository institutions to hold in the form of vault cash or deposits with the Fed.

Excess Reserves

Depository institutions often hold reserves in excess of what is required by the Fed. This difference between actual (legal) reserves and required reserves is called **excess reserves**. (Excess reserves can be negative, but they rarely are. Negative excess reserves indicate that depository institutions do not have sufficient legal reserves to meet their required reserves. When this happens, they borrow from other depository institutions or from a Federal Reserve district bank, sell assets such as securities, or call in loans.) Excess reserves are an important potential determinant of the rate of growth of the money supply, for as we shall see, it is only to the extent that depository institutions have excess reserves that they can make new loans. Because legal reserves produce no income, profit-seeking financial institutions have an incentive to minimize excess reserves, disposing of them either to purchase income-producing securities or to make loans with which they earn income through interest payments received. In equation form, we can define excess reserves in this way:

Excess reserves
The difference between legal reserves and required reserves.

Excess reserves = legal reserves - required reserves

In the analysis that follows, we examine the relationship between the level of reserves and the size of the money supply. This analysis implies that factors influencing the level of the reserves of the banking system as a whole will ultimately affect the size of the money supply, other things held constant. We show first that when someone deposits in one depository institution a check that is written on another depository institution, the two depository institutions involved are individually affected, but the overall money supply does not change. Then we show that when someone deposits in a depository institution a check that is written on the Fed, a multiple expansion in the money supply results.

Go to www.econtoday.com/chap16 to see Federal Reserve reports on the current amounts of required and excess reserves at U.S. depository institutions.

---

*The term *bank* will be used interchangeably with the term *depository institution* in this chapter because distinctions among financial institutions are becoming less and less meaningful.

THE RELATIONSHIP BETWEEN LEGAL RESERVES AND TOTAL DEPOSITS

To show the relationship between reserves and bank deposits, we first analyze a single bank (existing alongside many others). A single bank is able to make new loans to its customers only to the extent that it has reserves above the level legally required to cover the new deposits. When an individual bank has no excess reserves, it cannot make loans.

How a Single Bank Reacts to an Increase in Reserves

Balance sheet
A statement of the assets and liabilities of any business entity, including financial institutions and the Federal Reserve System. Assets are what is owned; liabilities are what is owed.

To examine the **balance sheet** of a single bank after its reserves are increased, let's make the following assumptions:

1. The required reserve ratio is 10 percent for all checkable deposits.
2. Checkable deposits are the bank's only liabilities; reserves at a Federal Reserve district bank and loans are the bank's only assets. Loans are promises made by customers to repay some amount in the future; that is, they are IOUs and as such are assets to the bank.
3. An individual bank can lend as much as it is legally allowed.
4. Every time a loan is made to an individual (consumer or business), all the proceeds from the loan are put into a checkable deposit account; no cash (currency or coins) is withdrawn.
5. Depository institutions seek to keep zero excess reserves because reserves do not earn interest. (Depository institutions are run to make profits; we assume that all depository institutions wish to convert excess reserves that do not pay interest into interest-bearing loans.)

Net worth
The difference between assets and liabilities.

6. Depository institutions have zero **net worth.** (In reality, all depository institutions are required to have some positive owners' equity, or capital, which is another name for net worth. It is usually a small percentage of the institutions' total assets.)

Look at the simplified initial position of Typical Bank in Balance Sheet 16-1. Liabilities consist of $1 million in checkable deposits. Assets consist of $100,000 in reserves and

BALANCE SHEET 16-1
Typical Bank

Assets			Liabilities	
Total reserves		$100,000	Checkable deposits	$1,000,000
Required reserves	$100,000			
Excess reserves	0			
Loans		900,000		
Total		$1,000,000	Total	$1,000,000

$900,000 in loans to customers. Total assets of $1 million equal total liabilities of $1 million. With a 10 percent reserve requirement and $1 million in checkable deposits, the bank has required reserves of $100,000 and therefore no excess reserves.

Assume that a depositor deposits in Typical Bank a $100,000 check drawn on another depository institution. Checkable deposits in Typical Bank immediately increase by $100,000, bringing the total to $1.1 million. Once the check clears, total reserves of Typical Bank increase to $200,000. A $1.1 million total in checkable deposits means that required reserves will have to be 10 percent of $1.1 million, or $110,000. Typical Bank now has excess reserves equal to $200,000 minus $110,000, or $90,000. This is shown in Balance Sheet 16-2.

BALANCE SHEET 16-2
Typical Bank

Assets			Liabilities	
Total reserves		$200,000	Checkable deposits	$1,100,000
Required reserves	$110,000			
Excess reserves	90,000			
Loans		900,000		
Total		$1,100,000	Total	$1,100,000

Effect on Typical Bank's Balance Sheet. Look at excess reserves in Balance Sheet 16-2. Excess reserves were zero before the $100,000 deposit, and now they are $90,000—that's $90,000 worth of assets not earning any income. By assumption, Typical Bank will now lend out this entire $90,000 in excess reserves in order to obtain interest income. Loans will increase to $990,000. The borrowers who receive the new loans will not leave them on deposit in Typical Bank. After all, they borrow money to spend it. As they spend it by writing checks that are deposited in other banks, actual reserves will fall to $110,000 (as required), and excess reserves will again become zero, as indicated in Balance Sheet 16-3.

BALANCE SHEET 16-3
Typical Bank

Assets			Liabilities	
Total reserves		$110,000	Checkable deposits	$1,100,000
Required reserves	$110,000			
Excess reserves	0			
Loans		990,000		
Total		$1,100,000	Total	$1,100,000

In this example, a person deposited a $100,000 check drawn on another bank. That $100,000 became part of the reserves of Typical Bank. Because that deposit immediately created excess reserves in Typical Bank, further loans were possible for Typical Bank. The excess reserves were lent out to earn interest. A bank will not lend more than its excess reserves because, by law, it must hold a certain amount of required reserves.

Effect on the Money Supply. A look at the balance sheets for Typical Bank might give the impression that the money supply increased because of the new customer's $100,000 deposit. Remember, though, that the deposit was a check written on *another* bank. Therefore, the other bank suffered a *decline* in its checkable deposits and its reserves. While total assets and liabilities in Typical Bank have increased by $100,000, they have *decreased* in the other bank by $100,000. The total amount of money and credit in the economy is unaffected by the transfer of funds from one depository institution to another.

The thing to remember is that new reserves for the banking system as a whole are not created when checks written on one bank are deposited in another bank. The Federal Reserve System can, however, create new reserves; that is the subject of the next section.

THE FED'S DIRECT EFFECT ON THE OVERALL LEVEL OF RESERVES

Now we shall examine the Fed's direct effect on the level of reserves, showing how a change in the level of reserves causes a multiple change in the total money supply. Consider the Federal Open Market Committee (FOMC), whose decisions essentially determine the level of reserves in the monetary system.

Federal Open Market Committee

Open market operations
The purchase and sale of existing U.S. government securities (such as bonds) in the open private market by the Federal Reserve System.

Open market operations are the purchase and sale of existing U.S. government securities in the open market (the private secondary U.S. securities market in which people exchange government securities that have not yet matured) by the FOMC in order to change the money supply. If the FOMC decides that the Fed should buy or sell bonds, it instructs the New York Federal Reserve Bank's Trading Desk to do so.[*]

A Sample Transaction

Assume that the Trading Desk at the New York Fed has determined that in order to comply with the latest directive from the FOMC, it must purchase $100,000 worth of U.S. government securities.[†] The Fed pays for these securities by writing a check for $100,000 drawn on its own account. This check is given to the bond dealer in exchange for the $100,000 worth of bonds. The bond dealer deposits the $100,000 check in a checkable account at a bank, which then sends the $100,000 check back to the Federal Reserve. When the Fed receives the check, it adds $100,000 to the reserve account of the bank that sent it the check. The Fed has created $100,000 of reserves. The Fed can create reserves because it has the ability to add to the reserve accounts of depository institutions whenever it buys U.S. securities. When the Fed buys a U.S. government security in the open market, it initially expands total reserves by the amount of the purchase.

Using Balance Sheets. Consider the balance sheets of the Fed and of the depository institution receiving the check. Balance Sheet 16-4 shows the results for the Fed after the bond purchase and for the bank after the bond dealer deposits the $100,000 check.[‡] The

---

[*]Actually, the Fed usually deals in Treasury bills that have a maturity date of one year or less.
[†]In practice, the Trading Desk is never given a specific dollar amount to purchase or to sell. The account manager uses personal discretion in determining what amount should be purchased or sold in order to satisfy the FOMC's latest directive.
[‡]Strictly speaking, the balance sheets that we are showing should be called the *consolidated balance sheets* for the 12 Federal Reserve district banks. We will simply refer to these banks as "the Fed," however.

Fed's balance sheet (which here reflects only account changes) shows that after the purchase, the Fed's assets have increased by $100,000 in the form of U.S. government securities. Liabilities have also increased by $100,000 in the form of an increase in the reserve account of the bank. The balance sheet for the bank shows an increase in assets of $100,000 in the form of reserves with its Federal Reserve district bank. The bank also has an increase in its liabilities in the form of a $100,000 deposit in the checkable account of the bond dealer. This is an immediate $100,000 increase in the money supply because the dealer's deposit is not offset by a withdrawal from another bank.

The Fed		Bank	
Assets	Liabilities	Assets	Liabilities
+$100,000 U.S. government securities	+$100,000 depository institution's reserves	+$100,000 reserves	+$100,000 checkable deposit owned by bond dealer

BALANCE SHEET 16-4
Balance sheets for the Fed and the bank when the Fed purchases a U.S. government security, showing changes only in assets and liabilities

Sale of a $100,000 U.S. Government Security by the Fed

The process is reversed when the account manager at the New York Fed Trading Desk sells a U.S. government security from the Fed's portfolio.

Sale of a Security by the Fed. When the individual or institution buying the security from the Fed writes a check for $100,000 and the check clears, the Fed reduces the reserves and deposits of the bank on which the check was written. The $100,000 sale of the U.S. government security leads to a reduction in reserves in the banking system and a reduction in checkable deposits. Hence the money supply declines.

Using Balance Sheets Again. Balance Sheet 16-5 shows the results for the sale of a U.S. government security by the Fed. When the $100,000 check clears, the Fed reduces by $100,000 the reserve account of the bank on which the check is written. The Fed's assets are also reduced by $100,000 because it no longer owns the U.S. government security. The bank's checkable deposit liabilities are reduced by $100,000 when that amount is deducted from the account of the bond purchaser, and the money supply is thereby reduced by that amount. The bank's assets are also reduced by $100,000 because the Fed has reduced its total reserves by that amount.

The Fed		Bank	
Assets	Liabilities	Assets	Liabilities
−$100,000 U.S. government securities	−$100,000 depository institution's reserves	−$100,000 reserves	−$100,000 checkable deposit balances

BALANCE SHEET 16-5
Balance sheets after the Fed has sold $100,000 of U.S. government securities, showing changes only in assets and liabilities

MONEY EXPANSION BY THE BANKING SYSTEM

Consider now the entire banking system. For practical purposes, we can look at all depository institutions taken as a whole. To understand how money is created, we must understand how depository institutions respond to Fed actions that increase reserves in the entire system.

Fed Purchases of U.S. Government Securities

Assume that the Fed purchases a $100,000 U.S. government security from a bond dealer. The bond dealer deposits the $100,000 check in Bank 1, which prior to this transaction is in the position depicted in Balance Sheet 16-6. The check, however, is not written on another depository institution; rather, it is written on the Fed itself.

BALANCE SHEET 16-6
Bank 1
This shows Bank 1's original position before the Federal Reserve's purchase of a $100,000 U.S. government security.

Assets			Liabilities	
Total reserves		$100,000	Checkable deposits	$1,000,000
Required reserves	$100,000			
Excess reserves	0			
Loans		900,000		
Total		$1,000,000	Total	$1,000,000

Now look at the balance sheet for Bank 1 shown in Balance Sheet 16-7. Reserves have been increased by $100,000 to $200,000, and checkable deposits have also been increased by $100,000. Because required reserves on $1.1 million of checkable deposits are only $110,000, the depository institution has $90,000 in excess reserves.

BALANCE SHEET 16-7
Bank 1

Assets			Liabilities	
Total reserves		$200,000	Checkable deposits	$1,100,000
Required reserves	$110,000			
Excess reserves	90,000			
Loans		900,000		
Total		$1,100,000	Total	$1,100,000

Effect on the Money Supply. The purchase of a $100,000 U.S. government security by the Federal Reserve from the public (a bond dealer, for example) increases the money supply immediately by $100,000 because checkable deposits held by the public—the bond dealers are members of the public—are part of the money supply, and no other bank has lost deposits.

The process of money creation does not stop here. Look again at Balance Sheet 16-7. Bank 1 has excess reserves of $90,000. No other depository institution (or combination of depository institutions) has negative excess reserves of $90,000 as a result of the Fed's bond purchase. (Remember, the Fed simply *created* the reserves to pay for the bond purchase.)

Bank 1 will not wish to hold non-interest-bearing excess reserves. Assume that it will expand its loans by $90,000. This is shown in Balance Sheet 16-8.

BALANCE SHEET 16-8
Bank 1

Assets		Liabilities	
Total reserves	$110,000	Checkable deposits	$1,100,000
Required reserves $110,000			
Excess reserves 0			
Loans	990,000		
Total	$1,100,000	Total	$1,100,000

The individual or business that has received the $90,000 loan will spend these funds, which will then be deposited in other banks. For the sake of simplicity, concentrate only on the balance sheet *changes* resulting from this new deposit, as shown in Balance Sheet 16-9. For Bank 2, the $90,000 deposit, after the check has cleared, becomes an increase in reserves as well as an increase in checkable deposits and hence the money supply. Because the reserve requirement is 10 percent, required reserves increase $9,000, so Bank 2 will have excess reserves of $81,000. But, of course, excess reserves are not income producing, so by assumption Bank 2 will reduce them to zero by making a loan of $81,000 (which will earn interest income). This is shown in Balance Sheet 16-10 on the next page.

BALANCE SHEET 16-9
Bank 2 (Changes Only)

Assets		Liabilities	
Total reserves	+$90,000	New checkable deposits	+$90,000
Required reserves +$9,000			
Excess reserves +$81,000			
Total	+$90,000	Total	+$90,000

Remember that in this example, the original $100,000 deposit was a check issued by a Federal Reserve bank to the bond dealer. That $100,000 constituted an immediate increase in the money supply of $100,000 when deposited in the bond dealer's checkable account. The deposit creation process (in addition to the original $100,000) occurs because of the fractional reserve banking system, coupled with the desire of depository institutions to

BALANCE SHEET 16-10
Bank 2 (Changes Only)

Assets		Liabilities	
Total reserves	+$9,000	Checkable deposits	+$90,000
Required reserves +$9,000			
Excess reserves 0			
Loans	+81,000		
Total	+$90,000	Total	+$90,000

maintain a minimum level of excess reserves. Under fractional reserve banking, banks must only hold a portion of new deposits as legal reserves, and in their quest to earn profits, they seek to transform excess reserves into holdings of loans and securities.

Continuation of the Deposit Creation Process. Look at Bank 3's simplified account in Balance Sheet 16-11, where again only *changes* in the assets and liabilities are shown. Assume that the firm borrowing from Bank 2 writes a check for $81,000 that is deposited in Bank 3; checkable deposits and the money supply increase by $81,000. Legal reserves of Bank 3 rise by that amount when the check clears.

BALANCE SHEET 16-11
Bank 3 (Changes Only)

Assets		Liabilities	
Total reserves	+$81,000	New checkable deposits	+$81,000
Required reserves +$8,100			
Excess reserves +$72,900			
Total	+$81,000	Total	+$81,000

Because the reserve requirement is 10 percent, required reserves rise by $8,100, and excess reserves therefore increase by $72,900. We assume that Bank 3 will want to lend all of those non-interest-earning assets (excess reserves). When it does, loans (and newly created checkable deposits) will increase by $72,900. This bank's legal reserves will fall to $8,100, and excess reserves become zero as checks are written on the new deposit. This is shown in Balance Sheet 16-12.

BALANCE SHEET 16-12
Bank 3 (Changes Only)

Assets		Liabilities	
Total reserves	+$8,100	New checkable deposits	+$81,000
Required reserves +$8,100			
Excess reserves 0			
Loans	+$72,900		
Total	+$81,000	Total	+$81,000

Bank	New Deposits	New Required Reserves	Maximum New Loans
1	$100,000 (from Fed)	$10,000	$90,000
2	90,000	9,000	81,000
3	81,000	8,100	72,900
4	72,900	7,290	65,610
.	.	.	.
.	.	.	.
.	.	.	.
All other banks	656,100	65,610	590,490
Totals	$1,000,000	$100,000	$900,000

TABLE 16-1

Maximum Money Creation with 10 Percent Required Reserves

This table shows the maximum new loans plus investments that banks can make, given the Fed's deposit of a $100,000 check in Bank 1. The required reserve ratio is 10 percent. We assume that all excess reserves in each bank are used for new loans or investments.

Progression to Other Banks. This process continues to Banks 4, 5, 6, and so forth. Each bank obtains smaller and smaller increases in deposits because 10 percent of each deposit must be held in required reserves; therefore, each succeeding depository institution makes correspondingly smaller loans. Table 16-1 shows the new deposits, possible loans, and required reserves for the remaining depository institutions in the system.

Effect on Total Deposits. In this example, deposits (and the money supply) increased initially by the $100,000 that the Fed paid the bond dealer in exchange for a bond. Deposits (and the money supply) were further increased by a $90,000 deposit in Bank 2, and they were again increased by an $81,000 deposit in Bank 3. Eventually, total deposits and the money supply will increase by $1 million, as shown in Table 16-1. The $1 million consists of the original $100,000 created by the Fed, plus an extra $900,000 generated by deposit-creating bank loans. The money multiplier process is portrayed graphically in Figure 16-2.

Increase in Total Banking System Reserves

Even with fractional reserve banking, if there are zero excess reserves, deposits cannot expand unless total banking system reserves are increased. The original new deposit in Bank 1, in our example, was in the form of a check written on a Federal Reserve district bank. It therefore represented new reserves to the banking system. Had that check been written on Bank 3, by contrast, nothing would have happened to the total amount of checkable deposits; there would have been no change in the total money supply. To repeat: Checks written on banks within the system, without any expansion of overall reserves within the banking system, represent transfers of reserves and deposits among depository institutions that do not affect the money supply. *Only when additional new reserves and deposits are created by the Federal Reserve System does the money supply increase.*

You should be able to work through the foregoing example to show the reverse process when there is a decrease in reserves because the Fed sells a $100,000 U.S. government security. The result is a multiple contraction of deposits and therefore of the total money supply in circulation.

FIGURE 16-2

The Multiple Expansion in the Money Supply Due to $100,000 in New Reserves When the Required Reserve Ratio Is 10 Percent

The banks are all aligned in decreasing order of new deposits created. Bank 1 receives the $100,000 in new reserves and lends out $90,000. Bank 2 receives the $90,000 and lends out $81,000. The process continues through banks 3 to 19 and then the rest of the banking system. Ultimately, assuming no leakages, the $100,000 of new reserves results in an increase in the money supply of $1 million, or 10 times the new reserves, because the required reserve ratio is 10 percent.

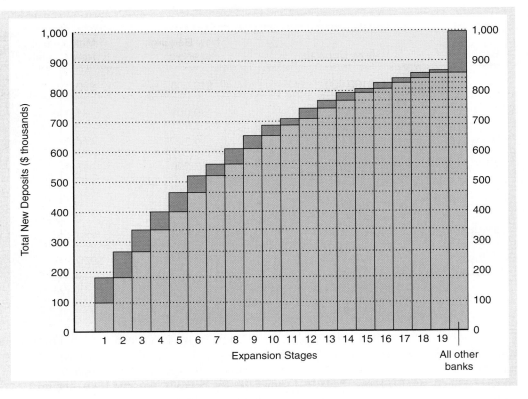

THE MONEY MULTIPLIER

In the example just given, a $100,000 increase in excess reserves generated by the Fed's purchase of a security yielded a $1 million increase in total deposits; deposits increased by a multiple of 10 times the initial $100,000 increase in overall reserves. Conversely, a $100,000 decrease in excess reserves generated by the Fed's sale of a security will yield a $1 million decrease in total deposits; they will decrease by a multiple of 10 times the initial $100,000 decrease in overall reserves.

We can now make a generalization about the extent to which the total money supply will change when the banking system's reserves are increased or decreased. The **money multiplier** gives the change in the money supply due to a change in reserves. If we assume that no excess reserves are kept and that all loan proceeds are deposited in depository institutions in the system, the following equation applies:

Money multiplier
The reciprocal of the required reserve ratio, assuming no leakages into currency and no excess reserves. It is equal to 1 divided by the required reserve ratio.

$$\text{Potential money multiplier} = \frac{1}{\text{required reserve ratio}}$$

That is, the maximum possible value of the money multiplier is equal to 1 divided by the required reserve ratio for checkable deposits. The *actual* change in the money supply—currency plus checkable account balances—will be equal to the following:

Actual change in money supply = actual money multiplier ∗ change in total reserves

Now we examine why there is a difference between the potential money multiplier—1 divided by the required reserve ratio—and the actual multiplier.

Forces That Reduce the Money Multiplier

We made a number of simplifying assumptions to come up with the potential money multiplier. In the real world, the actual money multiplier is considerably smaller. Several factors account for this.

Leakages. The entire loan (check) from one bank is not always deposited in another bank. At least two leakages can occur:

- *Currency drains.* When deposits increase, the public will want to hold more currency. Currency that is kept in a person's wallet remains outside the banking system and cannot be held by banks as reserves from which to make loans. The greater the amount of cash leakage, the smaller the actual money multiplier.
- *Excess reserves.* Depository institutions may wish to maintain excess reserves greater than zero. For example, a bank may wish to keep excess reserves so that it can make speedy loans when creditworthy borrowers seek funds. To the extent that banks want to keep positive excess reserves, the money multiplier will be smaller. The greater the excess reserves that banks maintain, the smaller the actual money multiplier.

Empirically, the currency drain is more significant than the effect of desired positive excess reserves.

Real-World Money Multipliers. The maximum potential money multiplier is the reciprocal of the required reserve ratio. The maximum is never attained for the money supply as a whole because of currency drains and excess reserves. Also, each definition of the money supply, M1 or M2, will yield a different money multiplier. For several decades, the M1 multiplier has stayed in a range between 2.5 and 3.0. The M2 multiplier, however, has shown a trend upward, ranging from 6.5 at the beginning of the 1960s to over 12 in the 2000s.

Other Ways That the Federal Reserve Can Change the Money Supply

As we have just seen, the Fed can change the money supply by directly changing reserves available to the banking system. It does this by engaging in open market operations. To repeat: The purchase of a U.S. government security by the Fed results in an increase in reserves and leads to a multiple expansion in the money supply. A sale of a U.S. government security by the Fed results in a decrease in reserves and leads to a multiple contraction in the money supply.

In principle, the Fed can change the money supply in two other ways, both of which will have multiplier effects similar to those outlined earlier.

Borrowed Reserves and the Discount Rate. If a depository institution wants to increase its loans but has no excess reserves, it can borrow reserves. One place it can borrow reserves is from the Fed itself. The depository institution goes to the Federal Reserve and asks for a loan of a certain amount of reserves. The Fed charges these institutions for any reserves that it lends them. The interest rate that the Fed charges is the **discount rate,** and

Discount rate
The interest rate that the Federal Reserve charges for reserves that it lends to depository institutions. It is sometimes referred to as the *rediscount rate* or, in Canada and England, as the *bank rate.*

Federal funds market
A private market (made up mostly of banks) in which banks can borrow reserves from other banks that want to lend them. Federal funds are usually lent for overnight use.

Federal funds rate
The interest rate that depository institutions pay to borrow reserves in the interbank federal funds market.

the borrowing is said to be done through the Fed's "discount window." Borrowing from the Fed increases reserves and thereby enhances the ability of the depository institution to engage in deposit creation, thus increasing the money supply.

Depository institutions actually do not often go to the Fed to borrow reserves. In years past, this was because the Fed would not lend them all they wanted to borrow. The Fed encouraged banks to tap an alternative source when they wanted to expand their reserves or when they needed reserves to meet a requirement. The primary source for banks to obtain funds is the **federal funds market.** The federal funds market is an interbank market in reserves, with one bank borrowing the excess reserves of another. The generic term *federal funds market* refers to the borrowing or lending of reserve funds that are usually repaid within the same 24-hour period.

Depository institutions that borrow in the federal funds market pay an interest rate called the **federal funds rate.** Because the federal funds rate is a ready measure of the price that banks must pay to raise funds, the Federal Reserve often uses it as a yardstick by which to measure the effects of its policies. Consequently, the federal funds rate is a closely watched indicator of the Fed's anticipated intentions.

For almost 80 years, the Fed tended to keep the discount rate unchanged for weeks at a time, and it typically set the discount rate slightly below the federal funds rate. Because this gave depository institutions an incentive to borrow from the Fed instead of from other banks in the federal funds market, the Fed established tough lending conditions. Often, when the Fed changed the discount rate, its objective was not necessarily to encourage or discourage depository institutions from borrowing from the Fed. Instead, altering the discount rate would signal to the banking system and financial markets that there had been a change in the Fed's monetary policy.

Today's Discount Rate Policy. In 2003, the Fed altered the way it lends to depository institutions. It now sets the discount rate *above* the federal funds rate. This discourages depository institutions from seeking loans unless they face significant liquidity problems. Currently, the Fed keeps the discount rate 1 percentage point higher than the market-determined federal funds rate. If the market federal funds rate is 2 percent, therefore, the discount rate is 3 percent. If the federal funds rate increases to 2.5 percent, the Fed automatically raises the discount rate to 3.5 percent.

In principle, the Fed can continue to use the discount rate as an instrument of monetary policy by changing the amount by which the discount rate exceeds the federal funds rate. For instance, if the Fed reduced the differential from 1 percentage point to 0.5 percentage point, this would reduce depository institutions' disincentive from borrowing from the Fed. As Fed lending increased in response, borrowed reserves would rise, and total reserves in the banking system would increase. The Fed has indicated that it does not plan to conduct monetary policy in this way, however.

As part of its new discount rate policy, the Fed announced that banks should not feel stigmatized if they borrow reserves directly from Fed district banks more often than in the past. Why do you think that banks have been slow to take the Fed up on its offer to lend more readily than in the past?

Policy E X A M P L E

The Discount Window Is Open, So Where Are the Banks?

When the Fed began maintaining the discount rate exactly 1 percentage point above the federal funds rate in early 2003, it also announced that it would be more willing to lend than in the past. Fed officials expected that this announcement would encourage banks to borrow larger amounts of reserves from the Fed and to borrow from the Fed more often.

During the following six months, however, the amount and frequency of discount-window borrowing by banks barely changed. So, in July 2003, the Fed made an effort to clarify and reiterate its openness to making larger and more frequent discount-window loans. It issued a press release cosigned by all other depository institution regulators—the Federal Deposit Insurance Corporation, the Office of the Comptroller of the Currency, the Office of Thrift Supervision, and the National Credit Union Administration. The press release stated that occasional use of the Fed's regular discount-window facilities "should be viewed as appropriate and unexceptional."

Nevertheless, banks have remained reluctant to borrow from the Fed. Some banking experts think that many banks still worry that outsiders may view heavier borrowing from the Fed as a possible sign of major liquidity problems. Others, however, think there is a more basic explanation for the banks' unwillingness to borrow very much or very often from the Fed: With the Fed's discount rate always set above the market federal funds rate, borrowing from the Fed simply isn't profitable.

For Critical Analysis

Under the new discount rate policy, what does the Fed have to gain from promoting more borrowing at the discount window?

Reserve Requirement Changes. Another method by which the Fed can potentially alter the money supply is by changing the reserve requirements it imposes on all depository institutions. Earlier we assumed that reserve requirements were fixed. Actually, these requirements are set by the Fed within limits established by Congress. The Fed can vary reserve requirements within these broad limits.

What would a change in reserve requirements from 10 to 20 percent do (if there were no excess reserves and if we ignore currency leakages)? We have already seen that the maximum money multiplier is the reciprocal of the required reserve ratio. If the required reserve ratio is 10 percent, then the maximum money multiplier is the reciprocal of $\frac{1}{10}$, or 10 (assuming no leakages). If, for some reason, the Fed decided to increase reserve requirements to 20 percent, the maximum money multiplier would equal the reciprocal of $\frac{1}{5}$, or 5. The maximum money multiplier is therefore inversely related to the required reserve ratio. If the Fed decides to increase reserve requirements, the maximum money multiplier will decrease. Therefore, with any given level of legal reserves already in existence, the money supply will contract.

In practice, open market operations allow the Federal Reserve to control the money supply much more precisely than changes in reserve requirements do, and they also allow the Fed to reverse itself quickly. In contrast, a small change in reserve requirements could, at least initially, result in a very large change in the money supply. Reserve requirement changes also impose costs on banks by restricting the portion of funds that they can lend, thereby inducing them to find legal ways to evade reserve requirements. That is why the Federal Reserve does not change reserve requirements very often.

Central banks in some countries adjust reserve requirements more often. What do you think that the People's Bank of China has attempted to accomplish by raising reserve requirements *only* for banks that it felt were making the riskiest loans?

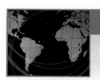

International Policy EXAMPLE

In China, Reserve Requirements Take Aim at High-Risk Banks

Since the early 2000s, the Chinese central bank, the People's Bank of China, has adjusted its reserve requirements several times. In late 2003, it raised the required reserve ratio for most deposits from 6.5 percent to 7.0 percent. The central bank intended for this change to reduce the money multiplier and slow the growth of the money supply.

In the spring of 2004, the People's Bank of China felt that it needed to do still more to rein in money supply growth. It began by raising the discount rate. In addition, it decided to boost reserve requirements once again. This time, however, it boosted required reserve ratios only for banks judged to be engaged in the riskiest lending activities. Thus the central bank used a change in reserve requirements to try to achieve two goals simultaneously: (1) to cut back on the money supply, and (2) to induce the riskiest banks to allocate fewer funds to risky loans.

For Critical Analysis
How does raising the required reserve ratio decrease the banking system's overall loan expansion as well as its total deposit expansion?

Sweep Accounts and the Decreased Relevance of Reserve Requirements

To many economists, reserve requirements are an outdated relic. They argue that reserve requirements might prove useful as a stabilizing tool if central banks really sought to achieve targets for the quantity of money in circulation, but they note that most central banks today pay little attention to variations in money growth. Hence, they contend, reserve requirements around the world should be reduced or even eliminated.

Table 16-2 shows that banks in many industrialized countries face lower required reserve ratios than they did a decade and a half ago. Relative to the required reserve ratios of other nations in the table, the official 10 percent ratio for transactions deposits in the United States stands out. This is misleading, however, because the *effective* U.S. required reserve ratio has been much lower than this since the mid-1990s.

The Great Reserve Requirement Loophole: Sweep Accounts. A key simplifying assumption in our example of the money creation process was that checkable deposits were

TABLE 16-2
Required Reserve Ratios in Selected Nations
Several nations have reduced their required reserve ratios in recent years.

Required Reserve Ratio	1989	2003
Checkable Deposits		
Canada	10.0%	0%
European Monetary Union*	—	2.0
Japan	1.75	1.2
New Zealand	0	0
United Kingdom	0.45	0.35
United States	12.0	10.0
Noncheckable Deposits		
Canada	3.0	0
European Monetary Union*	—	2.0
Japan	2.5	1.3
New Zealand	0	0
United Kingdom	0.45	0.35
United States	3.0	0

*The European Monetary Union was formed in 1999.
Sources: Gordon Sellon Jr. and Stuart Weiner, "Monetary Policy Without Reserve Requirements: Analytical Issues," Federal Reserve Bank of Kansas City *Economic Review* 81 (Fourth Quarter 1996), pp. 5–24; Bank for International Settlements.

the only bank liability that changes when total reserves change. Of course, banks also is-sue savings and time deposits. In addition, they offer *automatic transfer accounts.* In these accounts, which banks have offered since the 1970s, funds are automatically transferred from savings deposits to checkable deposits whenever the account holder writes a check that would otherwise cause the balance of checkable deposits to become negative. Auto-matic transfer accounts thereby protect individuals and businesses from overdrawing their checking accounts.

Beginning in 1993, several U.S. banks discovered a way to use automatic transfer ac-counts to reduce their required reserves. The banks shift funds *out of* their customers' checkable deposit accounts, which are subject to reserve requirements, and *into* the cus-tomers' savings deposits—mainly money market deposit accounts—which are *not* subject to reserve requirements. Automatic transfer accounts with provisions permitting banks to shift funds from checkable deposits to savings deposits to avoid reserve requirements are called **sweep accounts.** Banks gave the accounts this name because they effectively use them to "sweep" funds from one deposit to another.

As panel (a) of Figure 16-3 shows, total funds in U.S. sweep accounts exempt from the 10 percent required reserve ratio have increased dramatically since 1995. Panel (b) indi-cates that the immediate result was a decline in the reserves that U.S. banks hold at Fed-eral Reserve banks. Reserves have since risen but remain below previous levels.

Implications of Sweep Accounts for Measures of the Money Supply. Recall from Chapter 15 that there are two key measures of the U.S. money supply. One is M1, which consists of currency, transactions deposits, and traveler's checks. The other is M2, which is composed of M1 and various other liquid assets, such as savings accounts, money mar-ket deposit accounts, and small-denomination time deposits.

Sweep account
A depository institution account that entails regular shifts of funds from checkable deposits that are subject to reserve requirements to savings deposits that are exempt from reserve requirements.

To learn more from the Federal Reserve Bank of St. Louis about the growth of sweep accounts, go to www.econtoday.com/chap16, and scan down the page to "Retail and Deposit Sweep Program."

FIGURE 16-3
Sweep Accounts and Reserves of U.S. Depository Institutions at Federal Reserve Banks
Panel (a) depicts the growth of sweep accounts, which shift funds from transactions deposits subject to reserve requirements to savings deposits with no legal required reserve ratios. Panel (b) shows that sweep accounts induced an abrupt decline in reserve balances that depository institutions hold at Federal Reserve banks. Reserves have risen slightly since (with a brief jump after the 2001 terrorist attacks).

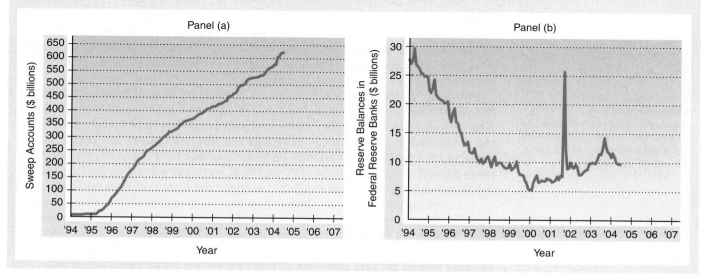

Between 1984 and 1993, M2 grew at an annual rate of just under 5 percent, and M1 grew at an annual rate of just over 8 percent. Since 1993, the average annual rate of growth in M2 has remained close to 5 percent, but the average annual rate of growth of M1 has been close to 1 percent. The reason is the widespread use of sweep accounts since 1993. When depository institutions began using sweep accounts to shift funds from checkable deposits into savings accounts, the growth of the funds in checkable deposits abruptly halted. Since 1993, M1 has increased by only a few billion dollars. Growth in M2 has continued, however, because funds that depository institutions shift from checkable deposits to savings accounts are already included in M2.

Sweep accounts have therefore artificially changed the behavior of the M1 measure of the money supply. From the Fed's perspective, this has made M1 a less useful way to track total liquidity in the United States. It now relies on M2 as its key measure of the money supply.

CONCEPTS in Brief

- The maximum potential money multiplier is equal to the reciprocal of the required reserve ratio. The actual multiplier is smaller than the maximum money multiplier because of currency drains and excess reserves voluntarily held by banks.

- The Fed can change the money supply through open market operations, in which it buys and sells existing U.S. government securities. This is the key way in which the Fed conducts monetary policy.

- In principle, the Fed can also conduct monetary policy by varying the discount rate to encourage changes in re-

serves. Starting in 2003, the Fed has automatically set the discount rate equal to the federal funds rate plus 1 percentage point.

- Finally, the Fed can change the amount of deposits created from reserves by changing reserve requirements, but it has rarely done so. Furthermore, since the mid-1990s, U.S. depository institutions have used sweep accounts to shift funds from checkable deposits to savings deposits that are exempt from reserve requirements, thereby reducing the relevance of reserve requirements for monetary policy.

To test your understanding of the concepts covered in this section, go to the Online Review at www.myeconlab.com/miller.

FEDERAL DEPOSIT INSURANCE

Federal Deposit Insurance Corporation (FDIC)
A government agency that insures the deposits held in banks and most other depository institutions; all U.S. banks are insured this way.

When businesses fail, they create hardships for creditors, owners, and customers. But when a depository institution fails, an even greater hardship results, because many individuals and businesses depend on the safety and security of banks. Figure 16-4 indicates that during the 1920s, an average of about 600 banks failed each year. In the early 1930s, during the Great Depression, that average soared to nearly 3,000 failures each year.

In 1933, at the height of such bank failures, the **Federal Deposit Insurance Corporation (FDIC)** was founded to insure the funds of depositors and remove the reason for ruinous runs on banks. In 1934, the Federal Savings and Loan Insurance Corporation (FSLIC) was established to insure deposits in savings and loan associations and mutual savings banks. In 1971, the National Credit Union Share Insurance Fund (NCUSIF) was created to insure deposits in credit unions. In 1989, the FSLIC was dissolved, and the Savings Association Insurance Fund (SAIF) was established to protect the deposits of those institutions.

As can be seen in Figure 16-4, bank failure rates dropped dramatically after passage of the early federal legislation. The long period from 1935 until the 1980s was relatively quiet. From World War II to 1984, fewer than nine banks failed per year. From 1985 until the beginning of 1993, however, 1,065 commercial banks failed—an average of nearly 120 bank failures per year, more than 10 times the average for the preceding 40 years! We

FIGURE 16-4
Bank Failures
During the Great Depression, a tremendous number of banks failed. Federal deposit insurance was created in 1933. Thereafter, bank failures were few until around 1984. Annual failures peaked at over 200 in 1989 and are now fewer than a dozen per year.

Source: Federal Deposit Insurance Corporation.

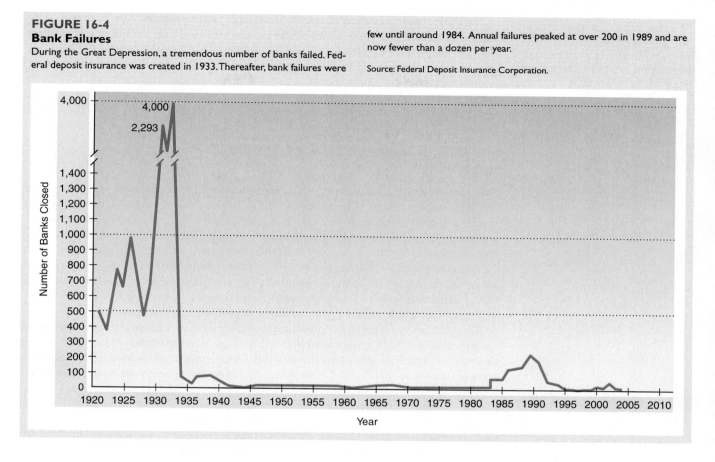

will examine the reasons shortly. But first we need to understand how deposit insurance works.

The Rationale for Deposit Insurance

The FDIC, FSLIC, and NCUSIF were established to mitigate the primary cause of bank failures, **bank runs**—the simultaneous rush of depositors to convert their demand deposits or time deposits into currency.

Consider the following scenario. A bank begins to look shaky; its assets may not seem sufficient to cover its liabilities. If the bank has no deposit insurance, depositors in this bank (and any banks associated with it) will all want to withdraw their funds from the bank at the same time. Their concern is that this shaky bank will not have enough assets to return their deposits to them in the form of currency. Indeed, this is what happens in a bank failure when insurance doesn't exist. Just as with the failure of a regular business, the creditors of the bank may not all get paid, or if they do, they will get paid less than 100 percent of what they are owed. Depositors are creditors of a bank because their funds are on loan to the bank. As we have seen, in a fractional reserve banking system, banks do not hold 100 percent of their depositors' funds in the form of reserves. Consequently, all depositors cannot withdraw all their funds simultaneously. Hence the intent of the legislation enacted in the 1930s was to assure depositors that they could have their deposits converted into cash when they wished, no matter how serious the financial situation of the bank.

Bank runs
Attempts by many of a bank's depositors to convert checkable and time deposits into currency out of fear that the bank's liabilities may exceed its assets.

To keep up with the latest issues in deposit insurance and banking with the assistance of the FDIC, go to www.econtoday.com/chap16.

The FDIC (and later the FSLIC, NCUSIF, and SAIF) provided this assurance. They charged insurance premiums to depository institutions based on their total deposits, and these premiums went into funds that would reimburse depositors in the event of bank failures. By insuring deposits, the FDIC bolstered depositors' trust in the banking system and provided depositors with the incentive to leave their deposits with the bank, even in the face of widespread talk of bank failures. In 1933, it was sufficient for the FDIC to cover each account up to $2,500. The current maximum is $100,000.

How Deposit Insurance Causes Increased Risk Taking by Bank Managers

Until very recently, all insured depository institutions paid the same small fee for coverage. (In 1996, the fee was reduced to zero for most banks.) The fee that they paid was completely unrelated to how risky their assets were. A depository institution that made loans to companies such as General Motors and Microsoft Corporation paid the same deposit insurance premium as another depository institution that made loans (at higher interest rates) to the governments of developing countries that were teetering on the brink of financial collapse. Although deposit insurance premiums for a while were adjusted somewhat in response to the riskiness of a depository institution's assets, they never reflected all of the relative risk. This can be considered a flaw in the deposit insurance scheme.

Because bank managers do not have to pay higher insurance premiums when they make riskier loans, they have an incentive to invest in more assets of higher yield, and therefore necessarily higher risk, than they would if there were no deposit insurance. The insurance premium rate is artificially low, permitting institution managers to obtain deposits at less than full cost (because depositors will accept a lower interest payment on insured deposits). Consequently, depository institution managers can increase their profits by using lower-cost insured deposits to purchase higher-yield, higher-risk assets. The gains to risk taking accrue to the managers and stockholders of the depository institutions; the losses go to the deposit insurer (and, as we will see, ultimately to taxpayers).

To combat these flaws in the financial industry and in the deposit insurance system, a vast regulatory apparatus was installed. The FDIC was given regulatory powers to offset the risk-taking temptations to depository institution managers; those powers included the ability to require higher capital investment; the ability to regulate, examine, and supervise bank affairs; and the ability to enforce its decisions. Still higher capital requirements were imposed in the early 1990s and then adjusted somewhat beginning in 2000, but the basic flaws in the system remain.

Normally, bank examiners based in government offices around the nation make periodic trips to visit the banks they supervise and audit. Why do you suppose that since 2002 federal banking regulators have adopted a more direct approach to examining the activities of the largest U.S. banks by stationing examiners on these banks' premises on a full-time basis?

Policy EXAMPLE

At a Few Banks, Supervisory Examinations Never End

Six banks in the United States—J.P. Morgan Chase, Bank of America, Citibank, Wachovia, Washington Mutual, and Wells Fargo—together account for about 40 percent of the assets of all U.S. depository institutions. From the perspective of federal banking regulators, therefore, about 40 percent of the risks that taxpayers face in providing deposit insurance are concentrated among these few banks.

Since 2002, the FDIC has given six of its banking examiners unique assignments: constant surveillance of the largest U.S. banks. The FDIC has stationed each of these individuals in an office located on the premises of the bank he or she examines. The examiners' daily presence at these banks gives the FDIC real-time information about the largest banks' activities and provides the agency with a specialist on the internal workings of the top banking organizations. The on-site examiners work together to produce weekly, quarterly, and annual reports

on the six banks they examine. Twice each week they participate in conference calls with other FDIC officials to discuss developing trends. In this way, the FDIC keeps constantly abreast of the banks' activities that pose the greatest potential risk of loss to the government's deposit insurance system.

For Critical Analysis
Who pays for the costs that government agencies incur in examining and supervising every bank in the United States?

Deposit Insurance, Adverse Selection, and Moral Hazard

As a deposit insurer, the FDIC effectively acts as a government-run insurance company. This means that the FDIC's operations expose the federal government to the same kinds of asymmetric information problems that other financial intermediaries face.

Adverse Selection in Deposit Insurance. One of these problems, as discussed in Chapter 15, is *adverse selection*, which arises when there is asymmetric information before a transaction takes place. Adverse selection is often a problem when insurance is involved because people or firms that are relatively poor risks are sometimes able to disguise that fact from insurers. It is instructive to examine the way this works with the deposit insurance provided by the FDIC. Deposit insurance shields depositors from the potential adverse effects of risky decisions and so makes depositors willing to accept riskier investment strategies by their banks. Clearly, this encourages more high-flying, risk-loving entrepreneurs to become managers of banks. Moreover, because depositors have so little incentive to monitor the activities of insured banks, it is also likely that the insurance actually encourages outright crooks—embezzlers and con artists—to enter the industry. The consequences for the FDIC—and for taxpayers—are larger losses.

Moral Hazard in Deposit Insurance and the U.S. Savings and Loan Debacle. As you learned in Chapter 15, *moral hazard* arises as the result of information asymmetry after a transaction has occurred. Moral hazard is also an important phenomenon in the presence of insurance contracts, such as the deposit insurance provided by the FDIC. Insured depositors know that they will not suffer losses if their bank fails. Hence they have little incentive to monitor their bank's investment activities or to punish their bank by withdrawing their funds if the bank assumes too much risk. This means that insured banks have incentives to take on more risks than they otherwise would—and with those risks come higher losses for the FDIC and for taxpayers.

For a variety of reasons, by the mid-1980s, the savings and loan (S&L) industry in the United States was facing disaster. What was occurring at that time was a perfect example of the perverse incentives that occur when government-provided deposit insurance exists. S&L institution managers undertook riskier actions than they otherwise would have because of the existence of deposit insurance. Moreover, because of the existence of deposit insurance, depositors in S&L associations had little incentive to investigate the financial dealings and stability of those institutions. Deposits were guaranteed by an agency of the federal government, so why worry? Households and firms had little incentive to monitor S&L institutions or even to diversify their deposits across institutions. From an S&L manager's point of view, as long as deposit insurance protected depositors, the manager could feel safer taking that risk. One result was an increase in the amount of high-risk, high-yielding assets purchased by many S&L associations.

Economics Front and Center

To consider how government deposit insurance can have moral hazard effects extending to any nation's banking system, consider the case study, **Deposit Insurance in an Expanded European Union,** on page 384.

The first year of the S&L crisis, 135 institutions failed. Over the next two years, another 600 went into receivership. By the end of the crisis, 1,500 thrift institutions had gone under. Politicians chose to solve the crisis by passing the Financial Institutions Reform, Recovery and Enforcement Act (FIRREA), popularly known as the Thrift Bailout Act of 1989. The estimated cost to U.S. taxpayers was about $200 billion. Congress followed up in 1991 by passing the FDIC Improvement Act (FDICIA). This law toughened regulatory standards and required the FDIC to close weak depository institutions promptly, rather than letting their managers continue to roll the dice with taxpayers' dollars at stake.

CONCEPTS in Brief

- To limit the fallout from system-wide failures and bank runs, Congress created the Federal Deposit Insurance Corporation (FDIC) in 1933. Since the advent of federal deposit insurance, there have been no true bank runs at federally insured banks.

- The FDIC's insurance of bank deposits insulates depositors from risks, so depositors are less concerned about riskier investment strategies by depository institutions. Thus bank managers have an incentive to invest in riskier assets to make higher rates of return.

- Failure to require depository institutions to limit risks to the U.S. deposit insurance system contributed to a savings and loan industry crisis in the 1980s. This induced Congress to give the FDIC greater authority to close weak institutions, but depository institutions continue to have incentives to take on greater risks than they would without deposit insurance.

To test your understanding of the concepts covered in this section, go to the Online Review at www.myeconlab.com/miller.

CASE STUDY: Economics Front and Center

Deposit Insurance in an Expanded European Union

Murphy has begun a new position with a multinational financial consulting firm. A German banking association has hired his firm to evaluate the effects that the recent addition of ten more countries will have on the European Union (EU) banking system. The firm has assigned Murphy to draft its initial report.

In 2004, banks located in ten nations—Cyprus, the Czech Republic, Estonia, Hungary, Latvia, Lithuania, Malta, Poland, Slovakia, and Slovenia—became a part of the EU banking system. Murphy has determined that, on average, these nations' governments provide deposit insurance guarantees nearly twice as large as in the original EU nations. In addition, the ratio of government bank examiners to the number of banks in these nations is much smaller than in the original EU countries. In general, bank regulators in these countries have fewer people per bank and smaller budgets available to perform their supervisory tasks. Murphy types on his computer keyboard, "The implications for moral hazard in these nations—and hence in the expanded European Union—are clear."

Points to Analyze

1. *How does a larger deposit insurance guarantee in a country such as Poland affect the likelihood of moral hazard problems in its banking system?*

2. *How does the relative lack of resources available to examine and supervise banks affect the potential for moral hazard problems at banks located in the EU's new member nations?*

Issues and Applications

Keeping Money Flowing Even When Electricity Cannot

Concepts Applied
- Reserves
- Open Market Operations
- Borrowed Reserves

When the lights went out in New York City and throughout much of the rest of the northeastern United States on August 14, 2003, thousands of banks and other depository institutions faced a significant liquidity problem. In principle, these financial institutions had funds available to honor their obligations, but with most of their computers unpowered and inoperable, many could not get access to funds for hours. The banking system did not grind to a complete stop, however. Banking gridlock was avoided in part because the Federal Reserve stood ready to serve as the banking system's lender of last resort.

Providing Emergency Liquidity at the Discount Window

When depository institutions could not power up their computer systems to retrieve and transmit funds they owed to other parties on August 14 and 15, a number of them turned to the Federal Reserve for credit. Using emergency facilities provided by the Fed, the institutions arranged for Federal Reserve banks to transmit immediately borrowed funds on their behalf. Once they were able to access their systems and transfer funds electronically again, the institutions repaid the Federal Reserve banks.

Figure 16-5 displays average nonseasonal borrowing from the Fed for several weeks preceding the power outage, the two weeks encompassing the power failure, and several weeks after the outage. As you can see, depository institutions' borrowings from the Fed were more than 20 times higher during the weeks of the power outage than during the preceding weeks.

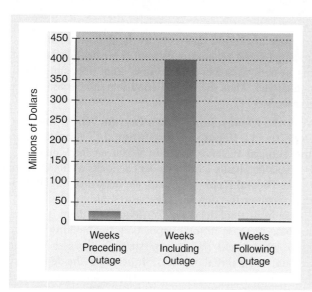

FIGURE 16-5

Average Federal Reserve Discount-Window Loans to Depository Institutions, Two-Week Intervals in July through September 2003

In the immediate aftermath of the massive power outage in the northeastern United States on August 14 and 15, 2003, the Federal Reserve significantly increased nonseasonal lending to depository institutions.

Source: Board of Governors of the Federal Reserve System.

A Big Power Outage, but a Relatively Small-Scale Test for the Fed

The increase in discount-window borrowing depicted in Figure 16-5 appears relatively dramatic. In comparison with earlier historical events, however, it was actually a minor blip in Fed lending at the discount window. For instance, within the 24 hours following the September 11, 2001, terrorist attacks in New York City, Washington, D.C., and Pennsylvania, the Fed extended more than *$45 billion* in credit.

Thus dealing with the 2003 failure in the northeastern power grid turned out to be just an out-of-the-ordinary day of business for the Federal Reserve System. We can hope that the Fed does not have to deal with many worse events for the U.S. financial system. Nevertheless, as the lender of last resort it stands ready to provide funds to all creditworthy depository institutions. At any given point in time, the Fed judges all but a few institutions to be creditworthy, so in principle the Fed could, in the worst extremity, temporarily bail out the entire banking system with loans from the discount window.

For Critical Analysis

1. Could an event such as the August 2003 power outage affect the money multiplier? If so, how? (Hint: How might it affect holdings of currency relative to checkable deposits?)
2. How might the Federal Reserve have maintained the money supply during the days following the August 14 blackout, even if it had not provided more credit at the discount window? (Hint: What are other methods of altering the money supply?)

Web Resources

1. How did the Fed respond to the two largest stock market crashes in history? Learn more about the 1929 and 1987 experiences in a 1987 essay by the then-president of the Federal Reserve Bank of Minneapolis via www.econtoday.com/chap16.
2. To find data on the discount-window borrowings and reserve deposits of depository institutions, go to www.econtoday.com/chap16.

Research Project

The founders of the Federal Reserve System said that a key duty of the institution was to provide an "elastic currency" in times of crisis. What do you think they meant by this? Is this what the Fed did during the power grid failure in August 2003? Have there been other instances when the Fed made sure that there was an "elastic currency"? Have there been times when the Fed has failed in this task? (Hint: For instance, the biggest stock market collapses were in 1929 and 1987, and the Fed responded to the crises very differently.)

SUMMARY DISCUSSION of Learning Objectives

1. **How the Federal Reserve Assesses Reserve Requirements:** The Federal Reserve establishes a required reserve ratio, which is currently 10 percent of nearly all checkable deposits at depository institutions. Legal reserves that depository institutions may hold to satisfy their reserve requirements include deposits they hold at Federal Reserve district banks and as cash in their vaults. Any legal reserves that a depository institution holds over and above its required reserves are called excess reserves.

2. **Why the Money Supply Does Not Change When Someone Deposits in a Depository Institution a Check Drawn on Another Depository Institution:** When an individual or a business deposits a check drawn on another party, two things occur. First, the depository institution on which the check was drawn experiences a reduction in its total deposits when the check clears. Second, the de-

pository institution that receives the deposit experiences an equal-sized increase in its total deposits. For the banking system as a whole, therefore, total deposits remain unchanged. Thus the money supply is unaffected by the transaction.

3. **Why the Money Supply Does Change When Someone Deposits in a Depository Institution a Check Drawn on the Federal Reserve System:** When an individual or a business (typically a bond dealer) deposits a check drawn on the Federal Reserve System, the depository institution that receives the deposit experiences an equal-sized increase in its total deposits. Consequently, there is an immediate increase in total deposits in the banking system as a whole, and the money supply increases by the amount of the initial deposit. Furthermore, the depository institution that receives this deposit can lend any reserves

in excess of required reserves, which will generate a rise in deposits at another bank. This process continues as each bank receiving a deposit has additional funds over and above required reserves that it can lend.

4. **The Maximum Potential Change in the Money Supply Following a Federal Reserve Purchase or Sale of U.S. Government Securities:** When the Federal Reserve buys or sells securities, the maximum potential change in the money supply occurs when there are no leakages of currency or excess reserves during the process of money creation. The amount of the maximum potential change is equal to the amount of reserves that the Fed injects or withdraws from the banking system times the reciprocal of the required reserve ratio.

5. **How the Fed Can and Does Influence the Money Supply:** In principle, the Fed can alter reserves and hence the money supply through open market operations, changing the discount rate, and adjusting reserve requirements. When the Fed engages in open market operations, it buys or sells existing U.S. government securities, thereby injecting reserves into or withdrawing reserves from the banking system. Altering the discount rate relative to the federal funds rate can encourage changes in borrowed reserves. Since early 2003, however, the Fed has kept the discount rate 1 percentage point above the federal funds rate, which discourages borrowing from the Fed and limits the Fed's ability to use the discount rate as a separate policy tool. Varying reserve requirements can change the amount of deposits created from bank reserves. The Fed has rarely conducted monetary policy in this way, and reductions in required reserves resulting from depository institutions' use of sweep accounts have made reserve requirements less relevant to monetary policy. Thus open market operations are the Fed's key tool of monetary policy.

6. **Features of Federal Deposit Insurance:** To help prevent runs on banks, the U.S. government in 1933 established the Federal Deposit Insurance Corporation (FDIC). This government agency provides deposit insurance by charging depository institutions premiums based on the value of their deposits, and it places these funds in accounts for use in closing failed banks and reimbursing their depositors. One difficulty associated with providing deposit insurance is the problem of adverse selection because the availability of deposit insurance can potentially attract risk-taking individuals into the banking business. Another difficulty is the moral hazard problem. This problem arises when deposit insurance premiums fail to reflect the full extent of the risks taken on by depository institution managers and when depositors who know they are insured have little incentive to monitor the performance of the institutions that hold their deposit funds.

KEY TERMS AND CONCEPTS

balance sheet (366)

bank runs (381)

discount rate (375)

excess reserves (365)

Federal Deposit Insurance Corporation (FDIC) (380)

federal funds market (376)

federal funds rate (376)

fractional reserve banking (364)

legal reserves (364)

money multiplier (374)

net worth (366)

open market operations (368)

required reserve ratio (365)

required reserves (365)

reserves (364)

sweep accounts (379)

PROBLEMS

Answers to the odd-numbered problems appear at the back of the book.

16-1. Identify each of the following as a commercial bank asset or liability.

 a. An auto loan to an individual
 b. Funds borrowed from a credit union in the federal funds market

 c. A customer's savings deposit
 d. The bank's required reserves

16-2. A bank's total assets equal $1 billion. Its liabilities equal $1 billion. Checkable deposits equal $500 million, loans equal $700 million, and securities equal $250 million.

a. If the bank's only other liabilities are savings deposits, what is the value of these savings deposits?

b. If the bank's only other assets are vault cash and reserve deposits with a Federal Reserve bank, what is the total amount of these assets?

16-3. A bank's only liabilities are $15 million in checkable deposits. The bank currently meets its reserve requirement, and it holds no excess reserves. The required reserve ratio is 10 percent. Assuming that its only assets are legal reserves, loans, and securities, what is the value of loans and securities held by the bank?

16-4. Draw an empty bank balance sheet, with the heading "Assets" on the left and the heading "Liabilities" on the right. Then place the following items on the proper side of the balance sheet:

a. Loans to a private company
b. Borrowings from a Federal Reserve district bank
c. Deposits with a Federal Reserve district bank
d. U.S. Treasury bills
e. Vault cash
f. Loans to other banks in the federal funds market
g. Checkable deposits

16-5. Suppose that the total liabilities of a depository institution are checkable deposits equal to $2 billion. It has $1.65 billion in loans and securities, and the required reserve ratio is 15 percent. Does this institution hold any excess reserves? If so, how much?

16-6. A bank has $120 million in total assets, which are composed of legal reserves, loans, and securities. Its only liabilities are $120 million in checkable deposits. The bank exactly satisfies its reserve requirement, and its total legal reserves equal $6 million. What is the required reserve ratio?

16-7. The Federal Reserve purchases $1 million in U.S. Treasury bonds from a bond dealer, and the dealer's bank credits the dealer's account. The required reserve ratio is 15 percent, and the bank typically lends any excess reserves immediately. Assuming that no currency leakage occurs, how much will the bank be able to lend to its customers following the Fed's purchase?

16-8. A depository institution holds $150 million in required reserves and $10 million in excess reserves. Its remaining assets include $440 million in loans and $150 million in securities. If the institution's only liabilities are checkable deposits, what is the required reserve ratio?

16-9. A bank has $260 million in total reserves, of which $10 million are excess reserves. The bank currently has $3.6 billion in loans, $1 billion in securities, and $140 million in other assets. The required reserve ratio for transactions deposits is 10 percent.

a. What is this bank's total amount of liabilities and net worth?

b. What additional amount of loans could this bank make to households and firms?

c. What is the current quantity of transactions deposits at this bank?

16-10. A bank has issued $4 billion in transactions deposits and $2 billion in time deposits and other nontransactions deposits. Its other liabilities and net worth equal $1 billion. The bank has $100 million in total reserves. The only reserve requirement that this and all other banks must satisfy is a 2 percent ratio that applies to transactions deposits.

a. What is the amount of the bank's total assets?

b. What is the amount of the bank's excess reserves?

c. What is the maximum potential money multiplier for the banking system?

16-11. A bank has $16 billion in total assets, of which $200 million are its total reserves. Customers initially hold a total of $9 billion in their transactions deposit accounts with this bank, but it has automatically transformed $8 billion of this amount into money market deposit accounts through its sweep account arrangements with these customers. The required reserve ratio for transactions deposits is 20 percent. The bank faces no other reserve requirement.

a. At present, does this bank meet its reserve requirement?

b. How much in excess reserves can this bank currently use to make loans or purchase securities?

c. What is the amount of this bank's contribution to the M1 measure of money?

16-12. Suppose that the value of the maximum potential money multiplier is equal to 4. What is the required reserve ratio?

16-13. Why is it that you cannot induce any net multiple deposit expansion in the banking system by buying a U.S. government security with a check, yet the Federal Reserve can do so?

16-14. Consider a world in which there is no currency and depository institutions issue only checkable deposits and desire to hold no excess reserves. The required reserve ratio is 20 percent. The central bank sells $1 billion in government securities. What happens to the money supply?

16-15. Assume a 1 percent required reserve ratio, zero excess reserves, and no currency leakages. What is the maximum potential money multiplier? How will total deposits in the banking system change if the Federal Reserve purchases $5 million in U.S. government securities?

ECONOMICS ON THE NET

E–Checks and the Money Supply In this chapter, you learned about how monetary policy actions of the Federal Reserve induce changes in total deposits in the banking system. Now let's think about monetary policymaking in a world with online checking.

Title: What Is eCheck?

Navigation: Go directly to the eCheck home page **echeck. commerce.net/overview** via **www.econtoday. com/chap16**, and click on *What Is eCheck?*

Application Read the discussion, and then answer the following questions.

1. Are e-checks substitutes for currency and coins, or are they substitutes for traditional paper checks? Does the answer to this question make a difference for how e-checks are likely to feature in the money multiplier process?

2. Suppose that there is widespread adoption of e-check technology by consumers and businesses. Would this affect the basic money multiplier model that we developed in this chapter? If so, how? If not, why not?

For Group Study and Analysis Divide the class into groups. Have each group evaluate the likely effects of e-check adoption, as well as widespread adoption of other forms of electronic retail payments mechanisms, on the money multiplier. Meet again as a class, and discuss the channels by which adoption of electronic moneys will potentially affect the money multiplier.

If your exam were tomorrow, would you be ready? For each chapter, MyEconLab Practice Tests and Study Plans pinpoint which sections you have mastered and which ones you need to study. That way, you are more efficient with your study time, and you are better prepared for your exams.

In addition to Practice Tests and your personalized Study Plan, you'll find the following media resources in MyEconLab:

1. *Graphs in Motion* animation of Figures 16-1 and 16-2.
2. An *Economics in Motion* in-depth animation of the Federal Reserve system and the banking system.
3. Videos featuring the author, Roger LeRoy Miller, on the following subjects:
    *   Depository Institution Reserves
    *   Deposit Insurance and Risk Taking

4. Links to the Web sites cited in the marginal Internet Resources, Issues and Applications feature, and Economics on the Net activity.
5. Audio clips of all key terms, additional practice problems, and a PDF version of the material from the print Study Guide.
6. eThemes of the Times, which is a New York Times article to help you understand the real-world applications of what you are learning.

To see how it works, turn to page 16 and then go to **www.myeconlab.com/miller**.

Get Ahead of the Curve

Domestic and International Dimensions of Monetary Policy

It was a rare public moment of disagreement between two members of the Federal Reserve's Board of Governors. In a conference discussion, one governor, Ben Bernanke, argued that the Fed should aim for a target rate of inflation, such as 2 percent per year. Another governor, Donald Kohn, disagreed. Kohn argued that an inflation rate target would hamstring the Fed. When the business downturn of 2001 began, he suggested, strict adherence to an inflation target would have prevented Fed officials from feeling free to let interest rates rapidly decline. In this chapter, you will learn more about the relationship between the money supply and the rate of inflation. In addition, you will find out how the money supply and the interest rate are related.

Media Resources

Refer to the end of the chapter for a full listing of the multimedia learning materials available in MyEconLab.

LEARNING OBJECTIVES

After reading this chapter, you should be able to:

1. Identify the key factors that influence the quantity of money that people desire to hold

2. Describe how the Federal Reserve's tools of monetary policy influence market interest rates

3. Evaluate how expansionary and contractionary monetary policy actions affect equilibrium real GDP and the price level in the short run

4. Understand the equation of exchange and its importance in the quantity theory of money and prices

5. Distinguish between the Keynesian and monetarist views on the transmission mechanism of monetary policy

6. Explain why the Federal Reserve cannot stabilize both the money supply and interest rates simultaneously

. . . studies have shown that Europe's euro currency notes are less durable than U.S. dollar notes and a number of other paper currencies? Euro notes wear out faster during regular use, and they break down more rapidly when they get wet—as when people accidentally leave the notes in pockets of clothing run through washing machines. The euro notes can also pose more problems for people who regularly handle money, such as bank tellers and store clerks, because constant skin contact with euro notes can cause more allergic reactions than with other nations' currencies.

Nevertheless, the euro's physical flaws are among the milder irritations facing the European Central Bank. This institution, after all, has broad responsibility for determining the overall money supply for the European Monetary Union, including checkable and other deposits in banks across the European subcontinent. Its policies must take into account the economic goals of a very diverse group of member nations.

In the United States, the Federal Reserve is responsible for conducting monetary policy, which entails varying the supply of money or the rate at which it grows in order to achieve national economic goals. When you were introduced to aggregate demand in Chapter 10, you discovered that the position of the aggregate demand curve is determined by the willingness of firms, individuals, governments, and foreign residents to purchase domestically produced goods and services. Monetary policy works in a variety of ways to change this willingness, both directly and indirectly.

Think about monetary policy in an intuitive way: An increase in the money supply adds to the amount of money that firms and individuals have on hand and so increases the amount that they wish to spend. The result is an increase in aggregate demand. A decrease in the money supply reduces the amount of money that people have on hand to spend and so decreases aggregate demand.

WHAT'S SO SPECIAL ABOUT MONEY?

By definition, monetary policy has to do, in the main, with money. But what is so special about money? Money is the product of a "social contract" in which we all agree to do two things:

1. Express all prices in terms of a common unit of account, which in the United States we call the dollar
2. Use a specific medium of exchange for market transactions

These two features of money distinguish it from all other goods in the economy. As a practical matter, money is involved on one side of every nonbarter transaction in the economy—and trillions of them occur every year. What this means is that something that changes the amount of money in circulation will have some effect on many transactions and thus on elements of GDP. If something affects the number of snowmobiles in existence, probably only the snowmobile market will be altered. But something that affects the amount of money in existence is going to affect *all* markets.

Holding Money

All of us engage in a flow of transactions. We buy and sell things all of our lives. But because we use money—dollars—as our medium of exchange, all *flows* of nonbarter transactions involve a *stock* of money. We can restate this as follows:

To use money, one must hold money.

Given that everybody must hold money, we can now talk about the *demand* to hold it. People do not demand to hold money just to look at pictures of past leaders. They hold it to be able to use it to buy goods and services.

The Demand for Money: What People Wish to Hold

Money balances
Synonymous with money, money stock, money holdings.

People have a certain motivation that causes them to want to hold **money balances.** Individuals and firms could try to do without non-interest-bearing money balances. But life is inconvenient without a ready supply of money balances. There is a demand for money by the public, motivated by several factors.

The Transactions Demand. The main reason people hold money is that money can be used to purchase goods and services. People are paid at specific intervals (once a week, once a month, and so on), but they wish to make purchases more or less continuously. To free themselves from having to make expenditures on goods and services only on payday, people find it beneficial to hold money. The benefit they receive is convenience: They willingly forgo interest earnings in order to avoid the inconvenience and expense of cashing in nonmoney assets such as bonds every time they wish to make a purchase. Thus people hold money to make regular, *expected* expenditures under the **transactions demand.** As nominal GDP rises, people will want to hold more money because they will be making more transactions.

Transactions demand
Holding money as a medium of exchange to make payments. The level varies directly with nominal GDP.

Precautionary demand
Holding money to meet unplanned expenditures and emergencies.

The Precautionary Demand. The transactions demand involves money held to make *expected* expenditures. People also hold money for the **precautionary demand** to make *unexpected* purchases or to meet emergencies. When people hold money for the precautionary demand, they incur a cost in forgone interest earnings that they balance against the benefit that having cash on hand provides. The higher the rate of interest, the lower the money balances people wish to hold for the precautionary demand.

The Asset Demand. Remember that one of the functions of money is to serve as a store of value. People can hold money balances as a store of value, or they can hold bonds or stocks or other interest-earning assets. The desire to hold money as a store of value leads to the **asset demand** for money. People choose to hold money rather than other assets for two reasons: its liquidity and the lack of risk.

Asset demand
Holding money as a store of value instead of other assets such as certificates of deposit, corporate bonds, and stocks.

The disadvantage of holding money balances as an asset, of course, is the interest earnings forgone. Each individual or business decides how much money to hold as an asset by looking at the opportunity cost of holding money. The higher the interest rate—which is the opportunity cost of holding money—the lower the money balances people will want to hold as assets. Conversely, the lower the interest rate offered on alternative assets, the higher the money balances people will want to hold as assets.

The Demand for Money Curve

Assume for simplicity's sake that the amount of money demanded for transactions purposes is fixed, given a certain level of income. That leaves the precautionary and asset demands for money, both determined by the opportunity cost of holding money. If we assume that the interest rate represents the cost of holding money balances, we can graph the relationship between the interest rate and the quantity of money demanded. In Figure 17-1, the demand for money curve shows a familiar downward slope. The horizontal axis measures the quantity of money demanded, and the vertical axis is the interest rate. In this sense, the interest rate is the price of holding money. At a higher price, a lower quantity of money is demanded, and vice versa.

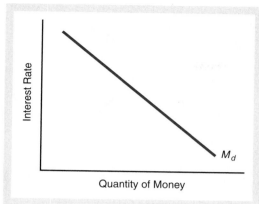

FIGURE 17-1
The Demand for Money Curve
If we use the interest rate as a proxy for the opportunity cost of holding money balances, the demand for money curve, M_d, is downward sloping, similar to other demand curves.

To see this, imagine two scenarios. In the first one, you can earn 20 percent a year if you put your cash into purchases of U.S. government securities. In the other scenario, you can earn 1 percent if you put your cash into purchases of U.S. government securities. If you have $1,000 average cash balances in a non-interest-bearing checking account, in the second scenario over a one-year period, your opportunity cost would be 1 percent of $1,000, or $10. In the first scenario, your opportunity cost would be 20 percent of $1,000, or $200. Under which scenario would you hold more cash instead of securities?

CONCEPTS in Brief

- To use money, people must hold money. Therefore, they have a demand for money balances.

- The determinants of the demand for money balances are the transactions demand, the precautionary demand, and the asset demand.

- Because holding money carries an opportunity cost—the interest income forgone—the demand for money curve showing the relationship between the quantity of money balances demanded and the interest rate slopes downward.

To test your understanding of the concepts covered in this section, go to the Online Review at www.myeconlab.com/miller.

THE TOOLS OF MONETARY POLICY

The Fed seeks to alter consumption, investment, and aggregate demand as a whole by altering the rate of growth of the money supply. The Fed has three tools at its disposal as part of its policymaking action: open market operations, discount rate changes, and reserve requirement changes.

Open Market Operations

The Fed changes the amount of reserves in the system by its purchases and sales of government bonds issued by the U.S. Treasury. To understand how the Fed does this, you must first start out in an equilibrium in which everybody, including the holders of bonds, is satisfied with the current situation. There is some equilibrium level of interest rate (and bond prices). Now if the Fed wants to conduct open market operations, it must somehow induce individuals, businesses, and foreign residents to hold more or fewer U.S. Treasury bonds. The inducement must be in the form of making people better off. So, if the Fed wants to buy bonds, it is going to have to offer to buy them at a higher price than exists in the marketplace. If the Fed wants to sell bonds, it is going to have to offer them at a lower

Go to www.econtoday.com/chap17 to learn about the Federal Reserve's current policy regarding open market operations. Click on "Meeting calendar statements, and minutes," and select the "Minutes" for the most recent month.

FIGURE 17-2
Determining the Price of Bonds
In panel (a), the Fed offers more bonds for sale. The price drops from P_1 to P_2. In panel (b), the Fed purchases bonds. This is the equivalent of a reduction in the supply of bonds available for private investors to hold. The price of bonds must rise from P_1 to P_3 to clear the market.

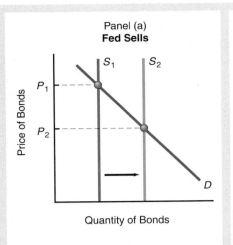
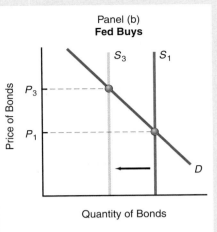

price than exists in the marketplace. Thus an open market operation must cause a change in the price of bonds.

Graphing the Sale of Bonds. The Fed sells some of the bonds in its portfolio. This is shown in panel (a) of Figure 17-2. Notice that the supply of bonds is shown here as a vertical line with respect to price. The demand for bonds is downward sloping. If the Fed offers more bonds it holds for sale, it shifts the supply curve from S_1 to S_2. It cannot induce people to buy the extra bonds at the original price of P_1, so it must lower the price to P_2.

The Fed's Purchase of Bonds. The opposite occurs when the Fed purchases bonds. You can view this purchase of bonds as a reduction in the stock of bonds available for private investors to hold. In panel (b) of Figure 17-2, the original supply curve is S_1. The new supply curve of outstanding bonds will end up being S_3 because of the Fed's purchases of bonds. To get people to give up these bonds, the Fed must offer them a more attractive price. The price will rise from P_1 to P_3.

Relationship Between the Price of Existing Bonds and the Rate of Interest. There is an inverse relationship between the price of existing bonds and the rate of interest. Assume that the average yield on bonds is 5 percent. You decide to purchase a bond. A local corporation agrees to sell you a bond that will pay you $50 a year forever. What is the price you are willing to pay for the bond? It is $1,000. Why? Because $50 divided by $1,000 equals 5 percent, which is as good as the best return you can earn elsewhere. You purchase the bond. The next year something happens in the economy, and you can now obtain bonds that have effective yields of 10 percent. (In other words, the prevailing interest rate in the economy is now 10 percent.) What has happened to the market price of the existing bond that you own, the one you purchased the year before? It will have fallen. If you try to sell it for $1,000, you will discover that no investors will buy it from you. Why should they when they can obtain the same $50-a-year yield from someone else by paying only $500? Indeed, unless you offer your bond for sale at a price of $500, no buyers will be forthcoming. Hence an increase in the prevailing interest rate in the economy has caused the market value of your existing bond to fall.

The important point to be understood is this:

The market price of existing bonds (and all fixed-income assets) is inversely related to the rate of interest prevailing in the economy.

Economics Front and Center

To consider an example of a situation in which an *anticipated* monetary policy action might cause both market interest rates and bond prices to change, see the case study, **What Might Happen to Bond Prices When the Fed Fails to "Telegraph" Its Intentions?** on page 407.

Changes in the Difference Between the Discount Rate and the Federal Funds Rate

When the Fed was founded in 1913, the most important tool in its monetary policy kit was changes in the discount rate, discussed in Chapter 16. The Fed originally relied on the discount rate to carry out monetary policy because it had no power over reserve requirements. More important, its initial portfolio of government bonds was practically nonexistent and hence insufficient to conduct a full range of open market operations. As the Fed has come increasingly to rely on open market operations, it has used the discount rate less frequently as a tool of monetary policy.

Recall that the discount rate is the interest rate the Fed charges depository institutions when they borrow reserves directly from the Fed. Since 2003, the Fed has kept the discount rate 1 percentage point above the market-determined federal funds rate. An increase in the discount rate relative to the federal funds rate would increase the cost of funds for depository institutions that seek loans from the Fed, in comparison to the cost of borrowing funds in the federal funds market. In principle, depository institutions that borrow from the Fed would pass at least part of this increased cost on to their borrowing customers by raising the interest rates they charge on loans.

Consequently, pushing up the discount rate relative to the federal funds rate could bring about a rise in market interest rates. Few depository institutions choose to borrow from the Fed at the higher discount rate, however, so this interest rate effect would likely be very small.

Changes in Reserve Requirements

Although the Fed rarely uses changes in reserve requirements as a form of monetary policy, it most recently did so in 1992, when it decreased reserve requirements on checkable deposits to 10 percent. In any event, here is how changes in reserve requirements can affect the economy.

If the Fed increases reserve requirements, banks must replenish their reserves by reducing their lending. To induce potential borrowers not to borrow so much, banks respond to an increase in reserve requirements by raising the interest rates they charge on the loans they offer. Conversely, when the Fed decreases reserve requirements, as it did in 1992, some depository institutions attempt to lend their excess reserves out. To induce customers to borrow more, depository institutions cut interest rates.

Of course, you learned in Chapter 16 that depository institutions can use sweep accounts to reduce their effective reserve requirements. This institutional change has muted the effects that variations in reserve requirements can have on market interest rates.

CONCEPTS in Brief

- Monetary policy consists of open market operations, discount rate changes, and reserve requirement changes undertaken by the Fed.

- When the Fed sells bonds, it must offer them at a lower price. When the Fed buys bonds, it must pay a higher price.

- There is an inverse relationship between the prevailing rate of interest in the economy and the market price of existing bonds and all fixed-income assets.

- In principle, the Fed can conduct monetary policy by varying the discount rate relative to the federal funds rate or altering reserve requirements, but it rarely does so.

To test your understanding of the concepts covered in this section, go to the Online Review at www.myeconlab.com/miller.

EFFECTS OF AN INCREASE IN THE MONEY SUPPLY

To understand how monetary policy works in its simplest form, we are going to run an experiment in which you increase the money supply in a very direct way. Assume that the government has given you hundreds of millions of dollars in just-printed bills that you load into a helicopter. You then fly around the country, dropping the money out of the window. People pick it up and put it in their pockets. Some deposit the money in their checking accounts. The first thing that happens is that they have too much money—not in the sense that they want to throw it away but rather in relation to other things that they own. There are a variety of ways to dispose of this "new" money.

Direct Effect

The simplest thing that people can do when they have excess money balances is to go out and spend them on goods and services. Here they have a direct impact on aggregate demand. Aggregate demand rises because with an increase in the money supply, at any given price level people now want to purchase more output of real goods and services.

Indirect Effect

Not everybody will necessarily spend the newfound money on goods and services. Some people may wish to deposit some or all of those excess money balances in banks. The recipient banks now discover that they have higher reserves than they wish to hold. As you learned in Chapter 16, one thing that banks can do to get interest-earning assets is to lend out the excess reserves. But banks cannot induce people to borrow more funds than they were borrowing before unless the banks lower the interest rate that they charge on loans. This lower interest rate encourages people to take out those loans. Businesses will therefore engage in new investment with the funds loaned. Individuals will engage in more consumption of durable goods such as housing, autos, and home entertainment centers. Either way, the increased loans have created a rise in aggregate demand. More people will be involved in more spending—even those who did not pick up any of the money that was originally dropped out of your helicopter.

How do you suppose that Zimbabwe's government learned that it is the total amount of money created that determines money supply growth?

International EXAMPLE

Zimbabwe Learns Smaller Bills Do Not Reduce Money Growth

In the summer of 2003, the government of Zimbabwe tried to reduce the rate of growth of its money supply, which at that time exceeded 300 percent per year. To pursue this objective, the government decided to stop printing the most popular and highest-denomination currency note, a bill worth 500 Zimbabwe dollars. What the government soon discovered, however, was that the people of Zimbabwe were willing to hold more lower-denomination notes instead. Thus the government found itself supplying so many low-denomination currency notes that its total money supply rose even faster than before. By the spring of 2004, the rate of growth of the total quantity of money in circulation in Zimbabwe had almost doubled, to more than 600 percent per year.

For Critical Analysis
Assuming that all other things besides the money supply were unchanged in Zimbabwe between the summer of 2003 and the spring of 2004, what must have happened to the nation's inflation rate?

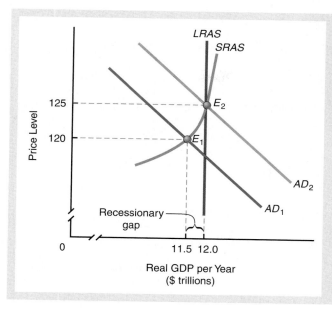

FIGURE 17-3
Expansionary Monetary Policy with Underutilized Resources
If we start out with equilibrium at E_1, expansionary monetary policy will shift AD_1 to AD_2. The new equilibrium will be at E_2.

Graphing the Effects of an Expansionary Monetary Policy

Look at Figure 17-3. We start out in a situation in which the economy is operating at less than full employment. You see a recessionary gap in the figure, which is measured as the horizontal difference between the *LRAS* curve and the current equilibrium. Short-run equilibrium is at E_1, with a price level of 120 and real GDP of $11.5 trillion. The long-run aggregate supply curve is at $12 trillion. Assume now that the Fed increases the money supply. Because of the direct and indirect effects of this increase in the money supply, aggregate demand shifts outward to the right to AD_2. The new equilibrium is at an output rate of $12 trillion of real GDP per year and a price level of 125. Here expansionary monetary policy can move the economy toward its *LRAS* curve sooner than otherwise.

Graphing the Effects of Contractionary Monetary Policy

Assume that there is an inflationary gap as shown in Figure 17-4 on the following page. There you see that the short-run aggregate supply curve, *SRAS*, intersects aggregate demand, AD_1, at E_1. This is to the right of the *LRAS* of real GDP per year of $12 trillion. Contractionary monetary policy can eliminate this inflationary gap. Because of both the direct and indirect effects of monetary policy, the aggregate demand curve shifts inward from AD_1 to AD_2. Equilibrium is now at E_2, which is at a lower price level, 120. Equilibrium real GDP has now fallen from $12.5 trillion to $12 trillion.

Note that contractionary monetary policy involves a reduction in the money supply, with a consequent decline in the price level (deflation). In the real world, contractionary monetary policy normally involves reducing the *rate of growth* of the money supply, thereby reducing the rate of increase in the price level (inflation). Similarly, real-world expansionary monetary policy typically involves increasing the rate of growth of the money supply.

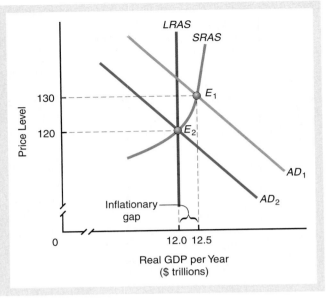

FIGURE 17-4
Contractionary Monetary Policy with Overutilized Resources

If we begin at an equilibrium at point E_1, contractionary monetary policy will shift the aggregate demand curve from AD_1 to AD_2. The new equilibrium will be at point E_2.

CONCEPTS in Brief

- The direct effect of an increase in the money supply arises because people desire to spend more on real goods and services when they have excess money balances.

- The indirect effect of an increase in the money supply works through a lowering of the interest rates, which en-

courages businesses to make new investments with the funds loaned to them. Individuals will also engage in more consumption (on consumer durables) because of lower interest rates.

To test your understanding of the concepts covered in this section, go to the Online Review at **www.myeconlab.com/miller.**

OPEN ECONOMY TRANSMISSION OF MONETARY POLICY

Go to www.econtoday.com/chap17 for links to central banks around the globe, provided by the Bank for International Settlements.

So far we have discussed monetary policy in a closed economy. When we move to an open economy, with international trade and the international purchase and sale of all assets including dollars and other currencies, monetary policy becomes more complex. Consider first the effect on exports of any type of monetary policy.

The Net Export Effect

When we examined fiscal policy, we pointed out that deficit financing can lead to higher interest rates. Higher (real, after-tax) interest rates do something in the foreign sector—they attract foreign financial investment. More people want to purchase U.S. government securities, for example. But to purchase U.S. assets, people first have to obtain U.S. dollars. This means that the demand for dollars goes up in foreign exchange markets. The international price of the dollar therefore rises. This is called an *appreciation* of the dollar, and it tends to reduce net exports because it makes our exports more expensive in terms of foreign currency and imports cheaper in terms of dollars. Foreign residents demand fewer of our goods and services, and we demand more of theirs. In this way, expansionary fiscal policy that creates deficit spending financed by U.S. government borrowing can lead to a reduction in net exports, which dampens the effect of fiscal policy on the economy.

But what about expansionary monetary policy? If expansionary monetary policy reduces real, after-tax U.S. interest rates, there will be a positive net export effect because foreign residents will want fewer U.S. financial instruments. Hence they will demand fewer dollars, thereby causing the international price of the dollar to fall. This makes our exports cheaper for the rest of the world, which then demands a larger quantity of our exports. It also means that foreign goods and services are more expensive in the United States, so we therefore demand fewer imports. We come up with two conclusions:

1. Expansionary fiscal policy may cause interest rates to rise and thereby attract international flows of financial capital. The resulting appreciation of the dollar causes net exports to decline, which offsets the effects of fiscal policy to some extent.

2. Expansionary monetary policy may cause interest rates to fall. Such a fall will induce international outflows of financial capital, thereby lowering the international value of the dollar and making U.S. goods more attractive. The net export effect of expansionary monetary policy will be in the same direction as the monetary policy effect, thereby amplifying the effect of such policy.

Why do you suppose that the Swiss National Bank, the central bank of Switzerland, has been relying solely on the net export effect to conduct monetary policy?

International Policy E X A M P L E

The Swiss Exchange Rate Fills in for the Interest Rate

In early 2003, nominal interest rates in Switzerland fell very close to zero percent per year. Market interest rates remained that low for more than a year. During this period, the nation found itself mired in its second recession of the 2000s, but the Swiss National Bank could not push *market* interest rates any lower.

Exports account for 45 percent of Switzerland's GDP. Consequently, the Swiss National Bank was able to take advantage of the net export effect created by an expansionary monetary policy. The resulting depreciation of the Swiss franc relative to the currencies of most other nations made Swiss exports less expensive for residents of those countries. Net exports in Switzerland rose, and this generated a rise in aggregate demand.

For Critical Analysis
Were Swiss real *interest rates necessarily equal to zero in 2003 and 2004?*

Contractionary Monetary Policy

Now assume that the economy is experiencing inflation and the Federal Reserve wants to pursue a contractionary monetary policy. In so doing, it will cause interest rates to rise in the short run, as discussed earlier. Rising interest rates will cause financial capital to flow into the United States. The demand for dollars will increase, and their international price will go up. Foreign goods will now look cheaper to U.S. residents, and imports will rise. Foreign residents will not want our exports as much, and exports will fall. The result will be a reduction in our international trade balance, that is, a decline in net exports. Again, the international consequences reinforce the domestic consequences of monetary policy.

Globalization of International Money Markets

On a broader level, the Fed's ability to control the rate of growth of the money supply may be hampered as U.S. money markets become less isolated. With the push of a computer button, billions of dollars can change hands halfway around the world. If the Fed reduces the growth of the money supply, individuals and firms in the United States can obtain dollars from other sources. People in the United States who want more liquidity can obtain their dollars from foreign residents. Indeed, it is possible that as world markets become increasingly integrated, U.S. residents, who can already hold U.S. bank accounts denominated in foreign currencies, may someday regularly conduct transactions using other nations' currencies.

CONCEPTS in Brief

- Monetary policy in an open economy has repercussions for net exports.

- If expansionary monetary policy reduces U.S. interest rates, there is a positive net export effect because foreign residents will demand fewer U.S. financial instruments, thereby demanding fewer dollars and hence causing the international price of the dollar to fall. This makes our exports cheaper for the rest of the world.

- When contractionary monetary policy causes interest rates to rise, foreign residents will want more U.S. financial instruments. The resulting increase in the demand for dollars will raise the dollar's value in foreign exchange markets, leading to a decline in net exports.

To test your understanding of the concepts covered in this section, go to the Online Review at www.myeconlab.com/miller.

MONETARY POLICY AND INFLATION

Most theories of inflation relate to the short run. The price index in the short run can fluctuate because of events such as oil price shocks, labor union strikes, or discoveries of large amounts of new natural resources. In the long run, however, empirical studies show a relatively stable relationship between excessive growth in the money supply and inflation.

Simple supply and demand analysis can explain why the price level rises when the money supply is increased. Suppose that there is a major oil discovery, and the supply of oil increases dramatically relative to the demand for oil. The relative price of oil will fall; now it will take more units of oil to exchange for specific quantities of nonoil products. Similarly, if the supply of money rises relative to the demand for money, more units of money are required to purchase specific quantities of goods and services. That is merely another way of stating that the price level increases or that the purchasing power of money declines. In fact, the classical economists referred to inflation as a situation in which more money is chasing the same quantity of goods and services.

The Equation of Exchange and the Quantity Theory

Equation of exchange
The formula indicating that the number of monetary units times the number of times each unit is spent on final goods and services is identical to the price level times real GDP.

Income velocity of money
The number of times per year a dollar is spent on final goods and services; equal to nominal GDP divided by the money supply.

A simple way to show the relationship between changes in the quantity of money in circulation and the price level is through the **equation of exchange,** developed by Irving Fisher (note that "≡" refers to an identity or truism):

$$M_s V \equiv PY$$

where M_s = actual money balances held by the nonbanking public

V = **income velocity of money,** which is the number of times, on average per year, each monetary unit is spent on final goods and services

P = price level or price index

Y = real GDP per year

Consider a numerical example involving a one-commodity economy. Assume that in this economy, the total money supply, M_s, is $5 trillion; the quantity of output, Y, is $12 trillion (in base-year dollars); and the price level, P, is 1.25 (125 in index number terms). Using the equation of exchange,

$$M_s V \equiv PY$$
$$\$5 \text{ trillion} \times V \equiv 1.25 \times \$12 \text{ trillion}$$
$$\$5 \text{ trillion} \times V \equiv \$15 \text{ trillion}$$
$$V \equiv 3$$

Thus each dollar is spent an average of three times a year.

The Equation of Exchange as an Identity. The equation of exchange must always be true—it is an *accounting identity.* The equation of exchange states that the total amount of money spent on final output, $M_s V$, is equal to the total amount of money *received* for final output, PY. Thus a given flow of money can be viewed from either the buyers' side or the producers' side. The value of goods purchased is equal to the value of goods sold.

If Y represents real GDP and P is the price level, PY equals the dollar value of national output of goods, and services, or *nominal* GDP. Thus

$$M_s V \equiv PY \equiv \text{nominal GDP}$$

The Quantity Theory of Money and Prices. If we now make some assumptions about different variables in the equation of exchange, we come up with the simplified theory of why the price level changes, called the **quantity theory of money and prices.** If we assume that the velocity of money, V, is constant and that real GDP, Y, is basically stable, the simple equation of exchange tells us that a change in the money supply can lead only to a proportionate change in the price level. Continue with our numerical example. Y is $12 trillion. V equals 3. If the money supply increases by 20 percent, to $6 trillion, the only thing that can happen is that the price level, P, has to go up from 1.25 to 1.5. In other words, the price level must also increase by 20 percent. Otherwise the equation is no longer in balance.

Quantity theory of money and prices
The hypothesis that changes in the money supply lead to proportional changes in the price level.

Empirical Verification. There is considerable evidence of the empirical validity of the relationship between monetary growth and high rates of inflation. Figure 17-5 tracks the

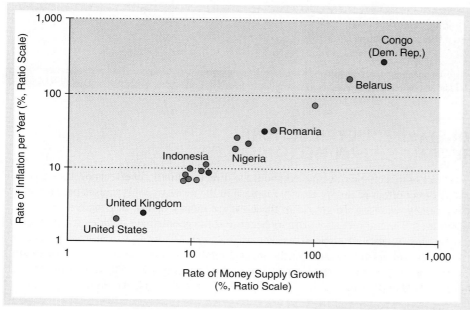

FIGURE 17-5
The Relationship Between Money Supply Growth Rates and Rates of Inflation
If we plot rates of inflation and rates of monetary growth for different countries, we come up with a scatter diagram that reveals an obvious direct relationship. If you were to draw a line through the "average" of the points in this figure, it would be upward sloping, showing that an increase in the rate of growth of the money supply leads to an increase in the rate of inflation.

Sources: International Monetary Fund and national central banks. Data are for latest available periods.

correspondence between money supply growth and the rates of inflation in various countries around the world.

How do you think that the quantity theory of money might help explain the deflation that Japan experienced during the early 2000s?

International Policy EXAMPLE

The Bank of Japan Forgets the Quantity Theory of Money

From 1999 through 2004, nominal interest rates in Japan were very close to zero. During the same period, the nation's price level fell. According to officials at the Bank of Japan, the Japanese central bank, the inability to push interest rates any lower meant that monetary policy could do little to raise aggregate demand. Thus, the officials argued, the Bank of Japan could not prevent Japan's deflation.

Aside from a four-month period in early 2002, the M2 measure of the quantity of money in circulation in Japan declined throughout the 1999–2004 period. Of course, the quantity theory indicates that a negative rate of growth of the

money supply will produce negative growth in the price level, or deflation. Application of the quantity theory of money, therefore, indicates that the Bank of Japan actually had a lot to do with Japan's deflationary situation. It also implies that raising the rate of money growth in Japan could ultimately have brought the deflationary experience to an end.

For Critical Analysis
How could an increase in the amount of money in circulation have caused the Japanese price level to rise even though nominal interest rates temporarily remained close to zero?

CONCEPTS in Brief

- The equation of exchange states that the expenditures by some people will equal income receipts by others, or $M_sV \equiv PY$ (money supply times velocity equals nominal GDP).

- Viewed as an accounting identity, the equation of exchange is always true, because the amount of money spent on final output of goods and services must equal the total amount of money received for final output.

- The quantity theory of money and prices states that a change in the money supply will bring about an equiproportional change in the price level.

To test your understanding of the concepts covered in this section, go to the Online Review at **www.myeconlab.com/miller.**

MONETARY POLICY IN ACTION: THE TRANSMISSION MECHANISM

At the start of this chapter, we talked about the direct and indirect effects of monetary policy. The direct effect is simply that an increase in the money supply causes people to have excess money balances. To get rid of these excess money balances, people increase their expenditures. The indirect effect occurs because some people have decided to purchase interest-bearing assets with their excess money balances. This causes the price of such assets—bonds—to go up. Because of the inverse relationship between the price of existing bonds and the interest rate, the interest rate in the economy falls. This lower interest rate induces people and businesses to spend more than they otherwise would have spent.

FIGURE 17-6
The Keynesian Money Transmission Mechanism

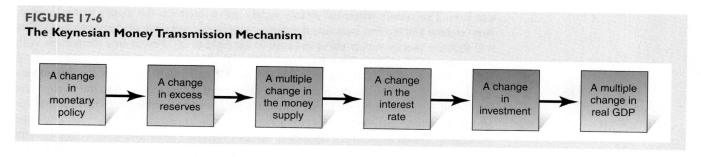

The Keynesian Transmission Mechanism

One school of economists believes that the indirect effect of monetary policy is the more important. This group, typically called Keynesian because of its belief in Keynes's work, asserts that the main effect of monetary policy occurs through changes in the interest rate. The Keynesian money transmission mechanism is shown in Figure 17-6. There you see that the money supply changes the interest rate, which in turn changes the desired rate of investment.

This transmission mechanism can be seen explicitly in Figure 17-7. In panel (a), you see that an increase in the money supply reduces the interest rate. The economywide demand curve for money is labeled M_d in panel (a). At first, the money supply is at M_s, a vertical line determined by our central bank, the Federal Reserve System. The equilibrium interest

FIGURE 17-7
Adding Monetary Policy to the Keynesian Model

In panel (a), we show a demand for money function, M_d. It slopes downward to show that at lower rates of interest, a larger quantity of money will be demanded. The money supply is given initially as M_s, so the equilibrium rate of interest will be r_1. At this rate of interest, we see from the

planned investment schedule given in panel (b) that the quantity of planned investment demanded per year will be I_1. After the shift in the money supply to M_s', the resulting increase in investment from I_1 to I_2 shifts the aggregate demand curve in panel (c) outward from AD_1 to AD_2. Equilibrium moves from E_1 to E_2, at real GDP of $12 trillion per year.

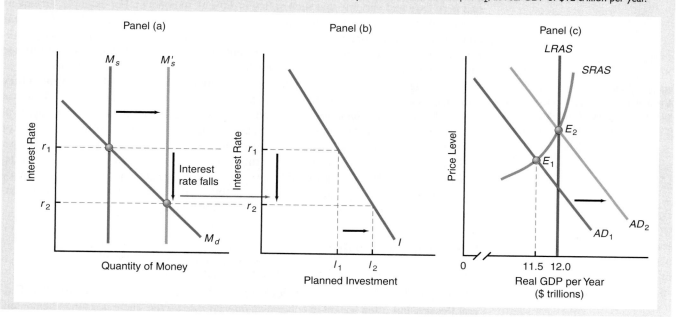

rate is r_1. This occurs where the money supply curve intersects the money demand curve. Now assume that the Fed increases the money supply, say, via open market operations. This will shift the money supply curve outward to the right to M'_s. People find themselves with too much cash (liquidity). They buy bonds. When they buy bonds, they bid up the prices of bonds, thereby lowering the interest rate. The interest rate falls to r_2, where the new money supply curve M'_s intersects the money demand curve M_d. This reduction in the interest rate from r_1 to r_2 has an effect on planned investment, as can be seen in panel (b). Planned investment per year increases from I_1 to I_2. An increase in investment will increase aggregate demand, as shown in panel (c). Aggregate demand increases from AD_1 to AD_2. Equilibrium in the economy increases from real GDP per year of $11.5 trillion, which is not on the *LRAS*, to equilibrium real GDP per year of $12 trillion, which is on the *LRAS*.

The Monetarists' Transmission Mechanism

Monetarists
Macroeconomists who believe that inflation in the long run is always caused by excessive monetary growth and that changes in the money supply affect aggregate demand both directly and indirectly.

Monetarists, economists who believe in a modern quantity theory of money and prices, contend that monetary policy works its way more directly into the economy. They believe that changes in the money supply lead to changes in nominal GDP in the same direction. An increase in the money supply because of expansionary open market operations (purchases of bonds) by the Fed leads the public to have larger money balances than desired. This excess quantity of money supplied induces the public to buy more of everything, especially more durable goods such as cars, stereos, and houses. If the economy is starting out at its long-run equilibrium rate of output, there can be only a short-run increase in real GDP. Ultimately, though, the public cannot buy more of everything; it simply bids up prices so that the price level rises.

Monetarists' Criticism of Monetary Policy

The monetarists' belief that monetary policy works through changes in desired spending does not mean that they consider such policy an appropriate government stabilization tool. According to the monetarists, although monetary policy can affect real GDP (and employment) in the short run, the length of time required before money supply changes take effect is so long and variable that such policy is difficult to conduct. For example, an expansionary monetary policy to counteract a recessionary gap may not take effect for a year and a half, by which time inflation may be a problem. At that point, the expansionary monetary policy will end up making the then-current inflation worse. Monetarists therefore see discretionary monetary policy as a potentially *destabilizing* force in the economy.

Monetary rule
A monetary policy that incorporates a rule specifying the annual rate of growth of some monetary aggregate.

According to the monetarists, policymakers should consequently follow a **monetary rule:** Increase the money supply *smoothly* at a rate consistent with the economy's long-run potential growth rate. *Smoothly* is an important word here. Increasing the money supply at 20 percent per year half the time and decreasing it at 17 percent per year the other half of the time would average out to about a 3 percent increase, but the results would be disastrous, say the monetarists. Instead of permitting the Fed to use its discretion in setting monetary policy, monetarists would force it to follow a rule such as "Increase the money supply smoothly at 3.5 percent per year" or "Abolish the Fed and replace it with a computer program allowing for a steady rise in the money supply."

FED TARGET CHOICE: INTEREST RATES OR MONEY SUPPLY?

It is not possible to stabilize the money supply and interest rates simultaneously. The Federal Reserve has often sought to achieve an *interest rate target*. There is a fundamental tension between targeting interest rates and controlling the money supply, however. Interest

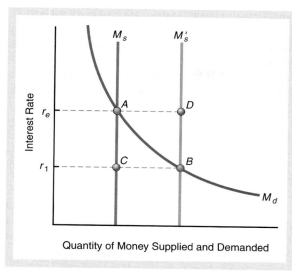

FIGURE 17-8

Choosing a Monetary Policy Target

The Fed, in the short run, can select an interest rate or a money supply target but not both. It cannot, for example, choose r_e and M'_s. If it selects r_e, it must accept M_s. If it selects M'_s, it must allow the interest rate to fall to r_1. The Fed can obtain point A or B. It cannot get to point C or D. It must therefore choose one target or the other.

rate targets force the Fed to abandon control over the money supply; money stock growth targets force the Fed to allow interest rates to fluctuate.

The Interest Rate or the Money Supply?

Figure 17-8 shows the relationship between the total demand for money and the supply of money. Note that in the short run (in the sense that nominal GDP is fixed), the demand for money is constant; short-run money supply changes leave the demand for money curve unaltered. In the short run, the Fed can choose either a particular interest rate (r_e or r_1) or a particular money supply (M_s or M'_s).

If the Fed wants interest rate r_e, it must select money supply M_s. If it desires a lower interest rate in the short run, it must increase the money supply. Thus, by targeting an interest rate, the Fed must relinquish control of the money supply. Conversely, if the Fed wants to target the money supply at, say, M'_s, it must allow the interest rate to fall to r_1.

Choosing a Policy Target

But which should the Fed target, interest rates or monetary aggregates? (And which interest rate or which money supply?) It is generally agreed that the answer depends on the source of instability in the economy. If the source of instability is variations in private or public spending, monetary aggregate (money supply) targets should be set and pursued because with a fixed interest rate, spending variations cause maximum volatility of real GDP. If the source of instability is an unstable demand for (or perhaps supply of) money, however, interest rate targets are preferred because the Fed's effort to keep the interest rate stable automatically offsets the effect of the money demand (or supply) change.

One perennial critic of the Federal Reserve, Milton Friedman, argues that no matter what, "the idea that a central bank can target interest rates is utterly false. Interest rates are partly a real magnitude, partly a nominal magnitude. The Federal Reserve cannot target real interest rates and has done great damage by trying to do so." Here Friedman is referring to the concept of the nominal rate of interest comprising the real interest rate plus the future expected inflation rate.

Consider the case in which the Fed wants to maintain the present level of interest rates. If actual market interest rates in the future rise persistently above the present (desired) rates,

Go to www.econtoday.com/chap17 for Federal Reserve news events announcing its latest monetary policy actions.

the Fed will be continuously forced to increase the money supply. The initial increase in the money supply will only temporarily lower interest rates. The increased money stock will eventually induce inflation, and inflationary premiums will be included in nominal interest rates. To pursue its low-interest-rate policy, the Fed must *again* increase the money stock because interest rates are still rising. Note that to attempt to maintain an interest rate target (stable interest rates), the Fed would have to abandon an independent money supply target.

THE WAY FED POLICY IS CURRENTLY IMPLEMENTED

No matter what the Fed is actually targeting, it currently announces an interest rate target. You should not be fooled, however. When the chair of the Fed states that the Fed is lowering "the" interest rate from, say, 2.75 percent to 2.25 percent, he really means something else. In the first place, the interest rate referred to is the federal funds rate, or the rate at which banks can borrow excess reserves from other banks. In the second place, even if the Fed talks about changing interest rates, it can do so only by actively entering the market for federal government securities (usually Treasury bills). So, if the Fed wants to lower "the" interest rate, it essentially must engage in expansionary open market operations. That is to say, it must buy more Treasury securities than it sells, thereby increasing the money supply. This tends to lower the rate of interest. Conversely, when the Fed wants to increase "the" rate of interest, it engages in contractionary open market operations, thereby decreasing the money supply (or the rate of growth of the money supply).

Laying Out the Fed Policy Strategy

Open market operations are the key means by which the Fed pursues its announced objective for the federal funds rate. Every six to eight weeks, the voting members of the Federal Open Market Committee (FOMC)—the seven Fed board governors and five regional bank presidents—determine the Fed's general strategy of open market operations.

The FOMC outlines its strategy in a document called the *FOMC Directive*. This document lays out the FOMC's general economic objectives, establishes short-term federal funds rate objectives, and specifies specific target ranges for money supply growth. After each meeting, the FOMC issues a brief statement to the media, which then prints stories about the Fed's action or inaction and what it is likely to mean for the economy. Typically, these stories run under headlines such as "Fed Cuts Key Interest Rate," "Fed Acts to Push Up Interest Rates," or "Fed Decides to Leave Interest Rates Alone."

Open Market Operations and the Federal Funds Rate

The FOMC leaves the task of implementing the Directive to officials who manage an office at the Federal Reserve Bank of New York known as the *Trading Desk*. The media spend little time considering how the Fed's Trading Desk conducts its policies, taking it for granted that the Fed can implement the policy action that it has announced to the public.

The Trading Desk's open market operations typically are confined within a one-hour interval each weekday morning. If the Trading Desk purchases government securities during this interval, it increases the quantity of reserves available to depository institutions. As you learned in Chapter 16, depository institutions may use the portion of these reserves not held as required reserves to expand their securities holdings and increase their lending. Among the loans that a number of depository institutions extend are overnight loans to other depository institutions in the federal funds market. Hence, depository institutions' receipts of new reserves via Fed open market purchases increase the supply of federal funds.

Other things being equal, an increase in the supply of federal funds at the currently prevailing federal funds rate results in an excess quantity of federal funds supplied at that rate. The market federal funds rate thereby falls until the quantity of federal funds supplied and demanded are once again equalized. In this way, open market purchases conducted by the Trading Desk induce a fall in the equilibrium federal funds rate.

CONCEPTS in Brief

- In the Keynesian model, monetary transmission operates through a change in interest rates, which changes investment, causing a multiple change in the equilibrium level of real GDP per year.

- Monetarists believe that changes in the money supply lead to changes in nominal GDP in the same direction. The effect is both direct and indirect, however, as individuals spend their excess money balances on cars, stereos, houses, and other items.

- Monetarists argue in favor of a monetary rule—increasing the money supply smoothly at a rate consistent with the economy's long-run potential growth rate. Monetarists do not believe in discretionary monetary (or fiscal) policy.

- The Fed can attempt to stabilize interest rates or the money supply, but not both.

To test your understanding of the concepts covered in this section, go to the Online Review at www.myeconlab.com/miller.

CASE STUDY: Economics Front and Center

What Might Happen to Bond Prices When the Fed Fails to "Telegraph" Its Intentions?

Cunningham is a new employee at the Federal Reserve Bank of New York. She works at the so-called Trading Desk, which is actually a suite of offices housing the Fed staffers who conduct the central bank's open market operations. During recent months, the Fed has held interest rates steady. The staff of the Trading Desk has just received information from the Fed's key policymaking committee, the Federal Open Market Committee (FOMC), indicating that it will certainly vote to push up market interest rates in a few weeks. The FOMC has also requested a draft for a press release announcing the rate hike.

Cunningham recalls that the Fed last induced an increase in market interest rates when she was still a university student. At that time, the Fed had surprised businesspeople by suddenly changing the wording of its announcements toward language indicating that higher interest rates might be in the offing. This sharp shift in tone had contrasted with previous Fed movements toward higher interest rates, which the central bank had tried to "telegraph" in advance via gradual changes in wording. The consequences of the Fed's failure to prepare financial markets in advance had been significant. Bondholders seeking to avoid capital losses when Treasury bond prices fell in response to the Fed's

move began to sell off their bonds. This fall in bond demand caused bond prices to fall rapidly. On the afternoon of the Fed's announcement, prices of both private and Treasury bonds dropped considerably, and market interest rates rose well above the level to which the FOMC had actually intended to push them. Thus the market responses to the Fed's simple announcement of a planned interest rate increase had exceeded the increase that the FOMC intended to generate.

Cunningham has been sitting quietly during the meeting. Now, however, she wonders if she should speak up about whether the Fed might want to consider doing some "telegraphing" in the next few weeks, in advance of the press release.

Points to Analyze

1. Why can widespread expectations that the Fed will conduct policies intended to push up market interest rates in the future cause bond prices to decline in the present?

2. If current bond prices decrease because of a market anticipation of higher interest rates in the future, what will happen to market interest rates in the present?

Using the Quantity Equation to Target the Inflation Rate

Concepts Applied

- Monetary Policy
- Quantity Theory of Money and Prices
- Income Velocity of Money

The list is long and growing, including such diverse nations as New Zealand, Mexico, Canada, the United Kingdom, the Philippines, Sweden, Israel, Australia, and the Czech Republic. In these and other nations, central banks announce and actively pursue targets for annual rates of inflation. If the Federal Reserve wished to add the United States to the list of countries with explicit inflation targets, how would it go about trying to achieve a target inflation rate?

How Inflation Targeting Works

In principle, the quantity theory of money and prices provides a guide for how the Fed could go about targeting the rate of inflation. As you learned in this chapter, the equation of exchange is $M_s V \equiv PY$. Thus, if the income velocity of money (V) and real GDP (Y) were to remain unchanged during the next year, the Fed could aim to attain a specific percentage change in the price level—that is, a target inflation rate—for that year by ensuring that the money supply grows at that rate.

The problem, of course, is that the velocity of money and real GDP rarely remain constant over time. For instance, variations in aggregate demand and aggregate supply unrelated to changes in the money supply can cause equilibrium real GDP to change over time. Achieving an inflation target, therefore, would require the Fed to make good predictions about likely variations in real GDP. Then the Fed could adjust the rate of money growth as necessary to offset those real GDP variations, thereby obtaining a percentage change in the price level consistent with its inflation target.

The Problem with Velocity

Even if the Fed were to do a good job of predicting and offsetting changes in real GDP, unexpected variations in velocity could still be a major hindrance to efforts to target the U.S. inflation rate. The average value of the income velocity of the M2 measure of money trended very slightly upward from about 1.6 in 1951 to about 1.7 in 1991. This small rise in average velocity over this period was not at all steady, however. Between 1960 and 1964, for instance, the M2 velocity suddenly declined from nearly 1.8 to 1.6, or by more than 2.5 percent per year. Between 1977 and 1981, the M2 velocity unexpectedly increased from just over 1.6 to 1.9, or by more than 3 percent per year.

Since 1991, the income velocity of money has been more volatile. Between 1991 and 1996, it rose at an average rate of almost 6 percent per year, from just under 1.8 to more than 2.1. Then velocity fell back again to a level just above 1.8 in the early 2000s.

Has the Fed Proved It Doesn't Require Inflation Targets?

In spite of the large velocity gyrations of the 1990s and early 2000s, however, the Fed managed to steadily reduce the average inflation rate from almost 3 percent per year in the early 1990s to less than 2 percent per year by the early 2000s. It accomplished this when velocity was rising in the early 1990s by holding annual money supply growth close to 3 percent. Then, when velocity was falling into the early 2000s, the Fed increased money growth to more than 7 percent per year.

The Fed has conducted monetary policy in the absence of a publicly announced target rate of inflation, but it apparently has found a way to adjust money supply growth to offset year-to-year changes in the rate of growth of real GDP and sudden variations in the annual rate of change in velocity. Even if the Fed has not aimed to target the inflation rate, its

success in keeping inflation low has proved that it probably could find a way to come close to attaining such a target if it really wanted to do so.

1. What kinds of factors do you suppose might contribute to variations in the income velocity of money?
2. From the perspective of aggregate demand–aggregate supply analysis, why might someone who believes that short-term stability of real GDP is more important than long-term price stability oppose Fed efforts to target the inflation rate? (Hint: If a sudden reduction in short-run aggregate supply caused real GDP to fall and the price level to rise, what would the Fed have to do to keep the price level stable, and how would this affect equilibrium real GDP?)

1. To learn about how the central bank of one nation, the Philippines, implements inflation targeting, go to www.econtoday.com/chap17.
2. For access to several detailed articles on inflation targeting in various nations, use the link available at www.econtoday.com/chap17.

Make a list of pros and cons associated with a Fed policy of announcing and aiming to achieve a target inflation rate. In your view, do the pros outweigh the cons, or vice versa? Why? If the Fed were to try to target the inflation rate, how would you recommend it go about determining what its inflation target should be?

SUMMARY DISCUSSION of Learning Objectives

1. **Key Factors That Influence the Quantity of Money That People Desire to Hold:** People generally make more transactions when nominal GDP rises, and they require more money to make these transactions. Consequently, they desire to hold more money when nominal GDP increases. People also hold money as a precaution against unexpected expenditures they may wish to make, and the interest rate is the opportunity cost of holding money for this purpose. In addition, money is a store of value that people may hold alongside bonds, stocks, and other interest-earning assets, and the opportunity cost of holding money as an asset is again the interest rate. Thus the quantity of money demanded declines as the market interest rate increases.

2. **How the Federal Reserve's Monetary Policy Tools Influence Market Interest Rates:** An open market purchase of government securities, a reduction in the discount rate, or a decrease in the required reserve ratio are all ways that the Federal Reserve can bring about an increase in total reserves in the banking system and an increase in the money supply. The rise in reserve levels that

banks have available to lend leads them to bid down interest rates on loans. Thus market interest rates tend to fall in response to any of these changes in the Fed's tools of monetary policy.

3. **How Expansionary and Contractionary Monetary Policies Affect Equilibrium Real GDP and the Price Level in the Short Run:** By pushing up the money supply and inducing a fall in market interest rates, an expansionary monetary policy action causes total planned expenditures to rise at any given price level. Hence the aggregate demand curve shifts rightward, which can eliminate a short-run recessionary gap in real GDP. In contrast, a contractionary monetary policy action reduces the money supply and causes an increase in market interest rates, thereby generating a fall in total planned expenditures at any given price level. This results in a leftward shift in the aggregate demand curve, which can eliminate a short-run inflationary gap in real GDP.

4. **The Equation of Exchange and the Quantity Theory of Money and Prices:** The equation of exchange is a truism that states that the quantity of money in circulation times

the average number of times a unit of money is used in exchange—the income velocity of money—must equal nominal GDP, or the price level times real GDP. According to the quantity theory of money and prices, we can regard the income velocity of money as constant and real GDP as relatively stable. Thus a rise in the quantity of money must lead to a proportionate increase in the price level.

5. **Keynesian and Monetarist Views on the Transmission Mechanism of Monetary Policy:** The Keynesian approach to the monetary policy transmission mechanism operates through effects of monetary policy actions on market interest rates, which bring about changes in desired investment and thereby affect equilibrium real GDP via the Keynesian multiplier effect. By contrast, mone-

tarists propose a transmission mechanism in which money supply changes directly influence total desired expenditures on goods and services.

6. **Why the Federal Reserve Cannot Stabilize the Money Supply and the Interest Rate Simultaneously:** To target a market interest rate, the Federal Reserve must be willing to adjust the money supply as necessary when there are variations in the demand for money. Hence stabilizing the interest rate typically requires variations in the money supply. To target the money supply, however, the Federal Reserve must be willing to let the market interest rate vary whenever the demand for money rises or falls. Consequently, stabilizing the money supply usually entails some degree of interest rate volatility.

KEY TERMS AND CONCEPTS

asset demand (392)

equation of exchange (400)

income velocity of money (400)

monetarists (404)

monetary rule (404)

money balances (392)

precautionary demand (392)

quantity theory of money and prices (401)

transactions demand (392)

PROBLEMS

Answers to the odd-numbered problems appear at the back of the book.

17-1. Let's denote the price of a nonmaturing bond (called a *consol*) as P_b. The equation that indicates this price is $P_b = I/r$, where I is the annual net income the bond generates and r is the market nominal interest rate.

a. Suppose that a bond promises the holder $500 per year forever. If the market nominal interest rate is 5 percent, what is the bond's current price?

b. What happens to the bond's price if the market interest rate rises to 10 percent?

17-2. Based on Problem 17-1, imagine that initially the market interest rate is 5 percent and at this interest rate you have decided to hold half of your financial wealth as bonds and half as holdings of non-interest-bearing money. You notice that the market interest rate is starting to rise, however, and you become convinced that it will ultimately rise to 10 percent.

a. In what direction do you expect the value of your bond holdings to go when the interest rate increases?

b. If you wish to prevent the value of your financial wealth from declining in the future, how should you adjust the way you split your wealth between bonds and money? What does this imply about the demand for money?

17-3. You learned in Chapter 11 that if there is an inflationary gap in the short run, then in the long run a new equilibrium arises when input prices and expectations adjust upward, causing the aggregate supply curve to shift upward and to the left and pushing equilibrium real GDP back to its long-run potential value. In this chapter, however, you learned that the Federal Reserve can eliminate an inflationary gap in the short run by undertaking a policy action that reduces aggregate demand.

a. Propose one monetary policy action that could eliminate an inflationary gap in the short run.

b. In what way might society gain if the Fed implements the policy you have proposed instead of simply permitting long-run adjustments to take place?

17-4. In addition, you learned in Chapter 11 that if there is a recessionary gap in the short run, then in the long run a new equilibrium arises when input prices and expectations adjust downward, causing the aggregate supply curve to shift downward and to the right and pushing equilibrium real GDP back to its long-run potential value. In this chapter, however, you learned that the Federal Reserve can eliminate a recessionary gap in the short run by undertaking a policy action that raises aggregate demand.

   a. Propose a monetary policy action that could eliminate a recessionary gap in the short run but uses a different tool of monetary policy than the one you considered in Problem 17-3.

   b. In what way might society gain if the Fed implements the policy you have proposed instead of simply permitting long-run adjustments to take place?

17-5. Explain why the net export effect of a contractionary monetary policy reinforces the usual impact that monetary policy has on equilibrium real GDP in the short run.

17-6. Suppose that the value of the U.S. dollar depreciates relative to foreign currencies.

   a. In the short run, what will happen to net exports in the United States?

   b. How will this affect U.S. aggregate demand and equilibrium real GDP in the short run?

   c. What policy action might the Federal Reserve take to prevent the dollar's depreciation from affecting equilibrium real GDP?

17-7. Use a diagram to illustrate how the Fed can reduce inflationary pressures by conducting open market sales of U.S. government securities.

17-8. Suppose that the quantity of money in circulation is fixed but the income velocity of money doubles. If real GDP remains at its long-run potential level, what happens to the equilibrium price level?

17-9. Suppose that following the events described in Problem 17-8, the Federal Reserve implements policies that cut the money supply in half. How does the price level now compare with its value before the income velocity of money and the money supply both changed?

17-10. Consider the following data: The money supply is equal to $1 trillion, the price level equals 2, and annual real GDP is $5 trillion in base-year dollars. What is the income velocity of money for this economy?

17-11. Consider the information in Problem 17-10. Suppose that the money supply increases by $100 billion and real GDP and the income velocity of money remain unchanged. According to the quantity theory of money and prices, what is the new price level after the increase in the money supply?

17-12. Answer the following based on your answer to Problem 17-11.

   a. What is the percentage increase in the money supply?

   b. What is the percentage change in the price level?

   c. How do the percentage changes in the money supply and price level compare?

17-13. Suppose that the Federal Reserve wishes to keep the nominal interest rate at a target level of 4 percent. Draw a money supply and demand diagram in which the current equilibrium interest rate is 4 percent. Explain a specific policy action that the Fed, using one of its three tools of monetary policy, could take to keep the interest rate at its target level if the demand for money suddenly declines.

17-14. Assuming that the Federal Reserve judges inflation to be the most significant problem in the economy and that it wishes to employ all three of its policy instruments, what should the Fed do with respect to each of these policy tools?

   a. Open market operations

   b. The discount rate relative to the federal funds rate

   c. Reserve requirements

17-15. Suppose that the Fed implements each of the policy changes you discussed in Problem 17-14. Now explain how the net export effect resulting from these monetary policy actions will reinforce their effects that operate through interest rate changes.

ECONOMICS ON THE NET

The Fed's Policy Report to Congress Congress requires the Fed to make periodic reports on the scope of its recent policy-making activities. In this application, you will study recent reports to learn about what factors affect Fed decisions.

Title: Monetary Policy Report to the Congress

Navigation: Go to www.econtoday.com/chap17 to view the Federal Reserve's Monetary Policy Report to the Congress (formerly called the Humphrey-Hawkins Report).

Application Read the report; then answer the following questions.

1. According to the report, what economic events played the most important role in shaping recent monetary policy actions?

2. Based on the report, what are the Fed's current monetary policy goals?

For Group Study and Analysis Divide the class into "domestic" and "foreign" groups. Have each group read the past four monetary policy reports and then explain to the class how domestic and foreign factors, respectively, appear to have influenced recent Fed monetary policy decisions. Which of the two types of factors seem to have mattered most during the past year?

Media Resources

If your exam were tomorrow, would you be ready? For each chapter, MyEconLab Practice Tests and Study Plans pinpoint which sections you have mastered and which ones you need to study. That way, you are more efficient with your study time, and you are better prepared for your exams.

In addition to Practice Tests and your personalized Study Plan, you'll find the following media resources in MyEconLab:
1. *Graphs in Motion* animation of Figures 17-2, 17-3, 17-4, 17-6, and 17-8.
2. Videos featuring the author, Roger LeRoy Miller, on the following subjects:
   ● Why People Wish to Hold Money
   ● The Quantity Theory of Money
   ● The Monetary Rule

3. Links to the Web sites cited in the marginal Internet Resources, Issues and Applications feature, and Economics on the Net activity.
4. Audio clips of all key terms, additional practice problems, and a PDF version of the material from the print Study Guide.
5. eThemes of the Times, which is a New York Times article to help you understand the real-world applications of what you are learning.

Get Ahead of the Curve

To see how it works, turn to page 16 and then go to www.myeconlab.com/miller.

Monetary Policy: A Keynesian Perspective

According to the traditional Keynesian approach to monetary policy, changes in the money supply can affect the level of aggregate demand only through their effect on interest rates. Moreover, interest rate changes act on aggregate demand solely by changing the level of real planned investment spending. Finally, the traditional Keynesian approach argues that there are plausible circumstances under which monetary policy may have little or no effect on interest rates and thus on aggregate demand.

Figure D-1 measures real GDP along the horizontal axis and total planned expenditures (aggregate demand) along the vertical axis. The components of aggregate demand are real consumption (C), investment (I), government spending (G), and net exports (X). The height of the schedule labeled $C + I + G + X$ shows total real planned expenditures (aggregate demand) as a function of real GDP. This schedule slopes upward because consumption depends positively on real GDP. Everywhere along the line labeled $Y = C + I + G + X$ real planned spending equals real GDP. At point Y^*, where the $C + I + G + X$ line intersects this 45-degree reference line, real planned spending is consistent with real GDP. At any real GDP level less than Y^*, spending exceeds real GDP, so real GDP and thus spending will tend to rise. At any level of real GDP greater than Y^*, real planned spending is less than real GDP, so real GDP and thus spending will tend to decline. Given the determinants of C, I, G, and X, total spending (aggregate demand) will be Y^*.

INCREASING THE MONEY SUPPLY

According to the Keynesian approach, an increase in the money supply pushes interest rates down. This reduces the cost of borrowing and thus induces firms to increase the level of investment spending from I to I'. As a result, the $C + I + G + X$ line shifts upward in

FIGURE D-1

An Increase in the Money Supply

An increase in the money supply increases real GDP by lowering interest rates and thus increasing investment from I to I'.

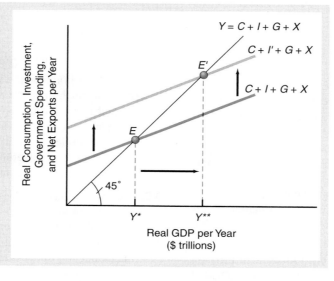

Figure D-1 by the full amount of the rise in investment spending, thus yielding the line $C + I' + G + X$. The rise in investment spending causes real GDP to rise, which in turn causes real consumption spending to rise, which further increases real GDP. Ultimately, aggregate demand rises to Y^{**}, where spending again equals real GDP. A key conclusion of the Keynesian analysis is that total spending rises by *more* than the original rise in investment spending because consumption spending depends positively on real GDP.

DECREASING THE MONEY SUPPLY

Not surprisingly, contractionary monetary policy works in exactly the reverse manner. A reduction in the money supply pushes interest rates up, which increases the cost of borrowing. Firms respond by reducing their investment spending, and this pushes real GDP downward. Consumers react to the lower real GDP by scaling back on their real consumption spending, which further depresses real GDP. Thus the ultimate decline in real GDP is larger than the initial drop in investment spending. Indeed, because the change in real GDP is a multiple of the change in investment, Keynesians note that changes in investment spending (similar to changes in government spending) have a *multiplier* effect on the economy.

ARGUMENTS AGAINST MONETARY POLICY

It might be thought that this multiplier effect would make monetary policy a potent tool in the Keynesian arsenal, particularly when it comes to getting the economy out of a recession. In fact, however, many traditional Keynesians argue that monetary policy is likely to be relatively ineffective as a recession fighter. According to their line of reasoning, although monetary policy has the potential to reduce interest rates, changes in the money supply have little *actual* impact on interest rates. Instead, during recessions, people try to build up as much as they can in liquid assets to protect themselves from risks of unemployment and other losses of income. When the monetary authorities increase the money supply, individuals are willing to allow most of it to accumulate in their bank accounts. This desire for increased liquidity thus prevents interest rates from falling very much, which in turn means that there will be virtually no change in investment spending and thus little change in aggregate demand.

PROBLEMS

The answer to this problem appears at the back of the book.

D-1. Suppose that each 0.1 percentage point decrease in the equilibrium interest rate induces a $10 billion increase in real planned investment spending by businesses. In addition, the investment multiplier is equal to 5, and the money multiplier is equal to 4. Furthermore, every $20 billion increase in the money supply brings about a 0.1 percentage point reduction in the equilibrium interest rate. Use this information to answer the following questions under the assumption that all other things are equal.

  a. How much must real planned investment increase if the Federal Reserve desires to bring about a $100 billion increase in equilibrium real GDP?

  b. How much must the money supply change for the Fed to induce the change in real planned investment calculated in part a?

  c. What dollar amount of open market operations must the Fed undertake to bring about the money supply change calculated in part b?

D-2. Suppose that each 0.1 percentage point increase in the equilibrium interest rate induces a $5 billion decrease in real planned investment spending by businesses. In addition, the investment multiplier is equal to 4, and the money multiplier is equal to 3. Furthermore, every $9 billion decrease in the money supply brings about a 0.1 percentage point increase in the equilibrium interest rate. Use this information to answer the following questions under the assumption that all other things are equal.

a. How much must real planned investment decrease if the Federal Reserve desires to bring about an $80 billion decrease in equilibrium real GDP?

b. How much must the money supply change for the Fed to induce the change in real planned investment calculated in part a?

c. What dollar amount of open market operations must the Fed undertake to bring about the money supply change calculated in part b?

D-3. Assume that the following conditions exist:

a. All banks are fully loaned up—there are no excess reserves, and desired excess reserves are always zero.

b. The money multiplier is 3.

c. The planned investment schedule is such that at a 6 percent rate of interest, investment is $1,200 billion; at 5 percent, investment is $1,225 billion.

d. The investment multiplier is 3.

e. The initial equilibrium level of real GDP is $12 trillion.

f. The equilibrium rate of interest is 6 percent.

Now the Fed engages in expansionary monetary policy. It buys $1 billion worth of bonds, which increases the money supply, which in turn lowers the market rate of interest by 1 percentage point. Indicate by how much the money supply increased, and then trace out the numerical consequences of the associated reduction in interest rates on all the other variables mentioned.

D-4. Assume that the following conditions exist:

a. All banks are fully loaned up—there are no excess reserves, and desired excess reserves are always zero.

b. The money multiplier is 4.

c. The planned investment schedule is such that at a 4 percent rate of interest, investment is $1,400 billion. At 5 percent, investment is $1,380 billion.

d. The investment multiplier is 5.

e. The initial equilibrium level of real GDP is $13 trillion.

f. The equilibrium rate of interest is 4 percent.

Now the Fed engages in contractionary monetary policy. It sells $2 billion worth of bonds, which reduces the money supply, which in turn raises the market rate of interest by 1 percentage point. Indicate by how much the money supply decreased, and then trace out the numerical consequences of the associated increase in interest rates on all the other variables mentioned.

Chapter *18*

Stabilization in an Integrated World Economy

I n August 2003, the Federal Reserve added a significant comment to its regular public statement about monetary policy. The Fed indicated that in light of the perceived threat of *deflation*, it intended to keep interest rates low for a "considerable period." Two months later, when the threat of deflation had receded, some Fed policymakers openly expressed their regret that this comment had been added. The comment, they feared, had led the public to anticipate expansionary monetary policy actions for some time to come. Acting on this expectation, the public raised total planned expenditures rapidly, thereby creating an *inflationary* threat. In this chapter, you will learn why expectations of policies can sometimes be as important as the policies themselves.

LEARNING OBJECTIVES

After reading this chapter, you should be able to:

1. Explain why the actual unemployment rate might depart from the natural rate of unemployment
2. Describe why there may be an inverse relationship between the inflation rate and the unemployment rate, reflected by the Phillips curve
3. Evaluate how expectations affect the actual relationship between the inflation rate and the unemployment rate
4. Understand the rational expectations hypothesis and its implications for economic policymaking
5. Identify the central features of the real-business-cycle challenge to active policymaking
6. Distinguish among alternative modern approaches to strengthening the case for active policymaking

Media Resources

Refer to the end of the chapter for a full listing of the multimedia learning materials available in MyEconLab.

...during the ten years prior to 2004 the average variability of U.S. real GDP was about 30 percent lower than it was during the ten years prior to 1994? In addition, average real GDP variability in the United States during the 1994–2003 period was more than 50 percent lower than it was between 1974 and 1983. Compared with the period stretching from 1910 to 1949, U.S. real GDP during the 1994–2003 decade was *83 percent* less variable.

To some observers, the reduction in variability of U.S. real GDP has obviously resulted from improved monetary and fiscal policymaking. Others, however, are not so sure that policymakers really deserve much of the credit.

ACTIVE VERSUS PASSIVE POLICYMAKING

Central to the debate about whether policymakers deserve a collective pat on the back is whether the credit for a generally more stable U.S. economy should be given to **active (discretionary) policymaking.** This is the term for actions that monetary and fiscal policymakers undertake in reaction to or in anticipation of a change in economic performance. On the other side of the debate is the view that the best way to achieve economic stability is through **passive (nondiscretionary) policymaking,** in which there is no deliberate stabilization policy at all. You have already been introduced to one nondiscretionary policymaking idea in Chapter 17—the *monetary rule,* by which the money supply is allowed to increase at a fixed rate per year. In the fiscal arena, passive (nondiscretionary) policy might be simply to balance the federal budget over the business cycle. Recall from Chapter 13 that there are lags between the time when the national economy enters a recession or a boom and the time when that fact becomes known and acted on by policymakers. Proponents of passive policy argue strongly that such time lags often render short-term stabilization policy ineffective or, worse, procyclical.

To take a stand on this debate concerning active versus passive policymaking, you first need to know the potential trade-offs that policymakers believe they face. Then you need to see what the data actually show. The most important policy trade-off appears to be between price stability and unemployment. Before exploring that, however, we need to look at the economy's natural, or long-run, rate of unemployment.

Active (discretionary) policymaking
All actions on the part of monetary and fiscal policymakers that are undertaken in response to or in anticipation of some change in the overall economy.

Passive (nondiscretionary) policymaking
Policymaking that is carried out in response to a rule. It is therefore not in response to an actual or potential change in overall economic activity.

THE NATURAL RATE OF UNEMPLOYMENT

Recall from Chapter 7 that there are different types of unemployment: frictional, cyclical, structural, and seasonal. *Frictional unemployment* arises because individuals take the time to search for the best job opportunities. Much unemployment is of this type, except when the economy is in a recession or a depression, when cyclical unemployment rises.

Note that we did not say that frictional unemployment was the *sole* form of unemployment during normal times. *Structural unemployment* is caused by a variety of "rigidities" throughout the economy. Structural unemployment results from factors such as these:

1. Union activity that sets wages above the equilibrium level and also restricts the mobility of labor
2. Government-imposed licensing arrangements that restrict entry into specific occupations or professions
3. Government-imposed minimum wage laws and other laws that require all workers to be paid union wage rates on government contract jobs
4. Welfare and unemployment insurance benefits that reduce incentives to work
5. A mismatch of worker training and skills with available jobs

Each of these factors reduces individuals' abilities or incentives to choose employment rather than unemployment.

Consider the effect of unemployment insurance benefits on the probability of an unemployed person's finding a job. When unemployment benefits run out, according to economists Lawrence Katz and Bruce Meyer, the probability of an unemployed person's finding a job doubles. The conclusion is that unemployed workers are more serious about finding a job when they are no longer receiving such benefits.

Frictional unemployment and structural unemployment both exist even when the economy is in long-run equilibrium—they are a natural consequence of costly information (the need to conduct a job search) and the existence of rigidities such as those noted. Because these two types of unemployment are a natural consequence of imperfect and costly information and rigidities, they are components of what economists call the *natural rate of unemployment*. As we discussed in Chapter 7, this is defined as the rate of unemployment that would exist in the long run after everyone in the economy fully adjusted to any changes that have occurred. Recall that real GDP tends to return to the level implied by the long-run aggregate supply curve (*LRAS*). Thus whatever rate of unemployment the economy tends to return to in long-run equilibrium can be called the natural rate of unemployment.

How has the natural rate of unemployment changed over the years?

E X A M P L E

The U.S. Natural Rate of Unemployment

In 1950, the unemployment rate was about 5 percent. By the early 2000s, it was close to 6 percent. These two endpoints of unemployment rates prove nothing by themselves. But look at Figure 18-1. There you see not only what has happened to the unemployment rate over that same time period but an estimate of the natural rate of unemployment. The line labeled "Natural rate of unemployment" is estimated by averaging unemployment rates from five years earlier to five years later at each point in time (except for the end period, which is esti-

mated). This computation reveals that until the late 1980s, the natural rate of unemployment was rising. But since then, a generally downward trend has taken hold.

For Critical Analysis
Of the various factors that create structural unemployment, which ones do you think explained the gradual trend upward in the natural rate of unemployment from the late 1940s until the 1990s in the United States?

Departures from the Natural Rate of Unemployment

Even though the unemployment rate has a strong tendency to stay at and return to the natural rate, it is possible for fiscal and monetary policy to move the actual unemployment rate away from the natural rate, at least in the short run. Deviations of the actual unemployment rate from the natural rate are called *cyclical unemployment* because they are observed over the course of nationwide business fluctuations. During recessions, the overall unemployment rate exceeds the natural rate; cyclical unemployment is positive. During periods of economic booms, the overall unemployment rate can go below the natural rate; at such times, cyclical unemployment is negative.

To see how departures from the natural rate of unemployment can occur, let's consider two examples. Referring to Figure 18-2, we begin in equilibrium at point E_1, with the associated price level P_1 and real GDP per year of level Y_1.

FIGURE 18-1
Estimated Natural Rate of Unemployment in the United States

As you can see in this figure, the actual rate of unemployment has varied widely in the United States in recent decades. If we estimate the natural rate of unemployment by averaging unemployment rates from five years earlier to five years later at each point in time, we get the line so labeled. It rose from the 1950s until the late 1980s and then gradually declined.

Sources: *Economic Report of the President; Economic Indicators*, various issues; author's estimates.

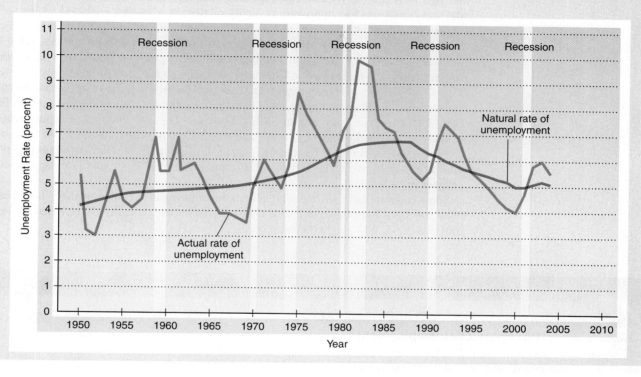

FIGURE 18-2
Impact of an Increase in Aggregate Demand on Real GDP and Unemployment

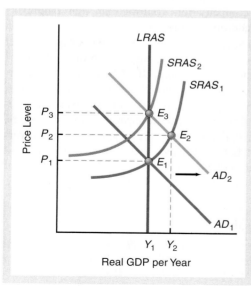

If the economy is operating at E_1, it is in both short-run and long-run equilibrium. Here the actual rate of unemployment is equal to the natural rate of unemployment. Subsequent to expansionary monetary or fiscal policy, the aggregate demand curve shifts outward to AD_2. The price level rises to P_2; real GDP per year increases to Y_2. The new short-run equilibrium is at E_2. The unemployment rate is now below the natural rate of unemployment. We are at a short-run equilibrium at E_2. In the long run, expectations of input owners are revised. The short-run aggregate supply curve shifts from $SRAS_1$ to $SRAS_2$ because of higher prices and higher resource costs. Real GDP returns to the *LRAS* level of Y_1 per year. The price level increases to P_3.

The Impact of Expansionary Policy. Now imagine that the government decides to use fiscal or monetary policy to stimulate the economy. Further suppose, for reasons that will soon become clear, that this policy surprises decision makers throughout the economy in the sense that they did not anticipate that the policy would occur. The aggregate demand curve shifts from AD_1 to AD_2 in Figure 18-2, so both the price level and real GDP rise to P_2 and Y_2, respectively. In the labor market, individuals would find that conditions had improved markedly relative to what they expected. Firms seeking to expand output will want to hire more workers. To accomplish this, they will recruit more actively and possibly ask workers to work overtime, so individuals in the labor market will find more job openings and more possible hours they can work. Consequently, as you learned in Chapter 7, the average duration of unemployment will fall and so will the unemployment rate. This unexpected increase in aggregate demand simultaneously causes the price level to rise to P_2 and the unemployment rate to fall. The *SRAS* curve will not stay at $SRAS_1$, however. The expectations of input owners, such as workers and owners of capital and raw materials, will be revised. The short-run aggregate supply curve shifts to $SRAS_2$ as input prices rise. We find ourselves at a new equilibrium at E_3, which is on the *LRAS*. Long-run real GDP per year is Y_1 again, but at a higher price level, P_3.

Some economists suggest that higher employer payments to cover workers' health care costs may have contributed to higher unemployment even as real GDP increased between 2001 and 2004. Why might this have occurred?

EXAMPLE

Have Higher Health Care Costs Boosted the Natural Rate of Unemployment?

When the last recession officially ended in the spring of 2001, government officials, businesspeople, and workers alike breathed a sigh of relief. Between 2000 and 2001, the unemployment rate had jumped from 4 percent to nearly 5 percent. Based on experiences during previous U.S. recoveries, many economists predicted a speedy rise in employment and a corresponding drop in the unemployment rate during 2002. Unemployment did not fall, however. It actually rose to 6 percent in 2002 and hovered close to this level throughout 2003 and into 2004.

Why didn't employment increase faster even as real GDP increased following the recession? Some economists suggest that rising employer-paid health care expenses were pushing up structural unemployment in the early 2000s even as cyclical unemployment was declining. They point out that for an employer, adding a worker makes sense only when the company can profit from the worker's labor. The overall cost of hiring an additional worker includes both wages and a number of nonwage costs. Nonwage expenses include contributions to Social Security, Medicare, and unemployment-compensation funds. Furthermore, the typical employer pays about two-thirds of the premiums required to fund the worker's private health insurance.

Between 2001 and 2004, average wages, payroll taxes, and unemployment-compensation contributions that employers paid to hire an additional worker rose by less than 7 percent. The health insurance premiums that employers paid to cover a typical worker and his or her family, in contrast, rose by 38 percent. As a consequence, since 2004 Federal Reserve surveys of employers have indicated that high health care costs, which now exceed employer-funded payroll taxes, have become the main structural barrier to hiring additional workers. As a consequence, rising health care expenses that employers pay on workers' behalf may have reduced the likelihood that unemployed workers will find jobs. If so, the natural rate of unemployment undoubtedly has increased.

For Critical Analysis
What could the government do to help reduce the costs that a typical employer faces when it considers hiring another worker?

The Consequences of Contractionary Policy. Instead of expansionary policy, the government could have decided to engage in contractionary (or deflationary) policy. As shown in Figure 18-3, the sequence of events would have been in the opposite direction of those in Figure 18-2. Again, beginning from an initial equilibrium E_1, an unanticipated reduction in aggregate demand puts downward pressure on both prices and real GDP; the price level falls to P_2, and real GDP declines to Y_2. Fewer firms will be hiring, and those that are hiring will offer fewer overtime possibilities. Individuals looking for jobs will find that it takes longer than predicted. As a result, unemployed individuals will remain unemployed longer. The average duration of unemployment will rise, and so will the rate of unemployment. The unexpected decrease in aggregate demand simultaneously causes the price level to fall to P_2 and the unemployment rate to rise. This equilibrium at E_2 is only a short-run situation, however. As input owners change their expectations about future prices, $SRAS_1$ will shift to $SRAS_2$, and input prices will fall. The new long-run equilibrium will be at E_3, which is on the long-run aggregate supply curve, LRAS. The price level will have fallen to P_3.

The Phillips Curve: A Rationale for Active Policymaking?

Let's recap what we have just observed. An *unexpected increase* in aggregate demand causes the price level to rise and the unemployment rate to fall. Conversely, an *unexpected decrease* in aggregate demand causes the price level to fall and the unemployment rate to rise. Moreover, although not shown explicitly in either diagram, two additional points are true:

1. The greater the unexpected increase in aggregate demand, the greater the amount of inflation that results, and the lower the unemployment rate.
2. The greater the unexpected decrease in aggregate demand, the greater the deflation that results, and the higher the unemployment rate.

The Negative Relationship Between Inflation and Unemployment. Figure 18-4 on the next page summarizes these findings. The inflation rate (*not* the price level) is measured along the vertical axis, and the unemployment rate is measured along the horizontal axis. Point A shows an initial starting point, with the unemployment rate at the natural rate,

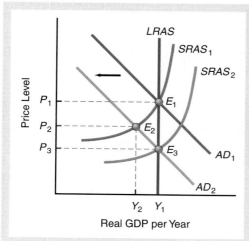

FIGURE 18-3

Impact of a Decline in Aggregate Demand on Real GDP and Unemployment

Starting from equilibrium at E_1, a decline in aggregate demand to AD_2 leads to a lower price level, P_2, and real GDP declines to Y_2. The unemployment rate will rise above the natural rate of unemployment. Equilibrium at E_2 is temporary, however. At the lower price level, the expectations of input owners will be revised. $SRAS_1$ will shift to $SRAS_2$. The new long-run equilibrium will be at E_3, with real GDP equal to Y_1 and a price level of P_3.

U^*. Note that as a matter of convenience, we are starting from an equilibrium in which the price level is stable (the inflation rate is zero). Unexpected increases in aggregate demand cause the price level to rise—the inflation rate becomes positive—and cause the unemployment rate to fall. Thus the economy moves upward to the left from A to B. Conversely, unexpected decreases in aggregate demand cause the price level to fall and the unemployment rate to rise above the natural rate—the economy moves from point A to point C. If we look at both increases and decreases in aggregate demand, we see that high inflation rates tend to be associated with low unemployment rates (as at B) and that low (or negative) inflation rates tend to be accompanied by high unemployment rates (as at C).

Is There a Trade-Off? The apparent negative relationship between the inflation rate and the unemployment rate shown in Figure 18-4 has come to be called the **Phillips curve,** after A. W. Phillips, who discovered that a similar relationship existed historically in Great Britain. Although Phillips presented his findings only as an empirical regularity, economists quickly came to view the relationship as representing a *trade-off* between inflation and unemployment. In particular, policymakers who favored active policymaking believed that they could *choose* alternative combinations of unemployment and inflation. Thus it seemed that a government that disliked unemployment could select a point like B in Figure 18-4, with a positive inflation rate but a relatively low unemployment rate. Conversely, a government that feared inflation could choose a stable price level at A, but only at the expense of a higher associated unemployment rate. Indeed, the Phillips curve seemed to suggest that it was possible for discretionary policymakers to fine-tune the economy by selecting the policies that would produce the exact mix of unemployment and inflation that suited current government objectives. As it turned out, matters are not so simple.

The NAIRU. If one accepts that a trade-off exists between the rate of inflation and the rate of unemployment, then the notion of "noninflationary" rates of unemployment seems appropriate. In fact, some economists have proposed what they call the **nonaccelerating inflation rate of unemployment (NAIRU).** The NAIRU is the rate of unemployment that corresponds to a stable rate of inflation. When the unemployment rate is less than the NAIRU, the rate of inflation tends to increase. When the unemployment rate is more than the NAIRU, the rate of inflation tends to decrease. When the rate of unemployment is equal to the NAIRU, inflation continues at an unchanged rate. If the Phillips curve trade-

---

Phillips curve
A curve showing the relationship between unemployment and changes in wages or prices. It was long thought to reflect a trade-off between unemployment and inflation.

Nonaccelerating inflation rate of unemployment (NAIRU)
The rate of unemployment below which the rate of inflation tends to rise and above which the rate of inflation tends to fall.

FIGURE 18-4
The Phillips Curve
Unanticipated changes in aggregate demand produce a negative relationship between the inflation rate and unemployment. U^* is the natural rate of unemployment.

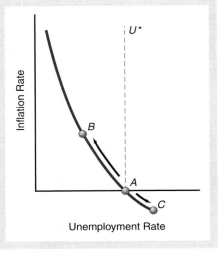

off exists and if the NAIRU can be estimated, that estimate will define the short-run trade-off between the rate of unemployment and the rate of inflation.

The Importance of Expectations

The reduction in unemployment that takes place as the economy moves from A to B in Figure 18-4 occurs because the wage offers encountered by unemployed workers are un-expectedly high. As far as the workers are concerned, these higher *nominal* wages appear, at least initially, to be increases in *real* wages; it is this perception that induces them to re-duce the duration of their job search. This is a sensible way for the workers to view the world if aggregate demand fluctuates up and down at random, with no systematic or pre-dictable variation one way or another. But if activist policymakers attempt to exploit the apparent trade-off in the Phillips curve, according to economists who support passive pol-icymaking, aggregate demand will no longer move up and down in an *unpredictable* way.

The Effects of an Unanticipated Policy.
Consider Figure 18-5, for example. If the Fed-eral Reserve attempts to reduce the unemployment rate to U_1, it must increase the money supply enough to produce an inflation rate of π_1. If this is an unexpected one-shot action in which the money supply is first increased and then held constant, the inflation rate will temporarily rise to π_1 and the unemployment rate will temporarily fall to U_1; but as soon as the money supply stops growing, the inflation rate will return to zero and unemploy-ment will return to U^*, its natural rate. Thus an unexpected one-shot increase in the money supply will move the economy from point A to point B, and the economy will move of its own accord back to A.

Adjusting Expectations and a Shifting Phillips Curve.
If activist authorities wish to prevent the unemployment rate from returning to U^*, they will conclude that the money supply must grow fast enough to keep the inflation rate up at π_1. But if the Fed does this,

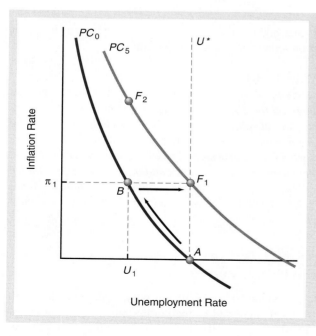

FIGURE 18-5
A Shift in the Phillips Curve
When there is a change in the ex-pected inflation rate, the Phillips curve (*PC*) shifts to incorporate the new expectations. PC_0 shows expec-tations of zero inflation. PC_5 reflects a higher expected inflation rate, such as 5 percent.

To try out the "bit/ed" Web site's virtual economy and use the Phillips curve as a guide for policymaking in the United Kingdom, go to www.econtoday.com/chap18.

argue those who favor passive policymaking, all of the economic participants in the economy—workers and job seekers included—will come to *expect* that inflation rate to continue. This, in turn, will change their expectations about wages. For example, suppose that π_1 equals 5 percent per year. When the expected inflation rate was zero, a 5 percent rise in nominal wages meant a 5 percent expected rise in real wages, and this was sufficient to induce some individuals to take jobs rather than remain unemployed. It was this expectation of a rise in real wages that reduced search duration and caused the unemployment rate to drop from U^* to U_1. But if the expected inflation rate becomes 5 percent, a 5 percent rise in nominal wages means *no* rise in *real* wages. Once workers come to expect the higher inflation rate, rising nominal wages will no longer be sufficient to entice them out of unemployment. As a result, as the *expected* inflation rate moves up from 0 percent to 5 percent, the unemployment rate will move up also.

In terms of Figure 18-5 on the previous page, as authorities initially increase aggregate demand, the economy moves from point A to point B. If the authorities continue the stimulus in an effort to keep the unemployment rate down, workers' expectations will adjust, causing the unemployment rate to rise. In this second stage, the economy moves from B to point F_1: The unemployment rate returns to the natural rate, U^*, but the inflation rate is now π_1 instead of zero. Once the adjustment of expectations has taken place, any further changes in policy will have to take place along a curve such as PC_5, say, a movement from F_1 to F_2. This new schedule is also a Phillips curve, differing from the first, PC_0, in that the actual inflation rate consistent with any given unemployment rate is higher because the expected inflation rate is higher.

To what extent do individuals and businesses take recent inflation into account when they make their predictions of future inflation?

Economics Front and Center

To think about the policy implications of the natural unemployment rate, the NAIRU, and the Phillips curve, contemplate the case study, **Can Central Banks Take All the Credit for Low Inflation?** on page 435.

International Policy EXAMPLE

The Effects of Higher Inflation on Inflation Expectations

Three economists at the Federal Reserve Bank of St. Louis, Andrew Levin, Fabio Natalucci, and Jeremy Piger, have attempted to measure the effects of a short-lived increase in actual inflation on expectations of future inflation. They considered what would happen to U.S., Japanese, and Euro-area inflation expectations if the actual inflation rate rose by 1 percentage point for just three years.

Their estimates imply that, other things being equal, even five years after this short-lived increase in inflation occurred the public would expect the future annual inflation rate to be about a third of a percentage point higher. As much as ten years later, the expected annual inflation rate would still be one-fourth of a percentage point higher. Thus the authors con-

clude that higher actual inflation has a significant holdover effect on long-term inflation expectations.

For Critical Analysis

The authors of this study also examined nations, such as Canada and the United Kingdom, in which central banks announce formal inflation targets. They concluded that in these nations a 1-percentage-point rise in actual inflation for three years would raise the expected future inflation rate by only 0.09 percentage point five years later and 0.01 percentage point ten years later. Why do you suppose that higher actual inflation has a smaller effect on inflation expectations when a central bank announces inflation targets?

The U.S. Experience with the Phillips Curve

In separate articles in 1968, Milton Friedman and E. S. Phelps published pioneering studies suggesting that the apparent trade-off suggested by the Phillips curve could not be exploited by activist policymakers. Friedman and Phelps both argued that any attempt to re-

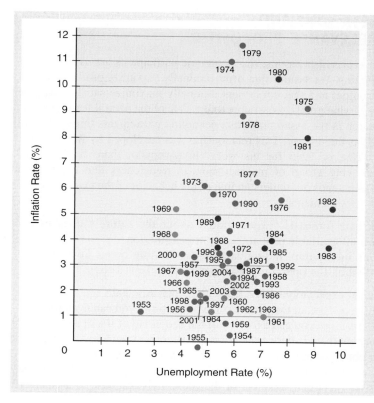

FIGURE 18-6
The Phillips Curve: Theory versus Data

If you plot points representing the rate of inflation and the rate of unemployment for the United States from 1953 to the present, there does not appear to be any Phillips curve trade-off between the two variables.

Sources: *Economic Report of the President; Economic Indicators*, various issues.

duce unemployment by inflating the economy would soon be thwarted by economic participants' incorporating the new higher inflation rate into their expectations. The Friedman-Phelps research thus implies that for any given unemployment rate, *any* inflation rate is possible, depending on the actions of policymakers. As reflected in Figure 18-6, the propositions of Friedman and Phelps were to prove remarkably accurate.

When we examine U.S. unemployment and inflation data over the past half century, we see no clear relationship between them. Although there seemed to have been a Phillips curve trade-off between unemployment and inflation from the mid-1950s to the mid-1960s, apparently once people in the economy realized what was happening, they started revising their forecasts accordingly. So, activist policymakers attempted to exploit the Phillips curve, and the presumed trade-off between unemployment and inflation disappeared.

CONCEPTS in Brief

- The natural rate of unemployment is the rate that exists in long-run equilibrium, when workers' expectations are consistent with actual conditions.

- Departures from the natural rate of unemployment can occur when individuals encounter unanticipated changes in fiscal or monetary policy. An unexpected rise in aggregate demand will reduce unemployment below the natural rate, whereas an unanticipated decrease in aggregate demand will push unemployment above the natural rate.

- The Phillips curve exhibits a negative relationship between the inflation rate and the unemployment rate that can be observed when there are *unanticipated* changes in aggregate demand.

- Activist policymakers seek to take advantage of a proposed Phillips curve trade-off between inflation and unemployment. Proponents of passive policymaking contend that, in fact, no trade-off exists because workers' expectations adjust to any systematic attempts to reduce unemployment below the natural rate.

To test your understanding of the concepts covered in this section, go to the Online Review at www.myeconlab.com/miller.

RATIONAL EXPECTATIONS AND THE POLICY IRRELEVANCE PROPOSITION

You already know that economists assume that economic participants act *as though* they were rational and calculating. We assume that firms rationally maximize profits when they choose today's rate of output and that consumers rationally maximize satisfaction when they choose how much of what goods to consume today. One of the pivotal features of current macro policy research is the assumption that economic participants think rationally about the future as well as the present. This relationship was developed by Robert Lucas, who won the Nobel Prize in 1995 for his work. In particular, there is widespread agreement among a growing group of macroeconomics researchers that the **rational expectations hypothesis** extends our understanding of the behavior of the macroeconomy. This hypothesis has two key elements:

Rational expectations hypothesis
A theory stating that people combine the effects of past policy changes on important economic variables with their own judgment about the future effects of current and future policy changes.

1. Individuals base their forecasts (expectations) about the future values of economic variables on all available past and current information.
2. These expectations incorporate individuals' understanding about how the economy operates, including the operation of monetary and fiscal policy.

In essence, the rational expectations hypothesis holds that Abraham Lincoln was correct when he said, "You may fool all the people some of the time; you can even fool some of the people all of the time; but you can't fool *all* of the people *all* of the time."

If we further assume that there is pure competition in all markets and that all prices and wages are flexible, we obtain what many call the *new classical* approach to evaluating the effects of maceconomic policies. To see how rational expectations operate in the new classical perspective, let's take a simple example of the economy's response to a change in monetary policy.

Flexible Wages and Prices, Rational Expectations, and Policy Irrelevance

Consider Figure 18-7, which shows the long-run aggregate supply curve (*LRAS*) for the economy, as well as the initial aggregate demand curve (*AD*$_1$) and the short-run aggregate supply curve (*SRAS*$_1$). The money supply is initially given by $M = M_1$, and the price level and real GDP are shown by P_1 and Y_1, respectively. Thus point A represents the initial long-run equilibrium.

Suppose now that the money supply is unexpectedly increased to M_2, thereby causing the aggregate demand curve to shift outward to AD_2. Given the location of the short-run aggregate supply curve, this increase in aggregate demand will cause real GDP and the price level to rise to Y_2 and P_2, respectively. The new short-run equilibrium is at B. Because real GDP is *above* the long-run equilibrium level of Y_1, unemployment must be below long-run levels (the natural rate), and so workers will soon respond to the higher price level by demanding higher nominal wages. This will cause the short-run aggregate supply curve to shift upward vertically, moving the economy to the new long-run equilibrium at C. The price level thus continues its rise to P_3, even as real GDP declines back down to Y_1 (and unemployment returns to the natural rate). So, as we have seen before, even though an increase in the money supply can raise real GDP and lower unemployment in the short run, it has no effect on either variable in the long run.

The Response to Anticipated Policy. Now let's look at this disturbance with the perspective given by the rational expectations hypothesis when wages and prices are flexible in a purely competitive environment. Suppose that workers (and other input owners) know

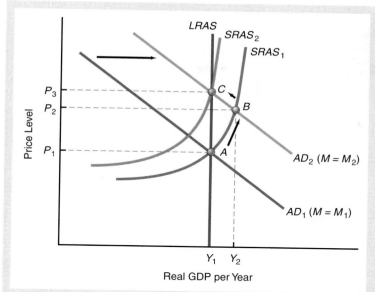

FIGURE 18-7

Response to an Unanticipated Rise in Aggregate Demand

Unanticipated changes in aggregate demand have real effects. In this case, the rise in demand causes real GDP to rise from Y_1 to Y_2 in the short run. Initial equilibrium is at point A. At point B, the price level is higher, so workers seek higher wages. The resulting fall in short-run aggregate supply produces a long-run equilibrium at point C.

ahead of time that this increase in the money supply is about to take place. Assume also that they know when it is going to occur and understand that its ultimate effect will be to push the price level from P_1 to P_3. Will workers wait until after the price level has increased to insist that their nominal wages go up? The rational expectations hypothesis says that they will not. Instead, they will go to employers and insist that their nominal wages move upward in step with the higher prices. From the workers' perspective, this is the only way to protect their real wages from declining due to the anticipated increase in the money supply.

The Policy Irrelevance Proposition. As long as economic participants behave in this manner, when we draw the *SRAS* curve, we must be explicit about the nature of their expectations. This we have done in Figure 18-8 on the next page. In the initial equilibrium, the short-run aggregate supply curve is labeled to show that the expected money supply (M_e) and the actual money supply (M_1) are equal ($M_e = M_1$). Similarly, when the money supply changes in a way that is anticipated by economic participants, the aggregate supply curve shifts to reflect this expected change in the money supply. The new short-run aggregate supply curve is labeled ($M_e = M_2$) to reveal this. According to the rational expectations hypothesis, the short-run aggregate supply curve will shift upward *simultaneously* with the rise in aggregate demand. As a result, the economy will move directly from point A to point C in Figure 18-8 without passing through B: The *only* response to the rise in the money supply is a rise in the price level from P_1 to P_3; neither output nor unemployment changes at all. This conclusion—that fully anticipated monetary policy is irrelevant in determining the levels of real variables—is called the **policy irrelevance proposition:**

> *Under the assumption of rational expectations on the part of decision makers in the economy, anticipated monetary policy cannot alter either the rate of unemployment or the level of real GDP. Regardless of the nature of the anticipated policy, the unemployment rate will equal the natural rate, and real GDP will be determined solely by the economy's long-run aggregate supply curve.*

Policy irrelevance proposition
The conclusion that policy actions have no real effects in the short run if the policy actions are anticipated and none in the long run even if the policy actions are unanticipated.

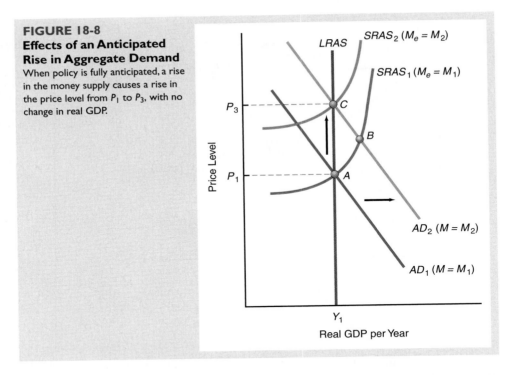

FIGURE 18-8

Effects of an Anticipated Rise in Aggregate Demand

When policy is fully anticipated, a rise in the money supply causes a rise in the price level from P_1 to P_3, with no change in real GDP.

What Must People Know? There are two important matters to keep in mind when considering this proposition. First, our discussion has assumed that economic participants know in advance exactly what the change in monetary policy is going to be and precisely when it is going to occur. In fact, the Federal Reserve does not announce exactly what the future course of monetary policy is going to be. Instead, the Fed tries to keep most of its plans secret, announcing only in general terms what policy actions are intended for the future. It is tempting to conclude that because the Fed's intended policies are not freely available, they are not available at all. But such a conclusion would be wrong. Economic participants have great incentives to learn how to predict the future behavior of the monetary authorities, just as businesses try to forecast consumer behavior and college students do their best to forecast what their next economics exam will look like. Even if the economic participants are not perfect at forecasting the course of policy, they are likely to come a lot closer than they would in total ignorance. The policy irrelevance proposition really assumes only that *people don't persistently make the same mistakes in forecasting the future.*

What Happens If People Don't Know Everything? This brings us to our second point. Once we accept the fact that people are not perfect in their ability to predict the future, the possibility emerges that some policy actions will have systematic effects that look much like the movements *A* to *B* to *C* in Figure 18-7 on page 427. For example, just as other economic participants sometimes make mistakes, it is likely that the Federal Reserve sometimes makes mistakes—meaning that the money supply may change in ways that even the Fed does not predict. And even if the Fed always accomplished every policy action it intended, there is no guarantee that other economic participants would fully forecast those actions. What happens if the Fed makes a mistake or if firms and workers misjudge the future course of policy? Matters will look much as they do in panel (a) of Figure 18-9, which shows the effects of an unanticipated increase in the money supply. Economic participants expect the money supply to be M_1, but the actual money supply turns out to be M_2. Be-

FIGURE 18-9
Effects of an Unanticipated Rise in Aggregate Demand
Even with rational expectations, an unanticipated change in demand can affect real GDP in the short run.

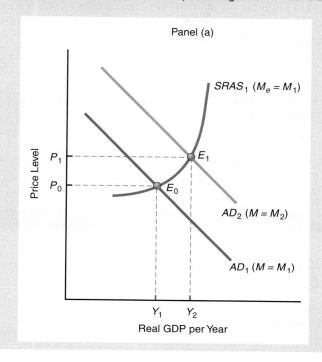

Panel (a)

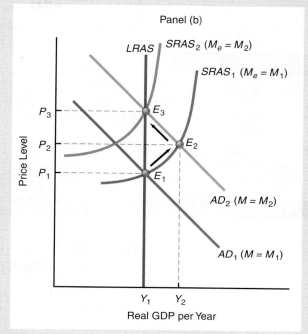

Panel (b)

cause $M_2 > M_1$, aggregate demand shifts relative to aggregate supply. The result is a rise in real GDP in the short run from Y_1 to Y_2. Corresponding to this rise in real GDP will be an increase in employment and hence a fall in the unemployment rate. So, even under the rational expectations hypothesis, monetary policy *can* have an effect on real variables in the short run, but only if the policy is unsystematic and therefore unanticipated.

In the long run, this effect on real variables will disappear because people will figure out that the Fed either accidentally increased the money supply or intentionally increased it in a way that somehow fooled individuals. Either way, people's expectations will soon be revised so that the short-run aggregate supply curve will shift upward. As shown in panel (b) of Figure 18-9, real GDP will return to long-run levels, meaning that so will the employment and unemployment rates.

The Policy Dilemma

Perhaps the most striking and disturbing feature of the policy irrelevance proposition is that it seems to suggest that only mistakes can have real effects. If the Federal Reserve always does what it intends to do and if other economic participants always correctly anticipate the Fed's actions, monetary policy will affect only the price level and nominal input prices. It appears that only if the Fed makes a mistake in executing monetary policy or people err in anticipating that policy will changes in the money supply cause fluctuations in real GDP and employment. If this reasoning is correct, the Fed is effectively precluded from using monetary policy in any rational way to lower the unemployment rate or to raise the level of real GDP. This is because fully anticipated changes in the money supply will lead to exactly offsetting changes in prices and hence no real effects. Many economists were disturbed at the prospect that if the economy happened to enter a recessionary period, policymakers would be powerless to push real GDP and unemployment back to long-run levels. As a result, they asked, in light of the rational expectations hypothesis, is it *ever* possible for systematic policy to have predictable real effects on the economy? The answer has led to even more developments in the way we think about macroeconomics.

CONCEPTS in Brief

- The rational expectations hypothesis assumes that individuals' forecasts incorporate all available information, including an understanding of government policy and its effects on the economy.

- If the rational expectations hypothesis is valid, there is pure competition, and all prices and wages are flexible, then the policy irrelevance proposition follows: Fully anticipated monetary policy actions cannot alter either the rate of unemployment or the level of real GDP.

- With rational expectations, flexible wages and prices, and pure competition, policies can alter real economic variables only if the policies are unsystematic and therefore unanticipated; otherwise people learn and defeat the desired policy goals.

To test your understanding of the concepts covered in this section, go to the Online Review at www.myeconlab.com/miller.

ANOTHER CHALLENGE TO POLICY ACTIVISM: REAL BUSINESS CYCLES

When confronted with the policy irrelevance proposition, many economists began to reexamine the first principles of macroeconomics with fully flexible wages and prices.

The Distinction Between Real and Monetary Shocks

Today, many economists argue that real, as opposed to purely monetary, forces might help explain aggregate economic fluctuations. An important stimulus for the idea that there are *real business cycles* was the economic turmoil of the 1970s. During that decade, world economies were staggered by two major disruptions to the supply of oil. The first occurred in 1973, and the second in 1979. In both episodes, members of the Organization of Petroleum Exporting Countries (OPEC) reduced the amount of oil they were willing to supply and raised the price at which they offered it for sale. Each time, the price level rose sharply in the United States, and real GDP declined. Thus each episode involving these aggregate supply shocks (see Chapter 11) produced a period of "stagflation"—real economic stagnation combined with high inflation. Figure 18-10 illustrates the pattern of events.

We begin at point E_1 with the economy in both short- and long-run equilibrium, with the associated supply curves, $SRAS_1$ and $LRAS_1$. Initially, the level of real GDP is Y_1, and the price level is P_1. Because the economy is in long-run equilibrium, the unemployment rate must be at the natural rate.

A reduction in the supply of oil, as occurred in 1973 and 1979, causes the $SRAS$ curve to shift to the left to $SRAS_2$ because fewer goods will be available for sale due to the reduced supplies. If the reduction in oil supplies is (or is believed to be) permanent, the $LRAS$ shifts to the left also. This assumption is reflected in Figure 18-10, where $LRAS_2$ shows the new long-run aggregate supply curve associated with the lowered output of oil.

In the short run, two adjustments begin to occur simultaneously. First, the prices of oil and petroleum-based products begin to rise, so the overall price level rises to P_2. Second, the higher costs of production occasioned by the rise in oil prices induce firms to cut back production, so real GDP falls to Y_2 in the short run. The new temporary short-run equilibrium occurs at E_2, with a higher price level (P_2) and a lower level of real GDP (Y_2).

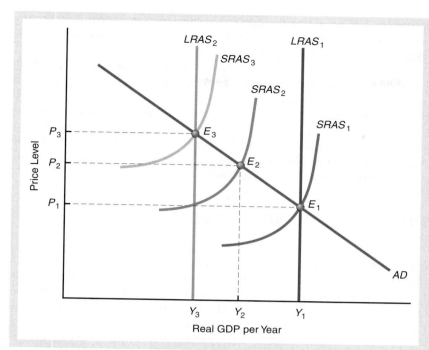

FIGURE 18-10
Effects of a Reduction in the Supply of Resources
The position of the *LRAS* depends on our endowments of all types of resources. Hence a reduction in the supply of one of those resources, such as oil, causes a reduction—an inward shift—in the aggregate supply curve from $LRAS_1$ to $LRAS_2$. In addition, there is a rise in the equilibrium price level and a fall in the equilibrium rate of real GDP per year.

Impact on the Labor Market

If we were to focus on the labor market while this adjustment from E_1 to E_2 was taking place, we would find two developments occurring. The rise in the price level pushes the real wage rate downward, even as the scaled-back production plans of firms induce them to reduce the amount of labor inputs they are using. So not only does the real wage rate fall, but the level of employment declines as well. On both counts, workers are made worse off due to the reduction in the supply of oil.

This is not the full story, however. Owners of nonoil inputs (such as labor) who are willing to put up with reduced real payments in the short run simply will not tolerate them in the long run. Thus, for example, some workers who were willing to continue working at lower wages in the short run will eventually decide to retire, switch from full-time work to part-time employment, or drop out of the labor force altogether. In effect, there is a reduction in the supply of nonoil inputs, reflected in an upward shift in the *SRAS* curve from $SRAS_2$ to $SRAS_3$. This puts additional upward pressure on the price level and exerts a downward force on real GDP. The final long-run equilibrium thus occurs at point E_3, with the price level at P_3 and real GDP at Y_3. (In principle, because the oil supply shock has had no direct effect on labor markets, the natural rate of unemployment does not change when equilibrium moves from E_1 to E_3.)

Generalizing the Theory

Naturally, the idea that the economy experiences real business cycles encompasses all types of real disturbances arising from aggregate supply shocks, such as sudden technological changes and shifts in the composition of the labor force. Moreover, a complete treatment of real shocks to the economy is typically much more complex than we have allowed for in our discussion. For example, an oil shock such as is shown in Figure 18-10 would likely also have effects on the real wealth of U.S. residents, causing a reduction in aggregate demand as well as aggregate supply. Nevertheless, our simple example still manages to capture the flavor of the real-business-cycle perspective, which indicates little role for policy activism to stabilize the economy.

The idea that aggregate supply shocks contribute to business cycles has improved our understanding of the economy's behavior, but economists agree that it alone is incapable of explaining all of the facets of business cycles that we observe. For example, it is difficult to imagine a real disturbance that could possibly account for the Great Depression in this country, when real income fell more than 30 percent and the unemployment rate rose to 25 percent. Moreover, the real-business-cycle approach continues to assume that all wages and prices are perfectly flexible and so fails to explain a great deal of the apparent rigidity of wages and prices throughout the economy.

MODERN APPROACHES TO RATIONALIZING ACTIVE POLICYMAKING

The policy irrelevance proposition and the idea that real shocks are primary causes of business cycles are major attacks on the desirability of trying to stabilize economic activity with activist policies. Both anti-activism suggestions arise from combining the rational expectations hypothesis with the assumptions of pure competition and flexible wages and prices. It should not be surprising, therefore, to learn that economists who see a role for activist policymaking do not believe that market clearing models of the economy can explain business cycles. They contend that the "sticky" wages and prices assumed by Keynes in his major work (see Chapter 11) remain important in today's economy. To explain how aggregate demand shocks and policies can influence a nation's real GDP and unemployment rate, these economists, who are sometimes called *new Keynesians,* have tried to refine the theory of aggregate supply. They have focused on providing alternative explanations for sources of stickiness in prices, wages, and unemployment.

Small Menu Costs and Sticky Prices

If prices do not respond to demand changes, two conditions must be true: someone must be consciously deciding not to change prices, and that decision must be in the decision maker's self-interest. One approach to explaining why many prices might be sticky in the short run supposes that much of the economy is characterized by imperfect competition (so firms are price searchers) and that it is costly for firms to change their prices in response to changes in demand. The costs associated with changing prices are called *menu costs,* and they include the costs of renegotiating contracts, printing price lists (such as menus), and informing customers of price changes.

Small menu costs
Costs that deter firms from changing prices in response to demand changes—for example, the costs of renegotiating contracts or printing new price lists.

Many such costs may not be very large, so economists call them **small menu costs.** Some of the costs of changing prices, however, such as those incurred in bringing together business managers from points around the nation or the world for meetings on price changes or renegotiating deals with customers, may be significant.

Firms in different industries have different cost structures. Such differences explain diverse small menu costs. Therefore, the extent to which firms hold their prices constant in the face of changes in demand for their products will vary across industries. Not all prices will be rigid. Nonetheless, some economists who promote policy activism argue that many—even most—firms' prices are sticky for relatively long time intervals. As a result, the aggregate level of prices could be very nearly rigid because of small menu costs.

Although most economists agree that such costs exist, there is considerably less agreement on whether they are sufficient to explain the extent of price rigidity that is observed.

Efficiency Wage Theory

An alternative modern approach to explaining why activist policymaking might affect real GDP and unemployment proposes that worker productivity actually *depends on* the wages that workers are paid, rather than being independent of wages. The idea is that higher real wages encourage workers to work harder, improve their efficiency, increase morale, and raise their loyalty to the firm. Across the board, then, higher wages tend to increase workers' productivity, which in turn discourages firms from cutting real wages because of the damaging effect that such an action would have on productivity and profitability.

Under highly competitive conditions, there will generally be an optimal wage—called the **efficiency wage**—that the firm should continue paying, even in the face of large fluctuations in the demand for its output. If the supply of labor increases, therefore, firms may continue to hold real wages steady at the efficiency wage level. Because new workers will not be able to find employment at the unchanged real wage rate, there will be an excess quantity of labor supplied, or unemployment.

Efficiency wage
The optimal wage that firms must pay to maintain worker productivity.

There are significant, valid elements in the idea of efficiency wages, but its importance in understanding national business fluctuations remains uncertain. For example, although the idea explains rigid real wages, it does not explain rigid prices. Moreover, the efficiency wage idea ignores the fact that firms can (and apparently do) rely on a host of incentives other than wages to encourage their workers to be loyal, efficient, and productive.

Effect of Aggregate Demand Changes on Output and Employment in the Long Run

Some economists who promote activist policymaking argue that a reduction in aggregate demand that causes a recession may affect output and employment even in the long run. They point out that workers who are fired or laid off may lose job skills during their period of unemployment. Consequently, they will have a more difficult time finding new employment later. Furthermore, those who remain unemployed over long periods of time may change their attitudes toward work. They may even have a reduced desire to find employment later on. For these reasons and others, a recession could permanently raise the amount of frictional unemployment.

As yet, little research has been done to quantify this theory. Why does the growth in self-employment and business incorporations in the aftermath of the last recession cast some doubt on the theory's relevance as an explanation for the behavior of all unemployed people?

EXAMPLE

No Jobs for Us? Let's Create Our Own Work

During 2002, following the recession that ended in 2001, the number of people classified as employed in the United States declined by more than 400,000. That year, the civilian labor force grew by just over 1.1 million, and the number of individuals counted as unemployed rose by about 1.5 million. On net, it was tempting for some media commentators at the time to conclude—and report—that the recession had caused 400,000 people to lose their jobs and kept 1.1 million people newly in the labor force from finding any work.

Of course, millions of individual stories underlie the aggregate statistics, so this conclusion is not necessarily justified. Indeed, one story that the media largely failed to cover was that during 2002 and 2003, the number of people who were self-employed—that is, those operating their own businesses—increased by more than 10 percent. The number of business incorporations rose by more than 7 percent. Some of this growth in self-employment and incorporated businesses surely reflected decisions by previously employed people to start their own firms. Undoubtedly, however, many who chose to start their own firms also were *unemployed* people who decided to try working for themselves instead of looking for paychecks from other firms. If prospects for traditional jobs are bleak, therefore, a number of people avoid unemployment by becoming self-employed.

For Critical Analysis
Why do you think that economists commonly view increases in the number of people who are self-employed and in the number of business incorporations as signals of higher future employment levels?

SUMMING UP: ECONOMIC FACTORS FAVORING ACTIVE VERSUS PASSIVE POLICYMAKING

To many people who have never taken a principles of economics course, it is apparent that the world's governments should engage in active policymaking aimed at achieving high and stable real GDP growth and a low and stable unemployment rate. As you have learned in this chapter, the advisability of policy activism is not so obvious.

Several factors are involved in assessing whether policy activism is really preferable to passive policymaking in the form of monetary rules and the like. Table 18-1 summarizes the issues involved in evaluating the case for active policymaking versus the case for passive policymaking.

Undoubtedly, you have heard about President Harry Truman's remark that he wished he could find a one-armed economist, so that he would not have to hear, "On the one hand. . .

TABLE 18-1
Issues That Must Be Assessed in Determining the Desirability of Active versus Passive Policymaking
Economists who contend that active policymaking is justified argue that evidence on each issue listed in the first column supports conclusions listed in the second column. In contrast, economists who suggest that passive policymaking is appropriate argue that evidence regarding each issue in the first column leads to conclusions listed in the third column.

Issue	Support for Active Policymaking	Support for Passive Policymaking
Phillips curve inflation-unemployment trade-off	Stable in the short run; perhaps predictable in the long run	Varies with inflation expectations; at best fleeting in the short run and nonexistent in the long run
Aggregate demand shocks	Induce short-run and perhaps long-run effects on real GDP and unemployment	Have little or no short-run effects and certainly no long-run effects on real GDP and unemployment
Aggregate supply shocks	Can, along with aggregate demand shocks, influence real GDP and unemployment	Cause movements in real GDP and unemployment and hence explain most business cycles
Pure competition	Is not typical in most markets, where imperfect competition predominates	Is widespread in markets throughout the economy
Price flexibility	Is uncommon because factors such as small menu costs induce firms to change prices infrequently	Is common because firms adjust prices immediately when demand changes
Wage flexibility	Is uncommon because factors such as wage effects on productivity lead firms to maintain relatively high real wages	Is common because nominal wages adjust speedily to price changes, making real wages flexible

but on the other hand" quite so often. The current state of thinking on the relative desirability of active or passive policymaking might make you as frustrated as President Truman was in the early 1950s. On the one hand, most economists agree that active policymaking is unlikely to exert sizable long-run effects on any nation's economy. Most also agree that aggregate supply shocks contribute to business cycles. Consequently, there is general agreement that there are limits on the effectiveness of monetary and fiscal policies. On the other hand, a number of economists continue to argue that there is evidence indicating stickiness of prices and wages. They argue, therefore, that monetary and fiscal policy actions can offset, at least in the short run and perhaps even in the long run, the effects that aggregate demand shocks would otherwise have on real GDP and unemployment.

These diverging perspectives help explain why economists reach differing conclusions about the advisability of pursuing active or passive approaches to macroeconomic policymaking. Different interpretations of evidence on the issues summarized in Table 18-1 will likely continue to divide economists for years to come.

CONCEPTS in Brief

- Even if all prices and wages are perfectly flexible, aggregate supply shocks such as sudden changes in technology or in the supplies of factors of production can cause national economic fluctuations. To the extent that these real business cycles predominate as sources of economic fluctuations, the case for active policymaking is weakened.

- Some economists suggest that small menu costs, efficiency wages, and potential long-term effects stemming from recessions make it possible for changes in aggregate demand to have real effects. These economists contend that these factors strengthen the case for policy activism.

To test your understanding of the concepts covered in this section, go to the Online Review at www.myeconlab.com/miller.

CASE STUDY: Economics Front and Center

Can Central Banks Take All the Credit for Low Inflation?

Bradshaw is a summer intern at a Federal Reserve bank. He has been asked to help with arrangements for the bank's annual symposium that features central bank officials and top economists from around the world. One of the benefits of Bradshaw's position is that from time to time he can take a seat in the audience and listen to the speakers.

This afternoon Bradshaw has been able to take a break from his duties and listen to a chief economist from the International Monetary Fund (IMF). As the presentation proceeds, Bradshaw notices that many of the central bank officials in the audience have begun to shift uncomfortably in their seats. The reason is clear: the IMF economist is suggesting that none of them can take full credit for the worldwide inflation reductions of the 1990s and 2000s. According to the speaker, it was easy for central banks to reduce inflation during this period because global deregulation and greater international business competition

were pushing down the natural unemployment rate. In fact, the speaker concludes, central banks missed a golden opportunity to reduce inflation rates close to zero.

Bradshaw thinks back on what he learned in his macroeconomics class about the natural rate of unemployment, the NAIRU, and Phillips curves. He wonders, "Could this IMF economist have a point?"

Points to Analyze

1. *How could deregulation and greater global competition lead to higher levels of employment, other things being equal, and thereby reduce the natural rate of unemployment and the NAIRU?*

2. *Why might it be "easier" for central bank officials to push inflation down during times when the natural unemployment rate and the NAIRU are falling than when they are rising?*

Issues *and* Applications

What the Fed Says Can Be Almost As Important As What It Does

I n the waning days of the summer of 2003, Federal Reserve officials announced an intention to keep interest rates low for a "considerable period." The officials did not define exactly how long this "considerable period" would be. As a consequence, within a matter of weeks, the Fed found itself in what one commentator called a "considerable pickle."

Concepts Applied

- Active Policymaking
- Anticipated Policies
- Unanticipated Policies

A Phillips Curve Interpretation of the Fed's Active Policymaking in the Early 2000s

After the 2001 recession, the unemployment rate remained stubbornly high. Consequently, during 2002 and 2003 the Federal Reserve embarked on active policymaking. Higher money supply growth pushed down interest rates. Lower interest rates, the Fed hoped, would induce the public to increase total planned spending, thereby raising aggregate demand and equilibrium real GDP. A decrease in unemploy-

ment would follow as businesses hired more workers to produce more goods and services.

As Figure 18-11 shows, inflation was relatively low in 2003. Although there was not a smooth short-run Phillips curve relationship, the downward-sloping curve that was the closest fit to the inflation-unemployment combinations experienced in recent years was not very steep. Thus Fed policymakers essentially made a bet that a relatively small increase in inflation would be sufficient to induce a relatively large decline in the unemployment rate.

FIGURE 18-11

Inflation and Unemployment Rates Since 1997

There has been an inverse, though not very smooth, relationship between inflation and unemployment since the late 1990s.

Sources: *Economic Report of the President*, 2004; *Economic Indicators*, various issues.

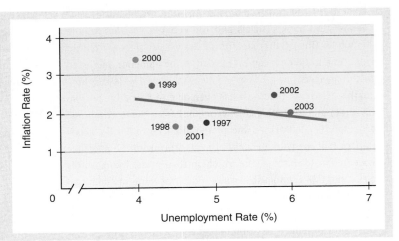

The Phillips Curve "Pickle" Caused by the Fed's Comment

Nevertheless, by August 2003, the Fed had kept interest rates low for more than a year, and the unemployment rate had not shown much downward movement. Fed officials, therefore, took the unusual step of adding the comment that the Fed planned to maintain low interest rates for a "considerable period." They hoped that this would truly convince the public to increase planned spending and thereby generate, at long last, a rise in aggregate demand and reduction in unemployment.

By late October, however, real GDP suddenly grew at an annualized rate exceeding 8 percent. The Fed officials' "considerable period" comment now came back to haunt them. If the economic expansion was already in progress, continuing to maintain high money supply growth in order to keep interest rates low for a "considerable period" would raise inflation expectations. This would cause the Phillips curve to shift out-

ward, resulting in higher inflation at any unemployment rate. Heading off rising inflation would require a reduction in the rate of growth of the money supply—and higher interest rates, which the Fed had just promised it would not allow. Yet, if the Fed did violate its promise by cutting back on money supply growth and allowing interest rates to rise, it could cause inflation to fall unexpectedly and generate a downward movement along the short-run Phillips curve in Figure 18-11. Then the unemployment rate would rise.

The Fed had discovered the power of its own words to influence the public's expectations. At their next meeting, Fed officials stated that the Fed "should not usually commit itself to a particular policy stance over some pre-established, extended time frame." The Fed's future policy stance, they concluded, "would be determined by the evaluation of the outlook, not the passage of time." In other words, the Fed began tactfully taking back its promise to pursue the same policy for a "considerable period."

For Critical Analysis

1. What do you suppose the Fed anticipated gaining, in the short run, from its efforts to convince households and firms that interest rates would remain low for some time? (Hint: How do consumers and businesses respond to low interest rates?)
2. Why did the Fed conclude that sticking indefinitely to a commitment to high money supply growth would eventually cause the short-run Phillips curve to shift outward?

Web Resources

1. To read Federal Reserve officials' latest statement about the Fed's monetary policy actions, go to the link available at www.econtoday.com/chap18.
2. To take a look at Fed officials' latest testimony before Congress and their semiannual reports submitted to Congress, go to www.econtoday.com/chap18.

Research Project

Consider, using an aggregate demand–aggregate supply diagram, the likely short-run and long-run effects of a public announcement by the Federal Reserve that it expects the inflation rate to be higher for the next several years. Do this first under the assumption that the Fed makes the announcement and simultaneously increases the money supply. Then redo your analysis assuming that the Fed simply announces that it expects higher inflation but then leaves the money supply unchanged. How do the short-run and long-run effects differ depending on whether the Fed increases the money supply? Why?

SUMMARY DISCUSSION of Learning Objectives

1. **Why the Actual Unemployment Rate Might Depart from the Natural Rate of Unemployment:** According to the basic theory of aggregate demand and short- and long-run aggregate supply, an unexpected increase in aggregate demand can cause real GDP to rise in the short run, which results in a reduction in the unemployment rate. Consequently, for a time the actual unemployment rate can fall below the natural rate of unemployment.

Likewise, an unanticipated reduction in aggregate demand can push down real GDP in the short run, thereby causing the actual unemployment rate to rise above the natural unemployment rate.

2. **The Phillips Curve:** An unexpected increase in aggregate demand that causes a drop in the unemployment rate also induces a rise in the equilibrium price level and, conse-

quently, inflation. Thus the basic aggregate demand–aggregate supply model indicates that, other things being equal, there should be an inverse relationship between the inflation rate and the unemployment rate. This downward-sloping relationship is called the Phillips curve, and it implies that there may be a short-run trade-off between inflation and unemployment.

3. **How Expectations Affect the Actual Relationship Between the Inflation Rate and the Unemployment Rate:** Theory predicts that there will be a Phillips curve relationship only when another important factor, expectations, is held unchanged. If people are able to anticipate policymakers' efforts to exploit the Phillips curve trade-off by engaging in inflationary policies to push down the unemployment rate, then basic theory also suggests that input prices such as nominal wages will adjust more rapidly to an increase in the price level. As a result, the Phillips curve will shift outward, and the economy will adjust more speedily toward the natural rate of unemployment. When plotted on a chart, therefore, the actual relationship between the inflation rate and the unemployment rate will not be a downward-sloping Phillips curve.

4. **Rational Expectations, Market Clearing, and Policy Ineffectiveness:** According to the rational expectations hypothesis, people form expectations of future economic variables such as inflation using all available past and current information and based on their understanding of how the economy functions. If pure competition prevails, wages and prices are flexible, and people form rational expectations, then only unanticipated policy actions can induce even short-run changes in real GDP. If people completely anticipate the actions of policymakers, wages and other input prices adjust immediately, so real GDP remains unaffected. A key implication of this expectations-based approach to macroeconomics is the policy irrelevance proposition, which states that the unemployment rate is unaffected by fully anticipated policy actions.

5. **The Real–Business-Cycle Challenge to Active Policymaking:** Even if pure competition prevails throughout the economy and prices and wages are flexible, technological changes and labor market shocks such as variations in the composition of the labor force can induce business fluctuations. To the extent that such aggregate supply shocks contribute to real business cycles, the case for active policymaking is weakened.

6. **Modern Approaches to Bolstering the Case for Active Policymaking:** Modern approaches to understanding the sources of business fluctuations highlight wage and price stickiness. Imperfectly competitive firms that face costs of adjusting their prices may be slow to change prices in the face of variations in demand, so real GDP may exhibit greater short-run variability than it otherwise would. Another idea is that worker productivity depends on the real wages that workers earn, which dissuades firms from reducing real wages below so-called efficiency wages. This results in widespread wage stickiness. Finally, some activist economists propose that short-term downturns in economic activity can affect the natural unemployment rate because people who lose their jobs in the short run also lose the opportunities to develop skills while unemployed or may change their attitudes toward work.

KEY TERMS AND CONCEPTS

active (discretionary) policymaking (417)

efficiency wage (433)

nonaccelerating inflation rate of unemployment (NAIRU) (422)

passive (nondiscretionary) policymaking (417)

Phillips curve (422)

policy irrelevance proposition (427)

rational expectations hypothesis (426)

small menu costs (432)

PROBLEMS

Answers to the odd-numbered problems appear at the back of the book.

18-1. Suppose that the government altered the computation of the unemployment rate by including people in the military as part of the labor force.

   a. How would this affect the actual unemployment rate?

   b. How would such a change affect estimates of the natural rate of unemployment?

   c. If this computational change were made, would it in any way affect the logic of the short-run and long-run Phillips curve analysis and its implications for policymaking? Why might the government wish to make such a change?

18-2. When Alan Greenspan was nominated for his third term as chair of the Federal Reserve's Board of Governors, a few senators held up his confirmation. One of them explained their joint action to hinder his confirmation by saying, "Every time growth starts to go up, they [the Federal Reserve] push on the brakes, robbing working families and businesses of the benefits of faster growth." Evaluate this statement in the context of short-run and long-run perspectives on the Phillips curve.

18-3. Economists have not reached agreement on how lengthy the time horizon for "the long run" is in the context of Phillips curve analysis. Would you anticipate that this period is likely to have been shortened or extended by the advent of more sophisticated computer and communications technology? Explain your reasoning.

18-4. The natural rate of unemployment depends on factors that affect the behavior of both workers and firms. Make lists of possible factors affecting workers and firms that you believe are likely to influence the natural rate of unemployment.

18-5. When will the natural rate of unemployment and the nonaccelerating inflation rate of unemployment (NAIRU) differ? When will they be the same?

18-6. People called "Fed watchers" earn their living by trying to forecast what policies the Federal Reserve will implement within the next few weeks and months. Suppose that Fed watchers discover that the current group of Fed officials is following very systematic and predictable policies intended to reduce the unemployment rate. The Fed watchers then sell this information to firms, unions, and others in the private sec-

tor. If pure competition prevails, prices and wages are flexible, and people form rational expectations, are the Fed's policies likely to have their intended effects on the unemployment rate?

18-7. Suppose that economists were able to use U.S. economic data to demonstrate that the rational expectations hypothesis is true. Would this be sufficient to demonstrate the validity of the policy irrelevance proposition?

18-8. Evaluate the following statement: "In an important sense, the term *policy irrelevance proposition* is misleading because even if the rational expectations hypothesis is valid, economic policy actions can have significant effects on real GDP and the unemployment rate."

18-9. The real-business-cycle approach attributes even short-run increases in real GDP largely to aggregate supply shocks. Rightward shifts in aggregate supply tend to push down the equilibrium price level. How, then, could the real-business-cycle perspective explain the low but persistent inflation that the United States has experienced in recent years?

18-10. Does the Federal Reserve have any role if real business cycles explain U.S. economic fluctuations? If so, what is that role?

18-11. Use an aggregate demand and aggregate supply diagram to illustrate why the existence of widespread stickiness in prices established by businesses throughout the economy would be extremely important to predicting the potential effects of policy actions on real GDP.

18-12. Economists have established that higher productivity due to technological improvements tends to push up real wages. Now suppose that the economy experiences a host of technological improvements. If worker productivity responds positively to higher real wages, will this effect tend to add to or subtract from the economic growth initially induced by the improvements in technology?

18-13. Normally, firms experience an increase in profits by adjusting their prices upward when aggregate demand increases. The idea behind the small-menu-cost explanation for price stickiness is that firms will leave their prices unchanged if their profit gain from adjusting prices is less than menu costs they would incur if they change prices. If firms anticipate that a rise in demand is likely to last for a long time, does this make them more or less likely to adjust their prices when they face small menu costs? (Hint: Profits are a flow that firms earn from week to week and month to month, but small menu costs are a onetime expense.)

18-14. What distinguishes the NAIRU from the natural rate of unemployment? (Hint: Which is easier to quantify?)

18-15. Suppose that more unemployed people who are classified as part of frictional unemployment decide to stop looking for work and start their own businesses instead. What is likely to happen to each of the following, other things being equal?

   a. The natural unemployment rate
   b. The NAIRU
   c. The economy's Phillips curve

ECONOMICS ON THE NET

The Inflation–Unemployment Relationship According to the basic aggregate demand and aggregate supply model, the unemployment rate should be inversely related to changes in the inflation rate, other things being equal. This application allows you to take a direct look at unemployment and inflation data to judge for yourself whether the two variables appear to be related.

Title: Bureau of Labor Statistics: Economy at a Glance

Navigation: Go to www.econtoday.com/chap18 to visit the Bureau of Labor Statistics Economy at a Glance home page.

Application Perform the indicated operations, and then answer the following questions.

   1. Click on the graph box next to *Consumer Price Index*. Take a look at the solid line showing inflation. How much has inflation varied in recent years? Compare this with previous years, especially the mid-1970s to mid-1980s.

   2. Back up to *Economy at a Glance*, and now click on the graph box next to *Unemployment Rate*. During what recent years was the unemployment rate approaching and at its peak value? Do you note any appearance of an inverse relationship between the unemployment rate and the inflation rate?

For Group Study and Analysis Divide the class into groups, and have each group search through the *Economy at a Glance* site to develop an explanation for the key factors accounting for the recent behavior of the unemployment rate. Have each group report on its explanation. Is there any one factor that best explains the recent behavior of the unemployment rate?

If your exam were tomorrow, would you be ready? For each chapter, MyEconLab Practice Tests and Study Plans pinpoint which sections you have mastered and which ones you need to study. That way, you are more efficient with your study time, and you are better prepared for your exams.

In addition to Practice Tests and your personalized Study Plan, you'll find the following media resources in MyEconLab:
   1. *Graphs in Motion* animation of Figures 18-1, 18-2, 18-4, 18-5, 18-8, and 18-10.
   2. Videos featuring the author, Roger LeRoy Miller, on the following subjects:
      ● The Natural Rate of Unemployment
      ● The New Keynesian Economics

   3. Links to the Web sites cited in the marginal Internet Resources, Issues and Applications feature, and Economics on the Net activity.
   4. Audio clips of all key terms, additional practice problems, and a PDF version of the material from the print Study Guide.
   5. eThemes of the Times, which is a New York Times article to help you understand the real-world applications of what you are learning.

To see how it works, turn to page 16 and then go to www.myeconlab.com/miller.

Get Ahead of the Curve

Chapter *19*

Policies and Prospects for Global Economic Growth

To start an officially recognized business in the United States, a person normally has to complete no more than four legal procedures, which usually take less than a week to finalize. The costs of formally registering the business amount to only a tiny fraction of the U.S. per capita income level. In contrast, Bolivia requires about three times as many legal procedures. These steps can rarely be finished in less than four months, and the costs of doing so normally add up to the equivalent of about 167 percent of the annual income earned by a typical Bolivian resident. In this chapter, you will learn why such relatively complicated, slow-moving, and expensive procedures for establishing business ownership are holding back economic growth in Bolivia and other developing nations.

LEARNING OBJECTIVES

After reading this chapter, you should be able to:

1. Explain why population growth can have uncertain effects on economic growth

2. Understand why the existence of dead capital retards investment and economic growth in much of the developing world

3. Describe how government inefficiencies have contributed to the creation of relatively large quantities of dead capital in the world's developing nations

4. Discuss the rationales for foreign financing of investment in developing nations and explain how developing countries benefit from international capital investment

5. Identify the key functions of the World Bank and the International Monetary Fund

6. Explain the basis for recent criticisms of policymaking at the World Bank and the International Monetary Fund

Media Resources

Refer to the end of the chapter for a full listing of the multimedia learning materials available in MyEconLab.

Did You Know That ...much of the world's housing is not legally owned and thus cannot easily be bought and sold? Estimates indicate that 57 percent of city dwellers and 67 percent of rural residents in the Philippines occupy homes to which no one has any clear legal title. In Haiti, approximately 68 percent of people who reside in cities and 97 percent of those in the countryside live in homes that have no official owner. In Egypt, unofficial structures house an estimated 92 percent of city dwellers and 85 percent of rural residents.

All told, the market value of real estate not legally registered in developing nations probably equals at least $9 trillion. This amount is nearly as high as the market value of all companies listed on the stock exchanges of the world's most developed nations. Because the ownership of unofficial properties in developing nations is not legally recognized by the nations' governments, people who own the properties have trouble putting them to their fullest possible use. For instance, members of a Philippines household who own an unregistered home cannot use the property as collateral if they wish to borrow funds to start a business. A Haitian owner of an unofficial dwelling cannot readily obtain insurance coverage, so she will be less likely to operate a garment shop from her home. If an Egyptian couple try to fund their child's education by renting a wing of their unofficial home to an individual who then fails to make promised rent payments, they will lack a clear legal right to evict the deadbeat tenant. Naturally, these and other problems restrict the usability and tradability of real estate, thereby limiting the potential contribution of this form of capital to economic growth in the Philippines, Haiti, and Egypt.

In the pages that follow, you will contemplate the prospects for economic growth in these and other nations of the world. You will learn about international institutions that the world's wealthier nations have established to promote global economic growth and about the policies of these institutions. You will also discover why prospects for economic growth remain bleak for many people around the globe, irrespective of the activities of these international institutions.

LABOR RESOURCES AND ECONOMIC GROWTH

You learned in Chapter 10 that the main determinants of economic growth are the growth of labor and capital resources and the rate of increase of labor and capital productivity. Human resources are abundant around the globe. Currently, the world's population increases by more than 75 million people each year. This population growth is not spread evenly over the earth's surface. Among the relatively wealthy nations of Europe, women bear an average of just over one child during their lifetimes. In the United States, a typical woman bears about 1.5 children. But in the generally poorer nations of Africa, women bear an average of six children.

Population growth does not necessarily translate into an increase in labor resources in a number of the poorest regions of the world, because many people in poor nations do not join the labor force or have trouble obtaining employment. Consequently, a common assumption is that high population growth in a less developed nation hinders the growth of its per capita GDP. Certainly, this is the presumption in China, where the government has imposed an absolute limit of one child per female resident. In fact, however, the relationship between population growth and economic growth is not really so clear-cut.

Population Growth and Economic Growth

Does a larger population contribute to or detract from economic growth? Given an unchanged level of aggregate real GDP, a higher population directly reduces per capita real GDP. After all, if there are more people, then dividing a constant amount of real GDP by a larger number of people reduces real GDP per capita.

This calculation works for growth rates too. We can express the growth rate of per capita real GDP in a nation as

$$\begin{array}{ccc}
\text{Rate of growth of} & = & \text{rate of growth} & - & \text{Rate of growth} \\
\text{per capita real GDP} & & \text{in real GDP} & & \text{of population}
\end{array}$$

Hence, if real GDP grows at a constant rate of 4 percent per year and the annual rate of population growth increases from 2 percent to 3 percent, the annual rate of growth of per capita real GDP will decline, from 2 percent to 1 percent.

How Population Growth Can Contribute to Economic Growth. Population growth can also increase the country's growth of labor resources. As you learned in Chapter 9, a higher rate of growth of labor resources contributes to increased growth of real GDP. For instance, suppose that a nation's rate of population growth increases as a result of increased immigration. The resulting growth in labor resources can boost the growth rate of real GDP. In addition, if the immigrants boost the nation's labor force participation rate, the resulting higher growth in real GDP can actually exceed the rate of population growth. The direct result of increased immigration, therefore, can be a net increase in the growth of real GDP per capita.

An increase in population via a higher birthrate obviously cannot immediately boost the rates of growth of labor resources and of real GDP, because years must pass before newborn individuals reach an age at which they are able to work. Nevertheless, over a period of years, it is still possible that increased population growth owing to a higher birthrate can also lead to a more rapid growth rate of total real GDP. This will occur directly as individuals enter the labor force when they reach working age. In addition, if the higher population growth causes an eventual increase in labor force participation in conjunction with technological improvements or increased capital accumulation, there can be an additional stimulus to growth. In principle, therefore, a higher rate of population growth can contribute to an overall rise in a nation's rate of growth of per capita real GDP.

Whether Population Growth Hinders or Contributes to Economic Growth Depends on Where You Live. On net, does an increased rate of population growth detract from or add to the rate of economic growth? Table 19-1 on the next page indicates that the answer depends on which nation one considers. In some nations that have experienced relatively high average rates of population growth, such as China, Hong Kong (a province of China), Singapore, and, to a lesser extent, India and Pakistan, economic growth has accompanied population growth. In contrast, in nations such as Saudi Arabia, Niger, and Zambia, there has been a negative relationship between population growth and per capita real GDP growth. Other factors apparently must affect how population growth and economic growth ultimately interrelate.

The Role of Economic Freedom

A crucial factor influencing economic growth is the relative freedom of a nation's residents. Particularly important is the degree of **economic freedom**—the rights to own private property and to exchange goods, services, and financial assets with minimal government interference—available to the residents of a nation.

Approximately two-thirds of the world's people reside in about three dozen nations with governments unwilling to grant residents significant economic freedom. The economies of these nations, even though they have the bulk of the world's population, produce only 13 percent of the world's total output. Several of these countries have experienced rates of economic growth at or above the 1.2 percent annual average for the world's nations during the past 30 years, but many are growing much more slowly. More than 30 of these countries have experienced negative rates of per capita income growth.

Economic freedom
The rights to own private property and to exchange goods, services, and financial assets with minimal government interference.

Go to www.econtoday.com/chap19 to review the Heritage Foundation's evaluations of the degree of economic freedom in different nations.

TABLE 19-1
Population Growth and Growth in Per Capita Real GDP in Selected Nations Since 1965

Country	Average Annual Population Growth Rate (%)	Average Annual Rate of Growth of Per Capita Real GDP (%)
China	1.5	6.8
Ghana	2.7	−1.0
Hong Kong	2.1	5.5
India	2.0	2.5
Jordan	4.3	−0.4
South Korea	1.4	7.2
Niger	3.3	−2.9
Pakistan	2.6	2.8
Saudi Arabia	4.1	−3.0
Sierra Leone	2.1	−1.4
Singapore	2.1	6.2
United States	1.0	1.4
Zambia	3.0	−2.1

Source: World Bank.

Only 17 nations, with 17 percent of the world's people, grant their residents high degrees of economic freedom. These nations, some of which have very high population densities, together account for 81 percent of total world output. All of the countries that grant considerable economic freedom have experienced positive rates of economic growth, and most are close to or above the world's average rate of economic growth.

The Role of Political Freedom

Interestingly, *political freedom*—the right to openly support and democratically select national leaders—appears to be less important than economic freedom in determining economic growth. Some countries that grant considerable economic freedom to their citizens have relatively strong restrictions on their residents' freedoms of speech and the press.

In fact, there is some evidence that greater democracy in a nation can sometimes modestly *reduce* economic growth. Perhaps this is because political freedom gives special-interest groups the chance to gain at the expense of society as a whole, because such groups find ways to pass laws that inhibit competition. For instance, business interests can band together to convince a legislature to prevent lower-priced goods from entering the country to compete with existing businesses. Such a reduction in competition then reduces the incentive for home businesses to innovate, stifling growth.

When nondemocratic countries have achieved high standards of living through consistent economic growth, they tend to become more democratic over time. This suggests that economic freedom tends to stimulate economic growth, which then leads to more political freedom. It is easy to understand, therefore, why nations with high population growth rates that fail to achieve significant economic freedom can fall into a terrible trap. Population growth via high birthrates reduces per capita incomes, and the lack of economic freedom inhibits real GDP growth. The lack of economic growth then perpetuates nondemocratic institutions. As a result, many people of the world continue to suffer from meager real GDP growth as well as from the absence of political and economic freedom.

CONCEPTS in Brief

- For a given rate of growth of aggregate real GDP, higher population growth tends to reduce the growth of per capita real GDP.

- To the extent that increased population growth leads to greater labor force participation that raises the growth of total real GDP, a higher population growth

rate can potentially boost the rate of growth in per capita real GDP.

- In general, the extent of political freedom does not necessarily increase the rate of economic growth. A greater degree of economic freedom, however, does have a positive effect on a nation's growth prospects.

To test your understanding of the concepts covered in this section, go to the Online Review at **www.myeconlab.com/miller.**

CAPITAL GOODS AND ECONOMIC GROWTH

A fundamental problem developing countries face is that a significant portion of their capital goods, or manufactured resources that may be used to produce other items in the future, is what economists call **dead capital.*** This term describes a capital resource lacking clear title of ownership. Dead capital may actually be put to some productive purpose, but individuals and firms face difficulties in exchanging, insuring, and legally protecting their rights to this resource. Thus dead capital is a resource that people cannot readily allocate to its *most efficient* use.

Dead capital
Any capital resource that lacks clear title of ownership.

In years past, observers of the plight of the world's poorest nations suggested that helping those countries address environmental problems they faced would encourage economic growth. As economists have dug deeper into the difficulties confronting residents of these nations, rather, they have found that dead capital is among the most significant impediments to growth of per capita incomes in these countries.

Why do you suppose that African nations are experiencing particularly low rates of growth in real GDP per capita?

International Policy EXAMPLE

Africa's Huge Dead Capital Problem

The average resident of the African continent earns about 5 percent of the per capita real GDP of a U.S. resident. Furthermore, his or her situation has not been improving. In 1970, 10 percent of the world's poorest people lived in Africa. Today, Africa is home to about 50 percent of the poorest people.

In light of the fact that the African continent possesses vast physical and human resources, what is holding back the region's economic growth? A fundamental factor is dead capital. Less than 10 percent of the continent's land is formally owned. Only about 10 percent of the residents of the region have legal title to the houses in which they reside. The total estimated value of informally occupied land and buildings in

Africa exceeds $1 trillion. This amount is almost 70 times the international aid that African nations receive each year.

African residents who do not own their land or their dwellings cannot borrow against the values of those items. They cannot readily sell them to others interested in starting productive businesses. Thus residents of almost an entire continent are residing on and within dead capital. Although dead capital is not the only reason for slow growth in Africa, it is surely among the most important.

For Critical Analysis
How might the assignment of property rights help to promote growth on the African continent?

---

*The term *dead capital* was coined by Hernando de Soto, who conducted the first studies of factors contributing to this problem in developing nations.

Dead Capital and Inefficient Production

Physical structures used to house both business operations and labor resources are forms of capital goods. As we noted at the beginning of this chapter, current estimates indicate that unofficial, nontransferrable physical structures valued at more than $9 trillion are found in developing nations around the world. Because people in developing countries do not officially own this huge volume of capital goods, they cannot easily trade these resources. Thus it is hard for many of the world's people to use capital goods in ways that will yield the largest feasible output of goods and services.

Go to www.econtoday.com/chap19 to read an article on dead capital in Cairo and elsewhere by Hernando DeSoto of Peru's Institute for Liberty and Democracy.

Consider, for instance, a hypothetical situation faced by an individual in Cairo, Egypt, a city in which an estimated 90 percent of all physical structures are unofficially owned and occupied. Suppose this person unofficially owns a run-down apartment building but has no official title of ownership of this structure. Also suppose that the building is better suited for use as a distribution center for a new import-export firm. The individual would like to sell or lease the structure to the new firm, but because he does not formally own the building, he is unable to do so. If the costs of obtaining formal title to the property are sufficiently high relative to the potential benefit—as they apparently are at present for about 9 out of every 10 Cairo businesses and households—this individual's capital resource will not be allocated to its most efficient use.

This example illustrates a basic problem of dead capital. People who unofficially own capital goods are commonly constrained in their ability to use them efficiently. As a result, large quantities of capital goods throughout the developing world are inefficiently employed.

Dead Capital and Economic Growth

Recall from Chapter 2 that when we take into account production choices over time, any society faces a trade-off between consumption goods and capital goods. Whenever we make a choice to produce more consumption goods today, we incur an opportunity cost of fewer goods in the future. This means that when we make a choice to aim for more future economic growth to permit consumption of more goods in the future, we must allocate more resources to producing capital goods today. This entails incurring an opportunity cost today because society must allocate fewer resources to the current production of consumption goods.

This growth trade-off applies to any society, whether in a highly industrialized nation or a developing country. In a developing country, however, the inefficiencies of dead capital greatly reduce the rate of return on investment by individuals and firms. The resulting disincentives to invest in new capital goods can greatly hinder economic growth.

Government Inefficiencies, Investment, and Growth. A major factor contributing to the problem of dead capital in many developing nations is significant and often highly inefficient government regulation. Governments in many of the world's poorest nations place tremendous obstacles in the way of entrepreneurs interested in owning capital goods and directing them to profitable opportunities.

In addition to creating a problem with dead capital, poorly administered government regulations tend to reduce investment in new capital goods. If newly produced capital goods cannot be easily devoted to their most efficient uses, there is less incentive to invest. In a nation with a stifling government bureaucracy regulating the uses of capital goods, newly created capital will all too likely become dead capital.

Thus government inefficiency can be a major barrier to economic growth. Figure 19-1 depicts the relationship between average growth of per capita incomes and index measures of governmental inefficiency for various nations. As you can see, the economies of coun-

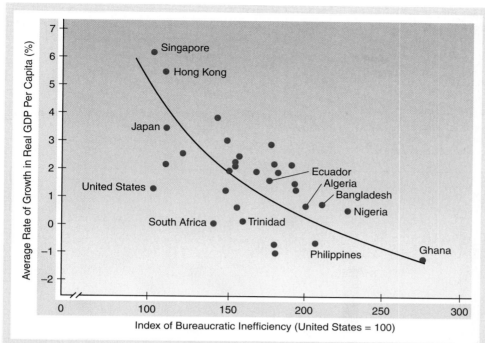

FIGURE 19-1
Bureaucratic Inefficiency and Economic Growth
Inefficiencies in government bureaucracies reduce the incentive to invest and thereby detract from economic growth.

Sources: International Monetary Fund; World Bank.

tries with less efficient governments tend to grow at relatively slower rates. The reason is that bureaucratic inefficiencies in these nations complicate efforts to direct capital goods to their most efficient uses.

Corruption and Growth. You might guess that in many nations plagued with inept governments generating large volumes of red tape, entrepreneurs will find ways to persuade officials to turn a blind eye to some regulations. Indeed, in many nations, bribery and graft are commonplace, and government officials selectively enforce the rules.

How much would you guess that it costs, as a percentage of per capita GDP, to enforce contracts in a typical nation?

International EXAMPLE

How Costly It Is to Enforce Contracts Depends on Where You Live

The World Bank estimates that in the United States, the average amount of time required to get through the 17 steps entailed in enforcing a typical contract is 365 days. That is a lot of steps and a lengthy period, but in the end the estimated cost is only 0.4 percent of U.S. per capita real GDP—equivalent to about one day's earnings in a regular U.S. workweek. Enforcing a contract in India takes the same number of steps and the same estimated time, but the cost that must be incurred amounts to 95

percent of India's per capita real GDP—essentially almost an entire year's earnings.

Figure 19-2 on the following page displays estimated contract-enforcement costs as percentages of per capita real GDP in these and various other nations, plus the world average, which is about 40 percent of per capita real GDP. Thus enforcing a contract currently requires the average resident of the world to spend the equivalent of more than four months of earned income. Of course, this person faces a smaller cost, relative to income, than someone living in the Dominican Republic, who typically must spend more than *four times* his or her annual earnings.

For Critical Analysis
What factors do you think contribute to contract-enforcement costs? (Hint: A nation's legal system governs the rules under which contracts are enforced.)

FIGURE 19-2
Contract-Enforcement Costs as a Percentage of Per Capita GDP in Selected Nations
In contrast to U.S. residents, for whom the average cost of enforcing a contract is a tiny fraction of per capita GDP, residents of most nations must spend much higher shares of their annual earned incomes to enforce a contract.

Source: World Bank.

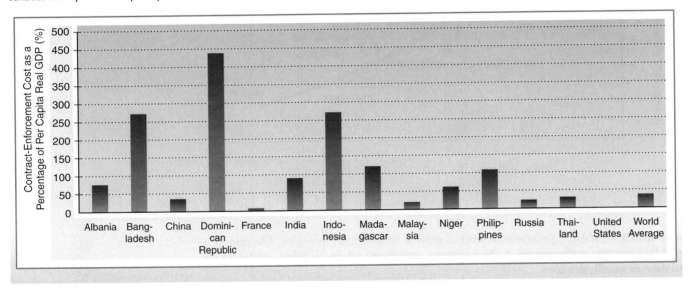

To the extent that the corruption of government officials permits entrepreneurs to avoid many sources of inefficiency, capital goods can be directed to more productive uses. Nevertheless, bribes and other inducements push up the costs of investing in and making use of capital goods, which reduces the net return on capital investment. In addition, corruption makes the return on capital dependent more on whims of individuals than on laws. This makes property rights less secure and thereby contributes to the dead capital problem.

CONCEPTS in Brief

- Dead capital is a capital resource without clear title of ownership. It is difficult for an owner to trade, insure, or maintain a right to use dead capital.

- The inability to put dead capital to its most efficient use contributes to lower economic growth, particularly in developing nations, where dead capital can be a relatively large portion of total capital goods.

- Inefficient government bureaucracies contribute to the dead capital problem, which reduces the incentive to invest in additional capital goods.

- Bribery and other forms of corruption detract from a nation's economic growth by pushing up the costs of investment and diminishing private property rights.

To test your understanding of the concepts covered in this section, go to the Online Review at www.myeconlab.com/miller.

PRIVATE INTERNATIONAL FINANCIAL FLOWS AS A SOURCE OF GLOBAL GROWTH

Given the large volume of inefficiently employed capital goods in developing nations, what can be done to promote greater global growth? One approach is to rely on private markets to find ways to direct capital goods toward their best uses in most nations. Another is to entrust the world's governments with the task of developing and implementing policies that enhance economic growth in developing nations. Let's begin by considering the market-based approach to promoting global growth.

Private Investment in Developing Nations

Each year since 1995, at least $150 billion in private funds have flowed to developing nations in the form of loans or purchases of bonds or stock. Of course, from year to year, international investors fail to renew loans to many developing nations and sell off quantities of bonds and stocks issued by these countries. When these international outflows of funds are taken into account, the *net* flows of funds to developing countries have averaged just over $100 billion per year since 1995. This is equivalent to more than one-tenth of the annual net investment that takes place within the United States.

Source of Foreign Funding for Capital Goods. Nearly all the funds that flow into developing countries do so to finance investment projects in those nations. Economists group these international flows of investment funds into three categories. One is loans from banks and other sources. The second is **portfolio investment,** or purchases of less than 10 percent of the shares of ownership in a company. The third is **foreign direct investment,** or the acquisition of sufficient stocks to obtain more than a 10 percent share of a firm's ownership.

Figure 19-3 displays percentages of each type of international investment financing provided to developing nations since the mid-1970s. As you can see, three decades ago, bank loans accounted for the bulk of international funding of investment in the world's less developed nations. Today, direct ownership shares in the form of portfolio investment and foreign direct investment account for most international investment financing.

Portfolio investment
The purchase of less than 10 percent of the shares of ownership in a company in another nation.

Foreign direct investment
The acquisition of more than 10 percent of the shares of ownership in a company in another nation.

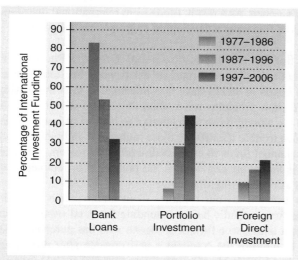

FIGURE 19-3

Sources of International Investment Funds
Since the mid-1970s, international funding of capital investment in developing nations has shifted from lending by banks to ownership shares via portfolio investment and foreign direct investment.

Source: International Monetary Fund (including estimates).

For a link to an Asian Development Bank analysis of the effects of foreign direct investment on developing nations, go to www.econtoday.com/chap19.

Why are international investors making fewer loans to residents of developing nations and instead choosing to direct more funds to portfolio investment and foreign direct investment? The dead capital problem helps explain this pattern. Foreign residents who lend to firms in developing countries must trust in the ability of domestic owners to avoid allowing their capital goods to become inefficiently employed. Foreign investors used to full ownership of capital will make sure that the resources they own in developing countries will be used efficiently. Thus foreign investors' incentives to avoid owning dead capital help to ensure that the resources they own in developing companies will not *become* dead capital.

How International Financial Flows Can Contribute to Global Growth. You may wonder why foreign investors are willing to finance investment in capital goods in developing nations in light of obstacles to their efficient use. Although these investments can be relatively risky, developing countries contain the bulk of the world's underutilized resources, including about 90 percent of its people. International investors who can find ways to put capital goods to productive use alongside the untapped talents and skills of residents of developing nations can anticipate earning significant returns on their investments. Sometimes these returns exceed the returns available in their own countries.

What do residents of developing nations stand to gain from issuing shares of ownership of capital goods to foreign investors? International investors typically reside in nations with fewer barriers to establishing proof of capital ownership. In addition, the developing nation's government may impose fewer rules on international investors. As a result, the capital they own is more likely to remain productive and will not become dead capital. In the long run, the development of more productive capital goods in developing nations translates into higher standards of living and higher rates of economic growth.

Obstacles to International Investment

There is an important difficulty with depending on international flows of funds to finance capital investment in developing nations. The markets for loans, bonds, and stocks in developing countries are particularly susceptible to problems relating to *asymmetric information* (see Chapter 15). International investors are well aware of the informational problems to which they are exposed in developing nations, so many stand ready to withdraw their financial support at a moment's notice. As a result, funds from international investors can be a potentially unstable means of financing a developing country's capital goods.

Asymmetric Information as a Barrier to Financing Global Growth. Recall from Chapter 15 that asymmetric information in financial markets exists when institutions that make loans or investors who hold bonds or stocks have less information than those who seek to use the funds. *Adverse selection* problems arise when those who wish to obtain funds for the least worthy projects are among those who attempt to borrow or issue bonds or stocks. If banks and investors have trouble identifying these higher-risk individuals and firms, they may be less willing to channel funds to even creditworthy borrowers. Another asymmetric information problem is *moral hazard*. This is the potential for recipients of funds to engage in riskier behavior after receiving financing.

In light of the adverse selection problem, anyone thinking about funding a business endeavor in any locale must study the firm carefully before extending financial support. The potential for moral hazard requires a lender to a firm or someone who has purchased the firm's bonds or stock to continue to monitor the company's performance after providing financial support. As you learned in Chapter 15, the difficulties that individuals face in these endeavors help explain why they might choose to entrust financial intermediaries with directing their funds to ultimate recipients.

By definition, financial intermediation is still relatively undeveloped in less advanced regions of the world. Consequently, individuals interested in financing potentially profitable investments in developing nations typically cannot rely on financial intermediaries based in these countries. Asymmetric information problems may be so great in some developing nations that very few private lenders or investors will wish to direct their funds to worthy capital investment projects. In some countries, therefore, concerns about adverse selection and moral hazard can be a significant obstacle to economic growth.

Incomplete Information and International Financial Crises. Those who are willing to contemplate making loans or buying bonds or stocks issued in developing nations must either do their own careful homework or follow the example of other lenders or investors whom they regard as better informed. Many relatively unsophisticated lenders and investors, such as relatively small banks and individual savers, rely on larger lenders and investors to evaluate risks in developing nations.

To some extent, therefore, a follow-the-leader mentality can influence international flows of funds. In extreme cases, the result can be an **international financial crisis.** This is a situation in which lenders rapidly withdraw loans made to residents of developing nations and investors sell off bonds and stocks issued by firms and governments in those countries.

International financial crisis
The rapid withdrawal of foreign investments and loans from a nation.

International financial crises can cause international financial flows to developing nations to slow to a trickle or even come to an abrupt halt, thereby harming affected nations' growth prospects for years afterward. This occurred, for instance, following an international bank lending crisis that affected many South American nations during the 1980s. Today, the growth prospects of developing nations continue to be in doubt in the wake of international financial crises that took place in Southeast Asia, Central Asia, and Latin America in the late 1990s and early 2000s. This undoubtedly helps explain why there has been a decline in flows of private funds to developing countries in recent years.

CONCEPTS in Brief

- On net, an average of about $100 billion in international investment funds flows to developing nations each year. In years past, bank loans were the source of most foreign funding of investment in developing countries, but recently portfolio investment and foreign direct investment have predominated.

- The primary motivation for foreign investment in developing nations is the potential for high rates of return on large amounts of untapped resources. International investors typically reside in nations where it is relatively easier to establish property rights to their capital goods, which may give them an advantage in avoiding the dead capital problem faced by many developing countries.

- Obstacles to private financing of capital accumulation and growth in developing nations include adverse selection and moral hazard problems, which can restrain and sometimes destabilize private flows of funds.

To test your understanding of the concepts covered in this section, go to the Online Review at www.myeconlab.com/miller.

INTERNATIONAL INSTITUTIONS AND POLICIES FOR GLOBAL GROWTH

There has long been a recognition that adverse selection and moral hazard problems can both reduce international flows of private funds to developing nations and make these flows relatively variable. Since 1945, the world's governments have taken an active role in supplementing private markets. Two international institutions, the World Bank and the International Monetary Fund, have been at the center of government-directed efforts to attain higher rates of global economic growth.

The World Bank

World Bank
A multinational agency that specializes in making loans to about 100 developing nations in an effort to promote their long-term development and growth.

The **World Bank** specializes in extending relatively long-term loans for capital investment projects that otherwise might not receive private financial support. When the World Bank was first formed in 1945, it provided assistance in the post–World War II rebuilding period. In the 1960s, the World Bank broadened its mission by widening its scope to encompass global antipoverty efforts.

Today, the World Bank makes loans solely to about 100 developing nations containing roughly half the world's population. Governments and firms in these countries typically seek loans from the World Bank to finance specific projects, such as improved irrigation systems, road improvements, and better hospitals.

The World Bank is actually composed of five separate institutions: the International Development Association, the International Bank for Reconstruction and Development, the International Finance Corporation, the Multinational Investment Guarantee Agency, and the International Center for Settlement of Investment Disputes. These World Bank organizations each have between 137 and 182 member nations, and on their behalf, the approximately 10,000 people employed by World Bank institutions coordinate the funding of investment activities undertaken by various governments and private firms in developing nations. Figure 19-4 displays the current regional distribution of nearly $20 billion in World Bank lending. Governments of the world's wealthiest countries provide most of the funds that the World Bank lends, although the World Bank also raises some of its funds in private financial markets.

The International Monetary Fund

International Monetary Fund
A multinational organization that aims to promote world economic growth through more financial stability.

Quota subscription
A nation's account with the International Monetary Fund, denominated in special drawing rights.

The **International Monetary Fund (IMF)** is an international organization that aims to promote global economic growth by fostering financial stability. At present the IMF has more than 180 member nations.

When a country joins the IMF, it deposits funds to an account called its **quota subscription.** These funds, which are measured in terms of an international unit of accounting called *special drawing rights,* form a pool of funds from which the IMF can draw to lend to members. Figure 19-5 displays current quota subscriptions for selected IMF member nations.

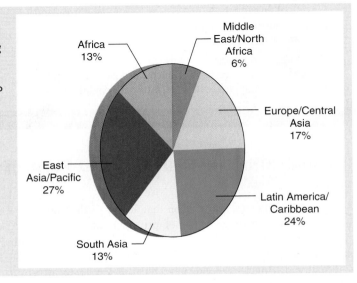

FIGURE 19-4
The Distribution of World Bank Lending Since 1990
Currently, about 40 percent of the World Bank's loans go to developing nations in the East Asia/Pacific and South Asia regions.

Source: World Bank.

Africa 13%

Middle East/North Africa 6%

Europe/Central Asia 17%

Latin America/ Caribbean 24%

South Asia 13%

East Asia/Pacific 27%

FIGURE 19-5
IMF Quota Subscriptions
The quota subscription of each member nation in the IMF, which is de-nominated in special drawing rights, determines its share of voting power within the IMF and how much it is eligible to borrow under standard IMF credit arrangements.

Source: International Monetary Fund.

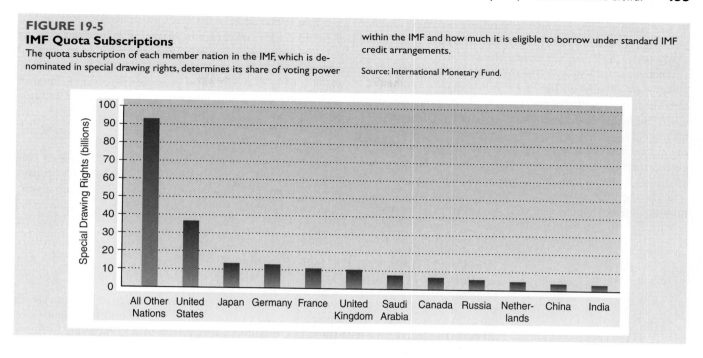

The IMF sets each nation's quota subscription based on the country's national income. The quota subscription determines how much a member can borrow from the IMF under the organization's standard credit arrangements. It also determines the member's share of voting power within the IMF. The U.S. quota subscription is just over 17 percent of the total funds provided by all member nations, so the U.S. government has an IMF voting share equal to that percentage.

The IMF assists developing nations primarily by making loans to their governments. Originally, the IMF's primary function was to provide so-called stand-by arrangements and short-term credits, and it continues to offer these forms of assistance.

After the 1970s, however, nations' demands for short-term credit declined, and the IMF adapted by expanding its other lending programs. It now provides certain types of credit directly to poor and heavily indebted countries, either as long-term loans intended to support growth-promoting projects or as short- or long-term assistance aimed at helping countries experiencing problems in repaying existing debts. Under these funding programs, the IMF seeks to assist any qualifying member experiencing an unusual fluctuation in exports or imports, a loss of confidence in its own financial system, or spillover effects from financial problems originating elsewhere.

Why do you suppose that some economists question the commonly heard claim that the U.S. government provides funds to the IMF at no cost?

International Policy EXAMPLE

The IMF's Cost to Taxpayers Is Surely More Than "One Dime"

In 1998, Robert Rubin, then the U.S. Treasury secretary, claimed that the billions of dollars the U.S. government regu-larly provides to the International Monetary Fund to make loans to other nations cost U.S. taxpayers "not one dime." The basis for this claim was that because the funds are used for loans that borrowing nations ultimately repay, there is no loss of the principal amount the U.S. government helps provide.

There is a problem with this reasoning, however. The U.S. government obtains all the funds that it makes available to the IMF from U.S. taxpayers. Many of these taxpayers could otherwise have saved those dollars at market interest rates, or they could have directly invested the funds in projects yielding market rates of return. The IMF pays interest to the U.S. government on these funds at short-term interest rates that are normally lower than the long-term interest rates at which it lends. The IMF also lends to countries at long-term interest rates that are below market levels. As a result, U.S. taxpayers earn lower interest from the U.S. government's "IMF investment" than they could earn by engaging in long-term saving and investing on their own. This difference is an implicit subsidy from U.S. taxpayers to the IMF and the nations to which it extends credit. Most estimates place the amount of this subsidy somewhere between $1.5 billion and $2 billion per year.

For Critical Analysis

Would U.S. taxpayers still be subsidizing the IMF and its borrowers if the IMF charged market rates of interest on its loans and repaid the U.S. government for the use of U.S. taxpayers' funds at market rates of interest?

The World Bank and the IMF: Part of the Solution or Part of the Problem?

Among the World Bank's client nations, meager economic growth in recent decades shows up in numerous ways. The average resident in a nation receiving World Bank assistance lives on less than $2 per day. Hundreds of millions of people in nations receiving its financial support will never attend school, and about 40,000 people in these countries die of preventable diseases every day. Thus there is an enormous range of areas where World Bank funds might be put to use.

The International Monetary Fund also continues to deal with an ongoing string of major international financial crisis situations. Countries most notably involved in such crises have included Mexico in 1995; Thailand, Indonesia, Malaysia, and South Korea in 1997; Russia in 1998; Brazil in 1999 and 2000; Turkey in 2001; and Argentina in 2001 and 2002.

Naturally, officials of both organizations conclude that world economic growth would have been even lower and financial instability even greater if the institutions did not exist. In recent years, however, economists have increasingly questioned World Bank and IMF policymaking.

Does the World Bank Really Have a Mission Anymore? In some nations, particularly in Africa, attracting private investment has proved difficult. Consequently, the World Bank has been a key source of credit for these nations. Nevertheless, as Figure 19-4 on page 452 indicates, only about 13 percent of lending by the World Bank since 1990 has been directed to African countries.

The World Bank's official mission is to make loans to developing nations that fund projects incapable of attracting private financing from investors at home or abroad. Nevertheless, the World Bank makes many of its loans to nations that have little trouble attracting private funds. Critics of such loans argue that they often interfere with the private market for capital goods and encourage the kind of inefficient investment that contributed to Asia's economic woes in the late 1990s and to Argentina's financial collapse in the early 2000s.

Some observers also contend that a number of countries that receive World Bank funds are inappropriate recipients of development assistance. For instance, China has reserves of currencies of other nations exceeding $400 billion, and its residents are net *lenders* of funds to other nations of the world. Nevertheless, the Chinese government and Chinese companies annually borrow between $2 billion and $3 billion from the World Bank.

Economics Front and Center

To consider whether China may be allocating too many resources to physical capital and not enough to human capital, read the case study, **Is China Overinvesting in Physical Relative to Human Capital?** on page 457.

Asymmetric Information and the World Bank and IMF. Like any other lenders, the World Bank and IMF encounter adverse selection and moral hazard problems. In an effort to address these problems, both institutions impose conditions that borrowers must meet to receive funds.

Officials of these organizations do not publicly announce all terms of lending agreements, however, so it is largely up to the organizations to monitor whether borrower nations are wisely using funds donated by other countries. In addition, the World Bank and IMF tend to place very general initial conditions on the loans they extend. They typically toughen conditions only after a borrowing nation has violated the original arrangement. By giving nations that are most likely to try to take advantage of vague conditions a greater incentive to seek funding, this policy worsens the adverse selection problem the World Bank and IMF face.

Some policymakers, economists, and other observers contend that the policies of the World Bank and the IMF have contributed to international financial crises. They argue that when the World Bank and the IMF provide subsidized credit for industries and governments, private lenders and investors anticipate that these two institutions will back up nations' debts. Thus private lenders and investors may lower their standards and make loans to, and buy bonds and stocks from, less creditworthy borrowers. Furthermore, if governments know that they can apply for World Bank and IMF assistance in the event of widespread financial failures, they have little incentive to rein in risky business practices.

Rethinking Long-Term Development Lending. Since the early 1990s, one of the main themes of development economics has been the reform of market processes in developing nations. Markets work better at promoting growth when a developing nation has more effective institutions, such as basic property rights, well-run legal systems, and uncorrupt government agencies.

Hence, there is considerable agreement that a top priority of the World Bank and the IMF should be to identify ways to put basic market foundations into place by guaranteeing property and contract rights. This requires constructing legal systems that can credibly enforce laws protecting these rights. Another key requirement is simplifying the processes for putting capital goods to work in developing countries.

A fundamental issue is what, if anything, international organizations such as the World Bank and the IMF can do to promote pro-growth institutional improvements in developing nations. From one standpoint, there may be little that the World Bank and the IMF can accomplish. After all, the forms of national legal institutions are largely political matters for the nations' leaders to decide. Nevertheless, a number of economists have suggested that the World Bank and the IMF should adopt strict policies against countries with institutional structures that fail to promote individual property rights, law enforcement, and anticorruption efforts. This would, they argue, give countries an incentive to shape up their institutional structures.

Other economists, in contrast, advocate direct financial assistance to governments attempting to implement such institutional reforms. Funds put to such use, they argue, could compensate those who lose power as a result of reform efforts, when shifting to a more capitalist system takes away a ruling group's dictatorial powers to control national resources. Such financial assistance could also help fund investments required to make reforms work. Those proposing this more active role for international lenders contend that the result could be much larger long-term returns for borrowing and lending nations alike. They argue that the overall return would be much greater than the sum of piecemeal payoffs from such projects as dams, power plants, and bridges.

To learn about the International Monetary Fund's view on its role in international financial crises, go to www.econtoday.com/chap19.

Alternative Institutional Structures for Limiting Financial Crises. There are also different views on the appropriate role for the International Monetary Fund in anticipating and reacting to international financial crises. In recent years economists have advanced a wide variety of proposals. Many of these proposals share common features, such as more frequent and in-depth releases of information both by the IMF and by countries that borrow from these institutions. Nearly all economists also recommend improved financial and accounting standards for those receiving funds from multinational lenders, as well as other changes that might help reduce moral hazard problems in IMF lending.

Nevertheless, many of the proposals for change diverge sharply. The IMF and its supporters have proposed maintaining its current structure but working harder to develop so-called early warning systems of financial crises so that aid can be provided to head off crises before they develop. Some economists have proposed establishing an international system of rules restricting capital outflows that might threaten international fianancial stability.

Other economists call for more dramatic changes. For instance, one proposal suggests creating a board composed of finance ministers of member nations directly in charge of day-to-day management of the IMF. Another suggests providing government incentives, in the form of tax breaks and subsidies, for increased private-sector lending that would supplement or even replace loans now made by the IMF.

Time to Replace the World Bank and the IMF? A few economists have called for completely eliminating both the World Bank and the IMF. Even economists who think these institutions should disappear, however, disagree on what should replace them. On the one hand, a proposal calls for reducing the current scope of government involvement in multinational lending by replacing the World Bank and the IMF with a single institution that would make only short-term loans to countries experiencing temporary financial difficulties. On the other hand, another proposal suggests broadening the roles of governments by developing a "global central bank" that would engage in open market operations using funds raised from new international taxes and other government funds.

So far, few proposals for altering the international financial architecture have led to actual change. The IMF has adopted some minor changes in its procedures for collecting and releasing information, and it has stiffened some of the financial and accounting standards that borrowers must follow to obtain credit. Naturally, the member nations of the IMF would have to agree to the adoption of more dramatic proposals for change. To date there has been little movement in this direction. Undoubtedly, consideration of proposals for an altered international financial structure will continue to generate global debate in the years to come.

CONCEPTS in Brief

- The World Bank is an umbrella institution for five international organizations, each of which has more than 130 member nations, which coordinate long-term loans to governments and private firms in developing nations.

- The International Monetary Fund is an organization with more than 180 member nations. It coordinates short-term and longer-term financial assistance to developing nations in an effort to stabilize international flows of funds.

- In principle, the World Bank's role is to provide loans to developing countries where asymmetric information problems deter private investment, but in recent years, the World Bank has provided funds to countries and companies that could have obtained financing from private investors.

- Like other lenders, the World Bank and the IMF confront adverse selection and moral hazard problems. Some observers worry that failure to deal with these problems has actually contributed to a string of international financial crises. Recently, there have been suggestions that both institutions should impose tougher preconditions on borrowers, such as requiring internal reforms that promote domestic investment.

To test your understanding of the concepts covered in this section, go to the Online Review at www.myeconlab.com/miller.

CASE STUDY : Economics Front and Center

Is China Overinvesting in Physical Relative to Human Capital?

Ghosal is a U.S. student participating in a university exchange program in Shanghai, China. She is amazed at how much activity she observes throughout the city, where construction cranes stretch across the horizon. She enjoys her daily rides on a new magnetic-levitation train, built at a cost exceeding $1 billion, which makes the trip from her apartment to the university in five minutes at speeds up to 250 miles per hour.

Ghosal has also noticed, though, that a lot of the physical capital in China is not used very efficiently. A considerable amount of capital equipment across Shanghai is rarely used and even sits idle for days at a time. Local news stories are replete with residents' complaints that when equipment breaks down, no one seems to know how to get it working again.

While doing research for a class project, Ghosal has found that China spends only 2.2 percent of its GDP on education, or the development of human capital. In contrast, education spending amounts to 5 percent of GDP in the United States, 4.2 percent of GDP in the Philippines, 3.5 percent of GDP in Russia, and 3.2 percent of GDP in India. Many children in rural areas of China receive at most a few years of education, and city schools often will not accept promising students from the countryside. How fast can China's per capita GDP continue to grow in the long term, Ghosal wonders, if its human resources do not become more productive?

Points to Analyze

1. *How can larger investments in human capital increase a nation's rate of economic growth?*

2. *Can you see any potential problem with Ghosal's basing her judgment of China's human capital investment in part on the share of its GDP devoted to education? (Hint: Does higher spending on education necessarily translate into better education?)*

I magine that you are a typical resident of Bolivia, and you are considering start-ing a legally incorporated business. Let's contemplate the hurdles that you will confront in getting your business officially approved, satisfying governmental authorities once it is in operation, and closing it if it fails to earn sufficient profit to justify keeping it in operation.

Concepts Applied

- Per Capita Income
- Dead Capital
- Economic Growth

The High Costs of Getting Off to a Slow Start

Table 19-2 shows the various procedures you must complete to get a Bolivian business going. As you can see, just getting a business officially started takes at least 127 days.

Before you even begin this process, however, you must save, and save, and save. Completing all these steps requires an amount equivalent to nearly $1,500. It takes the average Bolivian resident 20 months just to earn this amount; saving it takes much longer.

TABLE 19-2 **Legal Steps Required to Establish a Business in Bolivia** Setting up a Bolivian business re-quires 11 steps that take more than four months to complete.	First 20 Days	Next 40 Days	Next 67 Days
	1. Obtain formal approval of the business.	7. Obtain approval from two government business registration offices.	9. Prove that you have sufficient additional funds on deposit to cover your first payroll.
	2. Prepare and publish a legal application and initial account statement.	8. Register with the chamber of commerce.	10. Register with three government pension systems.
	3. Obtain a business tax registration card.		11. Gain approval of your payroll procedures from the Bolivian Ministry of Labor.
	4. Apply for legal commercial registration.		
	5. Provide evidence of sufficient funds to operate.		
	6. Obtain a business license.		

Source: World Bank.

Finally, You—and the Bolivian Government—Are in Business

Once your business goes into operation, you still have a lot to do to satisfy the Bolivian government. If your business earns profits, you must pay 25 percent of the profits to the government. If your business involves the exploitation of nonrenewable resources such as petroleum, you must pay the government an additional profits tax of 25 percent.

Your business must pay each employee a base wage amounting to at least $720 per year. After an employee completes a year of service, each year thereafter you must pay a "seniority bonus" equal to 5 percent of the employee's monthly wages. This annual bonus then increases with each additional year of service, reaching as high as 50 percent of a month's wages for an employee with 25 years of service. Every December, the government also requires your firm to pay a Christmas bonus equal to one month's wages.

Finally, if your business earns an annual profit, your company must also pay a further "production bonus" to each employee. This additional bonus usually must be equal to the wages the employee would normally earn in 45 days of work.

Failure Is Not an Option—At Least, Not for a While

What if your Bolivian firm operates for a while, but you ultimately decide that it is not earning sufficient profits to remain a viable business? In this case, you must give the firm's employees at least 30 days' notice of your intent to close the business, and you must pay them any bonuses to which they are legally entitled. If your company is bankrupt, perhaps because other businesses owe debts to your firm that you have been unable to collect during the more than 15 months it takes to enforce contracts in Bolivia, then it will probably take at least two years to formally close the business.

After contemplating these and other costs and delays associated with operating an officially incorporated Bolivian business, you may decide to go through the process. More likely, however, you will join the other "informal" companies that together account for an estimated 67 percent of all business earnings in Bolivia. You will be taking a chance, however, because your firm's legal rights will be limited. Thus, it will be very hard to sell your business in the future. Your investment, like those of many other owners of informal businesses, could well become dead capital. In addition, you probably will contribute, in your own small way, to a worsening of Bolivia's prospects for future economic growth.

For Critical Analysis

1. How might the fact that Bolivian companies are required to obtain many financial services only from other Bolivian firms further push up the costs of operating officially in that nation?
2. When faced with the certain high costs of operating legally in Bolivia, why do you suppose that so many business owners choose to operate informally, in spite of the risk that the investment may become dead capital as a result?

Web Resources

1. To access the World Bank's comparative information about the costs of going into business in many of the world's nations, go to the link available at www.econtoday.com/chap19.
2. For a monthly report by the World Bank on economic growth and development in the world's poorest nations, go to www.econtoday.com/chap19.

Research Project

Suppose that you have been hired by the World Bank to develop financial assistance programs geared toward promoting "self-help" on the part of aid recipients. In light of what you have learned in this chapter, what types of self-help would you recommend promoting? How would you recommend structuring World Bank financial assistance programs so that they would be consistent with this objective?

SUMMARY DISCUSSION of Learning Objectives

1. **Effects of Population Growth and Personal Freedoms on Economic Growth:** Increased population growth has contradictory effects on economic growth. On the one hand, for a given growth rate of real GDP, a higher rate of population tends to reduce growth of per capita real GDP. On the other hand, if increased population growth leads to a higher rate of labor force participation, the growth rate of real GDP can increase. The net effect can be an increase in the growth rate of per capita GDP. Greater political freedoms do not necessarily contribute to higher rates of economic growth. There is considerable evidence, however, of a positive relationship between the extent of economic freedom and the rate of growth of per capita incomes around the world.

2. **Why Dead Capital Deters Investment and Slows Economic Growth:** Relatively few people in less developed countries establish legal ownership of capital goods. These unofficially owned resources are known as dead capital. Even though they can be put to some productive use, inability to trade, insure, and enforce rights to dead capital make it difficult for unofficial owners to use these resources most efficiently. As a result, in many developing nations, there is a disincentive to accumulate capital, which tends to limit the economic growth prospects in these countries.

3. **Government Inefficiencies and Dead Capital in Developing Nations:** In many developing nations, government regulations and red tape impose very high costs on those who officially register capital ownership. The dead capital problem that these government inefficiencies create reduces investment and growth. This helps explain why there is a negative relationship between measures of government inefficiency and economic growth. In many nations, individuals and firms broaden their capability to use capital goods by engaging in bribery of government officials and other forms of corruption. The costs of corruption reduce the return on investment, however. In addition, corruption weakens the rule of law and thereby contributes to the dead capital problem. Greater corruption thereby reduces economic growth.

4. **Why Foreign Residents Invest in Developing Countries and How These Nations Benefit from International Investment:** The main incentive for foreign investment in developing countries is that foreign investors who are able to put underutilized resources in these nations to more efficient use can anticipate earning high rates of return. Foreign investors who establish rights of ownership to capital goods may be able to use them more efficiently than domestic residents, who are more constrained by their own governments. To the extent that international investors have this advantage over domestic residents, international flows of funds to developing nations can potentially do much to promote global economic growth.

5. **The Functions of the World Bank and the International Monetary Fund:** Adverse selection and moral hazard problems faced by private investors can both limit international flows of funds to developing countries and make these flows less stable. The World Bank's function is to finance capital investment in countries that have trouble attracting funds from private individuals and firms. A fundamental duty of the International Monetary Fund is to stabilize international financial flows. The IMF attempts to accomplish this mission by extending loans to countries caught up in international financial crises caused by sudden fluctuations in flows of funds across national borders.

6. **The Basis for Recent Criticisms of World Bank and IMF Policymaking:** Even though the World Bank's fundamental role is to make loans to developing countries that receive little private investment financing, recently it has extended credit to companies and governments that could have obtained funds in private loan markets. Critics also suggest that the World Bank and the IMF have failed to deal effectively with the adverse selection and moral hazard problems they face. This failure, critics suggest, has helped cause, rather than prevent, international financial crises. These concerns have motivated suggestions that the World Bank and the IMF should place more stringent conditions on access to credit, including requiring government borrowers to implement reforms that give domestic residents more incentive to invest.

KEY TERMS AND CONCEPTS

dead capital (445)

economic freedom (443)

foreign direct investment (449)

international financial crisis (451)

International Monetary Fund (IMF) (452)

portfolio investment (449)

quota subscription (452)

World Bank (452)

PROBLEMS

Answers to the odd-numbered problems appear at the back of the book.

19-1. A country's real GDP is growing at an annual rate of 3.1 percent, and the current rate of growth of per capita real GDP is 0.3 percent. What is the population growth rate in this nation?

19-2. The annual rate of growth of real GDP in a developing nation is 0.3 percent. Initially, the country's population was stable from year to year. Recently, however, a significant increase in the nation's birthrate has raised the annual rate of population growth to 0.5 percent.

    a. What was the rate of growth of per capita real GDP before the increase in population growth?

    b. If the rate of growth of real GDP remains unchanged, what is the new rate of growth of per capita real GDP following the increase in the birthrate?

19-3. During the 1990s, the average rate of growth of per capita real GDP in a developing country was 0.1 percent per year. Its average annual rate of population growth was 2.2 percent.

    a. What was the average annual rate of growth of real GDP in this nation during the 1990s?

    b. So far in the 2000s, a steady inflow of immigrants has caused the average annual rate of population growth to rise to 2.7 percent. If we assume that the average annual rate of growth of real GDP has remained unchanged, what has the average rate of per capita real GDP growth been during the 2000s?

    c. Suppose that in fact a number of immigrants have found employment and contributed to a 0.8 percentage point increase in the average annual rate of growth of the nation's real GDP. Given this additional information, what has been the net average rate of growth of per capita real GDP during the 2000s?

19-4. A developing country has determined that each additional $1 billion of legally registered investment in capital goods adds 0.01 percentage point to its long-run average annual rate of growth of per capita real GDP.

    a. Domestic entrepreneurs recently began to seek official approval to open a range of businesses employing capital resources valued at $20 billion. If the entrepreneurs undertake these investments, by what fraction of a percentage point will the nation's long-run average annual rate of growth of per capita real GDP increase, other things being equal?

    b. After weeks of effort trying to complete the first of 15 stages of bureaucratic red tape necessary to obtain authorization to start their businesses, a number of entrepreneurs decide to drop their investment plans completely, and the amount of official investment that actually takes place turns out to be $10 billion. Other things being equal, by what fraction of a percentage point will this decision reduce the nation's long-run average annual rate of growth of per capita real GDP from what it would have been if investment had been $20 billion?

19-5. Consider the estimates that the World Bank has assembled for the following nations:

Country	Legal Steps Required to Start a Business	Days Required to Start a Business	Cost of Starting a Business as a Percentage of Per Capita GDP
Angola	14	146	838%
Bosnia-Herzegovina	12	59	52%
Morocco	11	36	19%
Togo	14	63	281%
Uruguay	10	27	47%

Rank the nations in order starting with the one you would expect to have the highest rate of economic growth, other things being equal. Explain your reasoning.

19-6. The World Bank has also constructed index measures of the flexibility available to firms in hiring and firing workers. The higher the index number for the nation in the following table, the greater the degree of government regulation of the hiring and firing processes.

Country	Hiring Flexibility Index	Firing Flexibility Index
Brazil	78	68
Germany	63	45
Ireland	48	30
Mexico	81	70
Singapore	33	1
Yemen	33	28

Rank the nations in order starting with the one you would expect to have the highest rate of economic growth, other things being equal. Explain your reasoning.

19-7. Suppose that every $500 billion of dead capital reduces the average rate of growth in worldwide per capita real GDP by 0.1 percentage point. If there is $10 trillion in dead capital in the world, by how many percentage points does the existence of dead capital reduce average worldwide growth of per capita real GDP?

19-8. Assume that each $1 billion in investment in capital goods generates 0.3 percentage point of the average percentage rate of growth of per capita income, given the nation's labor resources. Firms have been investing exactly $6 billion in capital goods each year, so the annual average rate of growth of per capita income has been 1.8 percent. Now a corrupt government is in charge, and firms must make $100 million in bribe payments to gain official approval for every $1 billion in investment in capital goods. In response, companies cut back their total investment spending to $4 billion per year. If other things are equal and companies maintain this rate of investment, what will be the nation's new average annual rate of growth of per capita income?

19-9. During the past year, several large banks extended $200 million in loans to the government and several firms in a developing nation. International investors also purchased $150 million in bonds and $350 million in stocks issued by domestic firms. Of the stocks that foreign investors purchased, $100 million were shares that amounted to less than a 10 percent interest in domestic firms. This was the first year this nation had ever permitted inflows of funds from abroad.

   a. Based on the investment category definitions discussed in this chapter, what was the amount of portfolio investment in this nation during the past year?

   b. What was the amount of foreign direct investment in this nation during the past year?

19-10. Last year, $100 million in outstanding bank loans to a developing nation's government were not renewed, and the developing nation's government paid off $50 million in maturing government bonds that had been held by foreign residents. During that year, however, a new group of banks participated in a $125 million loan to help finance a major government construction project in the capital city. Domestic firms also issued $50 million in bonds and $75 million in stocks to foreign investors. All of the stocks issued gave the foreign investors more than 10 percent shares of the domestic firms.

   a. What was gross foreign investment in this nation last year?

   b. What was net foreign investment in this nation last year?

19-11. Identify which of the following situations currently faced by international investors are examples of adverse selection and which are examples of moral hazard.

   a. Among the governments of several developing countries that are attempting to issue new bonds this year, it is certain that a few will fail to collect taxes to repay the bonds when they mature. It is difficult, however, for investors considering buying government bonds to predict which governments will experience this problem.

   b. For several years foreign investors have owned stock in a company that, unknowingly to investors at the time of their investment, may have failed last year to properly establish legal ownership over a crucial capital resource.

   c. Companies in a less developed nation are issuing bonds to finance the purchase of new capital goods that the firms will own, and the companies will retain full ownership of these capital goods. There is considerable uncertainty among foreign investors who are considering the bond purchase, however, about whether the companies will establish legal ownership due to the maze of governmental rules and regulations they must satisfy.

   d. When the government of a developing nation received a bank loan three years ago, it ultimately repaid the loan but had to reschedule its payments after officials misused the funds for unworthy projects. Now the government, which still has many of the same officials, is trying to raise funds by issuing bonds to foreign investors, who must decide whether or not to purchase them.

19-12. Identify which of the following situations currently faced by the World Bank or the International Monetary Fund are examples of adverse selection and which are examples of moral hazard.

   a. The World Bank has extended loans to the government of a developing country to finance construction of a canal with a certain future flow of earnings. Now, however, the government has decided to redirect those funds to build a casino that may or may not generate sufficient profits to allow the government to repay the loan.

   b. The IMF is considering extending loans to several nations that failed to fully repay loans they re-

Chapter 33

Comparative Advantage and the Open Economy

I t is September 2003, and the global negotiations about international trade have begun in Cancún, Mexico. Representatives from the European Union (EU), the United States, and Japan have high hopes that they will be able to convince developing nations to open their borders to more imports of EU, U.S., and Japanese products. To their dismay, however, representatives of most developing nations have a different agenda. They want big cutbacks in EU, U.S., and Japanese agricultural subsidies. When the EU, U.S., and Japanese representatives balk, the meetings abruptly come to a conclusion, and a shadow has been cast over the future of global trade. In this chapter, you will learn why developing nations view subsidies to EU, U.S., and Japanese farmers as an issue relating to international trade.

LEARNING OBJECTIVES

After reading this chapter, you should be able to:

1. Discuss the worldwide importance of international trade
2. Explain why nations can gain from specializing in production and engaging in international trade
3. Distinguish between comparative advantage and absolute advantage
4. Understand common arguments against free trade
5. Describe ways that nations restrict foreign trade
6. Identify key international agreements and organizations that adjudicate trade disputes among nations

Media Resources

Refer to the end of the chapter for a full listing of the multimedia learning materials available in MyEconLab.

Did You Know That . . . in 2000, Ohio Art Company, the firm that sells Etch A Sketch toys, moved its production facilities from Ohio to China? Likewise, since 2001 Lionel Corporation, which once produced electric toy trains in New York, New Jersey, and Michigan, has manufactured its products in China. The Barbie dolls and other numerous toys that Mattell Corporation sells are no longer produced in the United States. Mattell now makes all of its toys in plants located in China, India, Indonesia, Italy, Malaysia, Mexico, and Thailand.

What economic forces have induced these and most other U.S. toy companies to choose to manufacture their products abroad instead of within the borders of the United States? The first thing you will learn in this chapter is that gains from specialization and international trade provide the fundamental economic motivation for determining where to produce any good or service. These gains ultimately explain why nearly all toys sold in the United States are now imported from other nations.

THE WORLDWIDE IMPORTANCE OF INTERNATIONAL TRADE

Look at panel (a) of Figure 33-1. Since the end of World War II, world output of goods and services (world real gross domestic product, or real GDP) has increased almost every year; it is now almost eight times what it was then. Look at the top line in panel (a). World trade has increased to more than 24 times what it was in 1950.

Go to www.econtoday.com/chap33 for the World Trade Organization's most recent data on world trade.

The United States figured prominently in this expansion of world trade. In panel (b) of Figure 33-1, you see imports and exports expressed as a percentage of total annual yearly income (GDP). Whereas imports added up to barely 4 percent of annual U.S. GDP in 1950, today they account for more than 14 percent. International trade has definitely become more important to the economy of the United States, and it may become even more so as other countries loosen their trade restrictions.

How has the ability of people around the world to buy and sell items using the Internet affected international trade?

E-Commerce EXAMPLE

The Internet Boosts International Trade

Caroline Freund of the World Bank and Diana Weinhold of the London School of Economics have examined how increased Internet use has affected international trade in the United States and 55 other nations. They found that greater Internet use by a nation's residents reduces their costs of engaging in international trade. As a consequence, the immediate effect of the takeoff in commercial sales on the Internet between 1997 and 1999 was a 1 percentage point increase in the average country's international trade. Since then, each 10 percentage point increase in Internet use by a nation's residents has resulted in a further 0.2 percentage point increase in trade with other nations.

For Critical Analysis
How might the ability to buy and sell items using the Internet reduce the costs of trading with other countries?

WHY WE TRADE: COMPARATIVE ADVANTAGE AND MUTUAL GAINS FROM EXCHANGE

You have already been introduced to the concept of specialization and mutual gains from trade in Chapter 2. These concepts are worth repeating because they are essential to under-

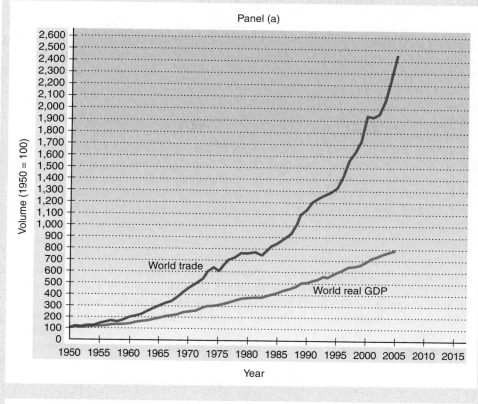

Panel (a)

FIGURE 33-1
The Growth of World Trade
In panel (a), you can see the growth in world trade in relative terms because we use an index of 100 to represent real world trade in 1950. By the mid-2000s, that index had increased to over 2,400. At the same time, the index of world real GDP (annual world real income) had gone up to only around 800. World trade is clearly on the rise: In the United States, both imports and exports, expressed as a percentage of annual national income (GDP) in panel (b), have generally been rising since 1950.

Sources: Steven Husted and Michael Melvin, *International Economics*, 3d ed. (New York: HarperCollins, 1995), p. 11, used with permission; World Trade Organization; Federal Reserve System; U.S. Department of Commerce.

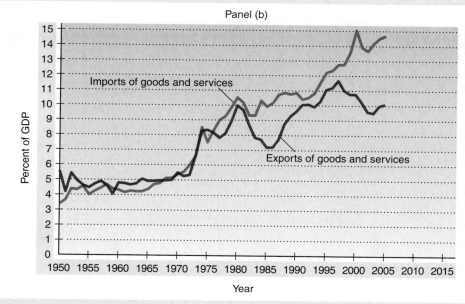

Panel (b)

standing why the world is better off because of more international trade. The best way to understand the gains from trade among nations is first to understand the output gains from specialization between individuals.

The Output Gains from Specialization

Suppose that a creative advertising specialist can come up with two pages of ad copy (written words) an hour or generate one computerized art rendering per hour. At the same time, a computer artist can write one page of ad copy per hour or complete one computerized art rendering per hour. Here the ad specialist can come up with more pages of ad copy per hour than the computer specialist and seemingly is just as good as the computer specialist at doing computerized art renderings. Is there any reason for the creative specialist and the computer specialist to "trade"? The answer is yes because such trading will lead to higher output.

Consider the scenario of no trading. Assume that during each eight-hour day, the ad specialist and the computer whiz devote half of their day to writing ad copy and half to computerized art rendering. The ad specialist would create eight pages of ad copy (4 hours × 2) and four computerized art renderings (4 × 1). During that same period, the computer specialist would create four pages of ad copy (4 hours × 1) and four computerized art renderings (4 × 1). Each day, the combined output for the ad specialist and the computer specialist would be 12 pages of ad copy and eight computerized art renderings.

If the ad specialist specialized only in writing ad copy and the computer whiz specialized only in creating computerized art renderings, their combined output would rise to 16 pages of ad copy (8 × 2) and eight computerized art renderings (8 × 1). Overall, production would increase by four pages of ad copy per day with no decline in art renderings.

The creative advertising employee has a comparative advantage in writing ad copy, and the computer specialist has a comparative advantage in doing computerized art renderings. **Comparative advantage** is simply the ability to produce something at a lower opportunity cost than other producers, as we pointed out in Chapter 2.

Why do you suppose that Argentina and Uruguay import electricity from Brazil?

Go to www.econtoday.com/chap33 for data on U.S. trade with all other nations of the world.

Comparative advantage
The ability to produce a good or service at a lower opportunity cost than other producers.

International EXAMPLE

Power Moves Across Borders in South America

Most South American nations produce about half of their electricity by burning natural gas to generate electric power. Natural gas is much easier to find, extract, and put to use in Brazil than in neighboring Argentina and Uruguay. Consequently, the opportunity cost of producing electricity is lower in Brazil. The lower opportunity cost of producing electricity in Brazil explains why both Argentina and Uruguay have been importing electricity from Brazil since early 2004.

For Critical Analysis
Why might Brazil someday import electricity from Argentina if recent discoveries of untapped natural gas in southern Argentina generate large increases in its stocks of this resource?

Specialization Among Nations

To demonstrate the concept of comparative advantage for nations, let's take the example of India and the United States. In Table 33-1, we show the comparative costs of production of commercial software programs and personal computers in terms of worker-days. This is a simple two-country, two-commodity world in which we assume that labor is the only factor of production. As you can see from the table, in the United States, it takes one worker-

Product	United States (worker-days)	India (worker-days)
Software program	1	1
Personal computer	1	2

TABLE 33-1
Comparative Costs of Production

day to produce one software program, and the same is true for one computer. In India, it takes one worker-day to produce one software program but two worker-days to produce one computer. In this sense, U.S. residents appear to be just as good at producing software programs as residents of India and actually have an **absolute advantage** in producing computers.

Absolute advantage
The ability to produce more output from given inputs of resources than other producers can.

Trade will still take place, however, which may seem paradoxical. How can trade take place if we can seemingly produce at least as many units of both goods as residents of India can? Why don't we just produce both ourselves? To understand why, let's assume first that there is no trade and no specialization and that the workforce in each country consists of 200 workers. These 200 workers are, by assumption, divided equally in the production of software programs and computers. We see in Table 33-2 that 100 software programs and 100 computers are produced per day in the United States. In India, 100 software programs and 50 computers are produced per day. The total daily world production in our two-country world is 200 software programs and 150 computers.

Now the countries specialize. What can India produce more cheaply? Look at the comparative costs of production expressed in worker-days in Table 33-1. What is the cost of producing one more software program? One worker-day. What is the cost of producing one more computer? Two worker-days. We can say, then, that in terms of the value of computers given up, in India the *opportunity cost* of producing software programs is lower than in the United States. India will specialize in the activity that has the lower opportunity cost. In other words, India will specialize in the activity in which is has a comparative advantage, which is the production of software programs.

According to Table 33-3 (page 782), after specialization, the United States produces 200 computers and India produces 200 software programs. Notice that the total world production per day has gone up from 200 software programs and 150 computers to 200 software programs and 200 computers per day. This was done without any increased use of resources. The gain, 50 "free" computers, results from a more efficient allocation of resources worldwide. World output is greater when countries specialize in producing the goods in which they have a comparative advantage and then engage in foreign trade. An-

Product	United States		India		
	Workers	Output	Workers	Output	World Output
Software programs	100	100	100	100	200
Personal computers	100	100	100	50	150

TABLE 33-2
Daily World Output Before Specialization
It is assumed that 200 workers are available in each country.

TABLE 33-3
Daily World Output After Specialization
It is assumed that 200 workers are available in each country.

Product	United States		India		World Output
	Workers	Output	Workers	Output	
Software programs	0	0	200	200	200
Personal computers	200	200	0	0	200

other way of looking at this is to consider the choice between two ways of producing a good. Obviously, each country would choose the less costly production process. One way of "producing" a good is to import it, so if in fact the imported good is cheaper than the domestically produced good, we will "produce" it by importing it. Not everybody, of course, is better off when free trade occurs. In our example, U.S. software producers and Indian computer makers are worse off because those two *domestic* industries have disappeared.

Some people are worried that the United States (or any country, for that matter) might someday "run out of exports" because of overaggressive foreign competition. The analysis of comparative advantage tells us the contrary. No matter how much other countries compete for our business, the United States (or any other country) will always have a comparative advantage in something that it can export. In 10 or 20 years, that something may not be what we export today, but it will be exportable nonetheless because we will have a comparative advantage in producing it. Consequently, the significant flows of world trade shown in Figure 33-2 will continue because the United States and other nations will retain comparative advantages in producing various goods and services.

Why has the island nation of Mauritius recently experienced a significant drop in exports of the key item it specializes in producing?

International EXAMPLE

Mauritius Searches for a New Comparative Advantage

For years, Mauritius, a nation located on an island in the Indian Ocean off the coast of Madagascar, specialized in the production of sugarcane. Beginning in the 1970s, however, textile firms discovered that the costs of hiring unskilled workers in Mauritius to operate clothing manufacturing equipment were very low. Textile companies rushed to establish factories on the island. By the mid-1990s one out of every five Mauritian workers had a job in the textile industry, and the Mauritian per capita income level had nearly doubled.

During the late 1990s and early 2000s, however, China and India emerged as new centers of clothing production. The Mauritian textile industry was unable to match these nations'

low production costs, and it began to shrink. By the mid-2000s, thousands of the island's residents, amounting to nearly 10 percent of its labor force, were out of work. Now Mauritian leaders are hoping that the improved education that accompanied higher incomes ultimately will help many unemployed workers find jobs in two new export industries: tourism and financial services.

For Critical Analysis
Why do changing relative opportunity costs across the world's nations cause comparative advantages to shift among nations over time?

FIGURE 33-2
World Trade Flows
International merchandise trade amounts to more than $7.5 trillion worldwide. The percentage figures show the proportion of trade flowing in the various directions throughout the globe.

Sources: World Trade Organization and author's estimates (data are for 2005).

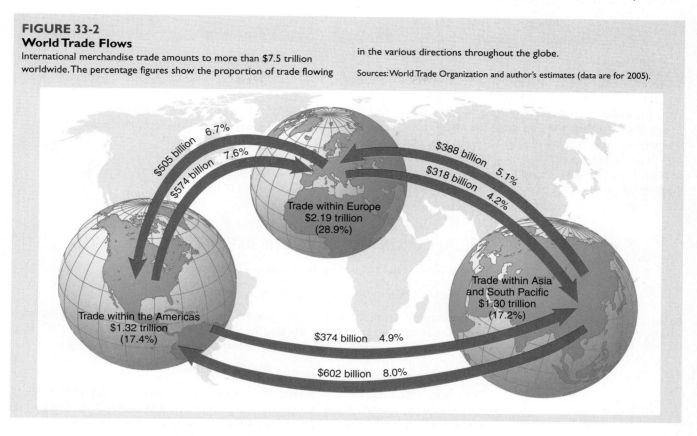

Other Benefits from International Trade: The Transmission of Ideas

Beyond the fact that comparative advantage results in an overall increase in the output of goods produced and consumed, there is another benefit to international trade. International trade bestows benefits on countries through the international transmission of ideas. According to economic historians, international trade has been the principal means by which new goods, services, and processes have spread around the world. For example, coffee was initially grown in Arabia near the Red Sea. Around A.D. 675, it began to be roasted and consumed as a beverage. Eventually, it was exported to other parts of the world, and the Dutch started cultivating it in their colonies during the seventeenth century and the French in the eighteenth century. The lowly potato is native to the Peruvian Andes. In the sixteenth century, it was brought to Europe by Spanish explorers. Thereafter, its cultivation and consumption spread rapidly. It became part of the North American agricultural scene in the early eighteenth century.

New processes have been transmitted through international trade. One of those involves the Japanese manufacturing innovation that emphasized redesigning the system rather than running the existing system in the best possible way. Inventories were reduced to just-in-time levels by reengineering machine setup methods.

All of the *intellectual property* that has been introduced throughout the world is a result of international trade. This includes new music, such as rock and roll in the 1950s and 1960s and hip-hop in the 1990s and 2000s. It includes the software applications and computer communications tools that are common for computer users everywhere.

How did international trade contribute to the development of the alphabet?

International EXAMPLE

International Trade and the Alphabet

Even the alphabetic system of writing that appears to be the source of most alphabets in the world today was spread through international trade. According to some scholars, the Phoenicians, who lived on the long, narrow strip of Mediterranean coast north of Israel from the ninth century B.C. to around 300 B.C., created the first true alphabet. It is thought that they developed the alphabet so that they could keep international trading records on their ships without having to take along highly trained scribes.

For Critical Analysis
Before alphabets were used, how might people have communicated in written form?

THE RELATIONSHIP BETWEEN IMPORTS AND EXPORTS

The basic proposition in understanding all of international trade is this:

> *In the long run, imports are paid for by exports.*[*]

Go to www.econtoday.com/chap33 to view the most recent trade statistics for the United States.

The reason that imports are ultimately paid for by exports is that foreign residents want something in exchange for the goods that are shipped to the United States. For the most part, they want U.S.-made goods. From this truism comes a remarkable corollary:

> *Any restriction of imports ultimately reduces exports.*

This is a shocking revelation to many people who want to restrict foreign competition to protect domestic jobs. Although it is possible to protect certain U.S. jobs by restricting foreign competition, it is impossible to make *everyone* better off by imposing import restrictions. Why? Because ultimately such restrictions lead to a reduction in employment in the export industries of the nation.

INTERNATIONAL COMPETITIVENESS

"The United States is falling behind." "We need to stay competitive internationally." Statements such as these are often heard in government circles when the subject of international trade comes up. There are two problems with such talk. The first has to do with a simple definition. What does "global competitiveness" really mean? When one company competes against another, it is in competition. Is the United States like one big corporation, in competition with other countries? Certainly not. The standard of living in each country is almost solely a function of how well the economy functions *within that country,* not relative to other countries.

Another problem arises with respect to the real world. According to the Institute for Management Development in Lausanne, Switzerland, the United States continues to lead the pack in overall productive efficiency, ahead of Japan, Germany, and the rest of the European Union. According to the report, the top-class ranking of the United States has

---

*We have to modify this rule by adding that in the short run, imports can also be paid for by the sale (or export) of real and financial assets, such as land, stocks, and bonds, or through an extension of credit from other countries.

been due to widespread entrepreneurship, more than a decade of economic restructuring, and information-technology investments. Other factors include the sophisticated U.S. financial system and large investments in scientific research.

How have information-technology investments affected the mix of exports in the United States?

E X A M P L E

U.S. Service Exports Gain on Merchandise Exports

Investments in new information technologies have increased U.S. efficiency in the production of many goods and services. Nevertheless, the most significant effect has been to reduce the opportunity cost of producing services in the United States relative to other nations. Figure 33-3 shows that a consequence has been considerable growth in the nation's exports of commercial services relative to its *merchandise exports*, or exports of physical goods. In 1980, U.S. exports of commercial services amounted to less than 18 percent of

U.S. merchandise exports. Today, U.S. exports of commercial services are more than 40 percent of U.S. merchandise exports.

For Critical Analysis
What would happen to U.S. exports of commercial services as a percentage of merchandise exports if nations such as India and Singapore were to gain a comparative advantage in providing commercial services?

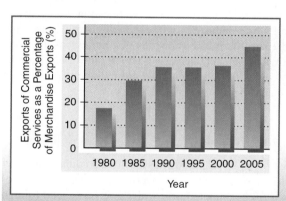

FIGURE 33-3

U.S. Exports of Commercial Services in Relation to U.S. Merchandise Exports

Since 1980, commercial service exports from the United States have more than doubled as a fraction of U.S. merchandise exports.

Source: U.S. Bureau of Economic Analysis.

CONCEPTS in Brief

- Countries can be better off materially if they specialize in producing goods for which they have a comparative advantage.

- It is important to distinguish between absolute and comparative advantage; the former refers to the ability to produce a unit of output with fewer physical units of input; the

latter refers to producing output that has the lowest opportunity cost for a nation.

- Different nations will always have different comparative advantages because of differing opportunity costs due to different resource mixes.

To test your understanding of the concepts covered in this section, go to the Online Review at www.myeconlab.com/miller.

ARGUMENTS AGAINST FREE TRADE

Numerous arguments are raised against free trade. They mainly focus on the costs of trade; they do not consider the benefits or the possible alternatives for reducing the costs of free trade while still reaping benefits.

The Infant Industry Argument

A nation may feel that if a particular industry is allowed to develop domestically, it will eventually become efficient enough to compete effectively in the world market. Therefore, the nation may impose some restrictions on imports in order to give domestic producers the time they need to develop their efficiency to the point where they can compete in the domestic market without any restrictions on imports. In graphic terminology, we would expect that if the protected industry truly does experience improvements in production techniques or technological breakthroughs toward greater efficiency in the future, the supply curve will shift outward to the right so that the domestic industry can produce larger quantities at each and every price. National policymakers often assert that this **infant industry argument** has some merit in the short run. They have used it to protect a number of industries in their infancy around the world.

Such a policy can be abused, however. Often the protective import-restricting arrangements remain even after the infant has matured. If other countries can still produce more cheaply, the people who benefit from this type of situation are obviously the stockholders (and specialized factors of production that will earn economic rents) in the industry that is still being protected from world competition. The people who lose out are the consumers, who must pay a price higher than the world price for the product in question. In any event, it is very difficult to know beforehand which industries will eventually survive. In other words, we cannot predict very well the specific infant industries that policymakers might deem worthy of protection. Note that when we speculate about which industries "should" be protected, we are in the realm of *normative economics*. We are making a value judgment, a subjective statement of what *ought to be.*

Infant industry argument
The contention that tariffs should be imposed to protect from import competition an industry that is trying to get started. Presumably, after the industry becomes technologically efficient, the tariff can be lifted.

Go to www.econtoday.com/chap33 for a Congressional Budget Office review of antidumping actions in the United States and around the world.

Countering Foreign Subsidies and Dumping

Another strong argument against unrestricted foreign trade has to do with countering other nations' subsidies to their own producers. When a foreign government subsidizes its producers, our producers claim that they cannot compete fairly with these subsidized foreign producers. To the extent that such subsidies fluctuate, it can be argued that unrestricted free trade will seriously disrupt domestic producers. They will not know when foreign governments are going to subsidize their producers and when they are not. Our competing industries will be expanding and contracting too frequently.

The phenomenon called *dumping* is also used as an argument against unrestricted trade. **Dumping** is said to occur when a producer sells its products abroad below the price that is charged in the home market or at a price below its cost of production. When a foreign producer is accused of dumping, further investigation usually reveals that the foreign nation is in the throes of a recession. The foreign producer does not want to slow down its production at home. Because it anticipates an end to the recession and doesn't want to hold large inventories, it dumps its products abroad at prices below home prices. U.S. competitors may also allege that it sells its output at prices below its full costs in an effort to cover at least part of its variable costs of production.

Dumping
Selling a good or a service abroad below the price charged in the home market or at a price below its cost of production.

Protecting Domestic Jobs

Perhaps the argument used most often against free trade is that unrestrained competition from other countries will eliminate jobs in the United States because other countries have lower-cost labor than we do. (Less restrictive environmental standards in other countries might also lower their private costs relative to ours.) This is a compelling argument, particularly for politicians from areas that might be threatened by foreign competition. For example, a representative from an area with shoe factories would certainly be upset about the possibility of constituents' losing their jobs because of competition from lower-priced shoe manufacturers in Brazil and Italy. But of course this argument against free trade is equally applicable to trade between the states within the United States.

Economists David Gould, G. L. Woodbridge, and Roy Ruffin examined the data on the relationship between increases in imports and the rate of unemployment. Their conclusion was that there is no causal link between the two. Indeed, in half the cases they studied, when imports increased, unemployment fell.

Another issue has to do with the cost of protecting U.S. jobs by restricting international trade. The Institute for International Economics examined just the restrictions on foreign textiles and apparel goods. U.S. consumers pay $9 billion a year more to protect jobs in those industries. That comes out to $50,000 *a year* for each job saved in an industry in which the average job pays only $20,000 a year. Similar studies have yielded similar results: Restrictions on imports of Japanese cars have cost $160,000 *per year* for every job saved in the auto industry. Every job preserved in the glass industry has cost $200,000 each and every year. Every job preserved in the U.S. steel industry has cost an astounding $750,000 per year.

Economics Front and Center

To contemplate how a nation's government might use product quality control as a pretext for restricting international trade in an effort to protect domestic jobs, read the case study, **A Looming Tequila Battle,** on page 792.

Emerging Arguments Against Free Trade

In recent years, two new antitrade arguments have been advanced. One of these focuses on environmental concerns. For instance, many environmentalists have suggested that genetic engineering of plants and animals could lead to accidental production of new diseases. These worries have induced the European Union to restrain trade in such products.

Another argument against free trade arises from national defense concerns. Major espionage successes by China in the late 1990s and early 2000s led some U.S. strategic experts to propose sweeping restrictions on exports of new technology.

Free trade proponents counter that at best these are arguments for the judicious regulation of trade. They continue to argue that by and large, broad trade restrictions mainly harm the interests of the nations that impose them.

CONCEPTS in Brief

- The infant industry argument against free trade contends that new industries should be protected against world competition so that they can become technologically efficient in the long run.

- Unrestricted foreign trade may allow foreign governments to subsidize exports or foreign producers to engage in dumping—selling products in other countries below their cost of production. To the extent that foreign export subsidies and dumping create more instability in domestic production, they may impair our well-being.

To test your understanding of the concepts covered in this section, go to the Online Review at www.myeconlab.com/miller.

WAYS TO RESTRICT FOREIGN TRADE

International trade can be stopped or at least stifled in many ways. These include quotas and taxes (the latter are usually called *tariffs* when applied to internationally traded items). Let's talk first about quotas.

Quotas

Quota system
A government-imposed restriction on the quantity of a specific good that another country is allowed to sell in the United States. In other words, quotas are restrictions on imports. These restrictions are usually applied to one or several specific countries.

Under a **quota system,** individual countries or groups of foreign producers are restricted to a certain amount of trade. An import quota specifies the maximum amount of a commodity that may be imported during a specified period of time. For example, the government might not allow more than 50 million barrels of foreign crude oil to enter the United States in a particular month.

Consider the example of quotas on textiles. Figure 33-4 presents the demand and supply curves for imported textiles. In an unrestricted import market, the equilibrium quantity imported is 900 million yards at a price of $1 per yard (expressed in constant-quality units). When an import quota is imposed, the supply curve is no longer S. Instead, the supply curve becomes vertical at some amount less than the equilibrium quantity—here, 800 million yards per year. The price to the U.S. consumer increases from $1.00 to $1.50. Thus the output restriction induced by the textile quota also has the effect of influencing the price that domestic suppliers can charge for their goods. This benefits domestic textile producers by raising their revenues and therefore their profits.

Voluntary restraint agreement (VRA)
An official agreement with another country that "voluntarily" restricts the quantity of its exports to the United States.

Voluntary Quotas. Quotas do not have to be explicit and defined by law. They can be "voluntary." Such a quota is called a **voluntary restraint agreement (VRA).** In the early 1980s, Japanese automakers voluntarily restrained exports to the United States. These restraints stayed in place into the 1990s. Today, there are VRAs on machine tools and textiles.

Voluntary import expansion (VIE)
An official agreement with another country in which it agrees to import more from the United States.

The opposite of a VRA is a **voluntary import expansion (VIE).** Under a VIE, a foreign government agrees to have its companies import more foreign goods from another

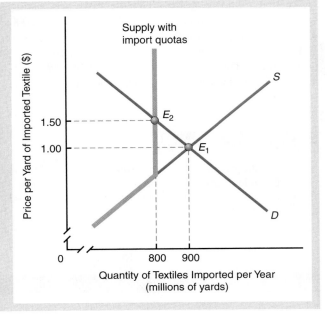

FIGURE 33-4
The Effect of Quotas on Textile Imports
Without restrictions, at point E_1, 900 million yards of textiles would be imported each year into the United States at the world price of $1.00 per yard. If the federal government imposes a quota of only 800 million yards, the effective supply curve becomes vertical at that quantity. It intersects the demand curve at point E_2, so the new equilibrium price is $1.50 per yard.

country. The United States almost started a major international trade war with Japan in 1995 over just such an issue. The U.S. government wanted Japanese automobile manufacturers voluntarily to increase their imports of U.S.-made automobile parts. Ultimately, Japanese companies did make a token increase in their imports of U.S. auto parts.

Tariffs

We can analyze tariffs by using standard supply and demand diagrams. Let's use as our commodity laptop computers, some of which are made in Japan and some of which are made domestically. In panel (a) of Figure 33-5, you see the demand and supply of Japanese laptops. The equilibrium price is $1,000 per constant-quality unit, and the equilibrium quantity is 10 million per year. In panel (b), you see the same equilibrium price of $1,000, and the *domestic* equilibrium quantity is 5 million units per year.

Go to www.econtoday.com/chap33 to take a look at the U.S. State Department's reports on economic policy and trade practices.

Now a tariff of $500 is imposed on all imported Japanese laptops. The supply curve shifts upward by $500 to S_2. For purchasers of Japanese laptops, the price increases to $1,250. The quantity demanded falls to 8 million per year. In panel (b), you see that at the higher price of imported Japanese laptops, the demand curve for U.S.-made laptops shifts outward to the right to D_2. The equilibrium price increases to $1,250, but the equilibrium quantity increases to 6.5 million units per year. So the tariff benefits domestic laptop producers because it increases the demand for their products due to the higher price of a close

FIGURE 33-5
The Effect of a Tariff on Japanese-Made Laptop Computers

Without a tariff, the United States buys 10 million Japanese laptops per year at an average price of $1,000, at point E_1 in panel (a). U.S. producers sell 5 million domestically made laptops, also at $1,000 each, at point E_1 in panel (b). A $500-per-laptop tariff will shift the Japanese import supply curve to S_2 in panel (a), so that the new equilibrium is at E_2, with price increased to $1,250 and quantity sold reduced to 8 million per year. The demand curve for U.S.-made laptops (for which there is no tariff) shifts to D_2, in panel (b). Domestic sales increase to 6.5 million per year, at point E_2.

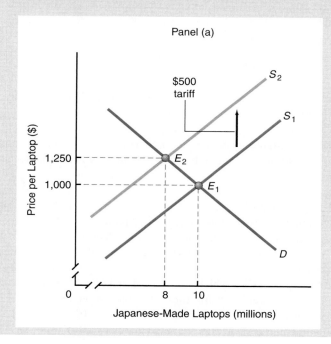

Panel (a)

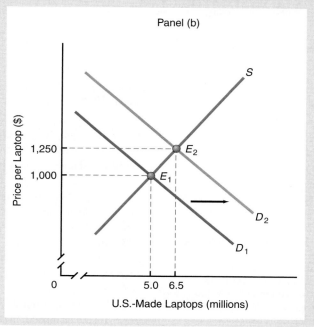

Panel (b)

FIGURE 33-6
Tariff Rates in the United States Since 1820

Tariff rates in the United States have bounced around like a football; indeed, in Congress, tariffs are a political football. Import-competing industries prefer high tariffs. In the twentieth century, the highest tariff was the Smoot-Hawley Tariff of 1930, which was about as high as the "tariff of abominations" in 1828.

Source: U.S. Department of Commerce.

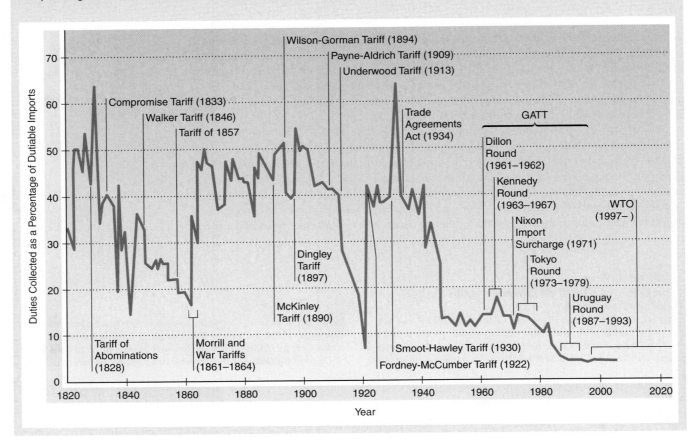

substitute, Japanese laptops. This causes a redistribution of income from Japanese producers and U.S. consumers of laptops to U.S. producers of laptops.

Tariffs in the United States. In Figure 33-6, we see that tariffs on all imported goods have varied widely. The highest rates in the twentieth century occurred with the passage of the Smoot-Hawley Tariff in 1930.

Current Tariff Laws. The Trade Expansion Act of 1962 gave the president the authority to reduce tariffs by up to 50 percent. Subsequently, tariffs were reduced by about 35 percent. In 1974, the Trade Reform Act allowed the president to reduce tariffs further. In 1984, the Trade and Tariff Act resulted in the lowest tariff rates ever. All such trade agreement obligations of the United States were carried out under the auspices of the **General Agreement on Tariffs and Trade (GATT),** which was signed in 1947. Member nations of GATT account for more than 85 percent of world trade. As you can see in Figure 33-6, there have been a number of rounds of negotiations to reduce tariffs. In 2002, the U.S. government proposed eliminating all tariffs on manufactured goods by 2015.

General Agreement on Tariffs and Trade (GATT)

An international agreement established in 1947 to further world trade by reducing barriers and tariffs. GATT was replaced by the World Trade Organization in 1995.

INTERNATIONAL TRADE ORGANIZATIONS

The widespread effort to reduce tariffs around the world has generated interest among nations in joining various international trade organizations. These organizations promote trade by granting preferences in the form of reduced or eliminated tariffs, duties, or quotas.

The World Trade Organization (WTO)

The most important international trade organization with the largest membership is the **World Trade Organization (WTO),** which was ratified by the Uruguay Round of the General Agreement on Tariffs and Trade at the end of 1993. The WTO, which as of 2005 had 147 member nations and included 33 observer governments, began operations on January 1, 1995. WTO decisions have concerned such topics as special U.S. steel tariffs imposed in the early 2000s, which the U.S. government withdrew after the WTO determined that they violated its rules. The WTO also adjudicated the European Union's "banana wars" and determined that the EU's policies unfairly favored many former European colonies in Africa, the Caribbean, and the Pacific at the expense of banana-exporting countries in Latin America. Now those former colonies no longer have a privileged position in European markets.

Why do you suppose that European nations continue to dispute WTO rules regarding the international trade of products that originated in those countries?

World Trade Organization (WTO)
The successor organization to GATT that handles trade disputes among its member nations.

International EXAMPLE

The European Union Starts a Food Fight

The European Union (EU) has pressed the WTO to create a global register of "geographically defined" food products it believes should be protected from alleged copycat products outside the EU. If the EU gets its way, firms around the globe will violate WTO rules if they sell food products named for European locales where the products first originated. Dairy products such as parmesan cheese and cheddar cheese and alcoholic beverages such as champagne, sherry, and madeira are among the 41 products on the EU's proposed list.

For Critical Analysis
Who would stand to benefit from the EU's efforts to prevent free trade of products with names originally derived from European locales?

On a larger scale, the WTO fostered the most important and far-reaching global trade agreement ever covering financial institutions, including banks, insurers, and investment companies. The more than 100 signatories to this new treaty have legally committed themselves to giving foreign residents more freedom to own and operate companies in virtually all segments of the financial services industry.

Regional Trade Agreements

Numerous other international trade organizations exist alongside the WTO. Sometimes known as **regional trade blocs,** these organizations are created by special deals among groups of countries that grant trade preferences only to countries within their groups. Currently, more than 140 bilateral or regional trade agreements are in effect around the globe. Examples include groups of industrial powerhouses, such the European Union, the North American Free Trade Agreement, and the Association of Southeast Asian Nations. Nations in South America with per capita real GDP nearer the world average have also formed re-

Regional trade bloc
A group of nations that grants members special trade privileges.

gional trade blocs called Mercosur and the Andean Community. Less developed nations have also formed regional trade blocs, such as the Economic Community of West African States and the Community of East and Southern Africa.

Some economists have worried that the formation of regional trade blocs could result in a reduction in members' trade with nations outside their own blocs. If more trade is diverted from a bloc than is created within it, then on net a regional trade agreement reduces trade. So far, however, most evidence indicates that regional trade blocs have promoted trade instead of hindering it. Numerous studies have found that as countries around the world have become more open to trade, they have tended to join regional trade blocs that promote even more openness.

CONCEPTS in Brief

- One means of restricting foreign trade is a quota system. An import quota specifies a maximum amount of a good that may be imported during a certain period.

- Another means of restricting imports is a tariff, which is a tax on imports only. An import tariff benefits import-competing industries and harms consumers by raising prices.

- The main international institution created to improve trade among nations was the General Agreement on Tariffs and

Trade (GATT). The last round of trade talks under GATT, the Uruguay Round, led to the creation of the World Trade Organization.

- Regional trade agreements among numerous nations of the world have established more than 140 regional trade blocs, which grant special trade privileges such as reduced tariff barriers and quota exemptions to member nations.

To test your understanding of the concepts covered in this section, go to the Online Review at www.myeconlab.com/miller.

CASE STUDY: Economics Front and Center

A Looming Tequila Battle

Corso is a mid-level official of the American Distilled Spirits Council (ADSC), a trade group composed of U.S. sellers of wines and other distilled alcoholic beverages. She has been assigned to investigate recent efforts by the Mexican government to regulate U.S. sales of tequila. At present, more than 80 percent of all tequila sold in the United States is transported from Mexico in bulk and then placed in containers by individual U.S. bottlers that wholesale it in their local areas.

Mexico's quasi-governmental Tequila Regulatory Council (TRC) has notified Corso that it has discovered evidence that bulk handlers on both sides of the border have tampered with tequila products. Some Mexican handlers, the TRC contends, have added water to certain tequilas, and a few U.S. handlers have blended different tequilas. In light of these alleged threats to the quality of tequilas, Corso has learned, the TRC is recommending to the Mexican government that it ban all bulk tequila shipments and require that tequila be bottled in Mexico.

After meeting with her superiors, Corso begins drafting a response to the TRC's claims and recommendation. "The TRC's recommendation," her draft response begins, "has less to do with quality control than with protecting jobs south of the U.S. border. If the Mexican government follows the TRC's recommendation, the ADSC will ask the U.S. government to file formal complaints with both the North American Free Trade Agreement and the World Trade Organization."

Points to Analyze

1. *Of the ways of restricting international trade discussed in this chapter, which method has the TRC recommended to the Mexican government?*

2. *How could the Mexican government discourage the cross-border shipment of bulk tequila without resorting to an outright ban on such shipments?*

Issues and Applications

Agricultural Subsidies Derail the WTO

As shown in Figure 33-7, by the mid-2000s membership of the World Trade Organization had grown to include about 50 percent more nations than had participated in the General Agreement on Tariffs and Trade in 1985. Global trade had more than tripled during the same period.

As trade among nations increased into the early 2000s, however, a dark cloud began to hover over the global trading system administered by the WTO. Developing nations were becoming increasingly skeptical of developed nations' true commitment to open trade. Even as the United States, the European Union, and Japan were pushing developing countries to lift tariff and quota barriers to U.S., EU, and Japanese exports, the governments of the developed nations were boosting subsidies to their domestic farmers producing agricultural goods. The subsidies allowed these farmers to sell their products at lower prices than they otherwise would have accepted. This, of course, gave agricultural producers in these developed nations an artificial advantage in world markets.

Concepts Applied

- World Trade Organization
- General Agreement on Tariffs and Trade
- Protectionism

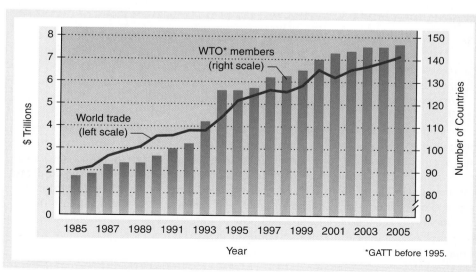

FIGURE 33-7

Growth in the World Trade Organization's Membership and in Global Trade

Both membership in the World Trade Organization and total international trade have increased considerably since the mid-1980s.

Source: World Trade Organization.

*GATT before 1995.

793

The Problem with Agricultural Subsidies

Naturally, those who have most to lose from agricultural subsidies are farmers residing in nations without government agricultural subsidies. By and large, these farmers live in developing countries. From their perspective, the U.S., EU, and Japanese subsidies amount to protectionist policies.

Consider, for instance, who is harmed by U.S. cotton subsidies. In 2002, Congress raised subsidies paid to U.S. cotton growers to nearly $4 billion per year. This gave U.S. cotton producers a significant advantage over their competitors elsewhere in the world. A number of these were farmers residing in poverty-stricken West Africa. Many of them were forced out of business by the lower cotton prices resulting from the influx of subsidized cotton exported by growers in the United States.

Agricultural Protectionism Slows the World Trade Locomotive

In 2003, U.S. agricultural subsidies were equal to nearly 20 percent of the total value of U.S. farming production. In the EU, subsidies amounted to 35 percent of the market value of agricultural output. The share of Japan's subsidies was even higher, at nearly 60 percent.

That year, many of the developing nations placed at a competitive disadvantage by these whopping agricultural subsidies drew a line in the sand. Most of these nations pulled out of WTO-sponsored global trade talks in Cancún, Mexico. More openness to trade on their part, they said, would depend on whether the developed nations slashed protectionist subsidies of agricultural production.

In late 2003, the U.S. government offered a proposal for joint reductions in agricultural subsidies by the United States, the European Union, and Japan. The governments of EU nations and Japan expressed some interest in considering the idea. Within months, however, negotiators faced a stalemate concerning exactly how to reduce subsidies without harming their U.S., EU, and Japanese farmers. As a consequence, so far the developed nations have not cut subsidies to their farmers, even though some economists estimate that eliminating the subsidies would add at least $100 billion annually to global GDP.

For Critical Analysis

1. Why do subsidies to U.S. cotton producers induce them to increase their supply of cotton for export to other nations? (Hint: How does a per-unit subsidy affect the marginal cost, and hence the short-run supply curve, of a perfectly competitive cotton producer?)
2. Who else besides West African cotton producers are harmed by U.S. government subsidies to cotton producers? (Hint: Who provides the funds for all the subsidies received by U.S. farmers?)

Web Resources

1. To learn more about why West African nations regard U.S. cotton subsidies as a protectionist policy, go to a link to the discussion provided by the Global Policy Forum at www.econtoday.com/chap33.
2. The Australia-Japan Research Foundation's analysis of Japan's world-leading agricultural subsidies is available at www.econtoday.com/chap33.

Research Project

Governments of developed nations typically argue that agricultural subsidies are domestic policies aimed solely at helping their farmers. Spillover effects in world markets, they claim, are not intentionally protectionist. Likewise, the U.S. government justifies its rules barring sales of certain European-manufactured pharmaceuticals as necessary to protect consumer safety. The EU bans all genetically modified U.S. crops on the same grounds. Yet these and other "domestic" policies adversely affect international trade. Suppose that you work for the WTO. You have been asked how to determine whether governments actually engage in such policies to protect domestic industries from foreign competition. How would you proceed? Why is this a tough question to answer?

SUMMARY DISCUSSION of Learning Objectives

1. **The Worldwide Importance of International Trade:** Total trade among nations has been growing faster than total world GDP. The growth of U.S. exports and imports relative to U.S. GDP parallels this global trend. Together, exports and imports now equal about one-fourth of total national production. In some countries, trade accounts for a much higher share of total economic activity.

2. **Why Nations Can Gain from Specializing in Production and Engaging in Trade:** A country has a comparative advantage in producing a good if it can produce that good at a lower opportunity cost, in terms of forgone production of a second good, than another nation. Because the other nation has a comparative advantage in producing the second good, both nations can gain by specializing in producing the goods in which they have a comparative advantage and engaging in international trade. Together they can then produce and consume more than they would have produced and consumed in the absence of specialization and trade.

3. **Comparative Advantage versus Absolute Advantage:** Whereas a nation has a comparative advantage in producing a good when it can produce the good at a lower opportunity cost relative to the opportunity cost of producing the good in another nation, a nation has an absolute advantage when it can produce more output with a given set of inputs than can be produced in the other country. Trade can still take place if both nations have a comparative advantage in producing goods that they can agree to exchange. The reason is that it can still benefit the nation with an absolute advantage to specialize in production.

4. **Arguments Against Free Trade:** One argument against free trade is that temporary import restrictions might permit an "infant industry" to develop to the point at which it could compete without such restrictions. Another argument concerns dumping, in which foreign companies allegedly sell some of their output in domestic markets at prices below the prices in the companies' home markets or even below the companies' costs of production. In addition, some environmentalists contend that nations should restrain foreign trade to prevent exposing their countries to environmental hazards to plants, animals, or even humans. Finally, some contend that countries should limit exports of technologies that could pose a threat to their national defense.

5. **Ways That Nations Restrict Foreign Trade:** One way to restrain trade is to impose a quota, or a limit on imports of a good. This action restricts the supply of the good in the domestic market, thereby pushing up the equilibrium price of the good. Another way to reduce trade is to place a tariff on imported goods. This reduces the supply of foreign-made goods and increases the demand for domestically produced goods, thereby bringing about a rise in the price of the good.

6. **Key International Trade Agreements and Organizations:** From 1947 to 1995, nations agreed to abide by the General Agreement on Tariffs and Trade (GATT), which laid an international legal foundation for relaxing quotas and reducing tariffs. Since 1995, the World Trade Organization (WTO) has adjudicated trade disputes that arise between or among nations. Now there are also more than 140 regional trade blocs that provide special trade preferences to member nations.

KEY TERMS AND CONCEPTS

absolute advantage (781)

comparative advantage (780)

dumping (786)

General Agreement on Tariffs and
   Trade (GATT) (780)

infant industry argument (786)

quota system (788)

regional trade bloc (791)

voluntary import expansion (VIE)
   (788)

voluntary restraint agreement (VRA)
   (788)

World Trade Organization (WTO)
   (791)

PROBLEMS

Answers to the odd-numbered problems appear at the back of the book.

33-1. The following hypothetical example depicts the number of calculators and books that Norway and Sweden can produce with one unit of labor.

Country	Calculators	Books
Norway	2	1
Sweden	4	1

If each country has 100 units of labor and the country splits its labor force evenly between the two industries, how much of each good can the nations produce individually and jointly? Which nation has an absolute advantage in calculators, and which nation has an absolute advantage in books?

33-2. Suppose that the two nations in Problem 33-1 do not trade.

a. What would be the price of books in terms of calculators in each nation?

b. What is the opportunity cost of producing one calculator in each nation?

c. What is the opportunity cost of producing one book in each nation?

33-3. Consider the nations in Problem 33-1 when answering the following questions.

a. Which country has a comparative advantage in calculators, and which has a comparative advantage in books?

b. What is the total or joint output if the two nations specialize in the good for which they have a comparative advantage?

33-4. Illustrate possible production possibilities curves (PPCs, see Chapter 2) for the two nations in Problem 33-1 in a graph with books depicted on the vertical axis and calculators on the horizontal axis. What do the differing slopes of the PPCs for these two nations indicate about the opportunity costs of producing calculators and books in the two countries? What are the implications for the comparative advantage of producing calculators or books in Norway and Sweden?

33-5. Suppose that initially the two nations in Problem 33-1 do not engage in international trade. Now they have decided to trade with each other at a rate where one

book exchanges for three calculators. Using this rate of exchange, explain, in economic terms, whether their exchange is a zero-sum game, a positive-sum game, or a negative-sum game. (Hint: Review Chapter 27 if necessary to answer this question.)

33-6. The marginal physical product of a worker in an advanced nation (MPP_A) is 100, and the wage (W_A) is $25. The marginal physical product of a worker in a developing nation (MPP_D) is 15, and the wage (W_D) is $5. Product prices are equal in all nations. As a cost-minimizing business manager in the advanced nation, would you be enticed to move your business to the developing nation to take advantage of the lower wage?

33-7. Consider the following table, which shows unspecialized productive capabilities of sets of workers in South Shore and neighboring East Isle, when answering the questions that follow.

Product	South Shore Workers	South Shore Output	East Isle Workers	East Isle Output
Modems	100	25	100	45
DVD drives	100	50	100	15

a. Which country has an absolute advantage in producing modems? DVD drives?

b. Which country has a comparative advantage in producing modems? DVD drives?

33-8. Refer to the table in Problem 33-7 to answer the following questions.

a. If each country has a total of 200 workers to devote to production of modems and DVD drives, what are the combined outputs of the two goods if these countries do not specialize in production according to comparative advantage?

b. What are the combined outputs if the two countries completely specialize in production according to comparative advantage? Measured in terms of outputs of modems and DVD drives, what are the gains from trade?

33-9. Consider the following table, which shows unspecialized productive capabilities of sets of workers in Northern Kingdom and Western Republic, neighboring countries that share a border, when answering the questions that follow.

Product	Northern Kingdom		Western Republic	
	Workers	Output	Workers	Output
Bushels of wheat	100	55	100	20
Surfboards	100	30	100	45

a. Which country has an absolute advantage in producing bushels of wheat? Surfboards?

b. Which country has a comparative advantage in producing bushels of wheat? Surfboards?

33-10. Suppose that each nation in Problem 33-9 currently specializes according to its comparative advantage, maximizes its production given the 200 workers each has available, and engages in trade with the other country. What do the two nations lose, in terms of outputs of bushels of wheat and surfboards, if one nation's government implements a law banning international trade?

33-11. You are a policymaker of a major exporting nation. Your main export good has a price elasticity of demand of −0.50. Is there any economic reason why you would voluntarily agree to export restraints?

33-12. The following table depicts the bicycle industry before and after a nation has imposed quota restraints.

	Before Quota	After Quota
Quantity imported	1,000,000	900,000
Price paid	$50	$60

Draw a diagram illustrating conditions in the imported bicycle market before and after the quota, and answer the following questions.

a. What are the total expenditures of consumers before and after the quota?

b. What is the price elasticity of demand for bicycles?

c. Who benefits from the imposition of the quota?

33-13 The following diagrams illustrate the markets for imported Korean-made and U.S.-manufactured televisions before and after a tariff is imposed on imported TVs.

a. What was the amount of the tariff per TV?

b. What was the total revenue of Korean television exports before the tariff? After the tariff?

c. What is the tariff revenue earned by the U.S. government?

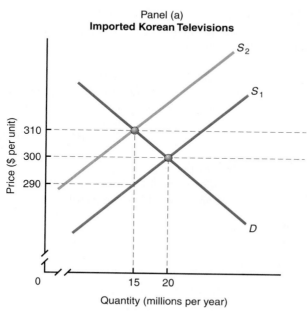

Panel (a)
Imported Korean Televisions

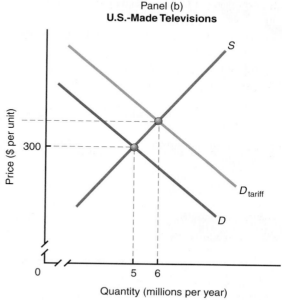

Panel (b)
U.S.-Made Televisions

33-14. Base your answers to the following questions on the graphs accompanying Problem 33-13.

   a. What was the revenue of U.S. television manufacturers before the tariff was imposed?

   b. What is their total revenue after the tariff?
   c. Who has gained from the tariff, and who is worse off?

ECONOMICS ON THE NET

How the World Trade Organization Settles Trade Disputes A key function of the WTO is to adjudicate trade disagreements that arise among nations. This application helps you learn about the process that the WTO follows when considering international trade disputes.

Title: The World Trade Organization: Settling Trade Disputes

Navigation: Go to www.econtoday.com/chap33 to access the WTO's Web page titled *Trading into the Future*, and click on *3. Settling Disputes*, in the left-hand margin.

Application Read the article; then answer the following questions.

1. As the article discusses, settling trade disputes often takes at least a year. What aspects of the WTO's dispute settlement process take the longest time?

2. Does the WTO actually "punish" a country it finds has broken international trading agreements? If not, who does impose sanctions?

For Group Study and Analysis Back up to *Trading into the Future*, and click on *4. Beyond the Agreements*. Have a class discussion of the pros and cons of WTO involvement in each of the areas discussed in this article. Which are most important for promoting world trade? Which are least important?

If your exam were tomorrow, would you be ready? For each chapter, MyEconLab Practice Tests and Study Plans pinpoint which sections you have mastered and which ones you need to study. That way, you are more efficient with your study time, and you are better prepared for your exams.

In addition to Practice Tests and your personalized Study Plan, you'll find the following media resources in MyEconLab:

1. *Graphs in Motion* animation of Figures 33-1, 33-4, and 33-5.
2. Videos featuring the author, Roger LeRoy Miller, on the following subjects:
   ● The Gains from Trade
   ● Arguments Against Free Trade

3. Links to the Web sites cited in the marginal Internet Resources, Issues and Applications feature, and Economics on the Net activity.
4. Audio clips of all key terms, additional practice problems, and a PDF version of the material from the print Study Guide.
5. eThemes of the Times, which is a New York Times article to help you understand the real-world applications of what you are learning.

To see how it works, turn to page 16 and then go to www.myeconlab.com/miller.

Get Ahead of the Curve

Chapter 34

Exchange Rates and the Balance of Payments

On this particular day, as on many others in the 2000s, the Japanese yen's value was rising relative to the U.S. dollar. Because yen were more expensive to obtain with dollars, U.S. residents faced higher dollar prices when they considered purchasing Japanese-made goods. In an effort to prevent a fall in exports to the United States that would weaken total spending on Japanese goods and services, the Japanese Finance Ministry hurriedly placed a very large order with a private Japanese bank to sell yen for dollars on its behalf. About 30 minutes later, the Finance Ministry canceled the order. Nevertheless, exactly as the Finance Ministry had planned, the yen's dollar value fell. Why did the Japanese Finance Ministry's apparent reversal of its sale of yen encourage a fall in the yen's dollar value? In this chapter, you will learn the answer to this question.

LEARNING OBJECTIVES

After reading this chapter, you should be able to:

1. Distinguish between the balance of trade and the balance of payments
2. Identify the key accounts within the balance of payments
3. Outline how exchange rates are determined in the markets for foreign exchange
4. Discuss factors that can induce changes in equilibrium exchange rates
5. Understand how policymakers can go about attempting to fix exchange rates
6. Explain alternative approaches to limiting exchange rate variability

Media Resources

Refer to the end of the chapter for a full listing of the multimedia learning materials available in MyEconLab.

Did You Know That ... when the value of the U.S. dollar in terms of other nations' currencies declines, foreign automakers often respond by shifting more of their production to the United States? For instance, when the dollar's world value declined between 2002 and 2004, Toyota cut back on vehicle output in Japan and increased production at its five U.S. plants. Likewise, DaimlerChrysler reduced its Mercedes output in Germany but nearly doubled production of Mercedes sport utility vehicles at its Alabama factory. Vehicles that these companies continued producing in Japan and Germany were priced in terms of yen and euros. Thus the 2002–2004 decline in the value of the dollar in terms of yen and euros caused vehicles still produced in those nations to be more expensive to U.S. consumers using dollars to buy them. By shifting production of more vehicles to the United States, Toyota, Daimler-Chrysler, and other foreign producers were able to avoid higher dollar prices that would have reduced their U.S. sales.

In this chapter, you will learn more about how changes in the dollar's value affect decisions of both sellers *and* buyers, both abroad *and* in the United States. Before we consider what causes variations in the value of the dollar and the more than 170 other currencies in circulation around the world, however, we will examine how we keep track of the international financial transactions that these currencies facilitate.

THE BALANCE OF PAYMENTS AND INTERNATIONAL CAPITAL MOVEMENTS

Governments typically keep track of each year's economic activities by calculating the gross domestic product—the total of expenditures on all newly produced final domestic goods and services—and its components. A summary information system has also been developed for international trade. It covers the balance of trade and the balance of payments. The **balance of trade** refers specifically to exports and imports of goods as discussed in Chapter 33. When international trade is in balance, the value of exports equals the value of imports. When the value of imports exceeds the value of exports, we are running a deficit in the balance of trade. When the value of exports exceeds the value of imports, we are running a surplus.

The **balance of payments** is a more general concept that expresses the total of all economic transactions between a nation and the rest of the world, usually for a period of one year. Each country's balance of payments summarizes information about that country's exports, imports, earnings by domestic residents on assets located abroad, earnings on domestic assets owned by foreign residents, international capital movements, and official transactions by central banks and governments. In essence, then, the balance of payments is a record of all the transactions between households, firms, and the government of one country and the rest of the world. Any transaction that leads to a *payment* by a country's residents (or government) is a deficit item, identified by a negative sign ($-$) when the actual numbers are given for the items listed in the second column of Table 34-1. Any transaction that leads to a *receipt* by a country's residents (or government) is a surplus item and is identified by a plus sign ($+$) when actual numbers are considered. Table 34-1 gives a listing of the surplus and deficit items on international accounts.

Accounting Identities

Accounting identities—definitions of equivalent values—exist for financial institutions and other businesses. We begin with simple accounting identities that must hold for families and then go on to describe international accounting identities.

Balance of trade
The difference between exports and imports of goods.

Balance of payments
A system of accounts that measures transactions of goods, services, income, and financial assets between domestic households, businesses, and governments and residents of the rest of the world during a specific time period.

Accounting identities
Values that are equivalent by definition.

Surplus Items (+)	Deficit Items (−)
Exports of merchandise	Imports of merchandise
Private and governmental gifts from foreign residents	Private and governmental gifts to foreign residents
Foreign use of domestically owned transportation	Use of foreign-owned transportation
Foreign tourists' expenditures in this country	U.S. tourists' expenditures abroad
Foreign military spending in this country	Military spending abroad
Interest and dividend receipts from foreign entities	Interest and dividends paid to foreign residents
Sales of domestic assets to foreign residents	Purchases of foreign assets
Funds deposited in this country by foreign residents	Funds placed in foreign depository institutions
Sales of gold to foreign residents	Purchases of gold from foreign residents
Sales of domestic currency to foreign residents	Purchases of foreign currency

TABLE 34-1
Surplus (+) and Deficit (−) Items on the International Accounts

If a family unit is spending more than its current income, such a situation necessarily implies that the family unit must be doing one of the following:

1. Reducing its money holdings or selling stocks, bonds, or other assets
2. Borrowing
3. Receiving gifts from friends or relatives
4. Receiving public transfers from a government, which obtained the funds by taxing others (a transfer is a payment, in money or in goods or services, made without receiving goods or services in return)

We can use this information to derive an identity: If a family unit is currently spending more than it is earning, it must draw on previously acquired wealth, borrow, or receive either private or public aid. Similarly, an identity exists for a family unit that is currently spending less than it is earning: It must be increasing its money holdings or be lending and acquiring other financial assets, or it must pay taxes or bestow gifts on others. When we consider businesses and governments, each unit in each group faces its own identities or constraints. Ultimately, net lending by households must equal net borrowing by businesses and governments.

Disequilibrium. Even though our individual family unit's accounts must balance, in the sense that the identity discussed previously must hold, sometimes the item that brings about the balance cannot continue indefinitely. *If family expenditures exceed family income and this situation is financed by borrowing, the household may be considered to be in disequilibrium because such a situation cannot continue indefinitely.* If such a deficit is financed by drawing on previously accumulated assets, the family may also be in disequilibrium because it cannot continue indefinitely to draw on its wealth; eventually, it will become impossible for that family to continue such a lifestyle. (Of course, if the family members are retired, they may well be in equilibrium by drawing on previously acquired assets to finance current deficits; this example illustrates that it is necessary to understand circumstances fully before pronouncing an economic unit in disequilibrium.)

Equilibrium. Individual households, businesses, and governments, as well as the entire group of households, businesses, and governments, must eventually reach equilibrium. Certain economic adjustment mechanisms have evolved to ensure equilibrium. Deficit households must eventually increase their income or decrease their expenditures. They will find that they have to pay higher interest rates if they wish to borrow to finance their deficits. Eventually, their credit sources will dry up, and they will be forced into equilibrium. Businesses, on occasion, must lower costs or prices—or go bankrupt—to reach equilibrium.

An Accounting Identity Among Nations. When people from different nations trade or interact, certain identities or constraints must also hold. People buy goods from people in other nations; they also lend to and present gifts to people in other nations. If residents of a nation interact with residents of other nations, an accounting identity ensures a balance (but not an equilibrium, as will soon become clear). Let's look at the three categories of balance of payments transactions: current account transactions, capital account transactions, and official reserve account transactions.

Current Account Transactions

Current account
A category of balance of payments transactions that measures the exchange of merchandise, the exchange of services, and unilateral transfers.

During any designated period, all payments and gifts that are related to the purchase or sale of both goods and services constitute the **current account** in international trade. Major types of current account transactions include the exchange of merchandise, the exchange of services, and unilateral transfers.

Merchandise Trade Exports and Imports. The largest portion of any nation's balance of payments current account is typically the importing and exporting of merchandise goods. During 2004, for example, as can be seen in lines 1 and 2 of Table 34-2, the United States exported an estimated $813.7 billion of merchandise and imported $1,406.5 billion. The balance of merchandise trade is defined as the difference between the value of merchandise exports and the value of merchandise imports. For 2004, the United States had a balance of merchandise trade deficit because the value of its merchandise imports exceeded the value of its merchandise exports. This deficit was about $592.8 billion (line 3).

Service Exports and Imports. The balance of (merchandise) trade has to do with tangible items—things you can feel, touch, and see. Service exports and imports have to do with invisible or intangible items that are bought and sold, such as shipping, insurance, tourist expenditures, and banking services. Also, income earned by foreign residents on U.S. investments and income earned by U.S. residents on foreign investments are part of service imports and exports. As can be seen in lines 4 and 5 of Table 34-2, in 2004, service exports were $336.7 billion and service imports were $255.0 billion. Thus the balance of services was about $81.7 billion in 2004 (line 6). Exports constitute receipts or inflows into the United States and are positive; imports constitute payments abroad or outflows of money and are negative.

When we combine the balance of merchandise trade with the balance of services, we obtain a balance on goods and services equal to −$511.1 billion in 2004 (line 7).

How much different would the balance on goods and services be if it was based on the locations of the owners of the firms that produce traded goods and services?

Current Account		
(1) Exports of goods	+ 813.7	
(2) Imports of goods	− 1,406.5	
(3) Balance of trade		− 592.8
(4) Exports of services	+ 336.7	
(5) Imports of services	− 255.0	
(6) Balance of services		+ 81.7
(7) Balance on goods and services [(3) + (6)]		− 511.1
(8) Net unilateral transfers	− 70.1	
(9) Balance on current account		− 581.2
Capital Account		
(10) U.S. private capital going abroad	− 795.1	
(11) Foreign private capital coming into the United States	+ 1,137.4	
(12) Balance on capital account [(10) + (11)]		+ 342.3
(13) Balance on current account plus balance on capital account [(9) + (12)]		− 238.9
Official Reserve Transactions Account		
(14) Official transactions balance		+ 238.9
(15) Total (balance)		0

TABLE 34-2
U.S. Balance of Payments Account, 2004 (in billions of dollars)

Sources: U.S. Department of Commerce, Bureau of Economic Analysis; author's estimates.
*Includes an approximately $25 billion statistical discrepancy, probably uncounted capital inflows, many of which relate to the illegal drug trade.

EXAMPLE

Taking Multinational Firms into Account in Trade Statistics

The U.S. balance on goods and services tracks the net flow of international trade of goods and services based on where traded items are produced. Thus the statisticians who tabulate this balance add only exports of goods and services *produced* within U.S. borders and subtract only U.S. imports of for-eign-*produced* goods and services. But this accounting does not include all activities of U.S. firms. Consider, for example, a U.S. multinational firm that owns a plant in Mexico where it produces a good or service that it sells to Canadian residents. Because the item is produced in Mexico and purchased by

Canadians, this transaction is not included in the U.S. balance on goods and services even though a U.S. firm was involved.

Recently, the U.S. Department of Commerce began report-ing a measure of the balance on goods and services based on the locations of the companies that own the resources utilized to produce internationally traded goods and services. This *ownership-based* U.S. balance on goods and services adjusts exports and imports to account for purchases and sales in-volving foreign affiliates of U.S. firms. Annual net receipts that U.S. parent companies derive from trade conducted by their foreign affiliates are always much larger than the net receipts foreign firms receive from their U.S. affiliates that engage in international trade. Consequently, the deficit in the ownership-based balance on goods and services averages about $60 billion per year less than the deficit in the official, production-based measure of this balance.

For Critical Analysis
Why might the fact that the balance of payments accounts were designed before multinational firms were very common help explain why the balances in these accounts are not based on ownership?

Unilateral Transfers. U.S. residents give gifts to relatives and others abroad, the federal government grants gifts to foreign nations, foreign residents give gifts to U.S. residents, and some foreign governments have granted funds to the U.S. government. In the current account, we see that net unilateral transfers—the total amount of gifts given by U.S. residents and the government minus the total amount received from abroad by U.S. residents and the government—came to an estimated −$70.1 billion in 2004 (line 8). The fact that there is a minus sign before the number for unilateral transfers means that U.S. residents gave more to foreign residents than foreign residents gave to U.S. residents.

Balancing the Current Account. The balance on current account tracks the value of a country's exports of goods and services (including military receipts plus income on investments abroad) and transfer payments (private and government) relative to the value of that country's imports of goods and services and transfer payments (private and government). In 2004, it was estimated to be −$581.2 billion.

Go to www.econtoday.com/chap34 for the latest U.S. balance of payments data from the Bureau of Economic Analysis.

If the sum of net exports of goods and services plus net unilateral transfers plus net investment income exceeds zero, a **current account surplus** *is said to exist; if this sum is negative, a* **current account deficit** *is said to exist. A* **current account deficit** *means that we are importing more goods and services than we are exporting. Such a deficit must be paid for by the export of money or money equivalent, which means a capital account surplus.*

Capital Account Transactions

Capital account
A category of balance of payments transactions that measures flows of real and financial assets.

In world markets, it is possible to buy and sell not only goods and services but also real and financial assets. These are the international transactions measured in the **capital accounts**. Capital account transactions occur because of foreign investments—either by foreign residents investing in the United States or by U.S. residents investing in other countries. The purchase of shares of stock in British firms on the London stock market by a U.S. resident causes an outflow of funds from the United States to Britain. The building of a Japanese automobile factory in the United States causes an inflow of funds from Japan to the United States. Any time foreign residents buy U.S. government securities, there is an inflow of funds from other countries to the United States. Any time U.S. residents buy foreign government securities, there is an outflow of funds from the United States to other countries. Loans to and from foreign residents cause outflows and inflows.

Line 10 of Table 34-2 on the previous page indicates that in 2004, the value of private capital going out of the United States was an estimated −$795.1 billion, and line 11 shows that the value of private capital coming into the United States (including a statistical discrepancy) was $1,137.4 billion. U.S. capital going abroad constitutes payments or outflows and is therefore negative. Foreign capital coming into the United States constitutes receipts or inflows and is therefore positive. Thus there was a positive net capital movement of $342.3 billion into the United States (line 12). This net private flow of capital is also called the balance on capital account.

There is a relationship between the current account and the capital account, assuming no interventions by the finance ministries or central banks of nations.

> *In the absence of interventions by finance ministries or central banks, the current account and the capital account must sum to zero. Stated differently, the current account deficit must equal the capital account surplus when governments or central banks do not engage in foreign exchange interventions. In this situation, any nation experiencing a current account deficit, such as the United States, must also be running a capital account surplus.*

This basic relationship is apparent in the United States, as you can see in Figure 34-1.

FIGURE 34-1
The Relationship Between the Current Account and the Capital Account

To some extent, the capital account is the mirror image of the current account. We can see this in the years since 1970. When the current account was in surplus, the capital account was in deficit. When the current account was in deficit, the capital account was in surplus. Indeed, virtually the only time foreign residents can invest in the United States is when the current account is in deficit.

Sources: International Monetary Fund; *Economic Indicators.*

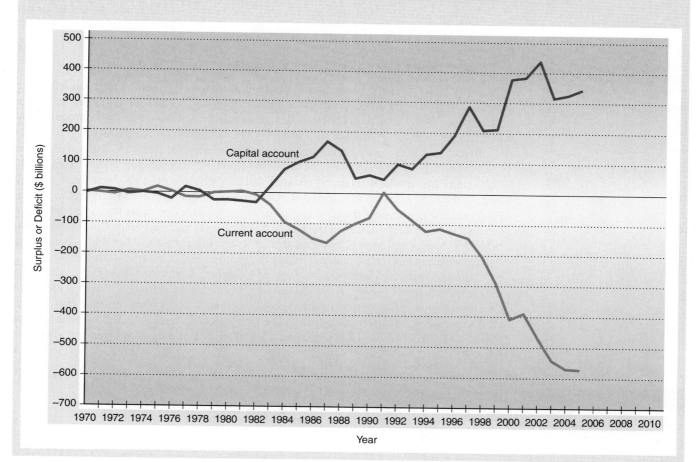

Official Reserve Account Transactions

The third type of balance of payments transaction concerns official reserve assets, which consist of the following:

Special drawing rights (SDRs)
Reserve assets created by the International Monetary Fund for countries to use in settling international payment obligations.

International Monetary Fund
An agency founded to administer an international foreign exchange system and to lend to member countries that had balance of payments problems. The IMF now functions as a lender of last resort for national governments.

1. Foreign currencies
2. Gold
3. **Special drawing rights (SDRs),** which are reserve assets that the **International Monetary Fund** created to be used by countries to settle international payment obligations
4. The reserve position in the International Monetary Fund
5. Financial assets held by an official agency, such as the U.S. Treasury Department

To consider how official reserve account transactions occur, look again at Table 34-2 on page 803. The surplus in the U.S. capital account was $342.3 billion. But the deficit in the U.S. current account was −$581.2 billion, so the United States had a net deficit on the combined accounts (line 13) of −$238.9 billion. In other words, the United States obtained less in foreign funds in all its international transactions than it used. How is this deficiency made up? By foreign central banks adding to their U.S. funds, shown by the +$238.9 billion in official transactions on line 14 in Table 34-2. There is a plus sign on line 14 because this represents an *inflow* of foreign exchange in our international transactions.

The balance (line 15) in Table 34-2 is zero, as it must be with double-entry bookkeeping. The U.S. balance of payments deficit is measured by the official transactions figure on line 14.

What Affects the Balance of Payments?

A major factor affecting any nation's balance of payments is its rate of inflation relative to that of its trading partners. Assume that the rates of inflation in the United States and in the European Monetary Union (EMU)—the nations that use the euro as their currency—are equal. Now suppose that all of a sudden, the U.S. inflation rate increases. EMU residents will find that U.S. products are becoming more expensive, and U.S. firms will export fewer of them to EMU nations. At the current dollar-euro exchange rate, U.S. residents will find EMU products relatively cheaper, and they will import more. The reverse will occur if the U.S. inflation rate suddenly falls relative to that of the EMU. All other things held constant, whenever the U.S. rate of inflation exceeds that of its trading partners, we expect to see a larger deficit in the U.S. balance of trade and payments. Conversely, when the U.S. rate of inflation is less than that of its trading partners, other things being constant, we expect to see a smaller deficit in the U.S. balance of trade and payments.

Another important factor that sometimes influences a nation's balance of payments is its relative political stability. Political instability causes *capital flight*. Owners of capital in countries anticipating or experiencing political instability will often move assets to countries that are politically stable, such as the United States. Hence the U.S. capital account balance is likely to increase whenever political instability looms in other nations in the world.

CONCEPTS in Brief

- The balance of payments reflects the value of all transactions in international trade, including goods, services, financial assets, and gifts.

- The merchandise trade balance gives us the difference between exports and imports of tangible items. Merchandise trade transactions are represented by exports and imports of tangible items.

- Included in the current account along with merchandise trade are service exports and imports relating to commerce in intangible items, such as shipping, insurance, and tourist expenditures. The current account also includes income earned by foreign residents on U.S. investments and income earned by U.S. residents on foreign investments.

- Unilateral transfers involve international private gifts and federal government grants or gifts to foreign nations.

- When we add the balance of merchandise trade and the balance of services and take account of net unilateral transfers and net investment income, we come up with the balance on the current account, a summary statistic.

- There are also capital account transactions that relate to the buying and selling of financial and real assets. Foreign capital is always entering the United States, and U.S. capital is always flowing abroad. The difference is called the balance on capital account.

- Another type of balance of payments transaction concerns the official reserve assets of individual countries, or what is often simply called official transactions. By standard accounting convention, official transactions are exactly equal to a nation's balance of payments but opposite in sign.

- A nation's balance of payments can be affected by its relative rate of inflation and by its political stability relative to other nations.

To test your understanding of the concepts covered in this section, go to the Online Review at www.myeconlab.com/miller.

DETERMINING FOREIGN EXCHANGE RATES

When you buy foreign products, such as a Japanese-made laptop computer, you have dollars with which to pay the Japanese manufacturer. The Japanese manufacturer, however, cannot pay workers in dollars. The workers are Japanese, they live in Japan, and they must have yen to buy goods and services in that country. There must therefore be some way of exchanging dollars for yen that the computer manufacturer will accept. That exchange occurs in a **foreign exchange market,** which in this case involves the exchange of yen and dollars.

The particular **exchange rate** between yen and dollars that prevails—the dollar price of the yen—depends on the current demand for and supply of yen and dollars. In a sense, then, our analysis of the exchange rate between dollars and yen will be familiar, for we have used supply and demand throughout this book. If it costs you 1 cent to buy 1 yen, that is the foreign exchange rate determined by the current demand for and supply of yen in the foreign exchange market. The Japanese person going to the foreign exchange market would need 100 yen to buy 1 dollar.

Now let's consider what determines the demand for and supply of foreign currency in the foreign exchange market. We will continue to assume that the only two countries in the world are Japan and the United States.

Demand for and Supply of Foreign Currency

You wish to purchase a Japanese-made laptop computer directly from the manufacturer. To do so, you must have Japanese yen. You go to the foreign exchange market (or your U.S. bank). Your desire to buy the Japanese laptop computer therefore causes you to offer (supply) dollars to the foreign exchange market. Your demand for Japanese yen is equivalent to your supply of U.S. dollars to the foreign exchange market.

> *Every U.S. transaction involving the importation of foreign goods constitutes a supply of dollars and a demand for some foreign currency, and the opposite is true for export transactions.*

In this case, the import transaction constitutes a demand for Japanese yen.

In our example, we will assume that only two goods are being traded, Japanese laptop computers and U.S. microprocessors. The U.S. demand for Japanese laptop computers

Foreign exchange market
A market in which households, firms, and governments buy and sell national currencies.

Exchange rate
The price of one nation's currency in terms of the currency of another country.

creates a supply of dollars and demand for yen in the foreign exchange market. Similarly, the Japanese demand for U.S. microprocessors creates a supply of yen and a demand for dollars in the foreign exchange market. Under a system of **flexible exchange rates,** the supply of and demand for dollars and yen in the foreign exchange market will determine the equilibrium foreign exchange rate. The equilibrium exchange rate will tell us how many yen a dollar can be exchanged for—that is, the dollar price of yen—or how many dollars (or fractions of a dollar) a yen can be exchanged for—the yen price of dollars.

The Equilibrium Foreign Exchange Rate

To determine the equilibrium foreign exchange rate, we have to find out what determines the demand for and supply of foreign exchange. We will ignore for the moment any speculative aspect of buying foreign exchange. That is, we assume that there are no individuals who wish to buy yen simply because they think that their price will go up in the future.

The idea of an exchange rate is no different from the idea of paying a certain price for something you want to buy. If you like coffee, you know you have to pay about 75 cents a cup. If the price went up to $2.50, you would probably buy fewer cups. If the price went down to 25 cents, you might buy more. In other words, the demand curve for cups of coffee, expressed in terms of dollars, slopes downward following the law of demand. The demand curve for yen slopes downward also, and we will see why.

Let's think more closely about the demand schedule for yen. Let's say that it costs you 1 cent to purchase 1 yen; that is the exchange rate between dollars and yen. If tomorrow you had to pay $1\frac{1}{4}$ cents ($0.0125) for the same yen, the exchange rate would have changed. Looking at such a change, we would say that there has been an **appreciation** in the value of the yen in the foreign exchange market. But another way to view this increase in the value of the yen is to say that there has been a **depreciation** in the value of the dollar in the foreign exchange market. The dollar used to buy 100 yen; tomorrow, the dollar will be able to buy only 80 yen at a price of $1\frac{1}{4}$ cents per yen. If the dollar price of yen rises, you will probably demand fewer yen. Why? The answer lies in looking at the reason you and others demand yen in the first place.

How do you suppose that a significant appreciation of the euro relative to the dollar affects U.S. imports of French wines?

International EXAMPLE

The Euro's Value Is Up, So French Wine Exports Are Down

Between 2002 and 2005, French wine exports to the United States dropped by nearly 18 percent. Some wine experts blamed part of the decline on what they perceived to be a drop in the overall quality of French wines. Others argued that during the 2001–2002 recession, U.S. residents seeking lower-priced wines had developed a taste for less expensive home-grown varieties. A few media commentators even attributed the drop to U.S. residents' unhappiness with the French government's foreign policies.

Economists offered a more fundamental explanation. During 2003, the dollar depreciated by almost 20 percent relative to the euro. Even if the euro price of a bottle of an elite

French Bordeaux wine held steady at around €200 between 2002 and 2003, U.S. residents had to give up nearly 20 percent more dollars to purchase it. The effective increase in the U.S. price of French wines generated a reduction in the quantity demanded by U.S. residents. Thus French wine exports to the United States declined.

For Critical Analysis
What do you predict will happen, other things being equal, to French exports of wine to the United States if the dollar appreciates considerably in relation to the euro?

Flexible exchange rates
Exchange rates that are allowed to fluctuate in the open market in response to changes in supply and demand. Sometimes called *floating exchange rates.*

Go to www.econtoday.com/chap34 for recent data from the Federal Reserve Bank of St. Louis on the exchange value of the U.S. dollar relative to the major currencies of the world.

Appreciation
An increase in the exchange value of one nation's currency in terms of the currency of another nation.

Depreciation
A decrease in the exchange value of one nation's currency in terms of the currency of another nation.

Appreciation and Depreciation of Japanese Yen. Recall that in our example, you and others demand yen to buy Japanese laptop computers. The demand curve for Japanese laptop computers, we will assume, follows the law of demand and therefore slopes downward. If it costs more U.S. dollars to buy the same quantity of Japanese laptop computers, presumably you and other U.S. residents will not buy the same quantity; your quantity demanded will be less. We say that your demand for Japanese yen is *derived from* your demand for Japanese laptop computers. In panel (a) of Figure 34-2 on the next page, we present the hypothetical demand schedule for Japanese laptop computers by a representative set of U.S. consumers during a typical week. In panel (b), we show graphically the U.S. demand curve for Japanese yen in terms of U.S. dollars taken from panel (a).

An Example of Derived Demand. Let us assume that the price of a Japanese laptop computer in Japan is 100,000 yen. Given that price, we can find the number of yen required to purchase up to 500 Japanese laptop computers. That information is given in panel (c) of Figure 34-2. If purchasing one laptop computer requires 100,000 yen, 500 laptop computers require 50 million yen. Now we have enough information to determine the derived demand curve for Japanese yen. If 1 yen costs 1 cent, a laptop computer would cost $1,000 (100,000 yen per computer × 1 cent per yen = $1,000 per computer). At $1,000 per computer, the representative group of U.S. consumers would, we see from panel (a) of Figure 34-2, demand 500 laptop computers.

From panel (c), we see that 50 million yen would be demanded to buy the 500 laptop computers. We show this quantity demanded in panel (d). In panel (e), we draw the derived demand curve for yen. Now consider what happens if the price of yen goes up to $1\frac{1}{4}$ cents ($0.0125). A Japanese laptop computer priced at 100,000 yen in Japan would now cost $1,250. From panel (a), we see that at $1,250 per computer, 300 laptop computers will be imported from Japan into the United States by our representative group of U.S. consumers. From panel (c), we see that 300 computers would require 30 million yen to be purchased; thus, in panels (d) and (e), we see that at a price of $1\frac{1}{4}$ cents per yen, the quantity demanded will be 30 million yen.

We continue similar calculations all the way up to a price of $1\frac{1}{2}$ cents ($0.0150) per yen. At that price, a Japanese laptop computer costing 100,000 yen in Japan would cost $1,500, and our representative U.S. consumers would import only 100 laptop computers.

Downward-Sloping Derived Demand. As can be expected, as the price of yen rises, the quantity demanded will fall. The only difference here from the standard demand analysis developed in Chapter 3 and used throughout this text is that the demand for yen is derived from the demand for a final product—Japanese laptop computers in our example.

Supply of Japanese Yen. Assume that Japanese laptop manufacturers buy U.S. microprocessors. The supply of Japanese yen is a derived supply in that it is derived from the Japanese demand for U.S. microprocessors. We could go through an example similar to the one for laptop computers to come up with a supply schedule of Japanese yen in Japan. It slopes upward. Obviously, the Japanese want dollars to purchase U.S. goods. Japanese residents will be willing to supply more yen when the dollar price of yen goes up, because they can then buy more U.S. goods with the same quantity of yen. That is, the yen would be worth more in exchange for U.S. goods than when the dollar price for yen was lower.

An Example. Let's take an example. Suppose a U.S.-produced microprocessor costs $200. If the exchange rate is 1 cent per yen, a Japanese resident will have to come up with 20,000 yen (= $200 at $0.0100 per yen) to buy one microprocessor. If, however, the exchange rate goes up to $1\frac{1}{4}$ cents for yen, a Japanese resident must come up with only

Panel (a)
**Demand Schedule for Japanese Laptop
Computers in the United States per Week**

Price per Unit	Quantity Demanded
$1,500	100
1,250	300
1,000	500
750	700

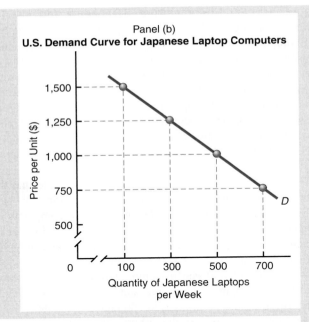

Panel (b)
U.S. Demand Curve for Japanese Laptop Computers

Panel (c)
**Yen Required to Purchase Quantity Demanded
(at *P* = 100,000 yen per computer)**

Quantity Demanded	Yen Required (millions)
100	10
300	30
500	50
700	70

Panel (d)
**Derived Demand Schedule for Yen in the
United States with Which to Pay for Imports of Laptops**

Dollar Price of One Yen	Dollar Price of Computers	Quantity of Computers Demanded	Quantity of Yen Demanded per Week (millions)
$ 0.0150	$1,500	100	10
0.0125	1,250	300	30
0.0100	1,000	500	50
0.0075	750	700	70

FIGURE 34-2
Deriving the Demand for Yen
In panel (a), we show the demand schedule for Japanese laptop computers in the United States, expressed in terms of
dollars per computer. In panel (b), we show the demand
curve, *D*, which slopes downward. In panel (c), we show the
number of yen required to purchase up to 700 laptop computers. If the price per laptop computer in Japan is 100,000
yen, we can now find the quantity of yen needed to pay for
the various quantities demanded. In panel (d), we see the
derived demand for yen in the United States in order to
purchase the various quantities of computers given in panel
(a). The resultant demand curve, D_1, is shown in panel (e).
This is the U.S. derived demand for yen.

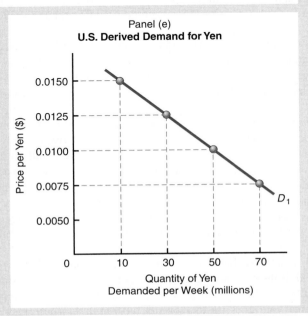

Panel (e)
U.S. Derived Demand for Yen

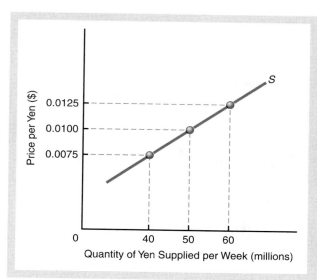

FIGURE 34-3
The Supply of Japanese Yen
If the market price of a U.S.-produced microprocessor is $200, then at an exchange rate of $0.0100 per yen (1 cent per yen), the price of the microprocessor to a Japanese consumer is 20,000 yen. If the exchange rate rises to $0.0125 per yen, the Japanese price of the microprocessor falls to 16,000 yen. This induces an increase in the quantity of microprocessors demanded by Japanese consumers and consequently an increase in the quantity of yen supplied in exchange for dollars in the foreign exchange market. In contrast, if the exchange rate falls to $0.0075 per yen, the Japanese price of the microprocessor rises to 26,667 yen. This causes a decrease in the quantity of microprocessors demanded by Japanese consumers. As a result, there is a decline in the quantity of yen supplied in exchange for dollars in the foreign exchange market.

16,000 yen (= $200 at $0.0125 per yen) to buy a U.S. microprocessor. At this lower price (in yen) of U.S. microprocessors, the Japanese will demand a larger quantity. In other words, as the price of yen goes up in terms of dollars, the quantity of U.S. microprocessors demanded will go up, and hence the quantity of yen supplied will go up. Therefore, the supply schedule of yen, which is derived from the Japanese demand for U.S. goods, will slope upward.*

We could easily work through a detailed numerical example to show that the supply curve of Japanese yen slopes upward. Rather than do that, we will simply draw it as upward sloping in Figure 34-3.

Total Demand for and Supply of Japanese Yen. Let us now look at the total demand for and supply of Japanese yen. We take all consumers of Japanese laptop computer and of U.S. microprocessors and put their demands for and supplies of yen together into one diagram. Thus we are showing the total demand for and total supply of Japanese yen. The horizontal axis in Figure 34-4 on the following page represents the quantity of foreign exchange—the number of yen per year. The vertical axis represents the exchange rate—the price of foreign currency (yen) expressed in dollars (per yen). The foreign currency price of $0.0125 per yen means it will cost you $1\frac{1}{4}$ cents to buy 1 yen. At the foreign currency price of $0.0100 per yen, you know that it will cost you 1 cent to buy 1 yen. The equilibrium, *E*, is again established at 1 cent for 1 yen.

In our hypothetical example, assuming that there are only representative groups of laptop computer consumers in the United States and microprocessor consumers in Japan, the equilibrium exchange rate will be set at 1 cent per yen, or 100 yen to one dollar.

---

*Actually, the supply schedule of foreign currency will be upward sloping if we assume that the demand for U.S. imported microprocessors on the part of the Japanese is price-elastic. If the demand schedule for microprocessors is inelastic, the supply schedule will be negatively sloped. In the case of unit elasticity of demand, the supply schedule for yen will be a vertical line. Throughout the rest of this chapter, we will assume that demand is price-elastic. It turns out that the price elasticity of demand tells us whether total expenditures by microprocessors purchasers in Japan will rise or fall when the yen drops in value. In the long run, it is quite realistic to think that the price elasticity of demand for imports is numerically greater than 1 anyway.

FIGURE 34-4

Total Demand for and Supply of Japanese Yen

The market supply curve for Japanese yen results from the total demand for U.S. microprocessors. The demand curve, D, slopes downward like most demand curves, and the supply curve, S, slopes upward. The foreign exchange price, or the U.S. dollar price of yen, is given on the vertical axis. The number of yen is represented on the horizontal axis. If the foreign exchange rate is $0.0125—that is, if it takes $1\frac{1}{4}$ cents to buy 1 yen—U.S. residents will demand 2 trillion yen. The equilibrium exchange rate is at the intersection of D and S, or point E. The equilibrium exchange rate is $0.0100 (1 cent). At this point, 3 trillion yen are both demanded and supplied each year.

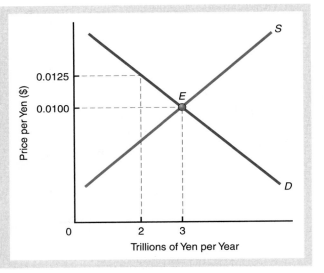

This equilibrium is not established because U.S. residents like to buy yen or because the Japanese like to buy dollars. Rather, the equilibrium exchange rate depends on how many microprocessors the Japanese want and how many Japanese laptop computers U.S. residents want (given their respective incomes, their tastes, and the relative price of laptop computers and microprocessors).*

A Shift in Demand. Assume that a successful advertising campaign by U.S. computer importers has caused U.S. demand for Japanese laptop computers to rise. U.S. residents demand more laptop computers at all prices. Their demand curve for Japanese laptop computers has shifted outward to the right.

The increased demand for Japanese laptop computers can be translated into an increased demand for yen. All U.S. residents clamoring for Japanese laptop computers will supply more dollars to the foreign exchange market while demanding more Japanese yen to pay for the computers. Figure 34-5 presents a new demand schedule, D_2, for Japanese yen; this demand schedule is to the right of the original demand schedule. If the Japanese do not change their desire for U.S. microprocessors, the supply schedule for Japanese yen will remain stable.

A new equilibrium will be established at a higher exchange rate. In our particular example, the new equilibrium is established at an exchange rate of $0.0120 per yen. It now takes 1.2 cents to buy 1 Japanese yen, whereas formerly it took 1 cent. This will be translated into an increase in the price of Japanese laptop computers to U.S. residents and as a decrease in the price of U.S. microprocessors to the Japanese. For example, a Japanese laptop computer priced at 100,000 yen that sold for $1,000 in the United States will now be priced at $1,200. Conversely, a U.S. microprocessor priced at $50 that previously sold for 5,000 yen in Japan will now sell for 4,167 yen.

What do you think has happened to the dollar price of South Africa's currency, the rand, as a result of increases in world demand for South African goods and financial assets?

---

*Remember that we are dealing with a two-country world in which we are considering only the exchange of U.S. microprocessors and Japanese laptop computers. In the real world, more than just goods and services are exchanged among countries. Some U.S. residents buy Japanese financial assets; some Japanese residents buy U.S. financial assets. We are ignoring such transactions for the moment.

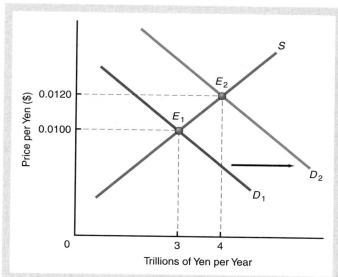

FIGURE 34-5
A Shift in the Demand Schedule
The demand schedule for Japanese laptop computers shifts to the right, causing the derived demand schedule for yen to shift to the right also. We have shown this as a shift from D_1 to D_2. We have assumed that the Japanese supply schedule for yen has remained stable—that is, Japanese demand for U.S. microprocessors has remained constant. The old equilibrium foreign exchange rate was $0.0100 (1 cent). The new equilibrium exchange rate will be E_2. It will now cost $0.0120 (1.2 cents) to buy 1 yen. The higher price of yen will be translated into a higher U.S. dollar price for Japanese laptop computers and a lower Japanese yen price for U.S. microprocessors.

International EXAMPLE

South Africa's Currency Appreciation

The global demand for gold and platinum, which are key South African export goods, has increased significantly since the end of 2001. In addition, South African interest rates rose relative to many other nations' interest rates after 2001, which induced residents of other nations to hold more South African financial assets. As people outside South Africa have sought to acquire more of its gold, platinum, and financial assets, the demand for its currency, the rand, has also increased. The result has been an increase in the dollar price of the rand. At the end of 2001, the rand's dollar price was only about $7\frac{1}{2}$ cents. Today, it is more than twice as high, at nearly $15\frac{1}{2}$ cents.

For Critical Analysis
As the rand's dollar price has increased, what has happened to the dollar price of gold and platinum produced in South Africa?

A Shift in Supply. We just assumed that the U.S. demand for Japanese laptop computers had shifted due to a successful ad campaign. Because the demand for Japanese yen is a derived demand by U.S. residents for laptop computers, this is translated into a shift in the demand curve for yen. As an alternative exercise, we might assume that the supply curve of Japanese yen shifts outward to the right. Such a supply shift could occur for many reasons, one of which is a relative rise in the Japanese price level. For example, if the prices of all Japanese-manufactured computer components went up 100 percent in yen, U.S. microprocessors would become relatively cheaper. That would mean that Japanese residents would want to buy more U.S. microprocessors. But remember that when they want to buy more U.S. microprocessors, they supply more yen to the foreign exchange market.

Thus we see in Figure 34-6 (p. 814) that the supply curve of Japanese yen moves from S to S_1. In the absence of restrictions—that is, in a system of flexible exchange rates—the new equilibrium exchange rate will be 1 yen equals $0.0050, or $\frac{1}{2}$ cent equals 1 yen. The quantity of yen demanded and supplied will increase from 3 trillion per year to 5 trillion

> **Economics Front and Center**
>
> To contemplate whether governments' announcements of their *preferred* levels of exchange rates can influence *actual* levels of exchange rates, read the case study, **Can Government Statements Move Exchange Rates?** on page 820.

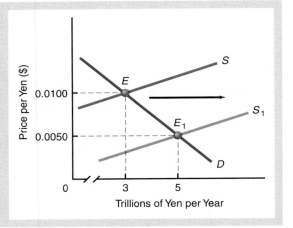

FIGURE 34-6
A Shift in the Supply of Japanese Yen
There has been a shift in the supply curve for Japanese yen. The new equilibrium will occur at E_1, meaning that $0.0050 ($\frac{1}{2}$ cent), rather than $0.0100 (1 cent), will now buy 1 yen. After the exchange rate adjustment, the annual amount of yen demanded and supplied will increase from 3 trillion to 5 trillion.

per year. We say, then, that in a flexible international exchange rate system, shifts in the demand for and supply of foreign currencies will cause changes in the equilibrium foreign exchange rates. Those rates will remain in effect until supply or demand shifts.

Market Determinants of Exchange Rates

The foreign exchange market is affected by many other variables in addition to changes in relative price levels, including the following:

● *Changes in real interest rates.* If the U.S. interest rate, corrected for people's expectations of inflation, abruptly increases relative to the rest of the world, international investors elsewhere will increase their demand for dollar-denominated assets, thereby increasing the demand for dollars in foreign exchange markets. An increased demand for dollars in foreign exchange markets, other things held constant, will cause the dollar to appreciate and other currencies to depreciate.

● *Changes in productivity.* Whenever one country's productivity increases relative to another's, the former country will become more price-competitive in world markets. At lower prices, the quantity of its exports demanded will increase. Thus there will be an increase in the demand for its currency.

● *Changes in consumer preferences.* If Germany's citizens suddenly develop a taste for U.S.-made automobiles, this will increase the derived demand for U.S. dollars in foreign exchange markets.

● *Perceptions of economic stability.* As already mentioned, if the United States looks economically and politically more stable relative to other countries, more foreign residents will want to put their savings into U.S. assets than in their own domestic assets. This will increase the demand for dollars.

CONCEPTS in Brief

● The foreign exchange rate is the rate at which one country's currency can be exchanged for another's.

● The demand for foreign exchange is a derived demand; it is derived from the demand for foreign goods and services

(and financial assets). The supply of foreign exchange is derived from foreign residents' demands for domestic goods and services.

- The demand curve of foreign exchange slopes downward, and the supply curve of foreign exchange slopes upward. The equilibrium foreign exchange rate occurs at the intersection of the demand and supply curves for a currency.

- A shift in the demand for foreign goods will result in a shift in the demand for foreign exchange, thereby changing the equilibrium foreign exchange rate. A shift in the supply of foreign currency will also cause a change in the equilibrium exchange rate.

To test your understanding of the concepts covered in this section, go to the Online Review at **www.myeconlab.com/miller.**

THE GOLD STANDARD AND THE INTERNATIONAL MONETARY FUND

The current system of more or less freely floating exchange rates is a recent development. We have had, in the past, periods of a gold standard, fixed exchange rates under the International Monetary Fund, and variants of the two.

The Gold Standard

Until the 1930s, many nations were on a gold standard. The value of their domestic currency was tied directly to gold. Nations operating under this gold standard agreed to redeem their currencies for a fixed amount of gold at the request of any holder of that currency. Although gold was not necessarily the means of exchange for world trade, it was the unit to which all currencies under the gold standard were pegged. And because all currencies in the system were linked to gold, exchange rates between those currencies were fixed. Indeed, the gold standard has been offered as the prototype of a fixed exchange rate system. The heyday of the gold standard was from about 1870 to 1914.

There was (and always is) a relationship between the balance of payments and changes in domestic money supplies throughout the world. Under a gold standard, the international financial market reached equilibrium through the effect of gold flows on each country's money supply. When a nation suffered a deficit in its balance of payments, more gold would flow out than in. Because the domestic money supply was based on gold, an outflow of gold to foreign residents caused an automatic reduction in the domestic money supply. This caused several things to happen. Interest rates rose, thereby attracting foreign capital and reducing any deficit in the balance of payments. At the same time, the reduction in the money supply was equivalent to a restrictive monetary policy, which caused national output and prices to fall. Imports were discouraged and exports were encouraged, thereby again increasing net exports.

Two problems plagued the gold standard. One was that by varying the value of its currency in response to changes in the quantity of gold, a nation gave up control of its domestic monetary policy. Another was that the world's commerce was at the mercy of gold discoveries. Throughout history, each time new veins of gold were found, desired expenditures on goods and services increased. If production of goods and services failed to increase proportionately, inflation resulted.

Bretton Woods and the International Monetary Fund

In 1944, as World War II was ending, representatives from the world's capitalist countries met in Bretton Woods, New Hampshire, to create a new international payment system to replace the gold standard, which had collapsed during the 1930s. The Bretton Woods Agreement Act was signed on July 31, 1945, by President Harry Truman. It created a new permanent institution, the International Monetary Fund (IMF), to administer the agreement and to lend to member countries that were experiencing significant balance of payments deficits. The arrangements thus provided are now called the old IMF system or the Bretton Woods system.

Member governments maintained the value of their currencies within 1 percent of the declared **par value**—the officially determined value. The United States, which owned most of the world's gold stock, was similarly obligated to maintain gold prices within a 1 percent margin of the official rate of $35 an ounce. Except for a transitional arrangement permitting a one-time adjustment of up to 10 percent in par value, members could alter exchange rates thereafter only with the approval of the IMF.

On August 15, 1971, President Richard Nixon suspended the convertibility of the dollar into gold. On December 18, 1971, the United States officially devalued the dollar—that is, lowered its official value—relative to the currencies of 14 major industrial nations. Finally, on March 16, 1973, the finance ministers of the European Economic Community (now the European Union) announced that they would let their currencies float against the dollar, something Japan had already begun doing with its yen. Since 1973, the United States and most other trading countries have had either freely floating exchange rates or managed ("dirty") floating exchange rates, in which their governments or central banks intervene from time to time to try to influence world market exchange rates.

FIXED VERSUS FLOATING EXCHANGE RATES

The United States went off the Bretton Woods system of fixed exchange rates in 1973. As Figure 34-7 indicates, many other nations of the world have been less willing to permit the values of their currencies to vary in the foreign exchange markets.

Fixing the Exchange Rate

How did nations fix their exchange rates in years past? How do many countries accomplish this today? Figure 34-8 shows the market for ringgit, the currency of Malaysia. At the initial equilibrium point E_1, U.S. residents had to give up $0.263 (26.3 cents) to obtain 1 ringgit. Suppose now that there is an increase in the supply of ringgit for dollars, perhaps because Malaysian residents wish to buy more U.S. goods. Other things being equal, the result would be a movement to point E_2 in Figure 34-8. The dollar value of the ringgit would fall to $0.200 (20 cents).

Par value
The officially determined value of a currency.

FIGURE 34-7
Current Foreign Exchange Rate Arrangements
Currently, 22 percent of the member nations of the International Monetary Fund have an independent float, and just over 22 percent have a managed float exchange rate arrangement. Among countries with a fixed exchange rate, more than 33 percent uses a fixed U.S. dollar exchange rate. Slightly over 21 percent of all nations use the currencies of other nations instead of issuing their own currencies.

Source: International Monetary Fund.

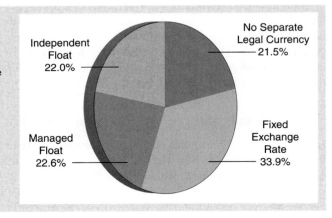

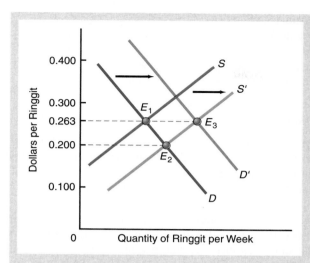

FIGURE 34-8
A Fixed Exchange Rate
This figure illustrates how the Bank of Malaysia could fix the dollar-ringgit exchange rate in the face of an increase in the supply of ringgit caused by a rise in the demand for U.S. goods by Malaysian residents. In the absence of any action by the Bank of Malaysia, the result would be a movement from point E_1 to point E_2. The dollar value of the ringgit would fall from $0.263 to $0.200. The Bank of Malaysia can prevent this exchange rate change by purchasing ringgit with dollars in the foreign exchange market, thereby raising the demand for ringgit. At the new equilibrium point, E_3, the ringgit's value remains at $0.263.

To prevent a ringgit depreciation from occurring, however, the Bank of Malaysia, the central bank, could increase the demand for ringgit in the foreign exchange market by purchasing ringgit with dollars. The Bank of Malaysia can do this using dollars that it has on hand as part of its *foreign exchange reserves*. All central banks hold reserves of foreign currencies. Because the U.S. dollar is a key international currency, the Bank of Malaysia and other central banks typically hold billions of dollars in reserve so that they can make transactions such as the one in this example. Note that a sufficiently large purchase of ringgit could, as shown in Figure 34-8, cause the demand curve to shift rightward to achieve the new equilibrium point E_3, at which the ringgit's value remains at $0.263. Provided that it has enough dollar reserves on hand, the Bank of Malaysia could maintain—effectively fix—the exchange rate in the face of the fall in the demand for ringgit.

This is the manner in which the Bank of Malaysia has maintained the dollar-ringgit exchange rate since 1999. This basic approach—varying the amount of the national currency demanded at any given exchange rate in foreign exchange markets when necessary—is also the way that *any* central bank seeks to keep its nation's currency value unchanged in light of changing market forces.

> *Central banks can keep exchange rates fixed as long as they have enough foreign exchange reserves to deal with potentially long-lasting changes in the demand for or supply of their nation's currency.*

What currencies do central banks most prefer to hold?

International EXAMPLE

Central Banks' Currencies of Choice

A central bank allocates its foreign exchange reserves based on its perception of which currencies are likely to prove most useful in altering the demand for its own nation's currency. Nearly 20 percent of all foreign exchange reserves held by all central banks are euros. Just over 15 percent of their foreign exchange reserves are Japanese yen, British pounds, and miscellaneous other currencies not including the U.S. dollar. Dollars account for the remaining 65 percent of all the foreign exchange reserves of all central banks. Clearly, central banks view the dollar as the most useful currency to utilize if they should desire to alter the demand for their respective currencies in the world's foreign exchange markets.

For Critical Analysis
Why might the extent of a foreign currency's use in global trade and finance affect a central bank's willingness to include it among its foreign exchange reserves?

Pros and Cons of a Fixed Exchange Rate

Why might a nation such as Malaysia wish to keep the value of its currency from fluctuating? One reason is that changes in the exchange rate can affect the market values of assets that are denominated in foreign currencies. This can increase the financial risks that a nation's residents face, thereby forcing them to incur costs to avoid these risks.

Foreign exchange risk
The possibility that changes in the value of a nation's currency will result in variations in the market value of assets.

Foreign Exchange Risk. The possibility that variations in the market value of assets can take place as a result of changes in the value of a nation's currency is the **foreign exchange risk** that residents of a country face because their nation's currency value can vary. For instance, if companies in Malaysia had many loans denominated in dollars but earned nearly all their revenues in ringgit from sales within Malaysia, a decline in the dollar value of the ringgit would mean that Malaysian companies would have to allocate a larger portion of their earnings to make the same *dollar* loan payments as before. Thus a fall in the ringgit's value would increase the operating costs of these companies, thereby reducing their profitability and raising the likelihood of eventual bankruptcy.

Limiting foreign exchange risk is a classic rationale for adopting a fixed exchange rate. Nevertheless, a country's residents are not defenseless against foreign exchange risk. In what is known as a **hedge,** they can adopt strategies intended to offset the risk arising from exchange rate variations. For example, a company in Malaysia that has significant euro earnings from sales in Germany but sizable loans from U.S. investors could arrange to convert its euro earnings into dollars via special types of foreign exchange contracts called *currency swaps.* The Malaysian company could likewise avoid holdings of ringgit and shield itself—*hedge*—against variations in the ringgit's value.

Hedge
A financial strategy that reduces the chance of suffering losses arising from foreign exchange risk.

The Exchange Rate as a Shock Absorber. If fixing the exchange rate limits foreign exchange risk, why do so many nations allow the exchange rates to float? The answer must be that there are potential drawbacks associated with fixing exchange rates. One is that exchange rate variations can actually perform a valuable service for a nation's economy. Consider a situation in which residents of a nation speak only their own nation's language. As a result, the country's residents are very *immobile:* They cannot trade their labor skills outside their own nation's borders.

Now think about what happens if this nation chooses to fix its exchange rate. Imagine a situation in which other countries begin to sell products that are close substitutes for the products its people specialize in producing, causing a sizable drop in worldwide demand for the nation's goods. Over a short-run period in which prices and wages cannot adjust, the result will be a sharp decline in production of goods and services, a falloff in national income, and higher unemployment. Contrast this situation with one in which the exchange rate floats. In this case, a sizable decline in outside demand for the nation's products will cause it to experience a trade deficit, which will lead to a significant drop in the demand for that nation's currency. As a result, the nation's currency will experience a sizable depreciation, making the goods that the nation offers to sell abroad much less expensive in other countries. People abroad who continue to consume the nation's products will increase their purchases, and the nation's exports will increase. Its production will begin to recover somewhat, as will its residents' incomes. Unemployment will begin to fall.

This example illustrates how exchange rate variations can be beneficial, especially if a nation's residents are relatively immobile. It can be difficult, for example, for a Polish resident who has never studied Portuguese to make a move to Lisbon, even if she is highly qualified for available jobs there. If many residents of Poland face similar linguistic or cultural barriers, Poland could be better off with a floating exchange rate even if its residents must incur significant costs hedging against foreign exchange risk as a result.

Splitting the Difference: Dirty Floats and Target Zones

In recent years, national policymakers have tried to soften the choice between adopting a fixed exchange rate and allowing exchange rates full flexibility in the foreign exchange markets by "splitting the difference" between the two extremes.

A Dirty Float.
One way to split the difference is to let exchange rates float most of the time but "manage" exchange rate movements part of the time. U.S. policymakers have occasionally engaged in what is called a **dirty float,** the active management of flexible exchange rates. The management of flexible exchange rates has usually come about through international policy cooperation.

Is it possible for nations to "manage" foreign exchange rates? Some economists do not think so. For example, economists Michael Bordo and Anna Schwartz studied the foreign exchange intervention actions coordinated by the Federal Reserve and the U.S. Treasury during the second half of the 1980s. Besides showing that such interventions were sporadic and variable, Bordo and Schwartz came to an even more compelling conclusion: Exchange rate interventions were trivial relative to the total trading of foreign exchange on a daily basis. For example, in April 1989, total foreign exchange trading amounted to $129 billion per day, yet the U.S. central bank purchased only $100 million in deutsche marks and yen during that entire month (and did so on a single day). For all of 1989, Fed purchases of marks and yen were only $17.7 billion, or the equivalent of less than 13 percent of the amount of an average day's trading in April of that year. Their conclusion is that foreign exchange market interventions by the U.S. central bank or the central banks of the other nations do not influence exchange rates in the long run.

Crawling Pegs.
Another approach to splitting the difference between fixed and floating exchange rates is called a **crawling peg.** This is an automatically adjusting target for the value of a nation's currency. For instance, a central bank might announce that it wants the value of its currency relative to the U.S. dollar to decline at an annual rate of 5 percent, a rate of depreciation that it feels is consistent with long-run market forces. The central bank would then try to buy or sell foreign exchange reserves in sufficient quantities to be sure that the currency depreciation takes place gradually, thereby reducing the foreign exchange risk faced by the nation's residents. In this way, a crawling peg functions like a floating exchange rate in the sense that the exchange rate can change over time. But it is like a fixed exchange rate in the sense that the central bank always tries to keep the exchange rate close to a target value. In this way, a crawling peg has elements of both kinds of exchange rate systems.

Target Zones.
A third way to try to split the difference between fixed and floating exchange rates is to adopt an exchange rate **target zone.** Under this policy, a central bank announces that there are specific upper and lower *bands,* or limits, for permissible values for the exchange rate. Within those limits, which define the exchange rate target zone, the central bank permits the exchange rate to move flexibly. The central bank commits itself, however, to intervene in the foreign exchange markets to ensure that its nation's currency value will not rise above the upper band or fall below the lower band. For instance, if the

Dirty float
Active management of a floating exchange rate on the part of a country's government, often in cooperation with other nations.

Crawling peg
An exchange rate arrangement in which a country pegs the value of its currency to the exchange value of another nation's currency but allows the par value to change at regular intervals.

Target zone
A range of permitted exchange rate variations between upper and lower exchange rate bands that a central bank defends by selling or buying foreign exchange reserves.

exchange rate approaches the upper band, the central bank must sell foreign exchange reserves in sufficient quantities to prevent additional depreciation of its nation's currency. If the exchange rate approaches the lower band, the central bank must purchase sufficient amounts of foreign exchange reserves to halt any further currency appreciation.

In 1999, officials from the European Union attempted to get the U.S. and Japanese governments to agree to target zones for the exchange rate between the newly created euro, the dollar, and the yen. So far, however, no target zones have been created, and the euro has floated freely.

Concepts in Brief

- The International Monetary Fund was developed after World War II as an institution to maintain fixed exchange rates in the world. Since 1973, however, fixed exchange rates have disappeared in most major trading countries. For these nations, exchange rates are largely determined by the forces of demand and supply in foreign exchange markets.

- Many other nations, however, have tried to fix their exchange rates, with varying degrees of success. Although fixing the exchange rate helps protect a nation's residents from foreign exchange risk, this policy makes less mobile residents susceptible to greater volatility in income and employment. It can also expose the central bank to spo-

radic currency crises arising from unpredictable changes in world capital flows.

- Countries have experimented with exchange rate systems between the extremes of fixed and floating exchange rates. Under a dirty float, a central bank permits the value of its nation's currency to float in foreign exchange markets but intervenes from time to time to influence the exchange rate. Under a crawling peg, a central bank tries to push its nation's currency value in a desired direction. Pursuing a target zone policy, a central bank aims to keep the exchange rate between upper and lower bands, intervening only when the exchange rate approaches either limit.

To test your understanding of the concepts covered in this section, go to the Online Review at www.myeconlab.com/miller.

CASE STUDY : Economics Front and Center

Can Government Statements Move Exchange Rates?

Martin is an employee of the U.S. Department of the Treasury. He has been assigned to assist the Group of Seven (G-7) finance ministers representing the governments of the United States, Japan, Germany, France, the United Kingdom, Italy, and Canada.

The latest G-7 meeting is under way. The German, French, and Italian finance ministers have proposed that the group issue a joint statement calling on China to allow its currency, the yuan, to rise in value relative to the dollar and the euro. These three finance ministers contend that making this statement will signal to traders in foreign exchange markets that the G-7 governments are serious in their view that there is a need for yuan appreciation. Traders, the finance ministers argue, will respond by purchasing yuan in anticipation of a future increase in the currency's value. Thus the market demand for China's currency will rise, and it will appreciate. In this way, the G-7 nations can bring about the desired outcome without actually having to sell dollars and euros for yuan in foreign exchange markets.

Martin thinks back to 2004, when the G-7 issued an essentially identical statement. What actually occurred afterward was an appreciation of the *euro* relative to both Asian currencies *and* the dollar. Martin wonders if the German, French, and Italian foreign ministers really understand that exchange rates are determined by demand and supply, rather than by politicians' whims.

Points to Analyze

1. *If the German, French, and Italian governments could convince the European Central Bank (ECB) to try to bring about an appreciation of Asian currencies relative to the euro, what would the ECB have to do?*

2. *How might the ECB and the Federal Reserve coordinate efforts to induce appreciations of Asian currencies relative to both the euro and the dollar?*

Japan's Finance Ministry Learns a New Currency Trick

Since 2002, there has been a general tendency for the U.S. dollar to lose value relative to the Japanese yen. This decline in the dollar's value vis-à-vis the yen has effectively raised the prices that U.S. consumers must pay to purchase Japanese goods and services. To try to keep this from occurring, the Japanese government has added billions of dollars to its foreign exchange reserves. The aim of purchasing dollars has been to raise the demand for dollars, increase the dollar's value in terms of yen, and reduce the U.S. prices of Japanese goods and services.

Traditionally, it was easy for economists to tell when the Japanese government was engaging in efforts to prop up the dollar's value in terms of yen. Lately, however, the Japanese government has found ways to hide its efforts to prevent the yen from appreciating.

Concepts Applied
- Exchange Rate
- Foreign Exchange Reserves
- Foreign Exchange Market

Selling Yen to Keep the Dollar–Yen Exchange Rate from Dropping

At first, Japanese efforts to prevent the yen's value from rising relative to the dollar entailed adding more dollars to the nation's roughly $700 billion in total foreign exchange reserves. Offering more yen in exchange for dollars increased the supply of yen in the foreign exchange market, which pushed the equilibrium dollar-yen exchange rate back downward. As a consequence, fewer dollars were required in exchange for yen so that the effective prices that U.S. residents paid for Japanese goods and services were lower once more.

Actions to sell Japanese yen for dollars in the foreign exchange market were coordinated by the Japanese government's Finance Ministry. Sometimes the Finance Ministry would instruct the Bank of Japan to purchase dollars directly on its behalf. At other times, it would direct the Bank of Japan to ask a private Japanese bank to buy dollars on its behalf. After the private bank had completed the transaction, the Finance Ministry would transmit more yen to the bank in exchange for the dollars than the bank had paid for the dollars in the foreign exchange market. In this way, the bank would profit from purchasing the dollars, and the Finance Ministry

would accomplish its aim of increasing the supply of yen in the foreign exchange market.

Inducing Private Banks to Prevent the Yen from Appreciating

In the face of ongoing pressure for a yen appreciation, the Japanese Finance Ministry found itself on the verge of buying dollars, through its accounts with the Bank of Japan or with private banks, almost continually. Because Japan officially had a floating exchange rate, the Finance Ministry did not want to give the impression that it was trying to fix the dollar-yen exchange rate. Therefore, it searched for a way to disguise its efforts to prevent the yen from appreciating.

The method Finance Ministry found entailed operating solely through private banks instead of the Bank of Japan. As before, the Finance Ministry would place an order with a private bank to purchase dollars with yen. It would place a very large order so that other banks would know that the government had to be involved. This caused the other Japanese banks to anticipate a decline in the value of the yen generated by the government's action, which encouraged them to buy dollars in hopes of profiting from selling them after the yen's value had declined. When numerous banks purchased dollars with yen, the yen started to depreciate against the dollar, just as the Finance Ministry desired. In the meantime, the Finance Ministry would cancel its order for the original bank to purchase dollars with yen. This bank would go along because it also would be able to profit from selling dollars for yen after the yen's depreciation.

In this way, neither the Japanese Finance Ministry nor the Bank of Japan was *officially* involved in efforts to prevent a yen appreciation. Foreign exchange market traders knew better, of course, but as long as private banks could profit from the Finance Ministry's actions, they were willing to participate in its not-so-transparent scheme to hide its activities.

For Critical Analysis

1. Why do you suppose that the Japanese Finance Ministry wished to keep the U.S. prices of Japanese-produced goods and services from increasing?
2. Why do you suppose economists commonly argue that actions to move exchange rates in desired directions are successful only if a government and the central bank or private banks operating on its behalf are able to profit from their efforts? (Hint: Would Japanese banks have been willing to sell yen for dollars if they expected that the yen would appreciate in the future?)

Web Resources

1. To read about the Bank of Japan's own perspective on its numerous foreign exchange interventions over the years, go to www.econtoday.com/chap34.
2. Go to the link available at www.econtoday.com/chap34 to learn more about U.S. interventions in foreign exchange markets from the Federal Reserve Bank of New York.

Research Project

Make a list of factors that are likely to influence whether a government's effort to alter the exchange value of its currency is likely to succeed in the near term. Why are the short-run effects of such efforts likely to be more pronounced than the long-run effects? Explain.

SUMMARY DISCUSSION of Learning Objectives

1. **The Balance of Trade versus the Balance of Payments:** The balance of trade is the difference between exports of goods and imports of goods during a given period. The balance of payments is a system of accounts for all transactions between a nation's residents and the residents of other countries of the world. In addition to exports and imports, therefore, the balance of payments includes cross-border exchanges of services and financial assets within a given time interval.

2. **The Key Accounts Within the Balance of Payments:** There are three important accounts within the balance of payments. The current account measures net exchanges of goods and services, transfers, and income flows across a nation's borders. The capital account measures net flows of financial assets. The official reserve transactions account tabulates cross-border exchanges of financial assets involving the home nation's government and central bank as well as foreign governments and central banks.

Because each international exchange generates both an inflow and an outflow, the sum of the balances on all three accounts must equal zero.

3. **Exchange Rate Determination in the Market for Foreign Exchange:** From the perspective of the United States, the demand for a nation's currency by U.S. residents is derived largely from the demand for imports from that nation. Likewise, the supply of a nation's currency is derived mainly from the supply of U.S. exports to that country. The equilibrium exchange rate is the rate of exchange between the dollar and the other nation's currency at which the quantity of the currency demanded is equal to the quantity supplied.

4. **Factors That Can Induce Changes in Equilibrium Exchange Rates:** The equilibrium exchange rate changes in response to changes in the demand for or supply of another nation's currency. Changes in desired flows of exports or imports, real interest rates, productivity in one

nation relative to productivity in another nation, tastes and preferences of consumers, and perceptions of economic stability are key factors that can affect the positions of the demand and supply curves in foreign exchange markets. Thus changes in these factors can induce variations in equilibrium exchange rates.

5. **How Policymakers Can Attempt to Keep Exchange Rates Fixed:** If the current price of another nation's currency in terms of the home currency starts to fall below the level where the home country wants it to remain, the home country's central bank can use reserves of the other nation's currency to purchase the home currency in foreign exchange markets. This raises the demand for the home currency and thereby pushes up the currency's

value in terms of the other nation's currency. In this way, the home country can keep the exchange rate fixed at a desired value, as long as it has sufficient reserves of the other currency to use for this purpose.

6. **Alternative Approaches to Limiting Exchange Rate Variability:** Today, many nations permit their exchange rates to vary in foreign exchange markets. Others pursue policies that limit the variability of exchange rates. Some engage in a dirty float, in which they manage exchange rates, often in cooperation with other nations. Some establish crawling pegs, in which the target value of the exchange rate is adjusted automatically over time. And some establish target zones, with upper and lower limits on the extent to which exchange rates are allowed to vary.

KEY TERMS AND CONCEPTS

accounting identities (800)

appreciation (808)

balance of payments (800)

balance of trade (800)

capital account (804)

crawling peg (819)

current account (802)

depreciation (808)

dirty float (819)

exchange rate (807)

flexible exchange rates (808)

foreign exchange market (807)

foreign exchange risk (818)

hedge (818)

International Monetary Fund (806)

par value (816)

special drawing rights (SDRs) (806)

target zone (820)

PROBLEMS

Answers to the odd-numbered problems appear at the back of the book.

34-1. Over the course of a year, a nation tracked its foreign transactions and arrived at the following amounts:

Merchandise exports	500
Service exports	75
Net unilateral transfers	10
Domestic assets abroad (capital outflows)	−200
Foreign assets at home (capital inflows)	300
Changes in official reserves	−35
Merchandise imports	600
Service imports	50

What is this nation's balance of trade, current account balance, and capital account balance?

34-2. Whenever the United States reaches record levels on its current account deficit, Congress flirts with the

idea of restricting imported goods. Would trade restrictions like those studied in Chapter 33 be appropriate if Congress desires mutual gains from trade?

34-3. Explain how the following events would affect the market for the Mexican peso.

a. Improvements in Mexican production technology yield superior guitars, and many musicians around the world desire these guitars.

b. Perceptions of political instability surrounding regular elections in Mexico make international investors nervous about future business prospects in Mexico.

34-4. Explain how the following events would affect the market for South Africa's currency, the rand.

a. A rise in U.S. inflation causes many U.S. residents to seek to buy gold, which is a major South African export good, as a hedge against inflation.

b. Major discoveries of the highest-quality diamonds ever found occur in Russia and Central Asia, causing a significant decline in purchases of South African diamonds.

34-5. Explain how the following events would affect the market for Thailand's currency, the baht.

    a. Market interest rates on financial assets denominated in baht decline relative to market interest rates on financial assets denominated in other nations' currencies.

    b. Thailand's productivity increases relative to productivity in other countries.

34-6. Suppose that the following two events take place in the market for Kuwait's currency, the dinar: The U.S. demand for oil, Kuwait's main export good, declines, and market interest rates on financial assets denominated in dinar decrease relative to U.S. interest rates. What happens to the dollar price of the dinar? Does the dinar appreciate or depreciate relative to the dollar?

34-7. Suppose that the following two events take place in the market for China's currency, the yuan: U.S. parents are more willing than before to buy action figures and other Chinese toy exports, and China's government tightens restrictions on the amount of U.S. dollar–denominated financial assets that Chinese residents may legally purchase. What happens to the dollar price of the yuan? Does the yuan appreciate or depreciate relative to the dollar?

34-8. On Wednesday, the exchange rate between the euro and the U.S. dollar was $1.20 per euro. On Thursday, it was $1.18. Did the dollar appreciate or depreciate against the euro? By how much?

34-9. On Wednesday, the exchange rate between the euro and the U.S. dollar was $1.17 per euro and the exchange rate between the Canadian dollar and the U.S. dollar was U.S. $0.79 per Canadian dollar. What is the exchange rate between the Canadian dollar and the euro?

34-10. Suppose that signs of an improvement in the Japanese economy lead international investors to resume lending to the Japanese government and businesses. Poli-

cymakers, however, are worried about how this will influence the yen. How would this event affect the market for the yen? How should the central bank, the Bank of Japan, respond to this event if it wants to keep the value of the yen unchanged?

34-11. Briefly explain the differences between a flexible exchange rate system, a fixed exchange rate system, a dirty float, and the use of target zones.

34-12. Explain how each of the following would affect Canada's balance of payments.

    a. Canada's rate of inflation falls below that of the United States, its main trading partner.

    b. The possibility of Quebec's separating from the federation frightens international investors.

34-13. Suppose that under a gold standard, the U.S. dollar is pegged to gold at a rate of $35 per ounce and the pound sterling is pegged to gold at a rate of £17.50 per ounce. Explain how the gold standard constitutes an exchange rate arrangement between the dollar and the pound. What is the exchange rate between the U.S. dollar and the pound sterling?

34-14. Suppose that under the Bretton Woods system, the dollar is pegged to gold at a rate of $35 per ounce and the pound sterling is pegged to the dollar at a rate of $2 = £1. If the dollar is devalued against gold and the pegged rate is changed to $40 per ounce, what does this imply for the exchange value of the pound?

34-15. Suppose that the Bank of China wishes to peg the rate of exchange of its currency, the yuan, in terms of the U.S. dollar. In each of the following situations, should it add to or subtract from its dollar foreign exchange reserves? Why?

    a. U.S. parents begin buying fewer Chinese-manufactured toys for their children.

    b. U.S. interest rates rise relative to interest rates in China, so Chinese residents seek to purchase additional U.S. financial assets.

    c. Chinese furniture manufacturers produce high-quality early American furniture and successfully export large quantities of the furniture to the United States.

ECONOMICS ON THE NET

Daily Exchange Rates It is an easy matter to keep up with changes in exchange rates every day using the Web site of the Federal Reserve Bank of New York. In this application, you will learn how hard it is to predict exchange rate movements, and you will get some practice thinking about what factors can cause exchange rates to change.

Title: The Federal Reserve Bank of New York: Foreign Exchange 12 Noon Rates

Navigation: Go to **www.econtoday.com/chap34** to visit the Federal Reserve Bank of New York's Statistics home page. Click on *Foreign Exchange 12 Noon Rates.*

Application Answer the following questions.

1. For each currency listed, how many dollars does it take to purchase a unit of the currency in the spot foreign exchange market?

2. For each day during a given week (or month), choose a currency from those listed and keep track of its value rel-

ative to the dollar. Based on your tabulations, try to predict the value of the currency at the end of the week *following* your data collections. Use any information you may have, or just do your best without any additional information. How far off did your prediction turn out to be?

For Group Study and Analysis Each day, you can also click on a report titled "Foreign Exchange 10 A.M. Rates," which shows exchange rates for a subset of countries listed in the noon report. Assign each country in the 10 A.M. report to a group. Ask the group to determine whether the currency's value appreciated or depreciated relative to the dollar between 10 A.M. and noon. In addition, ask each group to discuss what kinds of demand or supply shifts could have caused the change that occurred during this interval.

If your exam were tomorrow, would you be ready? For each chapter, MyEconLab Practice Tests and Study Plans pinpoint which sections you have mastered and which ones you need to study. That way, you are more efficient with your study time, and you are better prepared for your exams.

In addition to Practice Tests and your personalized Study Plan, you'll find the following media resources in MyEconLab:

1. *Graphs in Motion* animation of Figures 34-1, 34-3, 34-4, 34-5, and 34-6.
2. An Economics in Motion in-depth animation of Exchange Rates.
3. Videos featuring the author, Roger LeRoy Miller, on the following subjects:
   - Market Determinants of Foreign Exchange Rates
   - Pros and Cons of a Fixed Exchange Rate

4. Links to the Web sites cited in the marginal Internet Resources, Issues and Applications feature, and Economics on the Net activity.
5. Audio clips of all key terms, additional practice problems, and a PDF version of the material from the print Study Guide.
6. eThemes of the Times, which is a New York Times article to help you understand the real-world applications of what you are learning.

To see how it works, turn to page 16 and then go to **www.myeconlab.com/miller**.

Get Ahead of the Curve

Answers to Odd-Numbered Problems

CHAPTER 1

1-1. Economics is the study of how individuals allocate limited resources to satisfy unlimited wants.

    a. Among the factors that a rational, self-interested student will take into account are her income, the price of the textbook, her anticipation of how much she is likely to study the textbook, and how much studying the book is likely to affect her grade.

    b. A rational, self-interested government official will, for example, recognize that higher taxes will raise more funds for mass transit while making more voters, who have limited resources, willing to select replacement officials.

    c. A municipality's rational, self-interested government will, for instance, take into account that higher hotel taxes will produce more funds if as many visitors continue to stay at hotels, but the higher taxes will also discourage some visitors from spending nights at hotels.

1-3. Because wants are unlimited, the phrase applies to very high-income households as well as low- and middle-income households. Consider, for instance, a household that has a low income and unlimited wants at the beginning of the year. The household's wants will remain unlimited if it becomes a high-income household later in the year.

1-5. Sally is displaying rational behavior if all of these activities are in her self-interest. For example, Sally likely derives intrinsic value from volunteer and extracurricular activities and may believe that these activities, along with good grades, improve her prospects of finding a job after she completes her studies. Hence, these activities are in her self-interest even though they take away some study time.

1-7. If, for instance, your model indicates that each hour of study results in a 15 percentage-point gain on each test, you should spend 6 hours ($6 \times 15 = 90$) studying economics and 4 hours ($4 \times 15 = 60$) studying French.

1-9. **a.** Yes
    b. No
    c. Yes

1-11. Positive economic analysis deals with economics models with predictions that are statements of fact, which can be objectively proven or disproven. Normative analysis takes into account subjective personal or social values concerning the way things *ought* to be.

1-13. **a.** An increase in the supply of laptop computers, perhaps because of the entry of new computer manufacturers into the market, pushes their price back down.

    b. Another factor, such as higher hotel taxes at popular vacation destinations, makes vacation travel more expensive.

    c. Some other factor, such as a fall in market wages that workers can earn, discourages people from working additional hours.

APPENDIX A

A-1. **a.** Independent: price of a notebook; Dependent: quantity of notebooks

    b. Independent: work-study hours; Dependent: credit hours

    c. Independent: hours of study; Dependent: economics grade

A-3. **a.** above x axis; left of y axis
    b. below x axis, right of y axis
    c. on x axis; to right of y axis

A-5.

y	x
−20	−4
−10	−2
0	0
10	2
20	4

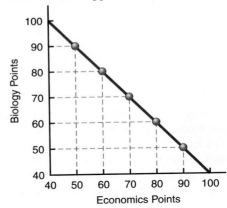

A-7. Each one-unit increase in *x* yields a 5-unit increase in *y*, so the slope given by the change in *y* corresponding to the change in *x* is equal to 5.

A-9. **a.** positive; each 1-unit rise in *x* induces a 5-unit increase in *y*.
  b. positive; each 1-unit rise in *x* induces a 1-unit increase in *y*.
  c. negative; each 1-unit rise in *x* induces a 3-unit decline in *y*.

CHAPTER 2

2-1. The opportunity cost of attending a class at 11:00 A.M. is the next-best use of that hour of the day. Likewise, the opportunity cost of attending an 8:00 A.M. class is the next-best use of that particular hour of the day. If you are an early riser, it is arguable that the opportunity cost of the 8:00 A.M. hour is lower, because you will already be up at that time but have fewer choices compared with the 11:00 A.M. hour when shops, recreation centers, and the like are open. If you are a late riser, it may be that the opportunity cost of the 8:00 A.M. hour is higher, because you place a relatively high value on an additional hour of sleep in the morning.

2-3. Each additional 10 points earned in economics costs 10 additional points in biology, so this PPC illustrates *constant* opportunity costs.

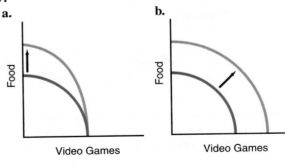

2-5. The $4,500 paid for tuition, room and board, and books are explicit costs and not opportunity costs. The $3,000 in forgone after-tax wages is the opportunity cost that the student incurs.

2-7.

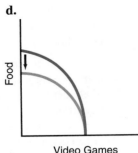

2-9. Because it takes you less time to do laundry, you have an absolute advantage in laundry. Neither you nor your roommate has an absolute advantage in meal preparation. You require 2 hours to fold a basket of laundry, so your opportunity cost of folding a basket of laundry is 2 meals. Your roommate's opportunity cost of folding a basket of laundry is 3 meals. Hence, you have a comparative advantage in laundry, and your roommate has a comparative advantage in meal preparation.

2-11. If countries produce the goods for which they have a comparative advantage and trade for those for which they are at a comparative disadvantage, then the distribution of resources is more efficient in each nation, yielding gains for both. Artificially restraining trade that otherwise would yield such gains thereby imposes social losses on residents of both nations.

2-13. a. If the two nations have the same production possibilities, then they face the same opportunity costs of producing consumption goods and capital goods. Thus, at present neither has a comparative advantage in producing either good.

  b. Because country B produces more capital goods today, it will be able to produce more of both goods in the future. Thus, country B's PPC will shift outward by a greater amount next.

  c. Country B now has a comparative advantage in producing capital goods, and country A now has a comparative advantage in producing consumption goods.

2-15. D

CHAPTER 3

3-1. The equilibrium price is $11 per CD, and the equilibrium quantity is 80 million CDs. At a price of $10 per CD, the quantity of CDs demanded is 90 million, and the quantity of CDs supplied is 60 million. Hence, there is a shortage of 30 million CDs at a price of $10 per CD.

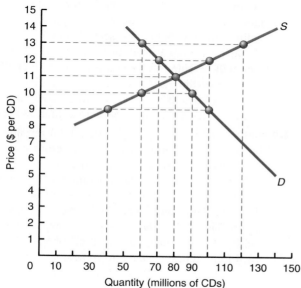

3-3. a. DSL and cable Internet access services are substitutes, so a reduction in the price of cable Internet access services causes a decrease in the demand for DSL high-speed Internet access services.

  b. A decrease in the price of DSL Internet access services generates an increase in the quantity of these services demanded.

  c. DSL high-speed Internet access services are a normal good, so a fall in the incomes of consumers reduces the demand for these services.

  d. If consumers expect that the price of DSL high-speed Internet services will fall in the future, then the demand for these services will tend to decrease today.

3-5. a. Complement: eggs; substitute: sausage

  b. Complement: tennis balls; substitute: racquetball racquets

  c. Complement: cream; substitute: tea

  d. Complement: gasoline; substitute: city bus

3-7. The increase in the market price of Roquefort cheese causes the demand for blue cheese to increase, so the demand curve for blue cheese shifts to the right. The market price of blue cheese increases, and the equilibrium quantity of blue cheese rises.

3-9. a. Because memory chips are an input in the production of laptop computers, a decrease in the price of memory chips causes an increase in the supply of laptop computers. The market supply curve shifts to the right, which causes the market price of laptop computers to fall and the equilibrium quantity of laptop computers to increase.

  b. Machinery used to produce laptop computers is an input in the production of these devices, so an increase in the price of machinery generates a decrease in the supply of laptop computers. The market supply curve shifts to the left, which causes the market price of laptop computers to rise and the equilibrium quantity of laptop computers to decrease.

  c. An increase in the number of manufacturers of laptop computers causes an increase in the supply of laptop computers. The market supply curve shifts rightward. The market price of laptop computers declines, and the equilibrium quantity of laptop computers increases.

  d. The demand curve for laptop computers shifts to the left along the supply curve, so there is a decrease in the quantity supplied. The market price falls, and the equilibrium quantity declines.

3-11. a. The demand for tickets declines, and there will be a surplus of tickets.

b. The demand for tickets rises, and there will be a shortage of tickets.

c. The demand for tickets rises, and there will be a shortage of tickets.

d. The demand for tickets declines, and there will be a surplus of tickets.

3-13. Ethanol producers will respond to the subsidy by producing more ethanol at any given price, so the supply of ethanol will increase, thereby generating a decrease in the price of ethanol.

a. Producers striving to supply more ethanol will consume more corn, an input in ethanol production. Hence, the demand for corn will increase, so the market price of corn will rise, and the equilibrium quantity of corn will increase.

b. A decline in the market price of ethanol, a substitute for gasoline, will cause the demand for gasoline to decline. The market price of gasoline will fall, and the equilibrium quantity of gasoline will decrease.

c. Ethanol and automobiles are complements, so a decline in the price of ethanol will cause an increase in the demand for autos. The market price of autos will rise, and the equilibrium quantity of autos will increase.

3-15. Aluminum is an input in the production of canned soft drinks, so an increase in the price of aluminum reduces the supply of canned soft drinks (option c). The resulting rise in the market price of canned soft drinks brings about an decrease in the quantity of canned soft drinks demanded (option b). In equilibrium, the quantity of soft drinks supplied decreases (option d) to an amount equal to the quantity demanded. The demand curve does not shift, however, so option b does not apply.

CHAPTER 4

4-1. To the band, its producer, and consumers, the market price of the CD provides an indication of the popularity of the band's music. If the market price rises relative to other CDs, then this signals that the band should continue to record its music for sale. If the market price falls relative to other CDs, then this signals that members of the band may want to consider leaving the recording industry.

4-3. The market rental rate is $500 per apartment, and the equilibrium quantity of apartments rented to ten-

ants is 2,000. At a ceiling price of $450 per month, the number of apartments that students wishing to live off campus wish to rent increases to 2,500 apartments. At the ceiling price, the number of apartments that owners are willing to supply decreases to 1,800 apartments. Thus, there is a shortage of 700 apartments at the ceiling price, and only 1,800 are rented at the ceiling price.

4-5. At the above-market price of sugar in the U.S. sugar market, U.S. chocolate manufacturers that use sugar as an input face higher costs. Thus, they supply less chocolate at any given price of chocolate, and the market supply curve shifts leftward. This pushes up the market price of chocolate products and reduces the equilibrium quantity of chocolate. U.S. sugar producers also sell surplus sugar in foreign sugar markets, which causes the supply curve for sugar in foreign markets to shift rightward. This reduces the market price of foreign sugar and raises the equilibrium quantity in the foreign market.

4-7. The market price is $400, and the equilibrium quantity of seats is 1,600. If airlines cannot sell tickets to more than 1,200 passengers, then passengers are willing to pay $600 per seat. Normally airlines would be willing to sell each ticket for $200, but they will be able to charge a price as high as $600 for each of the 1,200 tickets they sell. Hence, the quantity of tickets sold declines from 1,600, and the price of a ticket rises from $400 to as high as $600.

4-9. Before the price support program, total revenue for farmers was $5 million (the equilibrium price of $1.00 per bushel times the equilibrium quantity of 5 million bushels). After the program, total revenue is $10 million (the support price of $1.25 per bushel times the 8 million bushels demanded at the support price). The cost of the program for taxpayers is $5 million (the support price of $1.25 per bushel times the 4 million bushels the government must purchase that consumers do not wish to buy at the higher support price).

4-11. a. Because the minimum wage is above the equilibrium wage, more individuals who are currently now employed at fast-food restaurants will seek to work, but fast-food restaurants will desire to employ fewer workers than before. Consequently, there will be a surplus of labor, or unemployed workers, at the above-market minimum wage.

b. The wage rate is the price of an input, labor, so a rise in the wage pushes up the price of this input. This induces fast-food restaurants to reduce the quantity of hamburgers supplied at any given price of hamburgers, so the market supply curve shifts leftward. This brings about an increase in the market price of hamburgers and a reduction in the equilibrium quantity of hamburgers produced and consumed.

4-13. a. The rise in the number of wheat producers causes the market supply curve to shift rightward, so more wheat is supplied at the support price.

b. The quantity of wheat demanded at the same support price is unchanged.

c. Because quantity demanded is unchanged while quantity supplied has increased, the amount of surplus wheat that the government must purchase has risen.

CHAPTER 5

5-1. In the absence of laws forbidding cigar smoking in public places, people who are bothered by the odor of cigar smoke will experience costs not borne by cigar producers. Because the supply of cigars will not reflect these costs, the market cigar supply curve will likely be too far to the right from the perspective of society. The market price of cigars will be too low, and too many cigars will be produced and consumed.

5-3. Imposing the tax on pesticides causes an increase in the price of pesticides, which are an input in the production of oranges. Hence, the supply curve in the orange market shifts leftward. The market price of oranges increases, and the equilibrium quantity of oranges declines. Hence, orange consumers indirectly help to pay for dealing with the spillover costs of pesticide production by paying more for oranges.

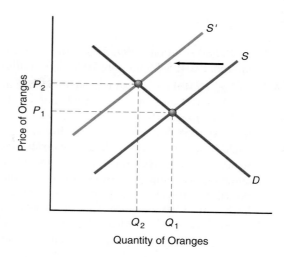

5-5. a. If the social benefits associated with bus ridership were taken into account, the demand for bus ridership would be greater, and the market price would be higher. The equilibrium quantity of bus rides would be higher.

b. The government could pay commuters a subsidy to ride the bus, thereby increasing the demand for bus ridership. This would increase the market price and equilibrium number of bus rides.

5-7. The government could provide schools and parents with subsidies to pay for computers and Internet access. This would increase the market price of Internet access and the equilibrium number of people, including children, with access to the Internet.

5-9. The problem is that although most people around the lighthouse will benefit from its presence, there is no incentive for people to voluntarily contribute if they believe that others ultimately will pay for it. That is, the city is likely to face a free-rider problem in its efforts to raise its share of the funds required for the lighthouse.

5-11. Because the marginal tax rate increases as workers' earnings decline, this tax system is regressive.

5-13. Seeking to increase budget allocations in future years and to make workers' jobs more interesting can be consistent with the profit-maximizing objectives of firms in private markets. Also, the government agency is promoting competition, which is analogous to behaving like a firm in a private market. Achieving these goals via majority rule and regulatory coercion, however, are aspects that are specific to the public sector.

CHAPTER 6

6-1. 1997: $300 million; 1999: $350 million; 2001: $400 million; 2004: $400 million; 2005: $420 million

6-3. During 2004 the tax base was an amount of income equal to $20 million/0.05 = $400 million. During 2005 the income tax base was equal to $19.2 million/0.06 = $320 million. Although various factors could have contributed to the fall in taxable income, dynamic tax analysis suggests that the higher income tax rate induced people to reduce their reported income. For instance, some people might have earned less income subject to city income taxes, and others might have even moved outside the city to avoid paying the higher income tax rate.

6-5. a. As shown in the diagram, if the supply and demand curves have their normal shapes, then the $2 per month tax on DSL Internet access services shifts the market supply curve upward by $2. The equilibrium quantity of DSL access services produced and consumed declines. In addition, the monthly market price of DSL access increases by an amount less than $2 per month. Consequently, consumers and producers share in paying the tax on each unit.

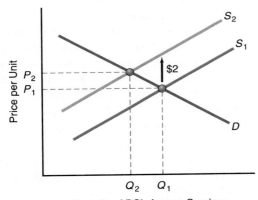

Quantity of DSL Access Services

b. If the market price of DSL Internet access for households rises by the full amount of the tax, then as shown in the diagram below, over the relevant range the demand for DSL access services by households is vertical. The quantity of services demanded by households is completely unresponsive to the tax, so households pay a monthly access rate that is exactly $2 higher, so they pay all of the tax.

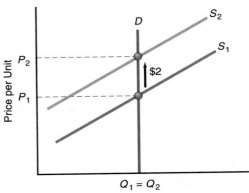

Quantity of DSL Access Services

c. If the market price of DSL access for businesses does not change, then as shown in the diagram below, over the relevant range the demand for Internet access services by businesses is horizontal. The quantity of services demanded by businesses is very highly responsive to the tax, so DSL access providers must bear the tax in the form of higher costs. Providers of DSL access services pay all of the tax.

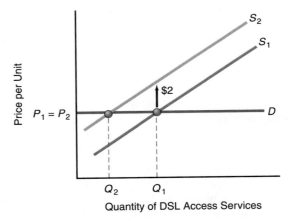

Quantity of DSL Access Services

6-7. Yes, public schools will lose students to private schools. The prices that public schools receive will also decline. Both of these changes will result in lower revenues for public schools.

6-9. a. $40 million
  b. The effective price of a DVD drive to consumers will be lower after the government pays the subsidy, so people will purchase a larger quantity.
  c. $60 million
  d. $90 million

6-11. a. 50 percent
   b. −20 percent

CHAPTER 7

7-1. By the time you would begin employment with employer B, the purchasing power of the salary you would earn from that job would have dropped by 5 percent. Thus, a year from now the purchasing power of the $25,000 salary will have dropped to $25,000/1.05 = $23,809.52. Furthermore, additional inflation during the following year will continue to erode the salary's purchasing power. In contrast, you anticipate that the purchasing power of the job offer from employer A will remain unchanged at $24,000. Hence, because you are indifferent between the jobs in other respects, you should accept job A.

7-3. The labor force equals the number employed plus the number unemployed, or 152 million + 8 million = 160 million. In percentage terms, therefore, the unemployment rate is 100 times 8 million/160 million, or 5 percent.

7-5. a. 30 people are always unemployed due to job changes each month, so the frictional unemployment rate is (30/1,000) × 100 = 3 percent.
   b. 20 people are structurally unemployed, and 30 people are frictionally unemployed, so that the total unemployment rate is (50/1,000) × 100 = 5 percent.
   c. Now 30 people are always unemployed due to job changes each month, so the frictional unemployment rate is (60/1,000) × 100 = 6 percent.
   d. 20 people are structurally unemployed, and 60 people are frictionally unemployed, so that the total unemployment rate is (80/1,000) × 100 = 8 percent.

7-7. a. 10 new people become unemployed each month, so the unemployment rate is (10/200) × 100 = 5 percent.
   b. one month
   c. two months
   d. Now a total of 20 people are unemployed each month, so the unemployment rate is (20/200) × 100 = 10 percent.

7-9. The price index for 2006 if 2004 is the base year is ($2,100/$2,000 × 100) =105.0

7-11. 2 percent

7-13. a. 2 percent
   b. 102.0

CHAPTER 8

8-1. Other things being equal, GDP will be lower, because the individual will no longer earn income in the marketplace, so this income will no longer be included in GDP.

8-3. a. GDP = $14.6 trillion; NDP = $13.3 trillion; NI = $12.5 trillion.
   b. GDP in 2010 will equal $13.5 trillion.
   c. If the value of depreciation were to exceed gross private domestic investment in 2011, then the nation's capital stock would decline. Because capital is a productive resource, the nation's future productivity likely would decline, and this decline would worsen if the situation were to continue beyond 2010.

8-5. a. Gross domestic income = $14.6 trillion; GDP = $14.6 trillion.
   b. Gross private domestic investment = $2.0 trillion.
   c. Personal income = $12.0 trillion; personal disposable income = $10.3 trillion.

8-7. a. Measured GDP declines.
   b. Measured GDP increases.
   c. Measured GDP does not change (the firearms are not newly produced).

8-9. a. The chip is an intermediate good, so its purchase in June is not included in GDP; only the final sale in November is included.
   b. This is a final sale of a good that is included in GDP for the year.
   c. This is a final sale of a service that is included in GDP for the year.

8-11. Price level index for 2005: 100.0
   Price level index for 2009: 127.1

8-13. The price index is (2008 nominal GDP/2007 real GDP) × 100 = ($88,000/$136,000) × 100 = 64.7.

8-15. The $1 billion expended to pay for employees and equipment and the additional $1 billion paid to clean up the oil spill would be included in GDP, for a total of $2 billion added to GDP in 2007. The rise in oil reserves increases the stock of wealth but is not included in the current flow of newly produced goods and services. In addition, the welfare loss relating to the deaths of wildlife is also not measured in the marketplace and thereby is not included in GDP.

CHAPTER 9

9-1. a. Y

b. X

9-3. The nation will maintain its stock of capital goods at its current level, so its output growth will be zero.

9-5. A: $8,250 per capita

B: $4,500 per capita

C: $21,000 per capita

9-7. 1.77 times higher after 20 years; 3.16 times higher after 40 years

9-9. 5 years

9-11. 4 percent

CHAPTER 10

10-1. The amount of unemployment would be the sum of frictional, structural, and seasonal unemployment.

10-3. The real value of the new full-employment level of nominal GDP is ($14.2 trillion/1.15) = $12.35 trillion, so the long-run aggregate supply curve has shifted rightward by $0.35 trillion.

10-5. This change implies a rightward shift of the long-run aggregate supply curve along the unchanged aggregate demand curve, so the long-run equilibrium price level will decline.

10-7. There are three effects. First, there is a real-balance effect, because the rise in the price level reduces real money balances, inducing people to cut back on their spending. In addition, there is an interest-rate effect as a higher price level pushes up interest rates, thereby reducing the attractiveness of purchases of autos, houses, and plants and equipment. Finally, there is an open-economy effect as home residents respond to the higher price level by reducing purchases of domestically produced goods in favor of foreign-produced goods, while foreign residents cut back on their purchases of home-produced goods. All three effects entail a reduction in purchases of goods and services, so the aggregate demand curve slopes downward.

10-9. a. At the price level P_2 above the equilibrium price level P_1, the total quantity of real goods and services that people plan to consume is less than the total quantity that is consistent with firms' production plans. One reason is that at the higher-than-equilibrium price level, real money balances are lower, which reduces real wealth and induces lower planned consumption. Another is that interest rates are higher at the higher-than-equilibrium price level, which generates a cutback in consumption spending. Finally, at the higher-than-equilibrium price level P_2, people tend to cut back on purchasing domestic goods in favor of foreign-produced goods, and foreign residents reduce purchases of domestic goods. As unsold inventories of output accumulate, the price level drops toward the equilibrium price level P_1, which ultimately causes planned consumption to rise toward equality with total production.

b. At the price level P_3 below the equilibrium price level P_1, the total quantity of real goods and services that people plan to consume exceeds the total quantity that is consistent with firms' production plans. One reason is that at the lower-than-equilibrium price level, real money balances are higher, which raises real wealth and induces higher planned consumption. Another is that interest rates are lower at the lower-than-equilibrium price level, which generates an increase in consumption spending. Finally, at the lower-than-equilibrium price level P_2, people tend to raise their purchases of domestic goods and cut back on buying foreign-produced goods, and foreign residents increase purchases of domestic goods. As inventories of output are depleted, the price level begins to rise toward the equilibrium price level P_1, which ultimately causes planned consumption to fall toward equality with total production.

10-11. This is a somewhat unsettled issue. It can be undesirable for some of the same reasons that anticipated inflation can be undesirable: People can incur costs as a result. For example, steady deflation could cause firms to incur menu costs, or costs of changing prices, when they adjust prices downward. Some economists (notably Milton Friedman), however, have argued that steady deflation equal to the real interest rate is desirable, because then people discount present and future at the same rate and consequently hold the "socially optimal" quantity of money.

10-13. a. The aggregate demand curve shifts leftward along the long-run aggregate supply curve; the equilibrium price level falls, and equilibrium real GDP remains unchanged.

b. The aggregate demand curve shifts rightward along the long-run aggregate supply curve; the equilibrium price level rises, and equilibrium real GDP remains unchanged.

c. The long-run aggregate supply curve shifts rightward along the aggregate demand curve; the equilibrium price level falls, and equilibrium real GDP increases.

d. The aggregate demand curve shifts rightward along the long-run aggregate supply curve; the equilibrium price level rises, and equilibrium real GDP remains unchanged.

CHAPTER 11

11-1. a. Because saving increases at any given interest rate, the desired saving curve shifts rightward. This causes the equilibrium interest rate to decline.

b. There is no effect on current equilibrium real GDP, because in the classical model the vertical long-run aggregate supply curve always applies.

c. A change in the saving rate does not directly affect the demand for labor or the supply of labor in the classical model, so equilibrium employment does not change.

d. The decrease in the equilibrium interest rate generates a rightward and downward movement along the demand curve for investment. Consequently, desired investment increases.

e. The rise in current investment implies greater capital accumulation. Other things being equal, this will imply increased future production and higher equilibrium real GDP in the future.

11-3. False. In fact, there is an important distinction. The classical model of short-run real GDP determination applies to an interval short enough that some factors of production, such as capital, are fixed. Nevertheless, the classical model implies that even in the short run the economy's aggregate supply curve is the same as its long-run aggregate supply curve.

11-5. a. The labor supply curve shifts rightward, and equilibrium employment increases.

b. The rise in employment causes the aggregate supply curve to shift rightward, and real GDP rises.

c. Because the immigrants have higher saving rates, the nation's savings curve shifts to the right along its investment curve, and the equilibrium interest rate declines.

d. The fall in the equilibrium interest rate induces a rise in investment, and saving also rises.

e. Capital accumulation rises, and more real GDP will be forthcoming in future years.

11-7. In the long run the aggregate supply curve is vertical because all input prices adjust fully and people are fully informed in the long run. Thus, the short-run aggregate supply curve is more steeply sloped if input prices adjust more rapidly and people become more fully informed within a short-run interval.

11-9. This event would cause the aggregate demand curve to shift leftward. In the short run, the equilibrium price level would decline, and equilibrium real GDP would fall.

CHAPTER 12

12-1. The completed table, which includes the answers to parts a and b, follows (all amounts in dollars):

Disposable Income	Saving	Consumption	APS	APC
200	−40	240	−0.20	1.20
400	0	400	0.00	1.00
600	40	560	0.07	0.93
800	80	720	0.10	0.90
1,000	120	880	0.12	0.88
1,200	160	1,040	0.13	0.87

For part c, the MPS is equal to $40/200 = 0.20$, and the MPC is equal to $160/200 = 0.8$.

12-3. a. Yes, because the rate of return on the investment exceeds the market interest rate.

b. No, because the rate of return on the investment is now less than the market interest rate.

12-5. a. The completed table follows (all amounts in dollars):

Real GDP	Consumption	Saving	Investment
2,000	2,000	0	1,200
4,000	3,600	400	1,200
6,000	5,200	800	1,200
8,000	6,800	1,200	1,200
10,000	8,400	1,600	1,200
12,000	10,000	2,000	1,200

MPC = 1,600/2,000 = 0.8; MPS = 400/2,000 = 0.2.

b. The graph appears below.

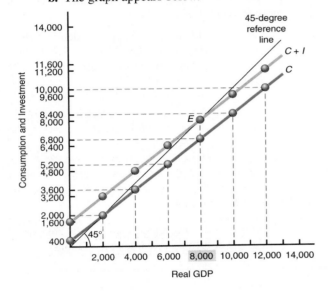

c. The graph appears below. Equilibrium real GDP on both graphs equals $8,000.

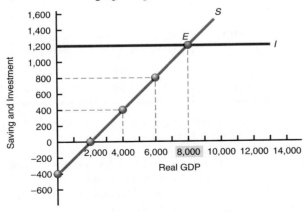

d. APS = $1,200/$8,000 = 0.15.

e. The multiplier is 1/(1 − MPC) = 1/(1 − 0.8) = 1/0.2 = 5. Thus if autonomous consumption were

to rise by $100, then equilibrium real GDP would increase by $100 times 5, or $500.

12-7. a. If Y = 0, autonomous consumption equals $800, which implies dissaving equal to $800, which is the amount of autonomous saving.

b. The marginal propensity to consume is 0.80, so the marginal propensity to save is 1 − MPC = 1 − 0.80 = 0.20.

c. The multiplier is 1/(1 − MPC) = 1/0.20 = 5.0.

12-9. The multiplier is 1/(1 − MPC) = 4, so 1 − MPC = 0.25, which implies that MPC = 0.75. Thus, consumption when real GDP equals $12 trillion is $1 trillion + (0.75 x $12 trillion) = $10 trillion.

12-11. The multiplier is 1/(1 − MPC) = 1/(1 − 0.75) = 4, so the increase in equilibrium real GDP is $250 billion × 4 = $1 trillion, and the level of real GDP at the new point on the aggregate demand curve is $11 trillion.

12-13. a. The MPS is equal to 1/3.

b. $0.1 trillion

CHAPTER 13

13-1. a. A key factor that could help explain why the actual multiplier effect may turned out to be lower is the crowding-out effect. Some government spending may have directly crowded out private expenditures on a dollar-for-dollar basis. In addition, indirect crowding out may have occurred. Because the government did not change taxes, it probably sold bonds to finance its increased expenditures, and this action likely pushed up interest rates, thereby discouraging private investment. Furthermore, the increase in government spending likely pushed up aggregate demand, which may have caused a short-run increase in the price level. This in turn, may have induced foreign residents to reduce their expenditures on U.S. goods. It also could have reduced real money holdings sufficiently to discourage consumers from spending as much as before. On net, therefore, real GDP rose in the short run but not by the full multiple amount.

b. In the long run, as the increased spending raised aggregate demand, wages and other input prices likely increased in proportion to the resulting increase in the price level. Thus, in the long run the aggregate supply schedule was vertical, and the increase in government spending induced only a rise in the price level.

13-3. Because of the recognition time lag entailed in gathering information about the economy, policymakers may be slow to respond to a downturn in real GDP. Congressional approval of policy actions to address the downturn may be delayed, hence an action time lag may also arise. Finally, there is an effect time lag, because policy actions take time to exert their full effects on the economy. If these lags are sufficiently long, it is possible that by the time a policy to address a downturn has begun to have its effects, real GDP might already be rising. If so, the policy action might push real GDP up faster than intended, thereby making real GDP less stable.

13-5. Situation *b* is an example of indirect crowding out because the reduction in private expenditures takes place indirectly in response to a change in the interest rate. In contrast, situations *a* and *c* are examples of direct expenditure offsets.

13-7. Situation *b* is an example of a discretionary fiscal policy action because this is a discretionary action by Congress. So is situation *d* because the president uses discretionary authority. Situation *c* is an example of monetary policy, not fiscal policy, and situation *a* is an example of an automatic stabilizer.

13-9. One possibility would be a government spending decrease of just the right amount to shift the aggregate demand curve leftward to a new equilibrium point on the long-run aggregate supply curve. Another would be a tax increase designed to achieve the same outcome.

13-11. Because the MPC is 0.80, the multiplier equals 1/(1 − MPC) = 1/0.2 = 5. Net of indirect crowding out, therefore, total autonomous expenditures must rise by $40 billion in order to shift the aggregate demand curve rightward by $200 billion. If the government raises its spending by $50 billion, the market interest rate rises by 0.5 percentage point and thereby causes planned investment spending to fall by $10 billion, which results in a net rise in total autonomous expenditures equal to $40 billion. Consequently, to accomplish its objective the government should increase its spending by $50 billion.

13-13. A cut in the tax rate should induce a rise in consumption and, consequently, a multiple short-run increase in equilibrium real GDP. In addition, however, a tax-rate reduction reduces the automatic-stabilizer properties of the tax system, so equilib-

rium real GDP would be less stable in the face of changes in autonomous spending.

APPENDIX C

C-1. a. The marginal propensity to consume is equal to 1 − MPS, or 6/7.

b. The required increase in equilibrium income is $0.35 trillion, or $350 billion. The multiplier equals 1/(1 − MPC) = 1/MPS = 1/(1/7) = 7. Hence, investment or government spending must increase by $50 billion to bring about a $350 billion increase in equilibrium income.

c. The multiplier relevant for a tax change equals −MPC/(1 − MPC) = −MPC/MPS = −(6/7)/(1/7) = −6. Thus the government would have to cut taxes by $58.33 billion to induce a rise in equilibrium equal to $350 billion.

C-3. a. The aggregate expenditure curve shifts up by $1 billion; equilibrium real income increases by $5 billion.

b. The aggregate expenditure curve shifts down by the MPC times the tax increase, or by 0.8 × $1 billion = 0.8 billion; equilibrium real income falls by $4 billion.

c. The aggregate expenditure curve shifts upward by (1 − MPC) times $1 billion = $0.2 billion. Equilibrium real income rises by $1 billion.

d. No change; no change.

CHAPTER 14

14-1. $0.4 trillion

14-3. A higher deficit creates a higher public debt.

14-5. The net public debt is obtained by subtracting government interagency borrowing from the gross public debt.

14-7. The gross public debt remains unchanged; the net public debt decreases.

14-9. a. Other things being equal, foreign dollar holders can be induced to hold more domestic government bonds used to finance domestic government deficits only if the domestic interest rate rises.

b. Immediately, the main source of dollars are the dollars that foreign residents otherwise would use to purchase exports.

14-11. The immediate effect would be only a change in accounting definitions. Proponents of capital budgeting argue that over time, this change would induce changes in government spending and taxation that might contribute to truly lower fiscal deficits.

14-13. Because real GDP rises at the current price level as a consequence of the upward shift in the $C + I + G + X$ curve, the aggregate demand curve shifts rightward. With unchanged short-run aggregate supply, the equilibrium price level rises, and equilibrium real GDP increases.

CHAPTER 15

15-1. Medium of exchange; store of value; standard of deferred payment.

15-3. Store of value; standard of deferred payment

15-5. M1 equals demand deposits and other checkable deposits plus currency plus traveler's checks, or $625 billion + $600 billion + $25 billion = $1,250 billion; M2 equals M1 + savings deposits plus small-denomination time deposits plus money market deposit accounts plus retail (non-institution) money market mutual funds, or $1,250 billion + $400 billion + $950 billion + $850 billion + $400 billion = $3,850 billion.

15-7. **a.** neither
   b. M2 only
   c. M1 and M2
   d. M2 only

15-9. In principle, each institution can match with each rationale; your explanations are the aspects of your answers that are most important.
   a. Insurance companies limit adverse selection by screening applicants for policies.
   b. Savings banks limit moral hazard by monitoring borrowers after loans have been made.
   c. Pension funds reduce management costs by pooling the funds of many future pensioners.

15-11. People who held international instruments did so in the anticipation that even if U.S. instruments were to earn low or negative returns in the future, many international instruments might earn relatively high returns, thereby yielding a positive return of their overall portfolio. Many of those who held many international instruments in 1997 and 1998 earned low or negative returns on those instruments, but by continuing to hold U.S. instruments that earned higher returns during this period, they earned a positive overall return on their portfolios. When U.S. instruments' returns fell in the early 2000s, some international returns were rising, which helped to compensate. Thus, international financial diversification is not necessarily a mistake; it is a way to try to smooth the overall return on one's portfolio.

15-13. In an extreme case in which the U.S. government were to close down the Federal Reserve System, it would have to compensate holders of Federal Reserve notes for the market value of those notes.

15-15. Back in 1913, the population was centered farther to the east. Thus, congressional representation was centered farther to the east, so political concerns together with a view that the Fed districts should be designed to best serve the existing population helped determine the geographic boundaries. These have not been redrawn since.

CHAPTER 16

16-1. **a.** asset
   b. liability
   c. liability
   d. asset

16-3. The bank's reserves are its required reserves, which equal $0.10 \times \$15$ million = $1.5 million. Total assets equal total liabilities, or $15 million. Hence, its remaining loans and securities must amount to its total assets of $15 million minus its reserves of $1.5 million, or $13.5 million

16-5. Yes, the bank holds $50 million in excess reserves. The bank's current total assets equal its $2 billion in total liabilities. It must hold 15 percent of its $2 billion in checkable deposits, or $0.30 billion as required reserves. Its total reserves equal $2 billion in total assets minus $1.65 billion in loans and securities, or $0.35 billion. Hence, the bank has $0.05 billion, or $50 million, in excess reserves.

16-7. The dealer's bank must hold 15 percent of the $1 million, or $150,000, as required reserves. Thus the bank can lend out the excess reserves of $850,000.

16-9. **a.** Total liabilities and net worth = total assets = $0.26 billion in total reserves + $3.6 billion in loans + $1 billion in securities + $0.14 billion in other assets = $5 billion.

b. The bank could lend its $10 million in excess reserves.

c. Transactions deposits equal required reserves of $0.25 billion/0.1 = $2.5 billion.

16-11. a. Yes

b. None, because the bank has $1 billion in current transactions deposits not "swept" to money market deposit accounts, so with a required reserve ratio of 0.20 the total amount of required reserves for the bank is the $200 million in reserves it currently holds.

c. Its $1 billion in transactions deposits are currently included in M1.

16-13. When you purchase a U.S. government security, you draw on existing funds in a deposit account and thereby redistribute funds already within the banking system; by way of contrast, the Federal Reserve creates funds that had not previously existed in the banking system.

16-15. The maximum potential money multiplier is 1/0.01 = 100, so total deposits in the banking system will increase by $5 million × 100 = $500 million.

CHAPTER 17

17-1. a. $500/0.05 = $10,000.

b. Its price falls to $500/0.10 = $5,000.

17-3. a. One possible policy action would be an open market sale of securities, which would reduce the money supply and shift the aggregate demand curve leftward. Others would be to increase the discount rate relative to the federal funds rate or to raise the required reserve ratio.

b. In principle, the Fed's action would reduce inflation more quickly.

17-5. Because a contractionary monetary policy causes interest rates to increase, financial capital begins to flow into the United States. This causes the demand for dollars to rise, which pushes up the value of the dollar and makes U.S. exports more expensive to foreign residents. They cut back on their purchases of U.S. products, which tends to reduce U.S. real GDP.

17-7.

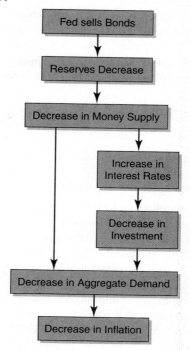

17-9. The price level remains at its original value. Because $M_s V = PY$, V has doubled, and Y is unchanged, cutting M_s in half leaves P unchanged.

17-11. $M_s V = PY$, so $P = M_s V/Y = ($1.1 \text{ trillion} \times 10)/$5 \text{ trillion} = 2.2$.

17-13. If the demand for money suddenly declines, then to keep the interest rate from falling the Fed should reduce the money supply via open market sales, an increase in the discount rate relative to the federal funds rate, or an increase in the required reserve ratio.

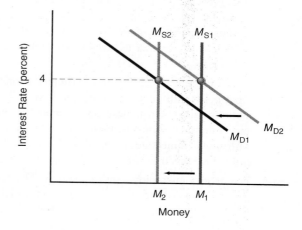

17-15. Any one of these contractionary actions will tend to raise interest rates, which in turn will induce international inflows of financial capital. This pushes up the value of the dollar and makes U.S. goods less attractive abroad. As a consequence, real planned total expenditures on U.S. goods decline even further.

APPENDIX D

D-1. **a.** $20 billion increase
b. $40 billion increase
c. $10 billion open market purchase

D-3. Through its purchase of $1 billion in bonds, the Fed increased reserves by $1 billion. This ultimately caused a $3 billion increase in the money supply after full multiple expansion. The 1 percentage-point drop in the interest rate, from 6 percent to 5 percent, caused investment to rise by $25 billion, from $1,200 billion to $1,225 billion. An investment multiplier of 3 indicates that equilibrium real GDP rose by $75 billion, to $12,075 billion, or $12.075 trillion.

CHAPTER 18

18-1. **a.** The actual unemployment rate, which equals the number of people unemployed divided by the labor force, would decline, because the labor force would rise while the number of people unemployed would remain unchanged.
b. Natural unemployment rate estimates also would be lower.
c. The logic of the short- and long-run Phillips curves would not be altered. The government might wish to make this change if it feels that those in the military "hold jobs" and thereby should be counted as employed within the U.S. economy.

18-3. The "long run" is an interval sufficiently long that input prices fully adjust and people have full information. Adoption of more sophisticated computer and communications technology provides people with more immediate access to information, which can reduce this interval.

18-5. The natural unemployment rate and the NAIRU are the same in a long-run equilibrium in which any short-run adjustments are concluded and in which

there is currently no tendency for the inflation rate to increase or decrease.

18-7. No. It could still be true that wages and other prices of factors of production adjust sluggishly to changes in the price level. Then a rise in aggregate demand that boosts the price level brings about an upward movement along the short-run aggregate supply curve, causing equilibrium real GDP to rise.

18-9. The explanation would be that aggregate demand has increased at a faster pace than the rise in aggregate supply caused by economic growth. On net, therefore, the price level has risen during the past few years.

18-11. If there is widespread price stickiness, then the short-run aggregate supply curve would be horizontal (see Chapter 11), and real GDP would respond strongly to a policy action that affects aggregate demand. By way of contrast, if prices are highly flexible, then the short-run aggregate supply curve slopes upward, and real GDP is less responsive to the change in aggregate demand.

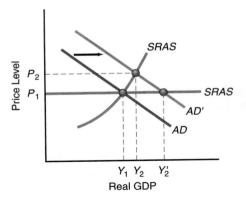

18-13. Increasing the price of a product in response to a long-lasting increase in demand will yield higher profits for several periods. The value of this stream of future profits is more likely to be sufficiently large to outweigh a small, one-time menu cost. In this situation, it is more likely that firms will raise their prices.

18-15. **a.** The measured unemployment rate when all adjustments will have occurred will now always be lower than before, so the natural unemployment rate will be smaller.
b. The unemployment rate consistent with stable inflation will now be reduced, so the NAIRU will be smaller.
c. The Phillips curve will shift inward.

CHAPTER 19

19-1. Population growth rate = real GDP growth rate − rate of growth of per capita real GDP = 3.1 percent − 0.3 percent = 2.8 percent.

19-3. a. Real GDP growth rate = rate of growth of per capita real GDP + population growth rate = 0.1 percent + 2.2 percent = 2.3 percent.
   b. Rate of growth of per capita real GDP = 2.3 percent − 2.7 percent = −0.4 percent.
   c. Rate of growth of per capita real GDP = 3.1 percent − 2.7 percent = +0.4 percent.

19-5. Morocco or Uruguay, then Bosnia-Herzegovina, Togo, and Angola. The cost of starting a business is slightly higher in Uruguay than in Morocco. Starting a business in Uruguay requires fewer legal steps. One of these two nations is likely to experience higher growth, other things being equal, than the others.

19-7. $10 trillion/$0.5 trillion × 0.1 = 2 percentage points.

19-9. a. Portfolio investment is equal to $150 million bonds plus $100 million in stocks representing ownership of less than 10 percent, or $250 million. (Bank loans are neither portfolio investment nor foreign direct investment.)
   b. Foreign direct investment is equal to $250 million in stocks representing an ownership share of at least 10 percent. (Bank loans are neither portfolio investment nor foreign direct investment.)

19-11. a. adverse selection
   b. moral hazard
   c. adverse selection
   d. adverse selection

19-13. a. The company had already qualified for funding at a market interest rate, so the World Bank is interfering with functioning private markets for credit. In addition, by extending credit to the company at a below-market rate, the World Bank provides an incentive for the company to borrow additional funds for less efficient investment.
   b. In this situation, the World Bank effectively is tying up funds in dead capital. There is an associated opportunity cost, because the funds could instead be allocated to another investment that would yield more immediate returns.
   c. In this case, the IMF contributes to a moral hazard problem, because the government has every

incentive not to make reforms that will enable it to repay this and future loans it may receive.

19-15. a. There is an incentive for at least some governments to fail to follow through with reforms, even if those governments might have had good intentions when they applied for World Bank loans.
   b. National governments most interested in obtaining funds to "buy" votes will be among those most interested in obtaining IMF loans. The proposed IMF rule could help reduce the number of nations whose governments seek to obtain funds to try to "buy" votes.

CHAPTER 33

33-1. Residents of Norway can produce 100 calculators and 50 books, while residents of Sweden can produce 200 calculators and 50 books. Their total output, therefore, is 300 calculators and 100 books. Sweden has an absolute advantage in calculators. Neither country has an absolute advantage in books.

33-3. a. Norway has a comparative advantage in the production of books, and Sweden has a comparative advantage in the production of calculators.
   b. If residents of both nations specialize, total production is 400 calculators and 100 books.

33-5. Without trade, Norway would have to forgo 1/2 of a book to obtain 1 calculator. With trade, however, Norway can obtain 1 calculator for 1/3 of a book. Without trade, Sweden would have to forgo 4 calculators to obtain 1 book. With trade, however, Sweden can obtain 1 book for 3 calculators. By trading, both nations can obtain the good at a price that is less than the opportunity cost of producing it. They are both better off with trade, so this is a positive-sum game.

33-7. a. East Isle has an absolute advantage in producing modems, and South Shore has an absolute advantage in producing DVD drives.
   b. The opportunity cost of producing one modem in South Shore is 2 DVD drives, and the opportunity cost of producing one modem in East Isle is 1/3 DVD drive. The opportunity cost of producing one DVD drive in South Shore is 1/2 modem, and the opportunity cost of producing one DVD drive in East Isle is 3 modems. Consequently, East Isle has a comparative advantage in produc-

ing modems, and South Shore has a comparative advantage in producing DVD drives.

33-9. **a.** Northern Kingdom has an absolute advantage in producing wheat, and Western Republic has an absolute advantage in producing surfboards.

b. The opportunity cost of producing one surfboard in Northern Kingdom equals 1.83 bushels of wheat, but it is only 0.45 bushels of wheat in Western Republic, so Western Republic has a comparative advantage in producing surfboards. The opportunity cost of producing one bushel of wheat in Northern Kingdom is 0.55 surfboard, but in Western Republic it is 2.25 surfboards, so Northern Kingdom has a comparative advantage in wheat production.

33-11. A price elasticity of demand less than unity indicates inelastic demand and, therefore, price and total revenue move in the same direction. If the nation restricts its exports, the price of the product rises and so does total revenue, even though the nation sells fewer units of output abroad.

33-13. **a.** Because the supply curve shifts by the amount of the tariff, the tariff is $20 per television.

b. Total revenue was $300 per unit times 20 million units, or $6 billion, before the tariff and $310 per unit times 15 million units, or $4.65 billion, after the tariff.

c. U.S. tariff revenue is $20 per unit times 15 million units, or $300 million.

CHAPTER 34

34-1. The trade balance is merchandise exports minus merchandise imports, which equals $500 - 600 = -100$, or a deficit of 100. Adding service exports of 75 and subtracting net unilateral transfers of 10 and service imports of 50 yields $-100 + 75 - 10 - 50 = -85$, or a current account balance of -85. The capital account balance equals the difference between capital inflows and capital outflows, or $300 - 200 = +100$, or a capital account surplus of 100.

34-3. **a.** The increase in demand for Mexican made guitars increases the demand for Mexican pesos, and the peso appreciates.

b. International investors will remove some of their financial capital from Mexico. The increase in the supply of the peso in the foreign exchange market will cause the peso to depreciate.

34-5. **a.** Investors shift their funds from Thailand to other nations where interest returns are higher, so the demand for the baht declines. The dollar-baht exchange rate falls, so the dollar appreciates. The baht depreciates.

b. The rise in Thai productivity reduces the price of Thai goods relative to goods in the United States, so U.S. residents purchase more Thai goods. This increases the demand for baht in the foreign exchange market, so the dollar-baht exchange rate increases. The dollar depreciates, and the baht appreciates.

34-7. The demand for Chinese yuan increases, and the supply of yuan decreases. The dollar-yuan exchange rate rises, so the yuan appreciates.

34-9. The Canadian dollar-euro exchange rate is found by dividing the U.S. dollar-euro exchange rate by the U.S. dollar-Canadian dollar exchange rate, or (1.17 $US/euro)/(0.79 $US/$C) = 1.48 $C/euro, or 1.48 Canadian dollars per euro.

34-11. A flexible exchange rate system allows the exchange value of a currency to be determined freely in the foreign exchange market with no intervention by the government. A fixed exchange rate pegs the value of the currency, and the authorities responsible for the value of the currency intervene in foreign exchange markets to maintain this value. A dirty float involves occasional intervention by the exchange authorities. A target zone allows the exchange value to fluctuate, but only within a given range of values.

34-13. When the U.S. dollar is pegged to gold at a rate of $35 and the pound at a rate of $17.50, the dollar-pound exchange rate equals $35/£17.50 = 2 ($/£).

34-15. **a.** The demand for yuan will decrease, which would begin to cause the equilibrium dollar-yuan exchange rate to decline. To prevent a yuan depreciation from occurring, the Bank of China can purchase yuan with dollars, thereby raising the demand for yuan to its previous level at the original exchange rate. Hence the Bank of China should reduce its dollar reserves.

b. To purchase more U.S. financial assets, Chinese residents must obtain more dollars, so they will increase the quantity of yuan supplied at each exchange rate. This would begin to cause the equilibrium dollar-yuan exchange rate to decline. To prevent a yuan depreciation from occurring, the bank of China can purchase yuan with dollars, thereby causing the demand for yuan to increase sufficiently to push the equilibrium exchange rate back to its original level. Thus the Bank of China should reduce its dollar reserves.

c. U.S. residents increase the quantity of yuan demanded at any given exchange rate in order to purchase Chinese furniture, so the demand for yuan increases. This would tend to cause the equilibrium dollar-yuan exchange rate to rise, resulting in a yuan appreciation. To keep this from happening, the Bank of China can purchase dollars with yuan, thereby increasing the supply of yuan and pushing back down the equilibrium exchange rate. Consequently, the Bank of China should increase its dollar reserves.

A

Absolute advantage The ability to produce more units of a good or service using a given quantity of labor or resource inputs. Equivalently, the ability to produce the same quantity of a good or service using fewer units of labor or resource inputs.

Accounting identities Values that are equivalent by definition.

Accounting profit Total revenues minus total explicit costs.

Action time lag The time between recognizing an economic problem and implementing policy to solve it. The action time lag is quite long for fiscal policy, which requires congressional approval.

Active (discretionary) policymaking All actions on the part of monetary and fiscal policymakers that are undertaken in response to or in anticipation of some change in the overall economy.

***Ad valorem* taxation** Assessing taxes by charging a tax rate equal to a fraction of the market price of each unit purchased.

Adverse selection The likelihood that individuals who seek to borrow money may use the funds that they receive for unworthy, high-risk projects.

Age-earnings cycle The regular earnings profile of an individual throughout his or her lifetime. The age-earnings cycle usually starts with a low income, builds gradually to a peak at around age 50, and then gradually curves down until it approaches zero at retirement.

Aggregate demand The total of all planned expenditures in the entire economy.

Aggregate demand curve A curve showing planned purchase rates for all final goods and services in the economy at various price levels, all other things held constant.

Aggregate demand shock Any event that causes the aggregate demand curve to shift inward or outward.

Aggregate supply The total of all planned production for the economy.

Aggregate supply shock Any event that causes the aggregate supply curve to shift inward or outward.

Aggregates Total amounts or quantities; aggregate demand, for example, is total planned expenditures throughout a nation.

Anticipated inflation The inflation rate that we believe will occur; when it does, we are in a situation of fully anticipated inflation.

Antitrust legislation Laws that restrict the formation of monopolies and regulate certain anticompetitive business practices.

Appreciation An increase in the exchange value of one nation's currency in terms of the currency of another nation.

Asset demand Holding money as a store of value instead of other assets such as certificates of deposit, corporate bonds, and stocks.

Assets Amounts owned; all items to which a business or household holds legal claim.

Asymmetric information Information possessed by one party in a financial transaction but not by the other party.

Automatic, or built-in, stabilizers Special provisions of certain federal programs that cause changes in desired aggregate expenditures without the action of Congress and the president. Examples are the federal progressive tax system and unemployment compensation.

Autonomous consumption The part of consumption that is independent of (does not depend on) the level of disposable income. Changes in autonomous consumption shift the consumption function.

Average fixed costs Total fixed costs divided by the number of units produced.

Average physical product Total product divided by the variable input.

Average propensity to consume (APC) Real consumption divided by real disposable income; for any given level of real income, the proportion of total real disposable income that is consumed.

Average propensity to save (APS) Real saving divided by real disposable income; for any given level of real income, the proportion of total real disposable income that is saved.

Average tax rate The total tax payment divided by total income. It is the proportion of total income paid in taxes.

Average total costs Total costs divided by the number of units produced; sometimes called *average per-unit total costs.*

Average variable costs Total variable costs divided by the number of units produced.

B

Balance of payments A system of accounts that measures transactions of goods, services, income, and financial assets between domestic households, businesses, and governments and residents of the rest of the world during a specific time period.

Balance of trade The difference between exports and imports of goods.

Balance sheet A statement of the assets and liabilities of any business entity, including financial institutions and the Federal Reserve System. Assets are what is owned; liabilities are what is owed.

Balanced budget A situation in which the government's spending is exactly equal to the total taxes and other revenues it collects during a given period of time.

Bank runs Attempts by many of a bank's depositors to convert checkable and time deposits into currency out of fear that the bank's liabilities may exceed its assets.

Barter The direct exchange of goods and services for other goods and services without the use of money.

Base year The year that is chosen as the point of reference for comparison of prices in other years.

Bilateral monopoly A market structure consisting of a monopolist and a monopsonist.

Black market A market in which goods are traded at prices above their legal maximum prices or in which illegal goods are sold.

Bond A legal claim against a firm, usually entitling the owner of the bond to receive a fixed annual coupon payment, plus a lump-sum payment at the bond's maturity date. Bonds are issued in return for funds lent to the firm.

Budget constraint All of the possible combinations of goods that can be purchased (at fixed prices) with a specific budget.

Bundling Offering two or more products for sale as a set.

Business fluctuations The ups and downs in business activity throughout the economy.

C

Capital account A category of balance of payments transactions that measures flows of real and financial assets.

Capital consumption allowance Another name for depreciation, the amount that businesses would have to save in order to take care of the deterioration of machines and other equipment.

Capital controls Legal restrictions on the ability of a nation's residents to hold and trade assets denominated in foreign currencies.

Capital gain The positive difference between the purchase price and the sale price of an asset. If a share of stock is bought for $5 and then sold for $15, the capital gain is $10.

Capital goods Producer durables; nonconsumable goods that firms use to make other goods.

Capital loss The negative difference between the purchase price and the sale price of an asset.

Capture hypothesis A theory of regulatory behavior that predicts that regulators will eventually be captured by special interests of the industry being regulated.

Cartel An association of producers in an industry that agree to set common prices and output quotas to prevent competition.

Central bank A banker's bank, usually an official institution that also serves as a country's treasury's bank. Central banks normally regulate commercial banks.

Certificate of deposit (CD) A time deposit with a fixed maturity date offered by banks and other financial institutions.

Ceteris paribus **[KAY-ter-us PEAR-uh-bus] assumption** The assumption that nothing changes except the factor or factors being studied.

Ceteris paribus **conditions** Determinants of the relationship between price and quantity that are unchanged along a curve; changes in these factors cause the curve to shift.

Checkable deposits Any deposits in a thrift institution or a commercial bank on which a check may be written, for all intents and purposes, a transactions account.

Closed shop A business enterprise in which employees must belong to the union before they can be hired and must remain in the union after they are hired.

Collective bargaining Bargaining between the management of a company or of a group of companies and the management of a union or a group of unions for the purpose of reaching a mutually agreeable contract that sets wages, fringe benefits, and working conditions for all employees in all the unions involved.

Collective decision making How voters, politicians, and other interested parties act and how these actions influence nonmarket decisions.

Common property Property that is owned by everyone and therefore by no one. Air and water are examples of common property resources.

Comparable-worth doctrine The belief that women should receive the same wages as men if the levels of skill and responsibility in their jobs are equivalent.

Comparative advantage The ability to produce a good or service at a lower opportunity cost than other producers.

Complements Two goods are complements if both are used together for consumption or enjoyment—for example, coffee and cream. The more you buy of one, the more you buy of the other. For complements, a change in the price of one causes an opposite shift in the demand for the other.

Concentration ratio The percentage of all sales contributed by the leading four or leading eight firms in an industry; sometimes called the *industry concentration ratio*.

Constant dollars Dollars expressed in terms of real purchasing power using a particular year as the base or standard of comparison, in contrast to current dollars.

Constant returns to scale No change in long-run average costs when output increases.

Constant-cost industry An industry whose total output can be increased without an increase in long-run per-unit costs; its long-run supply curve is horizontal.

Consumer optimum A choice of a set of goods and services that maximizes the level of satisfaction for each consumer, subject to limited income.

Consumer Price Index (CPI) A statistical measure of a weighted average of prices of a specified set of goods and services purchased by typical consumers in urban areas.

Consumption Spending on new goods and services out of a household's current income. Whatever is not consumed is saved. Consumption includes such things as buying food and going to a concert.

Consumption function The relationship between amount consumed and disposable income. A consumption function tells us how much people plan to consume at various levels of disposable income.

Consumption goods Goods bought by households to use up, such as food and movies.

Contraction A business fluctuation during which the pace of national economic activity is slowing down.

Cooperative game A game in which the players explicitly cooperate to make themselves better off. As applied to firms, it involves companies colluding in order to make higher than competitive rates of return.

Corporation A legal entity that may conduct business in its own name just as an individual does; the owners of a corporation, called shareholders, own shares of the firm's profits and enjoy the protection of limited liability.

Cost-of-living adjustments (COLAs) Clauses in contracts that allow for increases in specified nominal values to take account of changes in the cost of living.

Cost-of-service regulation Regulation that allows prices to reflect only the actual cost of production and no monopoly profits.

Cost-push inflation Inflation caused by decreases in short-run aggregate supply.

Craft unions Labor unions composed of workers who engage in a particular trade or skill, such as baking, carpentry, or plumbing.

Crawling peg An exchange rate arrangement in which a country pegs the value of its currency to the exchange value of another nation's currency but allows the par value to change at regular intervals.

Creative response Behavior on the part of a firm that allows it to comply with the letter of the law but violate the spirit, significantly lessening the law's effects.

Credence good A product with qualities that consumers lack the expertise to assess without assistance.

Cross price elasticity of demand (E_{xy}) The percentage change in the demand for one good (holding its price constant) divided by the percentage change in the price of a related good.

Crowding-out effect The tendency of expansionary fiscal policy to cause a decrease in planned investment or planned consumption in the private sector; this decrease normally results from the rise in interest rates.

Current account A category of balance of payments transactions that measures the exchange of merchandise, the exchange of services, and unilateral transfers.

Cyclical unemployment Unemployment resulting from business recessions that occur when aggregate (total) demand is insufficient to create full employment.

D

Dead capital Any capital resource that lacks clear title of ownership.

Decreasing-cost industry An industry in which an increase in output leads to a reduction in long-run per-unit costs, such that the long-run industry supply curve slopes downward.

Deflation A sustained decrease in the average of all prices of goods and services in an economy.

Demand A schedule of how much of a good or service people will purchase at any price during a specified time period, other things being constant.

Demand curve A graphical representation of the demand schedule; a negatively sloped line showing the inverse relationship between the price and the quantity demanded (other things being equal).

Demand-pull inflation Inflation caused by increases in aggregate demand not matched by increases in aggregate supply.

Demerit good A good that has been deemed socially undesirable through the political process. Heroin is an example.

Dependent variable A variable whose value changes according to changes in the value of one or more independent variables.

Depository institutions Financial institutions that accept deposits from savers and lend those deposits out at interest.

Depreciation A decrease in the exchange value of one nation's currency in terms of the currency of another nation; also, a reduction in the value of capital goods over a one-year period due to physical wear and tear and also to obsolescence.

Depression An extremely severe recession.

Derived demand Input factor demand derived from demand for the final product being produced.

Development economics The study of factors that contribute to the economic development of a country.

Diminishing marginal utility The principle that as more of any good or service is consumed, its extra benefit declines. Otherwise stated, increases in total utility from the consumption of a good or service become smaller and smaller as more is consumed during a given time period.

Direct expenditure offsets Actions on the part of the private sector in spending income that offset government fiscal policy actions. Any increase in government spending in an area that competes with the private sector will have some direct expenditure offset.

Direct marketing Advertising targeted at specific consumers, typically in the form of postal mailings, telephone calls, or e-mail messages.

Direct relationship A relationship between two variables that is positive, meaning that an increase in one variable is associated with an increase in the other and a decrease in one variable is associated with a decrease in the other.

Dirty float Active management of a floating exchange rate on the part of a country's government, often in cooperation with other nations.

Discount rate The interest rate that the Federal Reserve charges for reserves that it lends to depository institutions. It is sometimes referred to as the *rediscount rate* or, in Canada and England, as the *bank rate.*

Discounting The method by which the present value of a future sum or a future stream of sums is obtained.

Discouraged workers Individuals who have stopped looking for a job because they are convinced that they will not find a suitable one.

Diseconomies of scale Increases in long-run average costs that occur as output increases.

Disposable personal income (DPI) Personal income after personal income taxes have been paid.

Dissaving Negative saving; a situation in which spending exceeds income. Dissaving can occur when a household is able to borrow or use up existing assets.

Distribution of income The way income is allocated among the population.

Dividends Portion of a corporation's profits paid to its owners (shareholders).

Division of labor The segregation of a resource into different specific tasks; for example, one automobile worker puts on bumpers, another doors, and so on.

Dominant strategies Strategies that always yield the highest benefit. Regardless of what other players do, a dominant strategy will yield the most benefit for the player using it.

Dumping Selling a good or a service abroad below the price charged in the home market or at a price below its cost of production.

Durable consumer goods Consumer goods that have a life span of more than three years.

Dynamic tax analysis Economic evaluation of tax rate changes that recognizes that the tax base eventually declines with ever-higher tax rates, so that tax revenues may eventually decline if the tax rate is raised sufficiently.

E

Economic freedom The rights to own private property and to exchange goods, services, and financial assets with minimal government interference.

Economic goods Goods that are scarce, for which the quantity demanded exceeds the quantity supplied at a zero price.

Economic growth Increases in per capita real GDP measured by its rate of change per year.

Economic profits Total revenues minus total opportunity costs of all inputs used, or the total of all implicit and explicit costs.

Economic rent A payment for the use of any resource over and above its opportunity cost.

Economics The study of how people allocate their limited resources to satisfy their unlimited wants.

Economies of scale Decreases in long-run average costs resulting from increases in output.

Effect time lag The time that elapses between the implementation of a policy and the results of that policy.

Efficiency The case in which a given level of inputs is used to produce the maximum output possible. Alternatively, the situation in which a given output is produced at minimum cost.

Efficiency wage The optimal wage that firms must pay to maintain worker productivity.

Effluent fee A charge to a polluter that gives the right to discharge into the air or water a certain amount of pollution; also called a *pollution tax.*

Elastic demand A demand relationship in which a given percentage change in price will result in a larger percentage change in quantity demanded. Total expenditures and price changes are inversely related in the elastic region of the demand curve.

Empirical Relying on real-world data in evaluating the usefulness of a model.

Endowments The various resources in an economy, including both physical resources and such human resources as ingenuity and management skills.

Entitlements Guaranteed benefits under a government program such as Social Security, Medicare, or Medicaid.

Entrepreneurship The factor of production involving human resources that perform the functions of raising capital, organizing, managing, assembling other factors of production, and making basic business policy decisions. The entrepreneur is a risk taker.

Entry deterrence strategy Any strategy undertaken by firms in an industry, either individually or together, with the intent or effect of raising the cost of entry into the industry by a new firm.

Equation of exchange The formula indicating that the number of monetary units times the number of times each unit is spent on final goods and services is identical to the price level times nominal GDP.

Equilibrium The situation when quantity supplied equals quantity demanded at a particular price.

Excess reserves The difference between legal reserves and required reserves.

Exchange rate The price of one nation's currency in terms of the currency of another country.

Excise tax A tax levied on purchases of a particular good or service.

Exclusion principle The principle that no one can be excluded from the benefits of a public good, even if that person has not paid for it.

Expansion A business fluctuation in which the pace of national economic activity is speeding up.

Expenditure approach Computing GDP by adding up the dollar value at current market prices of all final goods and services.

Experience good A product that an individual must consume before the product's quality can be established.

Explicit costs Costs that business managers must take account of because they must be paid; examples are wages, taxes, and rent.

Externality A consequence of an economic activity that spills over to affect third parties; a situation in which a private cost (or benefit) diverges from a social cost (or benefit); a situation in which the costs (or benefits) of an action are not fully borne (or gained) by the two parties engaged in exchange or by an individual engaging in a scarce-resource-using activity.

F

Featherbedding Any practice that forces employers to use more labor than they would otherwise or to use existing labor in an inefficient manner.

Federal Deposit Insurance Corporation (FDIC) A government agency that insures the deposits held in banks and most other depository institutions; all U.S. banks are insured this way.

Federal funds market A private market (made up mostly of banks) in which banks can borrow reserves from other banks that want to lend them. Federal funds are usually lent for overnight use.

Federal funds rate The interest rate that depository institutions pay to borrow reserves in the interbank federal funds market.

Fiduciary monetary system A system in which money is issued by the government and its value is based uniquely on the public's faith that the currency represents command over goods and services.

Final goods and services Goods and services that are at their final stage of production and will not be transformed into yet other goods or services. For example, wheat is not ordinarily considered a final good because it is usually used to make a final good, bread.

Financial capital Funds used to purchase physical capital goods, such as buildings and equipment, and patents and trademarks.

Financial intermediaries Institutions that transfer funds between ultimate lenders (savers) and ultimate borrowers.

Financial intermediation The process by which financial institutions accept savings from businesses, households, and governments and lend the savings to other businesses, households, and governments.

Firm A business organization that employs resources to produce goods or services for profit. A firm normally owns and operates at least one "plant" in order to produce.

Fiscal policy The discretionary changing of government expenditures or taxes to achieve national economic goals, such as high employment with price stability.

Fixed costs Costs that do not vary with output. Fixed costs typically include such things as rent on a building. These costs are fixed for a certain period of time (in the long run, though, they are variable).

Fixed investment Purchases by businesses of newly produced producer durables, or capital goods, such as production machinery and office equipment.

Flexible exchange rates Exchange rates that are allowed to fluctuate in the open market in response to changes in supply and demand. Sometimes called *floating exchange rates*.

Flow A quantity measured per unit of time; something that occurs over time, such as the income you make per week or per year or the number of individuals who are fired every month.

Foreign direct investment The acquisition of more than 10 percent of the shares of ownership in a company in another nation.

Foreign exchange market A market in which households, firms, and governments buy and sell national currencies.

Foreign exchange rate The price of one currency in terms of another.

Foreign exchange risk The possibility that changes in the value of a nation's currency will result in variations in the market value of assets.

45-degree reference line The line along which planned real expenditures equal real GDP per year.

Fractional reserve banking A system in which depository institutions hold reserves that are less than the amount of total deposits.

Free-rider problem A problem that arises when individuals presume that others will pay for public goods so that, individually, they can escape paying for their portion without causing a reduction in production.

Frictional unemployment Unemployment due to the fact that workers must search for appropriate job offers. This takes time, and so they remain temporarily unemployed.

Full employment An arbitrary level of unemployment that corresponds to "normal" friction in the labor market. In 1986, a 6.5 percent rate of unemployment was considered full employment. Today, it is assumed to be around 5 percent.

G

Game theory A way of describing the various possible outcomes in any situation involving two or more interacting individuals when those individuals are aware of the interactive nature of their situation and plan accordingly. The plans made by these individuals are known as *game strategies*.

GDP deflator A price index measuring the changes in prices of all new goods and services produced in the economy.

General Agreement on Tariffs and Trade (GATT) An international agreement established in 1947 to further world trade by reducing barriers and tariffs. GATT was replaced by the World Trade Organization in 1995.

Goods All things from which individuals derive satisfaction or happiness.

Government budget constraint The limit on government spending and transfers imposed by the fact that every dollar the government spends, transfers, or uses to repay borrowed funds must ultimately be provided by the taxes it collects.

Government budget deficit An excess of government spending over government revenues during a given period of time.

Government budget surplus An excess of government revenues over government spending during a given period of time.

Government, or political, goods Goods (and services) provided by the public sector; they can be either private or public goods.

Gross domestic income (GDI) The sum of all income—wages, interest, rent, and profits—paid to the four factors of production.

Gross domestic product (GDP) The total market value of all final goods and services produced by factors of production located within a nation's borders.

Gross private domestic investment The creation of capital goods, such as factories and machines, that can yield production and hence consumption in the future. Also included in this definition are changes in business inventories and repairs made to machines or buildings.

Gross public debt All federal government debt irrespective of who owns it.

H

Health savings account (HSA) A tax-exempt health care account into which individuals can pay on a regular basis and out of which medical expenses can be paid.

Hedge A financial strategy that reduces the chance of suffering losses arising from foreign exchange risk.

Horizontal merger The joining of firms that are producing or selling a similar product.

Human capital The accumulated training and education of workers.

I

Implicit costs Expenses that managers do not have to pay out of pocket and hence do not normally explicitly calculate, such as the opportunity cost of factors of production that are owned; examples are owner-provided capital and owner-provided labor.

Import quota A physical supply restriction on imports of a particular good, such as sugar. Foreign exporters are unable to sell in the United States more than the quantity specified in the import quota.

Incentive structure The system of rewards and punishments individuals face with respect to their own actions.

Incentives Rewards for engaging in a particular activity.

Income approach Measuring GDP by adding up all components of national income, including wages, interest, rent, and profits.

Income elasticity of demand (E_i) The percentage change in demand for any good, holding its price constant, divided by the percentage change in income; the responsiveness of demand to changes in income, holding the good's relative price constant.

Income in kind Income received in the form of goods and services, such as housing or medical care; to be contrasted with money income, which is simply income in dollars, or general purchasing power, that can be used to buy *any* goods and services.

Income velocity of money The number of times per year a dollar is spent on fi-

nal goods and services; equal to nominal GDP divided by the money supply.

Income-consumption curve The set of optimal consumption points that would occur if income were increased, relative prices remaining constant.

Increasing-cost industry An industry in which an increase in industry output is accompanied by an increase in long-run per-unit costs, such that the long-run industry supply curve slopes upward.

Independent variable A variable whose value is determined independently of, or outside, the equation under study.

Indifference curve A curve composed of a set of consumption alternatives, each of which yields the same total amount of satisfaction.

Indirect business taxes All business taxes except the tax on corporate profits. Indirect business taxes include sales and business property taxes.

Industrial unions Labor unions that consist of workers from a particular industry, such as automobile manufacturing or steel manufacturing.

Industry supply curve The locus of points showing the minimum prices at which given quantities will be forthcoming; also called the *market supply curve*.

Inefficient point Any point below the production possibilities curve at which the use of resources is not generating the maximum possible output.

Inelastic demand A demand relationship in which a given percentage change in price will result in a less than proportionate percentage change in the quantity demanded. Total expenditures and price are directly related in the inelastic region of the demand curve.

Infant industry argument The contention that tariffs should be imposed to protect from import competition an industry that is trying to get started. Presumably, after the industry becomes technologically efficient, the tariff can be lifted.

Inferior goods Goods for which demand falls as income rises.

Inflation A sustained increase in the average of all prices of goods and services in an economy.

Inflation-adjusted return A rate of return that is measured in terms of real goods and services; that is, after the effects of inflation have been factored out.

Inflationary gap The gap that exists whenever equilibrium real GDP per year is greater than full-employment real GDP as shown by the position of the long-run aggregate supply curve.

Information product An item that is produced using information-intensive inputs at a relatively high fixed cost but distributed for sale at a relatively low marginal cost.

Informational advertising Advertising that emphasizes transmitting knowledge about the features of a product.

Innovation Transforming an invention into something that is useful to humans.

Inside information Information that is not available to the general public about what is happening in a corporation.

Interactive marketing Advertising that permits a consumer to follow up directly by searching for more information and placing direct product orders.

Interest The payment for current rather than future command over resources; the cost of obtaining credit. Also, the return paid to owners of capital.

Interest rate effect One of the reasons that the aggregate demand curve slopes downward: Higher price levels increase the interest rate, which in turn causes businesses and consumers to reduce desired spending due to the higher cost of borrowing.

Intermediate goods Goods used up entirely in the production of final goods.

International financial crisis The rapid withdrawal of foreign investments and loans from a nation.

International financial diversification Financing investment projects in more than one country.

International Monetary Fund An agency founded to administer an international foreign exchange system and to lend to member countries that had balance of payments problems. The IMF now functions as a lender of last resort for national governments.

Inventory investment Changes in the stocks of finished goods and goods in process, as well as changes in the raw materials that businesses keep on hand. Whenever inventories are decreasing, inventory investment is negative; whenever they are increasing, inventory investment is positive.

Inverse relationship A relationship between two variables that is negative, meaning that an increase in one variable is associated with a decrease in the other and a decrease in one variable is associated with an increase in the other.

Investment Any use of today's resources to expand tomorrow's production or consumption; spending by businesses on things such as machines and buildings, which can be used to produce goods and services in the future. The investment part of real GDP is the portion that will be used in the process of producing goods in the future.

J

Job leaver An individual in the labor force who quits voluntarily.

Job loser An individual in the labor force whose employment was involuntarily terminated.

Jurisdictional dispute A dispute involving two or more unions over which should have control of a particular jurisdiction, such as a particular craft or skill or a particular firm or industry.

K

Keynesian short-run aggregate supply curve The horizontal portion of the aggregate supply curve in which there is excessive unemployment and unused capacity in the economy.

L

Labor Productive contributions of humans who work, involving both mental and physical activities.

Labor force Individuals aged 16 years or older who either have jobs or who are looking and available for jobs; the number of employed plus the number of unemployed.

Labor force participation rate The percentage of noninstitutionalized working-age individuals who are employed or seeking employment.

Labor productivity Total real domestic output (real GDP) divided by the number of workers (output per worker).

Labor unions Worker organizations that seek to secure economic improvements for their members; they also seek to improve the safety, health and other benefits (such as job security) of their members.

Land The natural resources that are available from nature. Land as a resource includes location, original fertility and mineral deposits, topography, climate, water, and vegetation.

Law of demand The observation that there is a negative, or inverse, relationship between the price of any good or service and the quantity demanded, holding other factors constant.

Law of diminishing (marginal) returns The observation that after some point, successive equal-sized increases in a variable factor of production, such as labor, added to fixed factors of production, will result in smaller increases in output.

Law of increasing relative cost The observation that the opportunity cost of additional units of a good generally increases as society attempts to produce more of that good. This accounts for the bowed-out shape of the production possibilities curve.

Law of supply The observation that the higher the price of a good, the more of that good sellers will make available over a specified time period, other things being equal.

Leading indicators Events that have been found to exhibit changes before changes in business activity.

Legal reserves Reserves that depository institutions are allowed by law to claim as reserves—for example, deposits held at Federal Reserve district banks and vault cash.

Lemons problem The potential for asymmetric information to bring about a general decline in product quality in an industry.

Liabilities Amounts owed; the legal claims against a business or household by nonowners.

Limited liability A legal concept whereby the responsibility, or liability, of the owners of a corporation is limited to the value of the shares in the firm that they own.

Limit-pricing model A model that hypothesizes that a group of colluding sellers will set the highest common price that they believe they can charge without new firms seeking to enter that industry in search of relatively high profits.

Liquidity The degree to which an asset can be acquired or disposed of without much danger of any intervening loss in nominal value and with small transaction costs. Money is the most liquid asset.

Liquidity approach A method of measuring the money supply by looking at money as a temporary store of value.

Long run The time period during which all factors of production can be varied.

Long-run aggregate supply curve A vertical line representing the real output of goods and services after full adjustment has occurred. It can also be viewed as representing the real GDP of the economy under conditions of full employment—the full-employment level of real GDP.

Long-run average cost curve The locus of points representing the minimum unit cost of producing any given rate of output, given current technology and resource prices.

Long-run industry supply curve A market supply curve showing the relationship between prices and quantities after firms have been allowed the time to enter into or exit from an industry, depending on whether there have been positive or negative economic profits.

Lorenz curve A geometric representation of the distribution of income. A Lorenz curve that is perfectly straight represents complete income equality. The more bowed a Lorenz curve, the more unequally income is distributed.

Lump-sum tax A tax that does not depend on income. An example is a $1,000 tax that every household must pay, irrespective of its economic situation.

M

M1 The money supply, taken as the total value of currency plus checkable deposits plus traveler's checks not issued by banks.

M2 M1 plus (1) savings and small-denomination time deposits at all depository institutions, (2) balances in retail money market mutual funds, and (3) money market deposit accounts (MMDAs).

Macroeconomics The study of the behavior of the economy as a whole, including such economywide phenomena as changes in unemployment, the general price level, and national income.

Majority rule A collective decision-making system in which group decisions are made on the basis of more than 50 percent of the vote. In other words, whatever more than half of the electorate votes for, the entire electorate has to accept.

Marginal cost pricing A system of pricing in which the price charged is equal to the opportunity cost to society of producing one more unit of the good or service in question. The opportunity cost is the marginal cost to society.

Marginal costs The change in total costs due to a one-unit change in production rate.

Marginal factor cost (MFC) The cost of using an additional unit of an input. For example, if a firm can hire all the workers it wants at the going wage rate, the marginal factor cost of labor is the wage rate.

Marginal physical product The physical output that is due to the addition of one more unit of a variable factor of production; the change in total product occurring when a variable input is increased and all other inputs are held constant; also called *marginal product* or *marginal return*.

Marginal physical product (MPP) of labor The change in output resulting from the addition of one more worker. The MPP of the worker equals the change in total output accounted for by hiring the worker, holding all other factors of production constant.

Marginal propensity to consume (MPC) The ratio of the change in consumption to the change in disposable income. A marginal propensity to consume of 0.8 tells us that an additional $100 in take-home pay will lead to an additional $80 consumed.

Marginal propensity to save (MPS) The ratio of the change in saving to the change in disposable income. A marginal propensity to save of 0.2 indicates that out of an additional $100 in take-home pay, $20 will be saved. Whatever is not saved is consumed. The marginal propensity to save plus the marginal propensity to consume must always equal 1, by definition.

Marginal revenue The change in total revenues resulting from a change in output (and sale) of one unit of the product in question.

Marginal revenue product (MRP) The marginal physical product (MPP) times marginal revenue (MR). The MRP gives the additional revenue obtained from a one-unit change in labor input.

Marginal tax rate The change in the tax payment divided by the change in income, or the percentage of additional dollars that must be paid in taxes. The marginal tax rate is applied to the highest tax bracket of taxable income reached.

Marginal utility The change in total utility due to a one-unit change in the quantity of a good or service consumed.

Market All of the arrangements that individuals have for exchanging with one another. Thus, for example, we can speak of the labor market, the automobile market, and the credit market.

Market clearing, or equilibrium, price The price that clears the market, at which quantity demanded equals quantity supplied; the price where the demand curve intersects the supply curve.

Market demand The demand of all consumers in the marketplace for a particular good or service. The summation at each price of the quantity demanded by each individual.

Market failure A situation in which an unrestrained market operation leads to either too few or too many resources going to a specific economic activity.

Market share test The percentage of a market that a particular firm supplies; used as the primary measure of monopoly power.

Mass marketing Advertising intended to reach as many consumers as possible, typically through television, newspaper, radio, or magazine ads.

Medium of exchange Any asset that sellers will accept as payment.

Merit good A good that has been deemed socially desirable through the political process. Museums are an example.

Microeconomics The study of decision making undertaken by individuals (or households) and by firms.

Minimum efficient scale (MES) The lowest rate of output per unit time at which long-run average costs for a particular firm are at a minimum.

Minimum wage A wage floor, legislated by government, setting the lowest hourly rate that firms may legally pay workers.

Models, or theories Simplified representations of the real world used as the basis for predictions or explanations.

Monetarists Macroeconomists who believe that inflation in the long run is always caused by excessive monetary growth and that changes in the money supply affect aggregate demand both directly and indirectly.

Monetary rule A monetary policy that incorporates a rule specifying the annual rate of growth of some monetary aggregate.

Money Any medium that is universally accepted in an economy both by sellers of goods and services as payment for those goods and services and by creditors as payment for debts.

Money balances Synonymous with money, money stock, money holdings.

Money illusion Reacting to changes in money prices rather than relative prices. If a worker whose wages double when the price level also doubles thinks he or she is better off, that worker is suffering from money illusion.

Money market deposit accounts (MMDAs) Accounts issued by banks yielding a market rate of interest with a minimum balance requirement and a limit on transactions. They have no minimum maturity.

Money market mutual funds Funds of investment companies that obtain money from the public that is held in common and used to acquire short-maturity credit instruments, such as certificates of deposit and securities sold by the U.S. government.

Money multiplier The reciprocal of the required reserve ratio, assuming no leakages into currency and no excess reserves. It is equal to 1 divided by the required reserve ratio.

Money price The price that we observe today, expressed in today's dollars; also called the *absolute* or *nominal price.*

Money supply The amount of money in circulation.

Monopolist The single supplier of a good or service for which there is no close substitute. The monopolist therefore constitutes its entire industry.

Monopolistic competition A market situation in which a large number of firms produce similar but not identical products. Entry into the industry is relatively easy.

Monopolization The possession of monopoly power in the relevant market and the willful acquisition or maintenance of that power, as distinguished from growth or development as a consequence of a superior product, business acumen, or historical accident.

Monopoly A firm that has control over the price of a good. In the extreme case, a monopoly is the only seller of a good or service.

Monopsonist The only buyer in a market.

Monopsonistic exploitation Paying a price for the variable input that is less than its marginal revenue product; the difference between marginal revenue product and the wage rate.

Moral hazard The possibility that a borrower might engage in riskier behavior after a loan has been obtained.

Multiplier The ratio of the change in the equilibrium level of real GDP to the change in autonomous real expenditures; the number by which a change in autonomous real investment or autonomous real consumption, for example, is multiplied to get the change in equilibrium real GDP.

N

National income (NI) The total of all factor payments to resource owners. It can be obtained by subtracting indirect business taxes from NDP.

National income accounting A measurement system used to estimate national income and its components; one approach to measuring an economy's aggregate performance.

Natural monopoly A monopoly that arises from the peculiar production characteristics in an industry. It usually arises when there are large economies of scale relative to the industry's demand such that one firm can produce at a lower average cost than can be achieved by multiple firms.

Natural rate of unemployment The rate of unemployment that is estimated to prevail in long-run macroeconomic equilibrium, when all workers and employers have fully adjusted to any changes in the economy.

Near moneys Assets that are almost money. They have a high degree of liquidity and thus can be easily converted into money without loss in value. Time deposits and short-term U.S. government securities are examples.

Negative market feedback A tendency for a good or service to fall out of favor with more consumers because other consumers have stopped purchasing the item.

Negative-sum game A game in which players as a group lose at the end of the game.

Net domestic product (NDP) GDP minus depreciation.

Net investment Gross private domestic investment minus an estimate of the wear and tear on the existing capital stock. Net investment therefore measures the change in capital stock over a one-year period.

Net public debt Gross public debt minus all government interagency borrowing.

Net worth The difference between assets and liabilities.

Network effect A situation in which a consumer's willingness to purchase a good or service is influenced by how many others also buy or have bought the item.

New entrant An individual who has never held a full-time job lasting two weeks or longer but is now seeking employment.

New growth theory A theory of economic growth that examines the factors that determine why technology, research, innovation, and the like are undertaken and how they interact.

Nominal rate of interest The market rate of interest expressed in today's dollars.

Nominal values The values of variables such as GDP and investment expressed in current dollars, also called *money values;* measurement in terms of the actual market prices at which goods and services are sold.

Nonaccelerating inflation rate of unemployment (NAIRU) The rate of unemployment below which the rate of inflation tends to rise and above which the rate of inflation tends to fall.

Noncontrollable expenditures Government spending that changes automatically without action by Congress.

Noncooperative game A game in which the players neither negotiate nor cooperate in any way. As applied to firms in an industry, this is the common situation in which there are relatively few firms and each has some ability to change price.

Nondurable consumer goods Consumer goods that are used up within three years.

Nonincome expense items The total of indirect business taxes and depreciation.

Nonprice rationing devices All methods used to ration scarce goods that are price-controlled. Whenever the price system is not allowed to work, nonprice rationing devices will evolve to ration the affected goods and services.

Normal goods Goods for which demand rises as income rises. Most goods are normal goods.

Normal rate of return The amount that must be paid to an investor to induce investment in a business; also known as the *opportunity cost of capital.*

Normative economics Analysis involving value judgments about economic policies; relates to whether things are good or bad. A statement of *what ought to be.*

Number line A line that can be divided into segments of equal length, each associated with a number.

O

Oligopoly A market situation in which there are very few sellers. Each seller knows that the other sellers will react to its changes in prices and quantities.

Open economy effect One of the reasons that the aggregate demand curve slopes downward: Higher price levels result in foreign residents desiring to buy fewer U.S.-made goods, while U.S. residents now desire more foreign-made goods, thereby reducing net exports. This is equivalent to a reduction in the amount of real goods and services purchased in the United States.

Open market operations The purchase and sale of existing U.S. government securities (such as bonds) in the open private market by the Federal Reserve System.

Opportunistic behavior Actions that ignore the possible long-run benefits of cooperation and focus solely on short-run gains.

Opportunity cost The highest-valued, next-best alternative that must be sacrificed to obtain something or to satisfy a want.

Opportunity cost of capital The normal rate of return, or the available return on the next-best alternative investment. Economists consider this a cost of production, and it is included in our cost examples.

Optimal quantity of pollution The level of pollution for which the marginal benefit of one additional unit of clean air just equals the marginal cost of that additional unit of clean air.

Origin The intersection of the y axis and the x axis in a graph.

Outsourcing A firm's employment of labor outside the country in which the firm is located.

P

Par value The officially determined value of a currency.

Partnership A business owned by two or more joint owners, or partners, who share the responsibilities and the profits of the firm and are individually liable for all the debts of the partnership.

Passive (nondiscretionary) policymaking Policymaking that is carried out in response to a rule. It is therefore not in response to an actual or potential change in overall economic activity.

Patent A government protection that gives an inventor the exclusive right to make, use, or sell an invention for a limited period of time (currently, 20 years).

Payoff matrix A matrix of outcomes, or consequences, of the strategies available to the players in a game.

Perfect competition A market structure in which the decisions of *individual* buyers and sellers have no effect on market price.

Perfectly competitive firm A firm that is such a small part of the total *industry* that it cannot affect the price of the product it sells.

Perfectly elastic demand A demand that has the characteristic that even the slightest increase in price will lead to zero quantity demanded.

Perfectly elastic supply A supply characterized by a reduction in quantity supplied to zero when there is the slightest decrease in price.

Perfectly inelastic demand A demand that exhibits zero responsiveness to price changes; no matter what the price is, the quantity demanded remains the same.

Perfectly inelastic supply A supply for which quantity supplied remains constant, no matter what happens to price.

Personal Consumption Expenditure (PCE) Index. A statistical measure of average price using annually updated weights based on surveys of consumer spending.

Personal income (PI) The amount of income that households actually receive before they pay personal income taxes.

Persuasive advertising Advertising that is intended to induce a consumer to purchase a particular product and discover a previously unknown taste for the item.

Phillips curve A curve showing the relationship between unemployment and changes in wages or prices. It was long thought to reflect a trade-off between unemployment and inflation.

Physical capital All manufactured resources, including buildings, equipment, machines, and improvements to land that is used for production.

Planning curve The long-run average cost curve.

Planning horizon The long run, during which all inputs are variable.

Plant size The physical size of the factories that a firm owns and operates to produce its output. Plant size can be defined by square footage, maximum physical capacity, and other physical measures.

Policy irrelevance proposition The conclusion that policy actions have no real effects in the short run if the policy actions are anticipated and none in the long run even if the policy actions are unanticipated.

Portfolio investment The purchase of less than 10 percent of the shares of ownership in a company in another nation.

Positive economics Analysis that is strictly limited to making either purely descriptive statements or scientific predictions; for example, "If A, then B." A statement of *what is.*

Positive market feedback A tendency for a good or service to come into favor with additional consumers because other consumers have chosen to buy the item.

Positive-sum game A game in which players as a group are better off at the end of the game.

Precautionary demand Holding money to meet unplanned expenditures and emergencies.

Present value The value of a future amount expressed in today's dollars; the most that someone would pay today to receive a certain sum at some point in the future.

Price ceiling A legal maximum price that may be charged for a particular good or service.

Price controls Government-mandated minimum or maximum prices that may be charged for goods and services.

Price differentiation Establishing different prices for similar products to reflect differences in marginal cost in providing those commodities to different groups of buyers.

Price discrimination Selling a given product at more than one price, with the price difference being unrelated to differences in marginal cost.

Price elasticity of demand (E_p) The responsiveness of the quantity demanded of a commodity to changes in its price; defined as the percentage change in quantity demanded divided by the percentage change in price.

Price elasticity of supply (E_s) The responsiveness of the quantity supplied of a commodity to a change in its price; the percentage change in quantity supplied divided by the percentage change in price.

Price floor A legal minimum price below which a good or service may not be sold. Legal minimum wages are an example.

Price index The cost of today's market basket of goods expressed as a percentage of the cost of the same market basket during a base year.

Price leadership A practice in many oligopolistic industries in which the largest firm publishes its price list ahead of its competitors, who then match those announced prices. Also called *parallel pricing.*

Price searcher A firm that must determine the price-output combination that maximizes profit because it faces a downward-sloping demand curve.

Price system An economic system in which relative prices are constantly changing to reflect changes in supply and demand for different commodities. The prices of those commodities are signals to everyone within the system as to what is relatively scarce and what is relatively abundant.

Price taker A competitive firm that must take the price of its product as given because the firm cannot influence its price.

Price war A pricing campaign designed to capture additional market share by repeatedly cutting prices.

Price-consumption curve The set of consumer-optimum combinations of two goods that the consumer would choose as the price of one good changes, while money income and the price of the other good remain constant.

Principle of rival consumption The recognition that individuals are rivals in consuming private goods because one person's consumption reduces the amount available for others to consume.

Principle of substitution The principle that consumers and producers shift away from goods and resources that become priced relatively higher in favor of goods and resources that are now priced relatively lower.

Prisoners' dilemma A famous strategic game in which two prisoners have a choice between confessing and not confessing to a crime. If neither confesses, they serve a minimum sentence. If both confess, they serve a longer sentence. If one confesses and the other doesn't, the one who confesses goes free. The dominant strategy is always to confess.

Private costs Costs borne solely by the individuals who incur them. Also called *internal costs*.

Private goods Goods that can be consumed by only one individual at a time. Private goods are subject to the principle of rival consumption.

Private property rights Exclusive rights of ownership that allow the use, transfer, and exchange of property.

Producer durables, or capital goods Durable goods having an expected service life of more than three years that are used by businesses to produce other goods and services.

Producer Price Index (PPI) A statistical measure of a weighted average of prices of goods and services that firms produce and sell.

Product differentiation The distinguishing of products by brand name, color, and other minor attributes. Product differentiation occurs in other than perfectly competitive markets in which products are, in theory, homogeneous, such as wheat or corn.

Production Any activity that results in the conversion of resources into products that can be used in consumption.

Production function The relationship between inputs and maximum physical output. A production function is a technological, not an economic, relationship.

Production possibilities curve (PPC) A curve representing all possible combinations of total output that could be produced assuming (1) a fixed amount of productive resources of a given quality and (2) the efficient use of those resources.

Profit-maximizing rate of production The rate of production that maximizes total profits, or the difference between total revenues and total costs; also, the rate of production at which marginal revenue equals marginal cost.

Progressive taxation A tax system in which, as income increases, a higher percentage of the additional income is taxed. The marginal tax rate exceeds the average tax rate as income rises.

Property rights The rights of an owner to use and to exchange property.

Proportional rule A decision-making system in which actions are based on the proportion of the "votes" cast and are in proportion to them. In a market system, if 10 percent of the "dollar votes" are cast for blue cars, 10 percent of the output will be blue cars.

Proportional taxation A tax system in which, regardless of an individual's income, the tax bill comprises exactly the same proportion.

Proprietorship A business owned by one individual who makes the business decisions, receives all the profits, and is legally responsible for the debts of the firm.

Public debt The total value of all outstanding federal government securities.

Public goods Goods for which the principle of rival consumption does not apply; they can be jointly consumed by many individuals simultaneously at no additional cost and with no reduction in quality or quantity. Also no one who fails to help pay for the good can be denied the benefit of the good.

Purchasing power The value of money for buying goods and services. If your

money income stays the same but the price of one good that you are buying goes up, your effective purchasing power falls, and vice versa.

Purchasing power parity Adjustment in exchange rate conversions that takes into account differences in the true cost of living across countries.

Q

Quantity theory of money and prices The hypothesis that changes in the money supply lead to proportional changes in the price level.

Quota subscription A nation's account with the International Monetary Fund, denominated in special drawing rights.

Quota system A government-imposed restriction on the quantity of a specific good that another country is allowed to sell in the United States. In other words, quotas are restrictions on imports. These restrictions are usually applied to one or several specific countries.

R

Random walk theory The theory that there are no predictable trends in securities prices that can be used to "get rich quick."

Rate of discount The rate of interest used to discount future sums back to present value.

Rate of return The future financial benefit to making a current investment.

Rate-of-return regulation Regulation that seeks to keep the rate of return in an industry at a competitive level by not allowing prices that would produce economic profits.

Rational expectations hypothesis A theory stating that people combine the effects of past policy changes on important economic variables with their own judgment about the future effects of current and future policy changes.

Rationality assumption The assumption that people do not intentionally make decisions that would leave them worse off.

Reaction function The manner in which one oligopolist reacts to a change in price, output, or quality made by another oligopolist in the industry.

Real rate of interest The nominal rate of interest minus the anticipated rate of inflation.

Real values Measurement of economic values after adjustments have been made for changes in the average of prices between years.

Real-balance effect The change in expenditures resulting from a change in the real value of money balances when the price level changes, all other things held constant; also called the *wealth effect*.

Real-income effect The change in people's purchasing power that occurs when, other things being constant, the price of one good that they purchase changes. When that price goes up, real income, or purchasing power, falls, and when that price goes down, real income increases.

Recession A period of time during which the rate of growth of business activity is consistently less than its long-term trend or is negative.

Recessionary gap The gap that exists whenever equilibrium real GDP per year is less than full-employment real GDP as shown by the position of the long-run aggregate supply curve.

Recognition time lag The time required to gather information about the current state of the economy.

Recycling The reuse of raw materials derived from manufactured products.

Reentrant An individual who used to work full time but left the labor force and has now reentered it looking for a job.

Regional trade bloc A group of nations that grants members special trade privileges.

Regressive taxation A tax system in which as more dollars are earned, the percentage of tax paid on them falls. The marginal tax rate is less than the average tax rate as income rises.

Reinvestment Profits (or depreciation reserves) used to purchase new capital equipment.

Relative price The price of one commodity divided by the price of another commodity; the number of units of one commodity that must be sacrificed to purchase one unit of another commodity.

Rent control The placement of price ceilings on rents in particular cities.

Repricing, or menu, cost of inflation The cost associated with recalculating prices and printing new price lists when there is inflation.

Required reserve ratio The percentage of total deposits that the Fed requires depository institutions to hold in the form of vault cash or deposits with the Fed.

Required reserves The value of reserves that a depository institution must hold in the form of vault cash or deposits with the Fed.

Reserves In the U.S. Federal Reserve System, deposits held by Federal Reserve district banks for depository institutions, plus depository institutions' vault cash.

Resources Things used to produce other things to satisfy people's wants.

Retained earnings Earnings that a corporation saves, or retains, for investment in other productive activities; earnings that are not distributed to stockholders.

Ricardian equivalence theorem The proposition that an increase in the government budget deficit has no effect on aggregate demand.

Right-to-work laws Laws that make it illegal to require union membership as a condition of continuing employment in a particular firm.

S

Sales taxes Taxes assessed on the prices paid on a large set of goods and services.

Saving The act of not consuming all of one's current income. Whatever is not consumed out of spendable income is, by definition, saved. *Saving* is an action

measured over time (a flow), whereas *savings* are a stock, an accumulation resulting from the act of saving in the past.

Savings deposits Interest-earning funds that can be withdrawn at any time without payment of a penalty.

Say's law A dictum of economist J. B. Say that supply creates its own demand; producing goods and services generates the means and the willingness to purchase other goods and services.

Scarcity A situation in which the ingredients for producing the things that people desire are insufficient to satisfy all wants.

Search good A product with characteristics that enable an individual to evaluate the product's quality in advance of a purchase.

Seasonal unemployment Unemployment resulting from the seasonal pattern of work in specific industries. It is usually due to seasonal fluctuations in demand or to changing weather conditions, rendering work difficult, if not impossible, as in the agriculture, construction, and tourist industries.

Secondary boycott A boycott of companies or products sold by companies that are dealing with a company being struck.

Secular deflation A persistent decline in prices resulting from economic growth in the presence of stable aggregate demand.

Securities Stocks and bonds.

Services Mental or physical labor or help purchased by consumers. Examples are the assistance of physicians, lawyers, dentists, repair personnel, housecleaners, educators, retailers, and wholesalers; things purchased or used by consumers that do not have physical characteristics.

Share of stock A legal claim to a share of a corporation's future profits; if it is *common stock,* it incorporates certain voting rights regarding major policy decisions of the corporation; if it is *preferred stock,* its owners are accorded preferential treatment in the payment of dividends.

Share-the-gains, share-the-pains theory A theory of regulatory behavior that holds that regulators must take account of the demands of three groups: legislators, who established and oversee the regulatory agency; firms in the regulated industry; and consumers of the regulated industry's products.

Short run The time period during which at least one input, such as plant size, cannot be changed.

Shortage A situation in which quantity demanded is greater than quantity supplied at a price below the market clearing price.

Short-run aggregate supply curve The relationship between total planned economywide production and the price level in the short run, all other things held constant. If prices adjust incompletely in the short run, the curve is positively sloped.

Short-run break-even price The price at which a firm's total revenues equal its total costs. At the break-even price, the firm is just making a normal rate of return on its capital investment. (It is covering its explicit and implicit costs.)

Short-run economies of operation A distinguishing characteristic of an information product arising from declining short-run average total cost as more units of the product are sold.

Short-run shutdown price The price that covers average variable costs. It occurs just below the intersection of the marginal cost curve and the average variable cost curve.

Signals Compact ways of conveying to economic decision makers information needed to make decisions. A true signal not only conveys information but also provides the incentive to react appropriately. Economic profits and economic losses are such signals.

Slope The change in the *y* value divided by the corresponding change in the *x* value of a curve; the "incline" of the curve.

Small menu costs Costs that deter firms from changing prices in response to demand changes—for example, the costs of renegotiating contracts or printing new price lists.

Social costs The full costs borne by society whenever a resource use occurs. Social costs can be measured by adding external costs to private, or internal, costs.

Social Security contributions The mandatory taxes paid out of workers' wages and salaries. Although half are supposedly paid by employers, in fact the net wages of employees are lower by the full amount.

Special drawing rights (SDRs) Reserve assets created by the International Monetary Fund for countries to use in settling international payment obligations.

Specialization The division of productive activities among persons and regions so that no one individual or one area is totally self-sufficient. An individual may specialize, for example, in law or medicine. A nation may specialize in the production of coffee, computers, or cameras.

Standard of deferred payment A property of an asset that makes it desirable for use as a means of settling debts maturing in the future; an essential property of money.

Static tax analysis Economic evaluation of the effects of tax rate changes under the assumption that there is no effect on the tax base, so that there is an unambiguous positive relationship between tax rates and tax revenues.

Stock The quantity of something, measured at a given point in time—for example, an inventory of goods or a bank account. Stocks are defined independently of time, although they are assessed at a point in time.

Store of value The ability to hold value over time; a necessary property of money.

Strategic dependence A situation in which one firm's actions with respect to price, quality, advertising, and related changes may be strategically countered by the reactions of one or more other firms in the industry. Such dependence can exist only when there are a limited number of major firms in an industry.

Strategy Any rule that is used to make a choice, such as "Always pick heads."

Strikebreakers Temporary or permanent workers hired by a company to replace union members who are striking.

Structural unemployment Unemployment resulting from a poor match of workers' abilities and skills with current requirements of employers.

Subsidy A negative tax; a payment to a producer from the government, usually in the form of a cash grant per unit.

Substitutes Two goods are substitutes when either one can be used for consumption to satisfy a similar want—for example, coffee and tea. The more you buy of one, the less you buy of the other. For substitutes, the change in the price of one causes a shift in demand for the other in the same direction as the price change.

Substitution effect The tendency of people to substitute cheaper commodities for more expensive commodities.

Supply A schedule showing the relationship between price and quantity supplied for a specified period of time, other things being equal.

Supply curve The graphical representation of the supply schedule; a line (curve) showing the supply schedule, which generally slopes upward (has a positive slope), other things being equal.

Supply-side economics The suggestion that creating incentives for individuals and firms to increase productivity will cause the aggregate supply curve to shift outward.

Surplus A situation in which quantity supplied is greater than quantity demanded at a price above the market clearing price.

Sweep account A depository institution account that entails regular shifts of funds from checkable deposits that are subject to reserve requirements to savings deposits that are exempt from reserve requirements.

Sympathy strike A strike by a union in sympathy with another union's strike or cause.

T

Target zone A range of permitted exchange rate variations between upper and lower exchange rate bands that a central bank defends by selling or buying foreign exchange reserves.

Tariffs Taxes on imported goods.

Tax base The value of goods, services, incomes, or wealth subject to taxation.

Tax bracket A specified interval of income to which a specific and unique marginal tax rate is applied.

Tax incidence The distribution of tax burdens among various groups in society.

Technology Society's pool of applied knowledge concerning how goods and services can be produced.

Terms of exchange The conditions under which trading takes place. Usually, the terms of exchange are equal to the price at which a good is traded.

The Fed The Federal Reserve System; the central bank of the United States.

Theory of public choice The study of collective decision making.

Third parties Parties who are not directly involved in a given activity or transaction.

Thrift institutions Financial institutions that receive most of their funds from the savings of the public; they include mutual savings banks, savings and loan associations, and credit unions.

Tie-in sales Purchases of one product that are permitted by the seller only if the consumer buys another good or service from the same firm.

Time deposit A deposit in a financial institution that requires notice of intent to withdraw or must be left for an agreed period. Withdrawal of funds prior to the end of the agreed period may result in a penalty.

Tit-for-tat strategic behavior In game theory, cooperation that continues so long as the other players continue to cooperate.

Total costs The sum of total fixed costs and total variable costs.

Total income The yearly amount earned by the nation's resources (factors of production). Total income therefore includes wages, rent, interest payments, and profits that are received by workers, landowners, capital owners, and entrepreneurs, respectively.

Total revenues The price per unit times the total quantity sold.

Transaction costs All costs associated with making, reaching, and enforcing agreements.

Transactions accounts Checking account balances in commercial banks and other types of financial institutions, such as credit unions and mutual savings banks; any accounts in financial institutions on which you can easily write checks without many restrictions.

Transactions approach A method of measuring the money supply by looking at money as a medium of exchange.

Transactions demand Holding money as a medium of exchange to make payments. The level varies directly with nominal GDP.

Transfer payments Money payments made by governments to individuals for which in return no services or goods are rendered. Examples are welfare, Social Security, and unemployment insurance benefits.

Transfers in kind Payments that are in the form of actual goods and services, such as food stamps, subsidized public housing, and medical care, and for which in return no goods or services are rendered concurrently.

Traveler's checks Financial instruments purchased from a bank or a non-banking organization and signed during purchase that can be used as cash upon a second signature by the purchaser.

U

Unanticipated inflation Inflation at a rate that comes as a surprise, either higher or lower than the rate anticipated.

Unemployment The total number of adults (aged 16 years or older) who are willing and able to work and who are actively looking for work but have not found a job.

Union shop A legal environment in which businesses may hire nonunion members, conditional on their joining the union by some specified date after employment begins.

Unit elasticity of demand A demand relationship in which the quantity demanded changes exactly in proportion to the change in price. Total expenditures are invariant to price changes in the unit-elastic region of the demand curve.

Unit of accounting A measure by which prices are expressed; the common denominator of the price system; a central property of money.

Unit tax A constant tax assessed on each unit of a good that consumers purchase.

Universal banking An environment in which banks face few or no restrictions on their powers to offer a full range of financial services and to own shares of stock in corporations.

Unlimited liability A legal concept whereby the personal assets of the owner of a firm can be seized to pay off the firm's debts.

Util A representative unit by which utility is measured.

Utility The want-satisfying power of a good or service.

Utility analysis The analysis of consumer decision making based on utility maximization.

V

Value added The dollar value of an industry's sales minus the value of intermediate goods (for example, raw materials and parts) used in production.

Variable costs Costs that vary with the rate of production. They include wages paid to workers and purchases of materials.

Versioning Selling a product in slightly altered forms to different groups of consumers.

Vertical merger The joining of a firm with another to which it sells an output or from which it buys an input.

Voluntary exchange An act of trading, done on a voluntary basis, in which both parties to the trade are subjectively better off after the exchange.

Voluntary import expansion (VIE) An official agreement with another country in which it agrees to import more from the United States.

Voluntary restraint agreement (VRA) An official agreement with another country that "voluntarily" restricts the quantity of its exports to the United States.

W

Wants What people would buy if their incomes were unlimited.

Wealth The stock of assets owned by a person, household, firm, or nation. For a household, wealth can consist of a house, cars, personal belongings, stocks, bonds, bank accounts, and cash.

World Bank A multinational agency that specializes in making loans to about 100 developing nations in an effort to promote their long-term development and growth.

World index fund A portfolio of bonds issued in various nations whose individual yields generally move in offsetting directions, thereby reducing the overall risk of losses.

World Trade Organization (WTO) The successor organization to GATT that handles trade disputes among its member nations.

X

x **axis** The horizontal axis in a graph.

Y

y **axis** The vertical axis in a graph.

Z

Zero-sum game A game in which any gains within the group are exactly offset by equal losses by the end of the game.

MACROECONOMIC PRINCIPLES

Nominal versus Real Interest Rate

$$i_n = i_r + \text{expected rate of inflation}$$

where i_n = nominal rate of interest

i_r = real rate of interest

Marginal versus Average Tax Rates

$$\text{Marginal tax rate} = \frac{\text{change in taxes due}}{\text{change in taxable income}}$$

$$\text{Average tax rate} = \frac{\text{total taxes due}}{\text{total taxable income}}$$

GDP—The Expenditure and Income Approaches

$$GDP = C + I + G + X$$

where C = consumption expenditures

I = investment expenditures

G = government expenditures

X = net exports

$$GDP = \text{wages} + \text{rent} + \text{interest} + \text{profits}$$

Say's Law

Supply creates its own demand, or *desired* aggregate expenditures will equal *actual* aggregate expenditures

Saving, Consumption, and Investment

$$\text{Consumption} + \text{saving} = \text{disposable income}$$

$$\text{Saving} = \text{disposable income} - \text{consumption}$$

Average and Marginal Propensities

$$APC = \frac{\text{real consumption}}{\text{real disposable income}}$$

$$APS = \frac{\text{real saving}}{\text{real disposable income}}$$

$$MPC = \frac{\text{change in real consumption}}{\text{change in real disposable income}}$$

$$MPS = \frac{\text{change in real saving}}{\text{change in real disposable income}}$$

The Multiplier Formula

$$\text{Multiplier} = \frac{1}{MPS} = \frac{1}{1 - MPC}$$

$$\text{Multiplier} \times \begin{array}{c} \text{change in} \\ \text{autonomous} \\ \text{spending} \end{array} = \begin{array}{c} \text{change in} \\ \text{equilibrium level} \\ \text{of national income} \end{array}$$

Relationship Between Bond Prices and Interest Rates

The market price of existing (old) bonds is inversely related to "the" rate of interest prevailing in the economy.

Government Spending and Taxation Multipliers

$$M_g = \frac{1}{MPS}$$

$$M_t = -MPC \times \frac{1}{MPS}$$

Gresham's Law

Bad money drives good money out of circulation.

In this table we see historical data for the various components of nominal GDP. These are given in the first four columns. We then show the rest of the national income accounts going from GDP to NDP to NI to PI to DPI. The last column gives chain-weighted real GDP.

	The Sum of These Expenditures				Equals	Less	Equals	Plus	Less	Equals	Less			Plus	Equals	Less	Equals	
Year	Personal Consumption Expenditures	Gross Private Domestic Investment	Government Purchases of Goods and Services	Net Exports	Gross Domestic Product	Depreciation	Net Domestic Product	Net U.S. Income Earned Abroad	Indirect Business Taxes, Transfers, Adjustments	National Income	Undistributed Corporate Profits	Social Security Taxes	Corporate Income Taxes	Transfer Payments and Net Interest Earnings	Personal Income	Personal Income Taxes and Nontax Payments	Disposable Personal Income	Chain-Weighted Real GDP (2000 dollars)
1982	2077.3	517.2	680.5	-20.0	3255.0	426.9	2828.1	36.5	0.3	2864.3	65.4	208.9	66.5	251.8	2775.3	354.1	2421.2	5189.3
1983	2290.6	564.3	733.5	-51.7	3536.7	443.8	3092.9	37.1	45.8	3084.2	100.1	226.0	80.6	283.2	2960.7	352.3	2608.4	5423.8
1984	2503.3	735.6	797.0	-102.7	3933.2	472.6	3460.6	36.3	14.6	3482.3	130.3	257.5	97.5	292.5	3289.5	377.5	2912.0	5813.6
1985	2720.3	736.2	879.0	-115.2	4220.3	506.7	3713.6	26.5	16.7	3723.4	133.4	281.4	99.4	317.5	3526.7	417.4	3109.3	6053.7
1986	2899.7	746.5	949.3	-132.7	4462.8	531.1	3931.7	17.8	47.2	3902.3	103.7	303.4	109.7	336.9	3722.4	437.3	3285.1	6263.6
1987	3100.2	785.0	999.5	-145.2	4739.5	561.9	4177.6	17.9	21.8	4173.7	126.1	323.1	130.4	353.3	3947.4	489.1	3458.3	6475.1
1988	3353.6	821.6	1039.0	-110.4	5103.8	597.6	4506.2	23.6	-19.6	4549.4	161.1	361.5	141.6	368.5	4253.7	505.0	3748.7	6742.7
1989	3598.5	874.9	1099.1	-88.2	5484.4	644.3	4840.1	26.2	39.7	4826.6	122.6	385.2	146.1	415.1	4587.8	566.1	4021.7	6981.4
1990	3839.9	861.0	1180.2	-78.0	5803.1	682.5	5120.6	34.8	66.3	5089.1	123.3	410.1	145.4	468.3	4878.6	592.8	4285.8	7112.5
1991	3986.1	802.9	1234.4	-27.5	5995.9	725.9	5270.0	30.4	72.5	5227.9	131.9	430.2	138.6	523.8	5051.0	586.7	4464.3	7100.5
1992	4235.3	864.8	1271.0	-33.2	6337.7	751.9	5585.8	29.7	102.7	5512.8	142.7	455.0	148.7	595.6	5362.0	610.6	4751.4	7336.6
1993	4477.9	953.4	1291.2	-65.0	6657.4	776.4	5881.0	31.9	139.5	5773.4	168.1	477.7	171.0	601.9	5558.5	646.6	4911.9	7532.7
1994	4743.3	1097.1	1325.5	-93.6	7072.2	833.7	6238.5	26.2	142.4	6122.3	171.8	508.2	193.7	593.9	5842.5	690.7	5151.8	7835.5
1995	4975.8	1144.0	1369.2	-91.4	7397.7	878.4	6519.3	35.8	101.2	6453.9	223.8	532.8	218.7	673.7	6152.3	744.1	5408.2	8031.7
1996	5256.8	1240.3	1416.0	-96.2	7816.9	918.1	6898.8	35.0	93.7	6840.1	256.9	555.2	231.7	724.3	6520.6	832.1	5688.5	8328.9
1997	5547.4	1389.8	1468.7	-101.6	8304.3	974.4	7329.9	33.0	70.7	7292.2	287.9	587.2	246.1	744.1	6915.1	926.3	5988.8	8703.5
1998	5879.5	1509.1	1518.3	-159.9	8747.0	1030.2	7716.8	21.3	-14.7	7752.8	201.7	624.2	248.3	744.4	7423.0	1028.0	6395.0	9066.9
1999	6282.5	1625.7	1620.8	-260.5	9268.4	1101.3	8167.1	33.8	-35.8	8236.7	255.3	661.4	258.6	741.0	7802.4	1107.4	6695.0	9470.3
2000	6739.4	1735.5	1721.6	-379.5	9817.0	1187.8	8629.2	39.0	-127.0	8795.2	174.8	702.7	265.2	777.2	8429.7	1235.7	7194.0	9817.0
2001	7045.4	1607.2	1814.7	-366.5	10100.8	1266.9	8833.9	35.2	-112.1	8981.2	196.0	728.5	201.1	857.5	8713.1	1243.7	7469.4	9866.6
2002	7385.3	1589.2	1932.5	-426.3	10480.8	1288.6	9192.2	21.5	-77.1	9290.8	310.8	732.2	195.0	857.5	8910.3	1053.1	7857.2	10083.0
2003	7757.4	1670.6	2054.8	-495.0	10987.9	1373.5	9614.4	25.3	-26.4	9666.1	276.2	743.3	210.4	899.1	9335.3	1103.1	8232.2	10398.0
2004[a]	8220.5	1730.7	2176.4	-525.3	11602.3	1454.2	10148.1	23.5	-18.4	10190.0	265.4	766.0	232.6	844.4	9770.4	1160.4	8610.0	10670.1
2005[a]	8644.4	1861.9	2290.3	-550.5	12246.1	1539.7	10706.4	22.6	-37.3	10766.3	283.9	833.1	224.0	775.9	10201.2	1289.3	8911.9	10998.0

*Note: Some rows may not add up due to rounding errors.
[a]Estimates based on preliminary data.